Protecting User Privacy in Web Search Utilization

Rafi Ullah Khan
The University of Agriculture, Peshawar, Pakistan

A volume in the Advances in Information Security,
Privacy, and Ethics (AISPE) Book Series

Published in the United States of America by
IGI Global
Information Science Reference (an imprint of IGI Global)
701 E. Chocolate Avenue
Hershey PA, USA 17033
Tel: 717-533-8845
Fax: 717-533-8661
E-mail: cust@igi-global.com
Web site: http://www.igi-global.com

Library of Congress Cataloging-in-Publication Data

Names: Khan, Rafi Ullah, 1984- editor.
Title: Protecting user privacy in web search utilization / edited by Rafi
   Ullah Khan.
Description: Hershey, PA : Information Science Reference, 2023. | Includes
   bibliographical references and index. | Summary: "The objective is to
   publish both disciplinary, multidisciplinary and interdisciplinary works
   on questions related to experiences and phenomena that can or could be
   covered by concepts regarding the protection of privacy of web services
   users. Another major objective of this book is to highlight the
   importance of web search privacy to the readers and educate them about
   the recent developments. Privacy is a fundamental right, essential to
   autonomy and the protection of human dignity, serving as the foundation
   upon which many other human rights are built. Privacy is a meaningful
   way we seek to protect ourselves and society against arbitrary and
   unjustified use of power by reducing what can be known about us and what
   has been done to us while protecting us from others who may wish to
   exert control. This book will help students and the research community
   understand the current status of the privacy-aware web search mechanisms
   and help identify new challenges in the areas"-- Provided by publisher.
Identifiers: LCCN 2022044532 (print) | LCCN 2022044533 (ebook) | ISBN
   9781668469149 (h/c) | ISBN 9781668469156 (s/c) | ISBN 9781668469163
   (eISBN)
Subjects: LCSH: World wide web--Security measures. | Web browsing--Security
   measures. | Privacy, Right of. | Data privacy. | Data protection. |
   Internet users--Protection.
Classification: LCC TK5105.88813 .P783 2023 (print) | LCC TK5105.88813
   (ebook) | DDC 005.8--dc23/eng/20221128
LC record available at https://lccn.loc.gov/2022044532
LC ebook record available at https://lccn.loc.gov/2022044533

This book is published in the IGI Global book series Advances in Information Security, Privacy, and Ethics (AISPE) (ISSN: 1948-9730; eISSN: 1948-9749)

British Cataloguing in Publication Data
A Cataloguing in Publication record for this book is available from the British Library.

All work contributed to this book is new, previously-unpublished material. The views expressed in this book are those of the authors, but not necessarily of the publisher.

For electronic access to this publication, please contact: eresources@igi-global.com.

Advances in Information Security, Privacy, and Ethics (AISPE) Book Series

Manish Gupta
State University of New York, USA

ISSN:1948-9730
EISSN:1948-9749

MISSION

As digital technologies become more pervasive in everyday life and the Internet is utilized in ever in-creasing ways by both private and public entities, concern over digital threats becomes more prevalent.

The **Advances in Information Security, Privacy, & Ethics (AISPE) Book Series** provides cutting-edge research on the protection and misuse of information and technology across various industries and settings. Comprised of scholarly research on topics such as identity management, cryptography, system security, authentication, and data protection, this book series is ideal for reference by IT professionals, academicians, and upper-level students.

COVERAGE

- Data Storage of Minors
- Cookies
- IT Risk
- Internet Governance
- Telecommunications Regulations
- Security Information Management
- CIA Triad of Information Security
- Security Classifications
- Technoethics
- Tracking Cookies

IGI Global is currently accepting manuscripts for publication within this series. To submit a pro-posal for a volume in this series, please contact our Acquisition Editors at Acquisitions@igi-global.com or visit: http://www.igi-global.com/publish/.

Titles in this Series

For a list of additional titles in this series, please visit: www.igi-global.com/book-series

701 East Chocolate Avenue, Hershey, PA 17033, USA
Tel: 717-533-8845 x100 • Fax: 717-533-8661
E-Mail: cust@igi-global.com • www.igi-global.com

Frahan Ullah, *Northwestern Polytechnical University, Xi'an, China*
Kifayat Ullah, *University of Sao Paulo, Brazil*
Fazal Wahab, *Government of Khyber Pakhtunkhwa, Pakistan*
Abdul Waheed, *Seoul National University, South Korea*
Islam Zada, *International Islamic University, Islamabad, Pakistan*

Table of Contents

Chapter 1

Mohib Ullah, The University of Agriculture, Peshawar, Pakistan
Arbab Waseem Abbas, The University of Agriculture, Peshawar, Pakistan
Lala Rukh, The University of Agriculture, Peshawar, Pakistan
Kamran Ullah, The University of Agriculture, Peshawar, Pakistan
Muhammad Inam Ul Haq, Khushal Khan Khattak University Karak, Karak, Pakistan

Chapter 2

Rafi Ullah Khan, The University of Agriculture, Peshawar, Pakistan
Mohib Ullah, The University of Agriculture, Peshawar, Pakistan
Bushra Shafi, The University of Agriculture, Peshawar, Pakistan
Imran Ihsan, Air University, Islamabad, Pakistan

Chapter 3

Rafi Ullah Khan, The University of Agriculture, Peshawar, Pakistan
Mohib Ullah, The University of Agriculture, Peshawar, Pakistan
Bushra Shafi, The University of Agriculture, Peshawar, Pakistan

Chapter 4

Shaukat Ali, University of Peshawar, Pakistan
Shah Khusro, University of Peshawar, Pakistan
Mumtaz Khan, University of Peshawar, Pakistan

Detailed Table of Contents

Chapter 1

    Mohib Ullah, The University of Agriculture, Peshawar, Pakistan
    Arbab Waseem Abbas, The University of Agriculture, Peshawar, Pakistan
    Lala Rukh, The University of Agriculture, Peshawar, Pakistan
    Kamran Ullah, The University of Agriculture, Peshawar, Pakistan
    Muhammad Inam Ul Haq, Khushal Khan Khattak University Karak, Karak, Pakistan

Web search engine (WSE) is an inevitable software system used by people worldwide to retrieve data from the web by using keywords called queries. WSE stores search queries to build the user's profile and provide personalized results. User search queries often hold identifiable information that could compromise the user's privacy. Preserving privacy in web searches is the primary concern of users from various backgrounds. Many techniques have been proposed to preserve a person's web search privacy with time. Some techniques preserve an individual's privacy by obfuscating a user's profile by sending fictitious queries with the original ones. Others hide their identity and preserve privacy through unlinkability. However, a distributed technique preserves privacy by providing unlinkability and obfuscation. In distributed protocols, a group of users collaborate to forward each other queries to WSE, providing unlinkability and obfuscation. This work presents a survey of distributed privacy-preserving protocols. The benefits, limitations, and evaluation parameters are detailed in this work.

Chapter 2

    Rafi Ullah Khan, The University of Agriculture, Peshawar, Pakistan
    Mohib Ullah, The University of Agriculture, Peshawar, Pakistan
    Bushra Shafi, The University of Agriculture, Peshawar, Pakistan
    Imran Ihsan, Air University, Islamabad, Pakistan

Due to the exponential growth of information on the internet, web search engines (WSEs) have become indispensable for effectively retrieving information. Web search engines store the users' profiles to provide the most relevant results. However, the user profiles may contain sensitive information, including the user's age, gender, health condition, personal interests, religious or political affiliation, and others. However, this raises serious concerns for the user's privacy since a user's identity may get exposed and misused by third parties. Researchers have proposed several techniques to address the issue of privacy infringement while using WSE, such as anonymizing networks, profile obfuscation, and private information retrieval (PIR) protocols. In this chapter, the authors give a brief survey of the privacy attacks and evaluation models used to evaluate the performance of private web search techniques.

Rafi Ullah Khan, The University of Agriculture, Peshawar, Pakistan
Mohib Ullah, The University of Agriculture, Peshawar, Pakistan
Bushra Shafi, The University of Agriculture, Peshawar, Pakistan

Privacy quantification methods are used to quantify the knowledge the adverse search engine has obtained with and without privacy protection mechanisms. Thus, these methods calculate privacy exposure. Private web search techniques are based on many methods (e.g., proxy service, query modification, query exchange, and others). This variety of techniques prompted the researchers to evaluate their work differently. This section introduces the metrics used to evaluate user privacy (protection). Moreover, this section also introduces the metrics used to evaluate the performance of privacy attacks and theoretical evaluation approaches.

Shaukat Ali, University of Peshawar, Pakistan
Shah Khusro, University of Peshawar, Pakistan
Mumtaz Khan, University of Peshawar, Pakistan

The advancements in desktop computing technologies and widespread use of digital devices have enabled users to generate and store tons of contents on their computers, which creates an information overload problem. Therefore, users need applications to search and retrieve required stored data instantly and accurately. This attracted the software industry to develop desktop search engines using ideas of web search engines. However, selecting an effective desktop search engine is difficult for users. In this chapter, the authors have analyzed and compared available desktop search engines using a set of parameters including users' privacy and security. A generalized architecture for desktop search engines is presented for improving understanding and unification of development efforts. The new emerging trends, supporting users' privacy and security, and several open issues and challenges in the desktop search engines domain are also highlighted. The authors hope that this chapter will be helpful for researchers to find new research problems and users to select appropriate desktop search engines.

Tayyaba Riaz, City University of Science and Information Technology, Peshawar, Pakistan
Iftikhar Alam, City University of Science and Information Technology, Peshawar, Pakistan

Blockchain technology is the leading and revolutionary technology in this modern era of computing. Many countries around the world are diverting towards digital currency which is the initial popular service provided by blockchain technology e.g., Bitcoin, Litecoin, etc. The main feature of blockchain is to omit the central authority by introducing distributed ledger structures. The consensus protocols play a vital role in the performance and efficiency of blockchain-based frameworks. This study introduces the solution of different e-services and associated problems that are faced in developing countries for making the system transparent, smart, and secure. These features make Web 3.0 applications, which is the ultimate goal of blockchain-based technology. This study also explains the numerous aspects of blockchain-based e-services infrastructure, implementation issues, advantages, disadvantages, and challenges. This study may help practitioners for making smart, intelligent, highly secure, and robust applications even in developing countries.

Chapter 6

Today, with the changes and developments in software technologies, web applications have gained an important place by being actively used in many sectors. Due to the fact that web applications do not require installation costs and are easily accessible and operable, the increased usage rate in recent years makes these systems the target of cyber hackers. As a result of cyber attacks, services are blocked, and material and moral damages and data privacy violations are experienced. Within the scope of this study, web applications are explained, vulnerabilities that threaten software security and the measures that can be taken against these vulnerabilities are included. Particularly, security threats to web applications, security principles, secure software development lifecycles, test tools, and hardware and software products used for security are examined. In addition, SAMM and BSIMM models, which are maturity models used in secure software development, are discussed.

Chapter 7

For long-term relationships, the websites of various businesses store the PII and PHI of customers, which are mainly targeted by hackers. Cyber breaches mainly result in lack of customer trust and downfall of the business reputation. As a result, the customers become reluctant to share PII and PHI with online businesses until provided with the protection of sensitive data. The online resources of a business need to be in compliance with GDPR and PCI DSS. Companies undergo penetration testing of the infrastructure; for this, paid white hat hackers are hired under a legal contract. The companies also adopt RVDP program, where the Bug Bounty Platforms is one of the variants of RVDP. Security researchers are rewarded with an amount of bounty in the form of money or name in the hall of fame at official website for bugs' identification. Ideally, the security researcher would perform cyber security assessment. The vulnerabilities would be reported to intended stakeholders and the remediation measures with great deal of care so that PII and PHI won't be exploited by anyone.

Requirement engineering has gained tremendous popularity among the research and developers communities and comprises five activities, i.e., feasibility study, elicitation, analysis, specification, and validation. In the elicitation phase, the data is collected from different stakeholders. Hence, the overall system, process, and even data may be compromised and sometimes lead to privacy threats if the data is shared with a third party. To this end, this work proposes a comparative analysis of the eminent techniques, including privacy violation factors. The authors targeted 32 techniques for analysis from different project scenarios. This study may help the analysts with adequate knowledge and help project management teams to select the best and most secure elicitation techniques concerning the nature of projects.

This chapter assessed privacy and access of the liberation movements archives of South Africa. The study is based on personal experience of working with the liberation movement archives and review of literature on privacy and accessibility. The discussion was based on the liberation movements archives, privacy legislation, accountability, purpose specifications, donation of third party archives, information quality, confidentiality and security of archives, electronic records management systems, digitization of liberation movement archives, data subject participation, openness and transparency, public records, establishment of governance structure, raising awareness and training, partnership and collaboration, and access to liberation archives. Liberation movements are to ensure that they comply with the Protection of Personal Information Act 4 of 2013.

The current century has witnessed a prodigious expansion in scientific innovations contributing toward the betterment of humanity. The astonishing advancements in digital communications have facilitated various spheres of our lifestyle including the manufacturing sector. A plethora of cutting-edge technologies are rubbing shoulders to revolutionize manufacturing trends. Distributed system communications introduce a new concept of digital collaboration among a diversified range of scattered communication nodes. The individual resources of multiple nodes are intelligently integrated to formulate an aggregated impact that yields phenomenal productivity. The smart connectivity among various heterogeneous nodes may familiarize the network with an extended variety of potential security threats. The literature environs a bulk of security solutions proposed to overcome these challenges. This research study provides a comprehensive elaboration of these security threats along with the security practices designed to encounter such activities.

Chapter 11

Said Ul Abrar, The University of Agriculture, Peshawar, Pakistan
Kamran Ullah, The University of Agriculture, Peshawar, Pakistan
Saleem Zahid, The University of Agriculture, Peshawar, Pakistan
Mohib Ullah, The University of Agriculture, Peshawar, Pakistan
Irfan Ullah Khan, Imam Abdulrahman Bin Faisal University, Dammam, Saudi Arabia
Muhammad Inam Ul Haq, Khushal Khan Khattak University, Karak, Pakistan

Recently, electronics devices, cognitive computing, and sensing enable the deployment of internet-of-things (IoTs) with a huge application domain. However, resource constraints such as low computing powers or limited storage leave IoTs infrastructures vulnerable to a variety of cyber-attacks. In dark-net the address space developed as designated unrestricted internet address space anticipated to be used by trustworthy hosts anywhere in the world, therefore, any communication activity is presumed to be unwanted and particularly treated as a probe, backscatter, or miss-configuration. This chapter investigates and evaluates the operation of dark-net traffic detection systems in IoTs networks. Moreover, the most recent work done to ensure security in the IoTs network has been discussed. In particular, the areas of privacy provisioning, lightweight cryptographic framework, secure routing, robustness, and DoS attacks have been addressed. Moreover, based on the analysis of existing state-of-the-art protocols, the security requirements and challenges are highlighted along with identified open issues.

Chapter 12

Majida Khan Tareen, Institute of Space Technology, Islamabad, Pakistan
Altaf Hussain, Institute of Space Technology, Islamabad, Pakistan
Muhammad Hamad, Institute of Space Technology, Islamabad, Pakistan

The number of IoT devices connected to the global network is expected to be three times more, from 9.7 billion in 2020 to more than 29 billion in 2030. Globally connected IoT devices transmit enormous amounts of facts and figures daily via the internet for various purposes which is about users including important, intimate, or private information. As this data can be utilized for malevolent reasons, these devices constitute a privacy risk. IoT systems involved sensors gathering data from the environment, so known as cyber-physical systems which are highly vulnerable. Hence, user privacy issues such as password stealing, information and identity stealing, intruding, corrupting information, etc. are increasing day by day. Therefore, privacy experts and researchers are very much concerned about preventing user privacy issues and developed many PETs (blind signature, group signature, attribute-based credentials (ABCs), anonymous and pseudonymous data authentication, onion routing, encrypted communications, etc.) to prevent user privacy risks in IoT.

Chapter 13

Pedro Pina, Polytechnic Institute of Coimbra, Technology and Management School of
Oliveira do Hospital, Oliveira do Hospital, Portugal & SUScita - Research Group on
Sustainability Cities and Urban Intelligence, Portugal

The digital infrastructure of smart cities necessarily implies collecting big amounts of personal and its subsequent processing by software and applications designed to acquire analytical capabilities regarded to public spaces in order to enable efficient control over it. In the European Union legal context, aiming to densify the principle of informational self-determination, the general data protection regulation (GDPR) has provided citizens with greater power and control over their personal data, turning the responsibilities of smart cities administrators towards citizens much heavier. This chapter aims to analyse the impact on personal data and democratic public spaces derived from smart cities activities, to present the rights granted to individuals by the GDPR and its applicability to smart cities, and to make some recommendations regarding the implementation and the adaptation of the Regulation to the specific case of a smart city, not only to preserve a high-level level of privacy protection but also as a means to promote democratic solutions in public spaces.

Chapter 14

Danish Javeed, Northeastern University, China
Tianhan Gao, Northeastern University, China
Zeeshan Jamil, The University of Agriculture, Peshawar, Pakistan

The quality of human existence is improving day by day, and the internet of things (IoT) has arisen as a new world of technology in the last two decades. It has aided the world through its applications in many sectors. However, while delivering several benefits, the extreme expansion of IoT devices makes them a potential target of attacks, which jeopardise the organisation if left unchecked. Cyber security analysts have recently been using the DL-based model to detect and investigate malware in order to keep the organization secure from cyber-attacks. This work describes how AI-based techniques are utilized to identify cyber threats in the IoT environments better while considering these devices' heterogeneous and resource-constrained nature so that no extra burden is imposed on them. This work comprehensively evaluated the current solutions, challenges, and future directions in IoT security.

Foreword

The threat to privacy posed by centralized collections of user data by search engines is an issue that has been brought into sharp focus for the past several years. Data mining, intentional or accidental data leakage to third parties, and the concentration of personal information in the hands of a small number of centralized service providers have all aggravated to this problem.

Perhaps the most high-profile examples of this trend are the online social networks and social media sites that attract the lion's share of Internet users' time today. These sites offer a range of valuable services to individuals, but at the same time, they collect vast amounts of personal information about their users. This information includes not only the content that users themselves upload, but also patterns in their preferences and behavior, as well as their relationships with others. The providers of these services are logically centralized, which means that all this personally identifiable information is concentrated in the hands of a limited number of entities. These entities rely on large collections of extensive, detailed personal information to support their business model, which is primarily focused on targeted advertising.

Privacy infringement is a complex issue having significant implications for online services, as it exposes users to the risk of data breaches and other forms of misuse. It also raises important ethical questions about the appropriate use of personal data and the responsibilities of service providers in this area. The book encompasses the related topics comprehensively by discussing various aspects of privacy preserving technologies as well as analyzing corresponding evaluation strategies. Additionally, it includes sections focusing on state-of-the-art online security tools that prevent data leakage using traditional web technologies and Blockchain while considering conventional as well as IoT perspective. I appreciate all the authors for providing such an expert insight to important topics. The editors have also done an exceptional job by meticulously selecting the topic and chapters to ensure the wide-ranging coverage of the subject.

This book is a must-read for anyone interested in the field of online privacy and security. The research articles discussed in the book provide a solid foundation for understanding the complex issues related to privacy protection in today's interconnected world. I am confident that this book will help to raise awareness of the important issue and provide valuable insights into how research community can synergize its efforts to protect our privacy online. I highly recommend this book to anyone who is concerned about their online privacy and the need to protect it.

Muhammad Arshad Islam
National University of Computer and Emerging Sciences, Pakistan

Preface

Online user privacy is a delicate issue that has been unfortunately overlooked by technology corporations and especially the public since the birth of the internet. There is a misconception among people about the term "privacy." Usually, people think that privacy is the ability of an individual to isolate themselves or that it is a person's right to control access to their personal information. However, privacy is not just about revealing secret information; it also includes exploiting users' data, as the exploitation of personal data may lead to disastrous consequences. Online user privacy is the ability of individuals to control the information they disclose about themselves over the internet, as well as how that information is collected, stored, and used by online services and websites. With the increasing use of the internet and online services, privacy concerns have become more prevalent, and many people are concerned about the amount of personal data that is collected and shared without their knowledge or consent. The purpose of this book is to gather both multidisciplinary and interdisciplinary works on questions related to experiences and phenomena that can or could be covered by concepts regarding the protection and privacy of web service users. It further highlights the importance of web search privacy to the readers and educates them about recent developments in the field.

AN OVERVIEW OF BOOK CONTENT

Privacy is a fundamental right, essential to autonomy and the protection of human dignity, serving as the foundation upon which many other human rights are built. Privacy is a meaningful way we seek to protect ourselves and society against arbitrary and unjustified use of power by reducing what can be known about us and what has been done to us while protecting us from others who may wish to exert control. This book will help students and the research community understand the current status of privacy-aware web search mechanisms and help identify new challenges in the areas. This book has hot topics related to web privacy such as AI-based intrusion detection, desktop search engines, privacy risks, data leakage, web applications testing, secure cloud-based manufacturing, the status of user privacy in IoT, and GDPR for personal data protection.

TARGET AUDIENCE

This premier reference source is an essential resource for students and educators of higher education, data experts, privacy professionals and engineers, IT managers, software developers, government officials, archivists and librarians, privacy rights activists, researchers, and academicians.

SIGNIFICANCE OF THE BOOK

The book's contents appeal to anyone with an interest in web search privacy. This book will help raise awareness about privacy issues and educate individuals about how their personal information is collected, used, and shared by companies and organizations. Reading this book can help people to understand the importance of privacy and the risks associated with the misuse of personal information. This book can provide guidance on how to protect personal information, such as tips for securing online accounts, using privacy-enhancing tools, and avoiding scams and phishing attacks. This information can help individuals take proactive steps to protect their privacy. The knowledge contained in this book can empower individuals to take control of their personal information and make informed decisions about how it is used. By understanding their privacy rights, individuals can advocate for stronger privacy protections and demand more transparency from companies and organizations. This book can also help businesses and organizations understand their legal obligations regarding privacy and data protection. By following the best practices outlined in this book, businesses can ensure that they are complying with privacy laws and regulations. Moreover, this book can inspire new ideas and innovations for protecting privacy in a constantly evolving digital landscape. Reading about different privacy-enhancing technologies and strategies can help individuals and organizations develop new solutions for protecting personal information. Overall, this book is significant for raising awareness, protecting personal information, empowering individuals, promoting legal compliance, and inspiring innovation in privacy protection.

CHAPTER ORGANIZATION

The book comprises 14 chapters that aim to highlight hot topics related to web privacy, the impact of data privacy violations, privacy concerns in IoT, privacy laws, rules and regulations and applications.

Chapter 1, "State of the Art in Distributed Privacy-Preserving Protocols in Private Web Search," by Mohib Ullah, Arbab Waseem Abbas, Lala Rukh, Kamran Ullah, and Muhammad Inam Ul Haq discusses that Web Search Engine (WSE) is an inevitable software system used by people worldwide to retrieve data from the web by using keywords called queries. WSE stores search queries to build user profiles and provide personalized results. User search queries often hold identifiable information that could compromise the user's privacy. Preserving privacy in web searches is the primary concern of users from various backgrounds. Many techniques have been proposed to preserve a person's web search privacy with time. Some techniques preserve an individual's privacy by obfuscating a user's profile by sending fictitious queries with the original ones. Others hide their identity and preserve privacy through unlinkability. However, a distributed technique preserves privacy by providing unlinkability and obfuscation. In distributed protocols, a group of users collaborate to forward each other queries to WSE, providing unlinkability and obfuscation. This work presents a survey of distributed privacy-preserving protocols. The benefits and limitations of distributed privacy-preserving protocols and the evaluation parameters are detailed in this work.

Chapter 2, "A Survey On Performance Evaluation Mechanisms for Privacy-Aware Web Search Schemes" by Rafi Ullah Khan, Mohib Ullah, Bushra Shafi, and Imran Ihsan reveals that Due to the exponential growth of information on the Internet, Web Search Engines (WSEs) have become indispensable for effectively retrieving information. Web Search Engines store the users' profiles to provide the most relevant results. However, the user profiles may contain sensitive information, including the user's age, gender, health condition, personal interests, religious or political affiliation, and others. However, this raises serious concerns for the user's privacy since a user's identity may get exposed and misused by third parties. Researchers have proposed several techniques to address the issue of privacy infringement while using WSE, such as anonymizing networks, profile obfuscation, and private information retrieval (PIR) protocols. In this chapter, we give a brief survey of the privacy attacks and evaluation models used to evaluate the performance of private web search techniques.

Chapter 3, "Web Search Privacy Evaluation Metrics" by Rafi Ullah Khan, Mohib Ullah, and Bushra Shafi, discusses that privacy quantification methods are used to quantify the knowledge the adverse search engine has obtained with and without privacy protection mechanisms. Thus these methods calculate the privacy exposure. Private web search techniques are based on many methods (e.g., proxy service, query modification, query exchange, and others). This variety of techniques prompted the researchers to evaluate their work differently. This section introduces the metrics used to evaluate user privacy (protection). Moreover, this section also introduces the metrics used to evaluate the performance of privacy attacks and theoretical evaluation approaches.

Chapter 4, "Desktop Search Engines: A Review from User Perspective" by Shaukat Ali, Shah Khusro, and Mumtaz Khan, reveals that The advancements in desktop computing technologies and widespread use of digital devices have enabled users to generate and store tones of contents on their computers which creates information overload problem. Therefore, users need applications to search and retrieve required stored data instantly and accurately. This attracted the software industry to develop desktop search engines using the ideas of web search engines. However, selecting an effective desktop search engine is difficult for users. In this chapter, we have analyzed and compared available desktop search engines using a set of parameters including users' privacy and security. A generalized architecture for desktop search engines is presented for improving in understanding and unification of development efforts. The new emerging trends, supporting users' privacy and security and several open issues and challenges in the desktop search engines domain are also highlighted. We hope that this chapter will be helpful for researchers to find new research problems and for users to select appropriate desktop search engines.

Chapter 5, "Beyond Cryptocurrencies: A Review of Blockchain Technology for E-Services in Developing Countries" by Tayyaba Riaz and Iftikhar Alam, explores that Blockchain technology is a revolutionary technology in this modern era of computing. Many countries around the world are diverting towards digital currency, which is the initial popular service provided by Blockchain technology e.g., Bitcoin, and Lite coin. The features of Blockchain are to omit the central authority by introducing distributed ledger structures, ensuring transparency, and security. In developing countries, there are numerous issues in providing transparent, highly secure, and publically verifiable digital services. This makes it difficult to combat corruption and increases insecurity and lack of equity among citizens. This study reviews different e-services and associated problems that are faced in developing countries for making the system transparent, smart, secure, and verifiable. Moreover, this study explains several aspects of Blockchain-based e-services, and infrastructure, including implementation issues, advantages, disadvantages, and challenges. This study may help practitioners in developing smart, intelligent, highly secure, and robust e-service applications in developing countries.

Chapter 6, "Design, Development and Testing of Web Applications: Security Aspects" by Ufuk Uçak and Gurkan Tuna, explains that with the changes and developments in software technologies, web applications have gained an important place by being actively used in many sectors. Due to the fact that web applications do not require installation costs and are easily accessible and operable, the increased usage rate in recent years makes these systems the target of cyber hackers. As a result of cyber-attacks, services are blocked, material and moral damages and data privacy violations are experienced. Within the scope of this study, web applications are explained, vulnerabilities that threaten software security and the measures that can be taken against these vulnerabilities are included. Within the scope of the study, security threats to web applications, security principles, secure software development lifecycles, test tools and hardware and software products used for security are examined. In addition, SAMM and BSIMM models, which are maturity models used in secure software development, are discussed.

Chapter 7, "Data Leakage and Privacy Concerns in Public Bug Bounty Platforms" by Muhammad Hamad, Altaf Hussain and Majida Khan Tareen report that According to a recent survey, 63% of the overall world population use the internet and 90% of the world's online digital data is generated after 2019. This transformation has led businesses to establish their digital presence to leverage history's biggest potential market. To establish a long-term relationship, these websites store a lot of PII (Personally Identifiable Information) and PHI (Protected Health Information). The PII and PHI are often very lucrative targets for hackers and as a result, cyber-attacks happen every 39 seconds. Due to this, customers become reluctant to share PII and PHI with any online business and need some assurance that their sensitive data would stay safe. General Data Protection Regulation (GDPR) was created to resolve this issue. GDPR is considered to be one of the toughest user privacy laws in the world which bound businesses to ensure a certain set of practices for the handling of sensitive customer data. To ensure that customers' credit card information is secure with a specific business, Payment Card Industry Data Security Standard (PCI DSS) compliance is necessary. Bug Bounty is a public platform through which companies test their programs for penetration testing and reward testers/researchers/hackers with a certain amount of bounty. However, it has been observed that there is a very fine line between white, grey and black hat hackers and after finding some critical level bug, they could give a wrong report to the company and make more money by selling this zero-day bug on the dark web or black market. So again sanctity of business and assurance of customers' data privacy is again in question. This chapter would cover a detailed study and review of different cyber security compliance bodies, penetration testing processes and their types, hacker's types, public and private bug bounty processes and their platforms and would also help one in understanding legal bindings in case of deviation from standard document for "Rules of Engagement". The overall chapter will aid the businesses to maintain reputation and avoid cyber-attacks and also it would help customers with sensitive data to take intelligent decisions regarding PII.

Chapter 8, "On the Current State of Privacy Risks in Software Requirement Elicitation Techniques" by Zartasha Saeed, Shahab Haider, Zulfiqar Ali, Muhammad Arshad and Iftikhar Alam, explains that the requirement engineering encompasses five activities: feasibility investigation, elicitation, analysis, specification, and validation. Requirement engineering has achieved immense appeal among researchers and developers. During the elicitation step, data are gathered from several stack holders. Hence, if the data is shared with a third party, the integrity of the entire system, process, and data may be compromised, posing privacy risks. This paper proposes a comparative analysis of the prominent strategies, including privacy breach aspects, to achieve this objective. We picked 32 techniques from various project settings for examination. This study may assist analysts in acquiring the necessary knowledge and assist project management teams in selecting the most effective and secure elicitation approaches relative to the nature of projects.

Chapter 9, "Privacy and Accessibility of Liberation Movement Archives of South Africa" by Nkholedzeni Sidney Netshakhuma, assessed the privacy and access of the liberation movements archives of South Africa. The study is based on my personal experience of working with the liberation movement archives and a review of literature on privacy and accessibility. The discussion was based on the liberation movements archives, privacy legislation, accountability, purpose specifications, donation of third-party archives, information quality, confidentiality and security of archives, electronic records management systems, digitization of liberation movement archives, data subject participation, Openness and transparency, public records, the establishment of governance structure, raising awareness and training, partnership and collaboration and access to liberation archives. Liberation movements are to ensure that they comply with the Protection of Personal Information Act 4 of 2013.

Chapter 10, "SDSCCM: Secure Distributed System Communication for Cloud-based Manufacturing" by Danish Javeed, Tianhan Gao, Muhammad Shahid Saeed, Zeeshan Jamil and Rafi Ullah Khan, investigates that the current century has witnessed a prodigious expansion in scientific innovations contributing toward the betterment of humanity. The astonishing advancements in digital communications have facilitated various spheres of our lifestyle including the manufacturing sector. A plethora of cutting-edge technologies is rubbing shoulders to revolutionize manufacturing trends. Distributed system communications introduce a new concept of digital collaboration among a diversified range of scattered communication nodes. The individual resources of multiple nodes are intelligently integrated to formulate an aggregated impact that yields phenomenal productivity. The smart connectivity among various heterogeneous nodes may familiarize the network with an extended variety of potential security threats. The literature environs a bulk of security solutions proposed to overcome these challenges. This research study provides a comprehensive elaboration of these security threats along with the security practices designed to encounter such activities.

Chapter 11, "Security in Internet-of-Things, Requirements, Challenges and Open Issues" by Said Ul Abrar, Kamran Ullah, Saleem Zahid, Mohib Ullah, Irfan Ullah Khan, and Muhammad Inam Ul Haq, explores that electronic devices, cognitive computing and sensing enable the deployment of Internet-of-things (IoTs) with a huge application domain. However, resource constraints such as low computing powers, and limited storage IoT infrastructures are vulnerable to a variety of cyber-attacks. In Dark-Net the address space developed as designated unrestricted internet address space anticipated to be used by trustworthy hosts anywhere in the world, therefore, any communication activity is presumed to be unwanted and particularly treated as a probe, backscatter, or misconfiguration. This chapter investigates and evaluates the operation of Dark-Net Traffic Detection Systems in IoT networks. Moreover, the most recent work done to ensure security in the IoTs network has been discussed. In particular, the areas of privacy provisioning, lightweight cryptographic framework, secure routing, robustness and DoS attacks have been addressed. Moreover, based on the analysis of existing state-of-the-art protocols, the security requirements and challenges are highlighted along with identified open issues.

Chapter 12, "Users' Privacy in IoT" by Majida Khan Tareen, Altaf Hussain, and Muhammad Hamad, explains that the data gathered about individual users on IoT may include very intimate and private information. IoT devices are frequently distributed over the world, allowing for real-time communication between linked devices. Recently, a much broader range of IoT devices are connected to the network i.e., vehicles, household appliances, medical equipment, electric meters and controls, street lights, traffic controls, smart TVs, and digital assistants like Amazon Alexa and Google Home have all been targeted. These devices collect and transmit a huge amount of data daily via the Internet for various purposes. Users are mostly unaware of the fact that how much information is gathered and how it is utilized or shared with others. These devices constitute a privacy risk because this data can be utilized for malevolent reasons. Traditional cyber systems connect general-purpose computers, and IoT systems frequently connect highly specialized devices that are developed for specific purposes with limited programmability and customizability. Furthermore, unlike the highly centralized method of aggregating storage and processing power in huge data centres, IoT devices normally store and process data in a distributed manner. In addition, unlike traditional cyber systems, IoT systems also include sensors that collect data from the physical environment, so they are sometimes referred to as cyber-physical systems. With the presence of sensors and distributed nature of processing and storing data, IoT devices are highly vulnerable from a privacy point of view. Therefore, privacy experts are concerned about how data is gathered, used, and shared across various networked devices and data recipients to prevent user privacy risks. According to statista.com, the number of IoT devices is expected to triple, from 9.7 billion in 2020 to more than 29 billion in 2030. Hence as a result of these interconnected devices expanding day by day and user privacy issues (i.e., password stealing, information and identity stealing, intruding, corrupting information, etc), privacy experts and researchers are very much concerned about preventing user privacy issues. They developed many Privacy Enhancing Technologies (PETs) (i.e., Blind Signature, Group Signature, Attribute-Based Credentials (ABCs), Anonymous and pseudonymous data authentication, Onion routing, Encrypted Communications, etc.) to prevent user privacy risks in IoT. Even though there are numerous algorithms and schemes for overcoming privacy concerns, still there is a need for advanced methods to secure IoT devices and avoid breaches.

Chapter 13, "Adoption of GDPR for Personal Data Protection in Smart Cities" by Pedro Pina, reports that the digital infrastructure of smart cities necessarily implies collecting big amounts of personal and its subsequent processing by software and applications designed to acquire analytical capabilities regarded to public spaces to enable efficient control over it. In the European Union legal context, aiming to densify the principle of informational self-determination, the General Data Protection Regulation (GDPR) has provided citizens with greater power and control over their data, turning the responsibilities of smart city administrators towards citizens much heavier. This chapter aims to analyse the impact on personal data and democratic public spaces derived from smart cities activities, to present the rights granted to individuals by the GDPR and its applicability to smart cities, and to make some recommendations regarding the implementation and the adaptation of the Regulation to the specific case of a smart city, not only to preserve a high-level level of privacy protection but also as a means to promote democratic solutions in public spaces.

Chapter 14, "Artificial Intelligence (AI)-based Intrusion Detection System for IoT-enabled Networks: A State-of-the-art Survey" by Danish Javeed, TianHan Gao, and Zeeshan Jamil, explain that the quality of human existence is improving day by day, and the Internet of things (IoT) has arisen as a new world of technology in the last two decades. It has aided the world through its applications in many sectors. However, while delivering several benefits, the extreme expansion of IoT devices makes them a potential target of attacks, which jeopardize the organization if left unchecked. Cyber security analysts have recently been using the DL-based model to detect and investigate malware to keep the organization secure from cyber-attacks. This work describes how AI-based techniques are utilized to identify cyber threats in the IoT environments better while considering these devices' heterogeneous and resource-constrained nature so that no extra burden is imposed on them. This work comprehensively evaluated the current solutions, challenges, and future directions in IoT security.

Rafi Ullah Khan
The University of Agriculture Peshawar, Pakistan

Acknowledgment

In the name of Allah, the Most Gracious and the Most Merciful Alhamdulillah, all praises to Allah for the strengths and His blessing in completing this thesis. Peace and Blessing be upon the lovely prophet Mohammed (SALLALLAHOU ALAYHE WASALLAM).

This edited volume would not have been possible without the contributions of the talented authors who generously shared their research and insights. I want to express my gratitude to each and every one of them for their hard work and dedication.

I also want to thank my editorial advisory board, and reviewers, who provided valuable feedback and guidance. Their expertise and attention to detail ensured that this book met the highest standards of scholarship.

Special thanks go to our publisher, who believed in this project and provided us with the resources and support we needed to bring it to fruition. We are grateful for their commitment to academic excellence and their dedication to disseminating important research.

I would also like to acknowledge the support of our families and loved ones, who provided encouragement and understanding throughout the long process of editing this book. Your support was invaluable and greatly appreciated.

Finally, I want to acknowledge the scholars who came before us, whose groundbreaking research and insights laid the foundation for the work presented in this volume. Thank you for paving the way and inspiring us to continue pushing the boundaries of knowledge in our field.

Rafi Ullah Khan
The University of Agriculture, Peshawar, Pakistan

Chapter 1
State of the Art in Distributed Privacy–Preserving Protocols in Private Web Search

Mohib Ullah

The University of Agriculture, Peshawar, Pakistan

Arbab Waseem Abbas

The University of Agriculture, Peshawar, Pakistan

Lala Rukh

The University of Agriculture, Peshawar, Pakistan

Kamran Ullah

The University of Agriculture, Peshawar, Pakistan

Muhammad Inam Ul Haq

Khushal Khan Khattak University Karak, Karak, Pakistan

ABSTRACT

Web search engine (WSE) is an inevitable software system used by people worldwide to retrieve data from the web by using keywords called queries. WSE stores search queries to build the user's profile and provide personalized results. User search queries often hold identifiable information that could compromise the user's privacy. Preserving privacy in web searches is the primary concern of users from various backgrounds. Many techniques have been proposed to preserve a person's web search privacy with time. Some techniques preserve an individual's privacy by obfuscating a user's profile by sending fictitious queries with the original ones. Others hide their identity and preserve privacy through unlinkability. However, a distributed technique preserves privacy by providing unlinkability and obfuscation. In distributed protocols, a group of users collaborate to forward each other queries to WSE, providing unlinkability and obfuscation. This work presents a survey of distributed privacy-preserving protocols. The benefits, limitations, and evaluation parameters are detailed in this work.

DOI: 10.4018/978-1-6684-6914-9.ch001

INTRODUCTION

The world wide web (WWW) is a vast network of information and resources where users can access and search for a wide range of content, including text, images, videos, and audio (Khan & Ali, 2013; Khan, Ullah, Khan, Uddin, & Al-Yahya, 2021). Web search engines, such as Google and Bing, play a crucial role in helping users find the information they are looking for by processing large amounts of data and presenting relevant results based on their search queries. Search engines have become indispensable tools for Internet users as they allow easy and fast access to information on a global scale. Research has shown that people are becoming increasingly satisfied with the performance of search engines, but at the same time, they are also becoming increasingly concerned about their privacy (Ullah, 2020b). Using personalization algorithms by search engines to present search results and advertisements tailored to the user's interests is seen as both a strength and a weakness by different people.

On the one hand, personalized results can provide a more relevant and enjoyable experience for the user. On the other hand, it also raises privacy concerns as search engines collect and store large amounts of data about the user's activities, interests, and behaviours, which could be used for various purposes, including targeted advertising. Web search engines build a user profile based on various factors such as interests, preferences, and previous searches to provide more relevant results. This user profile can improve the accuracy of search results but also raises privacy concerns as it reveals sensitive information about the user. The user's profile contains their unique I.D., name, employer's details, location, and potentially sensitive information such as their health status, political views, religion, etc. (Cooper, 2008). As a result, users are often forced to trade off accuracy for privacy, which can result in less relevant search results (Dan & Davison, 2016). Search engines must balance the need for personalized results with user privacy protection.

A survey conducted in 2012 showed that many users were concerned about the privacy implications of web search engines recording their data and search queries (Ullah, 2020b). The query log, which records users' search activities, is a valuable resource for search engines as it helps them to provide more relevant results (Kaaniche, Masmoudi, Znina, Laurent, & Demir, 2020). However, the storage of query logs also poses a significant privacy threat, as this data can be disclosed to advertising agencies and media, potentially revealing sensitive information about users. The release of the AOL log in 2006, where twenty million queries generated by 658000 users over three months were published, is a well-known example of a privacy breach (Barbaro, Zeller, & Hansell, 2006; Wang, Liu, & Wang, 2020). This incident highlights the need for search engines to implement strong privacy policies and measures to protect user data and ensure users' privacy.

In some cases, web search engines may be required by court order to disclose individual queries as part of legal proceedings, such as divorce or civil lawsuits. These incidents have raised further concerns about the privacy of users' search data and the security of their personal information. The 2014 incident, where 80 million health records were lost by the second-largest insurance company in the U.S., highlights the need for better security measures to protect sensitive information (Mathews-Hunt, 2016; Yang, Onik, Lee, Ahmed, & Kim, 2019). These incidents have sparked a movement for privacy preservation among online community members and have led to questions about the privacy policies of the WSE. These incidents put a question mark on WSEs' policy regarding user privacy.

So far, many techniques have been proposed to protect users' privacy during their Web searches. These techniques can be classified into five major classes, i.e., distributed techniques, stand-alone methods, query scrambling, third-party infrastructure, and hybrid techniques. This chapter overviews the most prominent privacy-aware web search schemes and techniques. The classification of these privacy-preserving schemes and solutions is shown in Figure 1.

The chapter's organization, as described in sections 2, 3, and 4, helps to provide a clear overview of the current state of privacy-aware web search schemes, present a conclusive summary of these schemes, and discuss future directions in this field. This structured presentation can make it easier for readers to understand the key concepts and developments in privacy-aware web searches.

Figure 1. Taxonomy of private web search schemes

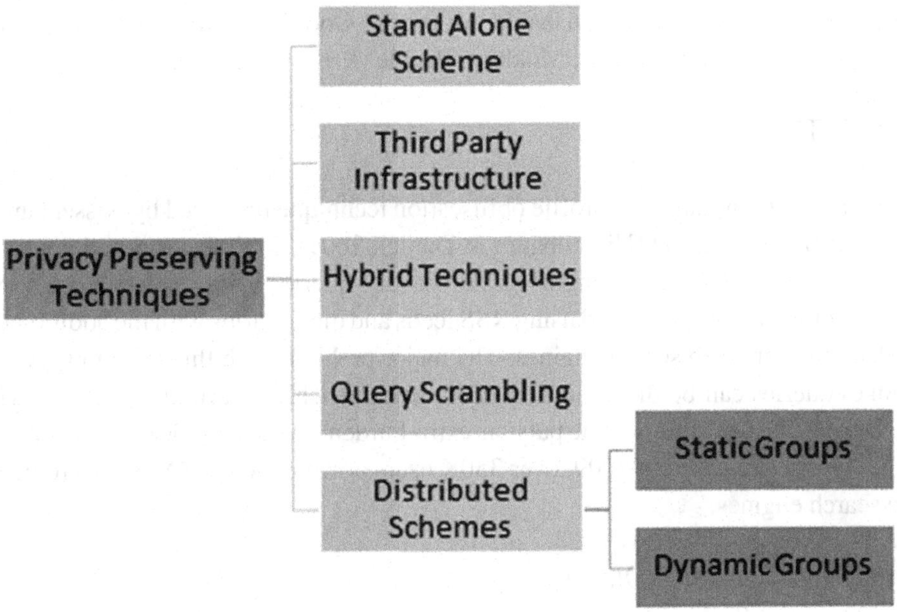

2. State of the Art

The importance of Web search privacy is undeniable and is an active research area. Many research efforts to preserve the user's privacy are made daily. Currently, many techniques and tools are available for privacy-preserved web searches. These techniques can be classified into five major classes, i.e. stand-alone methods, third-party infrastructure, hybrid techniques, query scrambling and distributed techniques. The stand-alone and query scrambling methods provide indistinguishability to the user by obfuscating their profile, whereas the third-party infrastructure and distributed techniques provide unlinkability between the user query and identity. The classification of these privacy-preserving schemes and solutions is shown in Figure 1. In this section, we present a brief description of each technique.

Stand-Alone Schemes

Stand-alone methods, also known as single-party systems, aim to achieve indistinguishability by sending fake queries alongside the original queries to mask the user's profile. They are often offered as browser plugins and have the advantage of not suffering from network delay. Some examples of stand-alone techniques are discussed in this section.

GooPIR

GooPIR is a user profile obfuscation technique proposed by Domingo-Ferrer et al. to hide the user-intended query from the web search engine (Domingo-Ferrer, Solanas, & Castellà-Roca, 2009). In GooPIR, the user query is broken down into several keywords, and then every keyword is masked with false keywords and submitted to the web search engine. These masking keywords are chosen to have a frequency similar to the target keywords. This technique was ineffective as the machine-generated mask words are easily detectable and distinguishable. Moreover, GooPIR is vulnerable to a similarity attack proposed by Petit et al. (Petit, Cerqueus, Mokhtar, Brunie, & Kosch, 2015).

Track Me Not (TMN)

Track Me Not (TMN) is another user profile obfuscation technique proposed by Nissenbaum and Howe as a user browser plugin in 2009 (Nissenbaum & Daniel, 2009). In their proposed approach, the user query is submitted to the web search engine and other fake queries to add noise to users' profiles. The fake queries are automatically generated using RSS feeds and dictionaries with the additional feature that TMN can select different web search engines. The major problem with this technique is that machine-generated (fake) queries can be distinguished easily using machine learning techniques (Khan, 2020; Peddinti & Saxena, 2010). Moreover, it puts an extra burden on communication (Ullah, 2020b). According to the statistics released in 2009, over 350K users downloaded TMN to ensure their privacy in front of web search engines.

Dissociating Privacy Agent (DisPA)

Dissociating Privacy Agent (DisPA) was proposed by Juarez and Torra (Juarez & Torra, 2015) in 2015 to hide users' intentions from the web search engine. DisPA creates a different profile of a single user, where each profile represents a specific user interest such as sports, health, recreation and others. The profiles are created using multiple cookies. Each user query is first evaluated by DisPA for profile selection and then submitted to the web search engine using recommended profile (cookies). DisPA aims to hide sufficient user information from Web search engines.

Stand-Alone Schemes Comparative Summary

Table 1 shows the comparison between stand-alone schemes presented in section 2.1. A qualitative comparison is indicated using the following five symbols: "❶"shows very bad, "❷"shows bad, "❸"shows neutral, "❹"shows good, and "❺"shows excellent scores. The "✓"shows the feature's availability while "✗" shows the non-availability of the feature. Whereas "N.A" shows that this feature does not apply to the selected scheme.

Table 1. Stand-alone schemes comparative summary

Technique	Fake Queries Source	Privacy	Personalized Result	Performance	Prone to Attacks	Previous Knowledge of fake queries	Scrambling Method
GooPIR	Dictionary	❸	❷	❺	✓	✗	NA
TrackMeNot	RSS Feeds	❸	❸	❺	✓	✓	NA
DisPa	-	❸	❹	❹	✓	✓	Generic Cookies

Third-Party Infrastructure

The third-party infrastructure offered unlinkability to the users from their queries in front of the web search engine. They are third-party service providers, some of which provide their infrastructure, such as proxy services like Anonymizer1 and Scroogle2, while some use the infrastructure of other willing users such as The Onion Routing (TOR) (Syverson, Dingledine, & Mathewson, 2004). Additionally, many web search service providers claim that they do not maintain user profiles such as Ixquick (Bradley, 2000), DuckDuckgo (Parsania, Kalyani, & Kamani, 2016) and others. Other examples of third-party infrastructure are VPN (Virtual Private Networks) (Seid & Lespagnol, 1998), Mixed Networks (Chaum, 1981), Web Mixes (Berthold, Federrath, & Köpsell, 2001), RAC (Mokhtar, Berthou, Diarra, Quéma, & Shoker, 2013) and others. This section will only discuss the popular solutions for personal web searches using the third-party infrastructure.

The Onion Routing (TOR)

The Onion Routing (TOR) was proposed by Dingledine et al. (Syverson et al., 2004) that uses a group of volunteer users who act as relay routers and provide privacy to the actual user. The TOR network consists of multiple proxies that hide the user's I.P. address (identity), but it is not specially designed to provide web search privacy to the users. The major problem with TOR is that it provides anonymity to the users at the Network layer of the OSI model. While the web search engine can identify the user at the application layer of the OSI model.

Scroogle

Scroogle was a privacy-aware third-party proxy service launched from 2003 till 2012 (Manoj & Jacob, 2012). Scroogle was a proxy service used to submit queries to Google on behalf of users. It was a popular service among users who wanted to retrieve data from Google privately, and before it went offline, it answered more than 350K daily queries. As a proxy service like ZenMate and Anonymizer, Scroogle also started profiling users like web search engines.

Third-Party Infrastructure Comparative Summary

Table 2 shows the comparison between selected Third-Party Infrastructure. A qualitative comparison is indicated using the following five symbols: "❶"shows very bad, "❷"shows bad, "❸"shows neutral,

"❹"shows good, and "❺"shows excellent scores. The "✓" shows the feature's availability while " ✗ " shows the non-availability of the feature.

Table 2. Third-party infrastructure comparative summary

Technique	Performance	Personalized Results	Anonymity		Tolerate Free-Riders	Prone to Attacks	Unlinkability
			Sender	Receiver			
Tor	❷	❷	✗	✗	✗	✓	✓
VPN	❸	❷	✗	✗	✗	✓	✓
Scroogle	❸	❷	✗	✗	✗	✓	✓
Web Mixes	❷	❷	✓	✓	✗	✓	✓
Mixed Network	❷	❷	✗	✗	✗	✓	✓
RAC	❶	❷	✓	✓	✓	✓	✓

Query Scrambling Techniques

The query scrambling technique was proposed by Arampatzis et al. (Arampatzis, Drosatos, & Efraimidis, 2015) to deceive web search engines into making users' actual profiles. Query scrambling is a self-privacy enforcing technique in which a user query is broken down and transformed into small and similar type multiple queries but with different terms. The result for each query is then collected and descrambled to get the answer. The major drawback of the query scrambling technique is poor quality results that loosely match the actual query. Moreover, it was not designed to hide the user's identity.

Hybrid Techniques

Hybrid privacy-aware web search techniques aim to provide the user with the utmost web search privacy by combining two or more techniques. The available hybrid web search privacy techniques usually combine indistinguishability and unlinkability techniques to achieve better privacy. This section discusses the most popular hybrid web search privacy preservation techniques.

PEAS (Private Efficient and Accurate Web Search)

Private Efficient and Accurate Web Search (PEAS) (Petit et al., 2015) is a hybrid web search privacy preservation technique proposed by Petit et al. in 2015. PEAS uses unlinkability (proxy server) and indistinguishability (fake queries) techniques. PEAS add a K number of fictitious queries with the user's original query using logical OR and then sends it to the web search engine using proxy services. According to the experimental results compared to GooPIR, less than 19% of queries were linked to the original users while using PEAS. However, even with this marvellous performance of PEAS compared to GooPIR, PEAS stood weak against adverse collaborating proxies servers.

X-Search

X-Search (Mokhtar et al., 2017) is another hybrid privacy-preserving solution successor to PEAS proposed by Mokhtar et al. in 2017. The working of the X-Search is the same as PEAS; they add fictitious queries with original user queries and send them through proxy servers. However, instead of untrusted proxy services, they used Software Guard Extensions (SGX), a secure proxy platform proposed by intel (Xing, Shanahan, & Leslie-Hurd, 2016). Using this trusted platform, they eliminate the problem of untrusted proxy services. However, according to Pires et al. (Pires et al., 2018), PEAS and X-Search are ineffective as the web search engine blocks them.

Privacy-Preserving Framework using DLT and TOR

Raza et al. proposed a hybrid web search privacy protection framework (Raza, Han, & Hwang, 2020) that is comprised of TOR (The Onion Routing) and DLT (Distributed Ledger Technology). Their proposed framework mainly addresses the question of whether web search engines can give biased results against user queries due to political, geo-political or any other reason that web search engines may track the user. To ensure user privacy, their proposed framework used TOR nodes and blockchain technology, where Tor nodes provide anonymity to the users, and the blockchain technology ensures protection from malicious users.

Hybrid Techniques Comparative Summary

Table 3 shows the comparison between selected Hybrid Techniques presented in section 2.4. A qualitative comparison is indicated using the following five symbols: "❶"shows very bad, "❷"shows bad, "❸"shows neutral, "❹"shows good, and "❺"shows excellent scores. The "✓ "shows the feature's availability while " ✗ " shows the non-availability of the feature. Whereas "N.A" and "N.T" are not applicable and not tested on the selected scheme.

Table 3. Hybrid techniques comparative summary

Technique	Personalized Result	Performance	Privacy	Prone to Attacks	Indistinguishability		Unlinkability				
					Fake Queries Source	Previous Knowledge of fake queries	Anonymity		Tolerate Free-Riders	Trusted Nodes System
							Sender	Receiver		
PEAS	❸	❹	❸	✓	Disjoint set of Group Profile	✓	✓	✓	✓	None
X-Search	❸	❸	❹	NT	Disjoint-set of Group Profile	✓	✓	✓	✓	SGX
DLT and TOR	❷	❷	❹	N.T.	N.A.	NA	✓	✓	✓	Blockchain

Distributed Schemes

Unlike stand-alone schemes, distributed web search privacy preservation schemes work with the co-operation of multiple users through which their queries are routed. There are two major categories in distributed web search privacy preserving schemes, i.e. indistinguishability and unlinkability. In the indistinguishability scheme, the user profile is obfuscated with actual queries of other users in distributed schemes. While in unlinkability, the user queries are submitted to the search engine by other group users. There are many distributed privacy preserve web search techniques available. This section will discuss the popular distributed web search privacy preservation schemes.

Unlinkability Solutions

Unlinkability is one of the popular privacy-preserved web search techniques aiming to dissociate users from their queries to mislead Web search engines. The prominent examples of Unlinkability solutions are UPIR and its different variants and CoWSA. This section will discuss the popular Unlinkability schemes for privacy-preserving web searches.

User Private Information Retrieval Protocol (UPIR)

User Private Information Retrieval (UPIR) was proposed by Domingo-Ferrer et al. in 2008 (Domingo-Ferrer & Bras-Amorós, 2008). They created a scenario of community (group) users who submit a query to the WSE on behalf of each other. The primary aim of this technique is to hide the user's intention from the web search engine and the other group members. For that purpose, they designated a shared memory location where the users place their queries. Other group members access the shared memory location, submit that query to the web search engine, and place the reply back on the same memory location where the query originator can retrieve it. For confidentiality purposes, the queries and replies are encrypted using symmetric key encryption techniques (Ullah, 2020a). The major weaknesses of this protocol are that query contents are visible to every group member due to shared encryption key, significant delay, and prone to intersection attack. Moreover, if the shared memory is compromised, it can link the queries to the users' I.P. addresses.

Optimal Configuration UPIR

Klara and Bras-Amoros (Stokes & Bras-Amorós, 2010) proposed an optimal configuration for the UPIR protocol to minimize the query response time delay and provide the user more privacy by adding multiple shared memory locations. In the previous version of UPIR, the privacy against the web search engine was satisfactory, but it was exposed to group members due to the shared encryption key. Klara and Bras-Amoros proposed a (v, b, r, k) - 1 design in which v represents the number of users, b represents shared memory location, and r represents the number of users accessing that memory location. K represents the number of users accessing that memory location. They proved that user anonymity is diffused among k(r-1) users.

Swanson and Stinson's UPIR Version

Swanson and Stinson found a crucial drawback in the optimal configuration version of UPIR, due to which the user's privacy can be significantly compromised (Swanson & Stinson, 2011). In the optimal configuration version, when v=r(k-1)+1, it shows that all the nodes in the group are the user's neighbour and webs; each engine can easily detect that all the users in the group submit the query, but the initiator node. Moreover, the protocol is also prone to intersection attacks. Swanson and Stinson proposed that original users must be allowed to submit their query to the web search engine with the probability of 1/v to avoid suspicion.

CoWSA

CoWSA is privacy-preserving cooperative computation for personalized web search applications proposed by Kaaniche et al. in 2020 (Kaaniche et al., 2020). CoWSA is a decentralized private web search solution that empowers the end-user to ensure his/her security, mitigate single-point failure and control his/her personal data. CoWSA comprises five entities, i.e. Web Search Engine, Client, User, trusted authorities and third parties. It is a proxy-based solution in which an interest-based group is created among users. The query is submitted using a randomly selected relay path and submitted to the web search engine using an aggregated profile of the final query submitting user.

Unlinkability Solutions in Distributed Schemes Comparative Summary

Table 4 compares selected Unlinkability Solutions in Distributed Schemes presented in section 2.5.1. A qualitative comparison is indicated using the following five symbols: "❶"shows very bad, "❷"shows bad, "❸"shows neutral, "❹"shows good, and "❺"shows excellent scores. Whereas "N.A" shows that this feature does not apply to the selected scheme.

Table 4. Unlinkability solutions in distributed schemes

Protocol	Group Type	Group Status	Vulnerability	Personalized Results	Privacy Protection	
					Peer	WSE
UPIR	S/M	Dynamic	Input-replacement, DoS	❸	❷	❸
UPIR Optimal Configuration	S/M	Static	Input-replacement, DoS, Intersection attack	❷	❷	❶
UPIR Swanson and Stinson	S/M	Dynamic	DoS, Intersection attack	❷	❸	❸
CoWSA	NA	NA	QuPiD Attack	❸	NA	❸

Indistinguishability Solutions

Indistinguishability is another popular privacy-preserved web search technique that aims to retrieve the required information from the web search engine or database and reveal the users' true intentions. The indistinguishability solutions use different strategies to preserve user privacy against web search engines or databases, such as submitting queries on behalf (Khan, Islam, Ullah, Aleem, & Iqbal, 2019; Reiter & Rubin, 1998; Romero-Tris, Viejo, & Castellà-Roca, 2015) of other users or accessing multiple copies of databases (Chor, Kushilevitz, Goldreich, & Sudan, 1998) and others. In this section, we will discuss the popular Indistinguishability schemes.

Private Information Retrieval

Private Information Retrieval (PIR was proposed by Chor et al. in 1998 for privacy-preserved information retrieval from public or private databases (Chor et al., 1998). The proposed solution was based on the supposition that multiple copies of the databases are available in different locations and accessible from anywhere. In the proposed technique, the user breaks their query into small queries and sends these queries to different copies of the databases. After retrieving the results from the different copies of the same database, the user performs the exclusive OR operation on the results to get the desired information. The same idea was proposed by Kushilevitz and Ostrovsky (Kushilevitz & Ostrovsky, 1997) for single databases by introducing algebraic properties and public key encryption.

Crowds

Another famous method in indistinguishability was Crowds, proposed by Reiter and Rubin (Reiter & Rubin, 1998) for retrieving data from web search engines without revealing the user's identity. They exploited the fact that WSE identifies the user by their I.P. address. So they proposed a collaborative environment, Crowds, in which a group of users is created using a server and a client-side user application, "Jando". The user's queries are then forwarded to a group for shuffling and submitted to the web search engine through a different user. The same track is followed to send the reply back to the user from the web search engine. They also proposed a privacy estimation mechanism called degree of anonymity (shown in Figure 2) to analyze the privacy exposure of the user. The major flaw of the Crowds was that it does not offer any privacy to the user query against the local eavesdropper; every node can see the contents of user queries.

Useless User Profile (UUP)

To solve the issue of local eavesdroppers Castella-Roca and Herrera-Joancomarti (Castellà-Roca, Viejo, & Herrera-Joancomartí, 2009) proposed Useless User Profile (UUP) technique in 2009. In UUP, the central server creates a group of users in which the query is forwarded and shuffled in an encrypted way anonymously. The query is then forwarded to the web search engine by any group member after receiving the results from the web search engine. The result is then broadcasted in the group to avoid linking the query results to the original user. They use the group key encryption technique proposed by El-Gamal (ElGamal, 1985). The major weaknesses of UUP were the failure of the protocol in case of a single adverse node. The results were broadcasted in clear text and latency.

Figure 2. Levels of degree of anonymity by Reiter and Rubin (Reiter & Rubin, 1998)

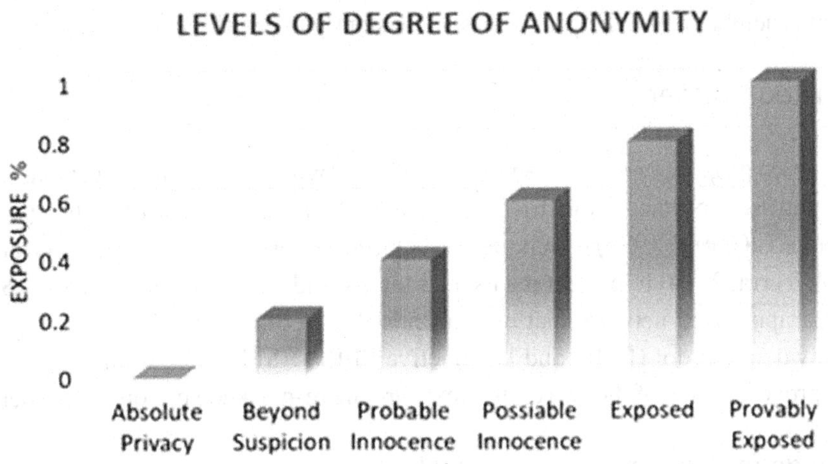

LEVELS OF DEGREE OF ANONYMITY

Lindell and Waisbard UUP

Lindell and Waisbard (Lindell & Waisbard, 2010) then evaluated the UUP from different aspects and found that UUP is secure in the case of semi-honest nodes but can be compromised even with a single adverse node. They further concluded that UUP is susceptible to Input-Tagging attacks, Stage skipping attacks, Input-Replacement attacks, Target public key attacks, and QuPiD attacks (Khan, 2020; Khan et al., 2020; Khan, Ullah, & Islam, 2016; Khan et al., 2021). To avoid these problems, they proposed the following steps in UUP: (i) query encryption and (ii) use of Mixnet (Chaum, 1981) for the query shuffling process. The Lindell and Waisbard version of UUP was very costly in terms of computational time, and it also introduced extra delay in the information retrieval process from the web search engine. Moreover, Liu and Yan (Cao, Liu, & Yan, 2016) reported that this improved version of UUP can be compromised in the verification stage and during the shuffling time, the actual query can be replaced by the fake query.

Private Web Search with Social Network

Viejo and Castella-Roca proposed a privacy-preserving web search technique that uses social network users (Viejo & Castellà-Roca, 2010). In their proposed technique, the user does not need to generate the group; instead, they use their social media contact as a group member. They shuffle their queries among their friends' circle and then submit them to the web search engine. As the group members are friends, there is very little probability of an adverse node entering the group. However, it is also one of the weaknesses of this protocol in case of multiple collaborators to find the query source. Furthermore, they did not use any encryption for query.

Erola et al. Social Network Private Web Search

Moreover, Erola et al. found a problem with a selfish node (a node that does not forward queries of other nodes) in this protocol (Erola, Castellà-Roca, Viejo, & Mateo-Sanz, 2011). To solve the problem of selfish nodes, Erola et al. proposed a selfishness function that calculates the node's selfishness level. However, the major weakness in that protocol was the static group because web search engines could easily find the group members, and the protocol was constantly under threat of intersection attacks.

UUP with Untrusted Partner

Viejo and Castella-Roca proposed an extended version of UUP with a novel idea of private web search in the presence of an untrusted partner (Romero-Tris, Castella-Roca, & Viejo, 2014). They used El-Gamal group key encryption (ElGamal, 1985) techniques and Optimized Arbitrary Size (OAS) Banes Network (Navarro-Arribas & Torra, 2014) to protect the user's identity and query contents. The OAS Banes Network is a directed graph-based network that uses all possible permutations for query shuffling. They used Plaintext Equivalence Proof (PEP), and Disjunctive PEP (DISPEP) functions as zero Knowledge proof technique to prove that one of the two cipher texts are the re-masked version of another cipher text.

Multiparty Methods for Privacy-Preserving Web Search

Viejo and Castella-Roca further improved their previous technique, i.e. UUP with an untrusted partner, by reducing the from 6.8 sec and 5.8 sec to 3.2 sec (Romero-Tris et al., 2015). They used the Optimized Arbitrary Size Banes Network for query shuffling, and every time a cipher text passed a switch, its value was re-masked and re-permuted, due to which the probability of finding the exact user is $1/n$. Their new proposed multiparty method is more secure and fast than its previous versions.

Co-Utile

Co-Utile is a self-enforcing protocol for privacy-preserved web searches proposed by Domingo-Ferrer et al. to promote social welfare (Domingo-Ferrer, Martínez, Sánchez, & Soria-Comas, 2018). Co-Utile comprises mutually beneficial users (agents) who have a common interest in getting the information privately from the web search engine. They used a game-theory model for a single-hop query submission game scenario for two agents and multi-hop for multiple users. Before submission, all users check the impact of their desired query on their privacy exposure using entropy. The major weaknesses of Co-Utile are no privacy between the agents and serious delay issues.

Poshida

Poshida is a distributed privacy-preserving protocol proposed by Ullah et al. to preserve a user's privacy in web searching (Ullah, Khan, & Islam, 2016b). Poshida claimed to ensure indistinguishability and provided profile obfuscation in web searching by sending queries of other group users. Poshida, as a distributed protocol, consisted of entities like a user, central server, Query Forwarding Node (QFN) and Web Search Engine (WSE). A user was a person who wanted to search data on WSE and preserve their privacy. C.S. was a dedicated machine that was supposed to supervise the working of Poshida, including group creation, QFN selection etc. A QFN, selected by C.S., was supposed to forward the queries of all group members to the WSE and broadcast encrypted results in the group.

Figure 3. Query sending and result retrieval process of Poshida (Ullah et al., 2016b)

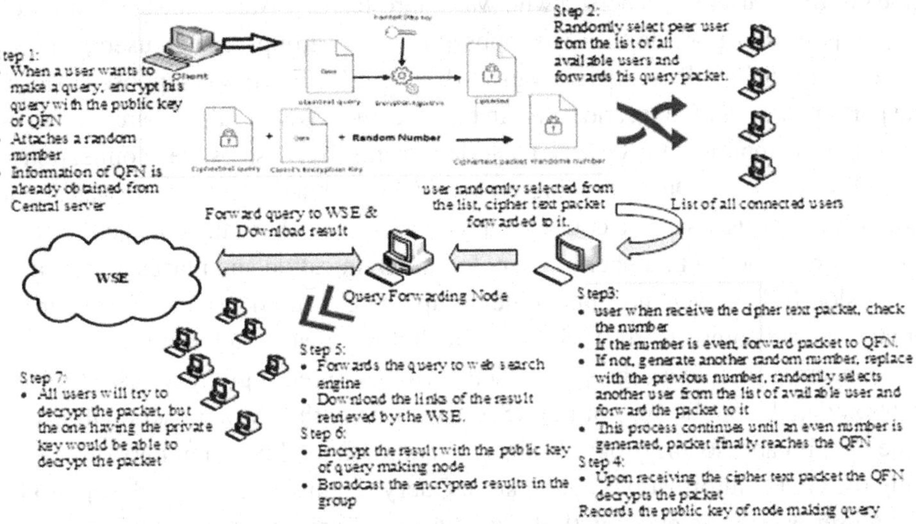

Similarly, WSE is a software system that searches Internet data and provides query results to the user (QFN). Poshida works in steps like group creation, query encryption & sending, query shuffling, query forwarding to WSE and results broadcasting. For a user to send a query, were required to connect to the central server first. The users had to send a connection request to the server. After receiving the 'n' number of requests, the central server created a group. Where 'n' was the size of the group. Poshida was tested for ten, twenty, and thirty users. After creating a group of n users, the C.S. also had to choose one user as a QFN. All users were supposed to be selected as QFN one by one.

A user selected as QFN had to provide a public key of the RSA algorithm for the encryption of the query. The C.S. then had to broadcast complete information about the group, including QFN details, the public key of QFN and others. Query sending and result retrieval process was the second step of Poshida the after the group creation process. For a user to send a query, they had to encrypt a query with the public key of QFN. The user then had to flip a coin to decide where to forward a query. If the flips resulted in the head, the query was forwarded to QFN. On the tail, a user had to forward it to a random group user. Such a process made the query shuffled among the group users. After receiving the query, the QFN decrypts it and sends it to WSE. After receiving the results from WSE, the QFN encrypted and broadcasted the results to the group members. The execution process of Poshida is shown in Figure 3.

Poshida ensured users' privacy such that no group member could see the query, as the query was encrypted with the public key of QFN. The QFN could not link a query with the user as the query was shuffled before arriving at the QFN. WSE could not build the actual profile of a user, as QFN had to forward the queries of all other group users. Hence, a user's profile is obfuscated with the profile of multiple users.

Poshida II

Ullah et al. introduced Poshida II, a multiple group's peer-to-peer protocol for private web search. Poshida II was an extension of Poshida, involving multiple groups (Ullah, Khan, & Islam, 2016a). Poshida II consisted of entities like users, a central server (C.S.), Group Query Forwarding Node (GQFN) and Web Search Engine (WSE). A user was a person who was interested in private web searching. Central Server was the core component of Poshida II. It is supposed to create groups, assign users, and participate in query shuffling and result broadcasting. Every group had their GQFN. It was supposed to forward queries to WSE, take part in query shuffling, and result in broadcasting. WSE is a software system that searches queries/data online and replies to the GQFN. Poshida II works in five steps, i.e., connection setup, group creation and GQFN selection, Query sending process, Query shuffling, query forwarding to WSE and results broadcasting. The user sends a connection request to the C.S. in the connection setup. The C.S. records the I.P. address and port number of users for communication and places a user in with a group having a vacant slot. If there were no slots in the group, the C.S. used to create a new group. Once the group count and size are complete, the C.S. selects a GQFN for each group.

Once the connection completes, the C.S. selects a GQFN for each group. A user selected as GQFN shares encryption details (public key) of the RSA algorithm with C.S. All users will act as GQFN no their turn. The C.S. broadcasts the group details (I.P. addresses and port numbers of each group member), including the GQFN information (public key). Query sending is the second step of Poshida II. To send a query, a user encrypts a query with the public key of any random GFQN and appends his/her encryption key, making a cipher packet. Figure 4 shows the query-sending process of Poshida II. The user then shuffles the query among the group member. The shuffling is performed in two phases, i.e., intra-group shuffling and inter-group shuffling. In the first phase, a user flips a biased coin to decide where to forward a query.

Figure 4. Query sending and intra-group shuffling process (Ullah, 2020b)

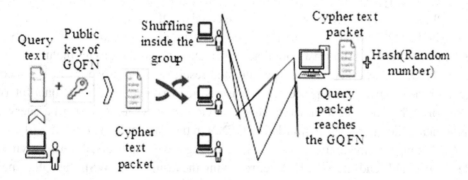

The probability of forwarding (pf) varies according to shuffle queries inside the group. When the result for coin tossing returns the head, the encrypted query packet is forwarded to the GQFN. Otherwise, the query packet is forwarded to a random group member. After a few shuffles, the packet reaches the GQFN. This shuffling disassociates the encrypted query from the users.

In the second shuffling phase, the query packet is shuffled among the GQFN to disassociate a query from the group. This shuffling is performed in the same way explained above. Each time a query packet arrives at GQFN, it decrypts it with the private key. The GQFN would only successfully decrypt the packet if encrypted with its public key. Figure 5 shows the encrypted query shuffling among the GQFNs.

The shuffling process concluded when the encrypted query packet arrived as destined GQFN. Query forwarding to the WSE and result retrieval is the next step of the Poshida II. After decrypting the cipher text, the GQFN forwards the query to the WSE. The WSE process the query and returns results to the GQFN. The GQFN encrypts the result with a user's encryption key and attaches the user's random number. The GQFN forwards the encrypted result packet to the C.S., which then forwards it to all GQFNs. The GQFNs forward the encrypted query packet to all users in the group. After checking the hash number, the user decrypts the encrypted result packet to retrieve the answer for the query sent.

Poshida II provided Privacy relative to the entities involved in forwarding queries to WSE, including group users, GQFNs, CS and WSE. Poshida II measured a user's profile privacy relative to the WSE through simulation using the privacy metric PEL. However, it did compute the privacy relative to the group users and C.S. in terms of probability.

Figure 5. Inter-group query shuffling (Ullah et al., 2016a)

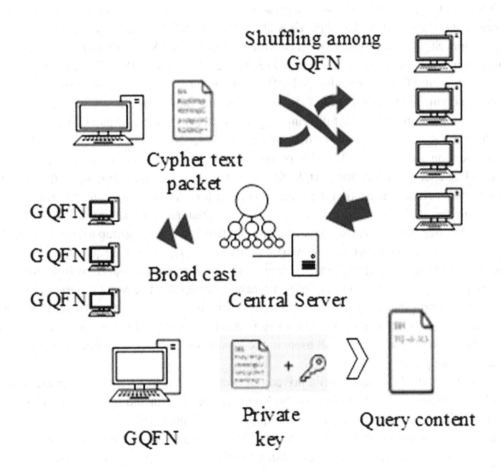

ObScure Logging (OSLo)

Ullah et al. proposed ObScure Logging (OSLo), another framework to protect and evaluate web search privacy in the healthcare domain (Ullah, Islam, Khan, Aleem, & Iqbal, 2019). OSLo is a distributed privacy-preserving protocol proposed to preserve and evaluate a user's local privacy and profile privacy. OSLo claims to preserve web search privacy relative to all entities forwarding queries to the WSE. Local privacy measures a user's privacy relative to the group users, CS and QFN, whereas profile privacy measures the privacy relative to the WSE. OSLo provides by making the query hidden from the group users through encryption and query shuffling. Profile privacy is achieved through obfuscation by forwarding queries of other group users. Local privacy is evaluated through the probabilistic advantage a curious entity has in linking a query with the user. Profile privacy computes the magnitude of profile obfuscation by forwarding the queries of other group users. Profile privacy is evaluated using a privacy metric, Profile Exposure Level (PEL).

OSLo consists of entities like users, Central Server (C.S.), a Search Query forwarding Client (SQFC) and Web Search Engine (WSE). A user is a person who wants to do the web search privately, and C.S. is the core entity of the OSLo. C.S. supervises all operations of OSLo, including connection setup and SQFC selection. SQFC is responsible for forwarding queries to the WSE and retrieving results. In contrast, WSE searches queries on the Internet and returns results to the QFN. OSLo executes in steps like connection setup, SQFC selection, Query shuffling and query sending & result retrieval process. First, a user sends a connection request to the C.S. After receiving the 'n' number of requests.

The C.S. creates a group. In the following step, the C.S. select one user as SQFC, who will be supposed to forward queries of all group members to the WSE. QFN share the public key, and port number for communication with the C.S. The C.S. broadcasts the details of users in the group and the SQFC information like encryption key and port details. To send a query, a user generates a query content, an encryption key for results encryption & a random number for verifying their query results and encrypts the query with the public key of SQFC, making an encrypted query packet. Shuffling is the next step of OSLo. In this step, the encrypted query packet is shuffled among the group user before reaching the SQFC. The user flips a coin to decide where to forward a query. The encrypted query packet is forwarded to a random user if the coin returns head. Otherwise, the encrypted query packet is forwarded to SQFC. After a few passes, the encrypted query packet reaches the SQFC. The SQFC decrypts the encrypted query packet, forwards the query to WSE, and retrieves the results for the query from WSE. The SQFC encrypts the results with a user's encryption key making an encrypted answer packet. The encrypted answer packet is broadcasted among all users in the group. The user with the decryption key would be able to decrypt the packet.

OSLo evaluates the local and profile privacy of a user. In Local Privacy, a user executing OSLo achieves both confidentiality and unlinkability. No group member, including users and C.S. apart from SQFC, could not see the query content, as the query is encrypted with the public key of SQFC. The probability of linking the query to the source from SQFC is given in Equation 1. Where n is the total number of users in the group, if C users collaborate with SQFC to link a query with the user, the probability of linking the query with the users is given in Equation 2.

$$Pr(S = Ui) = 1/(n-1) \tag{1}$$

$$Pr(S = Ui) = 1/(n-C) \tag{2}$$

In the case of profile privacy, the user is considered preserved if WSE cannot build an actual profile of a user. OSLo evaluates the profile privacy of a user for two situations, i.e. when self-query submission is allowed and when self-query submission is not allowed.

MG-OSLo

Multi-Group ObScure logging (MG OSLo) was proposed by Ullah et al. to preserve a user's privacy by employing multiple groups instead of a single group (Ullah et al., 2021). MG-OSLo was proposed to assess the local privacy for overlapping and non-overlapping group design and profile privacy when self-query submission is allowed and self-query submission is not permitted. MG-OSLo consists of entities like a user, Central server (CS), Query Forwarding Node (QFN) and Web Search Engine (WSE). MG-OSLo consists of 'b' groups, each with 'K' users. First, a user must connect to the C.S. The C.S. is responsible for group creation and management. Once the group count and size are complete, the C.S. select a QFN for each group and broadcasts the group details and its members to all users. To send a query to the WSE, a user first picks a QFN, then encrypts the query with the public key of the QFN and attaches their encryption keys with the encrypted query. After the query encryption process, the query is shuffled at two levels to disassociate the query and the user. The encrypted query is first shuffled among the group member by flipping a coin. Afterwards, the query is shuffled among the QFNs. These two shuffling levels make the query unlikable to the user or any group. The shuffling process completes when the query arrives at the terminus QFN. The QFN decrypts the query, forward it to the WSE and retrieves the results. The QFN encrypt the results with the user's encryption key and forwards it to all QFNs. Each QFN broadcasts the results in their respective group. The user with the decryption key would be able to decrypt the results. The query-sending and result-retrieval processes are depicted in figure 6.

MG-OSLo preserved local privacy through encryption, shuffling and profile privacy by forwarding queries of other group users. Local privacy is preserved if no entity can link a query with the users. As the query is encrypted with the public key of QFN, hence, no entity can see the query apart from the one public key utilized for encryption. Also, the query is shuffled among the group member and the QFNs making the query linkable with the user. As discussed above, there are two grouping approaches used in MG-OSLo, i.e., non-overlapping design and overlapping group design. In the non-overlapping group design, each user appears exactly in one group.

The performance of MG-OSLo is compared with OSLo and Co-utile in terms of PEL. Results show that MG-OSLo achieved 14.94% and 29% improved profile privacy than OSLo and Co-utile protocol for the group size of three users. A similar pattern has also been observed for higher group counts and sizes. MG-OSLo achieves better profile privacy because the profile is obfuscated with more users compared to both OSLo and co-utile. The chances of getting grouped with users with diverse interests are much higher.

PA-OSLO

All previously distributed privacy-preserving protocols performed random grouping of users. However, such groups can lead to a user grouping with people with similar interests. Such a case will not significantly obfuscate the user's profile. Profile Aware ObScure Logging (PaOSLo) was proposed by Ullah et al. to do a profile-aware grouping of users and to deal with the random grouping problem (Ullah et al., 2022). In PaOSLo, users are first clustered into groups having similar interests. In the following step, users from each cluster are selected to create a group of users having different interests. The rest of the group creation process is the same as of OSLo discussed above. The execution of PaOSLo share similarity with OSLo in the following ways. After the group has been created, the query-sending process, including encryption, query shuffling, query forwarding to WSE, results retrieval and result encryption and broadcasting, are the same as OSLo.

The experimentation of PaOSLo is performed with a subset of 1000 users of the AOL dataset. The similarity between the users' profiles is computed using the cosine similarity measure. After the similarity calculation, users are clustered into three, four and five clusters. Clustering is performed using the K-mean clustering algorithm. The experimentation of PaOSLo is performed for group sizes of three, four, and five users.

Results show that PaOSLo achieved 9.6% and 4.7% better privacy than the UUP and OSLo at the first degree of ODP (Open Directory Project) (Ullah et al., 2022). A similar pattern has been observed at the higher degrees of ODP. PaOSLo succeeded better in privacy because of the profile aware grouping than random grouping. Such groups made better profile obfuscation as users have different interests making the profile better obfuscated.

Figure 6. MG-OSLo: Query sending and result retrieval process (Ullah et al., 2021)

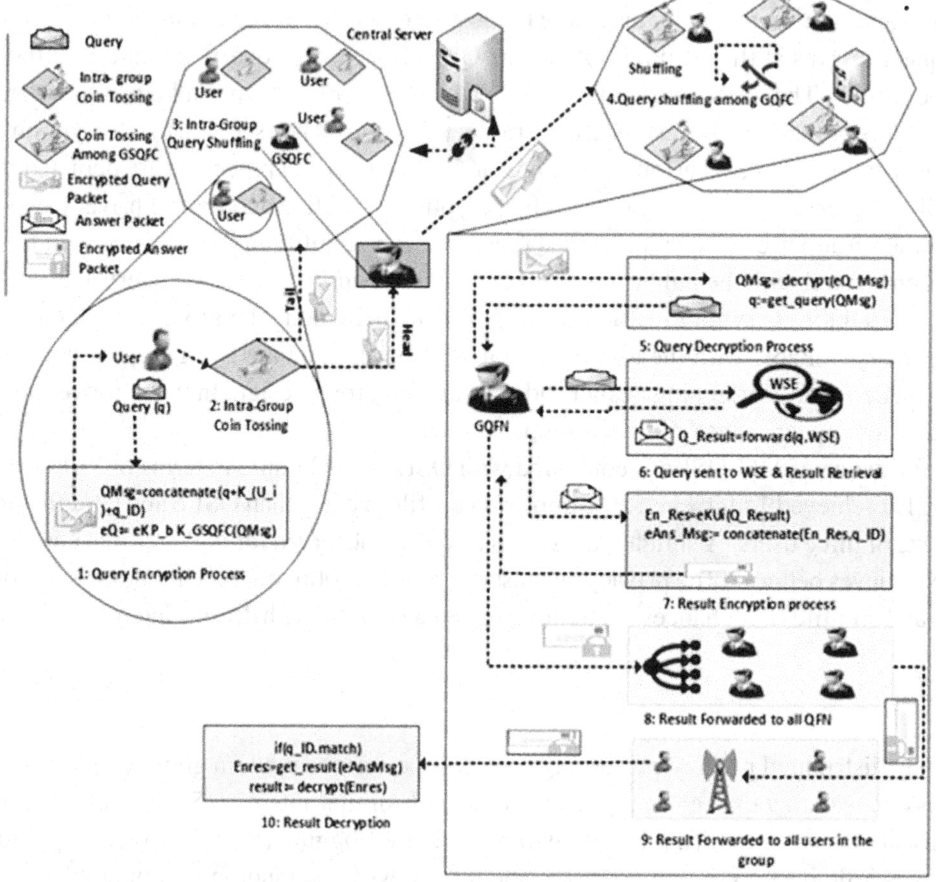

Indistinguishability Solutions in Distributed Schemes Comparative Summary

Table 4 compares selected Indistinguishability Solutions in Distributed Schemes presented in section 2.5.2. A qualitative comparison is indicated using the following five symbols: "❶"shows very bad, "❷"shows bad, "❸"shows neutral, "❹"shows good, and "❺"shows excellent scores. S shows a Single group, and S/M shows both Single and Multiple groups. Whereas "N.T" shows that this protocol is not tested for vulnerabilities.

Table 5. Indistinguishability solutions in distributed schemes comparative summary

Protocol	Group Type	Group Status	Encryption	Vulnerability	Personalized Results	Privacy Protection	
						Peer	WSE
Crowds	S	Static	Symmetric	Predecessor, DoS, Collaborating Peers	❸	❶	❶
UUP	S/M	Dynamic	No	DoS, Input Replacement, Targeted Public-key, Stage skipping, Input-tagging	❷	❶	❷
UUP Lindell et al.	S/M	Dynamic	Symmetric	Input-replacement, DoS, Verification stage attack	❷	❷	❷
UUP Social Network	S	Static	No	Predecessor, Denial of Service	❹	❶	❷
UUP Untrusted Partner	S/M	Dynamic	Asymmetric	Input-replacement, DoS, Intersection attack, Data Mining	❷	❹	❷
Co-Utile	S	Static	No	DoS	❸	❷	❷
Poshida	S	Dynamic	Asymmetric	NT	❸	❷	❷
Poshida II	S	Dynamic	Asymmetric	NT	❸	❷	❷
OSLo	S	Dynamic	Symmetric Asymmetric	NT	❷	❹	❸
MG-OSLo	M	Dynamic	Symmetric Asymmetric	NT	❷	❹	❸
PA-OSLo	S/M	Dynamic	Symmetric Asymmetric	NT	❶	❹	❹

CONCLUSION

Web searching is a vital part of our daily lives. Searching for data on the Internet is unavoidable these days. Web Search Engine (WSE)is the easiest way to find data on the Internet. However, WSEs record user searches as query logs and sell them to marketing agencies to generate revenue. The user searches (query logs) often contain sensitive information, and a leak of query logs can lead to serious privacy risks. This chapter discussed various privacy-preserving techniques, primarily focusing on distributed privacy-preserving techniques. This chapter discussed different methods of Web search privacy preservation schemes, including distributed schemes, query scrambling techniques, stand-alone schemes, third-party schemes and hybrid techniques.

Distributed protocols offer the advantages of unlinkability and indistinguishability, making them a promising approach to preserving privacy. However, some limitations to existing distributed protocols also need to be addressed. One limitation is the potential for significant delays in obtaining search results due to the distributed nature of the protocols. Another limitation is the potential for reduced result quality due to the anonymization of the query and the use of obfuscation techniques. Future research could explore the development of more efficient and scalable distributed protocols that can provide fast and accurate search results while preserving privacy to overcome the limitation. The balance of privacy and result quality may be achieved using new techniques such as secure multiparty computation and homomorphic encryption.

Distributed privacy-preserving protocols like UUP, Poshida, Poshida II, OSLo, MG-OSLo and PaO-SLo offer better protection to the users. Distributed privacy-preserving techniques provide both local Privacy (privacy relative to the group entities) and profile privacy (Privacy relative to the WSE). Local privacy in these protocols is achieved through encryption and query shuffling. In contrast, profile privacy is accomplished through obfuscation by forwarding other users' queries. UUP provided privacy relative to the group entities through encryption. However, UUP only computed the profile privacy using PEL, and it did not calculate the local privacy of a user. UUP is also vulnerable to machine learning attacks. Each UUP user could only forward a single query; afterwards, the group finishes.

Poshida provided privacy through encryption and profile obfuscation by employing a single group. The results in Poshida were also broadcasted in encrypted form, so no group member knows what has been searched. Poshida II used the concept of a multi-group. It has further improved the profile privacy of a user. OSLo also employed a single group but computed both a user's local privacy and the profile privacy of a user. Local privacy is achieved through both symmetric and asymmetric key cryptography. Local privacy is also computed using a probabilistic a curious entity has in linking a query with an individual. Profile privacy has been achieved by sending queries to the other group members. The results show that OSLo provided better obfuscation compared to the UUP. The MG-OSLo has addressed scalability by utilizing multiple groups. MG-OSLo provided and evaluated a user's local privacy and profile privacy of a user. MG-OSLo evaluated local privacy using overlapping and non-overlapping group designs. Balanced incomplete block design (BIBD) has been adapted to group users in MG-OSLo. Profile privacy achieved by MG-OSLo has also been compared with single group protocols (OSLo and UUP) for the situation when self-query submission is allowed and self-query submission is not permitted. The results show that MG-OSLo achieved better profile privacy than OSLo and UUP.

PaOSLo introduced profile-aware grouping compared to the random grouping of users. PaOSLo differs from existing single-group distributed protocols by clustering users having similar interests first. Later, creating a group of users having different interests. The results show that PaOSLo further improved the profile privacy of a user compared to the random group. Evaluating the privacy of distributed privacy-preserving by different machine learning-based attacks such as QuPiD and NN-QuPiD attacks is imperative.

FUTURE WORK

An alternative way of user profiling needs to be investigated in the future. The Web Search Engine maintains users' profiles in many ways to provide personalized results. A potential avenue for future research is the development of personalized privacy-preserving search protocols that can tailor search results to individual users while still protecting their privacy. More personalized search results while preserving privacy could be achieved using user profiling, contextual information, and machine learning techniques. It should also assess the trade-off between privacy and delay in distributed privacy-preserving protocols and compare their privacy with state-of-the-art protocols and stand-alone and hybrid schemes.

Similarly, investigating the impact of systematic grouping on the quality of the results is another crucial future effort, as there is an utmost need for privacy protection tools with that offer personalized results. The impact of profile-aware grouping on the search results and the delay caused by clustering needs to be measured in the future. The profile privacy shall also be examined with other privacy metrics such as K.L. divergence, standard deviation, and entropy. In summary, future research in this area should investigate alternative ways of user profiling that can provide personalized results while ensuring privacy.

REFERENCES

Arampatzis, A., Drosatos, G., & Efraimidis, P. S. (2015). Versatile query scrambling for private web search. *Information Retrieval Journal, 18*(4), 331–358. doi:10.100710791-015-9256-0

Barbaro, M., Zeller, T., & Hansell, S. (2006). A face is exposed for AOL searcher no. 4417749. *New York Times, 9*(2008), 8.

Berthold, O., Federrath, H., & Köpsell, S. (2001). *Web MIXes: A system for anonymous and unobservable Internet access.* Paper presented at the Designing privacy enhancing technologies. Springer. 10.1007/3-540-44702-4_7

Bradley, P. (2000). Search Engines:'Ixquick', a Multi-Search Engine With a Difference. *Ariadne, 23.*

Cao, Z., Liu, L., & Yan, Z. (2016). An Improved Lindell-Waisbard Private Web Search Scheme. *International Journal of Network Security, 18*(3), 538–543.

Castellà-Roca, J., Viejo, A., & Herrera-Joancomartí, J. (2009). Preserving user's privacy in web search engines. *Computer Communications, 32*(13-14), 1541–1551. doi:10.1016/j.comcom.2009.05.009

Chaum, D. L. (1981). Untraceable electronic mail, return addresses, and digital pseudonyms. *Communications of the ACM, 24*(2), 84–90. doi:10.1145/358549.358563

Chor, B., Kushilevitz, E., Goldreich, O., & Sudan, M. (1998). Private information retrieval. [JACM]. *Journal of the Association for Computing Machinery, 45*(6), 965–981. doi:10.1145/293347.293350

Cooper, A. (2008). A survey of query log privacy-enhancing techniques from a policy perspective. [TWEB]. *ACM Transactions on the Web, 2*(4), 1–27. doi:10.1145/1409220.1409222

Dan, O., & Davison, B. D. (2016). Measuring and predicting search engine users' satisfaction. [CSUR]. *ACM Computing Surveys, 49*(1), 1–35. doi:10.1145/2893486

Domingo-Ferrer, J., & Bras-Amorós, M. (2008). *Peer-to-peer private information retrieval.* Paper presented at the International Conference on Privacy in Statistical Databases. Springer. 10.1007/978-3-540-87471-3_26

Domingo-Ferrer, J., Martínez, S., Sánchez, D., & Soria-Comas, J. (2018). Co-utile P2P anonymous keyword search Co-utility (pp. 51-70). Springer.

Domingo-Ferrer, J., Solanas, A., & Castellà-Roca, J. (2009). h (k)-private information retrieval from privacy-uncooperative queryable databases. *Online Information Review*, *33*(4), 720–744. doi:10.1108/14684520910985693

ElGamal, T. (1985). A public key cryptosystem and a signature scheme based on discrete logarithms. *IEEE Transactions on Information Theory*, *31*(4), 469–472. doi:10.1109/TIT.1985.1057074

Erola, A., Castellà-Roca, J., Viejo, A., & Mateo-Sanz, J. M. (2011). Exploiting social networks to provide privacy in personalized web search. *Journal of Systems and Software*, *84*(10), 1734–1745. doi:10.1016/j.jss.2011.05.009

Juarez, M., & Torra, V. (2015). *Dispa: An intelligent agent for private web search Advanced research in data privacy.* Springer.

Kaaniche, N., Masmoudi, S., Znina, S., Laurent, M., & Demir, L. (2020). *Privacy preserving cooperative computation for personalized web search applications.* Paper presented at the Proceedings of the 35th Annual ACM Symposium on Applied Computing. ACM. 10.1145/3341105.3373947

Khan, R. (2020). *On the effectiveness of private information retrieval protocols.* Department of Computer Science, Capital University of Science and Technology.

Khan, R., Ahmad, A., Alsayed, A. O., Binsawad, M., Islam, M. A., & Ullah, M. (2020). QuPiD attack: Machine learning-based privacy quantification mechanism for PIR protocols in health-related web search. *Scientific Programming*, *2020*, 2020. doi:10.1155/2020/8868686

Khan, R., & Ali, S. (2013). Conceptual Framework of Redundant Link Aggregation. *arXiv preprint arXiv:1305.2708.*

Khan, R., Islam, M. A., Ullah, M., Aleem, M., & Iqbal, M. A. (2019). Privacy exposure measure: A privacy-preserving technique for health-related web search. *Journal of Medical Imaging and Health Informatics*, *9*(6), 1196–1204. doi:10.1166/jmihi.2019.2709

Khan, R., Ullah, M., & Islam, M. A. (2016). *Revealing pir protocols protected users.* Paper presented at the 2016 Sixth International Conference on Innovative Computing Technology (INTECH). IEEE. 10.1109/INTECH.2016.7845059

Khan, R., Ullah, M., Khan, A., Uddin, M. I., & Al-Yahya, M. (2021). NN-QuPiD attack: Neural network-based privacy quantification model for private information retrieval protocols. *Complexity*, *2021*, 2021. doi:10.1155/2021/6651662

Kushilevitz, E., & Ostrovsky, R. (1997). *Replication is not needed: Single database, computationally-private information retrieval.* Paper presented at the Proceedings 38th annual symposium on foundations of computer science. IEEE. 10.1109/SFCS.1997.646125

Lindell, Y., & Waisbard, E. (2010). *Private web search with malicious adversaries.* Paper presented at the International Symposium on Privacy Enhancing Technologies Symposium. IEEE. 10.1007/978-3-642-14527-8_13

Manoj, M., & Jacob, E. (2012). Design and development of a programmable meta search engine.

Mathews-Hunt, K. (2016). CookieConsumer: Tracking online behavioural advertising in Australia. *Computer Law & Security Review, 32*(1), 55–90. doi:10.1016/j.clsr.2015.12.006

Mokhtar, S. B., Berthou, G., Diarra, A., Quéma, V., & Shoker, A. (2013). *Rac: A freerider-resilient, scalable, anonymous communication protocol.* Paper presented at the In Proceedings of the 2013 IEEE 33rd International Conference on Distributed Computing Systems, ICDCS'13. IEEE.10.1109/ICDCS.2013.52

Mokhtar, S. B., Boutet, A., Felber, P., Pasin, M., Pires, R., & Schiavoni, V. (2017). *X-search: revisiting private web search using intel sgx.* Paper presented at the Proceedings of the 18th ACM/IFIP/USENIX Middleware Conference. IEEE. 10.1145/3135974.3135987

Navarro-Arribas, G., & Torra, V. (2014). *Advanced Research in Data Privacy* (Vol. 567). Springer.

Nissenbaum, H., & Daniel, H. (2009). TrackMeNot: Resisting surveillance in web search. In C. L. I. Kerr & V. Steeves (Eds.), *Lessons from the Identity Trail: Anonymity, Privacy, and Identity in a Networked Society.* Oxford University Press.

Parsania, V. S., Kalyani, F., & Kamani, K. (2016). A comparative analysis: DuckDuckGo vs. Google search engine. *GRD Journals-Global Research and Development Journal for Engineering, 2*(1), 12–17.

Peddinti, S. T., & Saxena, N. (2010). On the privacy of web search based on query obfuscation: A case study of trackmenot. Paper presented at the *Privacy Enhancing Technologies: 10th International Symposium, PETS 2010,* Berlin, Germany. 10.1007/978-3-642-14527-8_2

Petit, A., Cerqueus, T., Mokhtar, S. B., Brunie, L., & Kosch, H. (2015). *PEAS: Private, efficient and accurate web search.* Paper presented at the 2015 IEEE Trustcom/BigDataSE/ISPA. IEEE. 10.1109/Trustcom.2015.421

Pires, R., Goltzsche, D., Mokhtar, S. B., Bouchenak, S., Boutet, A., Felber, P., & Schiavoni, V. (2018). *CYCLOSA: Decentralizing private web search through SGX-based browser extensions.* Paper presented at the 2018 IEEE 38th International Conference on Distributed Computing Systems (ICDCS). IEEE. 10.1109/ICDCS.2018.00053

Raza, A., Han, K., & Hwang, S. O. (2020). A framework for privacy preserving, distributed search engine using topology of DLT and onion routing. *IEEE Access : Practical Innovations, Open Solutions, 8,* 43001–43012. doi:10.1109/ACCESS.2020.2977884

Reiter, M. K., & Rubin, A. D. (1998). Crowds: Anonymity for web transactions. [TISSEC]. *ACM Transactions on Information and System Security, 1*(1), 66–92. doi:10.1145/290163.290168

Romero-Tris, C., Castella-Roca, J., & Viejo, A. (2014). Distributed system for private web search with untrusted partners. *Computer Networks, 67,* 26–42. doi:10.1016/j.comnet.2014.03.022

Romero-Tris, C., Viejo, A., & Castellà-Roca, J. (2015). *Multi-party methods for privacy-preserving web search: survey and contributions Advanced research in data privacy.* Springer.

Seid, H. A., & Lespagnol, A. (1998). *Virtual private network: Google Patents.*

Stokes, K., & Bras-Amorós, M. (2010). Optimal configurations for peer-to-peer user-private information retrieval. *Computers & Mathematics with Applications (Oxford, England), 59*(4), 1568–1577. doi:10.1016/j.camwa.2010.01.003

Swanson, C. M., & Stinson, D. R. (2011). Extended combinatorial constructions for peer-to-peer user-private information retrieval. *arXiv preprint arXiv:1112.2762.*

Syverson, P., Dingledine, R., & Mathewson, N. (2004). *Tor: The secondgeneration onion router.* Paper presented at the Usenix Security.

Ullah, M. (2020a). *Obsecure logging: A framework to protect and evaluate the web search privacy.* [Ph. D. dissertation, Dept. Comput. Sci., Capital Univ., Telaiya, India].

Ullah, M., Islam, M. A., Khan, R., Aleem, M., & Iqbal, M. A. (2019). ObSecure Logging (OSLo): A framework to protect and evaluate the web search privacy in health care domain. *Journal of Medical Imaging and Health Informatics, 9*(6), 1181–1190. doi:10.1166/jmihi.2019.2708

Ullah, M., Khan, R., Haq, M. I. U., Khan, A., Alosaimi, W., Uddin, M. I., & Alharbi, A. (2021). Multi-group ObScure logging (MG-OSLo) A privacy-preserving protocol for private web search. *IEEE Access : Practical Innovations, Open Solutions, 9,* 79005–79020. doi:10.1109/ACCESS.2021.3078431

Ullah, M., Khan, R., & Islam, M. A. (2016a). *Poshida II, a multi group distributed peer to peer protocol for private web search.* Paper presented at the 2016 International Conference on Frontiers of Information Technology (FIT). IEEE. 10.1109/FIT.2016.022

Ullah, M., Khan, R., & Islam, M. A. (2016b). *Poshida, a protocol for private information retrieval.* Paper presented at the 2016 Sixth International Conference on Innovative Computing Technology (INTECH). IEEE. 10.1109/INTECH.2016.7845060

Ullah, M., Khan, R. U., Khan, I. U., Aslam, N., Aljameel, S. S., Ul Haq, M. I., & Islam, M. A. (2022). Profile Aware ObScure Logging (PaOSLo): A Web Search Privacy-Preserving Protocol to Mitigate Digital Traces. *Security and Communication Networks, 2022,* 2022. doi:10.1155/2022/2109024

Viejo, A., & Castellà-Roca, J. (2010). Using social networks to distort users' profiles generated by web search engines. *Computer Networks, 54*(9), 1343–1357. doi:10.1016/j.comnet.2009.11.003

Wang, H., Liu, W., & Wang, J. (2020). *Achieve web search privacy by obfuscation.* Paper presented at the Security with Intelligent Computing and Big-Data Services 2019: *Proceedings of the 3rd International Conference on Security with Intelligent Computing and Big-data Services (SICBS),* New Taipei City, Taiwan.

Xing, B. C., Shanahan, M., & Leslie-Hurd, R. (2016). Intel® software guard extensions (Intel® SGX) software support for dynamic memory allocation inside an enclave. *Proceedings of the Hardware and Architectural Support for Security and Privacy, 2016,* 1–9. doi:10.1145/2948618.2954330

Yang, J., Onik, M. M. H., Lee, N.-Y., Ahmed, M., & Kim, C.-S. (2019). Proof-of-familiarity: A privacy-preserved blockchain scheme for collaborative medical decision-making. *Applied Sciences (Basel, Switzerland)*, *9*(7), 1370. doi:10.3390/app9071370

ENDNOTES

[1]   http://www.anonymizer.com/
[2]   http://scroogle.org/

Chapter 2
A Survey on Performance Evaluation Mechanisms for Privacy-Aware Web Search Schemes

Rafi Ullah Khan
The University of Agriculture, Peshawar, Pakistan

Mohib Ullah
The University of Agriculture, Peshawar, Pakistan

Bushra Shafi
The University of Agriculture, Peshawar, Pakistan

Imran Ihsan
Air University, Islamabad, Pakistan

ABSTRACT

Due to the exponential growth of information on the internet, web search engines (WSEs) have become indispensable for effectively retrieving information. Web search engines store the users' profiles to provide the most relevant results. However, the user profiles may contain sensitive information, including the user's age, gender, health condition, personal interests, religious or political affiliation, and others. However, this raises serious concerns for the user's privacy since a user's identity may get exposed and misused by third parties. Researchers have proposed several techniques to address the issue of privacy infringement while using WSE, such as anonymizing networks, profile obfuscation, and private information retrieval (PIR) protocols. In this chapter, the authors give a brief survey of the privacy attacks and evaluation models used to evaluate the performance of private web search techniques.

DOI: 10.4018/978-1-6684-6914-9.ch002

INTRODUCTION

Online user privacy is a delicate issue and yet has been considered one of the significant and basic needs of the user by web service provider companies (Khan, 2020). Keeping records of users' queries and other activities on the Web by the service providers is not considered a misdeed. Many web service providers use this information for financial gains, such as targeted advertisement, market research and others (Khan, Islam, Ullah, Aleem, & Iqbal, 2019; Kulizhskaya, 2017; Petit, 2017). These companies claim that they use user behaviour tracking to improve product quality. However, collecting users' behavioural information and activity tracking without their knowledge is an indecent act and a direct violation of their fundamental rights (Raza, Han, & Hwang, 2020). Web Search Engine (WSE) is one of the prevalent web services used all over the globe. In the case of web search services, the issue of user privacy is more severe as it can unveil users' personal information (Khan, Ullah, Khan, Uddin, & Al-Yahya, 2021). Web search queries may contain users' queries related to their health condition, financial status, political affiliation, gender orientation, and others. These queries may unveil hidden implicit information about the users (Khan, 2020; Khan & Islam, 2017; Khan et al., 2019; Khan et al., 2021). In 2006, a privacy infringement case happened when America Online (AOL) (Adar, 2007; Barbaro, Zeller, & Hansell, 2006) published three months of queries from over 650K users, and New York Times managed to identify some of the users and their very personal information. Similarly, in the same year, Google was asked to submit the queries of their users to the United States Department of Justice (Khan, 2020). The Court of Justice of the European Union took this matter of user privacy seriously by introducing the "right to be forgotten" option and bound web service providers to its enforcement (Gibbs, 2016).

Due to the exponential growth in data and information on the internet, WSE has become essential for finding relevant information(Khan, 2020; Ullah, 2020; Ullah et al., 2022). WSE collects different information about the users and their profiles and uses these user profiles to retrieve the most relevant information according to the history and interests of the user (Stone, 2022a, 2022b). However, this user history and profile may contain explicit or implicit sensitive information about the user, which may lead to a privacy breach (Earp, Antón, Aiman-Smith, & Stufflebeam, 2005; Rostow, 2017). Furthermore, web service providers use this information for their other services (location, shopping, media, and others), due to which the target user receives recommendations from other services, which may lead to even more disastrous consequences (Citron & Solove, 2022).

Many new web search service providers took advantage of this situation and launched their WSE with privacy-preserving features. These web search service providers claim that they do not maintain users' profiles or any other activity tracking. However, the terms and conditions of these web search service providers affirm that they collect user queries only for result ranking purposes (Khan, 2020), and yet it may breach users' privacy, as happened in the case of AOL (Adar, 2007; Barbaro et al., 2006). Examples of these WSEs are Start-Page[1], Qwant[2], DuckDuckGo[3] and others.

Instead of server-side privacy preservation solutions, the researchers have proposed a client-side privacy preservation mechanism. The client-side privacy preservation mechanism does not rely upon service providers' privacy features; instead, they rely on their mechanism. These privacy preservation mechanisms can be classified into four major classes: Unlinkability solutions, Indistinguishability solutions, Hybrid Solutions and Private Information Retrieval Protocols (Khan, 2020). The details and examples of solutions for each class are given in the next section.

This chapter aims to survey performance evaluation mechanisms for privacy-aware web search schemes comprehensively. The performance evaluation mechanisms can be classified into two major classes, i.e. Privacy Attacks and Adverse Evaluation Models (Khan, 2020; Khan et al., 2019). The privacy attacks are further divided into two sub-classes, i.e., Active Attacks and Passive Attacks. In this chapter, we will discuss the working of these attacks in detail. The hierarchy of performance evaluation mechanisms for privacy-aware web search schemes is shown in figure 1.

The rest of the chapter is organized as follows: Section 2 briefly presents the privacy mechanisms proposed for private web searches. Section 3 discusses the attacks and adverse models developed for privacy schemes. In section 4, we present a conclusive summary of all the attacks, and in section 5, we discuss the relative future directions.

Figure 1. Hierarchy of performance evaluation mechanisms for privacy-aware web search schemes

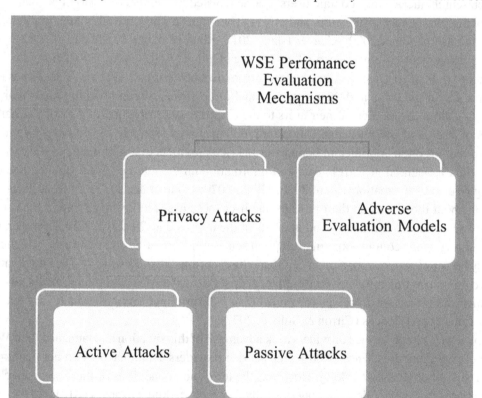

PRIVACY PRESERVE WEB SEARCH MECHANISMS

Privacy-preserving web solutions are used to overcome privacy infringement issues. These solutions can help users hide or minimize the connection between the queries and their identities. We classify these solutions into two significant types, i.e. server side and client side. We named the privacy solution provided by the web service providers a server-side solution. At the same time, the privacy solution users adopt for privacy preservation is named client-side solutions. Usually, the server side cannot be trusted. There are several examples (AOL (Adar, 2007; Barbaro et al., 2006) and Google (Frantziou, 2014; Khan et al., 2021; Newman, 2015)) where the user query log was published. Besides that, prevalent WSEs are not interested in providing such privacy features as their financial model works of users' history and activity (Khan, 2020).

We classify client-side privacy preservations techniques into four major classes: Unlinkability solutions, Indistinguishability solutions, Hybrid solutions and Private Information Retrieval Protocols. The details of these privacy preservation solutions are discussed in the following subsections.

Unlinkability Solutions

The primary aim of Unlinkability solutions is to break the bindings between users and their queries and thus hide users' true intentions from the curios WSE (Khan, 2020). WSE usually use IP addresses, HTTP/S headers, browsers cookies, device fingerprints and other unique identifiers to maintain users' profiles. The Unlinkability solutions use different techniques (such as cryptography) to alter the user identification information.

The prominent examples of these solutions are Virtual Private Networks or Proxy services (Dave, Sefika, & Campbell, 1992; Ezra et al., 2022; Shapiro, 1986). Users can submit their queries using these services to WSE and get perfect anonymity. However, in this case, the proxy server has its information. Other most common examples of Unlinkability solutions are RAC (Mokhtar, Berthou, Diarra, Quéma, & Shoker, 2013), The Onion Routing (Tor) (Syverson, Dingledine, & Mathewson, 2004), Web Mixes (Berthold, Federrath, & Köpsell, 2001), Mixed Network (Chaum, 1981) and others.

Indistinguishability Solutions

Indistinguishability solutions aim to distort users' profiles so that web search service providers cannot deduce users' interests correctly (Khan, 2020; Khan et al., 2019). The most predominant method in indistinguishability solutions is fake queries and profile obfuscations. Every user query is escorted with fake queries, due to which WSE cannot identify the intended initial query of the user. Different techniques are used to generate fake queries, such as query transformation (Juarez & Torra, 2015), query scrambling (Arampatzis, Efraimidis, & Drosatos, 2013), profile splitting (Juárez & Torra, 2013) and others. On the other hand, profile obfuscation techniques use multiple cookies to make different profiles of the same user on the WSE side.

The prominent examples of fake queries based solutions are Plausibly Deniable Search (PDS) (Murugesan & Clifton, 2009), Track Me Not (TMN) (Nissenbaum & Daniel, 2009), Privacy-Aware Web (PRAW) (Elovici, Glezer, & Shapira, 2005), Google Private Information Retrieval (GooPIR) (Domingo-Ferrer, Solanas, & Castellà-Roca, 2009), and others. While examples of profile obfuscation-based solutions are Dispa (Juarez & Torra, 2015) and UPS (Chen, Bai, Shou, Chen, & Gao, 2011).

Hybrid Solutions

Hybrid solutions are the combinations of unlinkability and indistinguishability techniques that provide adequate privacy to the user. These solutions' significant aims are to provide identity concealment and profile obfuscation to the user from the web search service providers. The prominent examples of hybrid solutions are X-Search (Mokhtar et al., 2017) and PEAS (Private, Efficient and Accurate Web Search) (Petit, Cerqueus, Mokhtar, Brunie, & Kosch, 2015).

Private Information Retrieval Protocols

In the previous section, we discuss single-user privacy preservation strategies (i.e. unlinkability, indistinguishability and hybrid). Private Information Retrieval protocol is a multiuser strategy that works in a group environment and provides users with privacy from adverse Web search service providers. In this solution, a group of users exchange their queries with other group members and then submit them to WSE on each other's behalf. After receiving results from the WSE, they forward them to the original query originator. In this way, the search engine cannot identify the true identity of the query originator and thus provide complete anonymity to the user.

The prominent examples of these protocols are Crowds (Reiter & Rubin, 1998), UPIR (User Private Information Retrieval) (Domingo-Ferrer & Bras-Amorós, 2008), UUP (Useless User Profile) (Castellà-Roca, Viejo, & Herrera-Joancomartí, 2009), Dissent (Wolinsky, Corrigan-Gibbs, Ford, & Johnson, 2012), Poshida (Ullah, Khan, & Islam, 2016b), Poshida II (Ullah, Khan, & Islam, 2016a), ObSecure Logging (OSLo) (Ullah, Islam, Khan, Aleem, & Iqbal, 2019), Multi-Group ObSecure Logging (MG-OSLo) (Ullah et al., 2021), Profile Aware ObSecure Logging (PA-OSLo) (Ullah et al., 2022) and others.

STATE-OF-THE-ART PRIVACY SCHEMES ATTACKS

The performance evaluation mechanisms are tools and techniques (such as attacks and adverse models) used to evaluate and compare the performance of the privacy preservation mechanisms (Khan, 2020; Khan et al., 2020; Khan & Islam, 2017; Khan et al., 2019; Khan et al., 2021). Privacy evaluation mechanisms can be divided into two major categories, i.e. Privacy Attacks and Privacy Evaluation models. The Privacy attacks are further divided into two sub-categories, i.e. Active Attacks and Passive Attacks. This section presents a detailed overview of all state of art privacy attacks and evaluation models.

Active Attacks

In active attacks, adverse web search service providers or other adverse entity attempts directly to breach the users' privacy by altering the runtime routine processes of communications (Khan, 2020). This section presents an overview and working of state-of-the-art active attacks.

Flooding Attack

The flooding attack aims to unveil the identity of a message's source (user) by flooding the whole anonymized network with service messages. This attack was proposed for Crowds, and Web Mixes privacy solutions (Berthold et al., 2001; Reiter & Rubin, 1998).

Timing Attack

A timing attack is used to disclose the identity of the originator user by measuring the access time of a recommended web page by the user. Most of the time, web browsers use the cache system to minimize response time and bandwidth requirements. Therefore, an adverse web search service provider can uncover the user's identity through repeated requests (Felten & Schneider, 2000).

Predecessor Attack

Predecessor attack (Wright, Adler, Levine, & Shields, 2004) was specially designed by Wright et al. for the Crowds system. According to the working of the attack, several adverse attacking nodes (users) join the Crowds network and record all the communication passing through them. After recording sufficient records, the attacking nodes find their victim node by comparing records.

Congestion Attack

Congestion attacks (Evans, Dingledine, & Grothoff, 2009) use network congestion strategy on different paths to identify the user's true identity. This attack is specially designed for identifying Tor users by introducing an adverse node and relay router. Once the communication path is identified, the anonymity of the user provided by Tor is broken.

Passive Attacks

In passive attacks, the web search service provider or adverse entity do not involve directly in unveiling the user identity. Instead, they use different tools and techniques to uncover users' identities from server logs (Khan, 2020). These attacks mostly use supervised and unsupervised machine learning algorithm-based models. The following sub-sections discuss the most prominent supervised and unsupervised machine learning algorithms used for passive attacks.

Logistic Regression

Logistic regression is a probability-based classifier usually used for binary classification (Cox, 1958). The probabilistic function is used to calculate the polarity of an event. While the classification model is built on features of past events. Equation 1 is used for data classification in Logistic Regression:

$$p\left(C_p|\vec{x}\right) = \frac{1}{1+e^{\theta_o + \vec{x}.\vec{\theta}}}$$

(1)

Where θ_o Represents the regression coefficient and error term. Moreover, the event classification is decided based on the threshold value, i.e. 0.5.

Vector Space Model

Vector Space Model (VSM) is a supervised machine learning algorithm that handles document classification problems efficiently (Schütze, Manning, & Raghavan, 2008). In VSM, a document is treated as a vector, and all the terms in a document are treated as vector components. VSM uses different similarity calculation methods (such as Cosine Similarity, Jaccard Similarity, Euclidian Distance and others) to find similarities between documents. In the case of privacy attacks, VSM is used to find similarities between users' queries and profiles. Equations 2 and 3 represent user-profiles and queries, while equation 4 represents the cosine similarity between user profiles and queries.

$$Profile_{User} = term_1, term_2, term_3, term_4, \ldots\ldots\ldots term_n \tag{2}$$

$$Query = qterm_1, qterm_2, qterm_3, qterm_4, \ldots\ldots\ldots qterm_n \tag{3}$$

$$Cos\theta = \frac{Profile_{user} \cdot}{\|Profile_{user}\| \ \|Query\|} \tag{4}$$

Support Vector Machine

Support Vector Machine (SVM) is a non-probabilistic, linear supervised machine learning algorithm (Dietrich, Opper, & Sompolinsky, 1999). It uses hyper-plane to detach two classes. The equation of hyper-plain is given in equation 5.

$$\vec{w}.\vec{x} - b = 0 \tag{5}$$

Where $\vec{w}$ represents the average vector and $\frac{b}{\|\vec{w}\|}$ Represents the distance from the origin. Vapnik and Cortes introduce a soft margin concept to separate two classes properly.

Alternating Decision Tree

Alternating Decision Tree is a classification algorithm that uses a decisions tree calculated using the previous events (Freund & Mason, 1999). The decision tree is developed using the rules where each rule has three components, i.e. preconditions, conditions and two scores. Where the preconditions are logical conjunction of conditions and conditions are facts. At the same time, the two values show the base condition and possible outcome. AD-Tree is a generalized form of voted decision stumps, decision trees and voted decision tree algorithms.

Random Forest

Random Forest is another tree-based supervised machine-learning algorithm that uses multiple decision trees for data classification (Breiman, 2001). For decision tree creation, random forest uses a randomly selected training subset and then uses votes input from multiple decision trees for event classification.

Zero Rule

Zero Rule (Zero R) is a supervised machine learning algorithm that learns and uses a rule-based model for data classifications. In this model, the rules evolve from the training data, ignoring all the predictors and relying on the target. Zero R is usually used as a benchmark classification algorithm that uses the most frequent value as a rule (Nasa & Suman, 2012).

Expectation Maximization Cluster

Expectation Maximization Cluster (EM Cluster) is an unsupervised machine learning algorithm that uses probability functions for event/data distribution in clusters. Usually, the EM cluster uses Gaussian Mixture to improve the density of the cluster (Arabie, Hubert, & De Soete, 1996).

K-Means

K-Means is another clustering algorithm that uses the distance function to place the data into the K number of clusters. Each cluster has a centroid, and data is distributed among the clusters based on the minimum distance from the centroid. For distance calculation, the most common functions are cosine similarity, Jaccard similarity, Euclidian distance and others. In a privacy protection attack, K-Means categorizes fake and users' original queries in different clusters.

Figure 2. Association rule mining attack with session windows
(Khan, Ullah, & Islam, 2016)

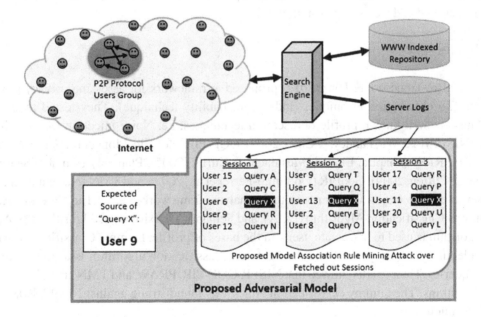

Association Rule Mining Attack

Association Rule Mining (ARM) technique-based attack was proposed by Khan et al. for popular PIR protocols User Private Information Retrieval (UPIR) and Useless User Profile (UUP) (Khan et al., 2016). Their proposed attack is used to find the source user of some queries of interest from the multiple session where the query of interest occurs in the WSE log. The session window (Khan, 2020; Khan et al., 2020; Khan & Islam, 2017; Khan et al., 2016; Khan et al., 2021) is the central part of their attack upon which the ARM is applied.

According to the working of the ARM attack, the attacker first creates the list of queries of interest. Then the attacker finds all the session windows where the queries of interest occur. The session window comprises a fixed number of entries in the WSE log that occurs before and after the query of interest (as shown in figure 2). After finding all the session windows, an ARM attack is applied to all sessions to find the frequent users using support and confidence metrics.

They tested the protocols with different parameter setting such as variable window size, number of queries and group size. The experiments are conducted with a subset of the AOL dataset containing queries submitted in a month. They concluded from the results that the more extensive group size of the protocol offers more security to the user but can be countered by a bigger window size. Similarly, user security and privacy are more vulnerable when they submit more than ten queries through the same group.

Adverse Evaluation Models for Privacy Schemes

The adverse evaluation model is a complete system comprised of data collection, cleansing, classification model (attack model), and data testing. For attack model creation, they usually use machine learning algorithms. The adverse evaluation models provide a privacy testing platform for private information retrieval protocols. This section gives a detailed discussion of adverse evaluation models for private information retrieval and web search solutions.

Balsa's Model

Balsa et al. (Balsa, Troncoso, & Diaz, 2012) proposed a framework for assessing privacy provided by prevalent profile obfuscation techniques (indistinguishability technique). They tested their proposed model against six well-known profile obfuscation techniques, i.e. Noise injection for Search Privacy Protection (NISPP) (Ye, Wu, Pandey, & Chen, 2009), OQF-PIR (Rebollo-Monedero, Forne, & Domingo-Ferrer, 2012), PRAW (Shapira, Elovici, Meshiach, & Kuflik, 2005), Plausibly Deniable Search (PDS) (Murugesan & Clifton, 2009), GooPIR (Domingo-Ferrer et al., 2009), and TMN (Nissenbaum & Daniel, 2009). They use three major algorithms in their analysis framework, i.e. Profile Filtering Algorithm (PFA), Dummy Classification Algorithm (DCA), and Semantic Classification Algorithm (SCA). Profile filtering algorithm is used to dissociate users on the bases of profile. Dummy Classification Algorithm is used to identify the fake queries, and the Semantic classification algorithm is used to semantically classify the queries. Their results showed that NISPP, OQF-PIR, PRAW, and TMN are vulnerable Profile filtering algorithms. The dummy classification attack was found strong against NISPP, PDS, GooPIR, and TMN techniques.

Peddinti and Saxena Model

Peddinti and Saxena proposed their model to evaluate the TMN and Tor as the most popular indistinguishability and unlinkability solutions (Peddinti & Saxena, 2010, 2011, 2014). Their model considered Web search service providers as adverse entities with the users' previous original profiles and curious to identify new users' queries. They adopted different strategies for both Tor and TMN. They developed a prediction model using machine learning algorithms and users' previous history. They used AOL's dataset for training and testing, which contained three-month queries of over 650k users. The first two months' data is ad training data, and last month's data is used as testing data. The details of their models with results are discussed as follows:

The Track Me Not (TMN) technique mainly aimed to differentiate between fake queries generated by the TMN and user-generated queries. The experiment was conducted with the data of 60 selected users. While RSS feeds and searches, results are used for fake query generations. They used unsupervised machine learning and supervised machine learning algorithms for model creation. They used EM-Cluster and K-Means algorithms for the clustering-based model and Zero-R, Random Tree, Random Forest, and ADT for the classification-based model. They reported that the classification-based model could identify 48.88% of original queries.

The Tor (unlinkability) technique mainly aimed to associate the incoming queries from the Tor nodes to the original users. This experiment used data from 60 selected users from the AOL dataset. They assume that the web search services provider has the list of potential Tor routers (nodes/users) and their activity information (cookies and search pattern). Then they simulated the Tor network under 100 and 1000 Tor nodes (router). They use SVM (Support Vector Machine), a supervised machine learning algorithm for user and query association. According to their experiment results, their proposed model identified 25.95% of queries in 100-node scenarios and 18.95% in 1000-node scenarios.

Gervais's Model

Unlike previous approaches, Gervais et al. proposed their attack model for the popular indistinguishability technique: Track Me Not (TMN) (Gervais, Shokri, Singla, Capkun, & Lenders, 2014). They proposed a Linkage Attack using similarity scores to find the relationship between users' queries and behavioural profiles. They used five parameters to model the user's behaviour, i.e. the identity of the user (Ui), user query (Q), user query time (Tq), the reply of query from a WSE (Rq), and set of web pages clicked (C). A set of all five parameters from one user is called an event, as shown in equation 6. Similarly, the association between two events is calculated using the Linkage function, as shown in equation 7.

$$Event_i = [Ui, Q, Tq, Rq, C] \tag{6}$$

$$Linkage\ Function(Event_i, Event_j) \tag{7}$$

SimAttack

SimAttack was proposed by Petit et al. for the performance evaluation of three well-known indistinguishability and unlinkability methods, i.e. GooPIR, Tor and TMN (Petit, 2017; Petit et al., 2016). Furthermore, they also assess the performance of the hybrid mechanism (i.e. combination of unlinkability and indistinguishability techniques) using SimAttack. Their attack model uses the supervised machine learning algorithm VSM (Vector Space Model) to calculate the similarity between the user query and their profiles. For similarity calculation, they used Dice Coefficient (equation 8), Jaccard Index (equation 9), and Cosine similarity (equation 10).

$$Dice's\ Cofficient(q, p) = 2. \frac{q.p}{\|q\|^2 + \|p\|^2} \tag{8}$$

$$Jaccard\left(q,p\right) = \frac{q \cdot p}{\left\|q\right\|^{2} + \left\|p\right\|^{2} - q \cdot p} \qquad (9)$$

$$Cosine\left(q,p\right) = \frac{q \cdot p}{\left\|q\right\| \cdot \left\|p\right\|} \qquad (10)$$

The aim of SimAttack, in the case of the unlinkability technique (Tor), was to identify the original requestor of a specific query. For identification of the original query requestor, they calculate the similarity between the profiles of users and the query. For experimentation, they made three subsets of 100, 200, and 300 users from the AOL dataset to find the impact of the number of users. According to the experiments' results, SimAttack could associate 36.8% to their original requestor with the 41.4% precision.

In the case of TMN and GooPIR (indistinguishability techniques), the primary aim of SimAttack was to detect fake queries submitted by the users. They used Dice's coefficient to calculate the similarity between queries and user profiles. The query with the slightest similarity to the user profile is considered fake. They used a dictionary for fake query generation in GooPIR, while TMN used RSS feeds. For testing, a subset of 100 users from the AOL dataset is used for both GooPIR and TMN. According to the results, SimAttack could detect 46.9% of queries with over 85% precision in the case of TMN. While in the case of GooPIR, SimAttack detected over 50% of queries correctly as fake queries.

Petit et al. also evaluated the performance of a hybrid technique (combination of unlinkability and indistinguishability) using SimAttack. They combine the strategy of Track Me Not (TMN) and Tor and create an anonymized web search log for experimentation. The results show that SimAttack could identify over 35% of user queries with 14.7% precision.

QuPiD Attack

Query to Profile Distance (QuPiD) Attack is another attack designed by Khan et al. to evaluate the privacy provided by the PIR protocols (Khan, 2020; Khan et al., 2020). In their attack, they considered the web search services provider as an adverse entity that wishes to identify users' original queries submitted through any PIR protocol. They assume that web search service providers already have the users' previous queries, and they wish to associate users with their original queries using machine learning techniques. They also used the session window concept, but instead of the query of interest, their session window is created based on the user of interest. The session window used in this attack is shown in figure 2.

The users' old profile data is used for model training, and data from the session window is used as testing data. For model training, they first acquire the query score from the uClassify service and then use these query scores as a feature vector for model creation. For comparative analysis of the model on different machine learning algorithms belongs to Lazy Learner, Tree, Rule, Bayesian and Metaheuristic families. The experiments are conducted on a subset of the AOL dataset having more than a hundred thousand queries. In contrast, the performance of the models is evaluated in terms of precision, recall and f-measure.

Figure 3. User of Interest-based Session Window used in QuPiD Attack
(Khan, 2020; Khan et al., 2020)

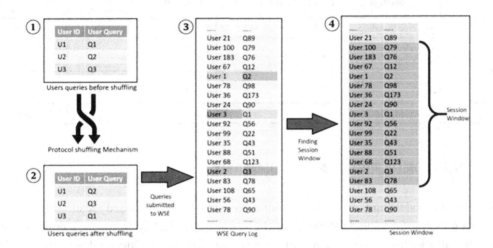

The results of the experiments illustrate that classification models built on IBK and Bagging performed marvelously compared to the other selected algorithms. IBK could associate 48% of queries to the original user with a precision of 83%. At the same time, Bagging could associate 45% of queries to the original user with a precision of 78%.

NN-QuPiD Attack

Neural Network-based Query to Profile Distance (NN-QuPiD) Attack (Khan et al., 2021) is an improved version of the QuPiD Attack (Khan, 2020; Khan et al., 2020) proposed by Khan et al. for better precision and recall rate. They used a subset of the AOL dataset consisting of 175911 queries of the selected active users for model building. Two third of the user data is used as training data, and the remaining one-third is used to create the simulated log of users for testing data. They used the same session window concept in the previous version of QuPiD Attack to fetch the users' sessions and used them as testing data. They used Multilayer Perceptron and Recurrent Neural Network (RNN) algorithms with its two variants LSTM (Long Short Term Memory) and BiLSTM (Bidirectional Long Short Term Memory) for model building. For model building they also used query score acquired from uClassify and query string.

According to the experimental results, Multilayer Perceptron performed poorly by associating 32.8% of queries to the original users with 41% precision. RNN LSTM associates 47% of queries to the original users with 93.2% precision, and RNN BiLSTM associates 51.2% of queries with original users with 92.3% precision. The performance of the NN-QuPiD attack is also compared with the IBK-based QuPiD Attack, which associates 49% of queries to the original users with 93.4% precision.

Table 1. Comparison of active attacks for privacy preserved web search techniques

Attack	Method	Indistinguishability	Unlinkability	PIR Protocol	Features used in the attack
Flooding Attack	Message Flooding	NA	Web Mixes	Crowds	User Message
Timing Attack	Repeated Request Time out	TMN	Tor	Crowds	User Query, Query Time
Predecessor Attack	Selfish and Adverse Nodes	NA	Tor	Crowds	User Query, User ID
Congestion Attack	Adverse Nodes	NA	Tor	NA	User Query, User ID

CONCLUSIVE COMPARISON AND SUMMARY

Adverse evaluation models and attacks are essential to evaluate the proposed techniques' performance and promote a more profound understanding of the system, specifically from a risk point of view. Understanding the attack and the adverse model mechanism provides a better understanding and insight into vulnerability in the privacy-preserving model. These attack and adverse models can help researchers to improve the privacy preservation technique. This chapter briefly introduces some significant attacks and adverse models proposed for privacy-preserved web search schemes. According to work, we divided web search privacy attacks into two classes, i.e. Privacy Attacks and Adverse Evaluation Models. While privacy attacks are further divided into two sub-classes, i.e. Active Attacks and Passive Attacks

In this section, we presented a conclusive comparison of all the types of attacks as mentioned earlier in three tables. In Table 1, we discussed the active attacks with their attack methods, target privacy-preserving techniques and features used in the attack. Similarly, Table 2 discussed passive attacks with all previously mentioned parameters. While in Table 3, we discussed the adverse models proposed for the privacy evolution of privacy-preserved web search schemes.

According to the details given in Table 1, most of the active attacks were designed for the most popular unlinkability Tor and Crowds protocol. The most common features in active attacks are users' IDs and queries. Similarly, according to Table 2, most passive attacks use machine learning techniques and users' history for building classification models. The most frequent data feature used in these attacks is users' queries. Passive attacks are designed for privacy-preserving solutions, but most targeted Tor OQF-PIR, NISSP, PRAW, PDS, TMN, and GooPIR. At the same time, most attacks and adverse models mentioned in Table 3 use supervised machine learning (classification) techniques to evaluate privacy mechanisms. These attacks and models were proposed for almost all famous privacy-preserved web search mechanisms, such as TMN, Tor, UUP, UPIR, and others.

Overall, from the information illustrated in Tables 1, 2, and 3, it is safe to conclude that machine learning-based attacks and adverse models are more generic so that they can be adapted for many types of private information retrieval solutions' evaluation with minor adoptions. These adverse models and attacks use users' previous information for model training and then use the hat model to identify the actual user of upcoming queries. These attacks and models were found more efficient than other active and passive attacks and can be efficiently used to evaluate all types of privacy-preserving web search techniques.

Table 2. Comparison of passive attacks for privacy preserved web search techniques

Attack	Method	Indistinguishability	Unlinkability	PIR Protocol	Features used in the attack
Logistic Regression	Classification	OQF-PIR, NISSP, PRAW, PDS, TMN, GooPIR	Tor	UUP, UPIR, Crowds	Query String, Time, Reply, Click page, User ID, uClassify Score
Vector Space Model	Classification	OQF-PIR, NISSP, PRAW, PDS, TMN, GooPIR	Tor	Crowds	Query String
Support Vector Machine	Classification	OQF-PIR, NISSP, PRAW, PDS, TMN, GooPIR	Tor	Crowds	Query String
Alternating Decision Tree	Classification	OQF-PIR, NISSP, PRAW, PDS, TMN, GooPIR	Tor	UUP, UPIR, Crowds	Query String
Random Forest	Classification	OQF-PIR, NISSP, PRAW, PDS, TMN, GooPIR	Tor	UUP, UPIR, Crowds	Query String, Time, Reply, Click page, User ID, uClassify Score
Zero Rule	Classification	OQF-PIR, NISSP, PRAW, PDS, TMN, GooPIR	Tor	UUP, UPIR, Crowds	Query String, Time, Reply, Click page, User ID, uClassify Score
Expectation Maximization (EM)	Clustering	TMN, GooPIR	Tor	NA	Query String, uClassify Score
K-Means	Clustering	TMN, GooPIR	Tor	UUP, UPIR, Crowds	Query String, uClassify Score
Khan et al.	Association Rule Mining (ARM)	NA	NA	UUP, UPIR, PBD	Query String, Time, User ID

Table 3. Comparison of adverse model for privacy preserved web search techniques

Adverse Model	Method	Algorithm	Indistinguishability	Unlinkability	PIR Protocol	Features used in the attack
Balsa's Model	Semantic Classification Algorithm, Dummy Classification Algorithm, Profile Filtering Algorithm	Similarity Function	OQF-PIR, NISSP, PRAW, PDS, TMN	NA	NA	Query String, RSS Feeds
Peddinti and Saxena Model	Classification	Zero R, Random Tree, Random Forest, Alternating Decision Tree, Logistic Regression	TMN	Tor	NA	Query String
Gervais's Model	Linkage Function	Similarity Function	TMN	NA	NA	Query String, Time, Reply, Click page, User ID
Petit et al.	SimAttack, Classification	Similarity Function Cosine, Jaccard, Dice Coefficient	TMN, GooPIR	Tor	NA	Query String
Khan et al.	QuPiD Attack, Classification	J.48, Decision Table, Logistic Model Tree, One R, JRip, K-Star, IBK, XG-Boost, Bagging, Bayes Net,	NA	NA	UUP, UPIR	uClassify Query Score
Khan et al.	NN-QuPiD Attack, Classification	MLP, RNN (LSTM), RNN (BiLSTM)	NA	NA	UUP, UPIR	uClassify Query Score, Query String

FUTURE RECOMMENDATIONS

We have concluded that machine learning-based models and attacks are effective against almost all privacy-preserving techniques. This conclusion unveiled the path for two primary future directions, i.e.

improving the machine learning-based attacks further by introducing better classification and similarity calculation mechanisms and improving the performance of privacy-preserving mechanisms as a countermeasure against these attacks.

For the attack improvement, Khan et al. suggested that the performance of the attack can be further improved by using novel neural network algorithms with fine-tuned parameters (Khan, 2020; Khan et al., 2021). Moreover, the researchers should also explore the algorithms from the new domain, such as graphs networks (Ahmad et al., 2020), computer semantics (ontology-based query classification (Ojha & Deepak, 2022)) and other methods for model building.

REFERENCES

Adar, E. (2007). *User 4xxxxx9: Anonymizing query logs.* Paper presented at the Proc of Query Log Analysis Workshop, International Conference on World Wide Web. IEEE.

Ahmad, Y., Ullah, M., Khan, R., Shafi, B., Khan, A., Zareei, M., Aldosary, A., & Mohamed, E. M. (2020). SiFSO: Fish swarm optimization-based technique for efficient community detection in complex networks. *Complexity, 2020,* 2020. doi:10.1155/2020/6695032

Arabie, P., Hubert, L., & De Soete, G. (1996). *Clustering and classification.* World Scientific. doi:10.1142/1930

Arampatzis, A., Efraimidis, P. S., & Drosatos, G. (2013). A query scrambler for search privacy on the internet. *Information Retrieval, 16*(6), 657–679. doi:10.100710791-012-9212-1

Balsa, E., Troncoso, C., & Diaz, C. (2012). *OB-PWS: Obfuscation-based private web search.* Paper presented at the 2012 IEEE Symposium on Security and Privacy. IEEE. 10.1109/SP.2012.36

Barbaro, M., Zeller, T., & Hansell, S. (2006). A face is exposed for AOL searcher no. 4417749. *New York Times, 9*(2008), 8.

Berthold, O., Federrath, H., & Köpsell, S. (2001). *Web MIXes: A system for anonymous and unobservable Internet access.* Paper presented at the Designing privacy enhancing technologies. 10.1007/3-540-44702-4_7

Breiman, L. (2001). Random forests. *Machine Learning, 45*(1), 5–32. doi:10.1023/A:1010933404324

Castellà-Roca, J., Viejo, A., & Herrera-Joancomartí, J. (2009). Preserving user's privacy in web search engines. *Computer Communications, 32*(13-14), 1541–1551. doi:10.1016/j.comcom.2009.05.009

Chaum, D. L. (1981). Untraceable electronic mail, return addresses, and digital pseudonyms. *Communications of the ACM, 24*(2), 84–90. doi:10.1145/358549.358563

Chen, G., Bai, H., Shou, L., Chen, K., & Gao, Y. (2011). *UPS: efficient privacy protection in personalized web search.* Paper presented at the Proceedings of the 34th international ACM SIGIR conference on Research and development in Information Retrieval. ACM. 10.1145/2009916.2009999

Citron, D. K., & Solove, D. J. (2022). Privacy harms. *BUL Rev., 102,* 793.

Cox, D. R. (1958). The regression analysis of binary sequences. *Journal of the Royal Statistical Society. Series B. Methodological, 20*(2), 215–232. doi:10.1111/j.2517-6161.1958.tb00292.x

Dave, A., Sefika, M., & Campbell, R. H. (1992). Proxies, application interfaces, and distributed systems *Proceedings of the Second International Workshop on Object Orientation in Operating Systems* (pp. 212-220): IEEE. 10.1109/IWOOOS.1992.252978

Dietrich, R., Opper, M., & Sompolinsky, H. (1999). Statistical mechanics of support vector networks. *Physical Review Letters, 82*(14), 2975–2978. doi:10.1103/PhysRevLett.82.2975

Domingo-Ferrer, J., & Bras-Amorós, M. (2008). *Peer-to-peer private information retrieval.* Paper presented at the International Conference on Privacy in Statistical Databases. 10.1007/978-3-540-87471-3_26

Domingo-Ferrer, J., Solanas, A., & Castellà-Roca, J. (2009). h (k)-private information retrieval from privacy-uncooperative queryable databases. *Online Information Review, 33*(4), 720–744. doi:10.1108/14684520910985693

Earp, J. B., Antón, A. I., Aiman-Smith, L., & Stufflebeam, W. H. (2005). Examining Internet privacy policies within the context of user privacy values. *IEEE Transactions on Engineering Management, 52*(2), 227–237. doi:10.1109/TEM.2005.844927

Elovici, Y., Glezer, C., & Shapira, B. (2005). Enhancing customer privacy while searching for products and services on the World Wide Web. *Internet Research, 15*(4), 378–399. doi:10.1108/10662240510615164

Evans, N. S., Dingledine, R., & Grothoff, C. (2009). *A Practical Congestion Attack on Tor Using Long Paths.* Paper presented at the USENIX Security Symposium. IEEE.

Ezra, P. J., Misra, S., Agrawal, A., Oluranti, J., Maskeliunas, R., & Damasevicius, R. (2022). Secured communication using virtual private network (VPN). *Cyber Security and Digital Forensics*, 309-319.

Felten, E. W., & Schneider, M. A. (2000). *Timing attacks on web privacy.* Paper presented at the Proceedings of the 7th ACM Conference on Computer and Communications Security. ACM.

Frantziou, E. (2014). Further Developments in the Right to be Forgotten: The European Court of Justice's Judgment in Case C-131/12, Google Spain, SL, Google Inc v Agencia Espanola de Proteccion de Datos. *Hum. Rts. L. Rev., 14,* 761.

Freund, Y., & Mason, L. (1999). The alternating decision tree learning algorithm. Paper presented at the *Proceedings of the Sixteenth International Conference on Machine Learning (ICML 1999),* Bled, Slovenia.

Gervais, A., Shokri, R., Singla, A., Capkun, S., & Lenders, V. (2014). *Quantifying web-search privacy.* Paper presented at the Proceedings of the 2014 ACM SIGSAC Conference on Computer and Communications Security. ACM. 10.1145/2660267.2660367

Gibbs, S. (2016). Google to extend 'right to be forgotten' to all its domains accessed in EU. *The Guardian, 11.*

Juárez, M., & Torra, V. (2013). *A self-adaptive classification for the dissociating privacy agent.* Paper presented at the 2013 Eleventh Annual Conference on Privacy, Security and Trust. IEEE.10.1109/PST.2013.6596035

Juarez, M., & Torra, V. (2015). *Dispa: An intelligent agent for private web search Advanced research in data privacy.* Springer.

Khan, R. (2020). *On the effectiveness of private information retrieval protocols.* Department of Computer Science, Capital University of Science and Technology.

Khan, R., Ahmad, A., Alsayed, A. O., Binsawad, M., Islam, M. A., & Ullah, M. (2020). QuPiD attack: Machine learning-based privacy quantification mechanism for PIR protocols in health-related web search. *Scientific Programming, 2020,* 2020. doi:10.1155/2020/8868686

Khan, R., & Islam, M. A. (2017). *Quantification of PIR protocols privacy.* Paper presented at the 2017 International Conference on Communication, Computing and Digital Systems (C-CODE). IEEE. 10.1109/C-CODE.2017.7918908

Khan, R., Islam, M. A., Ullah, M., Aleem, M., & Iqbal, M. A. (2019). Privacy exposure measure: A privacy-preserving technique for health-related web search. *Journal of Medical Imaging and Health Informatics, 9*(6), 1196–1204. doi:10.1166/jmihi.2019.2709

Khan, R., Ullah, M., & Islam, M. A. (2016). *Revealing pir protocols protected users.* Paper presented at the 2016 Sixth International Conference on Innovative Computing Technology (INTECH). ACM. 10.1109/INTECH.2016.7845059

Khan, R., Ullah, M., Khan, A., Uddin, M. I., & Al-Yahya, M. (2021). NN-QuPiD attack: Neural network-based privacy quantification model for private information retrieval protocols. *Complexity, 2021,* 2021. doi:10.1155/2021/6651662

Kulizhskaya, Y. (2017). *Snippet matching for click-tracking blocking.* Trinity College.

Mokhtar, S. B., Berthou, G., Diarra, A., Quéma, V., & Shoker, A. (2013). *Rac: A freerider-resilient, scalable, anonymous communication protocol.* Paper presented at the 2013 IEEE 33rd International Conference on Distributed Computing Systems. IEEE. 10.1109/ICDCS.2013.52

Mokhtar, S. B., Boutet, A., Felber, P., Pasin, M., Pires, R., & Schiavoni, V. (2017). *X-search: revisiting private web search using intel sgx.* Paper presented at the Proceedings of the 18th ACM/IFIP/USENIX Middleware Conference. 10.1145/3135974.3135987

Murugesan, M., & Clifton, C. (2009). *Providing privacy through plausibly deniable search.* Paper presented at the Proceedings of the 2009 SIAM International Conference on Data Mining. SAIM. 10.1137/1.9781611972795.66

Nasa, C., & Suman, S. (2012). Evaluation of different classification techniques for web data. *International Journal of Computers and Applications, 52*(9), 34–40. doi:10.5120/8233-1389

Newman, A. L. (2015). What the "right to be forgotten" means for privacy in a digital age. *Science, 347*(6221), 507–508. doi:10.1126cience.aaa4603 PMID:25635090

Nissenbaum, H., & Daniel, H. (2009). TrackMeNot: Resisting surveillance in web search.

Ojha, R., & Deepak, G. (2022). *SAODFT: Socially Aware Ontology Driven Approach for Query Facet Generation in Text Classification.* Paper presented at the International Conference on Electrical and Electronics Engineering. 10.1007/978-981-19-1677-9_14

Peddinti, S. T., & Saxena, N. (2010). *On the privacy of web search based on query obfuscation: A case study of trackmenot.* Paper presented at the International Symposium on Privacy Enhancing Technologies Symposium. IEEE. 10.1007/978-3-642-14527-8_2

Peddinti, S. T., & Saxena, N. (2011). *On the effectiveness of anonymizing networks for web search privacy.* Paper presented at the Proceedings of the 6th ACM Symposium on Information, Computer and Communications Security. ACM. 10.1145/1966913.1966984

Peddinti, S. T., & Saxena, N. (2014). Web search query privacy: Evaluating query obfuscation and anonymizing networks. *Journal of Computer Security, 22*(1), 155–199. doi:10.3233/JCS-130491

Petit, A. (2017). *Introducing privacy in current web search engines.* Université de Lyon; Universität Passau (Deutscheland).

Petit, A., Cerqueus, T., Boutet, A., Mokhtar, S. B., Coquil, D., Brunie, L., & Kosch, H. (2016). SimAttack: Private web search under fire. *Journal of Internet Services and Applications, 7*(1), 1–17. doi:10.118613174-016-0044-x

Petit, A., Cerqueus, T., Mokhtar, S. B., Brunie, L., & Kosch, H. (2015). *PEAS: Private, efficient and accurate web search.* Paper presented at the 2015 IEEE Trustcom/BigDataSE/ISPA. IEEE. 10.1109/Trustcom.2015.421

Raza, A., Han, K., & Hwang, S. O. (2020). A framework for privacy preserving, distributed search engine using topology of DLT and onion routing. *IEEE Access : Practical Innovations, Open Solutions, 8*, 43001–43012. doi:10.1109/ACCESS.2020.2977884

Rebollo-Monedero, D., Forne, J., & Domingo-Ferrer, J. (2012). Query profile obfuscation by means of optimal query exchange between users. *IEEE Transactions on Dependable and Secure Computing, 9*(5), 641–654. doi:10.1109/TDSC.2012.16

Reiter, M. K., & Rubin, A. D. (1998). Crowds: Anonymity for web transactions. [TISSEC]. *ACM Transactions on Information and System Security, 1*(1), 66–92. doi:10.1145/290163.290168

Rostow, T. (2017). What happens when an acquaintance buys your data: A new privacy harm in the age of data brokers. *Yale Journal on Regulation, 34*, 667.

Schütze, H., Manning, C. D., & Raghavan, P. (2008). *Introduction to information retrieval* (Vol. 39). Cambridge University Press Cambridge.

Shapira, B., Elovici, Y., Meshiach, A., & Kuflik, T. (2005). PRAW—A PRivAcy model for the Web. *Journal of the American Society for Information Science and Technology, 56*(2), 159–172. doi:10.1002/asi.20107

Shapiro, M. (1986). *Structure and encapsulation in distributed systems: The proxy principle.* Paper presented at the Int. Conf. on Distr. Comp. Sys.(ICDCS). IEEE.

Stone, M. (2022a). Understanding and Evaluating Search Experience. *Synthesis Lectures on Information Concepts, Retrieval, and Services, 14*(1), 1–105. doi:10.1007/978-3-031-79216-8

Stone, M. (2022b). *Units of Analysis: Query, Task, User Understanding and Evaluating Search Experience*. Springer. doi:10.1007/978-3-031-79216-8

Syverson, P., Dingledine, R., & Mathewson, N. (2004). *Tor: The secondgeneration onion router*. Paper presented at the Usenix Security.

Ullah, M. (2020). *'Obsecure logging: A framework to protect and evaluate the web search privacy* [Ph. D. dissertation, Dept. Comput. Sci., Capital Univ., Telaiya, India].

Ullah, M., Islam, M. A., Khan, R., Aleem, M., & Iqbal, M. A. (2019). ObSecure Logging (OSLo): A framework to protect and evaluate the web search privacy in health care domain. *Journal of Medical Imaging and Health Informatics, 9*(6), 1181–1190. doi:10.1166/jmihi.2019.2708

Ullah, M., Khan, R., Haq, M. I. U., Khan, A., Alosaimi, W., Uddin, M. I., & Alharbi, A. (2021). Multi-group ObScure logging (MG-OSLo) A privacy-preserving protocol for private web search. *IEEE Access : Practical Innovations, Open Solutions, 9*, 79005–79020. doi:10.1109/ACCESS.2021.3078431

Ullah, M., Khan, R., & Islam, M. A. (2016a). *Poshida II, a multi group distributed peer to peer protocol for private web search*. Paper presented at the 2016 International Conference on Frontiers of Information Technology (FIT). IEEE. 10.1109/FIT.2016.022

Ullah, M., Khan, R., & Islam, M. A. (2016b). *Poshida, a protocol for private information retrieval*. Paper presented at the 2016 Sixth International Conference on Innovative Computing Technology (INTECH). IEEE. 10.1109/INTECH.2016.7845060

Ullah, M., Khan, R. U., Khan, I. U., Aslam, N., Aljameel, S. S., Ul Haq, M. I., & Islam, M. A. (2022). Profile Aware ObScure Logging (PaOSLo): A Web Search Privacy-Preserving Protocol to Mitigate Digital Traces. *Security and Communication Networks, 2022*, 2022. doi:10.1155/2022/2109024

Wolinsky, D. I., Corrigan-Gibbs, H., Ford, B., & Johnson, A. (2012). *Dissent in numbers: Making strong anonymity scale*. Paper presented at the 10th USENIX Symposium on Operating Systems Design and Implementation (OSDI 12). IEEE.

Wright, M. K., Adler, M., Levine, B. N., & Shields, C. (2004). The predecessor attack: An analysis of a threat to anonymous communications systems. [TISSEC]. *ACM Transactions on Information and System Security, 7*(4), 489–522. doi:10.1145/1042031.1042032

Ye, S., Wu, F., Pandey, R., & Chen, H. (2009). *Noise injection for search privacy protection*. Paper presented at the 2009 International Conference on Computational Science and Engineering. ACM. 10.1109/CSE.2009.77

ADDITIONAL READING

Bashir, S., Lai, D. T. C., & Malik, O. A. (2022). Proxy-Terms Based Query Obfuscation Technique for Private Web Search. *IEEE Access: Practical Innovations, Open Solutions*, *10*, 17845–17863. doi:10.1109/ACCESS.2022.3149929

Hughes, K., Papadopoulos, P., Pitropakis, N., Smales, A., Ahmad, J., & Buchanan, W. J. (2021). Browsers' Private Mode: Is It What We Were Promised? *Computers*, *10*(12), 165. doi:10.3390/computers10120165

Kaaniche, N., Masmoudi, S., Znina, S., Laurent, M., & Demir, L. (2020, March). Privacy preserving cooperative computation for personalized web search applications. In *Proceedings of the 35th Annual ACM Symposium on Applied Computing* (pp. 250-258). 10.1145/3341105.3373947

Khandaker, M. R. (2020). *Protecting Cyberspace: Vulnerability Discovery and Mitigation* (Doctoral dissertation, The Florida State University).

Khandaker, M. R., Cheng, Y., Wang, Z., & Wei, T. (2020, March). COIN attacks: On insecurity of enclave untrusted interfaces in SGX. In *Proceedings of the Twenty-Fifth International Conference on Architectural Support for Programming Languages and Operating Systems* (pp. 971-985). 10.1145/3373376.3378486

Meyuhas, B., Gelernter, N., & Herzberg, A. (2020, December). Cross-Site Search Attacks: Unauthorized Queries over Private Data. In *International Conference on Cryptology and Network Security* (pp. 43-62). Springer, Cham. 10.1007/978-3-030-65411-5_3

PurandareB. (2020). Securing Private Webs.

Wolters, P. T. J. (2020). *Search Engines*. Digitalization and National Private Law.

Yekhanin, S. (2010). Private information retrieval. In *Locally Decodable Codes and Private Information Retrieval Schemes* (pp. 61–74). Springer. doi:10.1007/978-3-642-14358-8_4

ENDNOTES

[1]   www.startpage.com

[2]   www.qwant.com/?l=en

[3]   www.duckduckgo.com

Chapter 3
Web Search Privacy Evaluation Metrics

Rafi Ullah Khan
The University of Agriculture, Peshawar, Pakistan

Mohib Ullah
The University of Agriculture, Peshawar, Pakistan

Bushra Shafi
The University of Agriculture, Peshawar, Pakistan

ABSTRACT

Privacy quantification methods are used to quantify the knowledge the adverse search engine has obtained with and without privacy protection mechanisms. Thus, these methods calculate privacy exposure. Private web search techniques are based on many methods (e.g., proxy service, query modification, query exchange, and others). This variety of techniques prompted the researchers to evaluate their work differently. This section introduces the metrics used to evaluate user privacy (protection). Moreover, this section also introduces the metrics used to evaluate the performance of privacy attacks and theoretical evaluation approaches.

INTRODUCTION

Web search is the most dominant online activity due to the sheer abundance of information on the Web over the last two decades (El-Ansari, Beni-Hssane, Saadi, & El Fissaoui, 2021; Khan & Ali, 2013; Khan, Ullah, Khan, Uddin, & Al-Yahya, 2021; Preibusch, 2015). This abundance of information exceeds human processing abilities and prevent them from finding their desired contents (such as information, product, services and others) (Khan, 2020; Khan et al., 2021; Ullah, Islam, Khan, Aleem, & Iqbal, 2019). Web search engines provide the most relevant web content to the users based on their query, location, history (user profile) and other parameters (Khan et al., 2020; Khan & Islam, 2017; Ullah et al., 2021; Ullah et al., 2022). Usually, web search service providers claim that they offer their service free of cost and make

DOI: 10.4018/978-1-6684-6914-9.ch003

a profit with the advertisements displayed alongside query results (Khan & Islam, 2017; Khan, Islam, Ullah, Aleem, & Iqbal, 2019; Preibusch, 2015). However, maintaining user profiles may cause serious privacy breach concerns as these profiles may contain private and sensitive queries about users (Khan, 2020; Preibusch, 2015; Ullah et al., 2019). Eurobarometer reported in 2016 that 82% of European web users say that user activity monitoring tools should only be used with their permission (Monteleone, 2017; Zuiderveen Borgesius, Kruikemeier, Boerman, & Helberger, 2017).

Private web search and private information retrieval are the techniques for retrieving the desired information from web search engines or a database without disclosing the user's identity, intentions and other tracking information (Saint-Jean, 2005). These techniques are proposed to tackle the user privacy infringement problem (Khan et al., 2021). There are numerous techniques available to counter privacy infringement, such as proxy networks (Berthold, Federrath, & Köpsell, 2001; Mokhtar et al., 2017), profile obfuscation techniques (Nissenbaum & Daniel, 2009), query scrambling techniques (Arampatzis, Drosatos, & Efraimidis, 2015; Arampatzis, Efraimidis, & Drosatos, 2013), private information retrieval protocols (Reiter & Rubin, 1998; Romero-Tris, Castella-Roca, & Viejo, 2011; Romero-Tris, Viejo, & Castellà-Roca, 2015; Ullah et al., 2019; Ullah et al., 2021; Ullah, Khan, & Islam, 2016a, 2016b; Ullah et al., 2022; Viejo, Castella-Roca, Bernadó, & Mateo-Sanz, 2012) and others (Chen, Bai, Shou, Chen, & Gao, 2011; Mokhtar, Berthou, Diarra, Quéma, & Shoker, 2013; Mokhtar et al., 2017; Petit, Cerqueus, Mokhtar, Brunie, & Kosch, 2015; Shapira, Elovici, Meshiach, & Kuflik, 2005).

Performance evaluation metrics are vital tools to measure the effectiveness of the proposed procedures or methodologies and compare their performance against their state-of-the-art counterparts. The evaluation metrics are usually based on mathematical or statistical methods designed to simulate some events in a simulator or a mathematical model and collect the response values of these events. In computing, the usual metrics are algorithmic time and space complexity; however, different metrics are developed for different problems to evaluate the effectiveness of the tools proposed for the specific problems (Aslanpour, Gill, & Toosi, 2020). It is essential to select the right metric for evaluating the proposed techniques as it gives a sound idea about the behaviour and success of the technique on the field. Performance evaluation provides a systematic method to study a technique, practice, intervention or initiative to understand how well the proposed technique will achieve its goals. It also helps to determine which area of the proposed technique works fine and what could be improved. With the selection of appropriate metrics, one can demonstrate the impact of Research, suggest improvements, continue research efforts, and use used in other potential domains.

In private web searches and private information retrieval domains, various performance evaluation metrics are available to evaluate the performance of proposed techniques. Most researchers use statistical and mathematical functions, while some use simulation results and theoretical analysis of the mechanism. This chapter overviews the most prominent metrics used to evaluate privacy web search and private information retrieval techniques.

The rest of the chapter is organized as follows: Section 2 briefly presents the metrics proposed and used for private web search techniques evaluation. In section 3, we present a conclusive summary of all the attacks, and in section 4, we discuss the relative future directions.

PRIVATE WEB SEARCH EVALUATION METRICS

Private web search evaluation metrics are the methods and techniques used to evaluate the effectiveness of private web search or information retrieval methods. Most of these metrics use statistical methods and mathematical functions for performance evaluations of their proposed privacy-preserving techniques. However, some researchers also used simulation results and theoretical analysis of their proposed techniques. This section discusses the well-known privacy evolution metrics available for private web search and information retrieval methods.

Entropy

The entropy function calculates the quantity of information using a discrete random variable in the information theory domain (Khan, 2020). In the privacy quantification domain, the entropy function calculates the amount of user interest information learned by the adverse entity where the user interest is modelled as a discrete variable. Suppose we consider K as a set of user interests that contains keywords of user's interests [k1, k2, k3, ….. kn]. The entropy of H(K) will be mathematically shown in equation 1.

$$H(K) = E\left[-log_2\left(p(K)\right)\right] = -\sum_{j=1}^{n} p(k_j).log_2 p(k_j)$$

(1)

Where p represents a discrete random variable of the user of interest (UoI), the probability of each keyword used by UoI is represented as kj. This measure is used by PaOSLo (Ullah et al., 2022), Poshida (I, II) (Ullah et al., 2016a, 2016b), MG OSLo (Ullah et al., 2021), OSLo (Ullah et al., 2019), OQF-PIR (Rebollo-Monedero, Forne, & Domingo-Ferrer, 2012), and Balsa's Model (Balsa, Troncoso, & Diaz, 2012).

Cross Entropy Loss

Cross-Entropy Loss is a function designed to calculate the difference between two probability distributions. This function can be effectively used to calculate the privacy exposure of users from fake and actual (reference) profiles (Khan, 2020; Nissenbaum & Daniel, 2009). The equation for the Cross-Entropy Loss function is shown in equation 2. Where F represents the fake profile, and A represents the user's actual profile. This metric is used by Khan et al. for calculating user privacy exposure by their proposed method of Privacy Exposure Measure (Khan, 2020; Khan et al., 2019). This measure is used by Privacy Exposure Measure (PEM) (Khan, 2020; Khan et al., 2019) to evaluate their proposed scheme.

$$H(A,F) = -\sum_{j=1}^{m} (Aj).log(Fj)$$

(2)

Degree of Anonymity

The Degree of Anonymity is another measure that uses entropy to calculate the Anonymity of the user while using unlinkability techniques (Diaz, Seys, Claessens, & Preneel, 2002). This measure is used to calculate the ability of a WSE to connect the anonymized query to its original originator. As previously mentioned in the Entropy section, p(kj) represents probability kj is the original requestor of the query. The maximum entropy (HM) and degree of Anonymity, in that case, are shown in equations 3 and 4.

$$H_M = \log_2(n) \tag{3}$$

$$Degree_{Anonymity} = 1 - \frac{H_M - H(K)}{H_M} = \frac{H(K)}{H_M} \tag{4}$$

Where n represents the total number of users, the degree of Anonymity was first used by Reiter and Rubin in1998 for their proposed method Crowds (Reiter & Rubin, 1998) and was then adopted by Serjantov and Danezis (Serjantov & Danezis, 2002) and Diaz et al. (Diaz et al., 2002) as anonymity calculation function. The degree of Anonymity varies between 0 (maximum privacy) and 1 (minimum privacy), and Reiter and Rubin even developed a scale for privacy evaluation with various points shown in Figure 1.

Figure 1. Levels of degree of anonymity by Reiter and Rubin
(Reiter & Rubin, 1998)

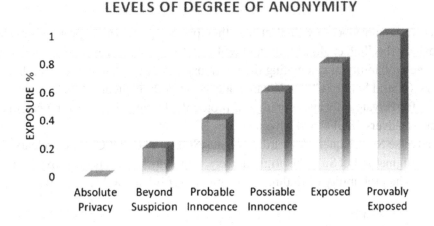

Standard Deviation

Standard deviation is a statistical measure used to calculate the average variation in a set of values. This measure is used by Khan et al. (Khan, 2020) to measure the amount of deviation by varying the number of queries in his proposed QuPiD Attack (Khan, 2020; Khan et al., 2020). They used Standard deviation of precision and recall in different scenarios. Mathematically standard deviation is shown in Equation 5.

$$Std\ Dev = \sqrt{\frac{\sum (xi - \mu)^2}{N}} \qquad (5)$$

Where N represents the size of the population (all values in the set), xi represents each value in the set, and μ is the population's mean.

Profile Exposure Level

Profile Exposure Level is a statistical measure used to estimate user profile exposure in front of adverse web search engines. In profile exposure level, the variation between users' obfuscated profile and original profile using mutual information entropy functions. The original user profile comprises users' original queries, while the obfuscated profile is created through any privacy-preserved web search mechanism. This metric is used by many prevalent Private information retrieval protocols such as PaOSLo (Ullah et al., 2022), MG-OSLo (Ullah et al., 2021), OSLo (Ullah et al., 2019), UUP (Juarez & Torra, 2015), Poshida-I (Ullah et al., 2016b), Poshida-II (Ullah et al., 2016a) and others. The mathematical formula of the Profile Exposure level is shown in Equation 6. The I(P,Q) function represents the mutual information, and the H(P) function represents the entropy.

$$Profile\ Exposure\ Level = \left(\frac{I(P,Q)}{H(P)} \times 100 \right) \qquad (6)$$

Local Privacy

Local Privacy metric was introduced by Ullah et al. in their privacy preservation protocols Poshida (Ullah et al., 2016b), Poshida II (Ullah et al., 2016a), and OSLo (Ullah et al., 2019). Local privacy measure is used to calculate the probability of calculating the relationship between the queries and their originator by other peer users, Central Server (CS) and Search query-forwarding client (SQFC). Local privacy was specially designed for Private information retrieval protocols. Local privacy can be calculated in two significant scenarios, adverse SQFC and adverse nodes.

In case of an adverse Search query-forwarding client (SQFC), the SQFC wants to learn the identity of a specific query originator. Let Su is the original query originator and Pu is the proxy user who passes the query to SQFC. The probability of finding the original user by the SQFC is shown in Equation 7.

$$Probability\ [Su\,|\,Pu] = \frac{1}{n-1} \qquad (7)$$

Where n shows the total number of peer nodes in the group excluding SQFC; similarly, if other nodes or Several adverse nodes also collaborate with SQFC to find the original query originator user, then the probability of finding the original user by the SQFC and Several adverse nodes is shown in Equation 8.

$$Probability\ [Su\,|\,Pu] = \frac{1}{n-A} \tag{8}$$

KL Divergence

KL- (Kullback-Leibler) divergence is a relative entropy calculation method used to find the difference between two probability distributions (Khan, 2020; Kullback & Leibler, 1951). Rebollo-Monedero and Jordi Forne (Parra-Arnau, Rebollo-Monedero, & Forné, 2014) and Khan et al. (Khan, 2020) used KL-Divergence to find the divergence of the user profile from the reference profile. This measure is also used to calculate the profile privacy leakage. The equation for the KL-Divergence is given in Equation 9. Where R and S are two probability distributions on Y space. This measure is used by Privacy Exposure Measure (PEM) (Khan, 2020; Khan et al., 2019) to evaluate their proposed scheme.

$$Div_{KL}(R\,||\,S) = \sum_{y \in Y} R(y) \log\left(\frac{R(y)}{S(y)}\right) \tag{9}$$

ProQSim Effect

ProQSim Effect is an unexpected behaviour of QuPiD attack discovered by Khan that significantly affects the performance of QuPiD attack (Khan, 2020). The ProQSim (Profile to Query Similarity) effect introduces irregular behaviour of the QuPiD attack in many cases, and upon investigation, three factors were found responsible. Limited user profile, Immense difference between user's profile and testing data, and user with similar interest and matching profile. Khan et al. used Euclidian distance to find the similarity between the profiles and explain the abovementioned factors. The Cosine similarity is shown in Equation 12. Similarly, a pixel map (Figure 2) illustrates the similarity between user profiles or between profiles and queries.

Privacy Exposure Measure (PEM)

The privacy Exposure Measure (PEM) was devised by Khan et al. (Khan et al., 2019) that allow users to set their privacy exposure threshold. PEM was proposed as a generic step in PIR protocols that enable users to protect their privacy. According to the design of PEM, the user is initially asked to set the privacy exposure threshold value. They called that value as maximum privacy exposure threshold or mpeT value. After setting the mpeT value, the similarity of every new query issued by the user is calculated with the profile value. If the similarity value is less than the mpeT value, then the query is forwarded to other peer nodes for shuffling. For similarity calculation, they used three well-known similarity measures, i.e. Euclidian Distance, Jaccard Similarity, and Cosine Similarity. Equations 10, 11, and 12 show the mathematical functions of Euclidian Distance, Jaccard Similarity, and Cosine Similarity.

$$Euclidean\ Distance\,(Qa, Pv) = \sqrt{\sum_{b=1}^{n}(Qab - Pvb)^2} \tag{10}$$

$$Jaccard\ Similarity(Qa, Pv) = \frac{\sum_b Min(Qab, Pvb)}{\sum_b Max(Qab, Pvb)} \tag{11}$$

$$Cosine\ Similarity(Qa, Pv) = \frac{\sum_{b=1}^{n} Qab.Pvb}{\sqrt{\sum_{b=1}^{n}(Qab)^2}\sqrt{\sum_{b=1}^{n}(Pvb)^2}} \tag{12}$$

Where Q represents the user queries and Pv represents the user profile vector.

Figure 2. User profile similarity Pixel map

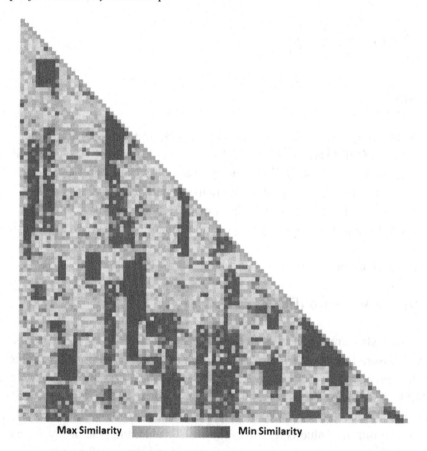

Max Similarity   Min Similarity

GooPIR Quality Assessment Measures

Domingo-Ferrer et al. proposed GooPIR, a private information retrieval technique that uses bogus keywords added to the user query to hide the user's true intentions (Domingo-Ferrer, Solanas, & Castellà-Roca, 2009). To evaluate the privacy provided by these queries, they developed three quality assessment measures Percentage of Coincidences, Average distance between coincidences, and Variance of the rank differences. They used the retrieved URLs obtained through regular communication and with GooPIR and compared them using the abovementioned quality assessment measures. Equations 13, 14 and 15 show the percentage of Coincidences, Average distance between coincidences, and Variance of the Rank differences, respectively.

$$Coincidences\% = \frac{Cardinality(S \cap S')}{N} \times 100 \tag{13}$$

$$Average\ Coincidences\ Distance(ACD) = \frac{\sum_{i \in S \cap S'} \left| Rank_S(i) - Rank_{S'}(i) \right|}{Card(S \cap S')} \tag{14}$$

$$Varience\ of\ Rank\ Diff = \frac{\sum_{i \in S \cap S'} \left(\left| Rank_S(i) - Rank_{S'}(i) \right| - ACD \right)^2}{Card(S \cap S')} \tag{15}$$

S represents the set of URLs obtained from regular communication, S' represents, and N represents the cardinality of S and S'.

Search Engine Results Analysis

Analysis of search engine results pages (or SERPs) is another method to evaluate and quantify the performance of the proposed web search privacy preservation method in terms of privacy protection. In this method, the evolution in the quality of the web search result pages is assessed with the introduction of fake queries. This method is used by TrackMeNot (TMN) (Khan, 2020; Nissenbaum & Daniel, 2009) to assess the evolving change in the user interest profile maintained on the server side. For experimentation, they used Yahoo! (search engine) user interest list.

Theoretical Analysis

Apart from the mathematical and statistical measures, some other methods use theoretical and algorithmic steps to evaluate the protocol's performance. These methods use Pi-Calculus (π-calculus) to verify the working of protocols. Examples of such protocol verifiers are ProVerif (Blanchet, 2001) and Avispa (Armando et al., 2005). These protocols are used to verify the properties of the protocols by devising all possible states. One of the major flaws of these protocol verifiers is the perfect modelling of the protocols.

Confusion Matrix

The Confusion Matrix is a widespread measure used to analyze the performance of a machine learning model (Khan, 2020; Kullback & Leibler, 1951). The confusion matrix is based on four major types of observations, i.e. True Negative (TN) observations, False Negative (FN) observations, True Positive

(TP) observations, and False Positive observations (FP) (Khan, 2020; Khan et al., 2020; Khan et al., 2021). The True Positive and True Negative are the observations correctly identified by the machine. In comparison, False Positive and False Negative are the observations incorrectly identified by the machine as positive or negative. These observations are classified into actual and predicted classes called Confusion Matrix, as shown in Figure 3. The confusion matrix is then used to create the essential metrics of the machine learning, i.e. Accuracy, Precision, Recall, and F1-Score (F-Measure).

Accuracy

The accuracy represents the score of correctly classified or identified observations out of all observations. The accuracy value is between 0 and 1, where 0 represents minimum accuracy or no observation classified correctly by the prediction or classification model, and 1 represents maximum accuracy, or all observations are classified correctly by the model. Accuracy is used in those cases where the data is well-balanced and has no class imbalance.

The equation for the accuracy is shown below (Equation 16):

$$Accuracy = \frac{TN + TP}{FN + TN + FP + TP} \qquad (16)$$

Figure 3. Confusion matrix
(Khan, 2020)

	Total Population	Actual Class	
		Condition Positive	Condition Negative
Predicted Class	Predicted condition positive	True Positive (TP)	False Positive (FP)
	Predicted condition negative	False Negative (FN)	True Negative (TN)

Precision

The precision metric is usually used to retrieve information and evaluate machine learning models. Precision shows the number of relevant observations out of the total retrieved or classified observations marked as relevant by the model. A precision metric is suitable for those cases where we want to be sure of our prediction. The equation for the precision is shown in Equation 17.

$$Precision = \frac{TP}{FP + TP} \qquad (17)$$

Recall

The recall is another popular metric usually used in information retrieval, but it is also used to evaluate machine learning models. Recall shows the number of relevant observations retrieved by the machine from the total relevant observations in the testing data. Recall metric is a good choice for those problems where we want to capture as many positives as possible. The equation for the precision is shown in Equation 18.

$$Recall = \frac{TP}{FN + TP} \tag{18}$$

F-Measure

F-Measure (or F1-Score) is the combination of the two measures, i.e. recall and precision. F-Measure gives the approximate average of recall and precision (Harmonic mean of recall and precision score) (Khan, 2020). The value of F-Measure is between 0 and 1, where 1 shows the perfect recall and precision, while 0 shows that one of the values in recall or precision is 0. F-Measure is used in cases where we want a model with good precision and recall. The equation for F-Measure is shown in equation 19.

$$F - Measure = 2 \times \frac{Recall \times Precision}{Recall + Precision} \tag{19}$$

Support

Khan et al. use the support metric in their proposed Association Rule Mining attack (Khan, Ullah, & Islam, 2016). They used the association rule mining technique to find the relationship between the user of interest (UoI) and their queries of interest (QoI) in the sessions of the obscure web search engine logs. The support metric shows the co-existence probability of the user and a query of interest in all retrieved sessions. The equation for support is shown in Equation 20.

$$Support(UoI) = \frac{frequency(UoI \cup QoI)}{Total\ Retrievd\ Sessions} \tag{20}$$

Confidence

Confidence is another metric used by Khan et al. in their proposed Association Rule Mining attack (Khan et al., 2016). They used the association rule mining technique to find the strength of the relationship between user appearance and the queries of interests in the sessions of the obscure web search engine logs. Confidence represents the conditional probability of the appearance of the user of interest with the queries of interest. The equation for support is shown in Equation 21.

$$Confidence\left(UoI \rightarrow QoI\right) = \frac{frequency\left(UoI \cup QoI\right)}{frequency\left(UoI\right)} \tag{21}$$

Group Visibility

Group visibility measure was designed by Khan et al. in their proposed Association Rule Mining attack (Khan et al., 2016). The measure is designed to find the percentage of visible group members of the private information retrieval (PIR) protocols during an Association Rule Mining attack. The group visibility is based on the frequency of users retrieved from the sessions of queries or users of interests with good confidence value (i.e. Confidence=>50%). The equation for the Group Visibility is shown in Equation 22.

$$Group\ Visibility = \frac{User\ with => 50\%Confidence}{Group\ Size} \tag{22}$$

CONCLUSION AND SUMMARY

Performance evaluation metrics are vital tools to measure the effectiveness of the proposed procedures or methodologies and compare their performance against their state-of-the-art counterparts. In computing, the usual metrics are algorithmic time and space complexity; however, different metrics are developed for different problems to evaluate the effectiveness of the tools proposed for specific problems. It is essential to select the right metric for evaluating the proposed techniques as it gives a sound idea about the behaviour and success of the technique on the field. In private web searches and private information retrieval domains, various performance evaluation metrics are available to evaluate the performance of proposed techniques. Most use statistical and mathematical functions, while some use simulation results and theoretical analysis of the mechanism. This chapter briefly introduces some significant performance evaluation metrics used to evaluate various well-known privacy-preserved web search and private information retrieval schemes.

This section presents a conclusive comparison of the performance evaluation metrics used to evaluate well-known privacy-preserved web search techniques. In Table 1, we discussed the evaluation metric and the core functions used in that evaluation metric. In most cases, Entropy and Profile Exposure Level (PEL) are used as evaluation metrics due to their versatile ability to handle information exposure or leak efficiently. Similarly, most techniques also used machine learning metrics, i.e. accuracy, recall, precision, and f-measure effectively. While in most cases, similarity functions are used to calculate the difference between users' original and anonymized profiles.

Table 1. Privacy metrics used to evaluate privacy preserved web search techniques

Protocol/Technique	Evaluation Metric	Core Function
Track Me Not (TMN)	Search Engine Results Pages (SERP) Matching	Set theory
RAC	Profile Exposure Level	Malicious Users Ratio
Web Mixes	Profile Exposure Level	Active Users Ratio
Plausibly Deniable Search (PDS)	Profile Similarity Percentage	Clustering, Cosine Similarity, Edit Distance
GooPIR	Coincidence Percentage, Average Coincidence distance, Variance of Rank Difference	Percentage, Variance, Distance
DisPa	Precision, Recall, F-Measure, True and False Positive	Clustering
OQF-PIR	Entropy	-
UPS	Precision, Recall	Classification
X-Search	Precision, Recall	Classification
PaOSLo	Profile Exposure Level (PEL), Local Privacy	Cosine Similarity, Entropy, Probability
Crowds	Probability	-
Poshida (I, II)	Profile Exposure Level (PEL), Local Privacy, Privacy Relative QFN, QGFN, Core Server, Group Users	Entropy, Probability
MG OSLo	Profile Exposure Level (PEL), Local Privacy, Privacy Relative QFN, QGFN, Core Server, Group Users	Entropy, Probability
OSLo	Profile Exposure Level (PEL), Local Privacy, Privacy Relative QFN, QGFN, Core Server, Group Users	Entropy, Probability
Query Profile Distance (QuPiD) Attack	Precision, Recall, F-Measure	Classification
SimAttack	Precision, Recall, F-Measure	Classification
Balsa's Model	Entropy	
Peddinti and Saxena Model	Accuracy, Misclassification, (FP, FN)	Classification
Neural Network-Query Profile Distance (NN-QuPiD) Attack	Precision, Recall	Classification
Association Rule Mining (ARM) Attack	Group Visibility, Accuracy, Support, Confidence	Association Rule Mining
Privacy Exposure Measure (PEM)	Precision, Recall, F-Measure, Profile Similarity, Cross-Entropy loss, Kullback-Liebler (KL) divergence	Cosine Similarity, Jaccard Similarity, Euclidian Distance

FUTURE RECOMMENDATIONS

We have concluded that in most cases, statistical metrics (Entropy, Probability, Profile Exposure Level (PEL) and other machine learning (accuracy, recall, precision, and f-measure) are effectively used in privacy evaluation. This conclusion unveiled the path for future directions, such as problems related to the statistical measure. As statistical measures are usually based on sample data and averages, they cannot draw a precise and clear picture of the problem. Instead, a Monte Carlo simulation method may better draw a clear picture of the problem. Moreover, the researchers should also need to research the area of theoretical assessments and protocol verification methods for privacy evolution.

REFERENCES

Arampatzis, A., Drosatos, G., & Efraimidis, P. S. (2015). Versatile query scrambling for private web search. *Information Retrieval Journal, 18*(4), 331–358. doi:10.100710791-015-9256-0

Arampatzis, A., Efraimidis, P. S., & Drosatos, G. (2013). A query scrambler for search privacy on the internet. *Information Retrieval, 16*(6), 657–679. doi:10.100710791-012-9212-1

Armando, A., Basin, D., Boichut, Y., Chevalier, Y., Compagna, L., Cuéllar, J., . . . Mantovani, J. (2005). *The AVISPA tool for the automated validation of internet security protocols and applications.* Paper presented at the International conference on computer aided verification. IEEE. 10.1007/11513988_27

Aslanpour, M. S., Gill, S. S., & Toosi, A. N. (2020). Performance evaluation metrics for cloud, fog and edge computing: A review, taxonomy, benchmarks and standards for future research. *Internet of Things, 12*, 100273. doi:10.1016/j.iot.2020.100273

Balsa, E., Troncoso, C., & Diaz, C. (2012). *OB-PWS: Obfuscation-based private web search.* Paper presented at the 2012 IEEE Symposium on Security and Privacy. IEEE. 10.1109/SP.2012.36

Berthold, O., Federrath, H., & Köpsell, S. (2001). *Web MIXes: A system for anonymous and unobservable Internet access.* Paper presented at the Designing privacy enhancing technologies. Springer.10.1007/3-540-44702-4_7

Blanchet, B. (2001). *An efficient cryptographic protocol verifier based on prolog rules.* Paper presented at the csfw. Springer. 10.1109/CSFW.2001.930138

Chen, G., Bai, H., Shou, L., Chen, K., & Gao, Y. (2011). *UPS: efficient privacy protection in personalized web search.* Paper presented at the Proceedings of the 34th international ACM SIGIR conference on Research and development in Information Retrieval. ACM. 10.1145/2009916.2009999

Diaz, C., Seys, S., Claessens, J., & Preneel, B. (2002). *Towards measuring anonymity.* Paper presented at the International Workshop on Privacy Enhancing Technologies. Springer.

Domingo-Ferrer, J., Solanas, A., & Castellà-Roca, J. (2009). h (k)-private information retrieval from privacy-uncooperative queryable databases. *Online Information Review, 33*(4), 720–744. doi:10.1108/14684520910985693

El-Ansari, A., Beni-Hssane, A., Saadi, M., & El Fissaoui, M. (2021). PAPIR: Privacy-aware personalized information retrieval. *Journal of Ambient Intelligence and Humanized Computing, 12*(10), 9891–9907. doi:10.100712652-020-02736-y

Juarez, M., & Torra, V. (2015). *Dispa: An intelligent agent for private web search Advanced research in data privacy.* Springer.

Khan, R. (2020). *On the effectiveness of private information retrieval protocols.* Department of Computer Science, Capital University of Science and Technology.

Khan, R., Ahmad, A., Alsayed, A. O., Binsawad, M., Islam, M. A., & Ullah, M. (2020). QuPiD attack: Machine learning-based privacy quantification mechanism for PIR protocols in health-related web search. *Scientific Programming, 2020*, 2020. doi:10.1155/2020/8868686

Khan, R., & Ali, S. (2013). Conceptual Framework of Redundant Link Aggregation. arXiv preprint arXiv:1305.2708.

Khan, R., & Islam, M. A. (2017). *Quantification of PIR protocols privacy.* Paper presented at the 2017 International Conference on Communication, Computing and Digital Systems (C-CODE). IEEE. 10.1109/C-CODE.2017.7918908

Khan, R., Islam, M. A., Ullah, M., Aleem, M., & Iqbal, M. A. (2019). Privacy exposure measure: A privacy-preserving technique for health-related web search. *Journal of Medical Imaging and Health Informatics*, *9*(6), 1196–1204. doi:10.1166/jmihi.2019.2709

Khan, R., Ullah, M., & Islam, M. A. (2016). *Revealing pir protocols protected users.* Paper presented at the 2016 Sixth International Conference on Innovative Computing Technology (INTECH). IEEE. 10.1109/INTECH.2016.7845059

Khan, R., Ullah, M., Khan, A., Uddin, M. I., & Al-Yahya, M. (2021). NN-QuPiD attack: Neural network-based privacy quantification model for private information retrieval protocols. *Complexity*, *2021*, 2021. doi:10.1155/2021/6651662

Kullback, S., & Leibler, R. A. (1951). On information and sufficiency. *Annals of Mathematical Statistics*, *22*(1), 79–86. doi:10.1214/aoms/1177729694

Mokhtar, S. B., Berthou, G., Diarra, A., Quéma, V., & Shoker, A. (2013). *Rac: A freerider-resilient, scalable, anonymous communication protocol.* Paper presented at the 2013 IEEE 33rd International Conference on Distributed Computing Systems. IEEE. 10.1109/ICDCS.2013.52

Mokhtar, S. B., Boutet, A., Felber, P., Pasin, M., Pires, R., & Schiavoni, V. (2017). *X-search: revisiting private web search using intel sgx.* Paper presented at the Proceedings of the 18th ACM/IFIP/USENIX Middleware Conference. ACM. 10.1145/3135974.3135987

Monteleone, S. (2017). *Reform of the e-Privacy Directive: EPRS.* European Parliamentary Research Service, Members' Research Service.

Nissenbaum, H., & Daniel, H. (2009). *TrackMeNot: Resisting surveillance in web search.* TrackMeNot.

Parra-Arnau, J., Rebollo-Monedero, D., & Forné, J. (2014). Measuring the privacy of user profiles in personalized information systems. *Future Generation Computer Systems*, *33*, 53–63. doi:10.1016/j.future.2013.01.001

Petit, A., Cerqueus, T., Mokhtar, S. B., Brunie, L., & Kosch, H. (2015). *PEAS: Private, efficient and accurate web search.* Paper presented at the 2015 IEEE Trustcom/BigDataSE/ISPA. IEEE. 10.1109/Trustcom.2015.421

Preibusch, S. (2015). The value of web search privacy. *IEEE Security and Privacy*, *13*(05), 24–32. doi:10.1109/MSP.2015.109

Rebollo-Monedero, D., Forne, J., & Domingo-Ferrer, J. (2012). Query profile obfuscation by means of optimal query exchange between users. *IEEE Transactions on Dependable and Secure Computing*, *9*(5), 641–654. doi:10.1109/TDSC.2012.16

Reiter, M. K., & Rubin, A. D. (1998). Crowds: Anonymity for web transactions. [TISSEC]. *ACM Transactions on Information and System Security, 1*(1), 66–92. doi:10.1145/290163.290168

Romero-Tris, C., Castella-Roca, J., & Viejo, A. (2011). *Multi-party private web search with untrusted partners.* Paper presented at the International Conference on Security and Privacy in Communication Systems. IEEE.

Romero-Tris, C., Viejo, A., & Castellà-Roca, J. (2015). *Multi-party methods for privacy-preserving web search: survey and contributions Advanced research in data privacy.* Springer.

Saint-Jean, F. (2005). *Java implementation of a single-database computationally symmetric private information retrieval (cSPIR) protocol.* Yale Univ New Haven Ct Dept Of Computer Science.

Serjantov, A., & Danezis, G. (2002). *Towards an information theoretic metric for anonymity.* Paper presented at the International Workshop on Privacy Enhancing Technologies. IEEE.

Shapira, B., Elovici, Y., Meshiach, A., & Kuflik, T. (2005). PRAW—A PRivAcy model for the Web. *Journal of the American Society for Information Science and Technology, 56*(2), 159–172. doi:10.1002/asi.20107

Ullah, M., Islam, M. A., Khan, R., Aleem, M., & Iqbal, M. A. (2019). ObSecure Logging (OSLo): A framework to protect and evaluate the web search privacy in health care domain. *Journal of Medical Imaging and Health Informatics, 9*(6), 1181–1190. doi:10.1166/jmihi.2019.2708

Ullah, M., Khan, R., Haq, M. I. U., Khan, A., Alosaimi, W., Uddin, M. I., & Alharbi, A. (2021). Multi-group ObScure logging (MG-OSLo) A privacy-preserving protocol for private web search. *IEEE Access : Practical Innovations, Open Solutions, 9,* 79005–79020. doi:10.1109/ACCESS.2021.3078431

Ullah, M., Khan, R., & Islam, M. A. (2016a). *Poshida II, a multi group distributed peer to peer protocol for private web search.* Paper presented at the 2016 International Conference on Frontiers of Information Technology (FIT). IEEE. 10.1109/FIT.2016.022

Ullah, M., Khan, R., & Islam, M. A. (2016b). *Poshida, a protocol for private information retrieval.* Paper presented at the 2016 Sixth International Conference on Innovative Computing Technology (INTECH). IEEE. 10.1109/INTECH.2016.7845060

Ullah, M., Khan, R. U., Khan, I. U., Aslam, N., Aljameel, S. S., Ul Haq, M. I., & Islam, M. A. (2022). Profile Aware ObScure Logging (PaOSLo): A Web Search Privacy-Preserving Protocol to Mitigate Digital Traces. *Security and Communication Networks, 2022,* 2022. doi:10.1155/2022/2109024

Viejo, A., Castella-Roca, J., Bernadó, O., & Mateo-Sanz, J. M. (2012). *Single-party private web search.* Paper presented at the 2012 Tenth Annual International Conference on Privacy, Security and Trust. IEEE. 10.1109/PST.2012.6297913

Zuiderveen Borgesius, F. J., Kruikemeier, S., Boerman, S. C., & Helberger, N. (2017). Tracking walls, take-it-or-leave-it choices, the GDPR, and the ePrivacy regulation. *Eur. Data Prot. L. Rev., 3*(3), 353–368. doi:10.21552/edpl/2017/3/9

ADDITIONAL READING

Afifi, M. H., Zhou, K., & Ren, J. (2018). Privacy characterization and quantification in data publishing. *IEEE Transactions on Knowledge and Data Engineering*, *30*(9), 1756–1769. doi:10.1109/TKDE.2018.2797092

Amos, R., Acar, G., Lucherini, E., Kshirsagar, M., Narayanan, A., & Mayer, J. (2021, April). *Privacy policies over time: Curation and analysis of a million-document dataset*. In *Proceedings of the Web Conference 2021* (pp. 2165-2176). 10.1145/3442381.3450048

Delgado-Santos, P., Stragapede, G., Tolosana, R., Guest, R., Deravi, F., & Vera-Rodriguez, R. (2022). A survey of privacy vulnerabilities of mobile device sensors. [CSUR]. *ACM Computing Surveys*, *54*(11s), 1–30. doi:10.1145/3510579

Jayaraman, B., & Evans, D. (2019). Evaluating differentially private machine learning in practice. In *28th USENIX Security Symposium (USENIX Security 19)* (pp. 1895-1912).

Jiang, H., Li, J., Zhao, P., Zeng, F., Xiao, Z., & Iyengar, A. (2021). Location privacy-preserving mechanisms in location-based services: A comprehensive survey. [CSUR]. *ACM Computing Surveys*, *54*(1), 1–36.

JohnsonG.ShriverS.GoldbergS. (2022). Privacy & market concentration: Intended & unintended consequences of the GDPR. *Available at* SSRN 3477686.

Wagner, I., & Eckhoff, D. (2018). Technical privacy metrics: A systematic survey. [CSUR]. *ACM Computing Surveys*, *51*(3), 1–38. doi:10.1145/3168389

Wu, Z., Li, G., Shen, S., Lian, X., Chen, E., & Xu, G. (2021). Constructing dummy query sequences to protect location privacy and query privacy in location-based services. *World Wide Web (Bussum)*, *24*(1), 25–49. doi:10.100711280-020-00830-x

Wu, Z., Shen, S., Zhou, H., Li, H., Lu, C., & Zou, D. (2021). An effective approach for the protection of user commodity viewing privacy in e-commerce website. *Knowledge-Based Systems*, *220*, 106952. doi:10.1016/j.knosys.2021.106952

Zhao, Y., & Chen, J. (2022). A survey on differential privacy for unstructured data content. [CSUR]. *ACM Computing Surveys*, *54*(10s), 1–28. doi:10.1145/3490237

KEY TERMS AND DEFINITIONS

Anonymity: Anonymity measures the ability of a system or process to protect the identity of individuals. It can be quantified using metrics such as k-anonymity and l-diversity, which evaluate the degree to which personal information can be linked to specific individuals.

Differential Privacy: Differential privacy measures the degree to which individual records in a dataset can be distinguished by an attacker. It is typically measured using metrics such as epsilon, which evaluates the amount of noise that must be added to a dataset to achieve a desired level of privacy.

Evaluation Metrics: Evaluation metrics are quantitative measures that are used to assess the performance of a model or algorithm. They are used to determine how well the model is performing in terms of accuracy, precision, recall, F1 score, and other measures. The choice of evaluation metrics depends on the type of problem being solved and the objectives of the model.

Information Leakage: Information leakage measures the amount of sensitive information that is exposed by a system or process. It can be quantified using metrics such as mutual information or entropy, which evaluate the amount of information that is revealed about an individual or a group of individuals.

Privacy Metrics: Privacy metrics are quantitative measures that are used to assess the level of privacy protection in a system or process. They help to evaluate the effectiveness of privacy-preserving mechanisms and to identify areas that need improvement.

Privacy Risk: Privacy risk measures the likelihood of a privacy breach or the potential harm that can result from a breach. It can be evaluated using metrics such as expected loss or probability of data breach.

Private Information Retrieval: Private Information Retrieval (PIR) is a cryptographic technique that allows a user to retrieve information from a database without revealing which information they are interested in. In traditional information retrieval systems, the user sends a query to the database, which then returns the relevant information. However, in PIR, the user sends a query to the database without revealing any information about the query or the data they are interested in.

Private Web Search Metrics: Private web search metrics are quantitative measures used to evaluate the effectiveness of privacy-preserving mechanisms in web search engines. These metrics help to assess the level of privacy protection provided by a search engine and identify areas for improvement.

Query Privacy: Query privacy measures the extent to which a search engine protects the queries made by the user. It can be quantified using metrics such as query uniqueness, which evaluates the degree to which queries can be linked to specific users.

Result Privacy: Result privacy measures the extent to which a search engine protects the search results. It can be quantified using metrics such as result diversity, which evaluates the degree to which the search results are unique for each user and the degree to which they protect the user's privacy.

Chapter 4
Desktop Search Engines:
A Review From User Perspectives

Shaukat Ali
University of Peshawar, Pakistan

Shah Khusro
University of Peshawar, Pakistan

Mumtaz Khan
University of Peshawar, Pakistan

ABSTRACT

The advancements in desktop computing technologies and widespread use of digital devices have enabled users to generate and store tons of contents on their computers, which creates an information overload problem. Therefore, users need applications to search and retrieve required stored data instantly and accurately. This attracted the software industry to develop desktop search engines using ideas of web search engines. However, selecting an effective desktop search engine is difficult for users. In this chapter, the authors have analyzed and compared available desktop search engines using a set of parameters including users' privacy and security. A generalized architecture for desktop search engines is presented for improving understanding and unification of development efforts. The new emerging trends, supporting users' privacy and security, and several open issues and challenges in the desktop search engines domain are also highlighted. The authors hope that this chapter will be helpful for researchers to find new research problems and users to select appropriate desktop search engines.

INTRODUCTION

The history of information retrieval (IR) has footprints long before the proliferation of internet. IR systems were needed when collection of data reached to a size beyond the strength of traditional cataloguing techniques. An IR system can search a vast collection of semi-structured and unstructured data (e.g., documents, web pages, images, videos, audios, etc.) to answer users' queries. IR systems were witnessed

DOI: 10.4018/978-1-6684-6914-9.ch004

in commercial and intelligence applications since 1960's. The integration of search into the fabric of desktop and mobile operating systems can be attributed to the success and high-level adoptability of the Web search engines (Sanderson & Croft, 2012).

Web technology has seen an incredible growth in the history of mankind since its inception in the mid 1990's. By September 2022, Google had indexed about 50 billion web pages. Success of the web gave rise to the problem of information overload, where finding required information is relatively a time consuming and cumbersome task. The increasing growth of information on the Web highlighted the importance of knowledge management. Several technologies have been investigated for this purpose including web search engines, and Semantic Web etc.

The evolution of computer hard drive technology has shown tremendous miniaturization and increase in the average size of storage capacity with the expense of decrease in the prices (Markscheffel, Büttner, & Fischer, 2011). The increasing number of varied application programs and the availability of new information sources has emerged new data formats, which significantly increased users' capability of storing different types of information and files on their PCs with an increase in their volume day by day. Therefore, PCs are suffering from the same information overload problem which was once experienced on the Web. Ultimately, finding/searching a required file on a PC is as hard as finding a needle in a haystack. To reduce search efforts, a painstaking user might organize his information in an advanced directory structure (Markscheffel, et al., 2011). However, studies have shown that traditional systems using desktop metaphor and folder hierarchy suffer from their limitations and might not provide adequate information management features specifically information retrieval (Jones & Dumais, 1986).

Most of the computer users normally act as "virtual pack rats" having the tendencies of hoarding their files in whatever drives space they may find (Farina, 2005). Thus, make it increasingly difficult for users to find quickly and accurately the exact locations of files on their PCs. To elevate the problem, ideas from the Web are leveraged into PCs, resulting into the development of desktop search engines (DSEs). DSEs are a new generation of desktop applications which enables users for quickly searching and retrieving required files simultaneously in multiple data sources (i.e., PCs, computers across the enterprise network, etc.) using a single query in the same way as web search engines are used for locating information on the Web (Noda & Helwig, 2005). A DSE works similarly to web search engines involving crawling, indexing, ranking, and searching activities (Narasimhan & Lowe, 2010).

Desktop search is an essential part of an operating system, but the search tools incorporated in operating systems are having certain limitations. To overcome these limitations, organizations especially the web giants such as Google, Yahoo, AOL, Microsoft, etc. have introduced their own DSEs during the last few years (Khusro, et al., 2017). However, the tools vary in cost, performance, user friendliness, and users' privacy and security (Khusro, et al., 2017). The web giants offered free of cost DSEs to convince users to use their web portals regularly. However, DSEs require new approaches because desktop files are normally different in structure than those on the Web. An average user selects a DSE that offers most attractive functionalities, which is easy-to-use, covers a variety of file types and support users' privacy and security (Cole, 2005; Khusro, et al., 2017; Narasimhan & Lowe, 2010). Similarly, due to different nature and complexities in desktop structure, desktop searching poses a number of challenges including (Cole, 2005): (1) limited capabilities of operating systems' built-in desktop search features due to keyword searching over a few file types, (2) structured files are easier to search as compared to unstructured files, (3) files of various desktop applications mostly differ structurally making search difficult and challenging, (4) IR approaches used in the Web search engines need to be incorporated for dealing with unstructured files, (5) metadata associated with files by authors requires to be extracted and utilized, (6) DSEs should be efficient at work and should not jeopardize system, and (7) DSEs have to use effective measures to deal with anticipated security and privacy problems which may arise.

In this chapter, we are presenting a comprehensive overview of the DSEs, highlighting their features, operations, and shortcomings. We have selected the different DSEs which are pioneers of the stream and used by a wide community of users. However, the DSEs with all of their innovations have resulted poorly due to: (1) using pure text-based ranking mechanisms (i.e., TF-IDF scores) which requires users to remember keywords contained in documents; (2) exact keyword matching for accomplishing searching processes effectively and (3) offering limited features and support users' privacy and security. Therefore, new generation of DSEs has been emerged which are indexing documents with more sophisticated ranking algorithms in addition to conventional TF-IDF scores with improved users' security and privacy considerations. These algorithms employ contextual information extraction form users' activities, associations between documents using semantic links and several others. The main contributions of this chapter include:

- A generalized architecture for DSEs has been proposed for helping readers to understand the phenomena.
- The key contribution is the critical investigation of the leading DSEs and highlighting their functionalities, limitations (i.e., both technological and non-technological) and their state-of-the-art. This analysis will help researchers in the area to find new research dimensions.
- A novel contribution is the enlisting of a set of evaluation parameters including users' privacy and security and making comparison of the selected DSEs using the evaluation criterion. Overall maturity score of the DSEs is shown in a tabular format describing their features and technical details.
- Another key contribution is the overview and classification of the new technologies emerging in the area for constructing sophisticated ranking algorithms to enhance the desktop search.
- Recommendation for incorporating users' privacy and security support in the DSEs. In addition, several issues and challenges are highlighted for finding new research dimensions.
- The on-hand knowledge is organized and presented in a way to boost up interest of the researchers/ readers in the area and provide them necessary initial knowledge to understand and add contributions to the area.

GENERALIZED DESKTOP SEARCH ENGINE FRAMEWORK

Although, current DSEs might be architecturally different from each other but there are some functions and features that are essential for each DSE. After keen analysis of the existing DSEs, we have presented a generalized three-layer framework for DSEs (shown in Figure 1.) in our previous research work (Khusro, et al., 2017). The three-layer framework is consisting of user interface layer, processing and extension layer, and storage layer. The integration and information flow among the various components of the framework from our previous research work (Khusro, et al., 2017) is depicted in Figure 2. For ease and helping in understanding the anatomy and operations of DSEs, each of these layers is explained under the following headings.

Figure 1. Generalized three-layer framework for DSEs
(Khusro, et al., 2017)

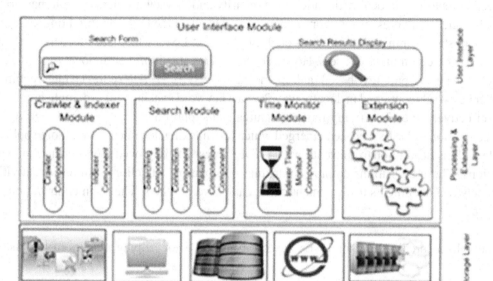

Figure 2. Integration and information flow among the components of the three-layer framework
(Khusro, et al., 2017)

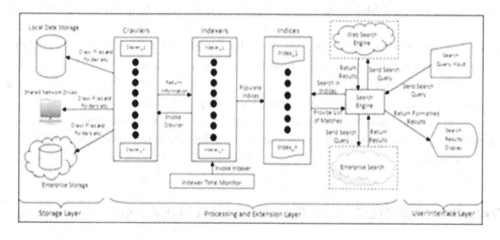

User Interface Layer

The user interface is the space indicating how interaction between users and applications take place. A good DSE should be easy to use and easy to understand while having lower learning curves and having professional aesthetics by requiring minimum steps to obtain the desired outputs. Thus, user interface marks usability of a DSE. The user interface layer should be composed of minimum two components: search form and search results display. A search form is where a user inputs his search query. A search form should contain an input field as well as other graphical components to help user in exploiting the valuable features of DSE for query generation such as advance options, etc. The files found matching a user's search query are to be displayed in the search results display part. The customization features should be provided to help users in displaying results in a variety of ways suitable to their needs. For example, the categorization features could display resulting files in organized collections according to their types and the tab controls could display a particular class of files, etc.

Processing and Extension Layer

This the technical layer where all search and retrieval operations are to be performed. It consists of four modules namely search module, crawler and Indexer module, time monitor module and extension module. The search module acts as a mediator and performs several functions essential for a DSE and could consist of searching component, connection component and results composition component. The search module receives search query from the search form component of the user interface module, searches the indices for finding matching files and forwards the search query to supporting web search engines (if available) and enterprise search (if available) for obtaining search results from remote machines. The DSEs can provide enterprise search to search and retrieve files in enterprise network as easily as from the local computer systems. The connection module establishes connections with remote web search engines and computers in an enterprise network for sending search query and receiving search results. The results composition module receives search results from local searching component and from remote machines (if available) and organize them into suitable order for presentation in the results display component of user interface layer. The crawler and indexer module is composed of two components namely crawler and indexer respectively. The indexer component is monitor responsible for initiating and controlling crawler component and populating index files (indices) with the information returned by the crawler component. The crawler component is responsible for searching and crawling files stored on local as well as remote drives such as files on enterprise network. The crawled files are handed over to indexer to extract and index more and more information related with files including name, location, extension, size, contents, date created, date modified, creator information and other related metadata to enable users for utilizing all possible search parameters during searching and retrieval. Once existing files are crawled and indexed, newly created files would be crawled and indexed in real time. A crawler component may maintain more than one crawler programs like web search engines to enhance crawling performance. The indexer determines the search accuracy of a DSE. The time monitor module is responsible for initiating and controlling indexer component. The crawling is a resource intensive task which could occupy much of the machine resources and could often result in jeopardizing the system. Therefore, indexer is controlled by indexer time monitor component of the module, which would initiate indexer when a system remains idle for a specific time or as per a user defined schedule. The extension module determines the methods (i.e., APIs, etc.) for extending and incorporating the capabilities of a DSE in other DSEs. Normally, DSEs with pluggable architecture allow third party developers to develop plug-ins to extend their capabilities.

Storage Layer

The storage layer refers to various storage drives which a DSE uses to crawl for information extraction and creating index files. The index files may be created locally on local hard drives or on remote drives in an enterprise network. The index files contain information received from the indexer component and could be used by the searching component. To enhance the technical efficiency, multiple index files may be maintained instead of a single large index file and multiple search functions can be executed in parallel by the searching component. The efficiency of a DSE can be measured in terms of memory usage, index file size, indexing time, and searching time (i.e., the lesser their values the higher the efficiency and vice versa). In addition to returning search results from these locations, the searching component can incorporate information in search results about files and folders located in computers which are accessible via the Web. A DSE should provide configuration features to users to properly define the types of files and folders to be indexed as well as the extent (i.e., local, enterprise, web, etc.) to which search should be carried out.

EVALUATION OF DESKTOP SEARCH ENGINES

Understanding the importance of DSEs, researchers have paid attention and compared several of the available engines by considering different aspects. However, the DSEs have got significant extensions in their available features as well as new remarkable features are added with the passage of time. Such enhancements and improvements need to be covered in the literature to give more current conclusions over the previous research. We have constructed a compact comparison criterion consisting of numerous parameters some of which might be inspired from the previous works; however, the conclusions derived are from explicit research, observations, and analysis. The DSEs used in this study (shown in Table 1) are selected are due to the following reasons:

- The DSEs are popular enough because of usage by a wide range of users for their search and retrieval functions.
- The DSEs provide foundation and inspiration for the new DSEs.
- The limitations of resources and time have restricted to the DSEs from an extended list. However, the study is generic enough can accommodate other DSEs.

Discussion of Desktop Search Engines

To do justice with the study, the DSEs are thoroughly analyzed and each of the features and functions claimed by the vendors are practically tested. During the study, the DSEs are found extremely useful and practical for healing the information overload problem on PCs. To present a comprehensive knowledge, not only various aspects of DSEs are discussed but their possible shortcomings are also highlighted.

AskJeeves Desktop Search (AJDS)

AJDS is a lightweight standalone DSE which can index and retrieve different types of file types (shown in Table 2) (Perez, 2004). AJDS presents a simple and standalone user interface (i.e., acquainted from desktop search company Tukaroo) which is divided into two panels: one for entering user query and another for viewing the retrieved results where most of the audio and videos can be previewed directly (Beal, 2004). The first few lines from a file are displayed in the preview pane to give users a clue about the file contents and making opening the file not necessary. The results are categorized into different categories using tab architecture such as pictures, office documents, bookmarks, etc. where each tab category lists the number of files being found. The tabs are quite useful for categorizing and fine tuning the search. Clicking web button on the interface could retrieve search results from the Web to be displayed in the DSE's web pane. Users can specify speed of indexing by defining the extent to which indexing should be performed on their computers hard drives.

Table 1. DSEs used in the study

Desktop Search Engines	Version
Ask Jeeves Desktop Search (Beta)	1.7.0
Copernic Desktop Search Professional	3.7
Google Desktop Search	5.9.1005.12335
Yahoo Desktop Search	1.2.5
Blinkx Desktop Search	3.5.5.1
dtSearch Desktop Search	7.71
Enfish Professional Search (Beta)	6.0
MSN Toolbar Suit (Beta)	2.0.0.1180
Beagle Desktop Search	0.3.9

Despite of so many user-friendly features, AJDS is limited to a few file formats and cannot index certain important file formats (i.e., PDF, ZIP, etc.), browser cache, emails and email attachments of Outlook Express, etc. It cannot render Microsoft Excel and PowerPoint files in its preview panel. Similarly, new files and folders cannot be manually added to heal the limitation. AJDS also thumbs its nose at indexing options customization by limiting users to scan either the My Documents and desktop folders or the entire disk but nothing in between.

Copernic Desktop Search (CDS)

Copernic Desktop Search (CDS) is another standalone DSE with easy-to-use, intuitive and promising user interface which looks very similar to AJDS but displays query results summary in an organized classified list using file types along with handy tabs at the top of the screen (Boutin, 2004). CDS extends windows taskbar with a search bar to access the DSE quickly instead of launching a separate desktop search window. CDS supports "search as you type", displaying results as a user type search query to make the search process quick but it needs to be explicitly turned on/off from the options menu. Users can narrow down their search results by selecting the kind of files they want to search by using toolbars at the top. User can enter advanced search queries encompassing boolean search terms (i.e., AND, OR, and NOT etc.), nested searches using parenthesis, fix keyword phrases using quotation marks in the search bar. CDS has preview pane to instantly preview a wide range of file types and highlights the location of search query terms within a file. The preview pane can display details of a selected item as well.

CDS is available in three versions: home, professional, and corporate which are varying in their functionalities. The home version is free to use and provides basic search functionalities. The professional and corporate versions are for commercial purposes, but their trial versions are also available. Since version 3.0 forward, network searching is only provided with professional and corporate versions. CDS can instantly index and search more than 150 file types (shown in Table 2). Users can extend the list by adding new file types. For better search experience, CDS is optimized for low memory footprint, lowest usage of computer resources, and low network load. It provides detailed index control (indexing range and indexing frequency). To improve performance, indexing schedule and resources utilization can be customized from options menu. To answer a user query, CDS must build an index in the background which is regularly updated as files are created, modified, or detected on the fly (called dynamic indexing). CDS start indexing the hard drive when the system remains idle for a predetermined time to compensate resource utilization and preventing the system from being jeopardized. CDS features of smart query spelling correction using "did you mean?", auto complete a search query as a user type few words, show pictures as thumbnails, and true wildcard supports makes it a rewarding experience (Winder, 2007).

For business use, Copernic has a spin-off company called Coveo which develops enterprise desktop search products with increases in security, network capabilities and manageability (Noda & Helwig, 2005). However, additional server software (e.g., Microsoft SharePoint, etc.) needs to be available for enterprise version to work. Like other counterparts, Copernic supports web search tool "Copernic Agent" within the CDS to get results from the Web along with desktop. However, Copernic Agent is not as much popular as Yahoo, Google, etc.

Google Desktop Search (GDS)

GDS is a freeware for Windows, MAC, and Linux operating systems and a powerful DSE with few extra features including sidebar for widgets, integrating local results with Google's standard web results, and integrating search results from users' other Google services (e.g., Gmail, Google Talk, etc.). GDS uses browser as a neat and uncluttered user interface and displays desktop search results in a layout resembling to the Google's web search. It acts like a Google.com for a user's hard drive which executes same search in parallel and integrates desktop search results with the Web search results and makes it transparent to realize if the results belong to the Web or hard drive. Using a web browser for user interface is advantageous because of local and web search results integration but have limitation of not leveraging the inherent power of DSEs (e.g., previewing of search results and instant results as the query is being typed etc.) (Kote, 2005). The explicit hyperlink must be used for previewing an item in the preview pane which does not show query terms highlighted. GDS support 'Search As You Type' feature in the deskbar and in the quick search box which can be tuned on/off by the users. In addition, GDS provides gadgets and sidebar to help in collecting and organizing new information from the Web. The sidebar is a vertical bar on the desktop which helps in organizing these gadgets. Google gadgets display weather, pictures, emails, and personalized news, etc. and are movable over the desktop.

GDS is a full text DSE which functions by first indexing files on a user hard drive (shown in Table 2). With the release of GDS's lighter and faster version 5.9 in 2009, it started supporting 64-bit Windows systems and latest browsers including Chrome, Firefox 3 and IE 8 (Kendall, 2013). GDS not only indexes files and folder on a user local hard drive but also of computers across network to let users search their home computer from their office computer quite easily and quickly (Agarwal, 2007). GDS updates its local index database continuously when PC is not busy to track any modification and creation of new files. GDS has cashing feature, where GDS will keep a copy of any webpage or file visited or stored locally on a user computer in his database which could be used for preview in the browser window without opening the required software. The Google provides an API for GDS to provide an environment for software developers to enhance and expand its functionality by creating new plug-ins/add-ins (Noda & Helwig, 2005). A floating deskbar is a distinguishing feature that enables users to input search query from any location on the screen.

GDS improves security by indexing control where privacy lover can specify folders to be indexed and can eliminate unwanted entries from the index. To improve in security, GDS does not support partial filename and Boolean operators as well as wild cards in the search query keywords. Despite of security efforts, GDS was plagued by security problems which could be exploited by hackers for searching a user's PC. Therefore, in September 2011 Google stopped GDS program and no new version is produced afterward (Kendall, 2013). Having heavier dependency on browser interface, query commands issued from deskbar or quick search box may not render any result if not connected with the Internet. To enable desktop search only, an explicit "search desktop" needed to be selected from the icon menu in taskbar. Despite of being very fast in providing a comprehensive search result, GDS lacks with previewing feature, which is a major feature provided by other competitors.

Yahoo Desktop Search (YDS)

Yahoo Desktop Search (YDS) also known as X1 Professional Client is a free, speedy, and convenient standalone DSE that uses and presents almost the same set of features of X1 search version 5 (i.e., an enterprise-level DSE from Idealab). YDS present an intuitive and user-friendly full screen interface consisting of two panes: the left pane responsible for search and display of search results and the right pane used for previewing purposes (Sherman, 2005). At start, YDS displays every file in the index but as a user keeps typing, the search results are narrowed down to the files matching search query keywords. The instant search-as-you-type is a YDS patent and is suffice for most of the searches (i.e., enabling search on prefix). YDS displays results in a Windows Explorer like columnar view displaying filenames with additional information. Results can be further narrowed to some well-defined categories including email, attachments, contacts, IM conversations, documents, pictures, music, files of all types, etc. for enabling users to view results in a specific category. To make search criteria more specific, YDS supports search on phrases, use of Boolean operators, and restrict results by using limiters such as filename, size, type, and data and time of creation etc. YDS emphasizes on email search while providing a separate tab for searching through attachments and handling emails instantly (Kote, 2005).

The right pane allows for a privacy-conscious preview so that the actual contents of any file type especially emails and attachments can be displayed in the same way as it would appear in its native application in milliseconds with matching words/phrases being highlighted (Kote, 2005). Graphics are displayed at full size rather than thumbnails and audio and video files are queued up in a mini-Windows Media player for enabling users to listen or watch files directly from YDS. The preview pane also contains a series of options for opening, printing, forwarding a file or replying to an email message.

YDS is available for Windows platforms only and supports indexing of more than 250 files formats (shown in Table 3). A unique feature of YDS is its capability of indexing MS Visio, AUTOCAD, CoralDraw and Adobe Illustrator drawing files. Yahoo! Instant messaging is the only chat tool supported by YDS (Tschabitscher, 2007a). It can index emails from yahoo email account. YDS searches and indexes what is inside the files relatively faster when a system becomes idle. A user has fine control over either manual index creation or defining policies for when and what should be indexed. YDS do not support real-time indexing to depict recent developments. In case the system is busy, indexing process is delayed and the newly created files would be indexed in the next indexing pass. Similarly, users can also define the location of the index file and can save queries for complex searches for reuse (Tschabitscher, 2007a).

Although, using the high valued features of X1, the YDS search results display is very confusing because of displaying too many columns in the vertical view and not sorting and organizing search results by relevancy (Noda & Helwig, 2005). As descended of X1, the main features found missing in YDS includes support for Eudora and Mozilla email clients, ability to index every type of Outlook data (i.e., appointments, tasks, and notes etc.) and support to index remote drives across network (Kote, 2005). It does not integrate web search results with desktop search results although a button is provided which will open "search.yahoo.com" in a separate instance of a web browser. As opposed to GDS and CDS, YDS does not incorporate dynamic indexing, web history caching and searching of web pages viewed. In addition to Yahoo! instant messaging no other chat tool is supported. A security problem was found in YDS that is it could index, and preview password protected emails archive file in Personal Folder (.PST). YDS is no longer available (Tschabitscher, 2007a).

Blinkx Desktop Search (BDS)

Blinkx Desktop Search (BDS) combines technologies of its own with Autonomy and is the smallest standalone DSE which searches and links information almost of any type (Claburn, 2006). Blinkx is ambitious about finding novel ways of searching and has achieved astonishing benchmarks in both technology and service. Blinkx runs as a background application which can be consulted upon need, or it can be started as a traditional standalone search engine either from the windows system tray or Blinkx toolbar appearing at the title bar. Blinkx toolbar updates users by coloring toolbar's icons about the finding of related web pages, web logs postings, local documents and emails, news, etc. in a subtle and useful way (Tschabitscher, 2007a). With its simple user interface, Blinkx returns search results simultaneously from various sources including local desktop, peer-to-peer network and Internet in response to users' queries. By default, local files are displayed sorted by date of creation; however, these can also be sorted by title, subject, etc. Similarly, options for filtering and displaying search results items and visualization feature for presenting a 3D view of the links tree structure is available for determining the approximate relevance of search results. Blinkx has built-in preview feature for previewing files and summary is presented by just hovering mouse over a file in the search result list. Clicking a file in the list would be opened directly in its native application. To limit search results, Blinkx supports keyword phrases enclosed in parenthesis and Boolean operators in the search criteria.

Instead of relying on keyword-based searches, Blinkx uses contextual information to flag files from local PC and Internet. Blinkx is compatible with majority of Windows applications and can index and search more than 255 file formats (shown in Table 3). Blinkx presents three files indexing modes. A mode can be selected by using the slide bar: stopped (left), active/inactive (middle), and fast (right). A mode determines the indexing speed subjected to the performance of the PC. Blinkx has pro-active search feature which uses contextual information to create links to information across various sources. While running in the background, Blinkx uses Autonomy's implicit query technology to implicitly generate search queries by parsing active files. Blinkx continuously reads a user's active screen, infer from the content of the current file, and generates links to related concepts available in various sources. The links are changed and refreshed continuously as a user continues in his session and can be retrieved from the Blinkx toolbar at the title bar. Blinkx has the feature of Smart Folders which automatically gets populated regularly with links to stuff on the PC or on the Internet based on content or certain keywords. Smart

Folders may contain any of the supporting file types and can be customized and narrowed down by users. Users are explicitly alerted by any change or update of a Smart Folder content. Smart Folders are of two types: customizable and shareable which allows emailing copies of content to people you want to share with and to deliver content via a website or blog. Another remarkable feature of Blinkx is SIS, an acronym for the phrase Stuff I've Seen, which maintains record of viewed files. Blinkx emphasizes on the use of range of enterprise-grade security methods for protecting users' privacy and data integrity. These methods use Windows Security profiles for strong user-authentication which enables multiple users to use the same computer unobtrusively and securely without seeing content of each other's files. Furthermore, all communication between Blinkx components and index files on local machine are encrypted to ensure confidentiality. Blinkx version 2.0 is also supporting querying peer-to-peer networks.

Although, Blinkx provides efficient methods for indexing control, but the indexing process creates extra load over CPU and is memory intensive. Therefore, it slows down the performance of computer system considerably. Blinkx preview viewer is distinctly of average quality and needs improvement. PDF and Word files are shown in plain text only and videos are handled superbly but image handling is poor. Furthermore, no search query keywords are highlighted in the search results files' contents in the preview making it difficult for user to trace required keywords. Blinks has lacking with thumbnail view or image scaling features which makes large images difficult to handle. No extra file formats plug-ins are required because of the already support of many file types.

dtSearch Desktop Search (DDS)

dtSearch (DDS) is a tremendously valuable desktop and network DSE that provides functionalities far beyond other standalone DSEs. dtSearch is a suite of tools which eradicates the plague associated with managing and searching terabytes of text across desktop, network, Internet and Intranet. dtSearch suite is composed of indexer, dtSearch desktop, CD wizard, and dtSearch web (Matzan, 2005). Based on users' specifications, the indexer creates indexes of the entire drives, folders, files, file types, email folders, web sites, etc. It can thoroughly index all popular file formats (shown in Table 3) and can even find readable text strings in binary files. The software logically groups information by maintaining different indexes such as email index, archived email index, index of My Documents folder (Heck, 2010). The index size varies and is typically limited to 1Teraybyte (1TB). However, by the introduction of meta index (i.e., index of indices) that has been included since version 7.01 this limit has also been removed (Matzan, 2005). Creating an index particularly initial index is a slow process depending on the size of data being indexed but 64-bit indexer reduces indexing time by about half (Heck, 2010). Comparatively updating an index takes less time and any change to index is notified in Windows task scheduler. Handling noise words, upper case and lower-case letters and words sensitivity of ascents also take place. An unlimited number of indices can be simultaneously searched in any combination. Files that are not indexed can also be searched in combination with indexed files. Unfortunately, dtSearch presents an antiquated user interface limiting to explore all its powers and user needs training before using it expertly. With proper configuration, dtSearch can be used as easily as using a web search engine (Matzan, 2005). However, dtSearch is practical for search professionals and not for newbies. The interface is rich enough providing multitude of functions to make effective indexing and searching operations. Search can be initiated by either using interface's button bar or opening the search dialog box. A scrolling word list appears as instant feedback as a user inputs search query in the search query box. In terms of search capabilities, dtSearch is more comprehensive and offers more than 24 indexed, un-indexed, fielded and full text search options including federated search, special forensics search options, advanced data classification objects and support for hundreds of international languages through Unicode. In addition to phrases and Boolean searches, the software offers an incredible number of search options including fuzzy, phonic, stemming, synonyms, wildcards, thesaurus, and proximity. The software offers variable terms weighting options of search terms. dtSearch has a large preview pane to display hits in native HTML, XML and PDF files with search words conveniently highlighted in the text and displaying links and images. The software does the same for Microsoft Office, OpenOffice, databases, emails and attachments, ZIP and unicodes files but they must be first converted into HTML format for display (Heck, 2010). From the list, files and messages can be launched in the default applications. The software has feature of exporting search results into various data formats for easy use with other programs. dtSearch has several options to sort federated and distributed search results including by relevance, date, number of hits, etc. In addition, different tabs are available in the main search dialog box to filter results to match (e.g., all DOC files etc.). The CD wizard creates a searchable index for backup of CDs and DVDs. Upon writing a CD/DVD project, CD wizard writes an index and self-contained DSE resembling a web browser on the disk. Once the CD is put into any Windows-based computer, the DSE automatically activates dtSearch engine interface to navigate CD content (Matzan, 2005). dtSearch web is a web-based search engine that converts all readable files into basic HTML pages for online viewing. The problem with this program is the requirements of IIS web server and Windows operating system for the server. For wide-scale corporate deployment, dtSearch uses active directory or Microsoft SMS where IT administrator can include a policy that specifies the index of shared network drives which eliminates users to crawl those repositories.

dtSearch is commercial software for Windows and Linux operating systems. dtSearch has been incorporated and used in hundreds of commercial applications by the developers. dtSearch has native 64-bit and 32-bit Win/Linux APIs for incorporating dtSearch directly into Java, C++, C#, ASP.NET, Delphi and .NET programs (Matzan, 2005). The APIs support SQL including BLOB data. Using APIs developers can have access to dtSearch integrated file parser, file formats supported and built-in HTML converter. The dtSearch spider supports static and dynamic web data like ASP.NET, MS SharePoint, CMS and PHP. The .NET spider API makes the full dtSearch spider functionality accessible to the developers.

dtSearch is more granular even than Copernic in setting search terms. For average users dtSearch can be expansive but not for small-businesses or corporate clients who want to locate data throughout their network, dtSearch can be a useful timesaving DSE. With all of sophistications, dtSearch requires robust storage particularly when sharing indexes over a network. It might require decent dedicated servers (i.e., SCSI or RAID) or dedicated cluster in case of sharing several large indexes. dtSearch also needs improvements in the time it takes to create indices and in its user interface.

Enfish Desktop Search (EDS)

Enfish (Enter, Find, and Share) (Jeremy, 2006) is an earliest personal information manager who presented the idea of searching files on a local machine was as simple and useful as searching the Web in 1998. Enfish legacy can be found in every DSE available today. It enables working with both Internet and desktop information simultaneously. Enfish is a shell program having the audacity of piggybacking on Internet Explorer and Outlook while considering them as the center of a user daily computing life. It does not mean of replacing them (i.e., they need to be present) but supplements them by integrating into a hub on a user computer (King, 2006). Enfish, however, does not provide features provided in

Internet Explorer and Outlook such as Outlook's spam filtering, etc. It offers a complex user interface which organizes information in different ways bringing disparate information into one place. The user interface contains several panels, present a list of broad categories on left-side in the form of tabs which offers flexibility by allowing users in customizing these tables. Any email, attachment, or document file indexed can be directly previewed in the preview panel in a comprehensive manner where search terms are highlighted in non-print-based files (e.g., DOC, PPT, etc.) but not in others (e.g., PDF, etc.). Enfish integrates email clients enabling users to not only open and preview massages directly but to start replies as well. The software provides unique features of saving complex search criteria in files called "Trackers" which could be easily launched from the sidebar and by cross-referencing information with a single click. These files can be given user friendly names and can be shared with other users. To make more customized and personal searches, Enfish supports tagging files (Jeremy, 2006). The software can be launched separately via toolbars in MS Office, or via the Windows taskbar.

Enfish uses Dex Engine to index both metadata and contents of files and messages (King, 2006). By default, Dex Engine can recognize more than 50 file types (shown in Table 4) including contacts, documents, emails, email attachments, etc. and displays information in the context of people and companies that a user knows and the projects he/she is working on. The software supports Microsoft Outlook, Outlook Express, Lotus Notes and AOL mail as email client. Enfish does not index instant messaging communication files. The software provides indexing control empowering users to determine which files, folders, or drives should be indexed, add more file types to cover legacy files and select folders to be excluded from indexing. However, the indexing control is limited as compared to others such as dtSearch Desktop, etc. Enfish indexes and cross references title, subject and complete content of all files on a user's digital disk, in network folders, in removable drives and in Internet and Intranet favorites. To keep information on any contact current, Enfish indexes and cross references information automatically and indexes supporting email clients in real time, whereas other documents are indexed as per schedule in the background (King, 2006). While providing numerous features to define criteria to filter and narrow down search results and sorting results by several criteria, the results returned lack with relevancy and precision. Enfish searches through vast amount of content very quickly and requires approximately 8% of the total hard disk space of items indexed for indexes.

Indeed, Enfish had brought a wealth of features on the table for finding and managing information, but the software suffered from instability, performance degradation, low understandability of user interface (King, 2006). Relationship with other Windows programs can be unstable. Enfish uses system resource extensively and could conflict with other third-party programs using Internet Explorer and Outlook, resulting in the system slowdown and crashes. Despite of being a strong earliest product, Enfish is crumbled because of lack with focusing on their strength: powerful indexing and flexible search. Enfish as a company and product does not exist now. In 2005, Enfish software decided to not sell their product any longer but would rather license its technology and patents to others (Jeremy, 2006). The Enfish technology has been licensed to "EasyReach" company.

MSN Toolbar Suite Desktop Search (MDS)

The MSN Toolbar Suite combines several search tools including MSN toolbar for Microsoft Office Outlook, the MSN Deskbar in the Windows taskbar, MSN toolbar for Internet Explorer and an MSN toolbar for Windows Explorer to help users a fast, simple and multi-context searching and surfing the Web. Each of these toolbars serve as an entry point to both local and web searching where users simply type what they are looking for. The MSN Deskbar supports both local and web searching directly from desktop and offers a bunch of unique features including word wheeling (auto complete) and aliases (Thurrott, 2004). The auto-complete technology (Microsoft called it word wheeling) delivers instant search results by listing relevant files above the Deskbar as soon as a user starts typing and the list gets narrow as a user type more characters, finally Deskbar isolates the file/information a user is looking for. Clicking an item in the list will open it directly in appropriate application. Aliases helps in accessing a list of commonly used shortcuts to applications, documents, frequently accessed web sites, etc. To access list of aliases-related hints and tips, "@" character must be typed in Deskbar text entry area. MSN Deskbar also serves as a supercharged Run dialog providing multiplicity of functionalities such as typing URL of a web page to open in browser, entering full pathname to open a file, prefixing a program name with "=" to launch it directly, etc. (Rubenking, 2005). From MSN Deskbar a user can directly look on the Web instead by clicking the Web button at the bottom of file list. The MSN Toolbar for Microsoft Office Outlook by default supports searching Outlook emails and attachments, and other items on the local drives as well as on the Web. For Outlook toolbar, Microsoft purchased Lookout software (Thurrott, 2004). MSM Outlook toolbar emulated its Lookout predecessor by utilizing experience and developments assets instead of code. MSN Internet Explorer toolbar offers a plethora of features including searching local desktop and the Web, highlighting search terms in the Web results, block pop-ups ads and form fill function. The pop-up blocker is XP SP 2-aware and requires a single click to block unwanted pop-up windows forever. An integrated viewer applet displays a miniature preview of web pages found and highlights by coloring each of the search terms hits to help in jumping between instances (Rubenking, 2005). Automatic form filling function needs to be preloaded with personal information, address, credit card information and username/password, which could be used to fill a form in a web page automatically by selecting "Fill Out Form" from the menu. A user's personal information is kept safe because of the password he/she created. The toolbar also contains links for quick access to MSN Messenger, MSN Hotmail and MSN Spaces, which enables users to start common communication tasks right from the bar including instant messaging, email and inserting URLs into Spaces blogs (Redmond, 2004). MSN Windows Explorer toolbar sits in all Explorer windows and provides searching capabilities identical to those found in Internet Explorer. The toolbar provides history of previous searches which could be accessed in Folder view (Thurrott, 2004). The main interface is extremely easy to use, enabling consumers to search desktop in a comfortable and familiar format, open files in their associated applications directly from their desktop search results and quick access to actions such as messaging, sharing, deleting and playing files. The main interface is divided into two panels namely the left panel that displays list of files found and the right panel contains preview display. The search results can be sorted in a variety of column headers (i.e., title, author, date, size, type and folder) and items from the search results presentation can be even drag and dropped onto the Windows desktop.

The MSN Deskbar indexes a variety of file types (shown in Table 4). However, it cannot index files contained within ZIP or other archives (Rubenking, 2005). The MSN toolbar suite needs to build index of a user's desktop-based data initially to provide instant search results in response to a search operation. The software provides indexing control where users can specify what and when to index. By default, the software indexes only when the system is idle to counter slowing work and killing performance, though a user can force it to "Index Now". Additionally, the software provides "Indexing Status" option in the menu for full details and "Snooze" option for snoozing indexing for a while to give users full power. The MSN Toolbar Suite is built on the current Windows security and privacy model and respects the privacy of multiple users on a single PC by utilizing Windows authentication and user account management infrastructure, providing consumers with a better-protected and more private desktop search experience (Redmond, 2004). Earlier it was thought that MSN Deskbar indexes encrypted Office documents, but investigation revealed a weakness in the Office program. Furthermore, the software does not cache version of file contents, so it would not reveal earlier versions of files, encrypted or otherwise (Rubenking, 2005).

In addition to searching both PC and the Web, the software provides more features as compared to other DSEs and is better integrated with Windows. The MSN Deskbar takes on other competitors, with some interesting features reminiscent of the powerful X1 search. However, its heavy reliance on Internet Explorer makes it less ideal choice for users of other browsers. Moreover, its lacks with indexing files inside ZIP archives, and full window search results with word wheeling needs immediate attention. Likewise, clicking "More" sometimes perversely yields results or none. Fixing these problems can make MSN Deskbar a good choice.

Beagle Desktop Search (BDS)

Beagle is one of the various graphical DSEs developed for Linux distribution. Beagle is desktop independent and can be used on GNOME, KDE, Enlightment, etc. requiring installation of few software packages including Mono and SQLlite. Beagle ships bundled with major Linux distributions including Debian, Ubuntu, Fedora Core, etc. Beagle grows out of Dashboard and early Mono-based systems and developed using Apple's MacOS X search functions as basic material (Schurmann, 2005). Beagle is a powerful indexing search engine which uses Lucene Indexing System to store data about files and folders stored on a computer for their quick retrieval (Wallen, 2010). Beagle has a full screen user friendly interface consisting of two panels: the top panel provides searching and search results display features and the bottom panel provides previewing features. Beagle has a "Find In" drop-down list to enable users for refining and narrowing their search criteria into 14 available categories including applications, media, pictures, mails, achieves, etc. However, Beagle displays eight items in each category while providing a tiny blue arrow for more results navigation. An item displayed in the result list can be opened, forwarded via e-mail, moved to a trash or opened in a file manager. However, the number of options for an item depends on its file type (Sharma, 2010). Furthermore, selecting a file in the results list will be previewed in the preview panel with words or partial sentences matching search query terms being highlighted within the file. However, apart from previewing, the preview panel also displays plethora of information about a file such as tile, path, date of last access or modified, etc. Users can use view menu to sort items in their result list using different criteria such as name, relevancy, date of last modified, etc. (Ayres et al., 2019). Beagle's user interface is not aesthetically pleasing as compared to other but the real beauty lies in its strength of complex search options such as searches are not case sensitive, prefixing a search term with minus to exclude from search, using OR for optional search terms, using root from of a search term while searching, using DATE operator to limit search within a date range, using double quotation marks (" ") for exact word or phrase searching and excluding common words (.i.e. a, the, and, is, etc.) from the search phrase (Ayres et al., 2019). In addition to user interface, Beagle has a suit of command line tools which could be used to create index and display search results (Sharma, 2010)).

Beagle is a full text DSE which works by first indexing files on a user's hard drive. Beagle comprises of three components (Schurmann, 2005). The Beagle demon runs in the background and provides the main search machine functionalities (Ayres et al., 2019). The Beagle demon scours the hard disk, analyses the known file types and records the findings in its database called index using the Lucene search engine by the Apache project. The Beagle demon constantly examines and detects any changes to the files and folders and updates its indexes accordingly in real time (Wallen, 2010). The Beagle client provides a convenient environment for the users to issue search query and receive a neat display of the results. These two components are deliberately set apart to enable other applications to leverage the Beagle search services. The D-Bus component provides a global communication infrastructure to transfer search query from Beagle client to Beagle demon as well as establish communication with various Linux system components (Ayres et al., 2019). Beagle, by default, indexes everything which is stored in home directory, excluding the default *, temp, etc. paths (Sharma, 2010). In addition to indexing files contents, Beagle indexes meta-data and tags associated with files and folders. Thus, making everything (i.e., documents, pictures, emails, etc.) searchable using names, meta-data and tags. Beagle can instantly index and search numerous file types (shown in Table 4). Beagle has a demon running in the background; however, Beagle's indexing can be very resources hungry, Therefore, to not jeopardize users' machines, Beagle provides search preferences window allowing users to customize for improving performance. Beagle provides users full indexing control by enabling users to customize when to start indexing and searching process, including and excluding directories to be indexed, listing file type from various data sources/applications to be indexed, and disabling Beagle on low-end computers (Wallen, 2010). Beagle supports network search option to extend desktop searches from a single machine to search files stored on multiple machines connected in a network (Ayres et al., 2019). Network search needs to be explicitly enabled from search preferences window. However, a remote machine can be accessed if it has Beagle installed with network search option enabled. A remote machine can be accessed using web-based interface while providing the IP address of the remote machine. A unique feature of Beagle is its capability of searching using files properties (i.e., meta-data) in addition to their contents. However, the number and type of properties varies for each file type. Therefore, one needs to be very careful while performing property search. Beagle has plug-ins to improve its functionalities such as plug-in for Firefox which can index information form web pages browsed with Firefox (Schurmann, 2005).

Beagle, despite of all its beauties, is plagued heavily by its resources usage critics. Beagle has been criticized by users in various forums for its instable appetite of memory and jeopardizing a machine's CPU entirely during its indexing process. Furthermore, Beagle's Mono requirement makes him a bit bloated especially for the users not using GNOME.

Comparison of Desktop Search Engines

Obviously, DSEs have turned searching a desktop as easy as searching the Web. A comprehensive overview of the selected DSEs is presented in previous section. In this section, the selected DSEs are compared using a compact comparison criterion consisting of several parameters to give more insight into knowledge. The results concluded and information derived for individual parameters after careful research, observation and analysis of the DESs A complete comparison of the DSEs using the criteria/parameters is depicted in Table 2, 3 and 4. An overview of the parameters is covered in the following sub-headings:

System Requirements

A DSE requires high level of computing resources to perform search at an acceptable speed. Resources requirements and utilizations are important issues to be considered especially for DSEs running in the background. DSEs vary in the amount of system resources requirements. To cater a catastrophic situation, one needs accurate information about the least level of system resources required by a DSE.

Operating Systems Support

A DSE's popularity and high-speed adaptability typically depends on its ability to support different operating systems. DSEs vary in this feature such as CDS works with Windows, but GDS works with Windows, MAC and Linux operating systems.

Searchable File Types

The utility of a DSE lies in its ability of supporting variety of file formats. Obviously, the more is the better. All these DSEs indexes and searches common file types, but few enable to define new ones for increasing the number of file types searchable by a DSE. DSEs vary in the number of file types supported such as YDS and Blinkx index and search more than 250 file types.

Operational Features

A system providing plethora of functions is likely the one to be adopted and used heavily. DSEs vary greatly in the number of features offering such as indexing options, email clients support and user interface. In addition to basic features, some DSEs are offering unique and special features as well. However, increase in functions should not be at the cost of increase in the complexity such as dtSearch desktop search provides sacks full of features but they are difficult to use because of its complex user interface.

Cost

Some of the DSEs are free, whereas others are commercial. Vendors provide free DSEs for availing certain other advantages such as earning revenue using advertisements. Free DSEs are either less powerful, (i.e., providing a very limited set of features), for the popularity, or increasing the number of users of a vendor's web search engines. Commercial DSEs charges cost while providing a rich set of features and functionalities. For example, functionally rich dtSearch DSE is commercial and charging $1000 for a single-server license, and $200 for the desktop-only version.

Enterprise Search Integration

Enterprise search systems index and integrate structured and unstructured data into their collection from a variety of sources such as file systems, Internet, databases, etc. Enterprise search systems are based on keywords or free text, where all business objects in a business role can be searched by keywords, IDs, or free text. DSEs vary by enterprise search integration support where some provide support while others do not.

Search Network Drives

A network drive is a drive or folder located on a remote computer that has been configured for sharing over a LAN. DSEs supporting network drives searching will index and search network drives in the similar fashion as indexing local drives. However, IT administrator can also define policy that specify the index of shared network drives which eliminates each user having to crawl these repositories (e.g., dtSearch desktop search).

Security and Privacy

Maintaining security and privacy is a major concern of successful DSEs as they deal with users' personal information located on their PCs. Therefore, a successful DSE will utilize measures for preventing unauthorized disclosure of user's personal information. Realizing the importance of users' security and privacy, desktop search DSEs vary in level of security and privacy protection such as AskJeeves suffers from privacy problem, but GDS encrypts index and data files, and Blinkx uses user authentication and encrypts all communication, index, and data files etc.

Consumer and Business

A DSE is targeted for the use of consumer, business or both. A consumer DSE is almost invariably aimed at the individuals and providing features and functions enough to satisfy the desktop searching needs of a single user. A business DSE caters to large and complicated organizations with many different processes and connections. A business DSE will contain enough set of features and functions to help business in getting profit and growth. A DSE should be powerful enough to satisfy needs of both consumers and businesses. For example, CDS, GDS and YDS are suitable enough for both consumer and business usage, whereas dtSearch is designed specifically for business usage.

Deskbar

Deskbar is an omnipresent versatile search interface embedded in taskbar near system tray. Deskbar lets users search their desktop using their search queries. A deskbar is supported by DSEs to help users initiating a search query without opening the DSE such as CDS, GDS and MSN Toolbar suit.

Plug-in Support

A plug-in is a software component that adds a specific feature to an existing software application. The applications supporting plug-ins enable customization. Only a few DSEs use plug-able architecture such as GDS.

Advance Search Options Support

The quality of a search result typically depends on the quality and number of keywords used in the search process. DSEs supporting advanced features such as Boolean expressions, wildcards, prefixes, stemming, phonic, fuzzy, synonym, etc. (e.g., dtSearch, and YDS.) enable users specifying complex search criteria for retrieving specific results. More strength can be added by defining multiple indices, searching un-indexed files and keeping track of complex queries (e.g., YDS and MSN Toolbar suit).

Web Support

DSEs supporting simultaneous or explicit web search provide more comprehensive and detailed search results. These DSEs vary in web support where few simultaneously search both PC and the Web for presenting collective results (e.g., GDS) while others support web search upon user selection (e.g., Enfish, and MSN Toolbar suit).

Enterprise Version

Some of the DSEs have enterprise version such as GDS, and CDS, which are more comprehensive and designed for teams and large organizations. Enterprise DSEs supports several features as compared to desktop applications such as indexing a vast number of file types, providing a wide variety of features and capable of not only indexing local computer drives but drives of computers connected in a network as well. Enterprise applications are designed to be more secure and have administration capabilities as compared to consumer level applications.

Patent

A desktop search application offers several features to help users in performing their daily searching tasks. However, some features are unique in their existence and can be filed as patent such as YDS has a patent of instant search-as-you-type (quick find) which is as a user type in the text-field the application searches instantly and narrows down the search as a user type more words.

Who is the Winner?

Undoubtedly, users who must meet tight deadlines to obtain and present files/information from a haystack of files/information will find DSEs extremely helpful. Several researchers have prioritized DSEs using their personal subjects of interests such as cost, search scope, etc. However, one cannot make a DSE superior over the others. In May 2005, the UW E-Business Consortium conducted a study and evaluated 12 DSEs along six attributes: usability, versatility, accuracy, security, efficiency and enterprise readiness and ranked Copernic DSE as the winner (Noda & Helwig, 2005). However, analysis of the results revealed that while the DSEs have shown great promises for significant productivity gains, most of the DSEs are still immature for significant business use due to lacks of privacy and security maturity and overall manageability (Noda & Helwig, 2005).

Despite of the fact that the DSEs are pretty much rich, competent and balanced to fulfill searching tasks beautifully; the DSEs have some shortcomings which are needed to be fixed.

- GDS provides the same environment for Google web search engine lovers. However, limitations of not organizing search results by relevancy and instant feedback during searching cannot be overlooked. Moreover, plagued by security and privacy problems which resulted in stopping the GDS production completely.

- The vast list of features provided by BDS makes him unmatchable. Smart Folders, SIS (Stuff I've Seen), strong user-authentication and encrypting index files are valuable features of BDS. However, limitations of effective preview pane, thumbnail view, image scaling features and enormous system requirements make BDS difficult to use.

- YDS provides the promising features of X1 at no cost. Features like previewing any file format in the same way as it would appear in its native application and instant search-as-you-type distinguishes YDS. Although, similar instant feedback systems are present in BDS and CDS, they are nowhere as quick as YDS. However, YDS is not suitable for users who want to index remote drives and use Mozilla and Eudora email client. Moreover, limitations of user interface clarity and organizing search results by relevancy cannot be overlooked.

- In typical Microsoft fashion, MDS is all eye candy and looks great. MDS strength is its tight integration with Outlook and Internet Explorer. MSN takes on other competitors using some interesting features reminiscent of the powerful X1. However, its lack of supporting Mozilla and Chrome applications and heavy reliance on Internet Explorer makes it less ideal choice for user of other browsers. Moreover, its lack of indexing files inside ZIP achieves needs improvements.

- EDS is the earliest DSE having the audacity of piggybacking on Internet Explorer and Outlook. Saving complex search criteria, cross-referencing information, contextual information display and adding new file types are the invaluable features of EDS. However, EDS was plagued by instability, performance degradation and greater commitment requirements of users. EDS uses system resources extensively and could conflict with other third-party programs using Internet Explorer and Outlook which results in slowing and crashing the system.

- DDS is a more granular desktop and network DSE providing functionalities to manage and search terabytes of text across domains. Indexing a vast number of file formats including binary files, maintain different indexes especially meta index, using indexes in any combination, index hidden files, creating indexes for backup storages and providing API for incorporation in other software are the remarkable features of DDS. However, requirement of robust storage, dedicated servers or dedicated clusters for large indexes sharing and improvement in the indexing time and user interface makes DDS difficult to use. More importantly, DDS is commercial and is expensive for average users but is suitable for corporate clients.

- CDS seems to be an excellent choice for home consumers due to being free and does the job beautifully. Its features such as marvelous user interface, support of file formats normally used at home, arranging search results by relevancy, suggesting alternatives to misspelled words, secure measures for protecting users' security and privacy, thumbnailing pictures in search results and more importantly of being free makes CDS an ideal choice for home user especially for ones using Firefox web browser. However, lacking with presenting emails search results like others such as X1 and supporting instant messaging (IM) chat messages are the areas where CDS needs improvements.

- BDS is a marvelous attempt from open-source community for desktop search. Its features such as simple to use and incorporation in Linux distributions make it the default choice for Linux based computer users. However, its intensive resources requirements for running demon in the background for real time indexing, slow indexing process, more memory storage requirements and dependency on Mono makes BDS a bit bloated for usage. Apart from them BDS also needs improvements in several of the other areas which are provided by its counterparts.

For a home consumer, a DSE should be powerful enough to crawl, index, and retrieve search query results from his single computer. For corporate (enterprise) users, a DSE should be capable of not only indexing local computer drives but network drives of computers connected in a network. All DSEs discussed above are suitable for home consumers and they are free to select DSE which could satisfy their needs beautifully. For corporate users, none of the DSEs discussed above is powerful enough to cater the varied needs of an organization. However, DDS in capable enough to cater small-business needs. For complete corporate operations, users would have to make a choice among the enterprise DSEs (e.g., Google Enterprise Search, X1 desktop Search and ISYS desktop search) which are commercial and provides tones of configuration options to improve performance and data protection from unauthorized access.

DESKTOP SEARCH AND NEW TRENDS

DSEs indexes files on PCs to fulfill the growing need of users to effectively search files on their PCs. The web search engines, on the other hand, have become more efficient with the implementation of more powerful ranking algorithms such as Page Rank and HITS. The DSEs with all their innovations have resulted poorly than the Web search engines even searching a small set of personal documents. The DSEs cannot directly adopt web's ranking mechanisms to personal computers due to lack of structural information in PCs files (i.e., hyperlinks between documents) which provide the basis for the ranking mechanisms. Current DSEs use pure text based ranking mechanisms (i.e., TF-IDF scores, a textual-relevance-based mechanism employed in conventional retrieval systems) which needs exact keywords matching to accomplish searching process effectively (Chen, Wu, Guo, & Wang, 2012; Chirita, Costache, Nejdl, & Paiu, 2006). However, TF-IDF scores cannot perform well due to certain reasons (Chen, et al., 2012): (1) it works only on keywords frequency (count of a keyword occurring in a file) and cannot handle ambiguous keywords (keywords having multiple meanings), and (2) if keywords are not ambiguous, a document with high TF-IDF score is not necessarily the specific one a user is trying to retrieve. Current DSEs work by the idea of teleporting - where users can get directly into their information target if they remember some of their keywords. A DSE might not retrieve at all if a user does not remember name of a file or any of its containing text. However, users might be remembering other things that go with the files such as context information and related files (Chau, Myers, & Faulring, 2008). The DSEs, therefore, needs enhancing simple indexing of data with more sophisticated ranking algorithms to relieve users from looking into jungle of result sets returned by their queries. Existing desktop file systems are architecturally lacking with the features to associate semantically related files. The idea of semantic desktop can fulfill the gap by exploring the missing ingredients. The semantically related files can be linked by gathering semantic information from users' contexts and associations among the documents (Chirita, et al., 2006).

Table 2. Detailed comparison of selected desktop search engines

Parameter	AskJeeves (AJDS)	Copernic (CDS)	Google (GDS)
System Requirements	400MHz CPU and 128 MB RAM minimum,1GHz and 256 MB RAM recd.	Not available	128MB of RAM and a 400MHz processor, 500MB free space vacant on hard drive
Operating System	Windows2000 and Windows XP	Windows 98/Me/NT/2000/XP/7/8	Windows 2000 and XP with Service Pack 3 or above, MAC, and Linux
Searchable File Types	Microsoft Office 2000 and higher files (MC), PDF files (M), ZIP archives (M), Bookmarks and web page history (MC), Outlook and Outlook Express emails and attachments (MC), image files (JPG, GIF and PNG formats) (M), music files (MP3, WMA, and WAV formats) (M), video files (MPEG and WMV formats) (M)	Microsoft Office 95 and higher files (MC), PDF and ZIP files (MC), OpenOffice files (MC), WordPrefect documents files (MC), Web pages (HTML, XHTML, and XML files) (MC), text files (ASCII, ANSI, UCS2, and UTF8) (MC), bookmarks and Web page history (MC), emails and attachments, and contacts (MC), image files (JPG, JPEG, GIF and PNG formats) (M), music files (MP3, OGC, WMA, and WAV formats) (M), video files (MPEG, MOV, ASF, and WMV formats) (M).	Microsoft Office 95 and higher files (MC), PDF and ZIP files (MC), OpenOffice files (MC), Web pages (HTML, XHTML, and XML documents) (MC), text files (ASCII, ANSI and others) (MC), bookmarks and web page history (MC), RSS reader, emails and attachments and contacts (MC), Gmail search (MC), AOL Instant Messaging (MC), image files (JPG, GIF, BMP, PNG, and other formats) (M), music files (MP3, WMA, WAV, and other formats) (M), video files (MPEG, MPG, AVI, WMV, and other formats) (M), and news clips (M).
Operational Features	File indexing, email indexing, image indexing, multimedia indexing, browser support (Internet Explorer 7.0+ on Windows, Firefox 3.6+ on Windows, and Google Chrome 17+ on Windows), email clients (Microsoft Outlook), limited indexing control, tab-based user interface, and preview pane.	File Indexing, email Indexing, image indexing, multimedia indexing, browser support (Microsoft Internet Explorer, Mozilla Firefox, Mozilla and Netscape 6x./7.x/8), full Indexing control, email clients (Microsoft Outlook, Outlook Express 5.x/6.x, Thunderbird, Eudora, and Windows Mail), tab based User Interface, preview pane, hyperlink for Web search, search as type search query (Quick find), indexing and resources utilization and customization, remember search terms, highlighting query keywords in the preview pane, query correction and auto-completion, and define index file location.	File indexing, email indexing, image indexing, multimedia indexing, browser support (Microsoft Internet Explorer, Mozilla Firefox, Netscape 7+, Google Chrome), email clients (Microsoft Outlook, Outlook Express, Netscape Mail, Mozilla Mail, Thunderbird, Gmail account), full indexing control, Web browser based user interface, sidebar, gadgets, integration of desktop and web search results, floating deskbar, search hidden files and folders, files and web pages cashing, quick search box, find deleted files, lock search, search as type search query (Quick find), encrypting index and data files, floating deskbar.
Cost	Free	Free	Free
Enterprise Search Integration	No	Yes	Yes
Search Network Drives	No	Yes	Yes
Security & Privacy	Privacy	Yes	Yes
Consumer or Business	Both	Both	Both
Deskbar	No	Yes	Yes
Plug-in Support	No	No	Yes
Advance Search Options	Yes	Yes	Yes
Web Support	No	Yes	Yes
Enterprise Version	No	Coveo Des. Search	Google Ent. Desktop
Patent	No	No	No
Search Query Functionality	Keywords phrase, filename, case insensitive, natural language query	Keywords phrase, filename, Boolean operators (AND, OR and NOT), nested sub-queries, case insensitive, wildcard, natural language query	Keywords phrases, case-insensitive, natural language query
Relevance Ranking	No	No	Yes

M = Metadata, C = Contents, MC = Metadata and Contents

Table 3. Detailed comparison of selected desktop search engines

Parameter	Yahoo (YDS)	Blinkx (BDS)	dtSearch (DDS)
System Requirements	128MB of RAM minimum, 256MB of RAM recommended	100 MB hard disk, 200 MHz CPU, and 64 MB RAM	30 MB hard disk, 256 MB RAM
Operating System	Windows 98 SE/ME, Windows 2000 SP3 or SP4, Windows XP	Windows 98/2000/ME/XP 2003, MAC OS X (10.2 & 3)	Windows 95/98/2000/NT/ME/XP 2003/ Vista/7, MS IIS, Linux
Searchable File Types	More than 250 file types: Microsoft Office files (MC), PDF and ZIP files (MC), Web pages (HTML, XHTML, and XML documents), Text files (ASCII, ANSI and others) (MC), emails an attachments and contacts (MC), Yahoo email, Yahoo! Instant Messaging files (MC), image files (JPG, GIF, BMP, PNG, and other formats) (M), music files (MP3, WMA, WAV, and other formats) (M), video files (MPEG, MPG, AVI, WMV, and other formats) (M).	More than 255 file types: Microsoft Office files (MC), Adobe PDF files (MC), Web pages (HTML files), text files (MC), achieve ZIP files (MC), emails and attachments and contacts (MC), AOL! Instant Messenger files (MC), image files (TIFF, JPG, GIF, BMP, and other formats) (M), music files (MP3, WAV, AAC, and other formats) (M), video files (MPEG, MPG, AVI, WMV, MOV etc.) (M).	Nearly every file type: Microsoft Office files (MC) and RTF files, OpenOffice files (MC), Adobe PDF files (MC), Web pages (HTML, XML documents), text files (MC), binary (Unicode) files, emails and attachments and contacts (MC), instant Messengers files (MC), image files (TIFF, JPG, GIF, BMP, and other formats) (M), music files (MP3, WAV, AAC, and other formats) (M), video files (MPEG, MPG, AVI, WMV, MOV and other formats) (M).
Operational Features	File indexing, email indexing, Image indexing, multimedia indexing, browser support (Microsoft Internet Explorer), email clients (Microsoft Outlook, Outlook Express, Thunderbird, Yahoo email account), full indexing control, standalone tab based user interface, privacy conscious preview pane, button for web search, save complex search queries for re-use and save search results for faster access, search as type search query (Quick Find), control indexing and resources utilization, highlighting query keyword in the search results in the preview pane, immediate answering and manipulating emails and other files, finding files, emails, and attachments etc. with speed and accuracy, and defining index file location.	File indexing, email indexing, image indexing, multimedia indexing, browser support (Microsoft Internet Explorer, Mozilla Firebird, Mozilla Firefox), email clients (Microsoft Outlook, Outlook Express, Eudora, Lotus Notes), full indexing control, standalone tab based user interface, using contextual information for searching, smart folders, stuff I've seen feature, search as type search query (Quick Find), control indexing and resources utilization, previewing search results in the preview pane, ensuring users' privacy and security, and data integrity and confidentiality, user authentication methods, indexing P2P network communication and index files encryption	File indexing, email indexing, image indexing, multimedia indexing, browser support (Microsoft Internet Explorer, Netscape, Opera), email clients (Microsoft Outlook, Outlook Express, Thunderbird, others), full indexing control, standalone tab based user interface, more than 24 indexed and unindexed and fielded, and full text search options, searching a number of indexes in any combinations, search history display, special forensic indexing and searching tools, browse and customize thesaurus options, previewing search results in the preview pane, providing APIs for developers, instant publishing and converting files contents into HTML format for display, indexing desktop, network, Internet and Intranet sites Exporting search results in a variety of data formats.
Cost	Free	Free	Commercial
Enterprise Search Integration	No	No	Yes
Search Network Drives	No	No	Yes
Security & Privacy	Yes	Yes	Yes
Consumer or Business	Both	Both	Business
Deskbar	No	No	No
Plug-in Support	No	No	No
Advance Search Options	Yes	Yes	Yes
Web Support	Yes	Yes	Yes
Enterprise Version	No	No	No
Patent	Instant Search-as-you-type	No	No
Search Query Functionality	Boolean operators (AND, OR, NOT), keywords phrases, word proximity, case-insensitive, natural language query, filename, size, date and time	Boolean operators (AND, OR, NOT), keywords phrases,, case-insensitive, natural language query	Boolean operators (AND, OR, NOT), keywords phrases, wildcards, fuzzy, phonics, stemming, word proximity, thesaurus, case-insensitive, synonyms, natural language query
Relevance Ranking	No	Yes	Yes

M = Metadata, C = Contents, MC = Metadata and Contents

Table 4. Detailed comparison of selected desktop search engines

Parameter	Enfish (EDS)	MSN (MDS)	Beagle (BDS)
System Requirements	300 MHz CPU, Hard Disk (30 MB), 256 MB RAM	500MHz CPU and 256 MB RAM	Depends on Linux distribution requirements
Operating System	Windows 98/NT (SP 3 or greater)/ 2000/ME/XP/Vista	Windows 2000 Service Pack 4 or later and XP	Linux, Unix, and Unix like systems
Searchable File Types	Microsoft Office files and Write and Professional Write Plus and RTF files (MC), Adobe PDF files (MC), Web pages (HTML, XML documents) (MC), text files (DOS, ANSI, Macintosh, Unicode character set) (MC), WordPerfect files (MC), emails and attachments and contacts (MC), image files (JPG, GIF, BMP, and Novell PerfectWorks) (M), music files (MP3, WAV, AAC, and other formats) (M), video files (MPEG, MPG, AVI, WMV, MOV and other formats) (M).	Microsoft Office files including OneNote files (MC), Adobe PDF files (MC), plain text files (MC), Outlook (email, contacts, calendar, tasks, and notes) files and attachments (MC), AOL and MSN Instant Messenger files (MC), Web pages (HTML, and XML documents) (MC), image files (GIF, JPG, and BMP) files (M), audio files (MP3) (M), video files (WMA, and AVI) (M).	Microsoft Office files (MC), OpenOffice files (MC), PDF files (MC), Archives (ZIP, TAR, GZIP, and BZIP) files (MC), Web pages (HTML, XHTML, and XML) files (MC), text files (TXT) (MC), bookmarks and web page history files (FireFox, Conqueror, and Epiphany) (MC), RSS feeds (MC), emails address book contacts (Evolution, Mozilla Thunderbird, and KMail) (MC), conversations (Pidgin, Kopete, and IRC logs) (MC), image files (PNG, JPG, TIFF, GIF, and SVG) (M), music files (MP3.OGG, FLAC) (M), video files (M), and source codes etc. (M).
Operational Features	File indexing, email indexing, image indexing, multimedia indexing, browser support, email clients, full indexing control, standalone tab based user interface, tabs addition and deletion and replacement, saving complex search criteria, indexing and cross-referencing information, special forensic indexing and searching tools, launch as a separate application via toolbars in MS Office and via Windows Taskbar, previewing search results in the preview pane, rolling all relevant information into one place, piggybacking on Internet Explorer and Outlook considering them as the center of a user daily computing life, indexing desktop and network and Internet and Intranet sites, sharing trackers with other users.	File indexing, email indexing, image indexing, multimedia indexing, browser support, email clients, full indexing control, word wheeling for instant search results, aliases for commonly used shortcuts, deskbar as a supercharged run dialog box, toolbars for Outlook and Deskbar and Internet Explorer and Windows Explorer to launch search from anywhere, searching both local desktop and Web, highlight search keywords in the search results, block pop-ups, fill function, history of previous searches, display search results in preview panel, cannot index ZIP or other archives, uses Windows authentication to provide security and privacy, searches as you type.	File indexing, email indexing, image indexing, multimedia indexing, browser support (FireFox and other Linux and Unix based web browsers), email clients (Evolution, Mozilla Thunderbird, and KMail), full indexing control, standalone user interface, browser-based user interface, previewing search results in the preview pane, property-based search, control indexing and resources utilization and customization, network computers search, real time indexing
Cost	Commercial	Free	Free
Enterprise Search Integration	Yes	Yes	Yes
Search Network Drives	Yes	No	Yes
Security & Privacy	Yes	Yes	No
Consumer or Business	Both	Both	Both
Deskbar	Yes	Yes	No
Plug-in Support	No	No	Yes
Advance Search Option	No	Yes	Yes
Web Support	Yes	Yes	No
Enterprise Version	No	No	No
Patent	No	No	No
Search Query Functionality	Keywords phrases, case-insensitive	Keywords phrases, (*) wildcards, case-insensitive	Boolean operators (AND, OR, NOT), sub-queries, keywords phrases, (*, ?) wildcards, word proximity, case-insensitive, natural language query
Relevance Ranking	No	No	Yes

M = Metadata, C = Contents, MC = Metadata and Contents

Context-Based Approaches

The DSEs can effectively leverage contextual information as compared to the web search engines (Chen, et al., 2012). The web search engines cannot capture contextual information automatically using web browsers due to security concerns. The DSEs are free of such security concerns and have extensive access rights to a local system. Therefore, they can capture great deal of contextual information which can be elegantly used to explore semantics of a query. It is believed that quality of keywords desktop search can be improved by contextualizing desktop search via leveraging the resource specific and semantic metadata captured from users' contexts and activities executed on their personal computers (Chen, et al., 2012; Chirita, et al., 2006).

Beagle++ (Chirita, et al., 2006) is a semantic desktop search prototype employing semantic and ranking mechanisms to improve conventional full text desktop search. The Beagle++ extends open-source Beagle desktop search infrastructure with additional metadata generators and ranking module for precise searching and ranking of resources on a desktop. The metadata generator extracts semantic metadata by exploiting contextual information to relate diverse desktop resources and ranking module (i.e., PageRank derived algorithm) computes ranking of resources for appropriate display of search results according to their importance (Ayres et al., 2019). Exploring contextual information and ranks computation will bring desktop search almost to the level of web search engines performance. RDFs ontology is employed for describing RDF metadata about a specific context. The metadata is generated either by direct extraction (i.e., information available with a resource) or by using appropriate associations rules along with some additional background knowledge. The metadata in RDF format is stored in metadata index. To answer a query, DSE uses metadata index in conjunction with full-text indexes. The ranking mechanism called ObjectRank is based on the Google's PageRank algorithm to rank the search results which could be more and more because of contextual metadata. The rank is calculated using the information obtained from context ontology and appropriate authority transfer annotations. The context ontology provides semantic relationships among resources and authority transfer schema graph (i.e., Object Ranking) expresses how importance propagates among the entities and resources inside the ontology. The Beagle++ not only relies on its ObjectRank mechanism but also take advantages of TF-IDF measure (i.e., default ranking mechanism used by Beagle) to determine resources existing on the desktop (Ayres et al., 2019). The ranking is, therefore, a two-step process: (1) ranks are computed with ObjectRank algorithm for all of the existing resources, and (2) the resultants ranks are integrated with the TF-IDF measures provided by Lucene.Net. It guarantees that a hit will have high rank score if it has high ObjectRank and TF-IDF score. The Beagle++ is compared with original Beagle systems and Beagle++ is found far more superior in both average precision and recall. However, Beagle++ is limited to specific desktop contexts (e.g., publications and web pages). The Beagle++ is restricted to extracting associations from predefined user actions between web pages, email messages and files, and not storing context information from continuous users' retrieval activities (Chen, et al., 2012).

The iMecho (Chen, et al., 2012) is a context-aware search framework emphasizing semantics of queries are context-aware (i.e., current activity state). The iMecho analyzes various access events recorded by various user activity monitors to infer the current task (i.e., activity state). The task mining algorithm detects tasks from the current access events which are used to initialize the user model. Hidden Markov Model (HMM) is used as a user model to record the relationship between user's current access event and possible task. HMM is selected because of its strength of relating one observable sequence with one hidden sequence and its fundamental speculation of relying current task on the previous task which is more practical in most cases of desktop activities. The model is created and frequently updated offline. To response a user's query at runtime, the model analyzes his current access events to infer the current task. iMecho context-aware ranking scheme is updated with the information returned from the model which will increase ranks of the items more closely relating to the current task. The effectiveness of context-aware ranking scheme is compared with the ranking schemes using TF-IDF scores in terms of average precision and average recall. After evaluations and statistical analysis, it has been deduced that context-aware ranking scheme is better than TF-IDF scores based ranking schemes in both precision and recall. iMecho, instead of depending on specific information types, uses more general information sources (i.e., file access pattern) which could be equally applied to any desktop resource.

The Stuff I've Seen (Dumais et al., 2003) facilitates users to locate information they have visited previously in a two-step process. Firstly, a unified index of information is built as they are seen by users on their computers. Secondly, rich contextual cues (i.e., author, thumbnail, time, previews, etc.) in combination with information obtained in first step are used for searching and presenting information. The SIS extends MS Search indexing architecture by five components: gatherer, filter, tokenizer, indexer, and retriever. The gather is the interface for accessing various information sources in their native formats (i.e., doc, PDF, HTML, etc.). The filter decodes information sources and extracts a stream of characters. The tokenizer breaks and organizes character stream into individual words using specialized linguistic processing (e.g., data normalization, stemming, etc.). The gatherer, filter and tokenizer components are extendable to accommodate new information sources and types. The indexer creates a standard inverted index for fast accessing. The retriever is the query language to be used for retrieving stored information. The retrievers make use of Boolean operators (i.e., AND, OR, NOT, +, -), advance search functions (i.e., phrase, proximity, wildcards, etc.) and best match retrieval on the full text and metadata properties. The Okapi's probabilistic ranking algorithm serves as the bases for the best match algorithm. All of the SIS components are executed on the client computer. The SIS, by default, indexes data sources where new data sources can be added and index once created is automatically updated as new files are created or downloaded. The SIS interface called the Top View provides several filters and refining attributes allowing users to specify search queries and to retrieve and manipulate results. The SIS is evaluated using both questionnaires and log files analysis and found that time, people and important retrieval cues are useful for finding information more easily using SIS.

Lamming et al., (Lamming & Newman, 1992) supports activity-based approach for enhancing information retrieval and suggested a system which employs activity monitors to gather a user's activities data and extracts contextual cues from the data to enhance retrieval. Rhodes (Rhodes, 1997) has followed the same approach and presented an agent-based system which analyzes users' physical activities to collect information relevant to the context.

Association-Based Approaches

Psychology research has proven that chains of associations are the vital weapon helping people in remembering things (Chen, Guo, Wu, & Xie, 2009). Human memory recall system works by remembering things using the associative memory fragments left in the brain along with the memory cues relating to the context of information capture or subsequent access. The computer users do not remember the location and names of files stored on their computers but they can remember other things associated with them. However, current desktop file systems do not support linking files semantically. In addition to teleporting, DSEs should support orienteering - where people might navigate to their target information in relatively few steps and each step will be representing an association (Chau, et al., 2008). Using the idea of multi-step associative retrieval of information on computers encourages researchers to come up with novel DSEs.

The Feldsper (Finding Elements by Leveraging Diverse Sources of Pertinent Associative Recollection) (Chau, et al., 2008) is multi-level associative information retrieval system which uses orienteering approach by letting users to add associations sequentially until the required target is found. The two novel characteristics of Feldsper are user interface and association information collection algorithm. The user interface provides interactive environment allowing users for creating multi-level associative retrieval query by incremental selections. Both query construction and query results presentation features are supported within a single user interface. User interface is composed of three parts: (1) navigation bar at the top for back and forward movements, (2) query area for creating queries visually and interactively, and (3) result area to visualize results. The Feldsper employees Google Desktop Search for creating database for indexing and tracking of the required data objects and access the database through Google Desktop Search API. To retrieve information about an item, the Google Desktop Search database is queried using its query API. The result object contains many relevant pieces of information about the item which are extracted and used by the Feldsper. The Feldsper stores association information about items in a graph data structure called association graph where vertices represent items and edges represents associations. The graph is directed one and implemented using the QuickGraph 2.0 open-source graph data structure. A separate module Graph Builder is developed for constructing the association graph. The Feldsper implements algorithms for generating results for a given query. The algorithms implement a results generator for each pair of associations in the query where the output a result generator is feed as input to the next result generator. The Feldsper is evaluated and both quantitative and qualitative analyses are found positive, confirming Feldsper is productive for users in several ways.

The XSearcher (Chen, et al., 2009) is associative memory-based desktop search system which enhances desktop search by exploiting associations and contexts of information to retrieve target item in the similar fashion as human associative memory builds and uses chains of associations to remember things. The XSearcher assumes that associations between desktop resources can be equivalent to links between web pages and ranking algorithm like PageRank can be used in desktop search. The XSearcher connects desktop resources though semantic links using information extracted from user activities and contexts. The semantic links provides basis for building and using memory fragments in a user mind during searching. In XSearch associations can be of three types: (1) content-based associations extracted from the content and attributes of resources, (2) explicit activity-based associations which are bound with specific user activities, and (3) implicit activity-based associations which can be discovered through user access pattern analysis and resource provenance analysis. The XSearcher architecture extends traditional desktop search with additional components for chasing user activities and constructing semantic links. The XSearcher has activity event monitor to store desktop event for generating semantic links by the association analyzer. A desktop ontology is employed for representing attributes of resources and their semantic associations. The resource associations and attributes are stored in RDF repository which can be searched for retrieving semantic links of a resource using RDF queries. The link based ranking algorithm uses both links and user's personal preferences to rank results by both relevance and importance. The XSearcher provides two ways to help users in refining and associate search results generated by the full text keyword search: (1) faceted search filters enable users to navigate in multi-dimensional information space by combining text search with a progressive narrowing of choices in each dimension, and (2) association graph navigation uses semantic links to explore associative links to extend the search results. The user interface uses two displays search results and associative context. The XSearcher is claimed superior to traditional desktop search because of its functioning being closer to human associative memory functioning.

Miscellaneous Approaches

Several of the personal information systems are proposed exploiting similarities of time of creations, location of creation, contents, author, etc. information to enhance search results. Dourish et al., (Dourish, Edwards, LaMarca, & Salisbury, 1999) has presented an attribute-based system like tagging to enable users to classify their personal information. The LifeStreams system (Fertig, Freeman, & Gelernter, 1996) is a time-based retrieval system which provides a single time-ordered stream of electronic documents and supports searching, filtering and summarization. The Ringel et al., (Ringel, Cutrell, Dumais, & Horvitz, 2003) has presented a timeline-based system enhances search results by displaying chief events which users could recognize and help them to retrieve personal information quite easily. Nardi et al., (Nardi & Barreau, 1997) has proposed a location-based information management system arguing people builds collection of documents which could be of same type, topics or proximity in creation time. The MyLifeBits (Gemmell, Bell, Lueder, Drucker, & Wong, 2002) focuses on locally storing multimedia files (i.e., videos, images, documents, etc.) of a user into collections and supports rich annotations for connecting resources within collections with links. The Haystack is a personal store which supports annotations for emphasizing relationships between individuals and their collections. The documents with similar contents are automatically connected and usage analysis is exploited to enhance and extend the search results set.

SECURITY AND PRIVACY ISSUES

The anticipated popularity of DSEs has become an industry hottest trend, promising to extend the success and ease of searching the Web for easily, comprehensively and quickly searching PCs. While enabling end-users in finding their files, enterprises are warned by analysts and IT executives about opting DSEs because of their potential security holes of revealing personal and confidential information on corporate computers (Hicks, 2004). The UW in their study concluded that most of DSEs are still immature for significant business use due to lack with mature security and overall manageability (Noda & Helwig, 2005). This conclusion worries desktop search companies and government investigation and intelligence authorities. If security is breached in anyway, prowlers can access sensitive information quickly.

New privacy issues could emerge where people would get shocked of easily discovering and accessing their personal information on the Web (Azzopardi, White, Thomas, & Craswell, 2020). Blaming DSEs is injustice because their sole purpose is making it easier to find and locate files or information on a particular computer (Sullivan, 2004). The problem is not because of the technology behind DSEs but rather the unintended consequences of being able to instantly locate previously hard-to-find data such as emails and cached web pages (Hicks, 2004). Several of real-world scenarios can be posted of users' security and privacy unintended violation such as:

- A child is involved in online unlawful activities (e.g., watching online porn web sites, etc.). A DSE using browser cache can help parents in exactly pinpointing which of the websites the child has been viewing.
- A researcher leaves his computer unattended for a short while of time (e.g., stepping out for bathroom, etc.) could be a nightmare. The competitors using DSEs can easily scan the researcher's computer for stealing, copying or destroying sensitive data quite effectively and easily.

The security concerns primarily arise due to two Ws: "What" sort of information should be indexed (i.e., it may include confidential or private information or not) and "Who" has access to the computer (Bradley, 2008; Ullah, Islam, Khan, Aleem, & Iqbal, 2019). DSEs centralize data by creating indexes of plenty of files which might contain personal, private or otherwise sensitive information which others should not have access to. The secure web pages require users to enter sensitive information such as username and password. Indexing such web pages enables revealing private and sensitive information as well as previous messages indexed in the cache on the local computer using simple search terms like "password" or "social security". The DSEs offer things which could be used by others (e.g., hackers, etc.) for useful searches such as Google's feature of searching a number range, etc. There are two ways to extract information from a user's machine using DSEs:

- To exploit a user's information security and privacy requires physical access to the machine which could expedite finding information using DSE (Bradley, 2008). Information could also be found using the old-fashioned hunt and peck way of searching through files.
- A hacker capable of accessing a machine from afar can also be of potential threat to data. A DSE centralizing its data (e.g., index files, etc.) could be helpful to hackers. A hacker could have nice fat target if he finds where a DSE keeps its data (Sullivan, 2004). Using a spyware module to access index files, hackers can theoretically search millions of PCs simultaneously.
- In integrated search engines hackers exploit local proxy server program on desktop either by Java or JavaScript-based man-in-the-middle attack that redirects search results intended for a user to an unauthorized location over the Web or by inserting an applet to open control channel for issuing queries to obtain private information (Cole, 2005).
- The Web integrated DSEs have a security hole where packets transmitted between client machine and web search engine can be spoofed easy and trick machine for delivering desktop search results to a remote machine over the Internet.
- The SSL encrypts anything sensitive for transmission while browsing secure web pages. However, the SSL encrypted web pages are decrypted before displaying in the browser. This is what cached by DSE and can be potentially exploited.

Realizing the importance of security and privacy problems, vendors have practiced several measures in their DSEs. These practices are worthy, but they need improvements and novel ideas to improve data security and privacy. The proposed methodologies include:

- The DSEs provide variable degree of indexing control by defining what files and folders, particular section of computer, email folders to index, etc. Likewise, searching for specific content types should also be disabled. The downside will be if something is not in desktop search index, it would not be only un-accessible to others but to the user as well. Likewise, anyone who has physical access to the machine can still access the required information.

- The public computers (e.g., computers at library, schools, internet cafes, etc.) are of more security concern because of random users. To secure public computers, administrator must ensure that information about web pages viewed, files created and any other should not linger form one user session to another.

- Emphasizing basic computer security using built-in controls in operating system (e.g., password protection, etc.) would make protection not mandatory. Using basic computer security would help in deciding who would have access to your computer which is difficult to decide.

- Encrypting secure web pages and other sensitive information can also promote protection. However, encrypting and decrypting information in real-time can reduce machine performance.

- The DSEs can be trained to not index places of computer system containing sensitive information such as web cache, MyDocuments folder, etc.

The deciding factors for monopolizing the DSEs marketplace includes the unique usability features they offer and how they deal with security and privacy issues that have emerged (Cole, 2005). Although it is appreciable that companies are coming up with innovative solutions for local corporate machines and exercising extreme caution to avoid creating any widespread security nightmare. It is generally suggested that until kinks have been removed, companies and individuals should avoid installing DSEs on machines containing sensitive information.

CONCLUSION AND FUTURE CHALLENGES

The remarkable developments in hardware and software technologies and the explosion of Web 2.0 have immersed users in an ocean of information. The decrease in average cost of data storage has encouraged users to create new content and download information from the Web to access contents 24/7. But the question is how to retrieve a particular file when there exists hundreds and thousands of files. The desktop search category is gaining a lot of attention especially after releasing DSEs by big players in the industry. DSEs were required due to growing demands of how to find a file effectively and easily among tones of files stored on a PC. To fulfill this growing need, dozens of competent, balanced and impressive DSEs are marketed by companies, varying in their appearances, functionalities and features. These DSEs work by creating an index database to help users in searching and retrieving files, emails, attachments, etc. quickly and easily. Among many other functions, the DSEs also help in organizing files without the need of moving the original files from their locations on the disk.

In this chapter, we have presented a comprehensive comparative overview of major DSEs and elaborated what features and functionalities they offer for solving information overload problem on PCs. These DSEs are fantastic in their capacity, providing unique methods to solve the underlying problem effectively and make it difficult to decide which one is the best. However, the race is not finished yet and desktop search space is still hot making it difficult to predict that what DSEs will provide in the coming years. The inclusion of giant web search engines companies has heat up the desktop search space. Some of the companies have developed their proprietary DSEs, whereas others have acquired the existing for their DSEs such as Mamma.com and AOL acquired Copernic technology for their DSEs. In the future, web search results will not include results from the public servers but would be able to search every hard drive on the planet with its application installed. Although, it is difficult to recognize how the web companies will make money out of the DSEs. Probably, they may integrate advertisements in the future or club the desktop search results with their Internet search engines. Whatever be the case, the consumer is the winner here.

Although DSEs were anticipated by leveraging the capabilities of web search engines to desktop computers, but desktop search is more complex than web search. Therefore, these DSEs face with several challenges requiring immediate attention of the research communities. These challenges include:

- The built-in desktop search features offered in existing operating systems and DSEs have fewer capabilities as compared to web search engines. They support simple keyword searches over a group of files of a single type.
- The desktop search is more complicated than web search because files differ structurally in a variety of ways. Furthermore, desktop files can be either structured or unstructured. The structured files are easier to search as compared to unstructured files.
- To deal with unstructured files, advance searching features and keyword-indexing algorithms must be incorporated into DSEs in the same way as used in web search engines.
- The DSEs must recognize and deal with multitude of file types which are increasing with the availability of new desktop applications. In addition, DSEs must derive any type of metadata associated by the authors with files.
- The DSEs should be efficient at work. Therefore, should not jeopardize PCs by enforcing a considerable processing and memory load.
- The DSEs must use effective measures to deal with the existing and anticipated security and privacy problems which may arise.

REFERENCES

Agarwal, A. (2007). *Best Desktop Search Software – Reviews and Comparison.* Labnol. https://www.labnol.org/internet/tools/best-desktop-search-software-reviews-and-comparison/553/

Ayres, D. L., Cummings, M. P., Baele, G., Darling, A. E., Lewis, P. O., Swofford, D. L., Huelsenbeck, J. P., Lemey, P., Rambaut, A., & Suchard, M. A. (2019). BEAGLE 3: Improved performance, scaling, and usability for a high-performance computing library for statistical phylogenetics. *Systematic Biology*, *68*(6), 1052–1061. doi:10.1093ysbioyz020 PMID:31034053

Azzopardi, L., White, R. W., Thomas, P., & Craswell, N. (2020). *Data-driven evaluation metrics for heterogeneous search engine result pages.* Paper presented at the Proceedings of the 2020 Conference on Human Information Interaction and Retrieval. ACM. 10.1145/3343413.3377959

Beal, A. (2004). First Look at Ask Jeeves Desktop Search. *Web Pro News.* https://www.webpronews.com/first-look-at-ask-jeeves-desktop-search-2004-12

Boutin, P. (2004). Keeper Finders. *Slate.* https://www.slate.com/articles/technology/webhead/2004/12/keeper_finders.html

Bradley, T. (2008). Desktop Search Tools. *Net Security*. http://netsecurity.about.com/od/secureyourcomputer/a/aa102904.htm

Chau, D. H., Myers, B., & Faulring, A. (2008). What To Do When Search Fails: Finding Information by Association. Paper presented at the *Proceedings of the SIGCHI Conference on Human Factors in Computing Systems,* Florence, Italy. 10.1145/1357054.1357208

Chen, J., Guo, H., Wu, W., & Xie, C. (2009). Search Your Memory! - An Associative Memory Based Desktop Search System. Paper presented at the *Proceedings of the 2009 ACM SIGMOD International Conference on Management of data,* Providence, Rhode Island, USA. 10.1145/1559845.1559992

Chen, J., Wu, W., Guo, H., & Wang, W. (2012). Context-Aware Search for Personal Information Management Systems. Paper presented at the *Proceedings of the 12th SIAM International Conference on Data Mining,* Anaheim, California, USA. 10.1137/1.9781611972825.61

Chirita, P.-A., Costache, S., Nejdl, W., & Paiu, R. (2006). *Beagle++: Semantically Enhanced Searching and Ranking on the Desktop.* Paper presented at the European Semantic Web Conference, Budva, Montenegro. http://www.springerlink.com/content/ 876p163v66873314/fulltext.pdf

Claburn, T. (2006). Blinkx Changes Desktop Search. *Information Week.* http://www.informationweek.com/blinkx-changes-desktop-search/184417400

Cole, B. (2005). Search Engines Tackle the Desktop. *Computer, 38*(3), 14–17. doi:10.1109/MC.2005.103

Dourish, P., Edwards, W. K., LaMarca, A., & Salisbury, M. (1999). Presto: An Experimental Architecture for Fluid Interactive Document Spaces. *ACM Transactions on Computer-Human Interaction, 6*(2), 133–161. doi:10.1145/319091.319099

Dumais, S., Cutrell, E., Cadiz, J., Jancke, G., Sarin, R., & Robbins, D. C. (2003). Stuff I've Seen: A System for Personal Information Retrieval and Re-Use. Paper presented at the *Proceedings of the 26th annual international ACM SIGIR conference on Research and development in informaion retrieval,* Toronto, Canada. 10.1145/860435.860451

Farina, P. A. (2005). *A Comparison of Two Desktop Search Engines: Google Desktop Search (Beta) vs. Windows XP Search Companion.* Paper presented at the *21th Annual Computer Science Conference Hartford,* USA.

Fertig, S., Freeman, E., & Gelernter, D. (1996). *Lifestreams: An Alternative to the Desktop Metaphor.* Paper presented at the *Conference Companion on Human Factors in Computing Systems,* Vancouver, British Columbia, Canada. 10.1145/257089.257404

Gemmell, J., Bell, G., Lueder, R., Drucker, S., & Wong, C. (2002). *MyLifeBits: Fulfilling the Memex Vision.* Paper presented at the *ACM international conference on Multimedia,* Juan-les-Pins, France. 10.1145/641007.641053

Heck, M. (2010). dtSearch Desktop, Version 7.64 Powerful, Enterprise-Level Search Tool. *Network World.* https://www.networkworld.com/reviews/2010/072610-desktop-search-tools-test-dtsearch.html

Hicks, M. (2004). Desktop Search: The Ultimate Security Hole? *eWeek.* https://www.eweek.com/c/a/Enterprise-Applications/Desktop-Search-The-Ultimate-Security-Hole/

Jeremy. (2006). The Fish That Was Ahead of Its Time. *Loose Wire Blog*. http://www.loosewireblog.com/2006/05/the_fish_that_w_1.html

Jones, W. P., & Dumais, S. T. (1986). The Spatial Metaphor for User Interfaces: Experimental Tests of Reference by Location versus Name. *ACM Transactions on Information Systems*, *4*(1), 42–63. doi:10.1145/5401.5405

Kendall, A. (2013). Best Free Desktop Search Utility. *Tech Support Alert*. https://www.techsupportalert.com/best-free-desktop-search-utility.htm

Khusro, S., Ali, S., Alam, I., & Ullah, I. (2017). Performance Evaluation of Desktop Search Engines Using Information Retrieval Systems Approaches. *Journal of Internet Technology*, *18*(5), 1043–1055.

King, N. (2006). Enfish Professional *Beta*. *PC Mag*. http://www.pcmag.com/article2/0,2817,939388,00.asp

Kote, T. (2005). Desktop Search Comparison. *The Jo*. http://thejo.in/2005/01/desktop-search-comparison/

Lamming, M. G., & Newman, W. M. (1992). *Activity-Based Information Retrieval: Technology in Support of Personal Memory*. Paper presented at the Proceedings of the IFIP 12th World Computer Congress on Personal Computers and Intelligent Systems. Springer.

Markscheffel, B., Büttner, D., & Fischer, D. (2011, December 11-14, 2011). Desktop Search Engines - A State of the Art Comparision. Paper presented at the *Proceedings of the 6th International Conference for Internet Technology and Secured Transactions (ICITST-2011)*, Abu Dhabi, UAE.

Matzan, J. (2005). dtSearch 7.0 Review. *Software in Review*. http://www.softwareinreview.com/search_tools/dtsearch_7.0_review.html

Narasimhan, V. L., & Lowe, M. (2010). *An Objective Comparison of Desktop Search and Visualization Tools*. Paper presented at the Proceedings of the 2nd International Conference on Trends in Information Sciences and Computing (TISC-2010). IEEE. 10.1109/TISC.2010.5714640

Nardi, B., & Barreau, D. (1997). "Finding and Reminding" Revisited: Appropriate Metaphors for File Organization at the Desktop. *SIGCHI Bull.*, *29*(1), 76–78. doi:10.1145/251761.248508

Noda, T., & Helwig, S. (2005). *Benchmark Sutdy of Desktop Search Tools*. UW E-Business Consortium, University of Misconsin.

Perez, J. C. (2004). Ask Jeeves Previews Desktop Search Tool. Utility Software. *PC World*. https://www.pcworld.com/article/118932/article.html

Redmond, W. (2004). Microsoft Introduces MSN Toolbar Suite Beta with Desktop Search. *Microsoft*. http://www.microsoft.com/en-us/news/press/2004/dec04/12-13searchtoolbarpr.aspx

Rhodes, B. J. (1997). The Wearable Remembrance Agent: A System for Augmented Memory. *Personal Technologies*, *1997*(1), 218–224. doi:10.1007/BF01682024

Ringel, M., Cutrell, E., Dumais, S. T., & Horvitz, E. (2003). *Milestones in Time: The Value of Landmarks in Retrieving Information from Personal Stores*. Paper presented at the INTERACT. http://dblp.uni-trier.de/db/conf/interact/interact2003.html#RingelCDH03

Rubenking, N. J. (2005). *MSN Toolbar Suite Beta.* Retrieved January 16, 2022, 2022, from http://www. pcmag.com/article2/0,2817,1741498,00.asp

Sanderson, M., & Croft, W. B. (2012). The History of Information Retrieval Research. *Proceedings of the IEEE, 100*(Special Centennial Issue), 1444-1451. 10.1109/JPROC.2012.2189916

Schurmann, T. (2005). The Beagle Desktop Search Engine SNIFFER DOG. *Linux Pro Magazine.* http:// www.linuxpromagazine.com/content/download/62688/485752/version/1/file/Beagle_Search_Tool.pdf

Sharma, S. (2010). Beagle. *Tech Radar.* http://www.techradar.com/news/software/applications/6-of-the-best-desktop-search-tools-for -linux-666158/2

Sherman, C. (2005). Yahoo Launches Desktop Search. *Search Engine Watch.* http://searchenginewatch. com/article/2048664/Yahoo-Launches-Desktop-Search

Sullivan, D. (2004). Privacy and Desktop Search: A Closer Look. *Search Engine Watch.* http://search-enginewatch.com/article/2065797/A-Closer-Look-At-Privacy-Desktop-Search

Thurrott, P. (2004). *MSN Toolbar Suite Preview.* Win SuperSite. http://winsupersite.com/windows-live/ msn-toolbar-suite-preview

Tschabitscher, H. (2007a). *Blinkx 2.0.5 - Email Search Tool.* Microsoft. http://email.about.com/od/ outlookaddons/gr/blinkx.htm

Tschabitscher, H. (2007b). *Enfish Find 6.1.3 - Email Search Tool.* Microsoft. http://email.about.com/od/ outlookaddons/gr/enfish_find.htm

Ullah, M., Islam, M. A., Khan, R., Aleem, M., & Iqbal, M. A. (2019). ObSecure Logging (OSLo): A Framework to Protect and Evaluate the Web Search Privacy in Health Care Domain. *Journal of Medical Imaging and Health Informatics, 9*(6), 1181–1190. doi:10.1166/jmihi.2019.2708

Wallen, J. (2010). *Efficient Desktop Searching with Beagle.* Linux. https://www.linux.com/news/software/ applications/277970:efficient-desktop-searching-with-beagle

Winder, D. (2007). *Yahoo Desktop Search review.* PC Pro. http://www.pcpro.co.uk/reviews/office/102280/ yahoo-desktop-search

Chapter 5
Beyond Cryptocurrencies:
A Review of Blockchain Technology for E-Services in Developing Countries

Tayyaba Riaz

City University of Science and Information Technology, Peshawar, Pakistan

Iftikhar Alam

City University of Science and Information Technology, Peshawar, Pakistan

ABSTRACT

Blockchain technology is the leading and revolutionary technology in this modern era of computing. Many countries around the world are diverting towards digital currency which is the initial popular service provided by blockchain technology e.g., Bitcoin, Litecoin, etc. The main feature of blockchain is to omit the central authority by introducing distributed ledger structures. The consensus protocols play a vital role in the performance and efficiency of blockchain-based frameworks. This study introduces the solution of different e-services and associated problems that are faced in developing countries for making the system transparent, smart, and secure. These features make Web 3.0 applications, which is the ultimate goal of blockchain-based technology. This study also explains the numerous aspects of blockchain-based e-services infrastructure, implementation issues, advantages, disadvantages, and challenges. This study may help practitioners for making smart, intelligent, highly secure, and robust applications even in developing countries.

1. INTRODUCTION

Blockchain is a prominent technology in the twenty-first century. In 1991, for the first time in history, a research team coined the term blockchain (Ahmad, Lutfiani, Ahmad, Rahardja, & Aini, 2021). The blockchain creator, Satoshi Nakamoto introduced the cryptocurrency name Bitcoin. Blockchain technology has revolutionary effects on different services in developed countries. It is now accepted that the deployment of blockchain technology in several sensitive activities can change the way it works by enhancing data security and efficiency (Salah, Rehman, Nizamuddin, & Al-Fuqaha, 2019). Numerous

DOI: 10.4018/978-1-6684-6914-9.ch005

blockchain-dependent applications have gained significant popularity in the last few years. For example, e-government, e-commerce, supply chain management systems, interbank transactions, healthcare applications, and many financial use cases are leading areas that focus on blockchain technology (Gao et al., 2021). However, in developing countries, the implementation of these services through blockchain is neither simple nor feasible due to the lack of infrastructure, required expenses, and trust by the layman.

Besides, in this chapter, we focus on blockchain-based e-services in developing countries as there are lots of issues regarding privacy, transparency, and security. The crux of the chapter is to describe blockchain technology from different aspects including brief yet comprehensive discussions on research gaps.

The rest of the chapter is divided into seven sections. Section 2 described the basic features. Section 3 discusses the basic flow and architecture of blockchain, types of blockchain are discussed in section 4, and the revolutionary applications of blockchain are highlighted in section 5. Section 6 discusses the theoretical findings and challenges. Section 7 concludes the chapter. References are enlisted in the end.

2. BASIC FEATURES OF BLOCKCHAIN

There are several key features of blockchain technology, such as decentralization, distributed ledgers, transparency, security, immutability, and independent network. These features make it different from any other network or database. In sub-sections, all these features are discussed in detail.

2.1 Decentralization

The blockchain contains multiple nodes having full access to sharing, creating, or uploading something new to their blocks. All miners have to trust the system instead of any third party to complete their work or to perform their transactions. We can take the bank system as an example, which is centralized, and everyone needs a bank to make secure their money as well as transactions upon this money i.e., transferring, depositing, withdrawing, and other services. Here, we can say that our money is secured. However, from another perspective, it may be a high risk because of the involvement of a third party (bank) in the middle. Therefore, a user wants to secure their money with little involvement from other parties. Here the technique, which truly works is called decentralization in the blockchain. The best examples of the financial use case of blockchain technology having the full implementation of decentralization are Bitcoin, Ethereum, Litecoin, etc.

Decentralization is the most important and basic feature of blockchain that works as a key component in a public-type network where decentralization is completely implemented. Previous studies show that the abstract view of a decentralized system and its implementation in a network of distributed information are two different platforms. Therefore, for every user, it is important to realize first whether they are working in a real decentralized system or not (Lee, Lee, Jung, Shim, & Kim, 2021). The public-type blockchain is an example of a decentralized system, where users or miners work in a truly independent environment. We can say it is more secure than the existing centralized systems. Figure 1 demonstrates the difference between decentralized and centralized systems.

Figure 1. Representation of centralize and decentralize system[1]

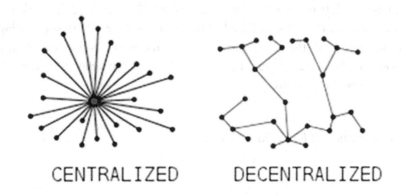

2.2 Distributed Ledger

Blockchain is the technology where all the nodes share the same electronic ledger and that are synchronized with each other with an interval of time and on each performed transaction. The data entered by a node will be equally distributed to all other remaining nodes of the specific network. Therefore, each node can easily monitor the activities done by the connected nodes from time to time. It maintains a sort of strong interaction between all members/nodes of a group. A common record is utilized to store transactions. A duplicate of the record is kept up with each user of the blockchain network. These duplicates are synchronized by ideal replication (Hughes, Park, Kietzmann, & Archer-Brown, 2019). It can help to improve transparency and security as well (Joo, Kim, Ghose, & Wilbur, 2023).

2.3 Transparency

The transparency in blockchain determines the level of access assigned to its users. In any network where the public is allowed to join it as a new node under some consensus. A transparent system maintains the history of transactions done between the nodes and also makes them visible to each node. With the help of transparency, the system ensures the prevention of any fraud because once any digital transaction occurs it is recorded in the ledger and after that, no one can change or delete it so that's why history is stored permanently. An open ledger can be visible to every participant node, so transparency could help up to a very large instant to make a trustable agreement. Moreover, many government use cases are highly recommended to deploy blockchain technology for their transparency (Tariq, Ibrahim, Ahmad, Bouteraa, & Elmogy, 2019).

2.4 Security

Blockchain technology provides improved security due to its mutual connectivity between all nodes. As we discussed that each node is having the hash of the previous node, for example, 1st block that is called the genesis block contains no previous hash because it is the first block of a network the 2nd block contains the hash of 1st block and 3rd block contains the hash of 2nd block and so on. If any peer tries to temper the value of a block it will make the value of all the remaining blocks invalid. It simply means that if the hacker wants to delete or alter the data of any block. The value of that targeted block's hash must also be changed. Because the value of a hash is the encrypted form of the consisting data, it automatically creates an alarm towards the next peer because of an error in its previous hash value. As each block is having previous hash so each current block hash should be matched with the value of the next block's previous hash as shown in Figure 2.

Figure 2. Simple demonstration of blockchain security

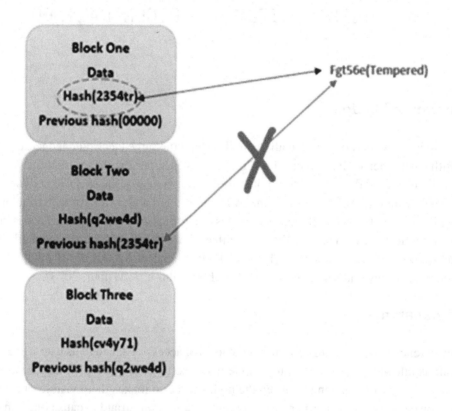

Talking about financial platforms in computer science technologies since 2005, blockchain leads the high level for providing much more space to defend important records or currency. In several types of applications and services security is the main issue due to which they are vulnerable to attacks (Khusro, Naeem, Khan, & Alam, 2018), that's why many researchers have used blockchain technology to resolve security issues (Chen, Yan, Guo, Ren, & Qi, 2022). Up-to-date news regarding financial technology says that over 700 types of cryptocurrencies exist. Therefore, it makes people attracted to blockchain technology.

2.5 Immutability

In the blockchain, immutability means the permanent existence of all the transactions and information stored in the distributed ledger. All nodes of a network are allowed to add the transaction record or any important data to the list of a block. No one can alter it even if a miner needs to update the already existing data, they would generate another transaction instead of updating or changing any consisting data. Blockchain having the fact of immutability provides data with much more security as well. Because of this fact, it is not possible to change the data of the ledger. Data cannot be deleted or tampered with. In case of any permission or private Peer-to-Peer network, a full node wants to delete any distributed/shared data, it is not guaranteed that node will still stay with the copy of that data (Casino, Politou, Alepis, & Patsakis, 2019). However, this feature has pros and cons regarding blockchain technology.

2.6 Independent Network

An independent network means that the bond created between all the members of a network has such a strong mutual understanding that any sort of fault occurred anywhere in the network can easily be tolerated. There is no effect on the whole performance of the network due to any fault occurring at any node. Instead, it will be going on as it is. This is because all the nodes are working together in a parallel way and faults could be tolerated easily, and that is a very strong feature to emerge our services.

Many governments, industrial, business, educational, and marketing, have begun applying this technology to ease their use. However, in developing countries, backtracking the service history for maintaining transparency, authenticity, and ease is a big issue. In the modern era of the 21st century, blockchain is one of the leading technologies which gave upgraded opportunities to the world of computer science. Furthermore, it enhances the functionality of digital services. For example, we can see the revolutionary impact of blockchain on cryptocurrency in the form of bitcoin as an initial application of it.

3. ARCHITECTURE AND WORKFLOW OF BLOCKCHAIN

The data in a blockchain is put away in cryptographically encoded lumps known as blocks. If a user wants to create a block in the existing network of chained blocks. First, it needs to go through some consensus protocols after that all the existing miners verify it so that one would be able to add its block. The following progressive block contains data about the past block and subsequently shapes a chain as shown in Figure 3.

Each block in a blockchain contains an extraordinary hash, exchange information, and hash of the past block. The underlying block is known as the genesis block. A genesis block doesn't contain a past hash. Members of the organization can be associations, people, or foundations that share a duplicate of the record that consecutively contains their legitimate exchanges (Pufahl, Ohlsson, Weber, Harper, & Weston, 2021).

Blockchain is the digitalization of something whether it is an asset or information regarding an asset. It is based on smart contracts between all the participating owners/miners. It can easily make any sort of complex workflow into a simple one (Shukla, Lin, & Seneviratne, 2022). They mine on their behalf and manage their records openly under special security that does not allow anyone to temper the block. Special security is all about creating a tight bond with the help of the hash of each block. Each block contains the hash and the hash of a previous block as well due to which tempering of any block is impossible because a huge number of calculations is needed there as shown inFigure 4.

There are also several types and categories of these consensus protocols i.e., Proof Of Work (POW), Proof Of Stack (POS), Proof Of Ownership (POO), etc. Any application, which used blockchain technology to move on its use cases purely depends on its consensus protocol and the measures which are important to run the needed consensus are the base for the production of a new block.

Figure 3. General demonstration of blockchain architecture

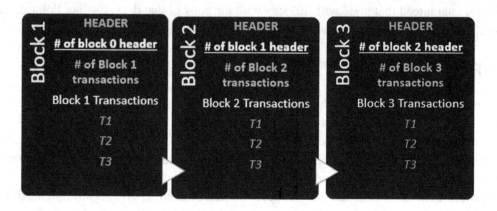

Figure 4. Simple representation of blockchain

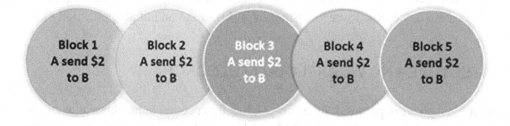

4. TYPES OF BLOCKCHAIN

Blockchain falls into three main types.

4.1 Public Blockchain/Permissionless Blockchain

It is a permissionless conveyed record on which anyone can join and go through exchanges. The advantage of a public blockchain is that it is trustable, secure, open, and transparent. Example of public blockchain is bitcoin ad Ethereum etc., (Gad, Mosa, Abualigah, & Abohany, 2022). It is a non-prohibitive type of record where each node has a duplicate. This implies that anybody with a web association can get to the public blockchain. It is worth mentioning here that to perform the tasks on a public type network respective node has to complete a computational activity. These complicated calculations should be performed to confirm changes and add them to the record. All the nodes are directly connected and work independently as shown in Figure 5.

On the blockchain network, no substantial record or exchange might be modified. Since the source code is normally open, anyone can look at the exchanges, reveal issues, and propose fixes.

Figure 5. Simple demonstration of public blockchain network

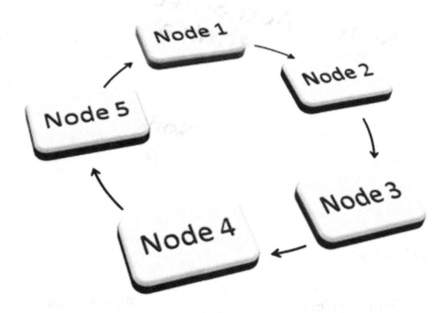

4.2. Private Blockchain/Permissioned Blockchain

In a private blockchain, the nodes are not directly or independently connected to the network, they need verification from the pre-selected authority (Gad et al., 2022). They are much of the time run on a little organization inside a firm or association as opposed to open to anyone who needs to contribute handling power. Permissioned blockchains and business blockchains are two additional terms for them. Figure 6 depicts the private blockchain network.

That authority is responsible for all the activities performed within the network. Here, the Blockchain is accessible for each hub to take part, the hub is limited and has severe power for the executives to get to the information.

4.3. Hybrid Blockchain

It is a blend of public and private Blockchains, as shown in Figure 7. When multiple private networks are joined to make a public network, it is a hybrid way of communication using blockchain technology. Additionally, it ordinarily has business-to-business organizations. The information can likewise be viewed as to some extent decentralized. Hybrid blockchain platforms are mainly used for the integration of IoT-based systems (Alkhateeb, Catal, Kar, & Mishra, 2022).

Figure 6. Simple demonstration of private blockchain network

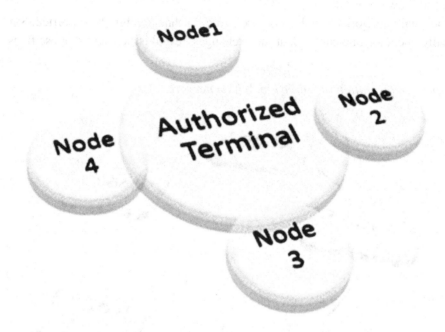

Figure 7. Hybrid blockchain[2]

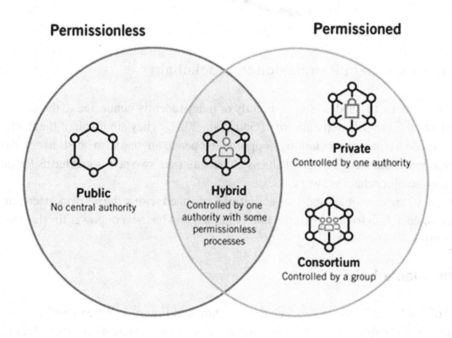

5. REVOLUTIONARY APPLICATIONS OF BLOCKCHAIN TECHNOLOGY

Currently, in all the public and private sectors either government departments or educational institutes, the data is recorded either manually or computerized. However, there are still many ambiguities that the government and its employees are facing. These traditional data sharing or management systems are far away from the leading challenges of security in these existing systems. All the previous work done in different areas like the transparency of vehicle records, FIR system, and medical reports using blockchain technology used either public or private types of blockchain. Blockchain has been globally involved in many non-financial and financial areas like data sharing, real estate, ownerships, copyright protection, food supply chain (as per food safety), creation of digital IDs, Smart property, automotive, digital currency, private markets, forecasting, public transport (ride-sharing) as well as cyber security, etc. The work done on public blockchain makes the system more expensive and energy-consuming. The use of only private blockchain makes the system not better and decentralized. The approach we followed would introduce a mutually effective environment.

Blockchain is the simple solution to all complications caused due to the trust problem. Using blockchain, all the records on distributed ledgers stayed immutable, maintaining a high level of security. Blockchain has been applied to various real-life use cases like promoting the banking system and money transactions in cryptocurrency. Improving the healthcare system is possible by maintaining the scalability of patient records. Blockchain has a significant impact on business and industrial areas by implementing supply chains for tracking information about products so customers can easily verify things and enhance trust. Job history is essential for counting experience, track record of promotions, transfers, performance, etc.

The beneficial characteristics of blockchain technology can help the government fight the fraud and corruption that comes either from internal or external entities because all types of crime in government departments lead to an increase in their expenditure. The nature of blockchain technology to be transparent can allow its use cases to extend over a large number in the future(Kassen, 2022). Perhaps all over the globe, the leaders of technologies have started work on deploying blockchain technology to make systems more and more decentralized (Durach, Blesik, von Düring, & Bick, 2021). Miners are allowed to create, upgrade, broadcast, and verify the records on behalf of some consensus protocol.

Blockchain is a peer-to-peer distributed network to share data among all the participating nodes (Tandon, Kaur, Mäntymäki, & Dhir, 2021). The impossible task to make changes or attack any block makes it more secure. A previous report from Statista 2020 shows that the world market for blockchain technology has gained much more popularity in the last three years and is expected to exceed USD 39 billion by 2025 (Tandon et al., 2021). In some other studies, till 2025, indications are up to $20 for the revenue against the enterprises' applications based on blockchain(Wang, Hua, Wei, & Cao, 2022). Initiatives towards e-government focus on public ease of access and decrease the other burdens related to administrative government employees (Nair, Ramesh, & Tyagi, 2023).

6. ISSUES AND CHALLENGES

A study says that with time, blockchains also have exposure to a lot of limitations(Wang et al., 2022). Special in energy applications the blockchain is leading toward true challenges. Currently, there are some limitations because of energy consumption. Although there are many outlooks to solve such problems in the coming future.

6.1 Issues related to Management and IoT Sensors

Blockchain has been valuable in different areas of innovation. For instance, it has been executed in IoT to further develop the security and proficiency of IoT-based gadgets. For instance, in the agriculture business, research shows that Blockchain permits food to be followed from farms to general stores in almost a few seconds. Thus, it helps in monitoring and finding unlawful attempts and delivery problems. but still, there is difficult to keep the data 100 percent safe from hackers. Data mining in Blockchain needs a lot of calculation and handling power. Most IoT gadgets don't have the necessary power to do as such (Nair et al., 2023). In another case, there is a lot of consumption of energy as well as generation of heat. The efforts that are applied to adopt super technologies lead to adverse effects sometimes. In the energy supply chain, one of the leading challenges is the "large amount of investment"(Almutairi et al., 2022).

6.2 Identification of Attacks in Blockchain

The publication of logical papers on blockchain security expanded quickly until 2020. The peak at present is in 2019, with 70 publications. The complete number of diary articles even significantly increased in that period. This perception shows the rising of research in the field of blockchain online protection. Moreover, the rising number of diary articles demonstrates that the examination joins toward a higher development level. A sum of 87 attacks has been extracted from the studies(Schlatt, Guggenberger, Schmid, & Urbach, 2022). At the same time, blockchain technology is going through a large number of cyberattack challenges. Furthermore, it also has many related risks (Mahmood, Chadhar, & Firmin, 2022).

6.3 Cyber Security Challenges

Cybersecurity challenges in blockchain technology are being investigated to enhance business processes and reshape business tasks. This checking audit paper was pointed toward investigating the ongoing literature reviews and categorizing different kinds of cybersecurity challenges in blockchain technology. Research journals like Elsevier, ResearchGate, IEEE, and ScienceDirect were looked through utilizing different terms, and after the screening, 51 exploration studies were viewed as significant (Mahmood et al., 2022). Another study has extracted and analyzed the 87 types of attacks and assaults from blockchain-based systems applications. Also highlights the way of the relationship between the developer, user, and attacker of that system(Schlatt et al., 2022).

In blockchain-based applications data is processed and collected on the cloud so almost vulnerability to attacks increases. Furthermore, public/permissionless blockchain is facing some limitations regarding confidentiality(Himeur et al., 2022). A study starts analyzing the cybersecurity for blockchain and proves the surety for the reliability of BCT with the aspects of cybersecurity. A total of 833 papers have been analyzed between 2013 and 2022. At the same time, 60 cyberattacks have also been detected for blockchain-based networks. Since the vulnerability has been seen in many areas, also various ways are introduced to fight against such threats. It is to be noticed that the cyberattacks, which are discussed usually, are for multi-purposes. There are a couple of highlights of Blockchain hacking practically, and all predefined attacks could disturb the framework or module work, but not this technology(Tanha, Hasani, Hakak, & Gadekallu, 2022).

6.4 Cyber Attacks on Blockchain Ledger

Decentralized cryptographic frameworks have become interesting targets for hackers/crackers because of significant benefit gains and huge rewards. Various attack models have been introduced in the recent couple of years (Ruan, Sun, Lou, & Li, 2022). The security level of the blockchain network directly corresponds to the complexity of the hash functioning power that runs the blockchain. As much as miners expand their mining system the more challenging the attack is for the attacker. Still, there are multiple ways a blockchain can be compromised (Aggarwal & Kumar, 2021).

In the sub-section, we will discuss the attacks experienced by the blockchain-based environment. Probably a lot of work has also been done to provide fault-tolerant peer-to-peer networks. But the vulnerabilities to some attacks come up sometime. For example:

6.4.1 Denial of Services (DoS)

One of the main growing up attacks in the services of network, the intensity of which is increasing day by day. Regardless of any study, some scholars of cryptography and security from Cornell university applied DoS attacks on ten types of blockchain-based ecosystems. So proved that such attacks can keep going on powerful cryptocurrencies and blockchain-based ecosystems(Raikwar & Gligoroski, 2022).

Another result from a study shows the DoS attacks on an Ethereum-based private blockchain environment with the consensus algorithm PoA (Proof of Authority). So, it has been proved that private blockchains can be vulnerable to DoS attacks(Battisti, Koslovski, Pillon, Miers, & Gonzalez, 2022). DoS attack avoid authentic users to access the services of their respective systems as shown in Figure 8. The same case is in DDoS (Distributed denial of services attacks) where the network is flooded with huge traffic of malware notifications or requests to make the system shut down.

Figure 8. Denial of service attack

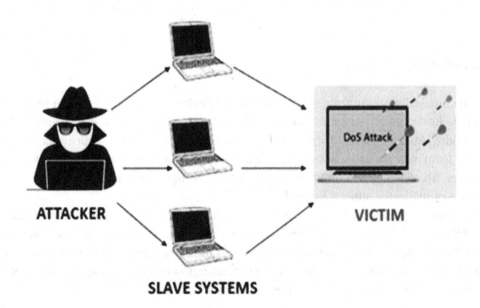

6.4.2 Sybil Attack

The Sybil attacks are the attacks in a situation where various numbers of fake identities attack the huge hub of linked nodes depicted in Figure 9. The hackers can place multiple fake users to become a huge part of a network to fetch the secrets in the ledger. although they prove these users as authentic nodes of the organization. by performing such blunders malware users can easily find out and modify the important part of existing transactions. In a Sybil attack, the hacker can misuse virtual machines, a few gadgets, or bogus (IP) addresses as a fake identity for the attack. A study for the investigation of multiple threats from Sybil attacks is analyzed by following some approaches (Hafid, Hafid, & Samih, 2022).

The permissionless blockchain protocols run the entire environment without any trustworthy authority. The blocks are increased and updated by themselves by following some ethics that have been specified contributions. These types of blockchain-based environments are probably vulnerable to Sybil attacks. Because anyone by following the specified rules and contributions can become part of a network whether it is a trustable person or a malicious person (Platt & McBurney, 2021).

Figure 9. Sybil attack

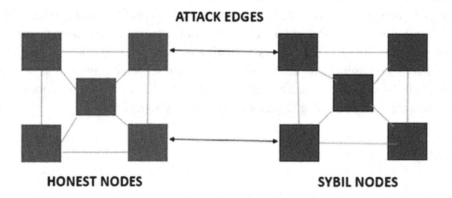

6.4.3 Eclipse Attack

The blockchain-based working frameworks are often popular for providing a high level of security. But also due to its decentralized nature some attacks such as eclipse attacks, can access the blockchain networks (Yıldız, Atmaca, Solak, Tursun, & Bahtiyar, 2022). Blockchain security has gained special consideration from industry and scholars because of its privileging and storage systems for applications in recent years. Since being a decentralized network, blockchain applications might be vulnerable to different kinds of malicious attacks(Xu et al., 2020).

In eclipse attacks, a single hub is disconnected from the distributed organization by the attackers. Like the Sybil attack, it doesn't go after the whole network. When the targeted node is disconnected, the attacker monitors all outer links of the respective node(Yıldız et al., 2022). From this point, the attacker can mishandle the services and components of the organization and releases several types of malicious activities on blockchain mining power. Figure 10 shows eclipse attacks.

Figure 10. Eclipse attack

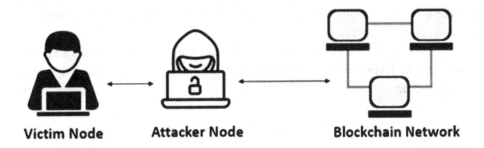

6.4.4 Routing Attack

In routing attacks, a message is targeted by the hacker in the blockchain network as depicted in Figure 11. The attacker intercepts and falsely modifies the message and sends it to its neighbors. More ever this attack is divided into further two types one is called a partitioning routing attack and the other is called a delay routing attack. In the category of partitioning attacks, it attacks an entire blockchain network in two ways or more (Saad, Cook, Nguyen, Thai, & Mohaisen, 2019). In a delay attack, the attacker fetches the information from the targeted network and tempers it, and resends it to the remaining nodes of the network.

Figure 11. Routing attack

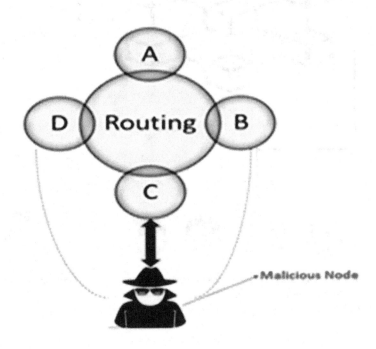

Consensus protocols are the bridge between the nodes of a network to build agreement systems and trust between them. For every consensus, there is a respective type to attack attempt by attackers. Any wireless sensor network framework can easily be tempered by routing attacks and degrade the overall performance of the network. A problem is detecting the malicious node that spread harm at high speed (Abd El-Moghith & Darwish, 2021).

Deep analysis by a study has been done to observe all well-known security issues and attacks related to blockchain technology. Several consensus mechanisms are categorized according to their vulnerability to attacks. Many of them are also vulnerable to DOS and routing attacks (Knudsen, Notland, Haro, Ræder, & Li, 2021).

6.4.5 The 51% Attack

The 51% attack is the type of attack in which a hacker or a team of attackers falsely gains access to almost 50 percent part of a targeted network. The concept is visualized in Figure 11. Due to owning 50 percent of nodes the attacker can easily modify and monitor the blockchain transactions or ledger. All the operations can easily be reversed or forwarded by having command of mining power as shown in Figure 12.

In the field of cryptocurrency, this attack can initiate a huge risk to the operations of the blockchain system (Hao, 2022). Still, to destroy bitcoin the attacker needs a lot of financial resources. In these cases, this attack is only applicable theoretically.

Figure 12. The 51% attack

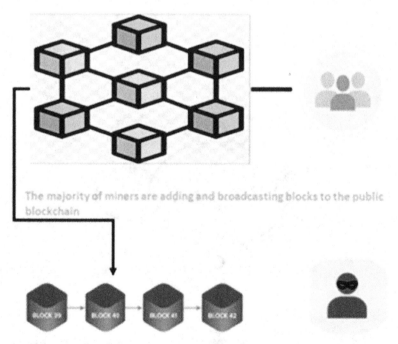

The majority of miners are adding and broadcasting blocks to the public blockchain

An attacker is adding blocks to private blockchain and not broadcasting them to the public blockchain

6.4.6 Double Spending Attack

Double spending attack was first of all introduced by Nakamoto in his historical studies (Nakamoto, 2008). In a double-spending attack, more than one transaction with a similar currency is performed by a client. This transaction is communicated to every hub in that organization. This transaction should be made sure by all other clients, this surety is time consumable. This specific time between every transaction can be an open window for the hacker to rapidly send off his/her attacks (Karpinski et al., 2021). Double spending attack is depicted in Figure 13.

Figure 13. Double spending attack

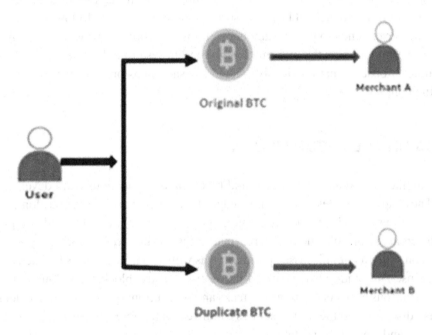

Nowadays several organizations have customized the blockchain system according to their needs and demands. Such type of systems is also prone to various type of attacks one among them being double-spending attack as well. This is just because the developers are not much familiar with the security risks and knowledge of these attacks while developing the systems (Iqbal & Matulevičius, 2021). Double spending attack is one of the major attacks that compromise the most of blockchain-based systems and have created much loss in the world of cryptocurrency (Begum et al., 2020).

6.4.7 Alternative History Attack

In an alternative-history attack, the attacker sent the transaction to the merchant falsely. Furthermore, double spending is already included by the attacker in an alternative history of assaults on blockchain systems (Malik, Gautam, Abidin, & Bhushan, 2019).

6.4.8 Race Attack

Another type of double spending attack is a race attack. In the race attack, the attacker makes two transactions. The main transaction is sent to the miner by the attacker. The particular product is sent by the miner without confirmation. In the meanwhile, the subsequent transaction is communicated by the attacker to invalidate the main transaction. Such types of attacks are a source of attacks launched against the integrity of blockchain technology (Anita & Vijayalakshmi, 2019).

6.4.9 Finney Attack

It is another type of double spending attack and withholding attack. In such a type of attack, the malicious miner buys a product from a merchant based on some amount through the following tricks(Aggarwal & Kumar, 2021). Miner pretends to pay the amount to himself within his private block. When the block has been mined the miner holds this information within his system only. When the merchant sent the product, the miner broadcast that previously created transaction as proof of payment and thus applies double spending here.

7. CONCLUSION AND FUTURE WORK

The chapter examines blockchain, its design, and blockchain applications from developing countries' perspectives. The chapter provides general knowledge about blockchain innovation alongside its applications in various regions. We give broad information on consensus methods utilized in digital currencies as well as in different regions like medical care, smart transportation frameworks, supply chains, banks, training, and so on. The chapter discussed permission as well as permissionless blockchain, private, and public blockchains. This study also discussed the features of the blockchain along with research and technical gaps in various projects. Moreover, attacks and precautionary measures for a blockchain-based projects are also discussed. In the future, studies can investigate more consensus protocols such as IoT, machine learning, and smart transportation.

REFERENCES

Abd El-Moghith, I. A., & Darwish, S. M. (2021). *A deep blockchain-based trusted routing scheme for wireless sensor networks.* Paper presented at the Proceedings of the International Conference on Advanced Intelligent Systems and Informatics 2020. Springer. 10.1007/978-3-030-58669-0_26

Aggarwal, S., & Kumar, N. (2021). Attacks on blockchain []: Elsevier.]. *Advances in Computers*, *121*, 399–410. doi:10.1016/bs.adcom.2020.08.020

Ahmad, D., Lutfiani, N., Ahmad, A. D. A. R., Rahardja, U., & Aini, Q. (2021). Blockchain technology immutability framework design in e-government. *Jurnal Administrasi Publik*, *11*(1), 32–41.

Alkhateeb, A., Catal, C., Kar, G., & Mishra, A. (2022). Hybrid blockchain platforms for the internet of things (IoT): A systematic literature review. *Sensors (Basel)*, 22(4), 1304. doi:10.339022041304 PMID:35214212

Almutairi, K., Hosseini Dehshiri, S. J., Hosseini Dehshiri, S. S., Hoa, A. X., Arockia Dhanraj, J., Mostafaeipour, A., Issakhov, A., & Techato, K. (2022). Blockchain Technology application challenges in renewable energy supply chain management. *Environmental Science and Pollution Research International*, 1–18. doi:10.100711356-021-18311-7 PMID:34989989

Anita, N., & Vijayalakshmi, M. (2019). *Blockchain security attack: A brief survey.* Paper presented at the 2019 10th International Conference on Computing, Communication and Networking Technologies (ICCCNT). Springer. 10.1109/ICCCNT45670.2019.8944615

Battisti, J. H., Koslovski, G. P., Pillon, M. A., Miers, C. C., & Gonzalez, N. M. (2022). *Analysis of an Ethereum Private Blockchain Network Hosted by Virtual Machines Against Internal DoS Attacks.* Paper presented at the Advanced Information Networking and Applications: Proceedings of the 36th International Conference on Advanced Information Networking and Applications (AINA-2022), Springer. 10.1007/978-3-030-99584-3_42

Begum, A., Tareq, A., Sultana, M., Sohel, M., Rahman, T., & Sarwar, A. (2020). Blockchain attacks analysis and a model to solve double spending attack. *International Journal of Machine Learning and Computing*, 10(2), 352–357.

Casino, F., Politou, E., Alepis, E., & Patsakis, C. (2019). Immutability and decentralized storage: An analysis of emerging threats. *IEEE Access : Practical Innovations, Open Solutions*, 8, 4737–4744. doi:10.1109/ACCESS.2019.2962017

Chen, J., Yan, Y., Guo, S., Ren, Y., & Qi, F. (2022). A system for trusted recovery of data based on blockchain and coding techniques. *Wireless Communications and Mobile Computing*, 2022, 1–12. doi:10.1155/2022/8390241

Durach, C. F., Blesik, T., von Düring, M., & Bick, M. (2021). Blockchain applications in supply chain transactions. *Journal of Business Logistics*, 42(1), 7–24. doi:10.1111/jbl.12238

Gad, A. G., Mosa, D. T., Abualigah, L., & Abohany, A. A. (2022). Emerging trends in blockchain technology and applications: A review and outlook. *Journal of King Saud University-Computer and Information Sciences*.

Gao, Y., Pan, Q., Liu, Y., Lin, H., Chen, Y., & Wen, Q. (2021). The notarial office in E-government: A blockchain-based solution. *IEEE Access : Practical Innovations, Open Solutions*, 9, 44411–44425. doi:10.1109/ACCESS.2021.3066184

Hafid, A., Hafid, A. S., & Samih, M. (2022). A tractable probabilistic approach to analyze sybil attacks in sharding-based blockchain protocols. *IEEE Transactions on Emerging Topics in Computing*.

Hao, Y. (2022). *Research of the 51% attack based on blockchain.* Paper presented at the 2022 3rd International Conference on Computer Vision, Image and Deep Learning & International Conference on Computer Engineering and Applications (CVIDL & ICCEA).

Himeur, Y., Sayed, A., Alsalemi, A., Bensaali, F., Amira, A., Varlamis, I., Eirinaki, M., Sardianos, C., & Dimitrakopoulos, G. (2022). Blockchain-based recommender systems: Applications, challenges and future opportunities. *Computer Science Review, 43*, 100439. doi:10.1016/j.cosrev.2021.100439

Hughes, A., Park, A., Kietzmann, J., & Archer-Brown, C. (2019). Beyond Bitcoin: What blockchain and distributed ledger technologies mean for firms. *Business Horizons, 62*(3), 273–281. doi:10.1016/j.bushor.2019.01.002

Iqbal, M., & Matulevičius, R. (2021). Exploring sybil and double-spending risks in blockchain systems. *IEEE Access : Practical Innovations, Open Solutions, 9*, 76153–76177. doi:10.1109/ACCESS.2021.3081998

Joo, M., Kim, S. H., Ghose, A., & Wilbur, K. C. (2023). Designing Distributed Ledger technologies, like Blockchain, for advertising markets. *International Journal of Research in Marketing, 40*(1), 12–21. doi:10.1016/j.ijresmar.2022.08.004

Karpinski, M., Kovalchuk, L., Kochan, R., Oliynykov, R., Rodinko, M., & Wieclaw, L. (2021). Blockchain Technologies: Probability of Double-Spend Attack on a Proof-of-Stake Consensus. *Sensors (Basel), 21*(19), 6408. doi:10.339021196408 PMID:34640729

Kassen, M. (2022). Blockchain and e-government innovation: Automation of public information processes. *Information Systems, 103*, 101862. doi:10.1016/j.is.2021.101862

Khusro, S., Naeem, M., Khan, M. A., & Alam, I. (2018). There is no such thing as free Lunch: An Investigation of Bloatware Effects on Smart Devices. *Journal of Information Communication Technologies and Robotic Applications*, 20-30.

Knudsen, H., Notland, J. S., Haro, P. H., Ræder, T. B., & Li, J. (2021). *Consensus in blockchain systems with low network throughput: A systematic mapping study.* Paper presented at the Proceedings of the 2021 3rd Blockchain and Internet of Things Conference. ACM. 10.1145/3475992.3475995

Lee, J., Lee, B., Jung, J., Shim, H., & Kim, H. (2021). DQ: Two approaches to measure the degree of decentralization of blockchain. *ICT Express, 7*(3), 278–282. doi:10.1016/j.icte.2021.08.008

Mahmood, S., Chadhar, M., & Firmin, S. (2022). Cybersecurity challenges in blockchain technology: A scoping review. *Human Behavior and Emerging Technologies, 2022*, 2022. doi:10.1155/2022/7384000

Malik, A., Gautam, S., Abidin, S., & Bhushan, B. (2019). *Blockchain technology-future of IoT: including structure, limitations and various possible attacks.* Paper presented at the 2019 2nd international conference on intelligent computing, instrumentation and control technologies (ICICICT). Springer. 10.1109/ICICICT46008.2019.8993144

Monrat, A. A., Schelén, O., & Andersson, K. (2019). A survey of blockchain from the perspectives of applications, challenges, and opportunities. *IEEE Access : Practical Innovations, Open Solutions, 7*, 117134–117151. doi:10.1109/ACCESS.2019.2936094

Nair, S. M., Ramesh, V., & Tyagi, A. K. (2023). *Issues and challenges (Privacy, security, and trust) in blockchain-based applications Research Anthology on Convergence of Blockchain, Internet of Things, and Security.* IGI Global.

Nakamoto, S. (2008). Bitcoin: A peer-to-peer electronic cash system. *Decentralized business review*, 21260.

Platt, M., & McBurney, P. (2021). Sybil attacks on identity-augmented Proof-of-Stake. *Computer Networks*, *199*, 108424. doi:10.1016/j.comnet.2021.108424

Pufahl, L., Ohlsson, B., Weber, I., Harper, G., & Weston, E. (2021). Enabling Financing in Agricultural Supply Chains Through Blockchain: Interorganizational Process Innovation Through Blockchain *Business Process Management Cases Vol. 2: Digital Transformation-Strategy, Processes and Execution* (pp. 41-56). Springer.

Raikwar, M., & Gligoroski, D. (2022). DoS Attacks on Blockchain Ecosystem. Paper presented at *the Euro-Par 2021: Parallel Processing Workshops: Euro-Par 2021 International Workshops*, Lisbon, Portugal. 10.1007/978-3-031-06156-1_19

Ruan, N., Sun, H., Lou, Z., & Li, J. (2022). A General Quantitative Analysis Framework for Attacks in Blockchain. *IEEE/ACM Transactions on Networking*, 1–16. doi:10.1109/TNET.2022.3201493

Saad, M., Cook, V., Nguyen, L., Thai, M. T., & Mohaisen, A. (2019). *Partitioning attacks on bitcoin: Colliding space, time, and logic.* Paper presented at the 2019 IEEE 39th international conference on distributed computing systems (ICDCS). IEEE. 10.1109/ICDCS.2019.00119

Salah, K., Rehman, M. H. U., Nizamuddin, N., & Al-Fuqaha, A. (2019). Blockchain for AI: Review and open research challenges. *IEEE Access : Practical Innovations, Open Solutions*, *7*, 10127–10149. doi:10.1109/ACCESS.2018.2890507

Schlatt, V., Guggenberger, T., Schmid, J., & Urbach, N. (2022). Attacking the trust machine: Developing an information systems research agenda for blockchain cybersecurity. *International Journal of Information Management*, 102470.

Shukla, M., Lin, J., & Seneviratne, O. (2022). Blockchain and IoT enhanced clinical workflow. Paper presented at the *Artificial Intelligence in Medicine: 20th International Conference on Artificial Intelligence in Medicine, AIME 2022*, Halifax, NS, Canada.

Tandon, A., Kaur, P., Mäntymäki, M., & Dhir, A. (2021). Blockchain applications in management: A bibliometric analysis and literature review. *Technological Forecasting and Social Change*, *166*, 120649. doi:10.1016/j.techfore.2021.120649

Tanha, F. E., Hasani, A., Hakak, S., & Gadekallu, T. R. (2022). Blockchain-based cyber physical systems: Comprehensive model for challenge assessment. *Computers & Electrical Engineering*, *103*, 108347. doi:10.1016/j.compeleceng.2022.108347

Tariq, U., Ibrahim, A., Ahmad, T., Bouteraa, Y., & Elmogy, A. (2019). Blockchain in internet-of-things: A necessity framework for security, reliability, transparency, immutability and liability. *IET Communications*, *13*(19), 3187–3192. doi:10.1049/iet-com.2019.0194

Wang, T., Hua, H., Wei, Z., & Cao, J. (2022). Challenges of blockchain in new generation energy systems and future outlooks. *International Journal of Electrical Power & Energy Systems*, *135*, 107499. doi:10.1016/j.ijepes.2021.107499

Xu, G., Guo, B., Su, C., Zheng, X., Liang, K., Wong, D. S., & Wang, H. (2020). Am I eclipsed? A smart detector of eclipse attacks for Ethereum. *Computers & Security*, *88*, 101604. doi:10.1016/j.cose.2019.101604

Yıldız, A. K., Atmaca, A., Solak, A. Ö., Tursun, Y. C., & Bahtiyar, S. (2022). *A Trust Based DNS System to Prevent Eclipse Attack on Blockchain Networks*. Paper presented at the 2022 15th International Conference on Security of Information and Networks (SIN). Springer. 10.1109/SIN56466.2022.9970533

ENDNOTES

[1]   https://en.wikipedia.org/wiki/Decentralised_system
[2]   https://www.foley.com/en/insights/publications/2021/08/types-of-blockchain-public-private-between

Chapter 6
Design, Development, and Testing of Web Applications:
Security Aspects

Ufuk Uçak
Ahmet Yesevi University, Turkey

Gurkan Tuna
Trakya University, Turkey

ABSTRACT

Today, with the changes and developments in software technologies, web applications have gained an important place by being actively used in many sectors. Due to the fact that web applications do not require installation costs and are easily accessible and operable, the increased usage rate in recent years makes these systems the target of cyber hackers. As a result of cyber attacks, services are blocked, and material and moral damages and data privacy violations are experienced. Within the scope of this study, web applications are explained, vulnerabilities that threaten software security and the measures that can be taken against these vulnerabilities are included. Particularly, security threats to web applications, security principles, secure software development lifecycles, test tools, and hardware and software products used for security are examined. In addition, SAMM and BSIMM models, which are maturity models used in secure software development, are discussed.

INTRODUCTION

Today, with the advancements in technology, traditional approaches are no longer used or effective in software development and software security. Security threats posed by software applications are increasing day by day. Security threats endanger the data security of corporations and organizations, as well as cause material and moral damages. Therefore, in recent years, software security has emerged to protect against cyber attacks on applications. Within the scope of software security, there are responsibilities

DOI: 10.4018/978-1-6684-6914-9.ch006

for both software developers and database managers. Accordingly, corporations and organizations need to change their software development methodologies.

Web applications are defined as computer programs that can perform some functions using web browsers as clients. Web applications have started to be used more and more each day as they replace existing traditional applications, and they have become very critical systems. Because businesses rely on web applications more and carry out their transactions using them. However, this trend has become a major concern (Shahid et al., 2022). Due to their various security vulnerabilities, cyber attackers can cause significant damage to business processes which typically lead to the loss of credibility and reputation, and cause data loss (Cumhurbaşkanlığı Dijital Dönüşüm Ofisi, 2021). Unauthorized access of cyber attackers may result in data breaches, and as a result of such access the cyber attackers may be able to view, copy, or share data. Therefore, it is necessary to identify the security vulnerabilities of web applications in use and then determine the precautions to be taken for these vulnerabilities (Handa, Negi, & Shukla, 2021). In addition to protecting computer networks using firewalls, intrusion prevention systems and anti-virus applications, these precautions involve keeping web applications up-to-date, updating software development methodologies, and using secure communication protocols.

In this chapter, based on an extensive literature review and using examples from our own application development experience, we first present the features of web applications, review how web applications are developed and deployed, identify the common security-related vulnerabilities of web applications. Then, we focus on the design principles of secure application development cycles by taking into consideration selected maturity models. Moreover, we try to explain how the measures to be taken in software development life cycles can address the well-known vulnerabilities of web applications against cyber attacks.

WEB APPLICATIONS

As the literature and news prove that web applications are inherently exposed to cyber threats. Therefore, the security vulnerabilities of web applications must be identified and then existing web applications must be secured with measures to be taken. As well as the existing web applications, future ones must be secured using secure application development practices.

A web client is a program that allows users to access web services, and with this access, they are processed and displayed in HyperText Markup Language (HTML) standards. Web clients are widely known examples of web browsers such as Google Chrome, Internet Explorer, and Mozilla Firefox. On the other hand, the web server processes Hypertext Transfer Protocol (HTTP) requests sent by web clients and sends their response back to the client. The web server responds to the request sent by the clients with HTTP in the same way. HTTP is used to transport information on the web and is used by clients to access web applications. Thanks to this protocol, all information can be accessed through the web server. The web client sends its requests using HTTP and the web server responds to the client using it, too. The way how content is sent to the clients by web servers is divided into two types as static and dynamic. Static content shows the page on the web server to the user as it is. It does not change according to the user's request. The HTML page prepared by the application is directly in front of the user.

It is necessary to point out the difference between web applications and websites here. Websites have a static structure. However, web applications have a dynamic structure and are basically software with user experience. Web applications are a bridge that connects to web servers running in the background through any browser. The clients are user computers that can receive service from a server. Web technologies rely on software languages such as HTML and JavaScript, which can process data and perform certain operations. Web applications have a number of advantages over traditional applications. Some of them are listed below.

- There is no need to use extra programs for user computers.
- They can be used regardless of underlying operating system.
- For the purpose of updating the application on the clients, the update made on the application running on the server is distributed to all clients. This way all clients are updated automatically
- They can run smoothly with all browsers.
- All clients do not experience compatibility problems because they have access to the current version.
- Since the hardware requirements of user computers are low compared to traditional applications, the end user costs are lower.

There are different types of web applications as listed below.

- **Client-executed Web applications:** Creating a client-side web application is pretty easy to use when there is no need to store user information for longer than a single session. For example, it can be used for easy games or image editors.
- **Web applications executed by the server:** If an application is built for being executed on a server, as a result of any change between form submissions, sections, and data updates, the server creates a new HTML file and the web page is reloaded.
- **Single page Web applications:** These applications are created using both front-end and back-end technologies. So these are more complex software that offers client-side and server-side and runs in the browser without page reloading.

Dynamic content can be described as pages created on request by a client. It depends on the user's request. Dynamic content is more complex than static content. In dynamic content, the HTML page is shaped according to the user's request (Nixon, 2021). In addition, the web server may need to create this page and make database connections in the background. The feature requested by the client is processed on the web server and receives the data from the database and presents it to the user. Due to the above reasons, dynamic content allows users and software developers to collaborate in a more functional structure.

The use of web applications is increasing day by day. When the convenience and productivity of web applications, which is widely used in many sectors and whose use is increasing, is considered, it is not surprising that they have become the focus of cyber attackers. Security vulnerabilities that lead to cyber attacks can be attributed to many reasons. However, it is not impossible to eliminate all of the security vulnerabilities and make all the web applications secure by taking some measures. Therefore, it is essential to focus on the principles and methods of how software development life cycles can be reorganized to ensure the security of web applications. In addition, it is necessary to raise awareness about software security in general.

SECURITY THREATS AND POLICIES TO SECURE SOFTWARE

One of the biggest problems of web applications is security. Although web applications are very useful, if their security problems are not addressed, they can cause consequences that can affect all systems the applications running on or located. The systems that can be affected include servers, networks, and other software and components running on.

Security Threats

There are different types of threats that target web applications. They can be broadly divided into three different types based on their targets or aims as the following.

- The ones that completely disable the software and prevent its use.
- The ones that enable the use of the software for different purposes by disrupting its operation.
- The ones that damage the whole system by exploiting the vulnerabilities found in the software.

In this context, principles should be established in accordance with the security of web applications, and they should be supported with designs and methods that ensure security.

In order to ensure software security, first of all, it is necessary to know the vulnerabilities used by cyber attackers. By knowing these vulnerabilities, security principles and methods are created in accordance with them. First of all, it is necessary to list common vulnerabilities of web applications.

Cross Site Scripting Vulnerabilities

Vulnerabilities that allow attackers to run JavaScript code on the target system are known as Cross Site Scripting (XSS). These vulnerabilities can be used by cyber attackers for harmful purposes because they can lead to perform many operations from accessing cookie information to accessing data on websites (Aydos et al., 2022). They rely on the permission given to the system because it is taken from a reliable source when the client accesses the data from the web browser, thanks to the malicious code pieces placed in the vulnerabilities in the plugins in the web application (Yan et al., 2022). In this way, the attacker gains access to a lot of browser-managed information on behalf of the user.

An example is as follows. There is a form element on a website that receives comments from users and saves this comment to the database, when the cyber attacker writes the following text in the comment data entry field; <script> alert("This is an example of malicious messages")</script>. It will be saved as a comment in the database in this way, but when the page is reloaded or another user attempts to open the page, the comment will be reflected in HTML, as it is in the <script></script> tags, it will be perceived by the browser as a JavaScript code and the message "This is an example of malicious messages" will appear in the alert box. Today, although most of the browsers and JavaScript frameworks take measures against some XSS vulnerabilities as standard, these measures can be bypassed by various methods and malicious codes can be injected into the pages.

SQL Injection

The dynamic contents and data of web-based applications are usually stored in databases. Having the data in the database is known as the place where cyber attackers want to reach. In some cases, some functions of web applications are also available on different systems. Cyber attackers try to get a database error with the special character they send to the search boxes. They detect the vulnerabilities of databases running in the background like this. Detecting these vulnerabilities, the attacker begins to manipulate the boxes where username and password are entered. In this way, it provides access to the database server and database.

SQL injection happens when data is sent by a program from an untrusted source and that data is used to dynamically generate an SQL query (Carter, 2018). The response is necessary for the attacker to understand the database architecture and access the application's secure information. With a specially crafted SQL command, the hacker can access all the information in the database by obtaining a response that provides a clear idea of the database structure. There are many types of SQL injection as the following.

- **Ones that depend on user inputs:** The attacker can inject form fields if filtering is not found before users' input reaches their database.
- **Cookies-based ones:** The cyber attacker can damage the database by adding malicious codes to the cookies on the user's computer, as if they were coming from the user's machine.
- **HTTP Header-based ones:** If a web application accepts input from HTTP headers, code is injected into the database with fake headers containing random SQL queries.

An example of SQL injections is as follows.

```
<form>
Your name: <input name="name" type="text" />
Your last name: <input name="surname" type="text" />
<button type="submit">Fetch Comments</button>
</form>
```

In the example code given above, the code will display all the comments sent by the user whose name and surname are written from the guest book on the page. In the input fields, the user can write the texts he/she wants.

In the program below, whose back-end side is coded with the .Net Core MVC infrastructure using C# programming language in the following area, when the user sends the information he/she has written in the form field to the server, the request sent in the controller mechanism is met and the user inputs are written directly to the database without any checking mechanism.

```
public IActionResultIndex(string name, string last name)
{
string queryString =
$"select * from guestbook where firstname = {firstname} and lastname = {last-
name}";
return View();
```

```
}
```

It does not pose a problem when the user acts as expected and sends name and surname information. However, when malicious cyber attackers notice such a designed system and enter data as follows;

```
<form>
Your name: <input name="name" type="text" value="ufuk'--" />
Your last name: <input name="surname" type="text" value="ucak" />
<button type="submit">Fetch Comments</button>
</form>
Query to be generated by the program:
string queryString =
$"select * from guestbook where first name = {ufuk--'} and last name = {ucak}";
Query to be run by SQL:
select * from guestbook where name='ufuk'--'' and last name ='ucak'
```

With -- syntax, all the following conditions are turned into comment lines. With ', the string closes the quotation in the column field, which can easily be guessed to be a data entry field, and turns the -- into a syntax that closes the query clauses that follow it. If the user had not added the - sign at the end, he would have sent a string expression where name = 'ufuk--' to the database. It would search for a user named ufuk-- in the database, and if it could not find it, it would return a null value. In this way, the user will be able to view the comments of all users in the database, although he is not authorized to query the user with the name horizon and surname plane and only see his comments.

Nowadays, Object-Relational Mapping (ORM) tools send the special SQL syntax in the fields where input is entered to the database as string expressions and can create a natural precaution against the attacks made using the abovementioned strategy (Torres et al., 2017).

Another type of injection attack seen in web-based applications is UNION attack. The UNION keyword allows creating another select query within a select query in SQL language (Zhang et al., 2022a). Some conditions must be met in order to perform a UNION attack. An example of these conditions is given below.

```
SELECT a,b FROM x UNION SELECT c,d FROM y
```

In the above code, table x has 2 columns in total. There are also 2 columns in the y table whose union query is sent. The first condition in the Union query is that the number of columns in the x and y tables must be equal to each other. If there are 4 columns in table x and 3 columns in table y, the union query will not work.

Cyber attackers can try a variety of information retrieval methods to find out how many columns there are in a table. The most commonly used method is the order by method. Order by can be used to sort the columns according to the results returned from the table.

```
SELECT * FROM x ORDER BY 1
SELECT * FROM x ORDER BY 2
```

By sending the queries to the system, it can be easily learned how many columns are in the table. The column name does not need to be known to order in SQL. It is possible to sort by columns as 1,2,3 as numeric. In this example, if there are 4 columns in the X table and a query like order by 5 is sent, an Out of Range error will be returned from the database.

The second condition is that the data types of the table columns are compatible with each other.

```
SELECT a,b FROM x UNION SELECT c,d FROM y
```

Data type *a* must be compatible with *c*, and data type *b* must be compatible with *d*. So if *a* is varchar, then *c* in the union syntax must also be varchar. If a varchar *c* integer, then the Union keyword will not work. After all the preparations are completed and the necessary information is obtained, the data can be retrieved by entering the code below into the form field.

```
UNION SELECT username, password FROM users--
```

Buffer Overflows

Data entered into web applications create buffer overflow problems when the size of information written to a memory location exceeds what it was allocated. Such entries sent by a cyber attacker may cause the servers to become full of memory, and the attacker can run code over the system in the meantime. It is detected if the attackers encounter errors by the server when they enter long entries sent from remote accesses.

Fuzzing

It is one of the most commonly used attack vectors by cyber hackers in web applications. It provides an error by sending long-character, complex-character word groups by the inputs to the remote server.

In some cases, the occurrence of errors causes the databases to overflow. On the other hand, in other cases, the data is deleted from the database. In addition, such sent words can make the server inoperable. Fuzzing attacks have stages as listed below.

- Detecting the system,
- Detecting entries,
- Creation of fuzzed data, i.e. characters,
- Execution of fuzzed data, and
- Waiting for the system's response.

Authentication

Client-side authentication methods of web applications are one of the security vulnerabilities (Zhang et al., 2022b). If the system does not have automated human or bot control tests, cyber attackers can use these vulnerabilities. Using this, attackers can access the systems through open ports, if the identity management and access permissions of unauthorized users to the system are not turned off. If the users registered in the application are not checked by the system and the connections of the users are not checked, it can lead to undesired results. Since there is no session management feature in HTTP, web applications have to keep the requests made by the users in session information. In cases where session management is not done properly or user-specific data is not kept in the session information, an attacker who obtains the user's session information can use it to replace the user.

Access Redundancy

If corporations and organizations do not determine the places where users can access, identities obtained due to the access redundancy may allow attackers to access sensitive information. In addition, due to the excess privileges defined for the users, the attacker using these privileges can also deactivate other systems.

Password Insecurities

If a password policy for users is not set, easy and mnemonic passwords can easily be solved with brute force attacks. Using brute force attacks on passwords, the cyber attacker uses the decoded passwords to access the system. Since web applications can work through any browsers, saving the passwords of the users in the browser makes it easier for the attacker to access these passwords. In addition, using passwords known in the IT industry, i.e. 123456789 and system123456, makes it easier to solve.

Brute - force attack can be summarized as cyber-attackers constantly attempting to login to the system through a word list (a list of various frequently used password examples) to obtain the user's password.

Multiple measures can be taken against brute force attacks. The most frequently used of these today is to prevent the request from being sent to the server without making this selection by placing a captcha in front of the login requests and selecting various symbols or numbers in the photo before the login request. This precaution prevents cyber attackers who make automatic login attempts to attack directly without analyzing the text in the photo. Another measure is the process of limiting the number of requests made within a certain period of time, called Rate Limiter.

In the example case, the user makes a request to the Controller mechanism. This request takes the user's name and password from a form element as input and passes the necessary checks to log in to the system. //Step 1,2,3, and 4 are marked in the code and the tasks of these marked areas are explained one by one.

```
public IActionResult Login([FromQuery] string userName, [FromQuery] string
Password)
{
//Step 1
        string remoteIp = HttpContext.Connection.RemoteIpAddress?.Map-
ToIPv4().ToString();
//Step 2
        var client = _inMemoryCache.GetOrCreate(remoteIp, (cache) =>
        {
            cache.AbsoluteExpirationRelativeToNow = TimeSpan.FromHours(1);
            return new LoginCheck {NumberofRequests = 0};
        });
//Step 3
```

```
if (client.NumberofRequests >= 3)
            { return Unauthorized();}
//Step 4
            else
{
//Check user
            bool isOk = CheckUserNamePasswordFromDatabase(userName, Pass-
word);
            if (isOk == false)
{
client.NumberofRequests+= 1;
}
}
            return View();
}
```

In step 1, the IP address of the incoming request is obtained.

In step 2, using CacheMemory, the IP address of the user who made the request is saved in the RAM on the server as a key. At this stage, if no record has been created before, a record that can be described as key:[192.168.1.1] NumberofRequests:[0] is created. cache.AbsoluteExpirationRelativeToNow = TimeSpan.FromHours(1);

The recording time of the incoming IP address as a key using syntax is limited to one hour. In this state, it will keep the requests made within one hour. For example, the user who makes two false attempts within one hour will have the right to try again three times, since his past requests will be reset after the 59th minute. The time can be increased or decreased according to the programmer's wish. If the IP address that made the request in Step 3 has made this attempt three or more times, it will be banned for one hour and the user will not be able to try to enter the username and password for one hour from that IP address, and the unauthorized page will be returned to the user. In step 4, the user name and password are verified, and if the user name and password are correct, if the user cannot log in to the system successfully, the number of requests property of the IP address kept as a key on CacheMemory is increased by one.

Fundamental Principles of Software Security

Software security has an important place in corporate policies. In order to establish this security, certain principles accepted in the literature are needed. These principles are used as a guiding map in the secure software development cycle.

- **Least Authority:** The minimum authorization is that the user or authorized person is defined with the minimum authorization to work with this policy and no more authorization is given. The places that users can access and the places that authorized personnel can access are separated. The places that are considered critical in terms of data privacy should be given to certain people. The advantages of this approach are as follows.
  - The changes that the application will make on the system are limited.

○   It cannot be used to infiltrate the rest of the system.

○   It reduces the chance of cyber attacks.

○   Distribution of malicious software is prevented.

- **Access Control:** Thanks to this policy, people who will access the web applications are controlled. For example, IT professionals have access to WEB servers, while database specialists can only access database servers. Audits are required when the IT professionals need to access the database servers. It determines people who will access the system and prevents other people from accessing the system. The benefits of this approach are as follows.

○   User identity verification is ensured.

○   Control of the authorizations of the users is ensured.

- **Separating Authentication and Access:** It is important to pass through authentication and provide access after that. In this way, direct access to important data will be prevented. In this way, the cyber attacker will not directly provide data that is important for web applications, but will need to authenticate. In addition, two-factor authentication (2FA) systems will further increase security in the authentication. If 2FA is in use, the user must first authenticate, and then provide another authentication for accessing the folders. After these stages, the user can access to the high-security folder.

- **Default Review:** The values considered by default during the deployment of web applications need to be checked to improve security. Things to check in this stage can be listed as follows.

○   Installing executable files so that anyone can write by default,

○   Setting up the application home directory so that everyone can read it,

○   Trace log files that anyone can write,

○   Presence of default passwords in publicly readable files,

○   Publicly readable directories,

○   Using default settings on devices that allow IP spoofing, and

○   Granted insecure rights on shared key files/databases.

- **Common Area Access Classification:** This policy uses common areas in accessing web software resources. For example, the files of the web applications should not be stored in the common areas shared with all users.

- **Detecting the Weakest Area:** During software development processes, it is expected to strengthen the identified vulnerabilities by identifying the weakest points of the software team and intensifying the work on this area.

- **Reducing the Attack Surface:** In this policy, other operations other than the necessary roles and applications on the server where the web application is located should be prevented. While attacking the server, the cyber attacker gains authority by using open ports and open applications. For this reason, it is necessary to remove all applications and roles that are more than necessary in the server.

- **Depth of Defense:** This policy is actually the support of purchased security products or software with different software and security products. In addition, system security should be integrated with software security.

- **Security Mechanism:** It is necessary to create a simplified and understandable security mechanism within organizations. This mechanism is topologized, visualizing error probabilities, making it easier to understand and correct. All security measures should be documented.

The complex structure of web server applications and possible SQL injection attacks on the database make it necessary to use security policies. In web applications, users must enter data, run code in the background and interact with databases. Therefore, security measures need to be taken into account during their development. The critical components that need to be designed in this context are listed in the following section.

SECURE SOFTWARE DEVELOPMENT LIFE CYCLE

Software development is basically realized through a series of processes. If the maturity of these processes is ensured, the quality and security of web applications can be guaranteed (TÜBİTAK-BİLGEM, 2018).

Requirements

The requirements are listed with the introduction of the software idea and then a software model suitable for these requirements is presented. Following this, security requirements should be listed and the design and following processes should be started based on the security requirements.

Design

At this stage, the design process is carried out in accordance with the requirements. All critical components should be taken into account by reviewing security requests. It should be designed by analyzing the threats that may occur and taking into account many factors such as network security, server security, and software security.

Development

The development phase is where the design turns into code with the design. The application created at this stage is made testable. Static analysis is performed at this stage. With static analysis, certain features of the software are tested without running. The requirements, source codes and files should be analyzed.

In the development processes, there are critical components that must be designed within the scope of security. These components are important for software security. Critical designs such as control of user inputs, coding of HTML outputs, database security, protecting data in motion and password security are required (Borky & Bradley, 2019). The database security, where the data is located, should be considered in more detail, especially in dynamically operating systems.

Control of User Inputs

Web applications interact with users. As a result of interactions, web servers process data and send the data to be stored in databases. It has been shown that malicious data entries can cause systems to malfunction. Taking advantage of the application's different responses, hackers can initiate processes up to stopping the system by using data entries. In this respect, controlling data that users enter is critical for security. Therefore, filtering solutions should be used for inputs and it is necessary to filter the user inputs by creating black and white lists. In addition, it is necessary to restrict multiple data entries and record user data entries. Furthermore, it is necessary to set the data types corresponding to the data on the database side accordingly. For example, the software should prevent writing a mobile-phone number in a column with a time-date data type. Input validation function, which is embedded in web development platforms for controlling user inputs, is an alternative module that helps to set rules and restrictions for each form field. In addition, corporations and organizations can test web applications with fuzzing attacks by using defensive cyber security tools. Fuzzing is an automatic error detection mechanism based on causing unexpected behavior, resource leaks, and crashes (Beaman et al., 2022). Fuzzing involves sending invalid, unexpected, or random data into a computer as input. Fuzzers repeat this process and monitor the environment until they detect security vulnerabilities (Sağıroğlu, 2019).

Encoding HTML Outputs

A web application does not only process data coming from its users. It processes data coming from the database or other services, too. In some cases, it becomes very difficult to filter the incoming data. Output coding systems enable the data to be converted into a suitable final format.

Database Security

Database security is one of the most important points to be designed. There are many operations that need to be done about the database. Since the data in the database is the last point that the cyber attacker can reach in the application, it is important to design it according to security procedures. First of all, web applications connect to databases and provide data processing, data entry or storage. For this reason, all unnecessary privileges of the user account to be connected to the application to be connected to the database should be revoked. If the user is captured by cyber attackers, it should be prevented from manipulating the data.

The second issue is that connection between a web application and the database must be built in an encrypted manner. The attacker who enters between the application and the database must not reach the data sent or viewed by the users by intervening. Keeping the data in the database encrypted is an important point for database security. Automation systems, such as alarms and disconnections, should be activated in case of blacklists determined to record data processing and queries on the database, and queries exceeding security protocols. Moreover, database servers must also be located in private networks in terms of network security. Finally, if the database queries coming from the web applications use merging or formatting methods, it should be avoided to create the resulting query with the input from the user (Aydoğdu & Gündüz, 2016).

Security of Data in Transit

Another important point to be mentioned after database security, which is one of the important points in terms of software security, is the security of data in transit. In web applications, clients cause data to move over the network. For this reason, the movement of data over the network is one of the measures to be taken in web applications.

It is necessary to use secure communication protocols when data travels over the network. It should be designed with protocols such as HTTPS, SSL and TLS, which provide strong encryption algorithms instead of simple and vulnerable communication protocols, such as HTTP and Telnet (Hughes, 2022). It is also necessary to create an encrypted traffic.

Password Security

Users on the client side of web applications have usernames and passwords that they use to log in to applications. Strong password policies are required to protect users. A strong password policy typically relies on the following.

- Changing at specific time intervals,
- Not allowed except for complex passwords,
- Preventing the use of passwords that will remind the user,
- Prohibition of passwords such as easily guessed passwords, i.e., 123456789,
- At least up to a certain number of characters,
- Preventing the use of previously set passwords, and
- Password policies of authorized users should contain stronger policies than normal users.

Secure Authentication

Passwords set by users alone are insufficient within the scope of security. In addition to strong passwords, Multi Factor Authentication (MFA) systems should be in use. When an MFA system is in use, in addition to the basic security provided by user names and passwords, additional security measures of logging in such as fingerprint, face recognition or SMS verification are used (Velásquez, Caro, & Rodríguez, 2018).

Test

In order to increase the security and quality of web applications, testing phase is started. At the end of the test, it should be seen that the web application is ready from all aspects and its distribution to the users can be started. There are many techniques available to reduce the vulnerabilities and bugs of web applications and increase security in web applications. The techniques used in this phase are as follows.

- **Random Testing (Fuzz Testing):** Random testing is used defensively for the institution. It is used to prove that user inputs to the database are filtered. This way, it is tested whether the database is sensitive to complex and special characters (Wang et al., 2020).
- **Dynamic Analysis:** Dynamic analysis allows to test all vulnerabilities related to dynamic components. When it is conducted, all vulnerabilities in network components, browsers, computers, servers and security products are tested.
- **Negative Test:** Negative test allows to test negative rules. All exceptions that are erroneous and do not comply with the security conditions are tested. For example, what happens when 10 digits are entered in the 11-digit place where the ID number should be entered. It is important to receive error messages in these tests.
- **Model Validation:** Security measures such as privacy, authentication, access control, server security, and database security are checked in the model validation process.

- **Logic Methods:** Logic methods allow to test whether there are logical errors in the codes in which web applications are written. The outputs of the codes are tested for security using AND and OR gates.
- **Code Retrofit:** Code retrofit is the formal strengthening of source code, file systems, and libraries of web applications with a pre-developed software security perspective.
- **Code with Proof:** It is tested that the web application codes, which are analyzed formally, are safe. Code pieces are checked line by line and security procedures are checked.
- **Application Container:** The access and authorization security of the computer files that the application runs are checked. This container is tested for resistance to software that damages it. In addition, container structure analysis and modeling are performed.
- **Authentication Tests:** For systems using authentication systems, the proper security operation of this system is tested. For example, in systems using MFA, it is checked whether the system responsible for SMS sending sends SMS to the right people.
- **Password Tests:** In a password test, specified password policies are tested. For example, it is a test for errors when at least 7-digit passwords and complex, 6-digit or non-complex passwords are tried to be set. In addition, another policy determined when setting a password is the absence of a reminder or password containing any private information.
- **Database Tests:** The operation and responsiveness of the database are tested with fuzz and other attack methods on the database. In this way, the vulnerabilities are addressed by looking at the answers given to the tests.
- **Data Privacy Test:** Data privacy test allows to check whether data entered by the user can be accessed by someone else until they reach the database. It is also a test whether it is encrypted even if there is a reach status.

Distribution

It means that the web application prepared during the distribution phase reaches the end user. In general, the distribution of web applications securely is critical.

Maintenance

After the web application is in use, measures should be taken to keep the application error-free and up-to-date. Information security vulnerabilities should be eliminated as quickly as possible.

USE OF MATURITY MODELS FOR SECURE SOFTWARE DEVELOPMENT

Secure software development maturity models are measurement models that show organizations the level of software security and are rated (Sarıman & Çelikten, 2021).

Software Assurance Maturity Model (SAMM)

The SAMM model shown in Figure 1 is tailored to the risks that organizations face and helps create and implement a software security strategy (OWASP, 2016). It includes management, communication, development, verification and their subcomponents. There are levels in this model. These levels indicate maturity levels.

- Level 0: The institution is in the initial state.
- Level 1: Security procedures have been understood, and trial practices to implement them have been made.
- Level 2: Security applications have started to be used effectively.
- Level 3: Security policies are fully implemented.

Figure 1. SAMM

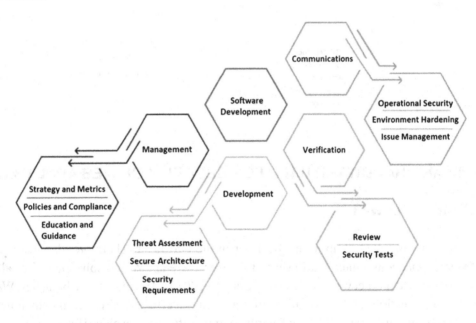

Building Security in Maturity Model (BSIMM)

The BSIMM model shown in Figure 2 is a tool to understand how the most advanced security teams and institutions and organizations conduct software security (BSIMM, 2008). It relies on a study of current software security initiatives. In this model, the application security practices of different organizations across industries, sizes, and geographies are quantified while the variations that make each organization unique are being identified.

Figure 2. BSIMM

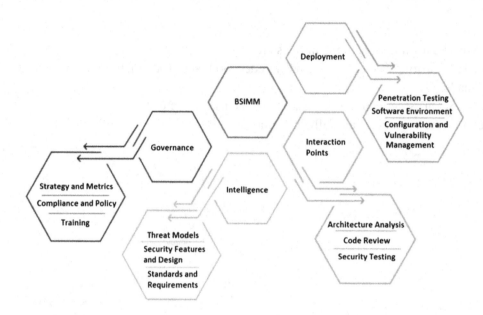

SOFTWARE AND HARDWARE USED FOR SECURITY OF WEB APPLICATIONS

Web Application Firewall

Firewall devices can only control up to the 4th layer in the OSI layer. Therefore, they cannot control the parts of web applications running at Layer 7. However, there are Web Application Firewall (WAF) solutions that control and protect web applications (Shugrue, 2017). To prevent data breaches, WAF solutions protect web applications and Application Programming Interfaces (APIs) from malicious internet traffic to servers. In addition, they allow the filtering and monitoring of web traffic and the distribution of incoming traffic to the web servers in accordance with the load distribution. Moreover, they scan and discover vulnerabilities in web applications that attackers can exploit, thereby they allow to address the discovered issues immediately.

MFA Solutions

MFA solutions that work where end users are located provide a secondary means of authentication. Even if there are usernames and passwords captured by the attacker, secondary authentication can prevent the attacker from infiltrating the system. In this way, end-user security, which is the beginning of security, is also controlled and managed with a centralized approach. MFA solutions provide a secondary user authentication method with authentication methods such as PIN, SMS, face recognition, etc.

Encryption Devices and Certificates

One of the indispensable products for ensuring data security is encryption devices. With the user's data entry or the beginning of the sending phase of the data in the database, the data must be transported securely. Encryption of data is done with the help of encryption devices or certificates. These two products enable the encrypted data to be opened by the end user or in the database. Generating certificates specifically for applications is an indispensable tool of data security.

Intrusion Detection Systems & Intrusion Prevention Systems

An Intrusion Detection System (IDS) detects and logs malicious activity within the system. In another sense, an IDS provides monitoring of all activities of the end user (Baykara & Daş, 2019). On the other hand, Intrusion Prevention System (IPS), tries to prevent malicious movements on the system by detecting them. It is necessary to monitor the actions of attackers through web applications and to prevent harmful codes. For this reason, IPS/IDS software is indispensable for these processes (Baykara & Daş, 2019).

STRATEGIES AGAINST CYBER THREATS

It is known that cyber attackers can take advantage of many different vulnerabilities existing in web applications. These vulnerabilities include end user errors, access redundancies, lack of strong password policies, cross-site scripting, database injection, memory overflows as a result of misconfiguration. The guide published by The Open Web Application Security Project (OWASP) in 2021 (OWASP, 2022) point out the following vulnerabilities as the most used ones.

- Access control,
- Encryption errors,
- Injections,
- Wrong designs and security configuration,
- Authentication errors,
- Cross-site scripting, and
- Software and data integrity errors.

It is known that if some principles are adopted and appropriate measures are taken, awareness of software security can be increased. These principles, which are at the top of the measures that can be taken against the specified vulnerabilities, are among the most important elements for security. These principles are:

- Minimum authority,
- Access control,
- Separating accesses,
- Reviewing defaults,
- Common access area access classification,
- Weak area detection,

- Reducing the attack surface,
- Depth of defense, and
- Security mechanisms.

As end-user security and misconfiguration in web applications threatens critical web applications, it is important to eliminate these vulnerabilities and take precautions. However, due to the continuous development of web applications and the state-of-the-art threats, the security levels of web applications need to be continuously checked and if necessary improved. For this reason, it is necessary to establish a secure software development cycle. There are stages in the secure software development cycle as Requirements, Design, Development, Testing, Deployment and Maintenance. During these stages, the development of web software is completed by considering security measures, and the security of the software is checked by performing tests on known vulnerabilities during the testing phase. In addition, the distribution of secure software, its maintenance stages and its transfer to the end users need to be examined.

Existing maturity models such as SAMM and BSIMM allow the developed software to reach a certain level of maturity. It provides the chance to control the software maturity level of institutions and organizations that develop web applications. The software and hardware used in providing security measures for web applications are:

- WAF,
- MFA,
- Encryption devices and certificates, and
- IDS/IPS.

The products and software used to increase web application security provide an additional layer and convenience in ensuring security. With the integration of these products and software into the existing web applications, the detection of malware and the ability to intervene immediately, as well as the safe transportation of data and secure access to the systems for the end users are provided. It also plays an important role in eliminating SQL injection vulnerabilities with WAF.

Although there are security vulnerabilities in web applications, it is possible to address these vulnerabilities and secure them with the security measures taken. However, certain procedures and measures need to be implemented to make this possible. In this study, the existing security vulnerabilities in the literature were presented, the security measures proposed against these vulnerabilities were listed, and the maturity models and the products used to support these measures were specified. However, considering that each day new and sophisticated threats emerge and new vulnerabilities are discovered, it is necessary to monitor and increase the security levels of web applications in a continuous manner.

Carrying out secure code reviews throughout the entire software development life cycle plays a key role as it helps to reduce the risk of inadvertently allowing code vulnerabilities to make their way through to production (Edmundson, 2013). A secure code review is basically a software quality assurance process that analyzes software source code to find out security-related weaknesses, correct flaws, fix logic errors, and scrutinize specification implementation. Therefore, it allows building application source code of the utmost security and quality. In addition, it ensures applications' compliance to existing regulations such as HIPAA, PCI-DSS, and FDA-11. In this way, it helps avoiding reputational harm and fines and to reduce the expense of fixing bugs that mostly occur at the early stages of the software development life cycle.

CONCLUSION

In the last decade, web applications have been taking place of traditional applications and have started to be widely used. In parallel with this trend, they have become the focus of cyber attackers. It is expected that attacks on these systems will increase with the developing technology. As cyber attackers have been targeting web applications and violating data security, keeping in mind the secure design principles in software development and measures to be taken to prevent cyber attacks plays a key role in web application security. In order to prevent cyber attacks, the application of security principles, the creation of secure designs and configurations, the determination of the products and software used in the configuration, their integration into the system, the creation of secure software cycles for continuously developed web applications, as well as the training of users who will use these systems and responding to these attacks is important.

In this chapter, the security vulnerabilities of web applications and the measures to be taken to eliminate these vulnerabilities were presented, and the roadmap of precautions and principles to be taken was created. Therefore, first, a through literature review was carried out to identify existing security threats that target web applications and potential solutions to deal with these threats. It is clear that web applications are vulnerable to a number of threats, but there are already solutions to these threats. As well as the solutions that aim to stop attacks already being made, it is needed to ensure the continuity of web applications with development-related measures. This can only be realized using secure software development life cycles. In this regard, maturity models play a key role to provide guidance to organizations and increase the awareness of software security. Taking into consideration the checklist provided by OWASP (OWASP, 2022) makes it easy to handle common threats targeting web applications. The list is updated every year and can be used as a reference guide. As well as this, an automated code review process can be helpful. Because it can compare source code to a standard set of guidelines to check for common sources of security threats.

ACKNOWLEDGMENT

Some parts of this chapter were produced from the first author's master's project. This research received no specific grant from any funding agency in the public, commercial, or not-for-profit sectors.

REFERENCES

Aydoğdu, D., & Gündüz, M. (2016). Web Uygulama Güvenliği Açıklıkları ve Güvenlik Çözümleri Üzerine Bir Araştırma. *Uluslarası Bilgi Güvenliği Mühendisliği Dergisi*, 2(1), 1–7. doi:10.18640/ubgmd.56836

Aydos, M., Aldan, Ç, Coşkun, E., & Soydan, A. (2022). Security testing of web applications: A systematic mapping of the literature. *Journal of King Saud University - Computer and Information Sciences, 34*(9), 6775-6792. doi:10.1016/j.jksuci.2021.09.018

Baykara, M., & Daş, R. (2019). Saldırı tespit ve engelleme araçlarının incelenmesi. *Dicle Üniversitesi Mühendislik Fakültesi Mühendislik Dergisi, 10*(1), 57–75. doi:10.24012/dumf.44905

Beaman, C., Redbourne, M., Mummery, J. D., & Hakak, S. (2022). Fuzzing vulnerability discovery techniques: Survey, challenges and Future Directions. *Computers & Security, 120*, 102813. doi:10.1016/j.cose.2022.102813

Borky, J. M., & Bradley, T. H. (2019). Protecting Information with Cybersecurity. In *Effective Model-Based Systems Engineering*. Springer., doi:10.1007/978-3-319-95669-5_10

BSIMM. (2008). *About the BSIMM*. BSIMM. https://www.bsimm.com/about.html

Carter, P. A. (2018). SQL Injection. In *Securing SQL Server*. Apress. doi:10.1007/978-1-4842-4161-5_10

Cumhurbaşkanlığı Dijital Dönüşüm Ofisi. (2021). Bilgi ve İletişim Güvenliği Denetim Rehberi. CDDO. https://cbddo.gov.tr/SharedFolderServer/Projeler/File/BG_Denetim_Rehberi.pdf

Edmundson, A., Holtkamp, B., Rivera, E., Finifter, M., Mettler, A., & Wagner, D. (2013). An Empirical Study on the Effectiveness of Security Code Review. In: Jürjens, J., Livshits, B., Scandariato, R. (eds) Engineering Secure Software and Systems. ESSoS 2013. Lecture Notes in Computer Science, vol 7781. Springer, Berlin, Heidelberg. doi:10.1007/978-3-642-36563-8_14

Handa, A., Negi, R., & Shukla, S. K. (Eds.). (2021). *Implementing enterprise cybersecurity with open-source software and standard architecture*. River Publishers. doi:10.1201/9781003338512

Hughes, L. E. (2022). SSL and TLS. In: Pro Active Directory Certificate Services. Berkeley, CA: Apress. doi:10.1007/978-1-4842-7486-6_11

Nixon, R. (2021). *Learning PHP, MySQL & JavaScript* (6th ed.). O'Reilly Media.

OWASP. (2016). *Software Assurance Maturity Model v1.5*. OWASP. https://owasp.org/www-pdf-archive/SAMM_Core_V1-5_FINAL.pdf

OWASP. (2021). *OWASP Top Ten*. OWASP. https://owasp.org/www-project-top-ten/ https://owasp.org/

Sağıroğlu, Ş. (Ed.). (2019). *Siber Güvenlik ve Savunma: Standartlar ve Uygulamalar*. Grafiker Yayınları.

Sarıman, G., & Çelikten, H. (2021). Yeni bir güvenli yazılım geliştirme uygulama modeli: GYG-MOD. *Uluslararası Teknolojik Bilimler Dergisi, 13*(1), 39–49.

Shahid, J., Hameed, M. K., Javed, I. T., Qureshi, K. N., Ali, M., & Crespi, N. (2022). A Comparative Study of Web Application Security Parameters: Current Trends and Future Directions. *Applied Sciences (Basel, Switzerland), 12*(8), 4077. doi:10.3390/app12084077

Shugrue, D. (2017). Fighting application threats with cloud-based WAFS. *Network Security, 2017*(6), 5–8. doi:10.1016/S1353-4858(17)30059-4

Torres, A., Galante, R., Pimenta, M. S., & Martins, A. J. (2017). Twenty Years of object-relational mapping: A survey on patterns, solutions, and their implications on application design. *Information and Software Technology*, *82*, 1–18. doi:10.1016/j.infsof.2016.09.009

TÜBİTAK-BİLGEM. (2018). Güvenli Yazılım Geliştirme Kılavuzu. Tübitak-Bilgem. Https://Siberaka-demi.Bilgem.Tubitak.Gov.Tr/Pluginfile.Php/6115/Mod_Page/Content/26/Sge-Klv-Guvenliyazilimge-listirmekilavuzu_R1.1.Pdf

Velásquez, I., Caro, A., & Rodríguez, A. (2018). Authentication schemes and methods: A systematic literature review. *Information and Software Technology*, *94*, 30–37. doi:10.1016/j.infsof.2017.09.012

Wang, Y., Jia, P., Liu, L., Huang, C., & Liu, Z. (2020). A systematic review of fuzzing based on machine learning techniques. *PLoS One*, *15*(8), e0237749. doi:10.1371/journal.pone.0237749 PMID:32810156

Yan, H., Feng, L., Yu, Y., Liao, W., Feng, L., Zhang, J., Liu, D., Zou, Y., Liu, C., Qu, L., & Zhang, X. (2022). Cross-site scripting attack detection based on a modified convolution neural network. *Frontiers in Computational Neuroscience*, *16*, 981739. doi:10.3389/fncom.2022.981739 PMID:36105945

Zhang, B., Li, J., Ren, J., & Huang, G. (2022b). Efficiency and Effectiveness of Web Application Vulnerability Detection Approaches: A Review. *ACM Computing Surveys*, *54*(9), 190. doi:10.1145/3474553

Zhang, W., Li, Y., Li, X., Shao, M., Mi, Y., Zhang, H., & Zhi, G. (2022a). Deep Neural Network-Based SQL Injection Detection Method. *Security and Communication Networks*, *2022*, 4836289. doi:10.1155/2022/4836289

ADDITIONAL READING

Hoffman, A. (2020). *Web application security: Exploitation and countermeasures for modern web applications*. O'Reilly.

Lepofsky, R. (2014). *The manager's guide to web application security: A concise guide to the weaker side of the web*. Apress. doi:10.1007/978-1-4842-0148-0

McClure, S., Scambray, J., & Kurtz, G. (2012). *Hacking exposed: Network security secrets and solutions*. McGraw-Hill/Osborne.

Scambray, J., Liu, V., & Sima, C. (2011). *Hacking exposed: Web application security secrets and solutions*. McGraw-Hill.

Shivakumar, S. K. (2015). *Architecting high performing, scalable and available enterprise web applications*. Morgan Kaufmann.

Takanen, A., DeMott, J., Miller, C., & Kettunen, A. (2018). *Fuzzing for software security testing and quality assurance*. Artech House.

KEY TERMS AND DEFINITIONS

Capability Maturity Model: A procedure used to develop and refine an organization's software development process.

Cyber Threat: A malicious act that is performed with the aim of damaging data, stealing data, or disrupting digital life in general.

Fuzzing: In software development, fuzzing is an automated software testing technique that involves providing invalid, unexpected, or random data as inputs to a computer program. The aim is to detect bugs automatically.

Software Development Life Cycle: The application of standard business practices to building software applications.

Web Application: A Web application is an application program that is stored on a remote server and delivered over the Internet through a web browser.

Chapter 7
Data Leakage and Privacy Concerns in Public Bug Bounty Platforms

Muhammad Hamad

Institute of Space Technology, Islamabad, Pakistan

Altaf Hussain

Institute of Space Technology, Islamabad, Pakistan

Majida Khan Tareen

Institute of Space Technology, Islamabad, Pakistan

ABSTRACT

For long-term relationships, the websites of various businesses store the PII and PHI of customers, which are mainly targeted by hackers. Cyber breaches mainly result in lack of customer trust and downfall of the business reputation. As a result, the customers become reluctant to share PII and PHI with online businesses until provided with the protection of sensitive data. The online resources of a business need to be in compliance with GDPR and PCI DSS. Companies undergo penetration testing of the infrastructure; for this, paid white hat hackers are hired under a legal contract. The companies also adopt RVDP program, where the Bug Bounty Platforms is one of the variants of RVDP. Security researchers are rewarded with an amount of bounty in the form of money or name in the hall of fame at official website for bugs' identification. Ideally, the security researcher would perform cyber security assessment. The vulnerabilities would be reported to intended stakeholders and the remediation measures with great deal of care so that PII and PHI won't be exploited by anyone.

DOI: 10.4018/978-1-6684-6914-9.ch007

INTRODUCTION

The computer is one of history's biggest inventions and has a huge impact on our lives. Computers are found to be excellent at performing computing tasks at a speed unmatchable by human beings. These computing devices made their way to each and every sector and reduced the human workload. After the advent of the Internet, the world became a global village and introduced the sense of being connected among people no matter in which geographical regions they live in. So broadly speaking, computers are a set of electronic circuits, along with software which defines how this hardware will operate and for communicating with other devices of same nature, it has an additional component for network establishment.

This paradigm shift opened new channels of collaboration and coexistence. The people from far apart regions became friends using social networking sites, researchers started working together on problems of mutual interest, and businessmen started trading on e-commerce sites.

So, for every other internet-connected task, a specific kind of software was required and then was created by IT Personnel. In the software requirement engineering process, both functional and nonfunctional requirements are discussed by stakeholders. The functional requirements are the core features of software for which it is about to get designed. Functional requirements clearly mention what kind of inputs the software should be capable of receiving, what processing it should perform on input data and what resultant output is required to be displayed. In contrast to this, non-functional requirements are mostly quality related things like user-experience, scalability, compatibility and security.

Like any other assets, this software is owned by some specific people e.g., Amazon multinational e-commerce company is owned by Jeffrey Preston Bezos and Facebook, a famous social media platform is owned by Mark Elliot Zuckerberg. According to a recent survey, there are 2.93 billion active Facebook users per month. Facebook has a huge database of private data associated with these 2.93 billion people. On the same lines Amazon, PayPal or any other Fintech company plays with lot of financial data of normal users. People now a days are very concerned about how the owner of respective software would manage, store, transmit and secure their critical/sensitive data. So, in the recent past, this concern of people has shifted security from non-functional requirement to functional requirement.

But there is a very peculiar difference between functional requirements (FR) and non-functional requirements (NFR), which is, that the explanation of FR is explicit and once the software is developed it is easy for client to assess if the objectives were truly met. In case of NFR, the extent to which certain requirements are fulfilled varies from person to person and there are no absolute criteria of quantification e.g., if the quality assessment of application is to be performed by multiple different persons at same time and their test case is to grade the usability of application, it seems definite that their grades won't match. The point here is to establish an idea that although security or cyber security switched from NFR to FR, still there is nothing like ultimate security and if someone has access to unlimited space and time every system ought to be breakable. So for better security assessment let's dissect the concept of information and cyber security and its 3 pillars.

Information Security Vs Cyber Security

Information security and cybersecurity are related but distinct concepts. Information security refers to the practice of protecting information and information systems from unauthorized access, use, disclosure, disruption, modification, or destruction. It focuses on safeguarding the confidentiality, integrity, and availability of information, whether in digital or non-digital form. Cybersecurity, on the other hand, is a subset of information security that specifically deals with protecting digital assets from cyber threats. It involves the use of various technologies, processes, and practices to safeguard devices, networks, systems, and information from digital attacks, theft, damage, or unauthorized access.

In summary, information security is a broader term that encompasses all aspects of protecting information, including physical and non-digital aspects. Cybersecurity is a subset of information security that focuses specifically on protecting digital assets from cyber threats. The explanation of some key terminologies in above definition are tabulated in Table 1.

Table 1. Definitions of key terms

Terms	Definitions
Asset	Asset is any digital or information system which has some monetary or reputation value.
Integrity	Integrity is to only allow authenticated user to modify or change the data at rest or in motion
Availability	Availability is to ensure that no malicious user is able to disrupt the services and system is reliable and trust worthy.

FACTS RELATED TO CYBER BREACHES

To establish the essence of how serious the issue of cyber breaches is, Institute performed a research (IBM, 2023) on 550 real breaches which was featured in IBM's annual cost of data breach report 2022. According to this research, there is 12.7% increase in average data breach cost since 2020 and the average cost of breach then was USD 3.86 million. According to another research (SearchLogistics, 2023), on average at least 280 days are required to identify a cyber-attack and in 2020 36 billion private records were exposed.

Data Driven Industries

Clive Humby, a British mathematician, in 2006 said that "Data is the new Oil". His statement aligns perfectly with the way industries operate now-a-days. With the increasing use of Artificial Intelligence and Data science algorithms, companies are in a race with each other to gain the competitive advantage, but what fuels these algorithms is actually the "Data". Online businesses have a high degree of control on user generated sensitive data. For example, websites collect personal information, financial information, user navigation patterns, confidential message and lot more. Also, it seems that the companies know more about the individuals than in actual knowing about their own data. Like oil, these extreme data collection procedures had also negatively affected the society, in a way that user's data has been utilized to shape custom ads and sell them things they don't want, and customer mind manipulation strategies shifted the control from user's hand to bigger data collection giants. Let's discuss different types of sensitive data and various consumer data privacy laws which can help the general public to have more control over their data. As most of these are state laws, organizations are under legal binding to abide by them. A few common types of sensitive data are tabulated in Table 2:

Table 2. Common types of sensitive data

Data Types	Details
Financial Information	Data related to bank accounts, credit and debit cards
Export Controlled Research	Data related to foreign policy and anti-terrorism
Federal Information Security Management Act (FISMA) Data	Data related to federal agencies who help companies with their cyber security implementation in US.
Personal Identifiable Information (PII)	Data used to identify a person e.g. Social security number, Birthdate, biometric Data, phone number, password, religion etc.
Protected Health Information (PHI)	Health related data e.g. medical history, medications, test etc.

IMPACTS OF SENSITIVE DATA LOSS

Biometric data is being collected by most smartphones for security purposes. If it is lost/ leaked, the criminals can use it to masquerade the identity of owner and can perform illicit activity of any kind. Sensitive data loss can have wide-ranging impacts, including financial losses, reputation damage, legal and regulatory consequences, personal and psychological impacts, and national security risks. It is essential to take measures to prevent data loss and to respond effectively if it does occur.

COMMON LAWS REGARDING SAFETY OF SENSITIVE CONSUMER DATA

Privacy Laws in US

If only the US laws regarding users' privacy are to be discussed, the most famous proposal is the American Data Privacy Protection Act (ADPPA). The Federal Trade Commission Act (FTC Act) delegates authority of customer data protection to FTC. FTC does not dictate commercial entities about what and how much data they are allowed to gather but only protect customers regarding misuse of their data. FTC takes action if the organization:

- Deviates from privacy policy
- Does not take appropriate measure regarding data security
- Mislead consumers about wrong claims of privacy and security.

Some common privacy laws about collection of online information are Children's Online Privacy Protection Act (COPPA) concerned with data collection policies about minors, Health Insurance Portability and Accounting Act (HIPAA) governs the health care information collection and Fair Credit Reporting Act (FCRA) that Regulates Credit and Debit card information.

Privacy laws in Europe

The General Data Protection Regulation (GDPR)

GDPR is one of the most famous laws regarding data privacy and is applicable to data of each member of 28 members of EU Union. It regulates data acquisition, storage, processing, communication and security. There are following key points in GDPR,

- Commercial entities are bound to ask for explicit permission for data collection and how the data would be used and shared across 3rd parties.
- In case of cyber-attack, stack holders must be notified in window of 72 hours.
- End user have control over their data and can ask to view, edit, delete or restrict the 3rd party communication of data

Some other common privacy laws in EU are Digital Services Act, Digital Markets Act, and E-Privacy Regulation.

Penetration Testing: A Compliance Requirement

As explained above, there exist certain laws which are very strict in nature and there are operating bodies which, in case of violation of these laws, penalize the businesses and thus companies may sometime end up in detrimental situations. So whichever companies collect and maintains user data, they try to be very careful and tries to avoid the penalties and legal issues. There exist many compliance and audit bodies, which performs inspection of cyber security implementation inside company and provide accreditations. To acquire these accreditations, there are certain practices the companies must ensure. One of those is, that the penetration testing of IT infrastructure is a must. Some common compliance bodies which demand penetration testing are (ERMProtect, 2023) are tabulated Table 3:

Table 3. Security compliance bodies

Security Compliance Bodies	Detail
ISO 2070001	As a part of risk management, companies must test their implemented security controls using penetration testing
PCI DSS	To ensure that, payment processing mechanisms are secure, companies must undergo penetration testing.
GDPR	Use penetration testing, to reveal the ways through which sensitive data of European citizens can be compromised.

TYPES AND PROCESSESS OF PENETRATION TESTING (PEN. TESTING)

Penetration testing is a method of assessing the security of a system, network, or application by simulating an attack to identify vulnerabilities that could be exploited by attackers. It is an offensive security approach; the tester actually mimics the thought process and strategy of adversary/hacker to launch a cyber-attack on assets of company under test in controlled and ethical manner.

Types of Pen. Testing

White Box

White box penetration testing is a type of ethical hacking approach that involves testing the security of a system or application with complete knowledge of its internal workings and architecture. In other words, the tester has access to the source code, design documents, network topology, and other technical details about the system being tested. This approach is often used when the tester is part of the development team or has been given a high level of access to the system for testing purposes. With this level of access, the tester can thoroughly analyze the system's vulnerabilities, assess its resilience against attacks, and provide detailed recommendations for improving its security posture. White box penetration testing is often contrasted with black box penetration testing, where the tester has no prior knowledge of the system being tested and must rely on external information gathering techniques to discover vulnerabilities. While black box testing can be useful for simulating real-world attacks, white box testing allows for a more comprehensive and targeted approach to identifying security weaknesses.

Grey Box

Grey box penetration testing is a type of ethical hacking approach that combines elements of both white box and black box testing. In a grey box testing scenario, the tester has some knowledge of the system being tested, but not complete access to its internal workings or architecture. For example, the tester may have access to a user account on the system or some limited access to the source code. This level of access allows the tester to conduct a more focused and targeted analysis of the system's security vulnerabilities, while still simulating the perspective of an external attacker who may have some insider knowledge or access. Grey box testing can be particularly useful when testing web applications or other complex systems, as it allows testers to gain a deeper understanding of the system's architecture and behavior without having to recreate it entirely. This approach can also help organizations identify vulnerabilities that might be missed in a purely black box testing scenario. Overall, grey box penetration testing can provide a more balanced and nuanced view of a system's security posture, helping organizations to identify and mitigate potential risks more effectively.

Black Box

Black box penetration testing is a type of ethical hacking approach that involves testing the security of a system or application without any prior knowledge of its internal workings or architecture. In other words, the tester has no access to the source code, design documents, network topology, or any other technical details about the system being tested. The goal of black box testing is to simulate a real-world attack by a hacker or malicious actor who has no prior knowledge of the system being targeted. The tester must use external information gathering techniques, such as network scanning and enumeration, to identify potential vulnerabilities and exploit them. Black box testing can be particularly useful for identifying security weaknesses that might be missed in other testing scenarios. Since the tester is approaching the system from the perspective of an external attacker, they are more likely to discover vulnerabilities that could be exploited by real-world attackers. However, black box testing can also be time-consuming and may not provide a comprehensive view of the system's security posture. Since the tester has no prior knowledge of the system being tested, they may miss important details that could impact its overall security. As a result, black box testing is often used in combination with other testing approaches, such as white box or grey box testing, to provide a more comprehensive view of a system's security.

Internal Network Penetration testing

Internal network penetration testing is a type of ethical hacking approach that involves testing the security of an organization's internal network, such as its LAN, WAN, and VPN infrastructure. The goal of internal network penetration testing is to identify potential vulnerabilities and security weaknesses that could be exploited by an attacker who gains access to the network. Internal network penetration testing typically involves simulating various types of attacks, such as phishing attacks, brute force attacks, and SQL injection attacks, to identify potential weaknesses in the network's security. The tester may also attempt to exploit known vulnerabilities in common network services and protocols, such as DNS, DHCP, and LDAP. One of the key benefits of internal network penetration testing is that it can help organizations identify security weaknesses that may not be apparent from external testing alone. For example, an attacker who gains access to an organization's internal network may be able to exploit vulnerabilities that are not visible from the public internet. By conducting internal network penetration testing, organizations can identify these potential vulnerabilities and take steps to mitigate them before an attacker can exploit them.

External Network Penetration Testing

External network penetration testing is a type of ethical hacking approach that involves testing the security of an organization's external-facing network, such as its internet-facing servers, websites, and applications. The goal of external network penetration testing is to identify potential vulnerabilities and security weaknesses that could be exploited by an attacker who is attempting to gain unauthorized access to the organization's network. External network penetration testing typically involves simulating various types of attacks, such as remote code execution, cross-site scripting, and SQL injection attacks, to identify potential weaknesses in the network's security. The tester may also attempt to exploit known vulnerabilities in common network services and protocols, such as HTTP, FTP, and SSH. One of the key benefits of external network penetration testing is that it can help organizations identify security weaknesses that are visible from the public internet and could be exploited by attackers from anywhere in the world. By conducting external network penetration testing, organizations can identify these potential vulnerabilities and take steps to mitigate them before an attacker can exploit them.

Web Application

Web application-based penetration testing is a type of ethical hacking approach that involves testing the security of a web application. The goal of web application-based penetration testing is to identify potential vulnerabilities and security weaknesses that could be exploited by an attacker who is attempting to gain unauthorized access to the web application or its associated data. Web application-based penetration testing typically involves simulating various types of attacks, such as cross-site scripting (XSS), SQL injection, and buffer overflow attacks, to identify potential weaknesses in the web application's security. The tester may also attempt to exploit known vulnerabilities in the web application's underlying architecture, such as outdated software versions or insecure coding practices. One of the key benefits of web application-based penetration testing is that it can help organizations identify security weaknesses that are specific to their web applications and may not be apparent from other types of testing. By conducting web application-based penetration testing, organizations can identify these potential vulnerabilities and take steps to mitigate them before an attacker can exploit them.

Mobile Application

Mobile application-based penetration testing is a type of ethical hacking approach that involves testing the security of a mobile application. The goal of mobile application-based penetration testing is to identify potential vulnerabilities and security weaknesses that could be exploited by an attacker who is attempting to gain unauthorized access to the mobile application or its associated data. Mobile application-based penetration testing typically involves simulating various types of attacks, such as injection attacks, insecure data storage, and man-in-the-middle attacks, to identify potential weaknesses in the mobile application's security. The tester may also attempt to exploit known vulnerabilities in the mobile application's underlying architecture, such as insecure API integrations or outdated software versions. One of the key benefits of mobile application-based penetration testing is that it can help organizations identify security weaknesses that are specific to their mobile applications and may not be apparent from other types of testing. By conducting mobile application-based penetration testing, organizations can identify these potential vulnerabilities and take steps to mitigate them before an attacker can exploit them.

TYPE OF HACKERS

White Hat

White hat hackers are individuals or organizations who engage in ethical hacking and cybersecurity testing to identify vulnerabilities and weaknesses in computer systems, networks, and applications. They are also known as ethical hackers or penetration testers. White hat hackers use their knowledge of security vulnerabilities and exploits to test the security of systems and applications, in order to identify weaknesses that can be exploited by malicious actors. They do this with the permission of the system or application owners, and follow a strict code of ethics to ensure that their testing activities do not cause harm or damage to the systems being tested.

Black Hat

Black hat hackers are individuals or groups who engage in illegal or malicious activities aimed at exploiting vulnerabilities in computer systems, networks, and applications. They use their knowledge of security vulnerabilities and exploits to gain unauthorized access to systems, steal sensitive data, or cause damage to systems and networks. Black hat hackers engage in a variety of illegal activities, including stealing personal and financial data, conducting cyber espionage, launching denial of service attacks, and installing malware on targeted systems. They often work anonymously and may be motivated by financial gain, political or ideological reasons, or simply the thrill of causing disruption and damage.

Grey Hat

Gray hat hackers are individuals who engage in both ethical and unethical hacking activities. They operate between the "white hat" and "black hat" hacker categories, and their motives can vary widely. Gray hat hackers typically use their knowledge and skills to identify and report security vulnerabilities and weaknesses in computer systems, networks, and applications. They may also offer to fix these vulnerabilities for a fee, even if they do not have permission from the system owner to do so. While gray hat hackers often have good intentions and may aim to help organizations improve their security, their actions can still be illegal and cause harm to the systems they are testing. They may also cross ethical boundaries by accessing sensitive data without permission or causing damage to systems.

PEN. TESTING PROCESS

According to Cyber Security Exchange, there are 5 major step in the process of penetration testing Reconnaissance, Scanning, Vulnerability Assessment, Exploitation, and Reporting (Cybersecurity Exchange, 2023). The details of these steps are given as follows:

1. **Reconnaissance**: This stage involves gathering information about the system or application being tested, including IP addresses, system architecture, and potential vulnerabilities about target using active and passive sources.
   a. Active Information Gathering: Target is probed to acquire information e.g. to eavesdrop, ping, or traceroute etc.
   b. Passive Information Gathering: The target is not engaged directly and information is acquired using Open Source Intelligence (OSINT) tools.
2. **Scanning**: Once the information is acquired using both active and passive sources, it time for now to scan the actual target to identify its workflow, running services, versions information, and service information. During this stage, the pen testers use various tools and techniques to scan the target system for vulnerabilities and weaknesses.
3. **Vulnerability Assessment**: In this step, pen tester finds potentially vulnerable areas and then test those using automated or manual penetration testing tools. Automated vulnerability scanning tools like Nessus or Burp suite pro.
4. **Exploitation**: In this stage, the pen testers attempt to exploit the vulnerabilities they have identified, using various tools and techniques to gain unauthorized access to the system. If the system is found vulnerable in last step, then in this step, it is required to see if the system is also exploitable. Vulnerability in most cases has a CVE or CVSS number associated with them and based on CVE number exploits can be downloaded from exploit dB website (Exploit-DB, 2023).
5. **Reporting**: After the testing is complete, the pen testers prepare a detailed report that includes the vulnerabilities that were identified, the severity of each vulnerability, and recommendations for remediation. The penetration testing report explicitly mentions executive summaries, vulnerabilities, proof of concepts, and other important information.

Limitations of Pen. Testing

Time-Boxed Approach

Based on how much time and information is provided to penetration tester, the results of test would change drastically. In situations of short time frame, only common attack vectors can be tested and in scenarios where time limit is not to short, pen tester can perform exhaustive security testing.

Rules of Engagement

With service disruption in mind, the client may restrict the pen tester to use only limited and safe set of tools. The problem here is that adversary can use any tool or strategy he wants so the pen tester report in this case will create "false sense of security".

Skills of a Penetration Tester

The skill, ability, and experience plays a vital role in success or failure of a penetration tester. As mentioned in previous section, there are different types of penetration testing based on information provided, location of tester, and type of application, so penetration tester skilled in one area might have rudimentary skills in the other ones.

Salaries of a Penetration Tester

According to some common employment oriented services, the salary range of a penetration tester is quite high. As per indeed.com the range is from $97,171 to $150,963 (Indeed, 2023). Another website, zipRecruiter.com has seen the salaries of pen tester as high as $179,317 (ZipRecruiter, 2023).

Zero Days

In most cases, pen tester only looks for known threats and run automatic payloads to exploit an application. Most penetration tests do not cover in-depth custom exploit research and creation for running/found services and due to which zero-days may still left unreported.

On-going Penetration Testing

Pen testing is always a snapshot of security posture of target at specific time. With threat landscape changing at every moment, an ongoing scheme of continuous penetration testing is required.

HOW TO OVERCOME LIMITATIONS OF PENETRATION TESTING?

The above stated limitations are nightmare for companies struggling with achievement of better security goals. So the challenge here was how to compete with the army of unlimited adversaries who have unlimited supplies at their disposal. By supplies, we mean unlimited time, skill, experience, and money.

To stand against these adversaries, an equal number of people with same resources were required. There comes the need of Vulnerability Disclosure Program and Bug Bounty Program.

Vulnerability Disclosure Program (VDP)

VDP is a systematic process/ program of accepting security reports against identified vulnerabilities from community and it also includes methods of report acceptance, triage, remediation and recognition. As there are certain laws associated with PII, PHI and other kinds of sensitive data, US Dept. of Justice's Criminal Division, Cybersecurity Unit mentions guidelines about how to conduct how to safely conduct security assessment and avoid litigation under CFFA (Computer Fraud and Abuse Act).

Components of VDP

Purpose/Promise Statement

It is an objective statement which represent that why the company is interested in a VDP program and how much they care for cyber security issues in their environment and also secrecy/privacy of company's data is important to them.

Scope

Organizations usually own more than one public facing assets and also have integrations with multiple 3rd party API's. So, this section clearly explains which assets are allowed for security researchers to conduct vulnerability assessment. Out of scope items must not be tested in any case without explicit permission of the owner.

Safe Harbor

This clarifies the ambiguities of security researcher that, if remains in scope and perform security assessment of only allowed sections in ethical manner, the security researcher won't get penalized under law.

Process Description

This defines the workflow and guides the community that how to interact with the organization in case of reporting. This step is paramount in understanding how the organization will respond on submission of bug and what should be in the reports and what are the additional documents or proof of concept the tester needs to submit. The description also includes the expected duration the researcher needs to wait before disclosure of bug on any public forum.

Bug Bounty Program (BBP)

A bug bounty program (BBP) is a crowdsourced security testing program that rewards individuals, often called "ethical hackers" or "white hat hackers," for identifying and reporting vulnerabilities or bugs in software, applications, or systems. The purpose of a bug bounty program is to incentivize and encourage individuals to report security issues to the organization, which can then fix them before they are exploited by malicious actors.

Bug bounty programs are typically offered by technology companies and organizations that rely on software or applications to run their operations. These programs may offer monetary rewards, such as cash, gift cards, or other incentives, to individuals who successfully identify and report security issues. In addition to monetary rewards, some programs may also offer recognition or public acknowledgment to participants who discover significant vulnerabilities.

Both the VDP and BBP programs receive bug reports against in scope items but unlike its counterpart, BBP needs to mention the explanation of what is that company offers and in what ways and it requires more settings than in VDP (VDP vs BBP:, 2023).

Types of Disclosure

Once the Pen Tester identifies some bug, he needs to report it or disclose it. Cybersecurity and Infrastructure Security Agency has created a policy template for vulnerability disclosure as per Binding Operational Directive 20-01 (CISA:, 2023). When it comes to disclosure there are 4 major options to choose from which are being discussed here.

Private Disclosure

In this model, pen tester is bound to share the details of bug in private with only the respective organization and no other entity is allowed to have or know about the bug regardless of its severity and importance. Only the organization have rights to share the data with whoever and whatever they feel necessary. The issue with this type is that, if the organization is unresponsive, not releasing appropriate patch or badly interacting with the tester, it makes him frustrated and this frustration can end up in the form of full disclosure.

Full Disclosure

In full disclosure, researchers publish the details of vulnerability, without even waiting for the patch to be available by respective organization. Full disclosure mostly includes details of vulnerable endpoints, proof of concept and there are cases where exploit code was also published. The positive aspect of full disclosure is it actually expedites the process of bug fixation because of reputation loss and crowd pressure and downside is that it gives equal opportunity to malicious actors to exploit the bug and perform the actions which they otherwise were not supposed to do.

Responsible Disclosure

Responsible disclosure is considered to be a middle ground between full and private disclosure. Testers are allowed to share the details of bug in public but only after it is fixed or patched by the organization. After an agreed upon time limit the researcher is allowed to share the details with the public even if the patch has not released yet.

Coordinated Disclosure

- The Overprotective neighbors

Remember the analogy of neighborhood watch, when the neighbors discover something bad, they'll let you know (as a responsible neighbor) but there is a problem. Not all of the neighbors would be right in their claims and when money or fame would be associated with reporting a correct issue, the company would receive an overwhelming response from community and most of them would be false positives. These false positives would eventually frustrate the security teams by continuously reading the incoming reports and this natural time wastage may lead to late replies to researchers with correctly identified issues with them. If the correct reports won't receive the timely response this can lead to Full Disclosure. That's why self-managed VDP is not considered to be a great idea and there exists a need for coordinated disclosure platforms.

- Coordinated disclosure platforms

As now a day, there is lot of 3rd party integration and multiple owners/users/stakeholders are involved in a product the coordinated disclosure platforms is one of the most suitable option. The reports submitted through these platforms are first verified/vetted by trusted professionals and then passed on to the organization. This process helps organizations get rid of working on unlimited false positives. The common examples of coordinated disclosure platforms are BugCrowd (BugCrowd, 2023), Hackerone (HackerOne, 2023) and Intigriti (INTIGRITI, 2023). BugCrowd even has their own objective rating standards which is also called Vulnerability Rating Taxonomy (VRT). This type of disclosure is

- No Disclosure

In this type, the researcher chooses not to disclose this vulnerability to any one not even the vendor of the product. This can occur because of many issues such as non-cooperative behavior of vendor, legal actions taken against researchers in past by vendor, difficult vulnerability reporting workflows and others.

The result of this non-disclosure is that the vulnerability is there but neither the vendor knows about it nor the end user is aware of the issue. There may be some adversaries other than researchers, who opted to not disclose the vulnerability, which are aware of this certain vulnerability and may use it against the company or end user. The adversaries may be state sponsored advanced persistent threats and they may hold hundreds of non-disclosed zero days also called as "government 0-day stockpiles". The government in this case can use these stockpiles against malicious actors who can also breach the privacy of general public behind the scene.

As we have seen different vulnerability disclosure program, and which method the researcher use is highly dependent on following key point:

- How severe the bug is?
- What could be the price of bug in dark web?
- What is the monetary compensation the pen test would receive?
- How much time researcher has spent in finding out this bug?
- How grateful the vendor would be on reporting?

- What are the legal issues he might have to face?

So, there are various questions that may pop up in researchers' minds and effective VDP always respect and consider these concerns and also take necessary actions to rectify them.

Price of Leaked Data in Dark Market

The price of leaked data in dark markets can vary widely depending on the type and quality of the data, as well as the demand for it. Some of the factors that can influence the price of leaked data include Type of data, Quality of data, Quantity of data, and Demand for data. According to various reports, the price of leaked data can range from a few cents to thousands of dollars per record. For example, credit card data can be sold for as little as $1 per record, while medical records can sell for as much as $1,000 per record. Ranging from zero days to leaked credit card numbers, there are hundreds of potential customers always ready to buy the sensitive stuff. These products includes zero day, forged documents, credit card numbers, hacked social media accounts, dumped credentials list etc. (PrivacyAffairs, 2023)

It's important to note that buying and selling leaked data is illegal and can have serious legal consequences. Additionally, individuals and organizations that have their data leaked may face financial and reputational damage, as well as other negative consequences.

DATA PRIVACY CONCERNS INVOLVED IN PENETRATION TESTING

Until this point, it has been established that for any ICT/ICS infrastructure, security assessment is a must to uncover hidden vulnerabilities. Also, it has been cleared that cyber security implementation is no longer a matter of choice but a basic component of any information system.

For cyber security assessment, the following two methodologies are discussed i.e. Penetration Testing and Vulnerability Disclosure Program. Both of these methods are very effective to reveal hidden weaknesses of the system but also have some inherent risks associated with them and because of these risks vendors feel reluctant to undergo any of above methods. Some of the natural thoughts against penetration testing or VDP are given in Table 4.

Table 4. Concerns of vendors against penetration testing and vulnerability disclosure program

Do I really need a cyber-security program in my company?
Should I hire internal security team for penetration testing?
Should I outsource cyber security testing of my resources?
If I launch VDP program, should I go with self-managed VDP or signup on coordinated disclosure services like Hackerone (HackerOne, 2023) or BugCrowd (BugCrowd, 2023)?
In VDP, among private and public bug bounty program, which one should I opt for?
How can I trust external pen test companies/teams/individuals in perspective of data privacy?
Will penetration testing disrupt my normal services?
Are there any legislations on which pen tester can be litigated if he goes out of scope?
How can I distinguish between legitimate traffic, ethical malicious test traffic and adversarial malicious traffic?

Along with many others, these above concerns of vendor left penetration tester in a paradoxical situation of to go or to not go for regular security assessment or penetration testing. Also from Penetration tester stand point he also has some concerns regarding his own safety while Pen testing and few of them are discussed in Table 5.

Table 5. Concerns of tester against penetration testing and vulnerability disclosure program

In most cases, management teams are non-technical and with them "Rules of Engagement" document is not as explicit as it should be and in the end the ambiguous areas create a lot of problem for tester's end.
Consider a case of web application in which backend database or server side code is not visible to pen tester, and usually pen tester takes steps based on his instinct and skill. There may be the case, when there are some backend queries or code exist which is based on some specific business logic requirement e.g. to delete the records of table-A on an occurrence of Event-1. While testing these type of applications some unwanted situation may arise and could be against the scope document. If that happens, Pen tester may have to face severe consequences.
While Pen testing, server/application or any related infrastructure get crashed followed by temporary down time or total disruption of service.
How much support vendor will provide in case of un-intentional out of scope achievements?

Both vendors and pen testers have some concerns in their minds regarding data security, organizational security, and individual security. We'll discuss solutions for each of them individually in following sections.

RECTIFICATION OF DATA PRIVACY CONCERNS OF VENDORS FOR SECURITY ASSESSMENT

As discussed already, vendor of the product is the one who actually owns the resource, collects/process and manages the private data of end users, thwart adversaries by implementing the required cyber security controls and need to avoid any litigations because of insecure handling of sensitive data. So because of this strategy of "defense in depth" or "security by design" must be followed. According to these schemes the security should be the part of architecture design in the very start of application development and every layer of application interaction must have some security measures in place. Let's consider that, application has already been developed by following "Security by design" principle, the next requirement now is to evaluate the loopholes and here the vendor has to make a decision about how to proceed with security assessment. Here the optimal methodology of security assessment is being discussed but before that let's understand the difference between in-house, outsource penetration testing and VDP style pen testing.

In-House Penetration Testing

In this model, either the company hires a resource person which works full time for a company or utilizes existing manpower to achieve an object. In house team is asked to perform pen test as a project and this team works under operational infrastructure of company. The pros and cons are discussed below:

Response Time

In house teams, better knows about the norms, culture and workflows of company and thus better able to understand the application and report the surface level bugs. Because of this they have relatively quicker response time than outsourced teams.

Data Privacy Risk for In-House Testing

In most companies, BYOD culture is discouraged, and employees need to use the organizational equipment to assess the security. Along with this, the organizations have strict codes of conduct on policy violations and actions of security teams are also monitored which makes them more careful and faithful than outsourced employees. So, the degree of data exfiltration risk is relatively lower than outsource pen testing.

Outsource Penetration Testing

An Outside individual or company is hired to carry out a penetration test of company. In outsourcing, the freelance individual is only in agreement with the organization on a project basis and does not have any long-term affiliation with the company. The vendor and researcher agree on a "Rules of engagement document" and discuss the process of carrying out procedure before the test actually starts. The pros and cons are discussed below:

Data Privacy Risk in Outsource Penetration Testing

Outsourcing has the risk of Data Privacy breach because in scenario where critical bug is found by the third party, he may not be able to disclose it and end up exploiting it for malicious purposes.

Cost Effective

Unlike in house teams, outsourcing is cost effective solution. In house teams has hefty price tags associated with them because they charge for man hours as for how much time they have to spend in company and company may not have every time new project for this team.

Realistic

External pen tests are more realistic in nature and these people are provided with the same level of access as any real hacker. In comparison with in house pen test this strategy is more realistic.

VDP Style Penetration Testing

The bug hunter is paid only if he finds a loophole in an application and does not cost a single penny to company otherwise. This model presumes a very week relationship between company and researcher. Vendor mentions the rules and scope regarding pen test of his application on some website but that doesn't bind the researcher to follow them all in true sense. Only when researcher claims for bounty, only then his actions may be cross verified but that is of very little use, because all the process has already been completed by researcher.

Data Exfiltration Risks Associated With Internal Network

Usually the internet facing assets are placed in DMZ and rest of internal network is behind the firewall. The asset placed in DMZ are supposed to be accessed by people from all over the world by using internet. The assets inside DMZ has large number of potential threat actors because of ease of access and hackers will tries to hack it, to use it only as pivot and to gain access to the internal network. This situation, if arise, would create a huge negative impact and may leads to high value of data exfiltration.

The possible solution of this issue is that before application deployment in DMZ a comprehensive cyber security testing of internal network must be performed. Through this security testing organization will be confident enough that in a worst case scenario if the application in DMZ gets compromised. The internal network's security would still be able to fight back.

OPTIMAL METHODOLOGY OF CARRYING OUT RISK FREE SECURITY ASSESSMENT

To carry out the security assessment procedure, a skilled pen test team is required. To make a decision about either in house or outsource security team would work some arguments are discussed in above paras. Apart from that, it is better to undergo both in house and outsource pen testing to leverage the advantage of both schemes and also overcome their disadvantages.

Level 1 Testing: Check Application Security for Common Data Entry and Exit Points

First step should be the pen testing from in house security team, so that obvious and surface level bugs should be immediately patched.

Level 2 Testing: Check Application Security for Sophisticated Data Leakage Chains

Once the in house team claims that the application is secure and there are no more bugs present in an application/infrastructure the application should be provided to outsource teams for further assessment. As the internal team has already performed certain security checks, chances are that outsource team will need to put more efforts and also demand relatively more time.

Level 3 Testing: Check Application Security Against Tricks Specific to Bug Hunters

As security is an ongoing process so no one can be sure that when and how someone is going to exploit a bug. So once the internal and external teams complete the task, create a vulnerability disclosure program using Hackerone (HackerOne, 2023), BugCrowd (BugCrowd, 2023) or Intigriti (INTIGRITI, 2023) and mention explicit VDP rules for researchers about how to perform the assessment and how and why to stay ethical during the test.

RECTIFICATION OF DATA PRIVACY CONCERNS OF PEN TESTERS FOR SECURITY ASSESSMENT

Pen testers are often required to access sensitive information during security assessments, which can raise data privacy concerns for the organization being tested. To address these concerns, there are several measures that pen testers can take to ensure the confidentiality and security of the organization's data:

- Obtain signed non-disclosure agreements (NDAs): Pen testers should obtain signed NDAs from the organization being tested, outlining the terms and conditions of the pen test and the confidentiality of the data accessed during the assessment.
- Use encrypted communication channels: All communication between the pen testers and the organization should be encrypted to ensure the confidentiality and security of the data being transmitted.
- Limit access to data: Pen testers should only access the data necessary for the assessment and should not retain any data that is not required for the test. They should also ensure that any data obtained during the assessment is securely destroyed after the test is complete.
- Implement access controls: Pen testers should implement access controls to ensure that only authorized personnel can access the data being tested. This may involve using role-based access controls or implementing multi-factor authentication.
- Use secure storage and transportation methods: Any data obtained during the assessment should be stored securely, using encryption and other security measures. If the data needs to be transported, it should be done so securely, using encryption and other security measures.

By taking these steps, pen testers can ensure that the data privacy concerns of the organization being tested are addressed, and that the confidentiality and security of the data are maintained throughout the assessment.

THREATS AGAINST RESEARCHERS

Researchers acting in good faith to test the product may face a situation when the things start getting wrong. There may be a situation when, without the evil intention of tester, some internal private data of company may be posted somewhere or data may get destroyed. This situation may lead tester into a situation he would never like to be in. As multiple stockholders are involved and related to data stores so they all tries to pressurize the researchers, and some common cases where researchers were threatened and litigated can be found here (ThreatsDisclose, 2023).

Electronic Frontier Foundation (EFF) Right for Researchers

The Electronic Frontier Foundation (EFF) is a non-profit organization that advocates for digital privacy, freedom of expression, and innovation. The EFF's Right to Research program aims to protect the rights of researchers to access information, conduct research, and share their findings. Under the Right to Research program, the EFF supports the following rights for researchers:

1. **Access to Information:** Researchers should have the right to access information and data necessary to conduct their research, without facing unnecessary restrictions or barriers.
2. **Freedom to conduct research:** Researchers should have the freedom to conduct research without fear of censorship or retaliation. This includes the ability to study controversial topics and express their findings without fear of retribution.
3. **Right to publish:** Researchers should have the right to publish their findings, without fear of censorship or retaliation. This includes the ability to publish research in open access journals and share their findings with others.
4. **Protection from legal threats:** Researchers should be protected from legal threats, such as lawsuits or criminal charges, related to their research activities. This includes protection from actions such as defamation suits or claims of intellectual property infringement.
5. **Transparency in research funding**: Researchers should be transparent about their funding sources and any potential conflicts of interest. This includes disclosing funding sources and any ties to industry or other organizations that may influence their research.

The EFF's Right to Research program is designed to support the important work of researchers and ensure that they have the freedom and protections necessary to conduct research and share their findings. To learn that how to get safe in situations of conflict, the researcher should learn about his rights from EFF Coders Rights Forum (EFF, 2023) and apply these practices while security assessment. The recommended best practices for researchers are as follow:

1. The researcher should inform vendor on the provided platform if he/she finds some critical bug.
2. The researcher must not share any kind of information related to bug on any platform without the vendor's consent.
3. The researcher must not try to disrupt the normal services of organization.
4. The researcher must not create a copy of data.
5. The researcher must not modify or delete data.

SUMMARY

The increased digitalization of assets in recent years has induced serious data privacy threats and may lead the people to life threatening situations. Apart from our physical existence everyone has an online existence and we share a lot of PII, PHI or highly sensitive data with companies online. If the organization, having our data, gets compromised then malicious actors would automatically have access to general public details as well. To analyze the impact, consider that a credit card database is somehow accessible to hackers, they will have lot of money at their disposal and they can do whatever they want with it. In case if biometric information is stolen by malicious actors they will have unrestricted access to everything and place the original user had access to. The laws exist, against which these hackers would penalized but only if they get caught and this seems too good to be true. So to gain better reputation and trust of public, organizations themselves have to act proactively and need to perform 3 levels of penetration testing as discussed in chapter. The security assessment would serve many purpose, first it would help organization to secure its infrastructure, and second it would help them get certified from accreditation bodies like ISO, and third is the trust of customers they gain. So overall this is a win-win situation. This chapter discussed various mechanisms of security assessment and risks associated with them. In the end an optimal methodology was discussed which recommends to undergo internal network pen testing before starting penetration testing of internet facing assets. The main reason for this is to make internal network capable enough to thwart any kind of breach which bypassed end user application. In the end, it is recommended to follow periodic security assessment exercises because there is nothing like ultimate security. The developers create the application and the hackers breaks it and this cycle goes on and on. So instead of only relying on ill-intentioned hacker to break the application, hire a hacker with positive mindset and ask if to find the loopholes before the hackers and fix it to avoid its illegitimate use.

REFERENCES

BugCrowd. (2023, February 28). Crowdsourced Cybersecurity Platform. https://www.bugcrowd.com/

CISA. (2023, Februrary 28). *Vulnerability Disclosure Policy Template*. CISA. https://www.cisa.gov/vulnerability-disclosure-policy-template

EC Council. (2023, February 28). *Understanding the Five Phases of the Penetration Testing Process*. EC Council. https://www.eccouncil.org/cybersecurity-exchange/penetration-testing/penetration-testing-phases/

EFF. (2023, Febraury 15). Coders' Rights Project. *EFF*. https://www.eff.org/issues/coders

ERMProtect. (2023, February 28). *Penetration Testing for Compliance*. ERMProtect. https://ermprotect.com/blog/penetration-testing-for-compliance/

OSEDA. (2023, February 28). *Exploit-DB*. Offensive Security's Exploit Database Archive. https://www.exploit-db.com/

HackerOne. (2023, February 28). *Bug Bounty*. Hacker Powered Security Testing. https://www.hackerone.com/

IBM. (2023, February 28). *Cost of a data breach 2022 - A million-dollar race to detect and respond*. IBM. https://www.ibm.com/reports/data-breach

Indeed. (2023, February 28). *Penetration tester salary in United States*. Indeed. https://www.indeed.com/career/penetration-tester/salaries

INTIGRITI. (2023, February 28). Bug Bounty & Agile Pentesting Platform. *Intigriti*. https://www.intigriti.com/

PrivacyAffairs. (2023, February 15). *Dark Web Price Index 2021 - Dark Web Prices of Personal Data.* Privacy Affairs. https://www.privacyaffairs.com/dark-web-price-index-2021/

SearchLogistics. (2023, February 28). Cybersecurity Statistics 2023: The Alarming Truth. *Search Logistics.* https://www.searchlogistics.com/grow/statistics/cybersecurity-statistics/

Statista. (2023, March 10). *Number of monthly active Facebook users worldwide as of 4th quarter 2022 (in millions).* Statistia. https://www.statista.com/statistics/264810/number-of-monthly-active-facebook-users-worldwide/

Threats Disclosed. (2023, February 15). Security Research Threats. https://threats.disclose.io/

VDP vs BBP. (2023, February 2023). HackerOne Platform. https://docs.hackerone.com/organizations/vdp-vs-bbp.html

ZipRecruiter. (2023, February 28). *Junior Penetration Tester Salary in LaCoste, TX.* ZipRecruiter. https://www.ziprecruiter.com/Salaries/Junior-Penetration-Tester-Salary-in-LaCoste,TX

Chapter 8
On the Current State of Privacy Risks in Software Requirement Elicitation Techniques

Zartasha Saeed
City University of Science and Information Technology, Peshawar, Pakistan

Shahab Haider
City University of Science and Information Technology, Peshawar, Pakistan

Zulfiqar Ali
City University of Science and Information Technology, Peshawar, Pakistan

Muhammad Arshad
City University of Science and Information Technology, Peshawar, Pakistan

Iftikhar Alam
City University of Science and Information Technology, Peshawar, Pakistan

ABSTRACT

Requirement engineering has gained tremendous popularity among the research and developers communities and comprises five activities, i.e., feasibility study, elicitation, analysis, specification, and validation. In the elicitation phase, the data is collected from different stakeholders. Hence, the overall system, process, and even data may be compromised and sometimes lead to privacy threats if the data is shared with a third party. To this end, this work proposes a comparative analysis of the eminent techniques, including privacy violation factors. The authors targeted 32 techniques for analysis from different project scenarios. This study may help the analysts with adequate knowledge and help project management teams to select the best and most secure elicitation techniques concerning the nature of projects.

DOI: 10.4018/978-1-6684-6914-9.ch008

INTRODUCTION

Research and development communities have witnessed a dramatic increase in demand for requirement engineering in recent years (Rasheed et al., 2021). Effective management of multiple operations in the requirement engineering phase is crucial to the success of a software development project, as requirement engineering includes five key activities: Feasibility analysis, Elicitation, Analysis, Specification, and Validation. Effective management of these five activities can help ensure that the final product is delivered on time, within budget, and meets user requirements. It is important to note that requirement engineering is an iterative process, and each activity may need to be revisited multiple times to ensure that the requirements are accurate, complete, and consistent (Kasauli et al., 2021). The selection of an appropriate techniques is challenging due to the presence of numerous requirement elicitation techniques.

Software engineering is a broad field that encompasses all phases of software development, from initial feasibility studies to system maintenance and support. The systematic procedure used in software engineering is known as the "software process." The software process provides a framework for developing software in a systematic, controlled, and efficient manner. The software process typically involves several phases: requirements analysis, design, implementation, testing, and maintenance. (Sommerville, 2011). It should provide a solid foundation for examining the product's prices, risks, and delivery times. Requirement validation verifies that the demands specified in the Software Requirements Specification (SRS) are accurate, reasonable, and compatible with the client's needs. It validates a client's requirements by eliminating Software Requirements (SR) ambiguities and inconsistencies (Sharma & Pandey, 2013).

As a result of several requirements-related failures, correcting problems during or after software development becomes more expensive and difficult (Pandey & Batra, 2013). It stresses the significance of paying more attention to the requirements elicitation process, as getting imprecise requirements from users can lead to subpar design and coding that may be difficult to rectify in the future (Schneider & Berenbach, 2013). It is vital to identify the relevant stakeholders from varied backgrounds and assess their requirements to ensure the success of the requirements elicitation process (Tsumaki & Tamai, 2006). This chapter will aid analysts in identifying the most efficient technique for getting critical information from stakeholders with various backgrounds and expectations regarding a software product or project. A complete comparison of prominent techniques is performed to help readers. We selected 32 techniques from several project contexts for analysis, such as user and system privacy breaches, problems, rewards, and drawbacks. This research may equip analysts with the necessary knowledge and aid project management teams in determining the most suitable ways to extract project characteristics.

The findings of the elicitation phase indicate that data is collected from different stakeholders. Therefore, the integrity of the entire system, process, and data may be jeopardized if the data is shared with a third party, raising privacy hazards. This chapter will also help analysts to enhance their skills and project management teams in determining the most effective and secure methods for eliciting requirements according to the nature of projects. The remaining portion of the chapter is divided into three significant sections. A relevant literature review is presented in Section II. Section III discusses the material's theoretical analysis, and Section IV concludes the chapter.

REVIEW OF LITERATURE

Requirement elicitation is collecting user requirements and presenting them to system experts. The quality of requirements is dependent on the elicitation method and strategies employed. To select the appropriate technique for demand elicitation, the analyst must understand the diverse backgrounds of the various stakeholders (Pandey & Batra, 2013). Several different elicitation approaches are discussed below for this purpose. Figure 1 depicts the required elicitation strategies as a word cloud.

Figure 1. Word-cloud of requirements elicitation

1. Interviews are undeniably the most well-known, influential, and widely used technique for determining requirements (Agarwal & Tanniru, 1990; Zowghi & Coulin, 2005). Since interviews are based on human interaction, they are informal, and the interview's effectiveness strongly depends on how well the participants get along. In-depth interviews are an efficient method for collecting a large amount of data. The effectiveness of the interviewer has a significant impact on the inter-

view results, particularly the usefulness of the information collected (Index, 1995). Unstructured interviews consist of dialogues that the interviewer is unable to control. One advantage is the development of original ideas and viewpoints (Goguen & Linde, 1993). In addition, the interviewer's effective conversational style may put the interviewee at ease, even if they are hesitant to answer the questions.

2. Task Analysis: This technique divides complex tasks into smaller, more manageable units, which are combined to make all actions and occurrences accessible. This strategy establishes a system and user roles hierarchy and the necessary skills. In addition to contextualizing the tasks, task analysis (Goguen & Linden, 1993) provides information on the user-system communications during the tasks. Due to the time and effort required to conduct extensive job research, choosing when and in what depth to evaluate key work components is crucial.

3. Questionnaires/Surveys: The initial stages of needs elicitation utilize questionnaires with both open-ended and closed-ended questions. Participants and the questionnaire author must specify and comprehend the concepts, ideas, and restrictions for the domain to be applicable. Focused questions are required to prevent the collection of copious amounts of redundant and unnecessary data. These are quick and straightforward methods for gathering information from many stakeholders, but the amount of information they can elicit is limited (Goguen & Linde, 1993).

4. Domain Analysis: Examining necessary, up-to-date documentation and applications, analyzing and assembling pertinent data, and identifying instances of reusable concepts and components can help build early needs. Documentation such as design reports, user manuals, printed copy structures, and files used in current business activities may be helpful in gathering requirements. Monitoring at upstream and downstream systems and harsh or comparable settings are common application themes (Goguen & Linde, 1993). Domain information, such as precise representations and models, can substantially impact the time required to elicit needs. Based on these findings, supplementary elicitation techniques and approaches are commonly applied (Sutcliffe & Maiden, 1998).

5. Introspection: The analyst must build system requirements based on what he or she believes the users and other stakeholders desire and want from the system (Goguen & Linde, 1993). Introspection is merely the first step in many elicitation endeavors. Introspection can only be entirely successful if the analyst is honest, like the framework's domain, focused, and aware of the client's professional measures (Carrizo, Dieste, & Juristo, 2014). Alternative elicitation techniques, such as protocol analysis and interviews, can be used alternatively when the investigator must use the Introspection strategy regularly. This strategy can be effectively used when the clients have limited knowledge of software systems employed at their work place.

6. Repertory grids: With repertory grids, stakeholders must develop and apply qualities to domain objects (Richardson et al., 1998). The structure can be shown as a grid by organizing the system segments, searching for occurrences of specific ordering, and giving appropriate values to each factor, despite the importance of recognizing and accounting for the similarities and differences across the different domain entities.

7. Card Sorting: Using their understanding of card sorting, stakeholders must categorize a collection of cards with the names of domain entities. In addition, the stakeholder must justify the card arrangement. To ensure the success of the card-sorting procedure, all parties must participate (Goguen & Linde, 1993). It is only achievable if the participants and the analyst possess subject-matter expertise. If the domain is unknown, a group can locate the objects (Nawaz, 2012). Card sorting approaches, such as CRC (Class Responsibility Collaboration) cards, can be utilized to discover

programmed classes in software codes. These cards are used to assign jobs to system components and persons.

8. Laddering: Laddering is a strategy for eliciting stakeholders' objectives, principles, and characteristics through an interview. Consumers are initially questioned about the product's essential characteristics. The interviewer uses his skills and other defining characteristics to elicit additional information about the customer's preferences. Due to their relative significance, the questions and answers are organized hierarchically. Using a tool and hiring a specialist are both viable options. Due to the substantial limitations, changes (such as additions/deletions) are challenging to implement at any level of the hierarchy. After a series of quick probing questions, stakeholders are invited to organize their responses via the laddering technique (Corbridge et al., 1994).

9. Group work: is prevalent and commonly utilized as a typical technique for achieving objectives (Aurum & Wohlin, 2005). Groups are convincing because they include, present, and encourage the engagement of all stakeholders. These activities are challenging to organize due to a large number of participants in each activity. A professional must monitor these sessions to guarantee that participants with diverse personalities can engage equally. Individual appeal and group cohesion substantially affect a group's efficiency (Karn et al., 2007).

10. Brainstorming: Participants from various stakeholder groups collaborate during an unstructured dialogue known as brainstorming (Paetsch et al., 2003) to produce as many ideas as possible without focusing on a single individual. It is essential to avoid in-depth inquiry or examination of concepts during this group exercise. This technique is typically employed to establish the initial mission statements for the project and target system. One advantage of brainstorming is that it stimulates independent thought and expression and generates innovative answers to problems. (Vieira et al., 2012).

11. Requirements Workshops: The phrase "requirements workshop" refers to a sequence of collaborative activities to identify and generate new software requirements. (Schalken & Van Vliet, 2004). Innovations that promote research are examples of requirements workshops. These include a multitude of players from various business industries. Focus Groups are an indispensable component of market research (Reed & Payton, 1997).

12. Joint Application Development (JAD): JAD has engaged all possible stakeholders in comprehensively discussing the issue and its solutions. (Liou & Chen, 1993). When all participants are present, the order can be maintained successfully, and problems can be resolved effectively. The primary distinction between JAD and brainstorming is that the system's objectives are determined before stakeholders are involved in JAD. JAD sessions include tasks, processes, and individual responsibilities organized and spelled out in writing (including concern specialists). The JAD conference focuses more on business-related than technical concerns.

13. Ethnography: This method helps analysts to collect relevant data while analyzing the behaviors of individuals of diverse cultures. This type of fieldwork requires observing a particular workplace, its personnel, and its interactions. The analyst immerses himself in the socio-organizational milieu to comprehend its needs (Richardson et al., 1998). Ethnography can be combined with other elicitation techniques, such as surveys and interviews, to collect detailed stakeholder responses (Goguen & Linde, 1993).

14. Observation: Observation is one sort of anthropological methodology (Richardson et al., 1998). Uninterrupted, an analyst observes a user's workspace. This approach is applied to maintain track of the project when the client cannot describe the project or the procedure is challenging to compre-

hend. Techniques such as task analysis and interviews are used in conjunction with it. Observational data should be uniquely identified to avoid confusion among analysts. It employs several methods, such as prototypes, interviews, and perspectives (Polyakov et al., 2013).

15. Protocol Analysis: Protocol analysis is doing an operation or task while defining the steps completed when employing the approach directly below them (Afflerbach, 2000; Alam et al., 2019a). This technique can provide comprehensive information and assist the analyst in completing the activities required by the goal system (Hernán & Robins, 2017). Due to the unique nature of speaking via action to complete a task, the confirmed relationship may not be addressed entirely or precisely.

16. *Apprenticing*: According to this method, the analyst instructs and executes process-related tasks under the supervision and direction of an expert (Beyer & Holtzblatt, 1995). Like protocol analysis, the analyst configures operational and financial indicators through observation, request, and execution. When the analyst is unfamiliar with the system's domain, and the user has difficulty describing their actions, it works effectively in both instances (Fuller & Davis, 2017). The emersion technique promotes this strategy by ensuring the expert is adequately involved in the business's operations.

17. Prototyping: It is appropriate to present prototypes of probable research solutions to stakeholders to collect comprehensive data and vital feedback. JAD and interviews are employed in addition to prototyping as elicitation tools. Prototypes are created using early specifications or examples of relevant technologies. This strategy is effective when designing human-computer interfaces or when stakeholders are uncertain about the current solution. Paper, evolutionary systems, throwaway, executable, storyboard, and paper prototypes are among the several prototyping methodologies accessible. Several levels of effort are required for each type (Jakkaew & Hongthong, 2017). The construction of models is a costly and time-consuming endeavor. This strategy has the advantage of allowing users to contribute to the development of requirements actively.

18. Goal-based approach: In the goal-based approach technique, high-level objectives that address system destinations are broken down into sub-objectives, which are then adjusted utilizing techniques such as AND connections and "Why" and "How" addressing to elicit specific requirements (Garg, Agarwal, & Khan, 2015). This technique can make it challenging to monitor goal modifications, and early errors in the system's high-level objectives might have a significant detrimental impact. Recent efforts to develop similar demand elicitation systems include the F3 project, the knowledge acquisition in automated specification meta-model, and the I framework. (Yu, 1997). (Dardenne et al., 1993; Bubenko & Wangler, 1993). Utilizing scenario-related objectives to evaluate requirements has also garnered significant interest.

19. Scenarios: Scenarios are detailed descriptions of how users interact with new and existing system operations to collect requirements (Kausar, Tariq, Riaz, & Khanum, 2010). Similar to use cases, scenarios disregard the system's underlying architecture, necessitating an inclusive and progressive development strategy (Du, Wang, & Feng, 2014; Khan et al., 2022). When utilizing scenarios, collecting all exceptions for each phase is usually a good idea (Alam, Khusro, & Khan, 2021; Jarke, 1999; Mishra, Mishra, & Yazici, 2008) illustrations of cooperative requirements engineering. The Inquiry Cycle, Scenario Plus, and system engineering are examples of systematic and exact elicitation approaches created by academic and industrial research organizations. Similar to how the construction of test cases helps understand and validate requirements, so are scenarios.

20. Viewpoints: Viewpoint approaches examine the domain from multiple vantage points to get an aggregate and constant of the planned system. One can, for instance, specify a system's operation,

implementation, and interfaces. The system can be seen from the perspectives of several customers or an existing system. Prioritizing needs and assisting the organization are two benefits of perspectives (Sohaib & Khan, 2010). It is expensive and challenging to describe non-functional requirements using this method. The multiperspective nature of Viewpoints enables them to elicit demands from a variety of sources (Van et al., 2012).

21. Functional Resonance Analysis Method (FRAM): FRAM is a systemic analysis-based tool for characterizing the processes of an extensive socio-technical system. (Erik, 2017). Applications for FRAM retrospective analysis identify any potential systemic issues or fundamental underpinnings of a specific work topic (Patriarca et al., 2020). FRAM requires more effort from the analyst to elicit requirements than conventional techniques such as interviews, observation, group work, and task analysis (Patriarca, Di Gravio, & Costantino, 2017). The main purpose is to attain more profound information on variability and how it might facilitate the specification and elicitation of requirements in complex socio-technical systems, such as building maintenance (Tian, Wu, Yang, & Zhao, 2016).

22. Contextually Adaptive (ACon): ACon is a data-mining method for addressing runtime uncertainty affecting contextual requirements (Carrizo, Dieste, & Juristo, 2017). Self-adaptive systems can respond instantaneously to alterations in user requirements, resource variations, and system faults (Cheng et al., 2014). Based on the most recent context data, a uses feedback loops to remain current on contextual requirements and how runtime uncertainty affects them. Adaptive systems do not, however, exist in a vacuum (Muoz-Fernández et al., 2018; Knauss et al., 2016). ACon examines and mines contextual data to (re-)operationalize context (Rodrigues et al., 2018). Thus, the comprehension of contextual requirements is updated (Zavala et al., 2015).

23. Quality Function Deployment (QFD): Throughout the product development process, QFD is a rigorous procedure for delivering product features based on customer feedback (Karlsson, 1997). It provides a reliable mechanism for evaluating customer feedback's effectiveness and ensuring product functionality's consistency and completeness to developers (Palomares et al., 2021; Khusro et al., 2018; Sousa-Zomer & Miguel, 2017). QFD has numerous advantages, including a more effective way of prioritizing and expressing software requirements, a stronger emphasis on customers and users, and handling non-functional requirements (Wu & Shieh, 2010).

24. *External Consultancy*: Involving requirements consultants enables businesses to discover and disclose the necessary and sufficient software and business needs for initiatives (Trujillo & Buzzi, 2016; Renault et al., 2009). A facilitator could manage the meeting, while a professional requirements consultant could provide the documentation, analysis, and validation activities during and following each session. *External Consultancy* would ensure that all specifications and models are precise, unambiguous, and complete (Santoro et al., 2000; Davey & Cope, 2009).

25. Ontologies: Ontologies have been utilized for many purposes, such as the development of a shared vocabulary in the field of requirements engineering (Aranda et al., 2008), the comprehension of a problem domain (Lefaix-Durand & Kozak, 2010), the restructuring and reuse of knowledge (Girardi & Leite, 2008), and the analysis of language expressivity ((Kilov & Sack, 2009). These methods are called requirement elicitation tactics (Valaski et al., 2014; Herlocker et al., 2004).

26. Business Process Model (BPM): These models gather requirements (Monsalve et al., 2012). BPM is used to evaluate the expressiveness of business process modeling notations. A business process model was created using Software Engineering Body of Knowledge (SWEBOK) and Business Analysis Body of Knowledge analyses (BABOK). The proposals are then validated by specialists

in business process visualization and software requirement elicitation (Sosnowski, Bereza, & Ng, 2021). (Ordóez et al., 2015) The method includes determining the requirements of an extensive software system that must be purchased based on the company's goals and underlying business processes.

27. Mind Mapping: Mind maps explain the authors' existing study technique conception (Crowe & Sheppard, 2012). Instead of offering a comprehensive picture of research issues, study design, sampling tactics, ethical considerations, data collection, data processing, and reporting findings, the fundamental parts of research operations are divided into seven categories (Mahmud & Veneziano, 2011). Even though selections made in one area of research may impact other areas, the mind maps exhibit no predetermined relationship between different areas (Liu, Tong, & Yang, 2018). They can teach, oversee, and outline research methodology issues, perhaps resulting in a complete study (Buran & Filyukov, 2015).

28. *Storytelling:* Everyone comprehends the logical structure of Storytelling (Boulila et al., 2011). When the system's activities are compared to a comprehensible narrative, information collecting and articulating needs increase rapidly (Derrick et al., 2013). Tales give life to the criteria that would otherwise be difficult to record or follow and could be overlooked (Gausepohl et al., 2016).

29. Ethnomethodology: Ethnomethodology explores how social interaction processes establish and preserve social order (Goguen and Linde, 1993). (Alam, Khusro, Rauf, & Zaman, 2014; Rouncefield, 2011). Incorporating critical infrastructures into a research environment and employing ethnomethodology as a technique for requirement elicitation has made it vital to appreciate knowledge and abilities. It is investigated by researchers in numerous fields (Elsey, 2021; Derrick et al., 2013).

30. Clear Language for Expressing Ordering (CLEO): The CLEO method is a revolutionary preference elicitation tool capable of recommending complicated configurable objects with preset discrete and continuous features and restrictions. (Campigotto et al. 2021). CLEO provides a practical approach to a suggestion by interactively optimizing the space of possible configurations in Hybrid domains (i.e., those with Boolean and numeric properties) while retaining uncertainty in the decision-utility maker and noisy feedback. (Franzle et al., 2006; Alam et al. 2019b;). Only one expert is knowledgeable about the selected system. It solicits preferences using the freshly developed learning modulo theory paradigm.

31. For CrowdRE research, prototypes are readily available. There are more ways to obtain feedback besides simply asking for it. However, development teams will specifically solicit user feedback. In contrast to monitoring, which provides crucial information on runtime events, online feedback systems allow end users to share their issues, experiences, and views. By merging the two data sources, requirement engineers acquired a deeper insight into end-user requirements (Oriol et al., 2018).

32. Gamification: A game-based environment will promote client inclusion in non-gaming scenarios (Ribeiro, Farinha, Pereira, & da Silva, 2014). Using gaming concepts in instances other than that video games has been proven to b Gamification is utilized in projects such as iThink and Architect's Use Case Diagram (AUCD) to accomplish benefits such as stakeholder communication, team conflict resolution, higher-quality requirements, and participants who are more adept at prioritizing.

THEORETICAL ANALYSIS OF ELICITATION TECHNIQUES

The quality of the need reflects the success of elicitation techniques. As a result, the requirement engineer can select the most suitable techniques for the developing project. A critical study of the methodologies is shown in Table 1.

Table 1. Privacy perspectives of elicitation techniques

Technique	Privacy Leakages	
	Protecting	RRemarks
Interview	×	Interview norms vary from person to person, especially in the case of a formal interview. The interviewee must have complete knowledge of the interviewer.
Repertory Grids	×	Due to the unfamiliarity of the technique, all parties concerned must confer with one another. As a result of the difficulties in comprehending the abstraction
Card Sorting	×	Confidentiality might be challenging to preserve because all parties are required to justify why they make specific card arrangements.
Questionnaires	√	No personal questions (such as name etc.) are requested in the surveys.
Group Work	×	Groups of stakeholders are asked to participate in the effort. When membership increases, the secret will become challenging to control.
Laddering	√	The questions answered in the laddering are exploratory; therefore, personal information such as the interview is redundant.
Brainstorming	√	History or Personal information of the participants is not required, as they are needed to provide unconventional suggestions.
Task Analysis	×	A hierarchy of system and user responsibilities and the requisite expertise.
JAD	√	Individual responsibilities are assigned to each user
Requirements for Workshops	×	All participants should work together in the workshop.
Domain Analysis	√	Study of the area where the proposed project would be carried out.
Introspection	√	There is no consultation needed for the user.
Apprenticing	×	No privacy since the analyst and expert would need all information about the expert to master the system.
Ethnography	×	Ethnography necessitates monitoring users at work; therefore, there is no privacy.
Observation	×	Ethnography like technique
Protocol Analysis	×	It is a method in which duties are completed in public with no privacy.
Scenarios	√	Sometimes it is challenging to turn situations into needs, notably functional and non-functional requirements.
Goal-Based Approaches	√	If the analyst is incompetent, they will encounter even more difficulties if the goals are unclear.
Prototyping	√	Users are only involved in requirement validation.
FARM	—	Need a specialized analyst, and only particular systems may utilize it.
Viewpoints	×	The perspective may be prejudiced.
ACon	—	Require an expert analyzer.
External Consultancy	×	Finding professional consultations is tough.
QFD	√	The development outlook is quite promising. However, the product appears to be deficient.
Ontologies	√	This method is always effective in tandem.

continues on following page

Table 1. Continued

Technique	Privacy Leakages	
	Protecting	**RRemarks**
Business Process Model	√	The business model should be carefully described for usage in the requirement.
Mind Mapping	√	It is an intriguing method for creative analysts to acquire requirement specifications.
Storytelling	×	Analyst occasionally struggles to convert the need.
Ethnomethodology	×	It is a highly participatory method, and sometimes the data gathered through social contact is meaningless.
Feedback	×	Depending on the response. Feedback can be anonymous. However, feedback that is not anonymous is treated more seriously.
CLEO	—	It is a highly specialized project, such as an adaptable project.
Gamification	√	Every project requires analysts to create a new game.

Interviews are predominantly interpersonal activities. Bringing together all parties for an interview is a difficult task. The abilities of the interviewer determine the quality of the information obtained. Throughout the interviewing process, respondents may be affected by prejudice. Clarification of information may demand follow-ups, during which participants may not recall information accurately (Goguen & Linde, 1993). (Index, 1995).

Repertory Grids involve requesting stakeholders to construct characteristics for a group of domain entities and assigning values to those qualities. The followings are the advantages and disadvantages of repertory grids. The risk perspectives of elicitation strategies are displayed in Table 2. It is a time-intensive method. A user must be an expert to employ this strategy. Both specialists and analysts must invest a great deal of effort and time.

Group Work: Group work can be an effective way for stakeholders to collaborate and achieve a common goal. By working together, stakeholders can share their knowledge, skills, and perspectives and use these to develop innovative solutions to complex problems. Group work can lead to better decision-making, increased creativity, and improved overall outcomes. Group work can also be more efficient and cost-effective than other methods of gathering information, such as individual interviews. We can quickly gather a large amount of information by working with a group of stakeholders at once. It can help us meet quality requirements quickly and at a lower cost. There may be complications when addressing delicate concerns if there is a possibility of trust issues among participants. The outcome may favour the room's dominant individual.

Task analysis is a technique that can be used to break down complex activities into smaller, more manageable sub-tasks. It can help identify the specific actions and events that comprise a more extensive process and the expertise and resources required to perform them. Task analysis can help establish a clear user and system duties hierarchy by dividing activities into smaller sub-tasks. It can also help identify the roles and responsibilities of different stakeholders and ensure that each task is assigned to the most appropriate individual or system. Task analysis can also simplify complex activities, making them easier to understand and perform. Breaking down tasks into smaller steps can help identify potential areas of confusion or difficulty and allow for improvements to be made to the overall process. Another benefit of task analysis is that it can help minimize redoing work. Identifying potential issues and areas for improvement early on in the process can help prevent errors and delays further down the line. Task analysis can also be used to enhance and improve existing systems.

Table 2. Risk perspectives of elicitation techniques

Technique	From Risk Perspectives		
	Time-Consuming	Costly	Remarks
Interview	×	×	The interview is inexpensive and quick compared to other methods.
Repertory Grids	√	√	More expensive, laborious, and time work consuming.
Card Sorting	√	√	Similar to repertory girds, but more time-consuming because they must additionally describe their unique card layout.
Questionnaires	×	×	Questionnaires are the most efficient method for quickly gathering requirements from a broad group.
Laddering	√	×	It is more expensive than an interview since a hierarchy of priority is established once an analyst conducts an interview. Automatic tools expedite the process.
Group Work	×	×	Group work can only be successful if everyone completes their assigned tasks on time.
Task Analysis	√	×	Work gets simpler when conducting a task analysis, but dividing large jobs into smaller ones takes more time.
Brainstorming	×	×	If not strictly moderated, brainstorming sessions can be drawn out and ineffective.
JAD	×	×	The presence of the customer facilitates the collection of necessities.
Domain Analysis	√	×	Expensive as studying the subject is time-consuming.
Ethnography	√	√	Observing the environment is a time-consuming job.
Requirements for Workshops	×	√	Requirement gathering is quick, but organizing a workshop could be expensive.
Introspection	×	×	It requires no time and is inexpensive but carries a significant danger. What if analyst assumptions are incorrect? The entire project would be flawed.
Observation	√	√	Observation takes time to gather requirements, which might be expensive.
Protocol Analysis	√	√	It is time-consuming, making it expensive.
Apprenticing	√	√	It takes considerable time and money to instruct analysts on their processes and oversee their use of them.
Prototyping	√	√	This technique is time-consuming and expensive, depending on rework and the sort of prototypes the analyst employs.
Goal-Based Approaches	√	×	Requirements extraction may be challenging, but it could be cheap if the technology is accessible.
Scenarios	√	√	Rework makes the scenarios expensive and time-consuming.
Viewpoints	√	√	The perspective may be uncertain, which may be pertinent.
FARM	×	√	Obtaining requirements from FRAM requires no additional time. System analysis can be expensive due to the enormous social-technical system involved.
ACon	×	√	Expensive due to the system's adaptability, expert opinion can be expensive
External Consultancy	×	√	While the presence of customers expedites the process,
QFD	√	×	Ontology creation is time-consuming and expensive.
Ontologies	×	×	Not expensive if the business process model is comprehensive.
Business Process Model	×	×	Mind maps are created meticulously and with great attention to detail, which is time-consuming and costly.

continues on following page

Table 2. Continued

Technique	From Risk Perspectives		
	Time-Consuming	**Costly**	**Remarks**
Mind Mapping	√	√	Rework makes it an expenditure
Storytelling	×	√	Social environment analysis is a highly time-consuming activity.
Ethnomethodology	×	×	Feedback collection can be pricey.
Feedback	×	√	This algorithm is difficult to implement.
CLEO	×	×	Collecting game requirements is quicker than making a game.
Gamification	×	×	Compared to other methods, it is inexpensive and quick.

Table 3. From usage perspectives

Technique	Advantages from usage perspectives					
	Easy	**Ambiguous**	**Comprehensiveness**	**Feasible for small projects**	**Repetition**	**Remarks**
Interview	√	√	√	√	√	That is simple and the most prevalent usage. The challenging aspect is establishing adequate interview standards
Card Sorting	×	×	×	×	√	Need expertise on both sides
Repertory Grids	×	×	×	×	×	Need expertise
Laddering	×	√	×	√	×	User involvement makes it difficult
Questionnaires	×	√	√	×	×	Simple to use and effective in case of appropriate questions.
Task Analysis	×	√	√	×	×	Reducing requirements into ever-smaller tasks is simple, but analysts must be mindful of coherence and coupling.
Group Work	×	×	√	√	√	Very successful when every group member works honestly.
JAD	√	×	×	√	×	Availability of Customers is always an issue
Brainstorming	√	×	√	×	×	The primary objective is to generate concepts without providing specifics. If any preceding points are invalid, that is not a thing.
Requirements for Workshops	×	√	√	×	×	Rearrangement of workshops is complicated sometimes
Domain Analysis	√	×	√	×	×	In case of non-availability of documentation
Introspection	√	×	√	√	√	The user's input will be omitted if an analyst relies solely on this method.
Ethnography	√	√	√	×	×	Simple to apply but challenges requirement collection as requirements are collected by observing the organization's social circle. It is not repetitive because altering the entire organizational environment is challenging.
Protocol Analysis	√	√	×	×	×	When a person does a task while describing it verbally, the distinction between them can be unclear.

continues on following page

Table 3. Continued

Technique	Advantages from usage perspectives					
	Easy	Ambiguous	Comprehensiveness	Feasible for small projects	Repetition	Remarks
Observation	√	×	√	×	√	It is simple to implement, contains no ambiguity, and is extremely thorough. It is only suitable for little projects because it can be time-consuming and repetitious.
Prototyping	√	√	√	×	√	Due to the repetitive nature of prototyping, it cannot be used for small projects.
Apprenticing	√	√	√	×	×	Not feasible for small projects, as training and monitoring analyst performance wastes time.
Scenarios	√	√	×	×	√	When users have explicit scenarios/visions for their project, scenario planning can be a successful strategy. Ambiguous scenarios cause confusion.
Goal-Based Approaches	×	√	×	×	×	The small organization y finds it challenging to gather requirements and establish objectives. Typically, a small project has no goal or a very general goal.
FARM	×	×	√	×	√	The expert needs to implement the FARM technique.
Viewpoints	√	√	×	×	×	Individuals can have various perspectives, which may lead to uncertainty and confusion regarding the requirements.
External Consultancy	×	×	×	×	√	A professional perspective can be beneficial. However, the major drawback is that finding an appropriate expert may require more consultation.
ACon	×	√	×	×	×	The expert needs to implement the technique
Ontologies	×	×	×	×	×	Creating ontologies can be challenging. This method usually works with other methods.
QFD	×	×	×	√	×	Obtaining quality criteria on the initial attempt can be challenging.
Mind Mapping	×	×	×	√	×	A higher risk factor, even a tiny error, can result in a significant issue.
Business Process Model	×	×	×	√	×	Understanding the business process model itself is challenging and might be confusing if it is not correctly stated.
Ethnomethodology	×	×	×	×	×	This technique is typically not very useful in the near term, but it can be pretty beneficial to research in the long term.
Storytelling	√	√	√	√	√	Due to the repetitive nature, ambiguity is possible. Because a second telling of a story might alter it
CLEO	×	×	×	×	×	Its specific algorithm
Feedback	√	√	×	√	√	Fewer feedback percentages are beneficial. More distinct feedback can increase ambiguity.
Gamification	×	×	×	×	√	Specific project

Analyzing the tasks that make up a process can help identify opportunities for automation or other process improvements. Task analysis can help determine the competencies and assets required to complete a project. Breaking down tasks into smaller sub-tasks can help identify the specific skills and resources needed to perform each task and ensure these are in place before work begins. (Bartlett & Toms, 2005). Depending on the level of deconstruction, the resulting data will be either comprehensive or rudimentary. With many participants, the task would be time-consuming. Moreover, data analysis could be challenging depending on the task analysis approach (hierarchical or cognitive).

Brainstorming is a method used to generate as many ideas as possible in a short amount of time. It is typically done in an informal, collaborative setting and involves stakeholders from diverse backgrounds and perspectives. One of the main benefits of brainstorming is its cost-effectiveness and minimal resource requirements. All that is needed is a group of stakeholders and a location for meeting. Brainstorming makes it an accessible technique for organizations with limited budgets or resources. Brainstorming encourages creativity and innovation by allowing stakeholders to express their ideas without fear of criticism or judgment freely. Encouraging various perspectives and ideas can lead to unique and novel solutions to complex problems. Each participant actively contributes to the procedure without requiring a high degree of qualification. Brainstorming facilitates the production of innovative concepts and facilitates the settlement of disputes. (Vieira et al., 2012). (Paetsch et al., 2003). It is unfit for addressing significant challenges. If not appropriately structured, time-consuming. Not often is the quantity of ideas indicative of their quality. If individuals are not paying close enough attention, ideas may be repeated. Introverts may struggle to participate in group talks due to their shyness.

JAD: In JAD, all parties will engage in an open discussion to evaluate the problems and their potential solutions. Decisions may be taken quickly when all parties are involved, and issues can be resolved without delay (Liou & Chen, 1993). JAD accelerates system design, quickly producing innovative ideas resulting in creative success. The workshop is interactive due to visual aids and case studies. Different perspectives within the team make staying focused on the objectives challenging. Time and money may be wasted without proper planning. Facilitators need training. Depending on the nature of the task, time efficiency may vary. JAD is only effective and fruitful if all parties are fully dedicated.

Domain Analysis: Examining current and relevant documentation and applications efficiently gather early requirements, comprehends and records domain knowledge, and discovers reusable concepts and components. In the absence of users and stakeholders, useful. Before engaging with stakeholders, assists business analysts in gaining a full grasp of the firm. It provides essential historical data, which helps construct interview questions. It allows prerequisites to be reused. It is a cost-effective technique (Sutcliffe & Maiden, 1998). (Goguen & Linden, 1993). Getting information from many documents involves a substantial amount of time. Pertinent information may be inaccessible in certain circumstances, such as outdated documents. Documentation must be updated periodically. If not, information or data may be missing or inaccurate (Rao, 2008).

A workshop is a group meeting focusing on creating and identifying software system requirements. Get superior criteria in less time. It is less expensive than doing individual interviews. Feedback is simple to receive. It helps stakeholders and analysts in developing confidence and understanding. In the workshop, participants collaborate to specify particular criteria. However, bringing the stakeholders and professionals together at the same table is a challenging task. Sometimes the workshop may be concluded with a comprehensive set of user requirements. However, it is usually concluded with partial criteria set of user requirements (Reed & Payton, 1997).

Analysts use ethnography to explore in-depth the behaviors of people from various cultures while collecting crucial data. It accelerates the process of identifying some aspects of a workplace. Facilitates comprehension of how people function and communicate inside an organization. Effectiveness requires limited resources. Contributes to the detection of important events that could otherwise go missed. Useful for ensuring that prerequisites are satisfied (Goguen & Linde, 1993). It depends solely on the ethnographer's skill, as there is no formal teaching on appropriately executing the ethnographic method. Engineers must have a great deal of experience to accomplish this. Unique and novel additions to the system may go unnoticed. Its diversified population prevents it from producing ideal results. It focuses primarily on end-users and is occasionally time-consuming. Diverse backgrounds among users and ethnographers may lead to communication issues (Richardson et al., 1998).

Using introspection, an analyst must develop system requirements based on what he/she believes stakeholders and users want from the system. Practically no expenses are associated with employing this method. Ethnography is an essential step to accomplish, and It might be an excellent step for gathering requirements (Carrizo et al., 2014). It is challenging for analysts to visualize the system's operational environment. It restricts stakeholder and other professional participation in discussions. Thus, it is only recommended when other tactics are used. Analysts and stakeholders must know the domain.

The analyst monitors the actual execution of current procedures by users without interfering. As the analyst evaluates the environment independently, it is authentic and believable. It is an efficient way of confirming and validating requirements collected through other means. The technique is economical from a financial standpoint. Provides a notion of how system users will interact. (Afflerbach, 2000). It may need many sessions to meet all the requirements, and a single session will not be enough (Richardson et al., 1998). Under active surveillance, users can act as they see fit when queries stop them. Passive observation makes it more difficult for analysts to determine why certain conclusions are made. It also requires a significant amount of time (Polyakov et al., 2013).

Protocol analysis is defined by Hernán and Robins (2017) as the execution of an activity or task while speaking aloud and discussing the underlying technological acts. Less expensive in terms of budget. No special equipment is necessary. This strategy can be pretty efficient for obtaining specific information. It illustrates the working of the system in real-time. It is very simple to implement, but it is ineffective for small projects. Moreover, users' absence may postpone the project and cause workplace disruptions (Beyer & Holtzblatt, 1995).

Apprenticeship: During the apprenticeship, the analyst instructs and does sub-process tasks under the guidance of an expert. It offers advantages that other data collection methods lack. Observing participant behavior can reveal attitude shifts. Participant observation produces information with a predictive element (Fuller & Davis, 2017). Participant observation poses a significant threat of adding bias to data entry. Participant strongly relies on the seasoned user's expertise. In most instances, the expert lacks time to train the analyst. It demanded extra time and effort (Jakkaew & Hongthong, 2017).

Prototyping: Presenting stakeholders with a solid foundation to examine prospective solutions is an effective way to collect thorough information and relevant input. Usually, prototypes are created under preliminary specifications or existing examples of comparable systems user participation in the design process. Early input from users can benefit the revision of criteria, reduces the time and expense required for the development. Analysts and users better comprehend the system (Garg et al., 2015). As consumers become accustomed to a system, they often resist change. According to previous estimations, estimated effort and costs may be excessive. Complex systems can be time-consuming to study.

Goal-based approach: Goal-based approaches and high-level system objectives are broken down into smaller sub-goals, then refined and elaborated upon until specific requirements are identified. This process can help establish connections between system objectives, domain objects, and requirements. One benefit of goal-based approaches is that they can help improve learning outcomes by allowing stakeholders to identify and address their knowledge gaps and deficiencies. By setting clear learning goals, stakeholders can track their progress and identify areas where they need additional support or practice. This strategy can help create a more self-directed learning experience and foster a sense of ownership and responsibility for one's learning.

Additionally, goal-based approach can enable individuals to receive consistent, constructive feedback, which can help them continue to develop and improve. By setting clear goals and objectives, individuals can receive specific, actionable, and focused feedback on their performance relative to their goals. The goal-based approaches can help create a more supportive learning environment and improve motivation and engagement. Goal-based approaches can effectively structure learning and development activities and improve performance and outcomes in other areas, such as system design and requirements engineering. Breaking down complex objectives into smaller, more manageable goals can help ensure everyone is aligned and working towards a shared vision while providing continuous learning and improvement opportunities. (Dardenne et al., 1993). (Bubenko & Wangler, 1993).

Scenarios: For requirements elicitation, a scenario is a detailed description of a specific interaction between the system and users and can be used to explore existing and new system operations. It is understandable by anyone with a user who does not have technological knowledge. They are simple to understand because they are written in natural languages. It contributes to the system's correct design by eliciting end-user requirements (Du et al., 2014). Building plausible scenarios requirement elicitation is a challenging task. Although it covers more criteria, it is still inappropriate for all projects. These do not entirely portray the future system, as they do not include all processes (Ram et al., 2011).

Viewpoints: Viewpoint approaches represent the domain from different perspectives to get a thorough and reliable sketch of the target system. Likewise, systems may be depicted from the perspective of several users or interconnected systems. Managing the massive amount of acquired data and prioritizing needs is difficult. If the description of a viewpoint in the proposed model is insufficiently broad, it will fail to account for all possible stakeholder and domain views. Frequently, suppliers of requirements lack the means or time to define needs in a manner other than their standard working notations (Van Heesch et al., 2012).

FRAM method is used to illustrate the activities of a complex socio-technical system. Instead of constructing a sequential cause-and-effect model of events over time, the FARM method considers system performance's non-linear nature (Erik, 2017). FARM emphasizes a broader view of socio-technical systems instead of a narrow perspective. It can reproduce any performance assessment activity, including itself (FRAM model). The FRAM is more concerned with the possibility of function variation than with the likelihood of failure or malfunction. It demands significant effort and is difficult to comprehend (Tian et al., 2016). (Patriarca et al., 2017).

ACon: ACon is an approach to requirements engineering that uses feedback loops to ensure that the system remains current with contextual requirements, even when runtime uncertainty affects those requirements. The basic idea behind ACon is to use feedback from the system's context to continuously monitor and adapt the system's behavior to changing requirements. It involves capturing contextual information about the user, the environment, and other relevant factors and adjusting the system's behavior and outputs. One of the critical benefits of ACon is its ability to adapt to changing requirements and contexts in real-time, which can help improve system performance, usability, and user satisfaction. By continuously monitoring and adapting to the user's needs and preferences. Moreover, it can create a more personalized and tailored user experience. However, implementing ACon can pose several challenges, such as ensuring the system can access accurate and relevant contextual information and managing the complexity of the feedback loops and adaptation mechanisms. Additionally, ensuring the system remains secure and compliant with relevant regulations and standards can be a significant challenge in adaptive systems. (Carrizo et al., 2017). ACon reduces data duplication and increases efficiency. Managing uncertainty affecting contextual runtime requirements while considering user input is vital. Furthermore, it can support systems in evaluating the environment to adapt to contextual requirements, and it augments earlier strategies for requirements monitoring by retaining the requirements monitoring specification. Hence, it reduces the time and cost associated with manual analysis, which is common in complex system contexts nowadays (Knauss et al., 2016). (Cheng et al., 2014). Its implementation does not require reasonable cost and time limitations. At the beginning of a project, developers cannot decide whether or not it is worthwhile of utilization. It requires analysts with methodological expertise (Zavala et al., 2015; Muoz-Fernández et al., 2018).

External Consultancy: Requirements Companies retain consultants for requirements elicitation sessions in which they quickly discover and report the critical and sufficient software and business requirements for the assigned projects. The external consultants have extensive professional experience in resolving similar problems in various sectors (Renault et al., 2009). Problem-solving fosters divergent and convergent cognitive processes. Their constant training may give them a better grasp of the modern, sophisticated problem-solving method (Trujillo & Buzzi, 2016). Using external advisors is often expensive. It took longer to comprehend the organization's structure and function and they are temporarily affiliated with the project (Santoro et al., 2000; Davey & Cope, 2009).

Ontologies are domain-specific frameworks that describe common and reusable knowledge. They serve as the foundation for modelling linked, high-quality, and coherent data due to their ability to describe high interconnectivity and relationships (Aranda et al., 2008). The ontological knowledge can be used to reorganize and reuse information in different secanrios. The study of the expressiveness of the language and accurate representation of the domain in the real world. Improve communications between specialists from diverse domains (Monsalve et al., 2012; Girardi & Leite, 2008). It is challenging to convert specific knowledge into ontologies. Several ontological languages exist. There are different ways to depict synonymy, which can lead to ambiguity and confusion (Zhang et al., 2007; Harzallah et al., 2012).

QFD is a way of implementing product functionality from the customer's standpoint. It provides a reliable mechanism for developers to assess client feedback's efficacy and confirm product features' consistency, completeness and improved communication among stakeholders (Karlsson, 1997). A more efficient way to prioritize requirements (Sousa-Zomer & Miguel, 2017; Palomares et al., 2021). It is challenging to distinguish between different and contradictory consumer expectations. Client unavailability may create difficulty. It may be challenging to bridge the divide between client and technical requirements. Developing and evaluating complicated matrices and analyses requires considerable time and effort (Wu & Shieh, 2010).

Creating a high-quality business process model is vital as the quality of the requirement specification decides the quality of the software. BPM assesses the expressiveness of business process modeling notations and aligns efforts with the company's central strategy (Monsalve et al., 2012). Improve communication during the entirety of the procedure. Enhance operational effectiveness. The potential for overanalysis. Probability of misinterpreting business objectives. Analysts have a limited amount of time to examine business process models.

Mind Mapping: A mind map helps represent project requirements graphically. It is a visual representation of the project's requirements. (Sosnowski et al., 2021; Ordóez et al., 2015). A mind map is a hierarchical graph of thinking and ideas demonstrating the connection between project components (Crowe & Sheppard, 2012). It facilitates the visualization of complex problems to simplify their understanding. It increases productivity. It encourages creativity (Mahmud & Veneziano, 2011; Liu et al., 2018). It might be challenging to differentiate between opinions and facts. Using mapped notes with other techniques, such as the Cornell or outline method, is common. A mind map requires excellent concentration. Regarding complex problems, mapping might be intimidating (Buran & Filyukov, 2015). Converting ideas and objectives into concrete tasks may be challenging without the necessary tools.

Storytelling is a logical process that is easily understandable by all group members. It is more convincing to correlate what the system accomplishes with a cohesive story, resulting in rapid data gathering and enhanced needs. A user story helps to understand and formulate the user's precise requirements and improves the collaboration with stakeholders (Boulila et al., 2011). Storytelling enables analysts to identify the oversights and scope growth rapidly.

Ethnomethodology: Utilizing ethnomethodology as a requirement elicitation tool, the significance of knowing the knowledge, abilities, and practices of researchers in many disciplines has been highlighted due to the extensive incorporation of infrastructures into research settings (Goguen & Linde, 1993). Ethnomethodology offers objective, unbiased observational methods (Rouncefield, 2011). When ethnomethodology is utilized without abstracting the conclusions, the result is countless observations but no generalizable conclusion that can be applied to situations of a similar nature. Time-consuming is the collection of data (Elsey, 2021; Derrick et al., 2013).

Online feedback platforms allow end-users to communicate their difficulties, experiences, and opinions while monitoring provides crucial information regarding runtime events. Supposedly, combining multiple inputs of user feedbacks can help requirements engineers understand the user expectation. Frequent feedback helps project teams to remain focused on client requirements and reduces the risk of misdirections during the project life cycle. Teams ensure the correct development and testing of certain system functions by incorporating early customer feedback. During the testing phase, evaluation metrics and user feedback might expose critical linkages between user behaviour and features (Oriol et al., 2018).

CLEO (Clear Language for Expressing Ordering): Compared to the previous practices, where the focus was on selecting the best instance in a database of alternatives, it uses interactive optimization in all possible configurations to provide a constructive approach to the recommendation (Campigotto et al., 2021). The speed with which CLEO can determine optimal configurations. It is possible to recover from initial errors (Sebastiani & Tomasi, 2015). This method requires an expert because its operations are challenging to comprehend (Campigotto et al., 2021; Franzle et al., 2006), as interpreting the outcomes is difficult.

Gamification: Non-gaming contexts will add gamification, a game-based atmosphere to improve customer engagement. It would assist in engaging and connecting stakeholders during elicitation, increasing their advantage in eliciting and settling framework requirements (Ribeiro et al., 2014). Gamification enhances inter-party communication, due to which prioritizing necessities become more effective.

CONCLUSION

Requirements engineering (RE) has become increasingly important in the software development industry over the past decade, as it plays a critical role in ensuring that software projects are completed on time and within budget while meeting stakeholders' needs and expectations. One of the critical challenges of the requirements phase of the software development life cycle (SDLC) is ensuring that the requirements are accurately and wholly captured, specified, and validated. This requires careful attention to the elicitation phase, where engineers and other stakeholders work together to identify and prioritize the system's functional and non-functional requirements. The selection of an appropriate elicitation methodology is critical to the project's success, as different techniques may be better suited to different project types or contexts. Moreover, these techniques should be used with care to avoid unnecessary privacy and security threats during elicitation process. Since the web breach can be done through various mechanism, so appropriate techniques should be adopted for different scenarios. The quality of the elicitation criteria is also an essential factor in determining the efficacy of the chosen methodology. Overall, practical requirements engineering is essential for ensuring the success of web-based software projects, as it enables teams to develop a clear and comprehensive understanding of the system's requirements and ensure that the final product meets the needs and expectations of stakeholders.

REFERENCES

Afflerbach, P. (2000). Verbal reports and protocol analysis. Handbook of reading research, 3, 163-179.

Agarwal, R., & Tanniru, M. R. (1990). Knowledge acquisition using structured interviewing: An empirical investigation. *Journal of Management Information Systems*, 7(1), 123–140. doi:10.1080/07421 222.1990.11517884

Alam, I., Khusro, S., & Khan, M. (2019a). Factors affecting the performance of recommender systems in a smart TV environment. *Technologies*, 7(2), 41. doi:10.3390/technologies7020041

Alam, I., Khusro, S., & Khan, M. (2019b). *Usability barriers in smart TV user interfaces: A review and recommendations.* Paper presented at the 2019 international conference on Frontiers of Information Technology (FIT). IEEE. 10.1109/FIT47737.2019.00069

Alam, I., Khusro, S., & Khan, M. (2021). Personalized content recommendations on smart TV: Challenges, opportunities, and future research directions. *Entertainment Computing*, 38, 100418. doi:10.1016/j. entcom.2021.100418

Alam, I., Khusro, S., & Naeem, M. (2017). *A review of smart TV: Past, present, and future.* Paper presented at the 2017 International Conference on Open Source Systems & Technologies (ICOSST). IEEE. 10.1109/ICOSST.2017.8279002

Alam, I., Khusro, S., Rauf, A., & Zaman, Q. (2014). Conducting surveys and data collection: From traditional to mobile and SMS-based surveys. *Pakistan Journal of Statistics and Operation Research*, 169-187.

Aranda, G. N., Vizcaíno, A., Cechich, A., & Piattini, M. (2008). *A Methodology for Reducing Geographical Dispersion Problems during Global Requirements Elicitation.* Paper presented at the WER. IEEE.

Aurum, A., & Wohlin, C. (2005). *Engineering and managing software requirements* (Vol. 1). Springer. doi:10.1007/3-540-28244-0

Bartlett, J. C., & Toms, E. G. (2005). Developing a protocol for bioinformatics analysis: An integrated information behavior and task analysis approach. *Journal of the American Society for Information Science and Technology*, *56*(5), 469–482. doi:10.1002/asi.20136

Beyer, H. R., & Holtzblatt, K. (1995). Apprenticing with the customer. *Communications of the ACM*, *38*(5), 45–52. doi:10.1145/203356.203365

Boulila, N., Hoffmann, A., & Herrmann, A. (2011). *Using Storytelling to record requirements: Elements for an effective requirements elicitation approach.* Paper presented at the 2011 Fourth International Workshop on Multimedia and Enjoyable Requirements Engineering (MERE'11). IEEE. 10.1109/MERE.2011.6043945

Bubenko, J. A., & Wangler, B. (1993). *Objectives driven capture of business rules and of information systems requirements.* Paper presented at the Proceedings of IEEE Systems Man and Cybernetics Conference-SMC. IEEE. 10.1109/ICSMC.1993.384821

Buran, A., & Filyukov, A. (2015). Mind mapping technique in language learning. *Procedia: Social and Behavioral Sciences*, *206*, 215–218. doi:10.1016/j.sbspro.2015.10.010

Campigotto, P., Teso, S., Battiti, R., & Passerini, A. (2021). Learning Modulo Theories for constructive preference elicitation. *Artificial Intelligence*, *295*, 103454. doi:10.1016/j.artint.2021.103454

Carrizo, D., Dieste, O., & Juristo, N. (2014). Systematizing requirements elicitation technique selection. *Information and Software Technology*, *56*(6), 644–669. doi:10.1016/j.infsof.2014.01.009

Carrizo, D., Dieste, O., & Juristo, N. (2017). Contextual attributes impacting the effectiveness of requirements elicitation Techniques: Mapping theoretical and empirical research. *Information and Software Technology*, *92*, 194–221. doi:10.1016/j.infsof.2017.08.003

Cheng, B. H., Eder, K. I., Gogolla, M., Grunske, L., Litoiu, M., Müller, H. A., & Rumpe, B. (2014). *Using models at runtime to address assurance for self-adaptive systems Models@ run. time.* Springer.

Corbridge, C., Rugg, G., Major, N., Shadbolt, N., & Burton, A. (1994). Laddering: Technique and tool use in knowledge acquisition. *Knowledge Acquisition*, *6*(3), 315–341. doi:10.1006/knac.1994.1016

Crowe, M., & Sheppard, L. (2012). Mind mapping research methods. *Quality & Quantity*, *46*(5), 1493–1504. doi:10.100711135-011-9463-8

Dardenne, A., Van Lamsweerde, A., & Fickas, S. (1993). Goal-directed requirements acquisition. *Science of Computer Programming*, *20*(1-2), 3–50. doi:10.1016/0167-6423(93)90021-G

Davey, B., & Cope, C. (2009). Consultants experience of requirements elicitation conversations-An empirical model.

Derrick, D. C., Read, A., Nguyen, C., Callens, A., & De Vreede, G.-J. (2013). *Automated group facilitation for gathering wide audience end-user requirements.* Paper presented at the 2013 46th Hawaii international conference on system sciences. IEEE. 10.1109/HICSS.2013.109

Du, J., Wang, J., & Feng, X. (2014). *A safety requirement elicitation technique of safety-critical system based on scenario.* Paper presented at the International Conference on Intelligent Computing. IEEE. 10.1007/978-3-319-09333-8_15

Elsey, C. (2021). *'This is my lesson': Ethnomethodological lessons in classroom order and social organization for adults with learning difficulties.* DeMontfort University.

Erik, H. (2017). *FRAM: the functional resonance analysis method: modelling complex socio-technical systems.* Crc Press. doi:10.1201/9781315255071

Fränzle, M., Herde, C., Teige, T., Ratschan, S., & Schubert, T. (2006). Efficient solving of large nonlinear arithmetic constraint systems with complex boolean structure. *Journal on Satisfiability. Boolean Modeling and Computation, 1*(3-4), 209–236.

Fuller, R. M., & Davis, C. J. (2017). *Requirements elicitation techniques as communication channels: a framework to widen the window of understanding Systems Analysis and Design.* Routledge.

Garg, N., Agarwal, P., & Khan, S. (2015). *Recent advancements in requirement elicitation and prioritization techniques.* Paper presented at the 2015 International Conference on Advances in Computer Engineering and Applications. IEEE. 10.1109/ICACEA.2015.7164702

Gausepohl, A, K., W Winchester, W., L Smith-Jackson, T., M Kleiner, B., & D Arthur, J. (. (2016). A conceptual model for the role of Storytelling in design: Leveraging narrative inquiry in user-centered design (UCD). *Health and Technology, 6*(2), 125–136. doi:10.100712553-015-0123-1

Girardi, R., & Leite, A. (2008). A knowledge-based tool for multi-agent domain engineering. *Knowledge-Based Systems, 21*(7), 604–611. doi:10.1016/j.knosys.2008.03.036

Goguen, J. A., & Linde, C. (1993). *Techniques for requirements elicitation.* Paper presented at the [1993] Proceedings of the IEEE International Symposium on Requirements Engineering. IEEE.

Harzallah, M., Berio, G., & Opdahl, A. L. (2012). New perspectives in ontological analysis: Guidelines and rules for incorporating modelling languages into UEML. *Information Systems, 37*(5), 484–507. doi:10.1016/j.is.2011.11.001

Herlocker, J. L., Konstan, J. A., Terveen, L. G., & Riedl, J. T. (2004). Evaluating collaborative filtering recommender systems. [TOIS]. *ACM Transactions on Information Systems, 22*(1), 5–53. doi:10.1145/963770.963772

Hernán, M. A., & Robins, J. M. (2017). Per-protocol analyses of pragmatic trials. *The New England Journal of Medicine, 377*(14), 1391–1398. doi:10.1056/NEJMsm1605385 PMID:28976864

Index, A. (1995). Communications of the ACM 1995 author index. *Communications of the ACM, 38*(12), 91–99. doi:10.1145/219663.219693

Jakkaew, P., & Hongthong, T. (2017). *Requirements elicitation to develop mobile application for elderly.* Paper presented at the 2017 International Conference on Digital Arts, Media and Technology (ICDAMT). IEEE. 10.1109/ICDAMT.2017.7905013

Jarke, M. (1999). *CREWS: towards systematic usage of scenarios, use cases and scenes Electronic Business Engineering.* Springer.

Karlsson, J. (1997). Managing software requirements using quality function deployment. *Software Quality Journal, 6*(4), 311–326. doi:10.1023/A:1018580522999

Karn, J. S., Syed-Abdullah, S., Cowling, A. J., & Holcombe, M. (2007). A study into the effects of personality type and methodology on cohesion in software engineering teams. *Behaviour & Information Technology, 26*(2), 99–111. doi:10.1080/01449290500102110

Kasauli, R., Knauss, E., Horkoff, J., Liebel, G., & de Oliveira Neto, F. G. (2021). Requirements engineering challenges and practices in large-scale agile system development. *Journal of Systems and Software, 172,* 110851. doi:10.1016/j.jss.2020.110851

Kausar, S., Tariq, S., Riaz, S., & Khanum, A. (2010). *Guidelines for the selection of elicitation techniques.* Paper presented at the 2010 6th International Conference on Emerging Technologies (ICET). IEEE. 10.1109/ICET.2010.5638476

Khan, B., Naseem, R., Alam, I., Khan, I., Alasmary, H., & Rahman, T. (2022). Analysis of Tree-Family Machine Learning Techniques for Risk Prediction in Software Requirements. *IEEE Access : Practical Innovations, Open Solutions, 10,* 98220–98231. doi:10.1109/ACCESS.2022.3206382

Khusro, S., Naeem, M., Khan, M. A., & Alam, I. (2018). There is no such thing as free Lunch: An Investigation of Bloatware Effects on Smart Devices. *Journal of Information Communication Technologies and Robotic Applications,* 20-30.

Kilov, H., & Sack, I. (2009). Mechanisms for communication between business and IT experts. *Computer Standards & Interfaces, 31*(1), 98–109. doi:10.1016/j.csi.2007.11.001

Knauss, A., Damian, D., Franch, X., Rook, A., Müller, H. A., & Thomo, A. (2016). ACon: A learning-based approach to deal with uncertainty in contextual requirements at runtime. *Information and Software Technology, 70,* 85–99. doi:10.1016/j.infsof.2015.10.001

Lefaix-Durand, A., & Kozak, R. (2010). Comparing customer and supplier perceptions of value offerings: An exploratory assessment. *Journal of Business Market Management, 4*(3), 129–150. doi:10.100712087-010-0038-0

Liou, Y. I., & Chen, M. (1993). Using group support systems and joint application development for requirements specification. *Journal of Management Information Systems, 10*(3), 25–41. doi:10.1080/07421222.1993.11518009

Liu, Y., Tong, Y., & Yang, Y. (2018). The application of mind mapping into college computer programming teaching. *Procedia Computer Science, 129,* 66–70. doi:10.1016/j.procs.2018.03.047

Mahmud, I., & Veneziano, V. (2011). *Mind-mapping: An effective technique to facilitate requirements engineering in agile software development.* Paper presented at the 14th International Conference on Computer and Information Technology (ICCIT 2011). IEEE. 10.1109/ICCITechn.2011.6164775

Mishra, D., Mishra, A., & Yazici, A. (2008). *Successful requirement elicitation by combining requirement engineering techniques.* Paper presented at the 2008 First International Conference on the Applications of Digital Information and Web Technologies (ICADIWT). IEEE. 10.1109/ICADIWT.2008.4664355

Monsalve, C., April, A., & Abran, A. (2012). *On the expressiveness of business process modeling notations for software requirements elicitation.* Paper presented at the IECON 2012-38th Annual Conference on IEEE Industrial Electronics Society. IEEE. 10.1109/IECON.2012.6389398

Muñoz-Fernández, J. C., Mazo, R., Salinesi, C., & Tamura, G. (2018). *10 challenges for the specification of self-adaptive software.* Paper presented at the 2018 12th International Conference on Research Challenges in Information Science (RCIS). IEEE.

Nawaz, A. (2012). A comparison of card-sorting analysis methods. Paper presented at *the 10th Asia Pacific Conference on Computer Human Interaction (Apchi 2012).* Matsue-city, Shimane, Japan.

Ordóñez, H., Villada, A. F. E., Vanegas, D. L. V., Cobos, C., Ordóñez, A., & Segovia, R. (2015). *An impact study of business process models for requirements elicitation in XP.* Paper presented at the International Conference on Computational Science and Its Applications. IEEE.

Oriol, M., Stade, M., Fotrousi, F., Nadal, S., Varga, J., Seyff, N., & Schmidt, O. (2018). *FAME: supporting continuous requirements elicitation by combining user feedback and monitoring.* Paper presented at the 2018 ieee 26th international requirements engineering conference (re). IEEE. 10.1109/RE.2018.00030

Paetsch, F., Eberlein, A., & Maurer, F. (2003). *Requirements engineering and agile software development.* Paper presented at the WET ICE 2003. Proceedings. Twelfth IEEE International Workshops on Enabling Technologies: Infrastructure for Collaborative Enterprises, 2003. IEEE. 10.1109/ENABL.2003.1231428

Palomares, C., Franch, X., Quer, C., Chatzipetrou, P., López, L., & Gorschek, T. (2021). The state-of-practice in requirements elicitation: An extended interview study at 12 companies. *Requirements Engineering, 26*(2), 273–299. doi:10.100700766-020-00345-x

Pandey, S., & Batra, M. (2013). Formal methods in requirements phase of SDLC. *International Journal of Computers and Applications, 70*(13), 7–14. doi:10.5120/12020-8017

Patriarca, R., Di Gravio, G., & Costantino, F. (2017). A Monte Carlo evolution of the Functional Resonance Analysis Method (FRAM) to assess performance variability in complex systems. *Safety Science, 91*, 49–60. doi:10.1016/j.ssci.2016.07.016

Patriarca, R., Di Gravio, G., Woltjer, R., Costantino, F., Praetorius, G., Ferreira, P., & Hollnagel, E. (2020). Framing the FRAM: A literature review on the functional resonance analysis method. *Safety Science, 129*, 104827. doi:10.1016/j.ssci.2020.104827

Polyakov, A., Efimov, D., Perruquetti, W., & Richard, J.-P. (2013). Output stabilization of time-varying input delay systems using interval observation technique. *Automatica, 49*(11), 3402–3410. doi:10.1016/j.automatica.2013.08.012

Ram, C., Montibeller, G., & Morton, A. (2011). Extending the use of scenario planning and MCDA for the evaluation of strategic options. *The Journal of the Operational Research Society*, *62*(5), 817–829. doi:10.1057/jors.2010.90

Rao, K. N. (2008). Application domain and functional classification of recommender systems—A survey. *DESIDOC Journal of Library and Information Technology*, *28*(3), 17–35. doi:10.14429/djlit.28.3.174

Rasheed, A., Zafar, B., Shehryar, T., Aslam, N. A., Sajid, M., Ali, N., Dar, S. H., & Khalid, S. (2021). Requirement engineering challenges in agile software development. *Mathematical Problems in Engineering*, *2021*, 2021. doi:10.1155/2021/6696695

Reed, J., & Payton, V. R. (1997). Focus groups: Issues of analysis and interpretation. *Journal of Advanced Nursing*, *26*(4), 765–771. doi:10.1046/j.1365-2648.1997.00395.x PMID:9354990

Renault, S., Méndez-Bonilla, Ó., Franch, X., & Quer, C. (2009). *PABRE: pattern-based requirements elicitation*. Paper presented at the 2009 Third International Conference on Research Challenges in Information Science. ACM.

Ribeiro, C., Farinha, C., Pereira, J., & da Silva, M. M. (2014). Gamifying requirement elicitation: Practical implications and outcomes in improving stakeholders collaboration. *Entertainment Computing*, *5*(4), 335–345. doi:10.1016/j.entcom.2014.04.002

Richardson, J., Ormerod, T. C., & Shepherd, A. (1998). The role of task analysis in capturing requirements for interface design. *Interacting with Computers*, *9*(4), 367–384. doi:10.1016/S0953-5438(97)00036-2

Rodrigues, A., Caldas, R. D., Rodrigues, G. N., Vogel, T., & Pelliccione, P. (2018). *A learning approach to enhance assurances for real-time self-adaptive systems*. Paper presented at the 2018 IEEE/ACM 13th International Symposium on Software Engineering for Adaptive and Self-Managing Systems (SEAMS). ACM. 10.1145/3194133.3194147

Rouncefield, M. (2011). Fieldwork, ethnography and ethnomethodology. LSCITS Socio-Technical Systems Engineering Handbook. University of St Andrews, 44-48.

Santoro, F. M., Borges, M. R., & Pino, J. A. (2000). *CEPE: cooperative editor for processes elicitation*. Paper presented at the Proceedings of the 33rd Annual Hawaii International Conference on System Sciences. IEEE. 10.1109/HICSS.2000.926587

Schalken, J., Brinkkemper, S., & van Vliet, H. (2004). *Assessing the effects of facilitated workshops in requirements engineering*. Paper presented at the Proceedings of the 8th Conference on Evaluation & Assessment in Software Engineering (EASE 2004), IEE Press. 10.1049/ic:20040406

Schneider, F., & Berenbach, B. (2013). A literature survey on international standards for systems requirements engineering. *Procedia Computer Science*, *16*, 796–805. doi:10.1016/j.procs.2013.01.083

Sebastiani, R., & Tomasi, S. (2015). Optimization modulo theories with linear rational costs. [TOCL]. *ACM Transactions on Computational Logic*, *16*(2), 1–43. doi:10.1145/2699915

Sharma, S., & Pandey, S. (2013). Revisiting requirements elicitation techniques. *International Journal of Computers and Applications*, *75*(12).

Sohaib, O., & Khan, K. (2010). *Integrating usability engineering and agile software development: A literature review.* Paper presented at the 2010 international conference on Computer design and applications. IEEE. 10.1109/ICCDA.2010.5540916

Sommerville, I. (2011). Software engineering 9th Edition. 18.

Sosnowski, M., Bereza, M., & Ng, Y. Y. (2021). *Business-Oriented Approach to Requirements Elicitation in a Scrum Project.* Paper presented at the International Conference on Lean and Agile Software Development. IEEE. 10.1007/978-3-030-67084-9_12

Sousa-Zomer, T. T., & Miguel, P. A. C. (2017). A QFD-based approach to support sustainable product-service systems conceptual design. *International Journal of Advanced Manufacturing Technology, 88*(1), 701–717. doi:10.100700170-016-8809-8

Sutcliffe, A., & Maiden, N. (1998). The domain theory for requirements engineering. *IEEE Transactions on Software Engineering, 24*(3), 174–196. doi:10.1109/32.667878

Tian, J., Wu, J., Yang, Q., & Zhao, T. (2016). FRAMA: A safety assessment approach based on Functional Resonance Analysis Method. *Safety Science, 85*, 41–52. doi:10.1016/j.ssci.2016.01.002

Trujillo, A., & Buzzi, M. C. (2016). *Participatory user requirements elicitation for personal menopause app.* Paper presented at the Proceedings of the 9th Nordic Conference on Human-Computer Interaction. IEEE. 10.1145/2971485.2996737

Tsumaki, T., & Tamai, T. (2006). Framework for matching requirements elicitation techniques to project characteristics. *Software Process Improvement and Practice, 11*(5), 505–519. doi:10.1002pip.293

Valaski, J., Reinehr, S., & Malucelli, A. (2014). *Environment for requirements elicitation supported by ontology-based conceptual models: a proposal.* Paper presented at the Proceedings of the International Conference on Software Engineering Research and Practice (SERP). IEEE.

Van Heesch, U., Avgeriou, P., & Hilliard, R. (2012). *Forces on architecture decisions-a viewpoint.* Paper presented at the 2012 Joint Working IEEE/IFIP Conference on Software Architecture and European Conference on Software Architecture. IEEE. 10.1109/WICSA-ECSA.212.18

Vieira, E. R., Alves, C., & Duboc, L. (2012). *Creativity patterns guide: support for the application of creativity techniques in requirements engineering.* Paper presented at the International Conference on Human-Centred Software Engineering. IEEE. 10.1007/978-3-642-34347-6_19

Wu, H.-H., & Shieh, J.-I. (2010). Applying repertory grids technique for knowledge elicitation in quality function deployment. *Quality & Quantity, 44*(6), 1139–1149. doi:10.100711135-009-9267-2

Yu, E. S. (1997). *Towards modelling and reasoning support for early-phase requirements engineering.* Paper presented at the Proceedings of ISRE'97: 3rd IEEE International Symposium on Requirements Engineering. IEEE. 10.1109/ISRE.1997.566873

Zavala, E., Franch, X., Marco, J., Knauss, A., & Damian, D. (2015). *SACRE: A tool for dealing with uncertainty in contextual requirements at runtime.* Paper presented at the 2015 IEEE 23rd International Requirements Engineering Conference (RE). IEEE. 10.1109/RE.2015.7320437

Zhang, H., Kishore, R., Sharman, R., & Ramesh, R. (2007). Agile Integration Modeling Language (AIML): A conceptual modeling grammar for agile integrative business information systems. *Decision Support Systems, 44*(1), 266–284. doi:10.1016/j.dss.2007.04.009

Zowghi, D., & Coulin, C. (2005). *Requirements elicitation: A survey of techniques, approaches, and tools Engineering and managing software requirements*. Springer.

Chapter 9
Privacy and Accessibility of Liberation Movement Archives of South Africa

Nkholedzeni Sidney Netshakhuma

Centre For African Studies, University of Cape Town, South Africa

ABSTRACT

This chapter assessed privacy and access of the liberation movements archives of South Africa. The study is based on personal experience of working with the liberation movement archives and review of literature on privacy and accessibility. The discussion was based on the liberation movements archives, privacy legislation, accountability, purpose specifications, donation of third party archives, information quality, confidentiality and security of archives, electronic records management systems, digitization of liberation movement archives, data subject participation, openness and transparency, public records, establishment of governance structure, raising awareness and training, partnership and collaboration, and access to liberation archives. Liberation movements are to ensure that they comply with the Protection of Personal Information Act 4 of 2013.

INTRODUCTION

Balancing privacy and access to information is highly evident in South Africa and has been of concern to liberation movements since the end of the apartheid. Therefore, this chapter assess liberation movements archives privacy and accessibility of repatriated from all over the world. These liberation movement archives offer unmatched views into the democractic South Africa. These liberation movement archives expand the history of South Africa. The chapter seeks to contribute to the debate on the privacy and accessibility of liberation movement archives. Most of these archives collection created, received and distributed contained privacy information and had security concerns. One of the challenges faced by the liberation movements was the treatment of privacy and confidential information. The liberation movements archives were collected before the enactment of the Protection of Personal Information Act

DOI: 10.4018/978-1-6684-6914-9.ch009

No 4 of 2013. These records were created in countries where the liberation movements seek refugees while their organisations were declared illegal by the apartheid government.

Given the emergent interest in the writings about privacy and access to political records across disciplines, the present study reviews the liberation movements archives repatriated from several parts of the world. There has been little if any, research undertaken on the assessment of privacy and access to liberation archives in South Africa. This book chapter fills gap on processing liberation movements archives containing personal information to protect privacy while facilitating access to archives .Analysis of records concentrated on the liberation movement archivists safeguarded privacy and access to liberation archives. Literature on the privacy and access has established the legal imperative for archivists to protect private information in certain cases Dowrey (2017, p. 5) . This chapter is based on the researcher personal experience of working on the liberation movement archives in 2004. I was responsible for selection, identification, processing archives materials repatriated from various mission offices. This chapter will be mostly based on personal encounter with liberation movements archives and review of literaterure on pirvacy and access to information. This chapter heading are structured as follows: liberation movements archives, privacy legislation, accountability, purpose specifications, donation of third party archives, information quality, confidentiality and security of archives, electronic records management systems, digitization of liberation movement archives, data subject participation, Openness and transparency, public records, establishment of governance structure, raising awareness and training, partnership and collaboration, access to liberation archives, conclustion and recommendation of the study.

LIBERATION MOVEMENTS ARCHIVES

The liberation movements commenced with the repatriation of ther archives after the unbanning of political organisations in 1990 by then President F.W De Klerk. The repatriation of archives was done with the aim of renewing dialogues around liberation movements archives. Liberaton movement for example the ANC developed an archives repatriation programme or project to repatriate liberation movements archives scattered all over the world. Consideration was taken that some of the repatriated archives contain private and confidential information which may damage image of organisation. These liberation movements archives not only document the historical, cultural and economic development of South Africa but provide basis for South Africa identity. South Africa public knowledge of the history of the liberation and oppression was part of heritage of South Africa.Citizens has the right to know the history of the South African liberation past. Hence there was a need to balance privacy and access to information on the liberation archives in South Africa. The liberation movements also provide evidence of the role played by military veterans of UMkhonto We Sizwe, military wing of the ANC. Therefore process and procedures were developed to control access to liberation movements archives.

Liberation movements referred to pollical organisations fought for the liberation for South Africa. In this study, the liberation movements include the ANC, Pan Africanist organisation (PAC) and Azanian People organisations (AZAPO). During the liberation struggle, they created or received various types of records such as memorandum, reports and minutes, audio visual materials. Most of the liberation movements archives repatriated were damaged which required to be repaired by professionals. Most of records need to be repaired and stored according to archives principles. The liberation movements were supposed to be responsible for their reparation of their liberation archives materials.The liberation movemen archives were created by South African nationalists fighting for a liberated nations(Ashie-Nikoi 2019, p. 147).

PRIVACY LEGISLATION

Privacy is a noteworthy but indefinable notion that is central to democratic government (Johnson, Regan, & Wayland, 2011). State is obliged in terms of the Protection of Personal Information Act No. 4 of 2013. to protect privacy information of its citizen. Privacy can be enforce through enactment of legislation protecting privacy of information. Most of the countries all over the world enacted privacy legislation to protect citizens rights. The enforcement was done because right to privacy is part of the human rights. This implies that secrecy and fundamental interest of the state cannot be allowed to override human and citizens right (Manceron & Morin 2021, p. 265). Organisations ensured that privacy of information should be protected all time. The literature on privacy recognises that privacy on archives collections was a matter of concern to the public (Donaldson & Bell, 2018). If organisation failed to protect privacy of individual may lead the organisation to litigations and other forms of legal disputes. The rights to individual would be destroyed if personal information was destroyed

After 2013, Political organisations in South Africa required to comply with the Protection of Personal Information Act no. 4 of 2013. It was the resposibility of the liberation movements to ensure that privacy of information is protected in compliance with the Protection of Personal Information Act No 4 of 2013. This Act was enacted in 2013 to protect privacy of individuals. This Act emanated from the Constitution of the Republic of South Africa which promote organisations to develop policies, processes and procedures to protect individual privacy. The Protection of Personal Information act No. 4 of 2013 was enacted to protect privacy of information created by public and private organisations. Therefore, political organisations as neither private and public entities protect privacy of individual information.

During the liberation struggle, liberation movements were not complying with any South Africa legislations bcause they were referred as illegal organisation. They were banned from participating to political activities. The apartheid monitored all political activites in South Africa and neighbouring countries. The apartheid raid liberations office based neither in Swaziland, Mozambigue and Botswana.

The liberation archives were created before 2013 of the enactment of the Protection of Personal Information Act of 1996. Liberation movements embarked on collection or identification of their archives before the enactment of the Protection of Personal Information Act No. 4 of 2013 in South Africa. Most of the liberation archives were created in 1960s after the banning of political movements. Political organisations banned by the apartheid government included ANC, South Africa Communist party (SACP) and PAC. These liberation movements were banned because of their stand against apartheid laws. The apartheid law were unjust. Consideration was not taken by the liberation movements to protect personal information even though their records were created underground. Records were protected against unauthorised used. This implies that by then political movements were not binded by the Protection of Personnel Information Act No. 4 of 2013. By then, South Africa has not planned personal data protection in the form of the Act. Legislation is only durable genuine application of privacy of information (Baloyi & Kotze 2017).

ACCOUNTABILITY

Political organsations elect a president and its national executive committee members during a national elective conference conducted every five years. The elected political leadership were given mandate by their members to drive political agenda of emancipation of marginalised communities. Political parties president is accountable for all records created, preserved and disseminated. The president is accountable for records created by political parties in pursuit of its political agenda, during election campaign and formulation of the party manifesto. The president, as the accounting officer is an Information Officer. The president of the party ensured that privacy statements, privacy policy developed and implemented in compliance with the Protection of Personal Information Act No 4 of 2013. The Protection of Personal Information act No. 4 of 2013 gave mandate the information officer to delegate more than two candidates as Deputy Information Officers. The president of the party may delegate to secretary general of deputy president or chairperson of the organisation. Secretary General of the party became Deputy Information Information of political organisation. Organisations were to ensure that both information and Deputy information officers registered with the Information Regulator of South Africa. The Information Regulator of South Africa established to enforce compliance with the Protection of Personal Information Act No. 4 of 2013. The executive committee of an organisation is responsible to ensure preservation of institution of political records. The decision regarding the type of records to be dissemination by organisation lied with the presidents and Secretary General. Hence other organisation prefer to appoit deputy president as information officer of the political organisation.

PURPOSE SPECIFICATION

The purpose limitation principle afford that any handling of personal information must be companion-able with the purpose stated and expression at the period of archives collection (Rauhofer 2014). This purpose specification of collection of data was also dependent on whether organisations were willing to embrace changes to protect privacy and personal information. Liberation movements records were created to pursuit liberation of South Africa. Most of the liberation archives contain information about the strategy to tackle the apartheid government, how the liberation movements access South Africa boundaries from other countries, educational activities, cooperation of liberation movements with other international organisations, anti – apartheid movements and other countries to increase solidairity with various countries, aid provided by the international organisations to support the liberation movements. Such records were created in the underground movements. Even though these liberation archives were collected and disseminated with the view to disseminate information.

DONATION OF THE THIRD PARTY ARCHIVES

Most of the liberation movements records associated with political, economc and social emancipation were created and donated by the third party organisations. According to Dowrey (2017, p. 7), the protection of third party privacy forms an central ethical coherent for controlling access to definite archives records in archives repository. Most of third parties had no say on how organisation interpreted and analysed their records. Archivist should have high intergrity when dealing with third parties records. In this chapter, the third parties organisations included the Anti- Apartheid movements, foreign governments (embassies), trade unions and non- profit organisations such as the Convention for a democracy of South Africa (CODESA) established in 1991 which were against the apartheid government. The CODESA was the afiliation of ninety-two organisations civic and local political organisation fighting against the apartheid. To fill the gap left by the ANC, South African Communist party, The Anti -Apartheid movements were established in the United Kingdom, Australia, Canada and United State of America. The Anti - Apartheid Movements also play prominent role on socio- economic development by providing educational bursaries to the liberation movements to study all over the world. The Anti – Apartheid movements played a role to aid liberation movements with educational. The Anti-Apartheid Movements advocated for economic, social and military sanctions against apartheid system of governance. The liberation movements were also assisted with military eguipment to fought against the apartheid. Sanctions or embargo against the apartheid government was promoted by the Anti- Apartheid movements. Anti – Apartheid movements created records about the role play by liberations movements in South Africa. Anti- apartheid movements stop their existence after 1994, when the democractic government came to power in 1994. Most of the Anti - Apartheid Movements repatriated archives materials to South African political organisations without restrictions attached to the collection. However, such collection were repatriation without identification of privacy and secrecy on the collection. It was up to political organisations to establish process and procedure to protect privacy of information. Political organisations was at the sympathy of third parties to advance archives management system. Donated archives materials extend archives management programme. This declaration is alluded to by Pekala (2017) who specified that original information communication technologies moulded the way archives provision information services. The topic of political parties' records privacy, as it concerns to organizational practices, holds thoughtful implications as universal computing and innovative technologies become plentiful. Poitical recods collected expanded through donation from the Anti- Apartheid movements. Anti -Apartheid movements are organisations established during the apartheid period to fought against the injustice systems of the apartheid government. The policy ensured that the aspirations of international donors are safe; this is another causal effect of the accessibility of ANC archives. Some of the archival records could not be accessed because of privacy, security, confidentiality, and copyright grade.

In most instances, political archives records with privacy topics leak to the public because most organisations lack policies, procesdure and processes to preserve such materials. Political parties know the integral value in their collection and hold, they encounter unforeseen challenges in stewarding that collection in methods that balance access and protection of privacy.

INFORMATION QUALITY

Records created by liberation movements supposed to be complete, accurate and relevant to advance democracy in South Africa. The questions was raised by the archives users or researchers as to whether liberation movement records repatriated were of quality. The characteristics of quality of archives materials is its completeness, its authenticity and original. The purpose of creation such records should be clearly started and Such records should contain metadata. Metatada included date of records creation, description of records, time of records creation, conditions of records, volume of records and others. Records should be reliable for decision making. During the struggle for independence, records were created without full metadata such as date of creation of records, the creator of records, time of the creation of records. Some of records were created without metadata and identities to afraid any traces to afraid any traces by the apartheid government. The creators of records were afraid in case if records fall in the hands of the apartheid agencies. This so because most of the political organisations lack standards and procedure during process such archives materials.

CONFIDENTIALITY AND SECURITY OF ARCHIVES

Most of the liberation movement archives were created underground by various organisations and individuals. This so because liberation fighters were afraid of their records to be raid by the apartheid police. Archives concerning liberation movements with privacy and security concerns were violated by the liberation movements had never never been transferred or catalogued to archives repository and consequently remained unavailable for consultation or research purposes. In some case, one of the arguments for destroying confidential and secret liberation movements was to prevent their indiscriminate use by the police or army in a democratic South Africa. The aim to destroy records was to ensure that records may not be used for now or in the future. However, destroying such records complicates the task of recording the history of the operations of liberation movements during the period of struggle. These records were also important because they document history of liberation movements. Such records may be used during the Truth and Reconcialliation (TRC) Commission established after democracy to promote reconicilaition of injustice during the apartheid period. "The TRC focused on the remaining records of the security system, despite the systematic destruction of a enormous bulk of state records and certification as measure of an effort to remove incrimintating evidence and sanitise the history of oppressive rule" (Dominy 2021 p. 141). The vicims of apartheid systems may use records to demand repatriation to the apartheid government. Most of the reports developed during the liberation struggle were intelligence reports containing confidential information which were not supposed to be seen by the apartheid government. Most of liberation movements records were classified information. Most of these records were not supposed to be seen by the apartheid government.

In 1996, the South African legislature in cabinet approved the Minimum Information Security Standards (MISS) policy to classify information.There are different levels of classification of records. Records may be classified as top sectret . This implied that such records may not be accessible by all parties, secret records are sentitive in nature. Such records may not be accessible by authorised users. There is restiricted information. This is an information which may not be access by any individuals. Any top records created by organisations and indivudals in pursuit of democracy were destroyed before were seen by the apartheid agents. Some records were created without metadata such as dates and time to prevent any traces of such records of liberation movements Protection of political records, through processes, to warrant confidentiality and security of evidence is a alarm to the world at large (Marutha & Mosweu 2020).

After democracy in South Africa, it was necessary for liberation movements to develop and establish proper archives management. The mission and vision statement of liberation movements is to collect archives related to liberation of South Africa, political, economic and social development in South Africa. Archives instituttions only accept records related to their mission statements. Therefore, liberation movements to develop donation policy. The policy provide framework on the type of records need to be collected. Archives materials are to be transferred to archives repository. The archives repository should be managed in terms of archives management principles. A qualified archivists with appropriate qualifications in archives, heritage and museum management should be appointed to manage all types of records. This implied that records with historical, cultural and scientific value were preserved in archives repository. Organisation developed long term preservation strategy to ensure long term preservation of archives materials. Archives repository should be build to control access of archives materials.

Issues about disposition and access to records are not exclusive to South Africa from a repressive past (Wisser and Blanco – River 2015 p. 4). Political organisations developed processes and procedures to disposed records without archival value due for disposal. The process of disposal of records was another way of the extentio of the protection of personal information. During the liberation struggle in South Afrca, liberation movements lacked archivist responsive for archives management. All correspondence records were place on archives boxes without being appraised to determine its value. This process promoted liberation movements to collect all records without identification of its value.

To avoid any political arrest, records with confidential and security information were destroyed. Liberation movements lack a systematic process to disposed records. Hence, the National Archives of South Africa recommended organisations to develop plan with the view to systematically dispose of records. The review of literatures shows that liberation movements lacked records and disposal schedule. This implies that records were not disposed in compliance with the National Archives and Records Services Act 43 of 1996. It was not easy to determine records without archival values.

It is essential for liberation movements to develop disposal of records procedures and processes to dispose records according to the records and archives management schedule. Liberation archives should be systematical disposed in a regularly basis. The disposal of records should be conducted after the appraisal of records. The appraisal of records determine records with archival values. Such records will be transferred to the National Archives of South Africa for peramanent preserveation. Physical or paper based records should be shredded permanently while electronic file should be totally disposed off. The certificate of disposal of records should be issued by the organisation as a proof or indication of records disposed off.

ELECTRONIC RECORDS MANAGEMEMENT SYSTEM

The role of liberation movements archives in the defence of secrecy and access to information must be consistence in electronic environment (Boel, Canavaggio & Quintana 2021, p. 87). This implied that liberation movements were to ensure that sensitive records were protected from unauthorised users. This means that organisation were to limit to preserve records in physical archives storage. This is so because the development and introduction of digital technologies have had impact on the preservation and dissemination of liberation movements records. Therefore, there is a need for an archivist to store and disseminate archives materials. This is so because records stored on physical environment. Data may be stored and processed on electronic information amangement systems or locations. It is the responssiblity of organisation to transform paper based records into electronic records management system with the view to promote access to information. Organisation are to ensure long term preservation of electronic records management system. The Information Communication Technology division ensured that software and hardware are structured to protect sensitive data. Electronic records management systems purchased by organisation should comply with the Protection of Personal Information Act No. 4 2013. Political organisations are to ensure that they comply with the electronic communication and transaction act of 2002. There should be proved of authenticity of records generated in an electronic environment. Political organisation are advised to develop electronic records management system to ensure that records created on electronic environement are protected from unauthorised use. The electronic records management sysem purchase by political organisation should be reliable and use by organisation on continuous basis.

DIGITIZATION OF LIBERATION MOVEMENTS ARCHIVES

When South Africa gained in independence in 1994, there was a need a need for liberation movements archives to be digitised to be able to be shared nationally and globally. Digitisation of archives materials gained momentum in the world, hoever privacy need to be considered during the process of digitising. However, the challenges on digitisation and making available of some records with orphans works (Truyen & Waelde 2016 p. 91). Because most of the liberation movements archives were created between 1960 to 1990, this implies that some of records were not traced back. Such orphan works were not indexed, catalogued, restoration or preservation. The review of literature shows lack of unified of specified liberation movements records. Therefore, intellectual property remain a challenge on political organisation.

Political organisations has a legal and ethical obligation to safeguard privacy during digitization project of their archives records. The digitization of the ANC archives projects commenced in 2003. Most of these digitisation project relied on the funding from international donors. Because of the demands of the liberation movements archives, liberation movements such as the ANC embarked on digitisation projects to ensure that their archives materials are accessible to various part of the world. The development toward digitization encompassed political records. It was necessary for liberation movements archives to be controlled against unauthorised users. This implies that digitisation projects was conducted in a manner to prevent confidentiality and privacy of information. Contributors requested whether they consider privacy during the digitization of liberation archives. The privacy of information was considered during the digitization of liberation archives. Participants indicated that they were aware that most archives records placed on online platforms are not secured hence there was a need to ensure the privacy of information. Organizations adhere to the security of information

DATA SUBJECT PARTICIPATION

Data created by organisations is linked to natural persons (Szekely, 2014). Natural persons are people linked during the creation of records. Creators of records should be informed about any decision with regards to the dissemination of information, appraisal and disposal of sch records. Prominent Individuals and various organisations created liberation movements archives. These individuals and organisations included member of political organisations, prominent political figures such as Thabo Mbeki, Walter Sisulu, Alfred Nzo, former anti- apartheid movements, organisations supporting the political organisations. These data subjects should have a say on all records created by political organisation. This implies that archivists to be sensitive of the concern of owner of data (Hayes &Truong, 2009, p. 172). However, the challenges with the liberation movements archives, is that majority of individuals and organisations created liberation movements records were already dead. Some of the non profit organisation and and Anti- apartheid movements stop to exist after the first democracy election in South Africa.. Therefore, it was necessary for archivist responsible for liberation movements to be familiar with the South Africa Copyright Act of 1978 and copyright legislation and privacy legislations of other countries to ensure that privacy of individuals are protected during the processing of archives materials. Furthermore, liberation movements were to engage in oral history. The oral history assisted liberation movements to assist

Data subjects are informed when records were shared or disseminated by the organisation. These archives are known as data subject. Therefore, it is the role of individuals to participate in the development and implementation of archives management systems.

OPENNESS AND TRANSPARENCY

The end of apartheid and the long road towards democracy change South Africa brought a advance wave of demand for oppeness and transparency. Openness and transparesses are the pillar of democratic state. Political movements are accountable to citizens because public played an important role to determine type of information disseminated to the public. Most organisations restricted public to access political records because of its nature of sensitivity. Most of political organisations did not want their records to be accessed because their afraid that their strategy may be copied. Citizens has a right to now their representatives in neither national, provincial and local legislation. Therefore, political organisations develop systems and process to promote access to the public information. Such information should be made available to various stakeholders. Public has the right to access political records. Hence processes and procedures need to be established by organisations for the information to be disseminate to the public.

PUBLIC RECORDS

Public records are created for the advancement of public affairs. In South Africa, public records are managed in compliance with the National Archives and Records Service Act 43 of 1996. The analysis of the National Archives and Records Service Act of 1996 shows a lack a clause of management of political records. There was a public concern as to whether liberation movements records to be preserved by private organisations or such records need cares and supervision of the National Archives of South Africa. This gaps raised a questions as to whether liberation movement records may be regarded as neither public or private records . Questions raise by most public as to whether political records are regarded as public records. The custody of records with public interest should ideally fall under the authority of the national Archives rather than under special repository (Wisser and Blanco-Rivera 2015 p. 3). Liberation movements archives may be placed on special repostiroy in a case where the national Archives of South Africa lack capacity to manage such collection. The review of literature shows that the National Archives of South Africa has limited staff members to carry tasks of archives management all over South Africa. This despite that few staff at the National Archives of South Africa possessed skills and knowledge in archives management. It seems that most of the public view political records especially liberation movements as part of the private collection. However, the fact that political parties serves the public interest their records are regarded as public records. South Africa has three sphere of the public. This include national, provincial and local government. Politicians are elected at national, provincial and local government. This means that the the importance of public archives for the rights an duties of citiznes in South Africa was given a boost. The public records are also subject to data protection control.

ESTABLISHMENT OF GOVERNANCE STRUCTURE

Information resources such as archives materials are regarded as an assets materials. Political organisations developed governance structure to manage personal information. This implies that organisations to establish Information management division. The division should be responsible for both archives, records and information management. The Records and Archives Management section should be responsible for the development of policies, procedures, process and filing and classification on the management of information.The governance structure is supposed to be managed by organisation. It is the responsible of political organisations to ensure that organisational structure of organisation is approved and implemented. The organisational structure should be reviewed on regular basis by an organisation. Ensuring that training and development of staff is conducted.

RAISING AWARENESS AND TRAINING

Political organisations developed program to train staff on archives management. Political organisations should conduct awareness and training with staff and its members on management on privacy of information. Awareness may be extended to the member of the public. The public should be taught to embrace liberation movement archives as history records which will contribute to the development of a nation. Archives materials may be used to promote reconcialition and build the nation. Therefore, archivists need to develop skills on management of archives materials to protect liberation archives. The review of the literature shows that archivists lack training on privacy (Donaldson & Bell 2018).

Political organisations may allocated resource (Human resources and finance) to ensure that access to privacy in organisation is maintained. Budget should be allocated to train staff on archives management. Budget would be allocated to train records. It was the responsiblity of organisation to ensure that allocation of resources is regular monitored on a regular basis.

PARTNERSHIP AND COLLABORATION

Liberation movements archives are scattered all over the world despite efforts by the liberation movements to embark on repatriation of archives projects. Some of archives materials are still preserved by the the mission offices. The mission offices were countries hosted former liberation movements when they were banned by apartheid government. Some of archives because of copyrights legislations of various countries were not repatriated to South Africa. Other organisations felt that they may not repatriation archives materials to South Africa as they want to maintain such records for future generations. Such information may be maintain by various organisations. Partnership and collaboration may be established at international level through diplomacy. South Africa government embarked on cultural diplomacy with countries held liberation movements archives materials all over the world.

Most of liberation movements partnered with university to preserve their liberation movements archives. For example, the University of Fort Hare partner with the former liberation movements such as the African Nation Congress, Azanian People's Organisation and Panist African National Congress to preserve archives materials. The university of Fort Hare is the official repository of the liberation movements of South Africa. The university holds a nuber of collection relating to liberation movement in South Africa. Personal paper which could could be explored include the Nelson Mandela collection. Liberation archives preserved by the University of Fort Hare are available for use for research purposes. These partnerships with the universities provide an opportunities for organisations to share resources and exchange of skills. Archivists from both organisations may share information and resources based.

ACCESS TO LIBERATION MOVEMENT ARCHIVES

Accessibility of archives highlighted socio-economic programme that emerged in South Africa after 1994 election. It was a clear intention of new democratic government came into existence. Hoever, there was a need for balance on privacy of information and provision of access to information in a democratic South Africa government. The enactment of the Protection of Personal Information Act No. 4 of 2013 provide right of individuals to access political records. Since the democractic commence of 1994, there have been attempts to access liberation archives that would provide an account of the actions of the liberation movements during the apartheid period. The factor that impact access to some liberation movements records include custody issues, political struggles and trust in the archival records (Wisser & Blanco-Rivera 2015 p. 12). Records with indivifuals and organisation provided consent may be accessible to various stakeholders. Individuals have a right to access records of political donations with regards to campaigns and other activities related to political activities. This legislation has implications on political organisation to develop systems to ensure privacy of information is protected within an organisation.

Even though South Africa value privacy, democracies deliver the access to information for the rational and responsible conduct of public affairs and to support organizations (Westin 2003). Political organisations conducted impact assessment to all information technologies purchased by to ensure compliance with the Protection of Personal Information Act No 4 of 2003. Conducting gap analysis assist organisations to identify privacy information gaps. Gaps found in the information communication technologies should be identified before the implementation of systems within political organisation. Technological developments exposed long-term access to archives and materials and compromised the privacy of information because systems become obsolete. Tough (2009, p.116) declares that the contests of digital records have many factors that work together to make them inaccessible. Inaccessible liberation archives caused by the changing technologies and information technologies, archives records that may once have been difficult to access. This technological change may also affect the accessibility of archives records.

Most archives materials preserved on online platform are not secured as alluded to by Cheng & Lai (2012, p. 243) stating that frauds and attacks by hackers may occur on a cloud system. Organisations are to ensure that user access cards are used in order to access archives materials.

This implies that publishing liberation archives on information communication technologies require that privacy be treasured and protected and cultural institutions support the copyright and intellectual property of individuals and corporations (Liebetrau 2005).

Languages is essential to determine access to archives materials. Archives materials should be written in a language understandable to research users. The review of literature shows that dominant language used on archives language was a foregin language. Most of liberation archives were repatriated from mission offices of the liberation movements such as the African National Congress and Pan African National Congress. Most of correspondence records were written in foreign language. Archives written in foreign language limit users to access archives materials. Some of archives collection were written in French, Spanish languages. In order for the archives materials to be understood by various stakeholders need to be interpreted and analysed. Therefore, it is essential for liberation movements to embark on a project of interpretation of archives materials.

CONCLUSION

This chapter provided a critical examination of balancing access and privacy of archives collection and during digitisation of archives materials. Despite that liberation movements archives has historical, cultural and social significance, privacy of such collection should be takne into consideration. Organisations are to develop policies, processes and procedures to ensure compliance with privacy policy such as Protection of Personal Information Act No. 4 of 2013. Archives may not be in the place where they originated.The chapter contends that for archives created in diaspora, often out of mullitple locations and cultural contexts, the question of privacy and access are not easily determined.

RECOMMENDATION

Archivists should strive to balance between access and privacy of information when dealing with liberation movements archives materials.

Privacy of information should be taken into consideration during the digitisation of liberation movement archives.

Liberation movements are to develop policies, procedures and guideline to ensure compliance with the legislations.

AREAS FOR FUTURE RESEARCH

The findings disseminated in this book chapter promoted the need for further research. Examining the privacy and accessibility can be extended to other non-profit organisations

REFERENCES

Abid, A., & Radoykov, B. (2003). *Access and preservation in the information society*. Blackwell.

Ambira, C & Kemoni, H. (2011). Records Management and risk management at Kenya Commercial Bank Limited, Nairobi. *Journal of Information Management. 13*(1), 475.

Ashie-Nikoi, D. E. (2019). Ghana's Cultural Records in Diaspora: Perspectives from Papers held at the Schomburg Centre for Research in Black Culture, New York. African Journal Library, Archives and Informatio Science, 29(2), 143 – 155.

Baloyi, N., & Kotze, P. (2017). Are Organisations in South Africa Ready to Comply with Personal Data Protection or Privacy Legislation and Regulations? IST Africa. *Conference Proceedings*. Counsil for Scientific and Industrial Research.

Boel, J., Canavaggio, P., & Quintana, G. A. (2021). Archives and human Rights. A close relationship. Boel, J Canavaggio, P and Quintana, A.G (ed). Archives and Human Right. Routledge Taylor and Francis Group.

Cheng, C. F., & Lai, W. H. (2012). The Impact of Cloud Computing Technology on Legal Infrastructure within the Internet – Focusing on the Protection of Information Privacy, *International Workshop on Information and Electronics Engineering. Procedia Engineering*, *29*, 241–251. doi:10.1016/j.proeng.2011.12.701

Dominy, G. (2021). A long walk to Justice. Archives and the truth and reconciliation process in South Africa. Boel, J Canavaggio, P and Quintana, A.G (ed). Archives and human Rights. London. Routledge Taylor and Francis Group.

Donaldson, R. D., & Bell, L. (2018). Security, Archivist, Digital Collections. *Journal of Archival Organization*, *15*(1-2), 1–19. doi:10.1080/15332748.2019.1609311

Dowrey, E. A. (2017). *Processing to Protect Privacy and Promote Access. A study of Archival Processing in Medical Archives, Health Sciences Collections, and Hisotry of Medicine Collections. A Master's Paper for the Masters of Science in Library Science degree*. University of North Caroline.

Hayes, R. G., & Truong, N. K. (2009). *Selective Archving: A model for privacy Sensitive Capture and Access Technologies* (A. Seniro, Ed.). Protecting Privacy in Video Surveillenance.

Johnson, G. D., Regan, M. P., & Wayland, K. (2011). *Campaign Disclosure, Privacy, and Transparency*, 19. Wm. & Mary Bill Rts. J. https://scholarship.law.wm.edu/wmborj/19, 4/7.

Liebetrau, C. P. (2005). Gearing up for change: Building digital resources in a South African cultural heritage context. *Innovation*, *30*, 22–30.

Manceron, G., & Morin, G. (2021). France and the archives of the Algerian War. In Boel, J Canavaggio, P and Quintana, A.G. (eds.) Archives and Human Rights. Routledge Taylor and Francis Group. doi:10.4324/9780429054624-23

Marutha, S. N., & Mosweu, O. (2020). *Confidentiality and Security of information in the public health -care facilities to curb HIV/AIDS trauma among patients in Africa. HIV/AIDS trauma among patients*. Global Knowledge, Memory, and Communication. doi:10.1108/GKMC-06-2020-0089

Pekala, S. (2017). Privacy and User Experience in 21st Century Library Discovery. *Information Technology and Libraries*, *36*(2), 48–58. doi:10.6017/ital.v36i2.9817

Rauhofer, J (2014). What do the proposed changes to the purpose limitation principle mean for public boides rights to access third party data?. *International Rev of Law, Computers and Technology*, *28* (2), 144 – 158: Doi:.2013.801592. doi:10.1080/13600869

Szekely, I. (2014). The right to be forgotten and the new archival paradigm. In Ghezzi A. Pereira, A. G., & Vesnic-Alujevic, L. (eds) The ethics of memory in a digital age. Interrogating the right to be foforgetten, pp 28 – 49. Palgrve Macmillan. doi:10.1057/9781137428455_3

Tough, AG. (2009). Archives in Sub–Saharan Africa Half a century after independence. *Archival Science 9*, 187–201.

Truyen, F., & Waelde, C. (2016). Copyright, cultural heritage and Photography: A Gordian Knot? Borowiecki, J.K; Forbes, N and Fresa, A (ed). Cultrual Heritage in a Changing World. Springer. doi:10.1007/978-3-319-29544-2_5

Westin, F. A. (2003). Social and Political Dimensions of Privacy. *The Journal of Social Issues*, *59*(2), 431–453. doi:10.1111/1540-4560.00072

Wisser, M. K., & Blanco-Rivera, A. J. (2015). Surveillance, Documentation and Privacy: An international comparative analysis of state intelligence records. *Archival Science*. doi:10.100710502-015-9240-x

KEY TERMS AND DEFINITIONS

African National Congress: This is the main political organization in South Africa established in 1912 to protect the right of disadvantaged groups such as black people.

Anit – Apartheid Movements: These are organisations established during the apartheid period to fight against the apartheid system.

Apartheid: It is a racial or discriminatory policies established by the National party in 1948, when they came to power to segregate people in terms of race or colour.

Archives: These are records which were permanently preserved by organisation because its records contains historical, cultural and social significance.

Archives repatriations: This is a process of retaining archives materials stored in the foreign countries and missions.

Liberation Movement Archives: These are Liberation movements Archives created within and outside South Africa between 1960 to 1960

Liberation Movements: These are political movements established to fought against the apartheid movements such as the African National Congress, Pan Afrinast Congress and Pan African Congress, Azanian People Organisation.

Missions Office: These are offices, as a sort of embassy, established by the liberation movements after they were banned.

Privacy: This is archives materials restricted to access by certain individuals in organizations.

Chapter 10
SDSCCM:
Secure Distributed System Communication for Cloud–Based Manufacturing

Danish Javeed
Northeastern University, China

Tianhan Gao
Northeastern University, China

Muhammad Shahid Saeed
Dalian University of Technology, China

Rafi Ullah Khan
Macquarie University, Sydney, Australia

Zeeshan Jamil
The University of Agriculture, Peshawar, Pakistan

ABSTRACT

The current century has witnessed a prodigious expansion in scientific innovations contributing toward the betterment of humanity. The astonishing advancements in digital communications have facilitated various spheres of our lifestyle including the manufacturing sector. A plethora of cutting-edge technologies are rubbing shoulders to revolutionize manufacturing trends. Distributed system communications introduce a new concept of digital collaboration among a diversified range of scattered communication nodes. The individual resources of multiple nodes are intelligently integrated to formulate an aggregated impact that yields phenomenal productivity. The smart connectivity among various heterogeneous nodes may familiarize the network with an extended variety of potential security threats. The literature environs a bulk of security solutions proposed to overcome these challenges. This research study provides a comprehensive elaboration of these security threats along with the security practices designed to encounter such activities.

DOI: 10.4018/978-1-6684-6914-9.ch010

1. INTRODUCTION

With the advent of scientific advancements, computer networks have also been evolved. These computer systems are performing miracles in every field of our lives and the industrial sector is a broader application domain of such networks. The implementation of computer networks in the industrial sector is exclusively increasing with the passage of time and such phenomenon gives birth to a wide range of technological attributes. The distributed systems communication is one of the prominent features of computer-based systems which has revolutionized the entire manufacturing industry. In such systems, the network components are not located at the same place. The communication among such nodes is being performed by specially designed network communication protocols. This concept gives birth to new manufacturing environments where manufacturing components work in a decentralized way and it also diminished the need for the presence of those components at the same place (Farzaneh, Montazeri, & Jamali, 2019). The specially designed network communication protocols enable those units to communicate efficiently and reliably. The concept of cloud-based communication also comes to put this idea beyond the brackets. Cloud-based services ensure the availability, integrity, and instant transmission of data across the network. The combination of these two technologies has now become the backbone of the industrial sector and modern manufacturing industries seem highly influenced by under contention combination (Sahay, Geethakumari, & Modugu, 2018).

1.1 Role of Distributed Systems

Computer networks are being modernized following the contemporary needs of society. Distributes networks are one of those systems that fall under the umbrella of modern computer networks. The distributed systems come with unique characteristics that make them entirely different from conventional computer networks. Such characteristics include resource sharing, concurrency, openness, scalability, fault tolerance, and transparency (Glissa, Rachedi, & Meddeb, 2016). The entire processing burden is divided among participant nodes of the network and hence each node participates according to its available resources. This mechanism creates an economically reasonable environment where each node doesn't need to be rich in terms of resources, rather it can use the required resources provided by the host node. This type of network is open and always ready to welcome new potential devices to be part of the network. As functionality and processing are divided among almost all the participant nodes of the network, so it becomes easy to diagnose the faults and miss happenings inside the network. There is no central authority upon with the component nodes have to depend in terms of monitoring, controls, and supervision (Airehrour, Gutierrez, & Ray, 2017). All this architecture gives birth to a transparent surrounding where the working of each device is observed by all component nodes. These exclusive characteristics of distributed networks make themselves an excellent choice for several sectors and the industrial manufacturing sector is one of them. All the core concepts of distributed networks are applied in manufacturing systems where devices are being deployed in a distributed pattern with no dependability upon a single authority (Hashemi & Shams Aliee, 2019). The automated communication among these nodes is ensured by specifically designed communication protocols. As the nodes are connected through reliable communication links so most of the time devices are not available in a single place like conventional network architecture. The resource sharing among these nodes can take place virtually with full transparency, scalability, and concurrency. As a result of this connectivity, the entire processing burden is divided among all nodes and a mutual harmonic scenario is created among the participant nodes (Hashemi & Shams Aliee, 2019).

1.2 Role of Cloud-Based Services

The availability of resources, reliability of communication, and instant interaction with desired data are the core requirements of an ideal computer network. Several technologies have been emerged to achieve these goals however, cloud-based technology has still made its prioritized position. The term cloud is used in terms of a third-party object which shares its resources and services with the mainstream network to enhance the functionality, efficiency, and potentiality of this network. In other words, we can also consider cloud as a vital part of the network where the cloud-based services are used very often (Mayzaud, Badonnel, & Chrisment, 2017). Now here comes the question of which services are provided by the cloud and how can they play a crucial role to enable a network to perform at its best? Starting from the top, the main service is availability. During the communication among a distributed network, the establishment of a chain process is a challenging task. To overcome this issue, the cloud ensures the availability of data to all nodes where they can systematically perform their individual tasks (Wang et al., 2018). The data is being updated on the cloud depends upon the requirements of the network. There are two main modes to update this data known as live updation and periodic updation respectively. In the first modes, the data is continuously being updated on the cloud, so it becomes available to all the component nodes of the network within no time. In the second mode, the data chunks are updated promptly, however, the application areas of such backups are less than the first one (Kunst et al., 2019). When the availability of data is provided by the cloud it becomes easy for nodes to maintain a chain process. Such a phenomenon also plays a crucial role to reduce processing time and end-to-end delay. The second major service is connectivity that comes to perform its functionality in terms of reliable sharing medium among the network components. The resource sharing can also be performed by such sort of heterogeneous communication links where the server and client can coordinate through this strategic architecture (Arora, Khanna, Rastogi, & Agarwal, 2017). The next major service provided by the cloud is storage. Cloud can efficiently store tons of data that is being processed across the network. This feature reduces the need for a bulk of storage devices and also makes the architecture as economic and sustainable. A node can simply interact with the cloud and can fetch its desired data within no time. Moreover, their storage mechanism provided by the cloud is not so complex. That phenomenon creates a reliable and scalable connectivity framework between the client node and cloud services to address the data backups (Ali et al., 2020).

1.3 Cyber-Attacks and its Countermeasure

The most crucial approaches for today are automation and remote control, by which the critical infrastructures can boost their efficiency and service standards. While the critical infrastructures' efficiency is clearly increased by the digital technologies used in these systems, there are also substantial problems connected to the continual attacks to the digital security of those infrastructures (Javeed, Gao, & Khan, 2021; Kolowrocki & Soszynska-Budny, 2018). These threats are described in the following subsections.

202

1.3.1 Phishing Attacks

It is one of popular attacks that are utilized to steal the delicate data of the users. It happens when an attacker, purporting to be a trustworthy entity (Javeed, Gao, Khan, & Ahmad, 2021; Roman et al., 2009), deceives the users to enter personal info into a phony website or downloading a malicious attachment, that may result in a virus installation or the revealing of sensitive information of the user. Specialized phishers aim for the absence of specialized active security measures by systems and the lack of knowledge or attentiveness of users with compromised attacks that combine social engineering and sophisticated tactics known as compromised attacks for critical infrastructures (Al Razib et al., 2022). Numerous articles concentrate on malicious website crawling based using sophisticed methods. (Chandrasekaran, Chinchani, & Upadhyaya, 2006) suggest a brand-new method called PHONEY, which instantly recognizes and evaluates phishing assaults. The tool underlying this strategy is a web browser plugin that displays data about the reliability of the sites, the security certifications they possess, and whether or not malicious code or deceptive urls have been proven to be present on them. A web browser prototype that was utilized as an agent to process data was developed by (Jain & Richariya, 2011). In a secure setting, the user opens the email in their web browser. If an attack is discovered, they are alerted and requested to delete the email. The authors of (Yan et al., 2020) introduced URL embedding (UE), a promising method. In order to determine correlation coefficients between various urls, this novel approach is utilized to look for correlations between various domain names. Furthermore, (Ma, Saul, Savage, & Voelker, 2009) investigated several machine learning techniques for categorising websites according to their features and content.

1.3.2 Ransomware Attacks

This style of attack introduces malware into the system in order to launch a dos attack. The users must pay a price to restore access to a service (dos) or personal data, and access (Javeed, Gao, Khan, & Shoukat, 2022). Industrial ransomware typically targets vital system entities in order to do as much harm as they can, in contrast to normal ransomware, which are dispersed widely (Javeed, Khan, et al., 2020). The authors of (Al-Hawawreh, Den Hartog, & Sitnikova, 2019) provide a thorough and organized study of the different hazards presented by these ransomwares and suggest some effective remedies. According to their investigation, such systems' edge gateways for industries are extremely susceptible to ransomware assaults. Using a dynamic machine, the authors of (Alhawi, Baldwin, & Dehghantanha, 2018) proposed a detection model learning methods for reliable detection of windows ransomware network assaults, such as conversation-based network traffic aspects. Their tests showed that the commercial database produced by these characteristics performs quite well in terms of accuracy.

1.3.3 System Attacks

Due to their prevalence and ease of use, SCADA systems are a target of one of the most frequent assaults on industrial infrastructure and are present in many industrial infrastructures throughout the world. Given the complication of the target devices, the variety of industrial networks, and the significance of the implementations in which these systems are placed, i.e., water, energy, and other networks, (Wahab et al., 2022) offered a study of how to attack devices while simultaneously studying, implementing, and proposing a specialized solution for their timely and accurate detection. Further, the attacker also alters the communication by performing Man in the middle attack (mitm) (Cekerevac et al., 2017; Conti, Dragoni, & Lesyk, 2016; Javeed et al., 2020; Khan, 2019; Maynard, mclaughlin, & Haberler, 2014). The attacker performs a covert sensor assault after creating mitm. This assault modifies the sensors' and actuators' settings to alter how some processes operate, but the system's monitoring components are blind to this change. Researchers proposed numerous intelligent frameworks for network traffic analysis between industrial devices and achieved a high success rate (Demertzis, Iliadis, & Bougoudis, 2020; Demertzis, Iliadis, & Anezakis, 2018; Javeed et al., 2020; Xing, Demertzis, & Yang, 2020). In order to find patterns that assist in the detection, identification, and prediction of anomalies without producing false alarms, additional technical or heuristic types of analysis related to anomaly detection is conducted in (Genge, Haller, & Enăchescu, 2019; Wahab et al., 2022).

1.3.4 Distributed Denial of Service attacks

Ddos attacks are simple to conduct but challenging to thwart. Cyber attackers frequently create a botnet, or a computers network, in order to launch a successful ddos attack. It can be divided in to two categories, i.e., Application-level ddos and Network level ddos attacks.

The Network level attacks primarily employ the ICMP, UDP, TCP, and DNS protocol packets and target the disruption of legitimate user connectivity by taking up all available bandwidth on the victim network (Zargar, Joshi, & Tipper, 2013). However, The Application-level attacks concentrate on overloading server resources (such as sockets, CPU, RAM, disk/database bandwidth, and I/O bandwidth) in order to interfere with the services provided to authorized users (Ranjan, Swaminathan, Uysal, & Knightly, 2006). The frequency of ddos attacks is significantly increasing as the network transitions to cloud computing settings. In cloud computing environments, traditional ddos assault protection systems confront numerous difficulties. Ddos attacks are serious dangers to cloud security, according to a recent Cloud Security Alliance survey (Jean-Francois, 2012; Yan et al., 2020). The rise and appearance of botnets is one key factor. Botnets are networks comprised of infected machines infested with malware. It is still challenging to contaminate a large number of machines in traditional networks. However, legitimate organizations might leverage the cloud's on-demand self-service features to easily add or subtract computing capacity, which could be used to instantly build a potent botnet (Ahmad et al., 2020).

With the flexibility and speed of cloud computing, attackers can not only conduct massive ddos attacks but also more sophisticated and flexible ddos attacks by utilizing a variety of client platforms. As attackers use botnets to overwhelm their victim's network infrastructure, ddos attacks have greatly increased in magnitude and frequency. The prevalence of mobile devices, including smartphones and tablets, is also anticipated to play a key role in the development of ddos assaults against cloud computing. Today's malicious attackers carry a potent attack tool that takes little training in the palm of their hands. In the next years, it is anticipated that the use of these attack tools would significantly rise due to how simple it is for mobile device users to sign up for ddos assault operations (Yu, Tian, Guo, & Wu, 2013). Since ddos assaults were launched against Yahoo, Amazon, and other well-known websites in 2000, experts have proposed numerous techniques to counteract ddos attacks. Several taxonomies of ddos attacks defense mechanisms have been presented in the literature (Ahmad, Liu, Javeed, & Ahmad, 2020; Bu, Yu, Liu, & Tang, 2011; Giotis et al., 2014). The focus of 's authors is on wired network systems' defenses against ddos flooding attacks.

1.3.5 Cross-Site-Scripting

Cloud-based manufacturing environments are by default insecure. The main cause of the theft of users' sensitive and personal information is that their developers don't set up safe development protocols (Rodríguez, Torres, Flores, & Benavides, 2020). This deficiency in ethical behaviour is regarded as a vulnerability. If the website is not properly created, a hacker can use this weakness to execute malicious code on the systems and spread throughout the entire organization's network. Due to the increase in Internet access, web browsers are currently the most common attack vector. The victim of this form of assault is the user, not the apps, according to the most recent report on security statistics in online applications (Gupta, Govil, & Singh, 2015). The second-most serious vulnerability, with about 38% of it being critical, is XSS. In conclusion, the following factors are taken into consideration while evaluating XSS: exploitability, business consequences, technical impacts, vulnerability detectability, and weakness prevalence. XSS frequently happens when (Elhakeem & Barry, 2013):

- A web application can accept untrusted data.
- This unreliable data is generated dynamically by the same web application.
- The victim accesses the webpage created by the malicious XSS script-infected web browser that had previously been contaminated with unreliable data.
- A server sent XSS script is performed within a web page, or more specifically, within the same domain as the web server.

This attack targets the web servers that host the web apps rather than utilizing flaws in any particular browser. There are three different sorts of attacks, per the literature (Kirda, Kruegel, Vigna, & Jovanovic, 2006). Document Object Model (DOM) XSS, non-persistent XSS, and persistent XSS. Any computing system has vulnerabilities that can be identified in the program, hardware, and even the developers. XSS attacks take advantage of the absence of systems to validate and filter the input fields in web forms to submit and execute malevolent scripts, which are deposited in text files as instructions that are translated line by line in real-time for their execution.

1.3.6 SQL Injection

Injecting a Web application is synonymous with accessing the data stored in the database. Data may be extremely important and vulnerable in some cases, such as financial transactions, financial secrets, or the internal mechanisms of a specific info system. Attackers may even utilize SQL injection attacks to attain subtle data pertaining to an industry security. SQL Injection could be quite harmful in numerous instances, liable on the platform from which the attack is launched and if it is effective in inoculating rogue users into the aimed system. There are many types of SQL injection attacks.

1. **Tautologies:** One or more conditional statements receive an injection of SQL queries that ensure their evaluation is always true.
2. **Logically Incorrect Queries:** using error messages that the database rejected to locate valuable information that helps with backend database injection.
3. **Piggy-Backed Queries:** An initial injected query has additional malicious queries added to it.

4. **Union Query:** An injected query is combined with a harmless query using the UNION keyword to retrieve data about additional tables from the application.

5. **Alternate Encodings:** It seeks to avoid being recognised by automated prevention methods and secure defensive coding. As a result, it aids the assailants in avoiding capture. Usually, it is used in conjunction with other offensive strategies.

6. **Stored Procedure:** They are frequently included in databases. To execute these built-in functions, the attacker employs malicious SQL Injection techniques.

To eliminate SQL Injection Vulnerabilities, the authors of (Thomas, Williams, & Xie, 2009) offer an automatic prepared statement generating process. Open source projects, i.e., I Net-trust, WebGoat, ITrust and Roller are used their research. About 94 percent of the SQLIVs in four open-source projects could be successfully replaced by their prepared statement code, according to the trial results. A static analysis framework is suggested by (Fu et al., 2007) as a way to identify SQL Injection Vulnerabilities. The authors proposed framework seeks to spot SQL Injection attacks at build time. There are two primary advantages to using this static analysis tool. A White-box Static Analysis is done first, followed by a Hybrid-Constraint Solver. In (Ruse, Sarkar, & Basu, 2010), the authors suggest a method for identifying SQL Injection Vulnerabilities using automatic test case generation. This framework's fundamental concept is built on developing a unique model that responds to SQL queries automatically. A reliable database testing model for Web applications is recommended by (Haixia & Zhihong, 2009). They suggest a few things, including first identifying probable entry points for SQL Injection, then automatically creating test cases, and identifying the vulnerability of the database by executing these test cases to create the attack simulation on an application. It is established that the suggested methodology is effective. The authors of (Shin, Williams, & Xie, 2006) advise using SQLUnitGen, an automated testing tool based on static analysis, to find input manipulation issues. The authors use the static analysis tool FindBugs in comparison to the SQLUnitGen tool. The absence of any false positives in the experiments demonstrates the effectiveness of the hypothesized mechanism. (Al-Hawawreh et al., 2019) emphasise the usage of manual procedures to guard against SQLI input manipulation flaws. Manual approaches employ code review and defensive programming. In defensive programming, an input filter is used to avoid users from entering potentially harmful phrases or characters. This is performed by using white or black lists. (Javeed et al., 2022) employ SQLCHECK in real time. It decides whether the input queries adhere to the programmer's specifications. A secret key is employed for the user input delimitation (Kunst et al., 2019). Finally, an IDS is suggested by (Javeed, Khan, et al., 2020) for the databases' backends. A prototype that operates at the session level namely DIWeDa is used to detect invasions in Web applications.

2. LITERATURE REVIEW

A plethora of scientific contributions are being made under the contention research domain, some of them are elaborated in this section.

Authors proposed a secure communicational framework to establish an anomaly free data communication in a distributed network of manufacturing nodes (Farzaneh et al., 2019). To be specific they have targeted Routing Protocol (RPL) for Low Power and Lossy Networks (LLNs) also known as RPL protocol that is an IPV6 routing protocol designed for resource constraint manufacturing environments. The proposed framework enables secure communication in RPL based distributed manufacturing systems by analyzing the flow of data that is being processed across the network. A HELLO-Flood attack is a commonly happened security attack in distributed manufacturing networks. The participant nodes show malicious behavior in the presence of such an attack and start sending a bulk of hello requests to neighbor nodes that tends to increase computational overhead within the network and finally this activity results in slowing down the entire communication process. The availability of data can be shacked by this malicious activity, so serious countermeasure needs to be done against such activities. The existence of such an attack can be identified by analyzing the data flow and that's exactly what the authors have proposed in this article. The proposed framework observes data flow in normal as well as attacking scenarios, if a particular node is identified to send an anonymous pattern of data then an alarming situation is flashed and the nodes are considered as a compromised node. The performance of this framework is checked in Contiki operating system based Cooja simulator were positive results seem to support the proposed idea in terms of efficient detection of HELLO-Flood attack in distributed system based manufacturing environments.

The RPL follows a specific and system friendly communication pattern to enable data transmission across the network. It makes a Destination Oriented Directed Acyclic Graph (DODAG) in which all the participant nodes follow a tree-based architecture to maintain a traffic flow towards the receiving node. The formation of this tree takes place by assigning a unique rank number to each node and this rank number is gradually decreased from sender to receiver node. When a gateway node is compromised, it shows a decreased rank number and asks previous nodes to send the data packet to it. Hence, the packet is sent to this malicious node that may result in part of full data loss. The authors presented a trust aware solution to counter such rank-based attack in which the rank number of each participant node is checked before every communication session (Sahay et al., 2018). The rank number is investigated and analyzed and abnormal allocation of rank number tends to declare this scenario as a legitimate activity. Hence, a new DODAG is instantly formed to prevent the happening of any injurious activity within the network. This framework is simulated in the Cooja simulator where it shows the effective detection of abnormal activities with less resource consumption in cloud-based distributed manufacturing networks. However, the instant formation of DODAG before and during each communication session sometimes may slow down the rapid communicational aspects of RPL protocol.

Another novel technique to counter security concerns in RPL is proposed named as secure RPL (SRPL) (Glissa et al., 2016). Two types of attack i.e sinkhole attack and blackhole attack have been addressed in this scientific work. When a node is compromised, it starts sending fake information regarding the rank number to its nearby nodes. As a result, the predefined data traveling path is finally manipulated and the data packets follow a new anonymous path. Partial packet loss or modification of data packets may occur as an outcome of such activity. The black hole attack has a close resemblance to the sinkhole attack. When a new path is adopted by a data stream, fully packet loss may also occur and that situation is referred to as a black hole attack. The authors have designed an investigation mechanism to identify the presence of sinkhole attack and black hole attack. The traffic stream is analyzed in terms of throughput and end-to-end transmission time. The decrement in throughput or an increment at the end-to-end transmission delay flashes an injurious scenario and the presence of compromised nodes are declared within the network. This technique is tested and processed in the Cooja simulator where it exhibits its strength regarding effective detection of attacks in distributed networks-based manufacturing units. However, this investigation mechanism consists of heavy processing that may tend to increase computational overhead. Nominal energy consumption in resource constraint distributed industrial units makes an ambiguous image of this proposed work.

RPL is generally susceptible to a variety of security attacks and a selective forwarding attack is one of them. During this attack, the compromised nodes disturb the predefined data flow path and rout the data stream to a new path (Airehrour et al., 2017). The unauthorized monitoring of data may occur as a result of this activity. Authors have addressed this issue and designed an identification technique to check the availability of attack in cloud-based distributed manufacturing environments. This technique works under the basic principles of the statistical count of throughput and end-to-end delay. By following a special means of calculation, the data packets are counted before and after each transmission session. The end-to-end delay of these packets is also calculated and analyzed. In a selective forwarding attack, most of the time only end-to-end delay increases, however, the statistical count of data packets remains the same. Still, such type of activities is not good for the network because it causes unnecessary delays in normal communication. The efficiency of this technique is tested in the cooja simulation environment in terms of True Positive Rate (TPR), False Positive Rate (FPR), and attack detection accuracy. This technique seems to prove its effectiveness on all the above-mentioned parameters that make it an ideal choice to be applicable in cloud-based distributed manufacturing networks.

A Dynamic and Comprehensive Testing Model (DCTM) is proposed that is capable to locate the presence of malicious activities in cloud-based distributed manufacturing systems (Hashemi & Shams Aliee, 2019). The rank attack, Sybil attack, and version number attack have been taken into consideration and the model is proposed to counter with such security challenges. The model works by analyzing the network behavior and dynamic checks have been implemented in this regard. The data flow, energy consumption of nodes, processing delay of nodes, and traffic pattern is analyzed in each random check. In critical cases, the periodic pattern of dynamic checks can also be implemented which makes the model more efficient and elegant. In Contiki operating system based Cooja simulator, authors have simulated the entire performance of this model where fast attack discovery can be observed by implementing this model, However, the model sometimes requires high computational resources that don't make it a perfect choice for limited resource distributed smart manufacturing environments.

RPL is a proactive distance-vector protocol that creates its routing table prior to beginning communication. DODAG formation is the core mechanism that is responsible for the working of this protocol. The architecture of DODAG is reestablished if a node dies or not responding well during a transmission session. So, the system has to formed new DODAG as well as Directed Acyclic Graphs (DAG) to maintain its error-free operations. A bulk of the system's energy is drained in such formation and continuous episodes of this formation may cause bad effects to the network health and its performance gradually goes down. To address this activity, authors have presented a monitoring strategy that checks whether there is a serious need to rebuild the DAG or not (Hashemi & Shams Aliee, 2019). In other words, it only allows the system to modify its DAGs and DODAG only in serious scenarios. Hence it differentiates between normal as well as attacking situations by keeping an eye on DODAG Information Solicitation (DIO) and DODAG Information Object (DIO) packets. During each formation of DODAG, the DIS and DIO packets are transmitted from bottom to upside and downside respectively. The transmission pattern of these packets helps to create a filter between normal and attacking scenario. The performance of this proposed framework is checked where efficient attack detection can be observed in small scale cloud-based industrial networks.

When a new DODAG is formed, it is labeled with a new version number. That greater number of version numbers shows the reconstruction cycles in original DODAG. So appropriate countermeasures need to be performed following its version numbers. However, sometimes compromised nodes send false information that results in the formation of the unnecessary formation of DODAG. This phenomenon tends to decrease network lifetime and high resource consumption may also occur. Such an attack is declared as a version number attack and to cater to this attack, a distributed monitoring strategy is designed (Mayzaud et al., 2017). The proposed model proves its effectiveness to stop the unnecessary formation of DODAG by checking the authenticity of demand.

Cloud-based manufacturing is catching ultimate attention and became a widely spreading concept in modern industries. The miracles of cloud-based manufacturing can be seen in almost every aspect of our lives. Such broader supplication areas also make it vulnerable to a variety of security concerns. Another monitoring strategy is proposed to reduce the happenings of malicious activities in cloud-based industrial manufacturing units (Wang et al., 2018). A combination of a distributed genetic algorithm (DGA) and manufacturing resource combinatorial optimization (MRCO) comes to design this monitoring mechanism. The DGA is divided into several modules to ensure high accuracy regarding malicious activity detection. A case study performance comparison of simple genetic algorithm (SGA) and Working procedure priority based algorithm (WPPBA) is performed in MATLAB simulation environments where the strengths of the proposed model can be noticed in terms of high accuracy regarding malicious activities detection in cloud-based manufacturing systems.

A quality of service (QoS) based technique is presented that is responsible to facilitate rapid, reliable, and secure communication in cloud-based distributed manufacturing units (Kunst et al., 2019). The concepts of cyber-physical systems CPS) gives an advanced life to cloud-based industries, with its immense functionalities, it also covers the security aspects in such type of environments. The proposed framework reduces the broader stream of data by enabling devices to perform multiple tasks. The devices with high resources have to perform more tasks as compared to devices with fewer resources. In this way, unnecessary to and fro movement of data packets is reduced to a notable extent that tends to increase rapid and secure communication. Hence the security checks can be applied on specific devices rather than to implement on the entire system. The effectiveness of the proposed framework is observed in MATLAB simulations environment where positive outcome appears to make the proposed technique as an ideal choice for cloud-based small industrial setups.

Data security is also one of the major security concerns in cloud-based manufacturing. The data is available on the cloud for where cloud performs a wide range of services, however, this data needs to be in an unusable form where it must be used only by the authorized parties. The authors proposed a cryptographic solution to secure this data. The solution is based on the combined effect of symmetric and asymmetric cryptographic and is named as Hybrid Cryptographic System (HCS) (Arora et al., 2017). The data is end-to-end and encrypted is also stored in the cloud in the same cryptographic form where it cannot be used by unauthorized authorities. This process ensures data security and end-to-end data integrity. The performance of the presented solution is tested in the CloudSim simulator where the strengths claim of the proposed model appears true, however, significant computational overhead may also cause by this model. The related work is summarized in the following Table 1:

Table 1. Limitations of the existing literature mechanisms

Ref	Proposed Solution	Strengths	Weakness	Parameters	Simulator
(Farzaneh et al., 2019)	Statistical count of DIS packets	Statistical count of DIS packets	Computation overhead increases	TPR, FPR	Cooja
(Sahay et al., 2018)	Packet delivery count based mechanism	Observation of rank attack and version number attack	High computation overhead	Packet Delivery Ratio, End to End delay	Cooja
(Glissa et al., 2016)	SRPL	Black hole and Sinkhole attack detection	High energy utilization is required	Low detection accuracy with a high computation overhead	Cooja
(Airehrour et al., 2017)	The periodic check based statistical count	Countermeasures against selective forwarding attack	End to end delay increases	Accuracy TPR FPR	Cooja
(Hashemi & Shams Aliee, 2019)	DCTM-RPL	Protection against rank, blackhole and Sybil attack	It requires high computation resource	Computational l Overhead	Cooja
(Hashemi & Shams Aliee, 2019)	DIS and DIO packets analysis	Detection of version number attack	High computation overhead	Attack detection accuracy	Cooja
(Mayzaud et al., 2017)	A distributed monitoring strategy	Prevention against version number attack	Requires high resources		Cooja
(Wang et al., 2018)	Manufacturing resource selection method	Reduction in the occurrence of chances of malicious activities	Not suitable for all sort of production units	Resource consumption, End to end delay	MATLAB
(Kunst et al., 2019)	QoS based analysis technique	Rapid and reliable communication	System sometimes slowdown		MATLAB
(Arora et al., 2017)	HCS	Data encryption	Requires higher resources	Data security, Data Integrity	CloudSim

3. CONCLUSION

Scientific innovations have productively transformed the conventional means of digital communications and have introduced various new cutting-edge technologies. Distributed systems communication is patronized over a general idea where identically heterogeneous nodes share their resources to contribute toward a gigantic task. The trend is impressively followed in the manufacturing sector and is revealing phenomenal performance over there as well. The involvement of multiple nodes enhances sometimes makes the network susceptible to an extensive catalogue of security risks that need to be overcome. These circumstances urge a valid need for some appropriate security measures to safeguard such networks against security threats. The domain is gaining significant attention, and several astonishing efforts are being made to secure distributed systems communication-based manufacturing environments. In this research study, we have classified the existing security threats and have discussed the security solutions made so far to address the under-contention research theme. In the future, the authors aims to discuss other security threats and the existing solutions to proactively detect the cyber threats in such systems.

REFERENCES

Ahmad, I., Liu, Y., Javeed, D., & Ahmad, S. (2020). *A decision-making technique for solving order allocation problem using a genetic algorithm.* Paper presented at the IOP Conference Series: Materials Science and Engineering. IOP Science. 10.1088/1757-899X/853/1/012054

Ahmad, I., Liu, Y., Javeed, D., Shamshad, N., Sarwr, D., & Ahmad, S. (2020). *A review of artificial intelligence techniques for selection & evaluation.* Paper presented at the IOP Conference Series: Materials Science and Engineering. 10.1088/1757-899X/853/1/012055

Airehrour, D., Gutierrez, J., & Ray, S. K. (2017). A trust-aware RPL routing protocol to detect blackhole and selective forwarding attacks. *Journal of Telecommunications and the Digital Economy*, *5*(1), 50–69. doi:10.18080/jtde.v5n1.88

Al-Hawawreh, M., Den Hartog, F., & Sitnikova, E. (2019). Targeted ransomware: A new cyber threat to edge system of brownfield industrial Internet of Things. *IEEE Internet of Things Journal*, *6*(4), 7137–7151. doi:10.1109/JIOT.2019.2914390

Al Razib, M., Javeed, D., Khan, M. T., Alkanhel, R., & Muthanna, M. S. A. (2022). Cyber Threats Detection in Smart Environments Using SDN-Enabled DNN-LSTM Hybrid Framework. *IEEE Access : Practical Innovations, Open Solutions*, *10*, 53015–53026. doi:10.1109/ACCESS.2022.3172304

Alhawi, O. M., Baldwin, J., & Dehghantanha, A. (2018). Leveraging machine learning techniques for windows ransomware network traffic detection. In *Cyber threat intelligence* (pp. 93–106). Springer. doi:10.1007/978-3-319-73951-9_5

Ali, S., Javaid, N., Javeed, D., Ahmad, I., Ali, A., & Badamasi, U. M. (2020). *A blockchain-based secure data storage and trading model for wireless sensor networks.* Paper presented at the International Conference on Advanced Information Networking and Applications. 10.1007/978-3-030-44041-1_45

Arora, A., Khanna, A., Rastogi, A., & Agarwal, A. (2017). *Cloud security ecosystem for data security and privacy.* Paper presented at the 2017 7th International conference on cloud computing, data science & engineering-confluence. IEEE. 10.1109/CONFLUENCE.2017.7943164

Bu, S., Yu, F. R., Liu, X. P., & Tang, H. (2011). Structural results for combined continuous user authentication and intrusion detection in high security mobile ad-hoc networks. *IEEE Transactions on Wireless Communications*, *10*(9), 3064–3073. doi:10.1109/TWC.2011.071411.102123

Cekerevac, Z., Dvorak, Z., Prigoda, L., & Cekerevac, P. (2017). Internet of things and the man-in-the-middle attacks–security and economic risks. *MEST Journal*, *5*(2), 15–25. doi:10.12709/mest.05.05.02.03

Chandrasekaran, M., Chinchani, R., & Upadhyaya, S. (2006). *Phoney: Mimicking user response to detect phishing attacks.* Paper presented at the 2006 International Symposium on a World of Wireless, Mobile and Multimedia Networks (WoWMoM'06). IEEE. 10.1109/WOWMOM.2006.87

Conti, M., Dragoni, N., & Lesyk, V. (2016). A survey of man in the middle attacks. *IEEE Communications Surveys and Tutorials*, *18*(3), 2027–2051. doi:10.1109/COMST.2016.2548426

Demertzis, K., Iliadis, L., & Bougoudis, I. (2020). Gryphon: A semi-supervised anomaly detection system based on one-class evolving spiking neural network. *Neural Computing & Applications*, *32*(9), 4303–4314. doi:10.100700521-019-04363-x

Demertzis, K., Iliadis, L. S., & Anezakis, V.-D. (2018). An innovative soft computing system for smart energy grids cybersecurity. *Advances in Building Energy Research*, *12*(1), 3–24. doi:10.1080/1751254 9.2017.1325401

Elhakeem, Y. F. G. M., & Barry, B. I. (2013). *Developing a security model to protect websites from cross-site scripting attacks using ZEND framework application.* Paper presented at the 2013 International Conference on Computing, Electrical and Electronic Engineering (Icceee). IEEE. 10.1109/IC-CEEE.2013.6634012

Farzaneh, B., Montazeri, M. A., & Jamali, S. (2019). *An anomaly-based IDS for detecting attacks in RPL-based internet of things.* Paper presented at the 2019 5th International Conference on Web Research (ICWR). IEEE. 10.1109/ICWR.2019.8765272

Fu, X., Lu, X., Peltsverger, B., Chen, S., Qian, K., & Tao, L. (2007). *A static analysis framework for detecting SQL injection vulnerabilities.* Paper presented at the 31st annual international computer software and applications conference (COMPSAC 2007). IEEE. 10.1109/COMPSAC.2007.43

Genge, B., Haller, P., & Enăchescu, C. (2019). Anomaly detection in aging industrial internet of things. *IEEE Access : Practical Innovations, Open Solutions*, *7*, 74217–74230. doi:10.1109/ACCESS.2019.2920699

Giotis, K., Argyropoulos, C., Androulidakis, G., Kalogeras, D., & Maglaris, V. (2014). Combining OpenFlow and sFlow for an effective and scalable anomaly detection and mitigation mechanism on SDN environments. *Computer Networks*, *62*, 122–136. doi:10.1016/j.bjp.2013.10.014

Glissa, G., Rachedi, A., & Meddeb, A. (2016). *A secure routing protocol based on RPL for Internet of Things.* Paper presented at the 2016 IEEE Global Communications Conference (GLOBECOM). IEEE. 10.1109/GLOCOM.2016.7841543

Gupta, M. K., Govil, M. C., & Singh, G. (2015). *Predicting Cross-Site Scripting (XSS) security vulnerabilities in web applications.* Paper presented at the 2015 12th International Joint Conference on Computer Science and Software Engineering (JCSSE). IEEE.

Haixia, Y., & Zhihong, N. (2009). *A database security testing scheme of web application.* Paper presented at the 2009 4th International Conference on Computer Science & Education. IOP Science.

Hashemi, S. Y., & Shams Aliee, F. (2019). Dynamic and comprehensive trust model for IoT and its integration into RPL. *The Journal of Supercomputing*, *75*(7), 3555–3584. doi:10.100711227-018-2700-3

Jain, A., & Richariya, V. (2011). Implementing a web browser with phishing detection techniques. *arXiv preprint arXiv.*

Javeed, D., Badamasi, U. M., Iqbal, T., Umar, A., & Ndubuisi, C. O. (2020). Threat detection using machine/deep learning in IOT environments. *International Journal of Computer Networks and Communications Security*, *8*(8), 59–65.

Javeed, D., Gao, T., & Khan, M. T. (2021). SDN-enabled hybrid DL-driven framework for the detection of emerging cyber threats in IoT. *Electronics (Basel)*, *10*(8), 918. doi:10.3390/electronics10080918

Javeed, D., Gao, T., Khan, M. T., & Ahmad, I. (2021). A hybrid deep learning-driven SDN enabled mechanism for secure communication in Internet of Things (IoT). *Sensors (Basel)*, *21*(14), 4884. doi:10.339021144884 PMID:34300623

Javeed, D., Gao, T., Khan, M. T., & Shoukat, D. (2022). A hybrid intelligent framework to combat sophisticated threats in secure industries. *Sensors (Basel)*, *22*(4), 1582. doi:10.339022041582 PMID:35214481

Javeed, D., Khan, M. T., Ahmad, I., Iqbal, T., Badamasi, U. M., Ndubuisi, C. O., & Umar, A. (2020). An efficient approach of threat hunting using memory forensics. *International Journal of Computer Networks and Communications Security*, *8*(5), 37–45. doi:10.47277/IJCNCS/8(5)1

Javeed, D., & MohammedBadamasi, U. (2020). Man in the middle attacks: Analysis motivation and prevention. *International Journal of Computer Networks and Communications Security*, *8*(7), 52–58. doi:10.47277/IJCNCS/8(7)1

Jean-Francois. (2012). Cloud Computing: Weapon of Choice for DDoS? Khan, T. U. (2019). Internet of Things (IOT) systems and its security challenges. *International Journal of Advanced Research in Computer Engineering and Technology*, *8*(12).

Kirda, E., Kruegel, C., Vigna, G., & Jovanovic, N. (2006). *Noxes: a client-side solution for mitigating cross-site scripting attacks.* Paper presented at the Proceedings of the 2006 ACM symposium on Applied computing. ACM. 10.1145/1141277.1141357

Kolowrocki, K., & Soszynska-Budny, J. (2018). *Critical Infrastructure Safety Indicators.* Paper presented at the 2018 IEEE International Conference on Industrial Engineering and Engineering Management (IEEM). IEEE.

Kunst, R., Avila, L., Binotto, A., Pignaton, E., Bampi, S., & Rochol, J. (2019). Improving devices communication in Industry 4.0 wireless networks. *Engineering Applications of Artificial Intelligence*, *83*, 1–12. doi:10.1016/j.engappai.2019.04.014

Ma, J., Saul, L. K., Savage, S., & Voelker, G. M. (2009). *Beyond blacklists: learning to detect malicious web sites from suspicious URLs.* Paper presented at the Proceedings of the 15th ACM SIGKDD international conference on Knowledge discovery and data mining. ACM. 10.1145/1557019.1557153

Maynard, P., McLaughlin, K., & Haberler, B. (2014). *Towards understanding man-in-the-middle attacks on iec 60870-5-104 scada networks.* Paper presented at the 2nd International Symposium for ICS & SCADA Cyber Security Research 2014 (ICS-CSR 2014) 2. IOP Science.

Mayzaud, A., Badonnel, R., & Chrisment, I. (2017). A distributed monitoring strategy for detecting version number attacks in RPL-based networks. *IEEE eTransactions on Network and Service Management*, *14*(2), 472–486. doi:10.1109/TNSM.2017.2705290

Ranjan, S., Swaminathan, R. P., Uysal, M., & Knightly, E. W. (2006). DDoS-Resilient Scheduling to Counter Application Layer Attacks Under Imperfect Detection. *Proceedings IEEE INFOCOM. 25TH IEEE International Conference on Computer Communications*, (pp. 1-13). IEEE. 10.1109/INFOCOM.2006.127

Rodríguez, G. E., Torres, J. G., Flores, P., & Benavides, D. E. (2020). Cross-site scripting (XSS) attacks and mitigation: A survey. *Computer Networks*, *166*, 106960. doi:10.1016/j.comnet.2019.106960

Roman, R., Fernandez-Gago, C., López, J., Chen, H. H., Gritzalis, S., Karygiannis, T., & Skianis, C. (2009). Trust and reputation systems for wireless sensor networks. In Security and Privacy in Mobile and Wireless Networking.

Ruse, M., Sarkar, T., & Basu, S. (2010). *Analysis & detection of SQL injection vulnerabilities via automatic test case generation of programs.* Paper presented at the 2010 10th IEEE/IPSJ International Symposium on Applications and the Internet. IEEE. 10.1109/SAINT.2010.60

Sahay, R., Geethakumari, G., & Modugu, K. (2018). *Attack graph—Based vulnerability assessment of rank property in RPL-6LOWPAN in IoT.* Paper presented at the 2018 IEEE 4th World Forum on Internet of Things (WF-IoT). IEEE. 10.1109/WF-IoT.2018.8355171

Shin, Y., Williams, L. A., & Xie, T. (2006). *SQLUnitgen: Test case generation for SQL injection detection.* Retrieved from Thomas, S., Williams, L., & Xie, T. (2009). On automated prepared statement generation to remove SQL injection vulnerabilities. *Information and Software Technology*, *51*(3), 589–598.

Wahab, F., Zhao, Y., Javeed, D., Al-Adhaileh, M. H., Almaaytah, S. A., Khan, W., Saeed, M. S., & Kumar Shah, R. (2022). An AI-Driven Hybrid Framework for Intrusion Detection in IoT-Enabled E-Health. *Computational Intelligence and Neuroscience*, *2022*, 2022. doi:10.1155/2022/6096289 PMID:36045979

Wahab, F., Zhao, Y., Javeed, D., Al-Adhaileh, M. H., Almaaytah, S. A., Khan, W., Saeed, M. S., & Kumar Shah, R. (2022). An AI-Driven Hybrid Framework for Intrusion Detection in IoT-Enabled E-Health. *Computational Intelligence and Neuroscience*, *2022*, 2022. doi:10.1155/2022/6096289 PMID:36045979

Wang, L., Guo, S., Li, X., Du, B., & Xu, W. (2018). Distributed manufacturing resource selection strategy in cloud manufacturing. *International Journal of Advanced Manufacturing Technology*, *94*(9), 3375–3388. doi:10.100700170-016-9866-8

Xing, L., Demertzis, K., & Yang, J. (2020). Identifying data streams anomalies by evolving spiking restricted Boltzmann machines. *Neural Computing & Applications*, *32*(11), 6699–6713. doi:10.100700521-019-04288-5

Yan, X., Xu, Y., Cui, B., Zhang, S., Guo, T., & Li, C. (2020). Learning URL embedding for malicious website detection. *IEEE Transactions on Industrial Informatics*, *16*(10), 6673–6681. doi:10.1109/TII.2020.2977886

Yu, S., Tian, Y., Guo, S., & Wu, D. O. (2013). Can we beat DDoS attacks in clouds? *IEEE Transactions on Parallel and Distributed Systems*, *25*(9), 2245–2254. doi:10.1109/TPDS.2013.181

Zargar, S. T., Joshi, J., & Tipper, D. (2013). A survey of defense mechanisms against distributed denial of service (DDoS) flooding attacks. *IEEE Communications Surveys and Tutorials*, *15*(4), 2046–2069. doi:10.1109/SURV.2013.031413.00127

Chapter 11
Security in Internet of Things:
Requirements, Challenges, and Open Issues

Said Ul Abrar
The University of Agriculture, Peshawar, Pakistan

Mohib Ullah
The University of Agriculture, Peshawar, Pakistan

Kamran Ullah
The University of Agriculture, Peshawar, Pakistan

Irfan Ullah Khan
Imam Abdulrahman Bin Faisal University, Dammam, Saudi Arabia

Saleem Zahid
The University of Agriculture, Peshawar, Pakistan

Muhammad Inam Ul Haq
Khushal Khan Khattak University, Karak, Pakistan

ABSTRACT

Recently, electronics devices, cognitive computing, and sensing enable the deployment of internet-of-things (IoTs) with a huge application domain. However, resource constraints such as low computing powers or limited storage leave IoTs infrastructures vulnerable to a variety of cyber-attacks. In dark-net the address space developed as designated unrestricted internet address space anticipated to be used by trustworthy hosts anywhere in the world, therefore, any communication activity is presumed to be unwanted and particularly treated as a probe, backscatter, or miss-configuration. This chapter investigates and evaluates the operation of dark-net traffic detection systems in IoTs networks. Moreover, the most recent work done to ensure security in the IoTs network has been discussed. In particular, the areas of privacy provisioning, lightweight cryptographic framework, secure routing, robustness, and DoS attacks have been addressed. Moreover, based on the analysis of existing state-of-the-art protocols, the security requirements and challenges are highlighted along with identified open issues.

DOI: 10.4018/978-1-6684-6914-9.ch011

1. INTRODUCTION

The emergence of internet of things (IoTs) has been made possible by the modern technological revolution in electronics, cognitive computing, and sensing, which has supplied essential infrastructure for a variety of applications. As the IoT domain expands, it is challenging to devise a reference design that can handle both present functionality and potential improvements. In IoTs, the data are acquired from multiple sources and processed by numerous entities, therefore, the IoTs architecture must be distributed in nature, scalable, interoperable, and capable of delivering Moreover, resource constraints such as limited computing power, storage capabilities and energy prohibit the deployment of sophisticated mechanisms. Therefore, the infrastructures used by IoTs are vulnerable to a variety of cyber-attacks. Likewise, traditional networking security solutions are not applicable in IoTs due to the specific architectural requirements and resource constraints. Therefore, light weighted and scalable solutions, under the resource constraints, are desirable to address the problems of privacy, Integrity, denial-of-service attacks detection, cryptographic framework, secure routing etc in IoTs.

Figure1 shows the security frame work in IoTs. The subsequent sections provide a brief detail of the current state-of-the-art solutions aross the sub domains. Finally, a detail discussion including the open research issues, challenges, requirements and future research directions, concludes each sub-domain.

Figure 1. Security framework in IoTs

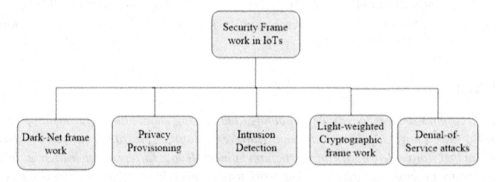

1.1 Dark-Net Traffic Detection Systems in IoTs

The Dark Web or Dark-net comprises a network of shared resources (i.e. websites, servers) open to public with hidden identifiers i.e. IPs. Accessing the shared resources needs special tools and applications. The Dark-net uses peer-to-peer networking with encapsulation where the data are transmitted in encrypted form. Likewise, the forwarding takes placed in a layered manner, where forwarding nodes decrypt layers of the encryption. In this manner, the intermediate nodes know only the position of immediate nodes before and after, this mechanism hides the identity of senders. The working principles of Dark-net make enables the users to carry out illegal activities. The most prominent literature exploits machine learning mechanisms to analyze the network traffic and detects Dark-net related activities (Abu Al-Haija et al., 2022; Demertzis et al., 2021). The employed machine learning techniques classify the different Dark-net traffics and detect certain patterns as malicious activities.

In general, due to the resource's constraints, the IoTs devices lack reasonable virus or malware detection software; therefore, these devices are vulnerable and easily become bots. Attackers take over control the device's routing and forwarding functions. In this manner, the compromised devices (also called, sinkholes or black holes) carry out malicious activities and, also infect other devices in the vicinity. Moreover, this crucial aspect has been addressed in (Pour et al., 2020), parameters such as packet interval timings, employed rates and geo distributions are considered. These features enable the identification of compromised devices (i.e. relay nodes for the Dark-net) to some extent. Likewise, the architectural standards and associated protocols have been overviewed in (Silva et al., 2018). It is pertinent to mention that existing work don not use common architecture and standards. Therefore, the issue of Dark-net traffic detection becomes more challenging and dynamic.

1.3 Intrusion Detection

Network Intrusion Detection Systems (NIDS), one of the most crucial aspect of IoTs, aims to identify harmful activities or intrusions (Abu Al-Haija et al., 2022) As a gatekeeper for the inter-connected devices, NIDS is crucial in thwarting cyber-attacks on various computing systems for businesses, people, and governments (Pour et al., 2020) Utilizing machine learning techniques to enhance NIDS performance has recently emerged as a viable avenue. These learning-based NIDSs have been shown to perform better than many other NIDSs. Machine learning techniques effectively extract and learn features from existing network data. When establishing an IoTs system, there are several factors to take into account, including security, power management, analytics techniques, and software application interoperability (Ogonji et al., 2020)[REMOVED HYPERLINK FIELD]. Since, the IoTs gadgets work without human operators. Therefore, a burglar might physically access these gadgets. Eaves dropping on wireless network utilized by IoTs devices, which frequently have a communication connection between them, allow intruders to access sensitive information. The IoTs devices are more vulnerable due to the limited resources and lack of sophisticated tools. The absence of sophisticated NIDS, IoTs devices are easily compromised and become relay for Dark-net. This limits the application domain of IoTs. Similarly, very few studies address Dark-net intrusion detection (Kanuparthi et al., 2013) in IoTs. In general, light weighted intrusion detections techniques such as (Ali et al., 2022) are needed.

1.4 Privacy in IoTs

Privacy, security threats, vulnerabilities with countermeasures and threat taxonomy have been thoroughly addressed in IoTs (Ogonji et al., 2020; Demertzis et al., 2021). Moreover, a detailed layered architecture of IoT along with threats to privacy and security are examined in-depth for each level of IoT architecture. Similarly, recent works covers eavesdropping, man-in-the-middle attacks, and other risks. These compromise the integrity and secrecy of the data while seizing control of specific components. Moreover, the work covers EU IoT regulations in addition to that. According to EU law, every level of architecture for an individual's information must be under their control. Further research questions necessitate a thorough examination of the technological underpinnings of this type of control. More in-depth research is needed on the concerns to privacy and energy factors.

In (Lin & Bergmann, 2016), the authors examined IoT privacy improvements across a range of application domains and examined the most important security challenges. Additionally, the authors offered an IoT-friendly security architecture. The gateway architecture best suits the resource constraints and ensures system availability. The design can run essential smart home services and executes complex management algorithms on a processor of reasonable power. Likewise, a middleware and cloud architecture are evaluated in IoTs. For the purpose of helping auto management, two technologies are discussed: the first is automated configuration assistance for strengthening system security, and the second is automatic system software and firmware updates to sustain continued secure system operation.

Existing work also covers security and privacy challenges in ad hoc networks (H. Yang et al., 2004). Security design faces a number of difficulties, including open architecture of P2P network, wireless medium shared network, constraints in resources, and frequently changing network topology. Given these difficulties, it is feasible to develop a multi-fence security system that provides both comprehensive protection and optimal network performance. Regarding the multi-hop transmission of packets among mobile nodes, security concerns and cutting-edge approaches are explored. The two levels and measures such as detection, prevention and reaction should be included in a comprehensive security system. Similarly, RFID is one of the promising technologies in IoTs for privacy provisioning (Khoo, 2011). RFID technology is seen as useful for inventory management and item monitoring. This needs to be applied to people, but there must be rules and regulations that are strictly enforced to assure acceptance because it might be misused. The authors draw the conclusion that both technological and societal difficulties must be overcome before RFID can be used to allow IoT. In Gutwirth et al. (2013), security of applications for mobile sensing has been explored. The authors highlighted possible advantages implied from the use of the specified application scenarios in this study. The authors looked at the data flow in the application architectures as well as the varied statistics that are currently obtained by mobile sensing apps. Threats to privacy are highlighted in particular. These dangers affect the fundamental data and sensor readings gathered from current mobile sensing installations. These readings include accelerometer data, sound samples, images, and spatial and temporal information. The temporal annotation of sensed data along with the spatiotemporal reading put the user's privacy in risk. Therefore, privacy preserving safeguards are crucial to avoid auto recording in private conversations and to preserve user privacy. This analogy can also be employed for pictures and videos.

Datagram Transport Layer Security (DTLS) and Host Identity Protocol (HIP) (Garcia-Morchon, Keoh, et al., 2013) introduce a secure architecture for the resource constrained IP-based IoTs. Likewise, pre-shared key management mechanisms (PSK) ensure secure access to the network. These measures preserve user privacy to a considerable level. However, the transmission and computational overheads are needed to be examined thoroughly.

In analysis (Sadeghi et al., 2015) With a thorough categorization and taxonomy of assaults, the examination of security needs, threat models, and security challenges in the IoTs is covered in detail. The article discusses current research questions and open problems. In the report, several directions for further research are also mentioned. The most recent attempt to categorize IoT security is found in (Lu et al., 2014). The authors put forth the Privacy Information Security Categorization paradigm, which is based on privacy and classification (PISC). There are three different degrees of privacy security. A breach of level-1 privacy involves the public disclosure of information that won't have a significant impact on the owner. Personal data that is anonymous or partially anonymous constitutes level-2 privacy. Information that directly relates to a user's identity is under level-3 privacy, including Internet IP address, fingerprint, and information from identification cards. False fingerprints cause important data to be stolen or lost. As a result, level-3 private information must be protected by intricate security protection procedures. However, protecting the various layers of private information needs multiple protection systems.

1.4.1 Requirements and Challenges

The privacy framework and solution in IoT should consider the following requirements.

- *Tracking and profiling*: A threat arises when an identity is linked to a specific person since this might result in surveillance and profiling. In order to avoid such activity in IoT, one of the main issues is to forbid it and implement certain preventative measures.
- *Locating and following.* An additional risk involves localization, where computers aim to monitor and document an individual's movements and locations. Developing protocols for IoT interactions that discourage this kind of behavior is one of the main challenges for IoT security solutions. In e-commerce scenarios, information about a person's profile is often utilized to deduce their interests by associating it with other profiles and data. Striking a balance between user privacy standards and business interests in profiling and data analysis poses a significant issue.
- *Finding and pursuing.* Localization, which happens when computers try to monitor and record a person's whereabouts over time and space, is another risk. One of the key challenges for security of IoT devices is creating rules for interactions with the internet of things that prohibit such behavior. Profiling information about a given individual is regularly combined with other profiles and data to infer interests. A significant challenge is balancing corporate interests in data analysis and profiling with user privacy norms.

1.5 The Cryptographic Framework in IoTs

IoTs pose additional challenges due to the resource constraints (i.e. energy, computing etc.) Therefore, light weighted cryptographic primitives are preferred for IoT applications, without sacrificing the necessary level of security. Therefore, lightweight cryptography has been a priority of the research community. In ISO/IEC 29192 and ISO/IEC JTC 1/SC 27, properties of light weighted cryptographies are covered. Additionally, a project for simple cryptography (ISO/IEC 29192) is being standardized. The ISO/IEC 29192 describes lightweight cryptography based on the size of chip and energy metrices.

1.5.1 Challenges and Solutions

IoT requires the development of a lightweight cryptographic framework due to hardware resource limitations. This can be done by suggesting that cryptographic graphic primitives are needed to be reviewed and redesigned with the limitations of IoT devices in mind.

A simple cryptographic architecture for IoTs is suggested in (Garcia-Morchon, Rietman, Shparlinski, et al., 2014). The suggested method operates in accordance with an IoT network's smart object's lifespan. TTP infrastructure is in charge of managing the keying materials. The suggested framework is utilized to produce the intelligent objects in a secure manner. A key distribution mechanism in Wireless Sensor Networks (WSNs) is proposed (Garcia-Morchon, Keoh, et al., 2013). The employed mechanism uses node identity in a distributed manner and manage key agreements under the resource constraints. The authors have (Garcia-Morchon, Rietman, Sharma, et al., 2014) suggested methods to simplify polynomial calculation for the Internet of Things. The work Brachmann et al. (2012) uncover security compromises at the transport layer which make the provision of end-to-end security difficult. Low-power and loss networks (LLNs) are nevertheless effective to face flooding attacks, replay attacks in end-to-end connections. Two strategies to lessen such attacks have been discussed by the authors. To start, implement DTLS or TLS at the application layer to assure end-to-end security and prevent 6LBR from gaining access to data in transit. Second, LLN is safeguarded via a DTLS-DTLS tunnel. There are simple key pre-distribution systems in (Garcia-Morchon, Gómez-Pérez, Gutiérrez, Rietman, Schoenmakers, et al., 2014). Such plans are put up for IoT. It is suggested in to increase the resource efficiency of such algorithms (Garcia-Morchon, Keoh, et al., 2013). In order to further improve the efficiency of the cryptographic procedures in IoT security provisioning (Garcia-Morchon, Gómez-Pérez, Gutiérrez, Rietman, & Tolhuizen, 2014) where the authors demonstrate how the MMO problem is analogous to locating nearby vectors in a lattice. A novel, effective ID-based key establishing strategy was presented by the authors (Garcia-Morchon et al., 2012). The identity-based system, with node's ID and a third party that securely transfers secret key to the node in the network tied to the device identifier. The other node's identity and secret keying material are utilized to create a standard pairing key for safe communication. For BSNs, the authors of (Morchón et al., 2006) have suggested a key management service (body sensor networks). The resources constraints are taken into account by the proposed scheme.

Heer et al. (2011) have discussed IoT communication security issues. The authors evaluate the architecture for secure IP-based IoT. When developing security architecture, the capabilities and lifetime of an IoT device should be taken into account. Another prerequisite is that the architecture should address the scalability concerns as well as transmission and computational overhead. The location of security at various IoT levels (link, network, or application layer) is another intriguing issue brought up by the authors. This is because each layer has distinct security needs and communication patterns. The network is vulnerable to assaults if security is provided only at the application layer. But concentrating on network or link layer security presents potential inter-application security risks. There have been attempts to present a lightweight security framework, and these efforts may be seen in (Hernandez-Ramos et al., 2015), where the suggested architecture offers a comprehensive security approach with limited smart object authentication and authorization features. To provide end-to-end security for the IoT, the authors of Peretti et al. (2015) suggested a lightweight architecture made up of the DTLS, CoAP, and Lo WPAN protocols. The authors' suggested framework, which helps the embedded software engineer choose the optimal encryption to meet application requirements, and efforts in assessing the lightweight cryptography framework, may be found in (Dinu et al., 2015). (Seitz et al., 2013) Provides a simple framework for implementing access control in the Internet of Things. For IoT devices, the authors suggested general authorization architecture. The suggested framework's evaluation is also included. A security architecture (Piro et al., 2014) complies with standards and the authors wanted to adapt it to the IoT paradigm in the future. In (Huang et al., 2016) is a related piece of work that also suggests an end-to-end security strategy for IoT. (Kothmayr et al., 2012) presented a security framework for IoTs based on accepted standards and current Internet standards with low power devices. However, the solution is excessively complex for low-power devices and ineffective in thwarting routing assaults. Likewise, end-to-end security concerns have not been addressed. Resources utilization has been examined, while security provision, among different state-of-the-art techniques in (Granjal et al., 2012). Similarly, a secure middleware is proposed in (Hameed et al., 2014) that address the security flaws in NFC-based devices. The middleware identifies rogue NFC tags or smart posters. Lightweight primitives were added to the middleware as a further extension to guarantee secrecy and integrity for any NFC application in (Hameed et al., 2015) (Hameed et al., 2016).

1.5.2 Open Issues and Future Direction

- *Prioritize Frameworks over the Cryptographic Algorithms:* The majority of the currently available research focuses improving the algorithmic stages in the cryptographic algorithms to carry out cryptographic operations. Whereas, the protocols that carry out simple activities to protect the IoT network is not taken into account in any of the recent studies. In contrast to WSN, IoT security provisioning is highly difficult due to the diverse nature of the devices. They are also placed in unsupervised situations that are more similar to people than WSN nodes. Likewise, in contrast to WSN, the IoT is anticipated to support IPv6, UDP and web. Therefore, in IoT, the security protocols should be light weighted and should address nodes diversity. Existing security protocols in WSN and IP networks cannot be used directly in IoTs. Because ordinary computer machines have adequate energy resources, processing power, and storage space, rather than being intrinsically built for resource-constrained devices, this is the main obstacle preventing the application of Internet security solutions in IoT.
- *Employing SDNs for Simple Security Provisioning:* In addition to cutting-edge IoT security solutions, the developing SDN paradigm, with its capacity to centralize routing operations, enables network monitoring and reconfiguration from a central location. This creates new opportunities for the SDN controller to design a thin cryptographic framework to address the resources constraints in IoTs.

1.6 Secure Routing in IoT

IP-based IoTs face range attacks including man in the middle, black-hole, neighbor discovery attack, spoofing, eavesdropping etc. attacks. All these well-known attacks are inherited from IPv4. Since it is anticipated that IoT would connect the physical world to the Internet, which raises a number of security problems, it follows that IoT needs the same security measures as necessary for IPv4. Threats from attacks can actually control the devices in an IoT network in addition to manipulating information. As more electronic systems, such as SCADA and Modbus, are integrated into IP-based systems, a sharp rise in threats is anticipated. As more diverse devices are integrated into the IoT network, this increases the security risks. In wireless mobile networks, the routes are established in a multi-hop fashion. Likewise, nodes are added and removed in the route maintenance phase. In this process, selfish and compromised nodes are added in the routing tables which interrupt the routing processes. Attacks from malicious nodes in the routing information are conceivable during this stage of route construction and discovery. By sending a tone of bogus route information to other nodes, for instance, one node might introduce a routing table overflow attack and cause the surrounding node's routing table to overflow. These methods populate the routing table with fictitious routes while preventing actual routes from using it.

1.6.1 Challenges

There are different key challenges, to be addressed, in secure routing.

- *Setup of a secure route.* Setting up a safe routing mechanism for data transfer in the Internet of Things is one of the major issues. Such a protocol needs to be capable of reliably guaranteeing a secure route between communication nodes and securely establishing a route. In order for the low-power IoT networks to function properly, computations that are done to route data should be lightweight.

- *Keeping malicious nodes apart.* Another difficulty is developing methods to rapidly and effectively identify rogue nodes and disconnect them from IoT networks. In order to reduce or completely prevent interruption in the routing process, the routing mechanisms should be capable to detect and isolate bad nodes in the routing process. The IoT current routing protocols are risky since the majority of IoT networks self-organize and frequently run without human intervention. Because hostile nodes may be very easily brought into the Internet of Things (IoT) network, it is necessary to create a protocol with tactics and procedures to prevent harmful nodes from entering the network or to identify them as soon as they begin engaging in malicious behavior.

- *Scalability*: The growing size of IoTs devices is challenging the deployment of routing protocols. The flooding-based routing protocols degrade performance as the network size increases. Likewise, transmission and computational overhead in the conventional routing protocols limit their applicability in resource constrained IoTs. Therefore, distributed mechanisms meeting the resource constraints are needed to deal with the scalability in IoTs. Moreover, distributed and scalable routing solutions such as (Zahid et al., 2018) (Zahid et al., 2022) are needed in IoTs. Light weighted distributed mechanisms with minimal transmission overhead are encouraged in the resources constrained environments. In the perspective of secure routing, the incorporated light weighted security measures should not introduce extra transmission overhead along with the employed routing procedures. Meanwhile, distributed, based on the local available information, routing procedure are scalable and best suits this particular domain.

1.6.2 Solution and Discussion

There exist several initiatives towards safe routing in IoTs. For the Internet of Things, (Tang et al., 2014) developed a reliable cost assurance routing protocol (CASER). Geographical routing rather than flooding is used in CASER to distribute routing information throughout the network. It stabilizes energy use and lengthens network lifetime. Additionally, it uses two routing techniques to convey messages: random wandering and deterministic routing. Two techniques are divided up according to certain security needs. By giving a probability to a variable that represents the security need and is reliant on the route's cost, the choice between two techniques is probabilistically controlled. A quantitative security study of CASER was given by the authors. However, details of CASER's software or component architecture are not covered. Advanced security attacks on routing may be discovered in (Lasla et al., 2014). According to the authors, node capture attacks involve capturing a valid node and turning it into a rogue node that executes harmful code by stealing cryptographic keys from the node. The infected node broadcasts a phony RREQ with a false info. (i.e., hop count) in order to attract traffic. In (Chze & Leong, 2014), secure multi-hop routing in IoTs is presented, with multilayer parameters included into the routing algorithm. The authors demonstrated that the suggested algorithm is appropriate for Internet of Things communication. Researchers have made multiple attempts to develop trust-aware routing algorithms. For example, in (Duan et al., 2014), authors claim to have developed a routing framework that is both lightweight and highly resistant to different assaults. The authors of (Bonetto et al., 2012) suggested secure methods for IoT devices with inadequate resources. (Wallgren et al., 2013) Provides a thorough examination of IoT security capabilities. The investigation is carried out by building and proving well-known routing attacks conducted in Lo WPAN networks running RPL. (Zhao & Ge, 2013) is a different paper that provides a thorough overview of security concerns in IoT. The authors spoke about the security measures used at various IoT architectural tiers.

1.6.3 Future Directions

- *Performance-Focused Routing Protocol Design for IoT Networks.* Despite several attempts to address the issue of safe routing and forwarding. However, studies are needed to evaluate the performance of such mechanisms, especially, in IoTs. Likewise, several sophisticated mechanisms in IoTs to find network assaults such as IDS. Nevertheless, these approaches do not consider the resource constraints of IoT devices. However, implementing a lightweight Intrusion Detection System (IDS) can aid in detecting malicious activity in an IoT network and thwarting routing attacks. It is important for the networking research community to focus on developing a new design for a lightweight IDS.
- *Control over routing operations that is both efficient and precise.* In addition to IoT lightweight IDS, centralized mechanism such as SDN, controlling the IoT network from a central location can efficiently monitor network activities. SDN controls and implement policies of security that may be swiftly revised in response to security risks. Therefore, cutting-edge security solutions using SDN are needed in IoTs.

1.7 Management of Robustness in IoT

The diverse range of IoTs devices make it hard to manage. Recently, because it supports the integration and management of various services, academics majorly focused on the service-oriented architecture (SOA) for managing IoTs (Priyantha et al., 2008). IoT application flaws are intolerable because they might interfere with users' daily activities or possibly put their lives in peril. To make matters worse, SOA is susceptible to all distributed system flaws (Bruning et al., 2007). Therefore, distributed systems' fundamental issues are present in SOA-based middleware for the Internet of Things. In addition to common IoT device errors, these faults can also arise from DoS attacks against IoT devices and services that stop IoT services from being provided to application users.

1.7.1 Challenges

Management of robustness faces several challenges as listed below:

- *Attack Tolerance:* IoTs require fresh and inventive network architectures that are intrinsically resilient to breaches and other nefarious assaults.
- *Early Attack Detection:* After an attack is initiated, the IoT network should have protocols and directives in place to swiftly detect the assault before it proliferates throughout the network and causes substantial damage.
- *Failure Recovery:* In the IoTs, failure recovery in a hurry becomes crucial. A prolonged interruption of IoT services might put people's lives in danger, especially if they are using disaster management applications. As a result, it is necessary that the middleware resource manager created for IoT networks quickly identify problems and take action to fix them. Failures of IoT devices may have a number of potential fixes. Replicating resources (Wang et al., 2009) and deploying them

in the same environment is one potential option. Due to the duplication of resources needed, this method is expensive.

1.7.2 Solution and Discussion

(Kuptsov et al., 2010) addressed the issue of a network node that was acting strangely. They produced a preliminary description of the Eco-Sec (Efficient Cooperative Security) protocol, which collaborates with other nodes using two voting mechanisms to govern the admission and revocation of nodes. The researchers also consider trust management to offer resilience in IoT. Likewise, the adopted parameters in Eco-Sec, for agreement, voting and revocation, have been examined in (Garcia-Morchon, Kuptsov, et al., 2013). Additional research on using context awareness and intelligence to solve similar problems may be found in (Garcia-Morchon & Wehrle, 2010) (Singhvi et al., 2005). The authors covered IoT resilience management in (Kamal et al., 2015). In (Misra et al., 2012), using cross-layer design approach, proposed a fault-tolerant routing protocol by exploiting machine learning. The AI-based algorithm selects the best course of action after dynamically adapting to the changing environment. The programmer also uses energy-conscious fault-tolerant routing. The sleep algorithm, which is controlled by a flexible and dynamic scheduling mechanism, conserves energy. Likewise, a self-learning based sensor defect detection method for monitoring industrial IoT is proposed in (Y. Liu et al., 2013). The self-learning module's responsiveness is neither assessed nor addressed. (Rajan et al., 2011) presented a self-optimizing and fault-tolerant network management paradigm for WSN. This approach does not address the expense of message forwarding middleware. Frameworks for cloud computing have been taken into consideration by researchers to give WSN fault tolerance, such as in (An, 2012). This study does not address the evaluation of sensor network configuration problems either. Similar work is done in (Fazio et al., 2014), where the authors offer a cloud-based framework to assess sensor network failures.

1.7.3 *Future Directions*

IoT network errors can be caused by both network assaults and energy exhaustion. There have been many attempts to address issues, but the most of them have not taken into account how resource-constrained IoT devices are. By centralizing the network view, fault-tolerant routing can be set up and failures across the IoT network may be regulated. It will be able to discover errors centrally because the controller will be the only one making routing decisions. The controller will make the choice to direct traffic to a different server or routing based on problem detection. So that steps may be made right away to tackle the problem by providing other choices, creative solutions that quickly identify flaws are necessary.

1.8 Denial of Service Attacks in IoTs

Attacks that cause a denial of service (DoS) have catastrophic implications for IoT applications (Mayer, 2009). The accessibility of IoT services and devices is crucial in IoT applications. DoS attacks obstruct the IoT services' regular functioning by rendering them unavailable. DDoS assaults are typically conducted simultaneously by several coordinated attackers, making it challenging to identify them before the services are rendered unavailable.

1.8.1 Challenges

There are a range of challenges in this particular domain. Some are listed below:

- *Efficient Counter measure resources:* Upon detecting a DoS attack, measures must be taken to minimize its impact. Due to the severe resource constraints of IoT networks, it is necessary to employ a lightweight and energy-efficient countermeasure strategy.
- *Detecting insider attacks on resources effectively:* In order to prevent insider attacks, permission should be granted to IoT nodes before they can join the network. It is crucial that techniques for detecting insider threats in IoT networks are both efficient and prompt. Failure to do so may lead to dire consequences, as insiders could compromise network nodes, expose confidential information, impair the functionality of the IoT network, or launch DDoS attacks.
- *Resource-effective DoS attack detection*: Detection systems for DoS attacks must be effective because these types of assaults are difficult to identify before they are launched. While there are existing methods for dealing with DDoS attacks on conventional internet networks, such as the one presented in (Moore et al., 2006), detecting DDoS attacks in IoT networks is a challenging task due to the significant differences in network and traffic characteristics. Additionally, detecting and implementing countermeasures for DDoS attacks under resource constraints is necessary for IoT networks. Such methods can be centralized, relying on monitoring IoT network traffic from a central location, or they can be distributed, enabling multiple IoT devices to collectively predict the likelihood of a DDoS attack on the network using statistical approaches.

1.8.2 Solution and Discussion

Researchers have focused on insider assaults, as seen in (Hu et al., 2014), where the authors suggested a system for managing the network employing a node that continuously monitors the network. By maintaining a dynamic threshold, the suggested algorithm operates. The threshold is changed based on a real-time evaluation of the total packet loss condition. Due to the loss caused by the false alert, this causes a fall in the detection rate. In (F. Liu et al., 2007), the authors presented a safe routing protocol based on a trust mechanism.

The history of research in IDS approaches is briefly covered in (D. Yang et al., 2006), which also provides a full explanation of IDS in IoTs. IoT based on 6LoWPAN when A denial of service assault frequently results in tragic circumstances. For 6LoWPAN-based IoT, the authors in (Kasinathan, Pastrone, et al., 2013) presented DoS detection architecture. However, the transmission overhead between the elements of the suggested architecture is not assessed. It also has a single point of failure because it has a centralized architecture. You can find broadcast protocol variants, such as the DoS-tolerant TESLA for IoT in (Ruan & Hori, 2012). Likewise, the authors suggested an IDS framework for IoT in (Kasinathan, Costamagna, et al., 2013). The components of the suggested framework are the monitoring system and detection engine. It is not mentioned how the suggested design performs when the size of the 6 Lo WPAN increases. The IDS framework's communication costs will rise when Lo WPAN size expands. Recent work on IDS for IoT may be found in (Pongle & Chavan, 2015), which also discusses the shortcomings of current IDS for IoT and potential IoT attacks.

1.8.3 Issues and Future Directions

The frameworks that have been suggested for dealing with insider and DDoS assaults are based on certain monitoring tools and detection engines. Because detection engines are based on AI algorithms, implementing one across an IoT network requires a lot of resources. Therefore, inventive, lightweight techniques are needed to identify DoS assaults. In addition to cutting-edge lightweight solutions, the developing SDN paradigm allows for controller-based network state monitoring. Algorithms for detecting DDoS assaults and other malicious behavior, such as insider attacks, can be implemented using the flows in the controller (Huang et al., 2016). Additionally, this will transfer responsibility for stopping DDoS assaults from IoT devices to a device with the necessary resources and an SDN controller, presumably the gateway device linking IoT devices. Integrating IoT gateways with cutting-edge SDN-based systems that are effective at detecting (Hameed & Ali, 2018) and mitigating (Hameed & Ahmed Khan, 2018) threats would be a viable hybrid solution.

Table 1. Security in IoTs

Sub-domain	Open Issues/Trends
Dark-Net	• *Resources Constraints:* *Due to resources constraints, the IoTs devices lack reasonable virus or malware detection software; therefore, these devices are vulnerable and easily become bots. Attackers take over control the device's routing and forwarding functions. In this manner, the compromised devices (also called, sinkholes or black holes) carry out malicious activities and, also infect other devices in the vicinity* • *Lack of common architecture:* *Existing work don not use common architecture and standards. Therefore, the issue of Dark-net traffic detection becomes more challenging and dynamic.*
Privacy	• *Tracking and profiling:* *A threat arises when an identity is linked to a specific person since this might result in surveillance and profiling. In order to avoid such activity in IoT, one of the main issues is to forbid it and implement certain preventative measures.* • *Locating and following:* *Localization is another threat that arises when computers try to track and record an individual's location and movements over a period of time. Creating protocols for IoT interactions that discourage this kind of activity is a primary challenge for IoT security solutions. In e-commerce scenarios, personal profiling data is often utilized to deduce interests by linking it with other profiles and data. However, balancing user privacy standards with business interests in profiling and data analysis poses a significant problem.* • *Finding and pursuing:* *Localization, which happens when computers try to monitor and record a person's whereabouts over time and space, is another risk. One of the main challenges for IoT security solutions is creating rules for interactions with the internet of things that prohibit such behavior. Profiling information about a given individual is regularly combined with other profiles and data to infer interests.* • *A significant challenge is balancing corporate interests in data analysis and profiling with user privacy norms.*
Intrusion Detection	• *Network Intrusion Detection System(NIDS): Due to resource constraints in IoT devices and lack of sophisticated tools, the IoTs is more vulnerable. The absence of sophisticated Network Intrusion Detection System(NIDS), IoTs devices are easily compromised and become relay for Dark-net. This limits the application domain of IoTs.* • *In general, light weighted intrusion detections techniques are needed.*
Cryptographic frame work	• *Cryptographic Framework:* *Existing research focuses improving the algorithmic stages in the cryptographic operations. Whereas, the protocols that carry out simple activities to protect the IoT network is the missing part.* • *Diversity: In IoT security provisioning is highly difficult due to the diverse nature of the devices. Moreover, the IoT is anticipated to support IPv6, UDP and web. Therefore, in IoT, the security protocols should be light weighted and should address nodes diversity. Existing security protocols in WSN and IP networks cannot be used directly in IoTs due to resources constraints.* • *SDN: In addition to cutting-edge IoT security solutions, the developing SDN paradigm, with its capacity to centralize routing operations, enables network monitoring and reconfiguration from a central location. This creates new opportunities for the SDN controller to design a thin cryptographic framework to address the resources constraints in IoTs.*

continues on following page

Table 1. Continued

Sub-domain	Open Issues/Trends
DoS attacks	• *Efficient **Counter measure** resources: Countermeasure strategy is required which is lightweight and energy-efficient in response to the DoS assaults.* • ***Detecting insider attacks:** Permission should be granted to IoT nodes before they can join the network to prevent insider attacks. The techniques employed for detecting insider threats in IoT networks should be efficient and prompt in response.* • ***Resource-effective DoS attack detection:** Due to the significant differences in network and traffic characteristics between traditional networks and IoT networks, detecting DDoS attacks in IoT is a challenging problem. Therefore, it is necessary to implement DDoS detection and other countermeasures under resource constraints in IoT. Centralized methods that rely on monitoring IoT network traffic from a central location may be used to determine the probability of a DDoS attack using statistical approaches. Alternatively, similar methods may be distributed, enabling multiple IoT devices to collectively predict the likelihood of a DDoS attack on the network.*
Secure Routing & Scalability	• ***Setup of a secure route.** Light weighted protocols capable of reliably guaranteeing a secure route between communication nodes and securely establishing a route. Routing mechanisms should be capable to detect and isolate bad nodes in the routing process. it is necessary to create a protocol with tactics and procedures to prevent harmful nodes from entering the network or to identify them as soon as they begin engaging in malicious behavior.* • ***Scalability:** The flooding-based routing protocols degrade performance as the network size increases. Likewise, transmission and computational overhead in the conventional routing protocols limit their applicability in resource constrained IoTs. Therefore, distributed mechanisms meeting the resource constraints are needed to deal with the scalability in IoTs*

1.9 Chapter Summary

The most recent work done to ensure security in the IoT network has been classified and discussed. There is a thorough discussion of efforts in the areas of privacy provisioning, lightweight cryptographic framework, secure routing robustness and management, denial of service, and insider threat detection. In the Internet of Things, privacy is essential, especially given that its features differ from those of a traditional Internet network. This study identifies and discusses such problems and demands. Table-1 highlights the open issues and trends. Lightweight cryptographic primitives appropriate for IoT networks are needed in addition to privacy to ensure security in the IoT network. Future steps are considered after compiling all the efforts made in this direction. Likewise, Context-aware approaches, lightweight protocols, and most recently virtualization techniques are offered to retain the integrity of the data while protecting privacy. Innovative solutions are needed for lightweight cryptographic primitives that should only use a small amount of an IoT mote's resources. In addition, the SDN solution provides centralized routing carried out at the SDN controller to build lightweight cryptographic solutions through IoT. IoT nodes are subject to a variety of network threats, which causes problems in the IoT network. Future perspective is highlighted while discussing efforts in this regard. Denial of service attacks executed by several coordinated nodes inside the IoT network may result in faulty nodes. Such errors are also common since insider attacks on the IoT network occur often. In order to quickly respond to malfunctioning nodes within the network and achieve fault tolerance in the IoT, centralized network state monitoring is necessary. SDN, a virtualization technology, allows centralizing network monitoring, which can help in recommending alternate servers or paths to maintain consistent service provisioning. In terms of DDoS in the IoT, a lightweight detection engine appropriate for the IoT is needed to quickly identify and mitigate DDoS. In an IoT network, centralized monitoring made possible by SDN can help identify DDoS attacks and help neutralize them. A centralized management structure that can cater for all the stated security concerns and needs within the IoT network is necessary for all the security requirements. SDN is a popular option that enables centralized network setting by the controller that oversees the network. You may find the first attempts made in this approach in (Huang et al., 2016). To establish a thorough centralized management framework for providing security via IoT, several possibilities and problems still need to be resolved. SDN must be carefully examined in order to be modified to offer management services across an IoT network.

REFERENCES

Abu Al-Haija, Q., Krichen, M., & Abu Elhaija, W. (2022). Machine-learning-based darknet traffic detection system for IoT applications. *Electronics (Basel)*, *11*(4), 556. doi:10.3390/electronics11040556

Ali, H., Batool, K., Yousaf, M., Islam Satti, M., Naseer, S., Zahid, S., Gardezi, A. A., Shafiq, M., & Choi, J.-G. (2022). Security Hardened and Privacy Preserved Android Malware Detection Using Fuzzy Hash of Reverse Engineered Source Code. *Security and Communication Networks*, *2022*, 1–11. doi:10.1155/2022/7972230

An, K. (2012). Resource management and fault tolerance principles for supporting distributed real-time and embedded systems in the cloud. *Proceedings of the 9th Middleware Doctoral Symposium of the 13th ACM/IFIP/USENIX International Middleware Conference*, (pp. 1–6). ACM. 10.1145/2405688.2405692

Bonetto, R., Bui, N., Lakkundi, V., Olivereau, A., Serbanati, A., & Rossi, M. (2012). Secure communication for smart IoT objects: Protocol stacks, use cases and practical examples. *2012 IEEE International Symposium on a World of Wireless, Mobile and Multimedia Networks (WoWMoM)*, (pp. 1–7). IEEE. 10.1109/WoWMoM.2012.6263790

Brachmann, M., Keoh, S. L., Morchon, O. G., & Kumar, S. S. (2012). End-to-end transport security in the IP-based internet of things. *2012 21st International Conference on Computer Communications and Networks (ICCCN)*, (pp. 1–5). IEEE.

Bruning, S., Weissleder, S., & Malek, M. (2007). A fault taxonomy for service-oriented architecture. *10th IEEE High Assurance Systems Engineering Symposium (HASE'07)*, (pp. 367–368). IEEE. 10.1109/HASE.2007.46

Chze, P. L. R., & Leong, K. S. (2014). A secure multi-hop routing for IoT communication. *2014 IEEE World Forum on Internet of Things (WF-Iot)*, (pp. 428–432). IEEE.

Demertzis, K., Tsiknas, K., Takezis, D., Skianis, C., & Iliadis, L. (2021). Darknet traffic big-data analysis and network management for real-time automating of the malicious intent detection process by a weight agnostic neural networks framework. *Electronics (Basel)*, *10*(7), 781. doi:10.3390/electronics10070781

Dinu, D., Biryukov, A., Großschädl, J., Khovratovich, D., Le Corre, Y., & Perrin, L. (2015). FELICS-fair evaluation of lightweight cryptographic systems. *NIST Workshop on Lightweight Cryptography*, 128. ACM.

Duan, J., Yang, D., Zhu, H., Zhang, S., & Zhao, J. (2014). TSRF: A trust-aware secure routing framework in wireless sensor networks. *International Journal of Distributed Sensor Networks*, *10*(1), 209436. doi:10.1155/2014/209436

Fazio, M., Celesti, A., Puliafito, A., & Villari, M. (2014). An integrated system for advanced multi-risk management based on cloud for IoT. *Advances onto the Internet of Things: How Ontologies Make the Internet of Things Meaningful*, 253–269.

Garcia-Morchon, O., Gómez-Pérez, D., Gutiérrez, J., Rietman, R., Schoenmakers, B., & Tolhuizen, L. (2014). HIMMO-A lightweight collusion-resistant key predistribution scheme. *Cryptology EPrint Archive*.

Garcia-Morchon, O., Gómez-Pérez, D., Gutiérrez, J., Rietman, R., & Tolhuizen, L. (2014). The MMO problem. *Proceedings of the 39th International Symposium on Symbolic and Algebraic Computation*, (pp. 186–193). IEEE. 10.1145/2608628.2608643

Garcia-Morchon, O., Keoh, S. L., Kumar, S., Moreno-Sanchez, P., Vidal-Meca, F., & Ziegeldorf, J. H. (2013). Securing the IP-based internet of things with HIP and DTLS. *Proceedings of the Sixth ACM Conference on Security and Privacy in Wireless and Mobile Networks*, (pp. 119–124). ACM. 10.1145/2462096.2462117

Garcia-Morchon, O., Kuptsov, D., Gurtov, A., & Wehrle, K. (2013). Cooperative security in distributed networks. *Computer Communications*, *36*(12), 1284–1297. doi:10.1016/j.comcom.2013.04.007

Garcia-Morchon, O., Rietman, R., Sharma, S., Tolhuizen, L., & Torre-Arce, J. L. (2014). DTLS-HIMMO: Efficiently securing a post-quantum world with a fully-collusion resistant KPS. *Cryptology EPrint Archive*.

Garcia-Morchon, O., Rietman, R., Shparlinski, I. E., & Tolhuizen, L. (2014). Interpolation and approximation of polynomials in finite fields over a short interval from noisy values. *Experimental Mathematics*, *23*(3), 241–260. doi:10.1080/10586458.2014.890918

Garcia-Morchon, O., Tolhuizen, L., Gomez, D., & Gutierrez, J. (2012). Towards full collusion resistant ID-based establishment of pairwise keys. *Extended Abstracts of the Third Workshop on Mathematical Cryptology (WMC 2012) and the Third International Conference on Symbolic Computation and Cryptography (SCC 2012)*, (pp. 30–36).

Garcia-Morchon, O., & Wehrle, K. (2010). Efficient and context-aware access control for pervasive medical sensor networks. *2010 8th IEEE International Conference on Pervasive Computing and Communications Workshops (PERCOM Workshops)*, (pp. 322–327). IEEE.

Granjal, J., Monteiro, E., & Silva, J. S. (2012). On the effectiveness of end-to-end security for internet-integrated sensing applications. *2012 IEEE International Conference on Green Computing and Communications*, (pp. 87–93). IEEE. 10.1109/GreenCom.2012.23

Gutwirth, S., Leenes, R., De Hert, P., & Poullet, Y. (2013). *European data protection: Coming of age* (Vol. 16). Springer. doi:10.1007/978-94-007-5170-5

Hameed, S., & Ahmed Khan, H. (2018). SDN based collaborative scheme for mitigation of DDoS attacks. *Future Internet*, *10*(3), 23. doi:10.3390/fi10030023

Hameed, S., & Ali, U. (2018). HADEC: Hadoop-based live DDoS detection framework. *EURASIP Journal on Information Security*, *2018*(1), 1–19. doi:10.118613635-018-0081-z

Hameed, S., Hameed, B., Hussain, S. A., & Khalid, W. (2014). Lightweight security middleware to detect malicious content in NFC tags or smart posters. *2014 IEEE 13th International Conference on Trust, Security and Privacy in Computing and Communications*, (pp. 900–905). IEEE.

Hameed, S., Jamali, U. M., & Samad, A. (2015). Integrity protection of NDEF message with flexible and enhanced NFC signature records. *2015 IEEE Trustcom/BigDataSE/ISPA, 1*, (pp. 368–375). IEEE.

Hameed, S., Jamali, U. M., & Samad, A. (2016). Protecting NFC data exchange against eavesdropping with encryption record type definition. *NOMS 2016-2016 IEEE/IFIP Network Operations and Management Symposium*, (pp. 577–583). IEEE.

Heer, T., Garcia-Morchon, O., Hummen, R., Keoh, S. L., Kumar, S. S., & Wehrle, K. (2011). Security Challenges in the IP-based Internet of Things. *Wireless Personal Communications, 61*(3), 527–542. doi:10.100711277-011-0385-5

Hernandez-Ramos, J. L., Pawlowski, M. P., Jara, A. J., Skarmeta, A. F., & Ladid, L. (2015). Toward a lightweight authentication and authorization framework for smart objects. *IEEE Journal on Selected Areas in Communications, 33*(4), 690–702. doi:10.1109/JSAC.2015.2393436

Hu, Y., Wu, Y., & Wang, H. (2014). Detection of insider selective forwarding attack based on monitor node and trust mechanism in WSN. *Wireless Sensor Network, 6*(11), 237–248. doi:10.4236/wsn.2014.611023

Huang, X., Craig, P., Lin, H., & Yan, Z. (2016). SecIoT: A security framework for the Internet of Things. *Security and Communication Networks, 9*(16), 3083–3094. doi:10.1002ec.1259

Kamal, R., Hong, C. S., & Choi, M. J. (2015). Autonomic Resilient Internet-of-Things (IoT) Management. *ArXiv Preprint ArXiv:1508.03975*.

Kanuparthi, A., Karri, R., & Addepalli, S. (2013). Hardware and embedded security in the context of internet of things. *Proceedings of the 2013 ACM Workshop on Security, Privacy & Dependability for Cyber Vehicles*, (pp. 61–64). ACM. 10.1145/2517968.2517976

Kasinathan, P., Costamagna, G., Khaleel, H., Pastrone, C., & Spirito, M. A. (2013). An IDS framework for internet of things empowered by 6LoWPAN. *Proceedings of the 2013 ACM SIGSAC Conference on Computer & Communications Security*, (pp. 1337–1340). ACM. 10.1145/2508859.2512494

Kasinathan, P., Pastrone, C., Spirito, M. A., & Vinkovits, M. (2013). Denial-of-Service detection in 6LoWPAN based Internet of Things. *2013 IEEE 9th International Conference on Wireless and Mobile Computing, Networking and Communications (WiMob)*, (pp. 600–607). IEEE.

Khoo, B. (2011). RFID as an Enabler of the Internet of Things: Issues of Security and Privacy. *2011 International Conference on Internet of Things and 4th International Conference on Cyber, Physical and Social Computing*, (pp. 709–712). IEEE. 10.1109/iThings/CPSCom.2011.83

Kothmayr, T., Schmitt, C., Hu, W., Brünig, M., & Carle, G. (2012). A DTLS based end-to-end security architecture for the Internet of Things with two-way authentication. *37th Annual IEEE Conference on Local Computer Networks-Workshops*, (pp. 956–963). IEEE. 10.1109/LCNW.2012.6424088

Kuptsov, D., Gurtov, A., Garcia-Morchon, O., & Wehrle, K. (2010). Brief announcement: Distributed trust management and revocation. *Proceedings of the 29th ACM SIGACT-SIGOPS Symposium on Principles of Distributed Computing*, (pp. 233–234). ACM. 10.1145/1835698.1835751

Lasla, N., Derhab, A., Ouadjaout, A., Bagaa, M., & Challal, Y. (2014). SMART: Secure Multi-pAths Routing for wireless sensor neTworks. *Ad-Hoc, Mobile, and Wireless Networks: 13th International Conference, ADHOC-NOW 2014, Benidorm, Spain.*

Lin, H., & Bergmann, N. W. (2016). IoT privacy and security challenges for smart home environments. *Information (Basel)*, *7*(3), 44. doi:10.3390/info7030044

Liu, F., Cheng, X., & Chen, D. (2007). Insider attacker detection in wireless sensor networks. *IEEE INFOCOM 2007-26th IEEE International Conference on Computer Communications*, (pp. 1937–1945). IEEE.

Liu, Y., Yang, Y., Lv, X., & Wang, L. (2013). A self-learning sensor fault detection framework for industry monitoring IoT. *Mathematical Problems in Engineering*, *2013*, 2013. doi:10.1155/2013/712028

Lu, X., Li, Q., Qu, Z., & Hui, P. (2014). Privacy information security classification study in internet of things. *2014 International Conference on Identification, Information and Knowledge in the Internet of Things*, (pp. 162–165). IEEE. 10.1109/IIKI.2014.40

Mayer, C. P. (2009). Security and privacy challenges in the internet of things. *Electronic Communications of the EASST, 17.*

Misra, S., Gupta, A., Krishna, P. V., Agarwal, H., & Obaidat, M. S. (2012). An adaptive learning approach for fault-tolerant routing in Internet of Things. *2012 IEEE Wireless Communications and Networking Conference (WCNC)*, (pp. 815–819). IEEE. 10.1109/WCNC.2012.6214484

Moore, D., Shannon, C., Brown, D. J., Voelker, G. M., & Savage, S. (2006). Inferring internet denial-of-service activity. [TOCS]. *ACM Transactions on Computer Systems*, *24*(2), 115–139. doi:10.1145/1132026.1132027

Morchón, O. G., Baldus, H., & Sánchez, D. S. (2006). Resource-efficient security for medical body sensor networks. *International Workshop on Wearable and Implantable Body Sensor Networks (BSN'06)*. IEEE. 10.1109/BSN.2006.45

Ogonji, M. M., Okeyo, G., & Wafula, J. M. (2020). A survey on privacy and security of Internet of Things. *Computer Science Review*, *38*, 100312. doi:10.1016/j.cosrev.2020.100312

Peretti, G., Lakkundi, V., & Zorzi, M. (2015). BlinkToSCoAP: An end-to-end security framework for the Internet of Things. *2015 7th International Conference on Communication Systems and Networks (COMSNETS)*, (pp. 1–6). IEEE.

Piro, G., Boggia, G., & Grieco, L. A. (2014). A standard compliant security framework for IEEE 802.15. 4 networks. *2014 IEEE World Forum on Internet of Things (WF-IoT)*, (pp. 27–30). IEEE.

Pongle, P., & Chavan, G. (2015). A survey: Attacks on RPL and 6LoWPAN in IoT. *2015 International Conference on Pervasive Computing (ICPC)*, (pp. 1–6). IEEE. 10.1109/PERVASIVE.2015.7087034

Pour, M. S., Mangino, A., Friday, K., Rathbun, M., Bou-Harb, E., Iqbal, F., Samtani, S., Crichigno, J., & Ghani, N. (2020). On data-driven curation, learning, and analysis for inferring evolving internet-of-Things (IoT) botnets in the wild. *Computers & Security*, *91*, 101707. doi:10.1016/j.cose.2019.101707

Priyantha, N. B., Kansal, A., Goraczko, M., & Zhao, F. (2008). Tiny web services: Design and implementation of interoperable and evolvable sensor networks. *Proceedings of the 6th ACM Conference on Embedded Network Sensor Systems*, (pp. 253–266). ACM. 10.1145/1460412.1460438

Rajan, M. A., Balamuralidhar, P., Chethan, K. P., & Swarnahpriyaah, M. (2011). A self-reconfigurable sensor network management system for internet of things paradigm. *2011 International Conference on Devices and Communications (ICDeCom)*, (pp. 1–5). IEEE. 10.1109/ICDECOM.2011.5738550

Ruan, N., & Hori, Y. (2012). DoS attack-tolerant TESLA-based broadcast authentication protocol in Internet of Things. *2012 International Conference on Selected Topics in Mobile and Wireless Networking*, (pp. 60–65). IEEE. 10.1109/iCOST.2012.6271291

Sadeghi, A.-R., Wachsmann, C., & Waidner, M. (2015). Security and privacy challenges in industrial internet of things. *Proceedings of the 52nd Annual Design Automation Conference*, (pp. 1–6). ACM. 10.1145/2744769.2747942

Seitz, L., Selander, G., & Gehrmann, C. (2013). Authorization framework for the internet-of-things. *2013 IEEE 14th International Symposium on" A World of Wireless, Mobile and Multimedia Networks"(WoWMoM)*, (pp. 1–6). IEEE.

Silva, B. N., Khan, M., & Han, K. (2018). Internet of things: A comprehensive review of enabling technologies, architecture, and challenges. *IETE Technical Review*, *35*(2), 205–220. doi:10.1080/02564602.2016.1276416

Singhvi, V., Krause, A., Guestrin, C., Garrett, J. H. Jr, & Matthews, H. S. (2005). Intelligent light control using sensor networks. *Proceedings of the 3rd International Conference on Embedded Networked Sensor Systems*, (pp. 218–229). IEEE. 10.1145/1098918.1098942

Tang, D., Li, T., Ren, J., & Wu, J. (2014). Cost-aware secure routing (CASER) protocol design for wireless sensor networks. *IEEE Transactions on Parallel and Distributed Systems*, *26*(4), 960–973. doi:10.1109/TPDS.2014.2318296

Wallgren, L., Raza, S., & Voigt, T. (2013). Routing attacks and countermeasures in the RPL-based internet of things. *International Journal of Distributed Sensor Networks*, *9*(8), 794326. doi:10.1155/2013/794326

Wang, X., Wang, J., Zheng, Z., Xu, Y., & Yang, M. (2009). Service composition in service-oriented wireless sensor networks with persistent queries. *2009 6th IEEE Consumer Communications and Networking Conference*, (pp. 1–5). IEEE.

Yang, D., Usynin, A., & Hines, J. W. (2006). Anomaly-based intrusion detection for SCADA systems. *5th Intl. Topical Meeting on Nuclear Plant Instrumentation, Control and Human Machine Interface Technologies (Npic&hmit 05)*, (pp. 12–16). IEEE.

Yang, H., Luo, H., Ye, F., Lu, S., & Zhang, L. (2004). Security in mobile ad hoc networks: Challenges and solutions. *IEEE Wireless Communications*, *11*(1), 38–47. doi:10.1109/MWC.2004.1269716

Zahid, S., Abid, S. A., Shah, N., Naqvi, S. H. A., & Mehmood, W. (2018). Distributed partition detection with dynamic replication management in a DHT-based MANET. *IEEE Access : Practical Innovations, Open Solutions*, *6*, 18731–18746. doi:10.1109/ACCESS.2018.2814017

Zahid, S., Ullah, K., Waheed, A., Basar, S., Zareei, M., & Biswal, R. R. (2022). Fault Tolerant DHT-Based Routing in MANET. *Sensors (Basel)*, *22*(11), 4280. doi:10.339022114280 PMID:35684901

Zhao, K., & Ge, L. (2013). A survey on the internet of things security. *2013 Ninth International Conference on Computational Intelligence and Security*, (pp. 663–667). IEEE. 10.1109/CIS.2013.145

Chapter 12
User Privacy in IoT

Majida Khan Tareen
Institute of Space Technology, Islamabad, Pakistan

Altaf Hussain
Institute of Space Technology, Islamabad, Pakistan

Muhammad Hamad
Institute of Space Technology, Islamabad, Pakistan

ABSTRACT

The number of IoT devices connected to the global network is expected to be three times more, from 9.7 billion in 2020 to more than 29 billion in 2030. Globally connected IoT devices transmit enormous amounts of facts and figures daily via the internet for various purposes which is about users including important, intimate, or private information. As this data can be utilized for malevolent reasons, these devices constitute a privacy risk. IoT systems involved sensors gathering data from the environment, so known as cyber-physical systems which are highly vulnerable. Hence, user privacy issues such as password stealing, information and identity stealing, intruding, corrupting information, etc. are increasing day by day. Therefore, privacy experts and researchers are very much concerned about preventing user privacy issues and developed many PETs (blind signature, group signature, attribute-based credentials (ABCs), anonymous and pseudonymous data authentication, onion routing, encrypted communications, etc.) to prevent user privacy risks in IoT.

INTRODUCTION

IoT (Internet of Things) is a system of connected devices, sensors, humans/animals, and objects provided by a unique identity. These can transfer and share data over the network independently. IoT can be human patient-wearing monitoring devices, animal-implanted chips, vehicles with GPS or sensors, and objects that are used to transfer information on the internet.

DOI: 10.4018/978-1-6684-6914-9.ch012

IoT has different definitions in different areas. Whitmore et al. (2015) note that IoT has no universal definition. According to IETF (Internet Engineering Task Force), IoT can be defined as the network of electronics, sensors, software, etc. embedded with physical objects that enable them to share and transfer data over the internet and other connected devices or person.

IoT technology is rapidly growing day by day. There were 7 billion IoT devices in 2018, in 2019 this increased to 26.6 million, and by 2013 connected IoT devices cross 31 billion [Statista.com].

This concept first emerges in the 1980s when university students amend Coca-Cola vending machines. They modified it to track its contents from distance. In 1999 Kevin Ashton devised the concept of IoT. During his work at Procter and Gamble, he purposed the concept of placing RFID chips on different products to track them via the supply chain (Aggarwal, 2012). This RFID technology then gained high fame and was adopted by the US Department of Defense and Walmart.

In the upcoming time as new IoT devices are introduced in industry and market, this technology gained a IoT of interest among people. The first smart refrigerator came into the market in 2000, apple launched 1st iPhone in the market in 2008 and the number of IoT devices keep on increasing day by day as technology advanced. Google played a significant role in this area, it tests 1st driverless car in 2009 and introduced Google's Nest smart thermostat which can control central heating from distance, in 2012. United Nations International Telecommunications Union reported that IoT has grown to be a huge deal (Perera).

In a decade or more, IoT has expanded into a larger spectrum of applications such as house-holds, transport, medical, etc. (Sundmaeker, 2010). IoT has made astride towards fully integrated internet from static internet with the help of wireless tech such as Bluetooth, WiFi etc. according to Gubbi in (Tavares, 2014), creating smart environment by connecting these objects will be the upcoming revolution.

Architecture of IoT

The architecture of IoT (Internet of Things) can be divided into four layers:

1. **Perception Layer**: This layer is responsible for collecting data from physical objects using sensors and other devices. These sensors may include temperature sensors, motion sensors, cameras, and more.
2. **Network Layer**: This layer is responsible for transmitting the data collected by the perception layer to the cloud or other remote servers. The network layer may use Wi-Fi, Bluetooth, cellular networks, or other communication protocols to send the data.
3. **Application Layer**: This layer is responsible for processing the data received from the network layer. The application layer may involve machine learning algorithms or other types of data analysis tools to make sense of the data.
4. **Business Layer**: This layer is responsible for creating value from the data processed by the application layer. The business layer may involve creating reports, triggering alerts, or taking actions based on the insights gained from the data.

Overall, the IoT architecture is designed to enable communication between physical objects and the digital world. By collecting data from sensors and other devices, processing that data, and creating value from it, IoT systems can enable a wide range of applications, from smart homes to industrial automation (Rajendran, 2020).

Benefits and Applications of IoT

IoT makes our environment, houses, offices, and cars smarter, extra measurable, and chatter. It is probably surprising to observe numerous things linked to the internet, and what kind of profit humans can originate from examining the data (Luong, 2016). A few examples of IoT devices that have an influence on industries are (Grant-Muller, 2014): Intelligent transportation systems help to reduce traffic congestion, reduce fuel usage, schedule vehicle repairs on a priority basis and save lives. Smart electric grids, electric system reliability, and customer charge policy on basis of less usage. Intelligent and prioritize pending maintenance problems, repairing instruments etc. and Smart waste management system, intelligent law enforcement system etc. (Mwasilu, 2014).

Data-driven systems are being built into the infrastructure of 'smart cities making it easier for municipalities to run waste management, law enforcement, and other programs more efficiently. IoT shows enhancements on an intimate level. Linked devices are used in market along with industry and business such as sending low on milk alert to user on way home by the smart refrigerator, checking safety alarms and set temperature of home before arrival and many other things.

Consumer Applications

Smart Home: In smart homes, the IoT played an important role. There are many advance applications used in smart homes for different purposes such as smart door locks, automatic alarm systems, remote temperature setting, and smart TV and refrigerator etc. one of the example of such efficient devices are energy efficient devices, for example in smart home such device decided when to switch on the lights depending upon the number of person present in that room or external weather conditions. Many other devices used for different important purposes like smart cameras for security, gas sensor to sense leakage, smoke detector to detect weather there is fire broke off etc. (Bhat, 2017).

Eldercare: There are different types of helpful IoT devices used by elder or disable people. It make their life easy, for example they can control different devices at home with their voices.

Commercial Applications

Medical and Healthcare: IoT devices play a very important role in the health department, such as distant monitoring of patients and sending notifications in case of emergency. Patients are embedded with different IoT sensors e.g. pacemakers, hearing devices, etc. Such devices monitored patient health continues e.g. taking vitals, taking temperature, and sending these readings to the concerned department or person. In hospitals smart beds are used, these beds can adjust according to patients' movements. Another example is smart medical fridges, these fridges contain different medicines, and etc. temperature of these fridges can be controlled remotely via IoT devices (Sharma, 2016).

Media and Entertainment: another advantage of IoT is generating data of high quality and creating ads for the purpose of marketing in the industry, which is according to the customer requirements.

Transportation: another considerable part of IoT devices is in transportation. Many devices are used to sustain the health of vehicles, maintain parking in parking lots, manage traffic loads, etc.

Building and Home automation: numerous IoT apps are being used for evaluating the condition of homes as well as to control safety, temperature, humidity, and other things. These applications are installed on IoT devices and make sure to access sensor data to maintain temperature, light, humidity, door locks, etc. remotely. Also, it is possible to control different smart appliances like fridges AC, TV, etc. from anywhere.

Industrial Applications

Manufacturing: innovative goods manufacturing becomes easy due to IoT devices. These devices help in the delivery of goods automatically in the actual time frame with the help of IoT devices, sensors, network gadgets, etc.

Agriculture: numerous IoT apps are used in agriculture department for different purposes such as collection of rainfall data, outdoor temperature, speed of wind and other factors as well. This information is used for multiple benefits such as simplifying agricultural practices, decreasing human efforts, taking cultivated decisions, improving quality of crops, increasing quantity, etc. the farmers can not only track the temperate and humidity but can also decide which fertilizers or parasitic sprays will be used for improving crops.

Infrastructure

Energy Management: sensing devices and actuation techs are used for the purpose of improving energy usage and consumption. IoT sensors are being used in equipment related to energy usage for better utilization of energy.

Environmental Monitoring: IoT sensors are also part of environmental surveillance. These sensors sense the environment situations such as movement of animal in surroundings their habitats, etc.

Military Applications

Internet of Military Things (IoMT): one of the important applications of IoT devices is IoMT. Different sensors are used for the purpose of surveillance in times of war. These applications are helpful for handling combat activities in remote areas, also advances technologies are used in biometrics, drones, robots, etc. to manage security of the country.

User Privacy in IoT

Privacy is very brad concept, in literature there are many definitions of privacy according to different aspects (Ramgovind, 2010). From history point of view, privacy is defined as corporal, regional, communicational, and mass media privacy. As digital data is growing day by day along with the advancement of technology, privacy concerns becomes the most dominating issues of these days. In 1968 Westin defined data privacy as "it is the right of each person, that he/she can decide what information about him/her will be shared and to whom" (Westin, 1968). Although this definition is about non-digital data still it is valid. The appropriate definition of privacy in IoT depends upon following three factors (Ziegeldorf, 2014).

1. An individual has control over the information.
2. An individual must be aware of the personal information used by other parties.
3. An individual must be well aware of the privacy risks of using IoT devices

Privacy Challenges in IoT

Privacy is becoming a big concern as the internet is rapidly involved in our day-to-day to day life. People share a lot of personal information over the internet like their pictures, locations, videos, documents, etc. every person has the right to share personal information and is aware of the fact that this information is used by whom at what time, and for which purpose (Ziegeldorf, 2014).

IoT devices are connected to the internet, so privacy is a major concern. A third party can collect personal information about an individual as it is present on the internet. This information can be used for any purpose by a third party. In this scenario private information of an individual must be secured, Individuals should be aware that this private information is used by which party and for what purpose, also without the permission of the individual, information cannot be gathered. Maintaining privacy in this scenario where a massive amount of private data is shared on daily basis is a difficult thing (Vikas, 2015).

Basic architecture of IoT is based on three layers named, physical, network, and application layers. At the first layer (physical) many sensors and IoT devices are installed, and these devices collect an enormous amount of data from the surroundings. This data is collected in three steps i.e. in first step, data is collected by IoT devices and sensors. Then the data is aggregated, in which data is processed to make information. While in third step, different techniques are applied to analyze data to extract real information from raw/ aggregated data.

This data collection, processing and transmission process is the most critical thing, information has many privacy threats during these steps. For example, in health care department, patient wear IoT sensors for health monitoring purpose, if intruder gain access to patient data, alter it, steal it or create fake patient with this information, this create serious issue.

Need for Privacy

User privacy in IoT is defined by Internet security glossary as "every person has right to decide how much it will engage with its surroundings, including how much information about itself the entity is prepared to share with others" (Shirey, 2000). Networks of smart devices gather information from the surroundings and transmit it to applications present on servers. During this process, data privacy is a major concern at different levels such as device, storage processing, and during communication. User privacy in IoT is one of the emerging agenda these days.

Privacy Requirements (Use Cases)

With the advancement of IoT in our day-to-day life privacy vulnerabilities are also increasing rapidly. Following are some of the examples of IoT devices where users experience problems.

Two researchers in late 2015 discovered that about 68000 medical devices were online exposed and 12000 of these devices are related to the healthcare organization (Patton, 2014; Srinivasan, 2008). This research concluded that the major reason for privacy risk in these devices is that, these devices used old version of Window XP to connect with the internet. It has a lot of vulnerabilities regarding data privacy. This dated version of windows is still in use in many legacy systems hence causing future privacy issues for devices connected to these systems. Researchers use a search-engine called Shodan which online searches IoT devices attached to the internet. They found different medical devices such as pacemakers, MRI scanners, cardiology devices, anesthesia equipment, infusion system, etc. connected to the internet with the help of Shodan. These devices are very easy to hack with hard-coded logins or brute force attacks. But there is no such evidence that hackers cause any kind of damage to this data via changing it or stealing IoT.

In smart homes, the FATS attack is one of the famous attacks (Henze, 2014). These attacks are based on wireless network traffic, such as acknowledging different activities on WiFi, classification of sensors, data traffic from home sensor networks, etc.

Forbes tinted magazine publish an article recently in which Noam Rotem and Ran Locar did the research. In their research they expose a chines company Orvibo, this company claims to run a platform that manages IoT devices. The database of this company is easily retrieved by straight connection, which exposes 2 billion records of users including their passwords, payment information, codes, and smart camera recordings.

Assisted living is another imported development in IoT, privacy risks involved in this use case are presented in (Kong, 2019). Senior citizens in assisted living use different IoT devices that measure their vital signs by using unobtrusive sensors and this information is then delivered to the cloud where it is remotely and fast accessed by their family or doctors. There are two types of user privacy risks first is related to senior citizens' medical records and the second to his/her data. IoT devices using clouds for fast access give birth to more user privacy risks.

In the internet of vehicles (IoV) presented in (Solanas, 2014) many sensors and control devices, etc. are attached to the vehicles to enforce autonomous control in it. There is a greater risk that intruded inject false massage by a malicious vehicle that endangers the system. With this advanced development in IoV, it is necessary to provide user privacy by applying privacy mechanisms to ensure that IoV BigData collected is trusted and not tempered.

Consider the smart health (s-Health) system in IoT presented in (Finn, 2013). The s-Health is mainly used for monitoring health issues and measuring vital signs, it gathers a huge amount of sensitive data and stores it to cloud storage which can be easily exposed to a third party. The s-Health not only mitigate health-related issue, but it also gathers personal information in the context of citizen habits, social media activities, daily life routine, religion, etc. this system is related to safety management such as (helmet detection, glasses, etc.) is monitored and traced. Kumar and Patel highlighted seven privacy issues (Kumar, 2014):

1. Person privacy: an individual has right to keep personal information private
2. Behavioral privacy: an individual has right to keep sensitive issue private.
3. Communicational privacy: an individual ha right that personal communication is secure.
4. Data and image privacy: individual's private data and images are secured.
5. Thoughts and feelings privacy: an individual has right to keep his actions, thoughts and feelings private and share with whom it concerned.
6. Location privacy: an individual has complete right not to expose his current location.
7. Association privacy: an individual has right to be with whoever he wants to be.

2.3 Privacy Threats in IoT Applications

IoT is becoming an essential part of our day-to-day life. There are numerous applications mentioned above where IoT devices play important roles. These IoT devices collect massive amount of data from surroundings and transmit it via cloud or wireless medium to other parties for different purposes, so there is huge risk of user's personal data misuse which eventually leads to different privacy issues. Privacy of user's data is important, so IoT architecture needs to provide promising user privacy over the internet. Tracking tags on the internet is not possible for user, so user has no knowledge that his/her private data is used by whom and when for which purpose. Similarly many organizations such as marketing companies collect user information from surroundings without user's knowledge and used it for different purposes (Evans, 2012). Different threats that IoT devices faced daily are as follow:

- **User Privacy:** User privacy is the most emerging issue in IoT these days, one of the mechanism proposed for user data privacy is data tagging in (Cao, 2010). K-anonymity model in (Wang, 2011) is presented for the reason of reserve personal data. An analysis on privacy issues and risks are presented in (Lv, 2011), which explain the scenario in which domain name is fixed for specific nodes of IoT.
- **Device Privacy:** Device privacy is one of the important factors in users' data privacy. An unauthorized user can access hardware to influence users' data. There are many algorithms that provide devices, one of the algorithms is the Multi Routing Random Walk algorithm which is used for WSNs. This algorithm uses Quick Response Code Technique (Evans, 2012) to provide device privacy by adding noise and preventing private information from the intruder.
- **Communication Privacy:** The greatest privacy threat to user data is during communication. Generally, data is transmitted through the medium after encryption by using many encryption methods. During communication, pseudonyms are used to provide secure communication. There are few communication protocols used for providing secure data communication over medium and cloud. Devices that are connected to the network communicate only when required and after completion, it should disconnect it from the network, also for communication purpose future this device will be re-authenticate before joining the network (Babar, 2010).
- **Secure Data Communications:** Communication of secure data is important in user privacy issue. Data should be transferred only to authentic user with confidentiality. Also the identity of sender should be secure (Daubert, 2015).
- **Identity Management:** Different techniques are used at administrative level to provide unique identification for each user and identify the user to provide protection in network (Daubert, 2015).
- **Privacy in Storage:** Storage privacy is also very important concept. Stored data must be protected and transmitted only when required to authorize entity. To hide the identity of stored data anonymization technique is used. Also different noise techniques are used to hide data in database from anonymous access (Evans, 2012).
- **Privacy at Processing:** Sensitive data processing must be accurate an appropriate. Such data is processed carefully, DRM system provides data exchange rules which are very important. In case of sensitive data processing, owner of data must be aware of each aspect, when data is shared, to which party, and for what purpose this data will be used (Evans, 2012).
- **Resilience to Attacks:** In this era of IoT, where everyone is connected to network and sharing massive amount of data on daily basis, intruder can attack and use this private data for any purpose. There are many internal and external attacks that cause harm to users' private data. So there must be resilience to such attacks.
- **Trust:** In IoT trust is the basic factor for users' data privacy. Trust can be categorized into many thing such as trust on hardware, trust on software, trust upon user and data (Miao, 2012).

- **Mobile Security:** In the network of mobile IoT, nodes are continuously moving from one cluster to the other. This cause a great danger of node identification, authentication and internal attacks. Protocols based on cryptography are commonly used to provide these nodes protection. An ad-hoc protocol is used in the scenario where node move from one cluster and join the other (Balte, 2015) (Ziegeldorf J. H., 2014).
- **Secure Middleware:** Middleware is used to provide security in IoT, as in these networks different devices interact with each other. So there is a need of multiple middle layers to provide security to data (Miao, 2012).
- **Localization and Tracking:** The user's location information is very important, and this information cannot be shared with a third party without his/her permission. The IoT devices such as smartphones record user's location and the attacker can intrude the device and check the current location of user (Balte, 2015).
- **Inventory Attack:** Inventory attacks cause harm in different areas, in the IoT environment, these attacks are harmful specifically in healthcare. In this attack, the attacker sends many queries to the entity to guess his interest by his responses (Ziegeldorf J. H., 2014).

Legislations for IoT Users' Privacy

With the upsurge in the use of IoT, the demand for user privacy also increases. A massive quantity of raw figures about users is collected by the devices on daily basis. This raw data is about location, s-health, identity, accounts, and much more. There are different types of IoT devices used in routine every day such as in the COVID-19 pandemic, smart thermometers, and rings are used. Many organizations for producing revenue and gaining market control collect user data continually. There is a greater need for the law to prevent consequences.

Privacy legislations are made to apply limitations on the organizations that collect user data daily for different purposes, also these laws forced privacy on users' private data leakage. Universal Declaration of Human Rights in 1948 first time acknowledged privacy as an important human right, and this act is part of constitutional law in many countries. Fair information practices (FIPs) were established when in 1974 US Privacy Act approved the legislation on data privacy. The FIPs include five principles (OECD, 1980).

1. There must be no undisclosed systems for individual data.
2. The individuals must know how his/her data is used.
3. The individuals have the right to stop secondary use.
4. The individuals have the right to change data.
5. Data must be protected from misapplication.

The U.S. Privacy Act of 1974 only works with the federal government. It did not include general data privacy legislation. So the Organization for Economic Co-operation and Development (OECD), improved these rules to avoid trade barriers from ever more varied privacy legislation (Fromholz, 2000). In their directive, they embedded FIPs add rules according to which data is only collected with the permission of the user.

OECD extended FIPs into eight principles that later on became the foundation of EU privacy law (Commerce., 2012).

1. **Collection Limitation:** data collection must be according to the law, by fair means, and with the permission of the user.
2. **Data Quality:** data must be related, correct, comprehensive, and up to date.
3. **Purpose Specification:** before collecting and processing data, the purpose must be specified.
4. **Use Limitation:** personal data must not be revealed, accessible, and utilized for non-specified reasons.
5. **Security Safeguards:** security safeguards must be used to protect private data.
6. **Openness:** There must be a strategy that specify expansions for private data.
7. **Individual Participation:** the individual must have the right to access data whenever required, and must be informed before collecting erasing, or modifying his/her data.
8. **Accountability:** for complying with all these principles data controllers will be accountable.

This legislation has a greater impact: the EU data directives not only effectively ensured standards of data protection, but also encourage international efforts for data privacy e.g. the Safe Harbor agreement (Linn, 2021).

The EU privacy laws were enforced in the member countries, so the non-EU countries developed their own privacy legislation such as the Privacy Shield framework (Minssen, 2020). Later, in 2016 EU embraced the general data protection regulation (GDPR) (De Hert, 2012) which is the successor of Directive 95/46/EC (Cha, 2018). GDPR changes Directive 95/46/EC and embedded six rules shown in Table 1 (Cha, 2018).

Table 1. GDPR privacy rules for IoT

Consent	Consent must be vibrant, unique, and easy to withdraw.
Breach Notification:	The breach notification must be sent within 72hr.
Right to Access:	Individual has the right to access information.
Right to Be Forgotten:	Erase personal data if no longer required for any valid purpose.
Data Portability:	User has the right to receive his/her uploaded data in a machine-readable form and can transmit it to other data controllers.
Privacy-by-Design(PbD)	The controller implements suitable techniques at the time of processing data.

Currently, data protection legislation focused on protecting data in cloud computing, web user tracking, etc. However, the protection presented by legislation is inadequate, as data spills and privacy breaches increase daily. The IoT will undeniably generate new grey areas to avoid loopholes in legislative boundaries. There is a greater need of implementing the legislation properly and work on privacy enhancing technologies to provide IoT users complete privacy.

PRIVACY ENHANCING TECHNOLOGIES (PETS)

Categorization of Privacy Issues

User privacy issues have been studied by many researchers in their studies (Lopez, 2017). Three main privacy problems were highlighted by Lopezet in (Malina, 2019) are: user privacy, context privacy, and content privacy. Khan divided 12 privacy issues reported by different researchers into 3 classes (Khan, 2019):

1. **Privacy Threats:** this class shows faults and problems at the IoT system and services level, it could be used by other parties that can cause different internal and external attacks.
2. **Privacy Leakage:** this class shows the threats of a direct breach of user information that can be misused by intruders.
3. **Privacy Attacks:** this class highlights internationally performed issues by attackers that intrude into the system steal users' private data and misuse it for criminal purposes.

The general privacy prevention and protection methods are Data Minimization, Data Anonymization, Data Security, Data Control, Identity Management, Secure Communication, and User Awareness/ Transparency about their personal data information sharing.

Categorization of PETs for IoT

According to Khan-2019, privacy enhanced technologies for IoT are categorized into four categories i.e. Device level implementation, Used as applications, Applied in networks, and Applied in data storage, cloud, and back-end servers (Khan, 2019). Whereas, the basic privacy features provided by privacy enhanced technologies PETs are Anonymity (the user is unidentifiable), Pseudonymity (the user is recognizable only to issuers), Un-linkability (activities performed by the same user cannot be linked), Un-traceability (users' personal information such as credentials cannot be tracked and backed by issuers), Revocation (the user can only be removed by the authenticated issuer) and Data privacy (any type of user's private data such as identities, credentials, vitals, etc. are not exposed to a third party.)

PETs for IoT Devices

Privacy-Enhancing Technologies (PETs) can play an essential role in protecting the privacy and security of IoT devices. The use of PETs can help to protect the privacy and security of IoT devices and the data they generate. By implementing the technologies, organizations can ensure that personal data is collected and processed in a responsible and ethical manner. There are different types of privacy enhancement techniques that are used to provide privacy to IoT users. In this section, we will discuss different types of PETs used by IoT devices.

Blind Signature (BS)

Blind signature is a digital signature that blinded the massage before it is signed. So that, the signer will not know the message content. Then this signed message will be unblended afterward. At this instant, it is like a normal digital signature and can be checked against the original message. BS can be implemented using many public-key encryption schemes.

Group Signature (GS)

Group digital signature uses a digital signature algorithm and a challenge-response identification protocol that offers operative authentication. It is based on the public key structure; group members first generate public keys. Then designed authority generates their identity code (ID), identity mark, and secret key. Every group member retains his/her private key and the ID for signing. These parameters ensure that only members can make signatures and provide data authenticity for the signer.

Attribute-Based Credentials (ABCs)

Attribute-Based Credentials (ABC) define decryption ability that is based on a user's attributes. In a multi-authority ABC mechanism, multiple attribute authorities check different sets of attributes to issue matching decryption keys to users, and encryptors need a user to obtain keys for suitable attributes from each authority before message decryption.

Anonymous and Pseudonymous Data Authentication

In pseudonym systems, users are permitted to have contact with many organizations anonymously. This system is operative in an anonymous way. Each organization knows one user with different pseudonyms. These pseudonyms cannot be linked and guarantee the data anonymity. In an anonymous and pseudonymous data authentication system, processes are applied to user and organization interactions.

The Onion Touting

Onion routing technique is for private communication over a public network. It provides anonymous connections. These connections are strongly resilient to eavesdropping and traffic analysis. Its anonymous connections are bidirectional, real-time, and used anywhere. Identifying information that must be in the data stream is carried over an anonymous connection. An onion is a data structure that acted as the destination address by onion routers; so, it is used to create an anonymous connection. Onions appear different for each onion router and also for network observers. It is the same for data carried over the connections established by these onions. Web browsers and e-mail clients, require no change to use onion routing, they do this through a series of proxies.

Encrypted Communications

When two entities are communicating and do not want a third party to intercept their communication it's encrypted communications. It means people can share information with confidence that no one can intercept what they said. Data transmitted over the internet is broken into discrete packets, these packets flow over the internet from one computer to computer, guided about their destination. These packets have multiple ways to flow from point A to point B, so any computer along the way can snoop these packets on their way towards their destination. There are many types of encryption techniques used to secure data on the internet.

Symmetrical Encryption

Symmetrical encryption system implicates a single cryptographic key, which is known to both sender and the receiver. Both parties can encrypt and decrypt this data.

Public Key Encryption

Public key encryption system includes a special pair of keys. One key is public and the other is private. The sender uses a pair of public and private keys to encode the messages, and the receiver has the opposite pair of these keys for decoding the message.

Mix Networks

Mix networks are multistage system, it provides anonymity by using cryptography and permutations. Mix network changes the appearance and removes the order of arrival for a batch of inputs to provide anonymity for the batch of inputs. The main component of mix net is the stage; it performs the mixing of batch input by applying cryptographic transformation using encryption or decryption. It changes the appearance of input, then it is followed by permutation.

Crowds

This scheme grouped users into a large geographically diverse group called a crowd. This group issues request collectively on the behalf of group members. In this way, Web servers are not able to locate the true source from where the request is generated. Even the cooperating crowd members cannot distinguish from which member request originated.

Homomorphic Encryption

Homomorphic encryption is an encryption technique that applies computation on cipher texts. It generates an encrypted text which is decrypted to the plain text again. This technique is used in modern communication system architecture. RSA is a public-key encryption technique that used homomorphic encryption properties.

Polymorphic Encryption and Pseudonymization (PEP)

The PEP algorithm is a novel method that secures personal and sensitive data privacy. In traditional encryption methods, only one key is used to decrypt the encrypted data. This approach is a big hurdle in the case of big data analytics. PEP is a new cryptographic method that is used to overcome this issue, it secures the privacy of data, especially in areas such as healthcare, medical data collection via different self-measurement apps and devices, big data analytics, and identity management. PEP work in three steps.

1. Newly generated data is encrypted in a polymorphic manner and stored. For example, PEP enables the self-measurement application to store all the measurement data in the polymorphic encrypted form in the database.
2. Then later it can be decided based on the policy in which the data subject plays an important role that who can decrypt this data.
3. The decryption of this encrypted data is done by a trusted specific party who knows how to decrypt the cipher texts and for whom.

Attribute-Based Encryption Scheme (ABE)

ABE encryption scheme is used for the privacy of data for different kinds of attacks such as unauthorized authentication, fabrication, interruption, alteration, and illegal access to data. In this scheme certificated authority (CA) generates public or secret keys based on a set of attributes

Data Splitting

Data splitting mechanisms detect pieces of data that cause privacy risks and split them into chunks on local premises to avoid privacy risks. The clear chunks of data are stored separately in the cloud where no external entities can access them.

Differential Privacy

Differential privacy mechanisms used mathematical functions to ensure the privacy of data. This method assumes that the attacker has maximum background knowledge and secondly it consists of a strict quantitative evaluation mechanism that uses the objective function of the ε-differential privacy distribution optimization technique to ensure privacy.

SDN-Enabled Hybrid DL-Driven Framework

As IoT is extensively emerging these days, along with other threats risk of cyber-attacks on IoT devices is also increasing day by day. There is a different mechanism to detect and mitigate these cyber threats to provide privacy to user data using IoT devices. To provide security and cater to privacy issues in IoT SDN-enabled hybrid DL-driven threat detection system is purposed its threat detection accuracy is 99.74% (Al Razib, 2022).

SDN-Enabled DNN-LSTM Hybrid Framework

For the detection of cyber threats in a smart environment deep learning-based SDN is purposed that enable IDS for threat detection. This technique is capable of detecting even common and less occurring cyber threats (Al Razib, 2022).

SUMMARY

User privacy in IoT is an emergent concern in today's world. With the increase in technology specifically the IoT world has witnessed that different IoT devices are connected to the internet every day and this connectivity is increasing day by day. The vast amount of user data is collected and processed on daily basis causing privacy concerns. So users' right to privacy is an important and basic need for developing users' trust in IoT. To mitigate these privacy concerns legislation is made along with privacy-enhanced techniques. Legislation is implemented to provide users their privacy rights, whereas PETs are used to solve the privacy issues faced by users in different areas using IoT devices. For this reason, privacy issues are categorized into three classes (privacy threats, privacy leakage, and privacy attacks) and then PETs are also categorized based on these three classes to provide users with secure and private connections over the internet and secure them for different privacy threats and attacks. For example, blocking a device or asking user permission of taking action against a potential privacy attack may be dangerous in certain situations. Consider a door-unlock application, it unlocks the door when there is smoke in the house because of certain reasons upon the user's approval. It asks the user permission to unlock the door when there is smoke in the house, in case the user cannot respond the notification door remained locked which might be dangerous in certain circumstances. To avoid such dangers IoT devices must be implanted by different response disciplines to maintain integrity. IoT as an emerging technology faces many technical and non-technical challenges so the development of a standard IoT privacy framework is hindered. It is concluded that user privacy protection is the mutual responsibility of all parties, they must take active participation and cooperate to ensure user privacy and develop user trust in IoT. IoT devices must be designed by manufacturers with integrated privacy measures. IoT-oriented methods must be used on the infrastructure level to avoid privacy leaks, also users must be notified by IoT applications that what data is collected and for what purpose and ask the user's permission before. IoT users must also be careful about authorities asking for their data and understand the consequences that may result in misuse of their private information.

REFERENCES

Aggarwal, R. a. (2012). RFID security in the context of" internet of things. *The First International Conference on Security of Internet of Things* (pp. 51-56). Association for Computing Machinery (ACM). 10.1145/2490428.2490435

Al Razib, M. J. (2022). Cyber threats detection in smart environments using SDN-enabled DNN-LSTM hybrid framework. *IEEE Access : Practical Innovations, Open Solutions*, *10*, 53015–53026. doi:10.1109/ACCESS.2022.3172304

Babar, S. M. (2010). *Proposed security model and threat taxonomy for the Internet of Things (IoT)*. In Recent Trends in Network Security and Applications: Third International Conference, CNSA 2010, (pp. 420-429). Springer Berlin Heidelberg.

Balte, A. K. (2015). Security issues in Internet of things (IoT): A survey. *International Journal of Advanced Research in Computer Science and Software Engineering*, *5*(4).

Bhat, O. S. (2017). Implementation of IoT in smart homes. *International Journal of Advanced Research in Computer and Communication Engineering, ●●●,* 149–154.

Cao, J. C. (2010). Castle: Continuously anonymizing data streams. *IEEE Transactions on Dependable and Secure Computing, 8*(3), 337–352.

Cha, S. C., Hsu, T.-Y., Xiang, Y., & Yeh, K.-H. (2018). Privacy enhancing technologies in the Internet of Things: Perspectives and challenges. *IEEE Internet of Things Journal, 6*(2), 2159–2187. doi:10.1109/JIOT.2018.2878658

USD Commerce. (2012). *The U.S.-EU & U.S. - Swiss Safe Harbor Frameworks.* Retrieved from US Department of Commerce http://export.gov/safeharbor/

Daubert, J. W. (2015). A view on privacy & trust in IoT. *In 2015 IEEE International Conference on Communication Workshop (ICCW)* (pp. 2665-2670). IEEE. 10.1109/ICCW.2015.7247581

De Hert, P., & Papakonstantinou, V. (2012). The proposed data protection Regulation replacing Directive 95/46/EC: A sound system for the protection of individuals. *Computer Law & Security Review, 28*(2), 130–142. doi:10.1016/j.clsr.2012.01.011

Evans, D. &. (2012). Efficient data tagging for managing privacy in the internet of things. *In 2012 IEEE International Conference on Green Computing and Communications* (pp. 244-248). IEEE. 10.1109/GreenCom.2012.45

Finn, R. L. (2013). Seven types of privacy. . *European data protection: coming of age,* 3-32.

Fromholz, J. M. (2000). The European Union data privacy directive. *Berk. Tech. LJ, 15,* 461.

Grant-Muller, S., & Usher, M. (2014). Intelligent Transport Systems: The propensity for environmental and economic benefits. *Technological Forecasting and Social Change, 82,* 149–166. doi:10.1016/j.techfore.2013.06.010

Hassan, A. N., Nihad, M., & Nife, N. (2019). The Internet of Things Privacy. *Journal of Computational and Theoretical Nanoscience, 16*(3), 1007–1018. doi:10.1166/jctn.2019.7990

Henze, M. H. (2014). User-driven privacy enforcement for cloud-based services in the internet of things. *International Conference on Future Internet of Things and Cloud.,* (pp. 191–196). IEEE. 10.1109/FiCloud.2014.38

Khan, T. U. (2019). Internet of Things (IOT) systems and its security challenges. [IJARCET]. *International Journal of Advanced Research in Computer Engineering and Technology,* 12.

Kong, Q. L., Lu, R., Ma, M., & Bao, H. (2019). A privacy-preserving sensory data sharing scheme in Internet of Vehicles. *Future Generation Computer Systems, 92,* 644–655. doi:10.1016/j.future.2017.12.003

Kumar, J. S. (2014). 2014 A survey on internet of things: Security and privacy issues. *International Journal of Computers and Applications, 90*(11).

Linn, E. (2021). *A Look into the Data Privacy Crystal Ball: A Survey of Possible Outcomes for the EU-U.S.* Privacy Shield Agreement 50. *Vanderbilt Law Review,* 1311.

Lopez, J. R., Rios, R., Bao, F., & Wang, G. (2017). Evolving privacy: From sensors to the Internet of Things. *Future Generation Computer Systems, 75*, 46–57. doi:10.1016/j.future.2017.04.045

Luong, N. C., Hoang, D. T., Wang, P., Niyato, D., Kim, D. I., & Han, Z. (2016). Data collection and wireless communication in Internet of Things (IoT) using economic analysis and pricing models: A survey. *IEEE Communications Surveys and Tutorials, 18*(4), 2546–2590. doi:10.1109/COMST.2016.2582841

Lv, J. Y. (2011). A new clock synchronization architecture of network for internet of things. In *International Conference on Information Science and Technology.* (pp. 685-688). IEEE.

Malina, L. S. (2019). A privacy-enhancing framework for internet of things services. In Network and System Security. *13th International Conference, NSS 2019* (pp. 77-97). Sapporo, Japan: Springer International Publishing. 10.1007/978-3-030-36938-5_5

Miao, J., & Wang, L. (2012). Rapid identification authentication protocol for mobile nodes in internet of things with privacy protection. *Journal of Networks, 7*(7), 1099. doi:10.4304/jnw.7.7.1099-1105

Minssen, T. S., Seitz, C., Aboy, M., & Corrales Compagnucci, M. (2020). The EU-US Privacy Shield Regime for Cross-Border Transfers of Personal Data under the GDPR: What are the legal challenges and how might these affect cloud-based technologies, big data, and AI. *EPLR, 4*(1), 34–50. doi:10.21552/eplr/2020/1/6

Mwasilu, F. J.-K.-W., Justo, J. J., Kim, E.-K., Do, T. D., & Jung, J.-W. (2014). Electric vehicles and smart grid interaction: A review on vehicle to grid and renewable energy sources integration. *Renewable & Sustainable Energy Reviews, 34*, 501–516. doi:10.1016/j.rser.2014.03.031

OECD. (1980). Recommendation of the council concerning guidelines governing the protection of privacy and trans border flows of personal data. Organisation for Economic Co-operation and Development (OECD).

Patton, M. G. (2014). Uninvited connections: a study of vulnerable devices on the internet of things (IoT). *In 2014 IEEE Joint Intelligence and Security Informatics Conference* (pp. pp. 232-235). IEEE.

PereraG. T. (n.d.). Identification of the Optimum Light Conditions and Development of an Iot Based Setup to Monitor a Household Indoor Hydroponic Tomato Cultivation. *Available at:* SSRN 4167457. doi:10.2139/ssrn.4167457

Rajendran, S. S. (2020). Security and Privacy for Internet of Things (IoT): Issues and Solutions. [IJS-REM]. *International Journal of Scientific Research in Engineering and Management, 4*(11).

Ramgovind, S. M. (2010). The management of security in cloud computing. 2010 Information Security for South Africa, (pp. 1-7). IEEE.

Sharma, V. a. (2016). A review paper on "IOT" & It's Smart Applications. *International Journal of Science, Engineering and Technology Research (IJSETR)*, (pp. 472-476). ACM.

Shirey, R. (2000). *RFC 2828: Internet Security Glossary.*.

Solanas, A. P.-B., Patsakis, C., Conti, M., Vlachos, I., Ramos, V., Falcone, F., Postolache, O., Perez-martinez, P., Pietro, R., Perrea, D., & Martinez-Balleste, A. (2014). Smart health: A context-aware health paradigm within smart cities. *IEEE Communications Magazine, 52*(8), 74–81. doi:10.1109/MCOM.2014.6871673

Srinivasan, V. S. (2008). Protecting your daily in-home activity information from a wireless snooping attack. *In Proceedings of the 10th International Conference on Ubiquitous Computing*, (pp. 202-211).

Sundmaeker, H. G. (2010). Vision and challenges for realising the Internet of Things. *Cluster of European research projects on the internet of things. European Commision, 3*(3), 32–36.

Vikas, B. O. (2015). Internet of things (iot): A survey on privacy issues and security. *International Journal of Scientific Research in Science, Engineering and Technology*, 168–173.

Wang, Y. (2011). *A privacy enhanced dns scheme for the internet of things.*

Westin, A. F. (1968). Privacy and freedom. *Washington and Lee Law Review*, 166.

Whitmore, A., Agarwal, A., & Da Xu, L. (2015). The Internet of Things—A survey of topics and trends. *Information Systems Frontiers, 17*(2), 261–274. doi:10.100710796-014-9489-2

Ziegeldorf, J. H., Morchon, O. G., & Wehrle, K. (2014). Privacy in the Internet of Things: Threats and challenges. *Security and Communication Networks, 7*(12), 2728–2742. doi:10.1002ec.795

Ziegeldorf, J. H., Morchon, O. G., & Wehrle, K. (2014). Privacy in the Internet of Things: Threats and challenges. *Security and Communication Networks, 7*(12), 2728–2742. doi:10.1002ec.795

Chapter 13
Adoption of GDPR for Personal Data Protection in Smart Cities

Pedro Pina

Polytechnic Institute of Coimbra, Technology and Management School of Oliveira do Hospital, Oliveira do Hospital, Portugal & SUScita - Research Group on Sustainability Cities and Urban Intelligence, Portugal

ABSTRACT

The digital infrastructure of smart cities necessarily implies collecting big amounts of personal and its subsequent processing by software and applications designed to acquire analytical capabilities regarded to public spaces in order to enable efficient control over it. In the European Union legal context, aiming to densify the principle of informational self-determination, the general data protection regulation (GDPR) has provided citizens with greater power and control over their personal data, turning the responsibilities of smart cities administrators towards citizens much heavier. This chapter aims to analyse the impact on personal data and democratic public spaces derived from smart cities activities, to present the rights granted to individuals by the GDPR and its applicability to smart cities, and to make some recommendations regarding the implementation and the adaptation of the Regulation to the specific case of a smart city, not only to preserve a high-level level of privacy protection but also as a means to promote democratic solutions in public spaces.

INTRODUCTION

In cyberworld, the clash between digital technology and personal data protection rights is an evident reality. Smart cities are one of the most recent fields where the referred conflict takes place. The notable development of digital information and communication technologies (ICT), especially the Internet of Things (IoT) or cloud computing, and its application to activities of planning and administration of the cities, even if merged with traditional infrastructures, is the genesis of the concept of smart cities that use ICT to enhance the quality of daily life and the efficiency of services provided by the municipality, in a sustainable way, ensuring that the needs of present and future generations will be safeguarded with

DOI: 10.4018/978-1-6684-6914-9.ch013

respect to a multidimensional approach involving economic, environmental, cultural, educational or social (International Telecommunication Union, 2016).

Smart cities comprise various components related to urban services, energy, e-economy, smart living or smart environment (Magare et al, p. 40) that are related not only to the administration of the city itself but also to the optimization of different aspects of each individual's daily life. As envisioned by the National League of Cities (2016, p. 5), in a smart city of the future, a community member will wake up in a house where an artificial intelligence will automatically control smart and connected household appliances, monitoring light levels, temperature, food stock or even the resident's health. A multi-modal transportation system where different means of smart transports will be interconnected providing and processing real-time data will minimize the risks of accidents or traffic jams. A network of smart streetlights embedded sensors will be used also for safety purposes and will be able to detect violent activities or to flash their lights in case of emergencies. Collecting and processing quantitative data related to rain level, solar light level or others will smart cities to save and to use energy resources in a sustainable and efficient way (p. 6). From traffic surveillance to efficient energy consumption or 24/7 healthcare services, smart cities may offer an optimized and enhanced living experience.

The digital infrastructure of a smart city necessarily implies collecting big amounts of heterogeneous information, including citizens' personal data or measurements provided by IoT devices, and its subsequent processing by software and applications designed to acquire analytical capabilities regarded to public spaces in order to enable efficient control over it. Big Data systems are required to mine data, to collect, to store and to process information not only on quantitative aspects of the city but also on personal data such as the identity, health or personal tastes of citizens, capable of tracing the profile of each one. Smart cities will be able to recognize digital identity wallets and interoperable digital identities for their residents. Therefore, transactions made by digital citizens in smart cities will be observable, which will create abundance of data on user behavior on an unprecedented scale. Such heterogeneous information will be needed to improve different smart city services and will be considered by programmers and decision-makers when planning for the expansion of smart city services and resources (Al Nuaimi et al., 2015).

Privacy concerns may arise from the use of ubiquitous surveillance technology. In the European Union (EU), the activities of collecting and processing personal data must comply with the provisions of the General Data Protection Regulation (Regulation (EU) 2016/679) (GDPR), a legal document that foresees the fundamental right of each individual to informational and communicational self-determination. The GDPR has recognized citizens the power to be in control of their personal information, which may clash with technological solutions that smart city planners intend to implement.

Some civil society organizations have also questioned possible misuses of the technology given the fact that it provides smart cities' authorities or programmers the capability to monitor and register the behaviors, the transactions, and the routine of the user (#WhyID, n.d.). The ubiquity of the technology provides multifaceted uses related to the behavior of the individual in his/her private sphere but also in public spaces, which will promote a panoptic surveillance system that may not comprise with fundamental rights and freedoms of a democratic society.

This chapter is composed of three primary sections. It starts with a brief analysis of the impact on personal data and democratic public spaces derived from smart cities' technology. Then, it will present the rights granted to individuals by the GDPR and the corresponding obligations that collectors and processors of personal data must apply to their practices and its applicability to smart cities. Finally, some recommendations regarding the implementation and the adaptation of GDPR to the specific case of a smart city will be made, not only to preserve a high-level level of privacy protection but also as a means to promote democratic solutions in public spaces.

DATAFIED SMART CITIES: RISKS TO PRIVACY AND TO THE PUBLIC INTEREST

Main Features of Smart Cities

Smart cities have been promoted in the last two decades as places where urban life is made identifiable and manageable and the efficiency of urban services is enhanced through the collection, processing, and analysis of digital data. ICTs are the foundation pillar of smart cities. Digital technologies are implemented to collect data to monitor and enhance urban infrastructures such as transportation, waste management, energy or water consumption, and emergency response given the ability to monitor urban activities and behaviors through pervasive, interconnected sensors, perceptive things and Internet networks that convert activities from the urban space into data (Halegoua, 2020b). Cities are considered smart not only because of the mere implementation of digital technology but mainly given the fact that the use of ICTs must be functionally oriented to enhance urban systems in order to provide more efficient global services to citizens (Marsal-Llacuna et al., 2014; Hall, 2000; Chen, 2010; Albino, Berardi & Dangelico, 2015).

In this context, a city can be described as smart where a balance between economic, environmental and social development elements may be found and where the referred dimensions are linked through decentralized processes to manage resources, assets, and urban flows for real-time processes in a more efficient way (Ismagilova et al, 2022). Smart cities rely on ecosystems of multiple key layers of sectorial networks (e.g. for smart parking, smart transportation, smart e-health, smart energy consumption, etc) that must be concerted to become ubiquitous and to provide citizens a daily life full range of rational and sustainable solutions and experiences. A smart city integrates multiple systems composed of task-oriented applications that provide services to citizens while evolving with all the dimensions of the city through digital, analytical and automated data-driven means (Alnahari & Ariaratnam, 2022, p. 979).

Metaphorically, the smart city may be seen as sentient complex structure similar to a body with a brain and organs that follow common functions such as seeing, hearing, knowing and responding to residents (Halegoua, 2020a) or, ideally and from a technological perspective, an entity acting like a computer. To act as so, smart cities rely on promising technologies such as the Internet of Things (IoT), cloud computing, or artificial intelligence (AI). The IoT may be described as a network of physical objects (the things) embedded and working with sensors, software, processors, mobile cloud computing, and machine learning technologies organized to connect and exchange data with other machines and systems over the internet (Singh et al. 2019; Ismagilova et al., 2019). Everyday devices like cars, home appliances or other machines can use sensors to collect and process data shared within an automated network to subsequently provide secure and efficient services and to intelligently respond to users. Lin et al. (2017, 1125), identify two major features in IoT: working as an extension of the Internet, it implies the coexistence of various and interconnected and interoperable networks where information may flow and be delivered to support different applications; the things connected in such interconnected net of networks are not limited anymore to physical objects or devices, since information such as measurements, non-personal data or human behaviors and preferences can also be used.

The transmission of quantitative and personal data collected by IoT sensors and devices through interconnected digital networks allows the interoperability between applications related to smart cities' key features: smart industry and economy, smart living, smart education, smart governance, smart mobility, and smart environment (Manville & Kotterink, 2014; Lombardi et al., 2012).

Collecting and Processing Personal Data in Smart Cities

The rise of Big Data is ineluctably linked to the concept of smart cities (Taylor & Richter, 2015, 175). According to the so-called model of the 3 V's proposed by Laney (2001), in order to promote enhanced perception, subsequent decision making, and cost-effective innovative automated processes and functions, Big Data implies a high-level of volume, velocity and variety of information (Gartner, n.d.). In this Big Data framework where smart cities stand, a huge number of diverse kinds of personal data or measurements must be gathered, processed, and analyzed, coming from a surfeit of sources at maximum velocity (Theodorou & Sklavos, 2019, 25).

Smart cities's sensors, devices, and software such as traffic cameras, road sensors, connected vehicles, smartphones and connected infrastructures are designed to collect and to process a vast volume of data, whether of personal nature or not, through sensors, and its online transmission aiming at a real-time response of the system.

The legal concept of personal data includes any information related to a natural person. That person may already be identified but, for legal purposes, it is enough that he/she is identifiable. An identifiable person is one who can be identified, directly or indirectly, by reference to one or a set of personal identifiers that may include names, identification numbers, online identifiers, or location data, but also to one or more aspects related to the physical, genetic, mental, cultural, economic, or social identity of the natural person (Article 4 (1) GDPR). Non-personal data may be perceived as information not linked to an identified or identifiable individual, that is any other information than personal data as specified in the GDPR. Both kinds of data constitute an important tool for the implementation of the smart cities. According to the needs of a specific application, different kinds of data will be treated.

A smart irrigation management system implanted in public parks and gardens, for instance, will need to collect more quantitative non-personal data, like the rain level or the natural drainage capacity of the city in a specific moment than personal data from citizens. An e-health application will have to collect personal sensitive data from the user like age, gender, race, health, or genetic data.

Interoperability and interconnection of data and applications are being designed to improve the individual user experience within a smart city. People-centered smart cities' interconnected applications may give a resident a full range of comfortable and efficient solutions: for instance, one can self-drive a smart car connected to the city traffic platform that will indicate at a real-time the best or the fastest route to the destiny, where to park, how many spots are available in a parking garage; the interconnection of smart cars will prevent accidents to happen; healthcare applications connected to the smart car can detect symptoms of an heart attack during the drive and automatically set a new route to the nearest hospital restaurants or inform the user that the order in a restaurant he/she is about to make is not adequate to his/her blood sugar or cholesterol level.

A system that provides for such kind of users' experiences involves the treatment of data that must be considered personal (name, age, address, gender, health, personal preferences, etc). Moreover, given the fact that applications must be interconnected to give the referred broad daily life experience, personal data will have to transmitted and shared between the providers of the different applications. The collector or the responsible for treating data may be the city government or public or private enterprises that provide, for instance, parking lot services, electricity, water, or healthcare to citizens, which brings the not only political but also corporate interests to the picture (Viitanen & Kingston, 2014).

From this perspective, smart cities' sensors generate intelligence for the use by companies and governments that frequently build and finance smart cities under Public-Private Partnerships (PPP), which can be defined as long-term contractual agreements concluded between a public entity and a private partner according to which the latter finances and provides public services, with shared risks and management functions (OECD, 2012). Consequently, the multipolarity of interconnected smart cities' service providers will imply constant flows of information previously collected by public or private entities enabling access to a huge amount of data, whether personal or not, data collected by one and others in the system.

Risks to Privacy and to the Public Interest

By using smart cities applications, citizens may release their identities, location or consumption information and preferences that can be used to infer user behavior and to create consumers' profile; additionally, excessive collection of data and knowledge over-mining may disclose sensitive information that data subjects are unwilling to reveal (Qu et al., 2019, 81) and that can be transferred to other providers within the system without individuals' consent or control.

Drones and cameras can be used as surveillance tools in the public space, making it possible to constantly control or monitor people's activities and preferences. Moreover, since personal data is stored, transferred, and processed by multiple agents in the network, there will be always a risk of security breach and leakage, malware attacks, or other vulnerabilities giving unauthorized access to third parties, namely untrusted entities and criminals (Ismagilova et al., 2022, 400; Rosadi et al., 2021). For such reasons, citizens are increasingly becoming aware of the potential risks for their privacy derived from the implementation of smart cities applications and slowly gaining interest for the risks derived from data processing activities. Citizen protests have been taking place in several locations where smart cities initiatives and programs have been implemented, such as San Diego, Nashville, Philadelphia, Amsterdam, Nice or Marseille. Citizens are starting to show some resistance to the rollout of smart cities' data driven technology mainly because of their concern around unauthorized collection of data, the control, and the power of private companies over the collected data and the ensuing loss of privacy. Furthermore, citizens fear the creation of a surveillance city and the implementation of a discriminatory and totalitarian system derived from the control of privacy in public spaces.

The intended large-scale (personal) data collecting, and processing creates a high level of privacy and security risk to individuals. However, despite the above-mentioned protests, surveys and studies suggest that majority of current city residents and visitors are not familiarized with the concept of smart city or Big Data and what it implies (Van Zoonen, 2016, 473; Thomas et al, 2015). For instance, according to Cró & Roegiers (2021, p. 36), a recent survey showed that, in Lisbon, almost 20% of the participants were not aware of the collection and analysis of personal data. 71.6% of the answers revealed discomfort by knowing their personal data were being used. The respondents explained that they were afraid of data leakage and that data could be hacked, and that they were distressed with idea that someone else could be using their personal information without consent, especially in the case of sensitive data. More visible and ostentatious equipment such as drones, surveillance cameras or sensor-equipped streetlights directly attract the attention of citizens giving them the feeling that they are being permanently controlled and monitored.

From the public interest point of view, the loss of privacy derived from the constant monitoring of multiple activities may have real and serious consequences for democracies, undermining the right to freely express, to dissent and protest.

Williams (2021) identifies the following Smart City Cautionary Trends:

- Totalitarianism, considering the deployment of intrusive technology without a prior democratic discussion; by dismissing people's participation in favor of technocraticism; and by the possible creation of a surveillance police state;
- Panopticonism enabled by the erosion of privacy, by the possibility of unauthorized searches and apprehensions; and by considering the augmented risk of security and data breaches;
- Discriminatory surveillance by targeting minorities and other marginalized communities; intensifying discrimination and (in)visibility; and promoting different access to digital services;
- Privatization of public services and infrastructures, by the increase of through public procurement or PPP agreements, favoring corporate decision-making in detriment of democratic procedures; avoiding legal and constitutional safeguards; and intensifying surveillance monopolies;
- Technological "solutionism", by solving moral or political problems with technology that quantifies, tracks or gamifies behavior.

Unregulated smart cities projects may become a threat to citizens' individual rights and to a democratic society as a whole. The clash between technology and human rights is not new. Although it might have been opaque and unperceived in the beginning of the implementation of smart cities, it is today unquestionable that national or local legislators must take the phenomenon in consideration in order to respect fundamental rights, freedoms and guarantees related to the private sphere of each citizens or collective rights in the public space.

SMART CITIES AND DATA PROTECTION IN THE EU

The General Data Protection Regulation (GDPR)

In the EU, the *acquis communautaire* legislation traditionally perceives privacy rights in a broad manner and predicts a strengthened guarantee of personal data. Privacy rights are perceived not only as "the right to be left alone" (Warren & Brandeis, 1890) but also as a right of permanent control over personal data. Ensuing a seminal decision of the German Constitutional Court ruling that the individual must be protected against unrestricted collection, storage, use and disclosure of his/her personal information, the referred activities must be encompassed by constitutional provisions foreseeing personal rights' (BVerfGE, 1983). The recognized fundamental right guarantees the legal power of everyone to determine how or when to disclose and to use their personal data. The European approach and perception of the right of the individual to personal data is not restricted to a mere defensive guarantee of privacy as a fundamental right with a positive content is foreseen. According to the described conception, the right to privacy, named as the right to informational and communicational self-determination is constituted by two different but complementary dimensions. The first dimension is similar to the right conceptualized by Warren & Brandeis as it comprehends a negative content and presents a defensive and reactive protection of the rightsholder against intrusion by the State and/or by individuals or corporations who collect and treat digital or analogical personal information. From this perspective, one's personal information is protected from public scrutiny in similar ways to the guarantee of the secrecy or privacy of correspondence and of other types of private communication. The right to informational and communicational self-determination has a second dimension which can be qualified as a right with a positive nature, since it comprises the power of each individual to be in constant control of his/her own personal information, granting him/her the ability to dispose of it and on what conditions, and to determine at every moment what information about his/her respect others know, collected or have been processing.

Article 8 of the Charter of Fundamental Rights of the EU (CFREU) comprises the two above-mentioned dimensions, as it predicts the right to the protection of personal data concerning each data subject and that such information must be treated fairly for specified purposes under the consent of the rightsholder or when justified by other legitimate reason established by law. In accordance with that article, every individual has the right to access his/her personal data which has been collected and the right to have it rectified.

The right to communicational and informational self-determination is regulated in more concrete terms by the Directive on privacy and electronic communications (Directive 2002/58/EC) and, specially, by the GDPR.

Considering the mentioned pieces of EU legislation, the following basic principles must be respected so that the activity of collecting, and processing of personal data may be considered legitimate:

- The principle of lawfulness: this principle, assuming that the activities of collecting and processing personal data constitute a restriction of a fundamental right, means that such activities shall only be accepted and found legitimate within the limits of the law and, particularly, when carried out under the data subjects' free, prior and informed consent, unless if based on a specific public interest (Article 6). The GDPR distinguishes (ordinary) personal data from sensitive data. According to Article 9 (1) personal data is to be considered sensitive when revealing information concerning a natural persons' health, genetic data, biometric data for the unique purpose of identifying a natural person, race and ethnicity, sexual orientation, sex life, political opinions, philosophical or religious beliefs, or trade union membership. Processing of sensitive data is prohibited, unless the data subject has given explicit, meaningful and informed consent to the processing of such sensitive information for one or more specified and previously communicated purposes, and also in cases where sensitive data processing is necessary to protect the vital interests of the rightsholder or of a third person in cases when the data subject is legally or physically incapable of giving consent; or when it is objectively required for the pursuit of a specific and significant public interest.
- The finality or purpose limitation principle, which means that the collection and the processing of personal information can only be carried out following a well-defined and specific purpose that must be identified or be identifiable in every moment of the activity. The purpose limitation is complemented with the principles of objective and temporal limitation.
- The principle of objective limitation, according to which the specific use of personal information must be compatible to the purpose that justified the collection and also that such use must be adequate, proportional, and objectively required to the previously declared finality.
- The principle of time limitation imposes that personal data shall only be kept for the time needed to accomplish the lawful finality behind its processing.
- The data quality principle, indicating that the collected data must be accurate and permanently updated.

- The principle of transparency and access to data, which implies that the individual may freely access to his/her collected personal data for purposes such as knowing the existence of the actual collection, what is being stored, to whom were data eventually transferred and processed, rectifying, erasing or blocking the information when inexact or incomplete.
- The accountability principle, which foresees that the controller must not only ensure but also demonstrate at any time compliance with the Regulation.
- The security principle, related to the prevention of data breach, predicts that, in order to protect personal information against accidental or illegitimate loss or destruction, unauthorized access or disclosure, particularly where data is transmitted over a network, the controller is obliged to implement appropriate organizational and technical measures.
- The confidentiality principle, according to which the controller shall ensure the secrecy of communications and the correlated traffic data, as it is forbidden to tap, listen, interception or to carry out other kinds of surveillance of communications, without the consent of the data subjects', except when legally authorized or obliged to do so (Pina, 2011, 247).

Deepening and densifying the discriminated principles, the GDPR predicts that, when planning activities of collecting, and processing of personal data, protection by design and by default solutions must be adopted by programmers and controllers. Operational applications of privacy by design principles to IoT must include present the following functions and procedures: predict privacy challenges and eradicate chances of abuse; set up privacy solutions by default; embedding data reliability and integrity into all layers of IoT; optimize user experiences to maximum functionality while protecting user interests; clarify messages and solutions to promote user awareness; temper effective control with responsible and transparent monitoring; respect users and consumers as stakeholders to leverage trust (Cavoukian & Popa, 2016). Data collectors are therefore obliged to design and build personal data treatment systems with privacy in mind as an aid to improving protection (Stefanouli & Economou, 2019, 750).

In this context, where processing is liable to result in a high risk to fundamental rights, guarantees and freedoms of natural persons, the GDPR requires that, prior to the processing, controllers promote a Data Protection Impact Assessment (DPIA) (Tikkinen-Piri et al., 2017, 143).

Moreover, the Regulation obliges controllers to respect several procedural steps when carrying out their activities.

According to Article 24, in any moment of the processing, the controller is obliged to guarantee and to be able to demonstrate that the activity is being performed in accordance with the GDPR.

The controller must implement by default solutions to ensure that only personal data which are needed for the specific purpose of the activity are processed. Moreover, the controller must ensure that personal information is not made accessible without human intervention to an undetermined number of natural persons (article 25 GDPR).

Controllers also fall under an obligation foreseen in Article 32 to adopt adequate measures for the security of processing, namely the encryption and pseudonymisation of personal information; the capacity to ensure the continuing integrity, confidentiality, resilience and availability of services and processing systems; in the occasion of a incident, the ability to promptly restore the availability and access to personal data; to regularly test, assess and evaluate the efficiency of the measures that were taken for ensuring the security of the processing.

No later than 24 hours after having become aware of data breaches, controllers must notify the occurrence to the supervisory authority (Article 33) and, after that and without undue delay, to data subjects in case the breach is likely to harmfully affect their personal data.

Procedural questions were taken very serious in the GDPR. The controller is obliged to designate a data protection officer (DPO) if the processing is carried out by an authority or body of the public sector (Article 37); otherwise, the existence of a DPO is not mandatory except when controllers or processors carry out processing operations demanding systematic and regular monitoring on a large scale as their core activities.

Controllers are obliged to ensure the timely and properly involvement of the DPO in all matters related to the protection of personal data.

According to Article 39, the DPO will be responsible for:

- informing and advising controllers, processors and employees of their obligations according to the GDPR;
- monitoring compliance with the Regulation of the controller or processor's policies related to the protection of personal data, particularly the ones related to data protection by design or by default solutions;
- monitoring communications of personal data breaches;
- monitoring the DPIA's performance and the application for prior authorization or consultation;
- acting as the contact point for the national supervisory authority;
- co-operating with the supervisory authority at the latter's request or on the data protection officer's own initiative.

In reactive and punitive terms, Article 83 (5) of the GDPR foresees that infringements of its main provisions will be subject to extremely high administrative fines that can go up to 20 000 000 EUR. However, in the case of an undertaking, the fine can go up to 4% of the total worldwide annual turnover of the previous financial year, if higher.

In EU, considering the activities of collecting, processing and transmitting personal data within smart cities' platforms, the legal framework prescribed by the GDPR will necessarily be applicable and respected.

Smart Cities and the GDPR

Smart cities are a unique special case that represent the synthesis of all the problems derived from the clash between privacy and IoT, big data, or even the fainting of the boundaries between private and public spaces (Edwards, 2015, pp. 8-9).

With the GDPR, personal data in the EU has reached a high level of protection. Since smart cities deal with people in their urban environment and considering their daily behaviors, personal data collection comes to as inevitable (Vojković, 2018, 1497). Using data collected by smart cities technologies, local governments can make an efficient and sustainable use of public resources and enhance the use of public infrastructures and spaces, while residents are directed to make better or more rational choices.

The multiple services' network of a smart city implies that a myriad of personal data collectors and controllers may act. The complexity of the networks, the heterogenous nature of collectors and controllers (public agents, private corporations, etc), and the different finalities inherent to their activities or the transmission of data over the network system make it a very complex task to foresee all possible uses of a collected personal data, if the above-mentioned principles, namely the finality or the objective and temporal limitation principles, are to be respected.

From the rightsholder's point of view, to know in a specific moment which specific provider in the network has access to the collected data and if its usage is lawful will a very complex task. To identify who will be responsible to react in case of a data breach is also a difficult task since all the system depends on a complex network of different providers constantly collecting, processing and exchanging information and personal data.

This scenario leads to the inescapable conclusion that the implementation of a smart city system implies personal data processing activities that will probably result in a high risk for privacy and personal information security (Bu-Pasha, 2020). Therefore, smart city initiatives and projects need to be preceded by a DPIA to preventively evaluate the legitimacy and fairness of the processing, to identify risks, to eventually find existing alternatives and, when likely, to mitigate those risks by proposing appropriate measures (Autoritei Persoonsgegevens, 2021, 13).

According to the Dutch Data Protection Authority, activities for which a DPIA is mandatory includes:

- The ones carried out with the use of IoT, since it comprises extensive processing and systematic monitoring and transmission of personal data over the network.
- Exchanging personal data through PPP's or other public or private parties.
- Large-scale and systematic processing or monitoring of public/open spaces or location data related to natural persons, namely with the use of surveillance cameras or other kinds of sensors (Autoritei Persoonsgegevens, 2021, 13).

In the referred operations, the Dutch Data Protection Authority includes, for instance, sensors following people in public spaces, information nodes, cameras, webcams, bodycams or drones, smartphones, etc. In other words, the implementation of smart cities will for sure imply a prior DPIA.

Conducting a DPIA is an essential activity to gain awareness of the risks to personal data associated with a smart city and its sectorial operations. The compliance of proposed technical solutions with the above-mentioned principles and norms will have to be questioned and analysed.

A minimum content of the DPIA is foreseen in Recitals 84 and 90 and in Article 35(7) of the GDPR. The document must demonstrate compliance with the Regulation and describe the envisioned processing operations and its purposes. It must contain an evaluation of the necessity and proportionality of the processing and indicate the risks that the operation may pose to the rights and freedoms of data subjects as well as and the appropriate measures that shall be taken to mitigate them.

A DPIA may represent an important support for controllers to incorporate protection by design or by default solutions into the diverse projects that, together, constitute the smart city network. As previously said, the purpose that was considered when personal data are going to be collected must be clearly defined, lawfully justified, minimized to the strictly necessary to pursue the purpose of the collection so that data shall always be processed in a way compatible with that purpose.

The DPIA may eventually impose embedded privacy by anonymisation or pseudonymisation of personal data. When personal data is to be transferred to another controller, such operation must be justified and comply with GDPR principles. Any new use of personal information within the network, namely the use of transferred data, will have to be re-evaluated since it will have to comply with the finality, the necessity, and the limitation principles. The above stated means that data may have to be de-identified in case of new uses even if the original one a broader collection of personal data was lawful and justified.

Sharing and re-using personal data are particularly challenging activities for controllers and entail substantial risks for data subjects. Describing the information flow within the complex network of a smart city is a key task that must be considered in the DPIA to constantly comply with the GDPR demands. For instance, certain personal information collected for a specific purpose may not be lawfully used by another controller to whom it was transmitted if he/she does not need the full amount of personal information to execute his/her activity; otherwise, the objective limitation principle will be violated.

Implementing a DPIA is also an excellent opportunity to promote the participation of citizens in the multipolar relationship embodied by a smart city. Privacy for public space concerns (Galič, 2019) and the complex dichotomy between private (personal) rights - public interest are matters that have been gaining attention recently.

Technological solutions for the public space of a smart city must not forget the impact they may have on public matters touching basic democratic principles, freedoms and guarantees like non-discrimination, equal access to cultural, educational or health services. Given the complexity of personal data processing systems in the framework of smart cities, when conducting a DPIA, the involvement and the participation of citizens is, therefore, fundamental. However, article 35(9) of the GDPR only states that the views of data subjects shall only be considered when the controller finds it appropriate. The Regulation leaves room for the controller to choose when to open the DPIA to citizen´s participation or not, namely for the *a priori* undetermined cases that are found appropriate.

After the implementation of the DPIA, the execution of data-based smart cities applications by municipalities and/or private corporations must be monitored and followed by DPO's who must exercise the competences given by Article 39.

Limitations of the GDPR When Applied to Smart Cities

The GDPR was not elaborated with the special multipolar case of smart cities in mind.

In a complex network like the one related to a smart city it may not be an easy task to acquire a prior, free and informed consent by data subjects to lawfully process their personal data. As Edwards (2015, p. 33) points out, the IoT exacerbates the lack of motivation, opportunity or resources to give meaningful consents in the current online environment. Considering the purpose limitation derived from the finality principle, it will be an almost impossible task to predict the entire chain or flow of data transmissions to other smart cities' services providers. A free, informed, and unequivocal acquiescence from the data subject to the processing of his/her personal data will be a chimera. Even though some personal data, especially the collected in open spaces, like the one collected by CCTV or by traffic light's sensors, may be found lawful for public interest reasons, the possibility of transmission within the complex network and its subsequent use by other smart services will not share the same validation.

For such reason, some authors, mainly from the USA, where, as above mentioned, the right to privacy has a more restrict meaning than in the EU, have been proposing a pragmatic solution according to which, in the IoT and the smart cities context, it would be preferable to concentrate efforts on data use in detriment of data collection. In this perspective, it would be mor efficient to cede legal control over the latter, in favour of accepting protection whenever data are used (Mundie, 2014; Rai, 2018; Cheung, 2018).

In the smart cities' context, it will also be very difficult to identify who will be responsible and accountable for an eventual and specific data breach or data leakage. Probably for such reason, the Regulation does not foresee the necessary articulation between municipal and private corporations DPO's. These officers are not directly responsible for the compliance of smart city activities with the GDPR. They play, however, a key role in the context of privacy by design solutions as they must stand in a position that allows them to achieve knowledge of activities and practices in order to be capable to offer advice and proficient guidance and supervision" (Autoritei Persoonsgegevens, 2021, 31).

Moreover, the GPDR does not predict a local supervisory authority, an intermediate instance of control between the national supervisory authority, the DPO's and the controllers, with supervising competences and with direct knowledge of the specific smart city. The referred authority could suppress the lack of integrated monitoring of the system. To obtain an effective protection of personal data within the smart cities context and to fulfill the requirements of a democratic society, both in the moment of the implementation of the DPIA and during the execution of its applications, it would be advised to adapt GDPR provisions to the specific case of smart cities and to involve the whole community and their representatives in all the moments of its creation and implementation.

SOLUTIONS AND RECOMMENDATIONS

The benefits coming from the creation of smart cities must be obtained in a way that cities do not become a discriminatory, surveilled, and panoptic space. Following Peter van de Crommert, rather than 'Big brother is watching you', it is preferable to build a smart city infrastructure and network where we can declare that 'Big brother is helping you' (Naafs, 2018). Pragmatic technology-centered perspectives may be functional from the perspective of the efficiency of the infrastructure but it comprises the risk of creating a surveillance society. Changing the focus of regulation and enforcement to the moment when data is used in detriment of the time of collecting data gives open and arbitrary space to providers to gather personal information of citizens.

Innovation is not incompatible with the respect for human rights. Although freedom of investigation and innovation is the default policy for scientific and technological investigation in a democratic and free society, such freedom doesn't mean that innovation shall be completely unregulated or completely permissionless. A regulatory framework of innovation is important to guarantee that human rights are not violated and that innovators will not cause any potential harms or disruptions. A balance between this precautionary principle and innovation must be constantly found, especially in the framework of smart cities. Excessive regulation may lead to evasive entrepreneurialism and civil disobedience (Thierer, 2020); lack of regulation may result in human rights (like freedom, privacy or non-discrimination) violation.

If balance is not achieved, there will be a risk that technology will create a golden cage: probably an upgraded place to live if efficiency and comfort are the basis for the evaluation, but, at the same time, a place with pervasive and ubiquitous surveillance where the individual's sphere of development, his/her personality and privacy rights are not respected.

Smart cities initiatives may collapse without public acceptance and the respect of fundamental rights. Therefore, adapting and complementing GDPR provisions to IoT, Big Data and smart cities is advised, since in its current version it may not be a self-sufficient tool to ensure the legality of processing (Christofi, Wauters & Valcke, 2021. p. 29).

One important recommendation would be to foresee a smart city trust board of representatives of diverse and multiple interests in stake, including the city council, private corporations, and citizens. The board would work next to the municipal executive board and would have consultive competences regarding the DPIAs or monitoring the system in order to assure that meaningful consent is complemented by a system of data-driven accountability (Cheung, 2018, p. 12). Considering the importance of PPP in the smart cities' context, such board would be the perfect place to promote accountability and responsibilities and to construct the relationship between public authorities, private enterprises and citizens to enable an effective balance between the the protection of fundamental rights and public interest-based initiatives (Christofi, 2021, p. 89).

With the involvement of citizens as a goal, conducting a DPIA must have participatory moments where the impact for privacy and democracy can be discussed and prevented. Acting in preventive terms with the participation of all the stakeholders will allow to identify risks, to prevent or minimize, improves transparency in the process of decision-making and promotes citizens' acceptance of the implemented system. The higher the potential risks may be, the more pressing is the need for the involvement of citizens in preventing perceived infringement in order to minimize potential damages. Citizens must not be objectified and seen as mere consumers or data providers: they (must) play a critical role in delineating a fair system where their personal data is essential.

As Judith Veenkamp points out, it is possible to strengthen democracy with the use of technology designed to control and monitor public space. However, the focus has to be directed to smart citizens in detriment of smart cities. If citizens are given an equal place since the drawing table of a smart city, with their knowledge about themselves and their neighborhood, they can play a constructive and undeniable role, takin the application to a more substantive democratic level (Autoritei Persoonsgegevens, 2021, 29).

The recommended board would also have competences in matters of transparency, facilitating rights-holders the access to their personal information: which data were collected, the finality of collecting and processing data, who the controllers are, data flow/transmission, etc. In a network where personal data may be used by several controllers it would facilitate the exercise of the right to access information, to correct or to erase data by data subjects. Moreover, in the event of data breach, right after the mandatory notification by DPOs, an intermediate instance like the proposed board, between the national supervisor and smart city controllers, would be able to act faster and with direct knowledge of the network, preventing damage.

CONCLUSION

It is undeniable that smart cities show the potential to improve the quality of life of individuals while finding rational, sustainable, and efficient solutions to different dimensions of the city like energy, environment, transportation, healthcare, public safety, economy, or education. Simultaneously, the technology used also has the potential to promote harmful uses that may put at risk fundamental rights, guarantees and freedoms related to privacy or to democratic public participation since it requires collecting, processing, and transmitting huge quantities of personal data of residents through a network of a myriad of service providers. The data collected may be used as means to a panoptic surveillance society where the individual, his/her private sphere or public activities become completely observable and controlled, leaving no room for privacy, to freedom of expression in public spaces and to democratic participation. Such activities directly collide with the right to informational and communicational self-determination foreseen in the CFREU and in the GDPR.

Without trust, security and guarantees of a lawful and non-discriminatory use of the collected data, the public will not peacefully accept the use of smart cities' technology and applications, which will endanger the success of its implementation.

Beyond technological solutions, participation and collaboration are the keys for the success of smart cities and its acceptance by citizens.

Making the system privacy-friendly, transparent, democratic, and participated; turning citizens co-responsible for the implementation of smart cities instead of mere data providers or consumers of services; conciliating public and private interests within the network: these are key notes to impede that smart cities become Orwellian cities. Smart cities need the collaboration of smart citizens to become fully democratic spaces and efficient and trustworthy ecosystems.

Compliance with the GDPR may be a way to achieve a smart city since, on the one hand, the Regulation imposes privacy by designs solutions and, on the other hand, requires that serious procedures take place in case of data breach.

However, the GDPR was enacted taking in consideration generic uses of personal data and not the specific case of a smart city.

The special multipolar nature of smart cities and the complexity of its network requires a regulation implementing and adapting the GDPR.

The future will show if smart cities will be created, implemented, and developed following a people-centric or a mere technological-centric vision.

Responses:

I would like to thank the reviewer for all the objective comments that were made.

I tried to incorporate the suggestions in the text.

Following the reviewer's suggestion, the title of the manuscript shall be changed to Adoption of GDPR for User Data Protection in Smart Cities.

REFERENCES

Al Nuaimi, E., Al Neyadi, H., Mohamed, N., & Al-Jaroodi, J. (2015). Applications of Big Data to smart cities. *Journal of Internet Services and Applications, 6*(25), 25. doi:10.118613174-015-0041-5

Albino, V., Berardi, U., & Dangelico, R. M. (2015). Smart Cities: Definitions, Dimensions, Performance, and Initiatives. *Journal of Urban Technology, 22*(1), 1, 3–21. doi:10.1080/10630732.2014.942092

Alnahari, M. S., & Ariaratnam, S. T. (2022). The Application of Blockchain Technology to Smart City Infrastructure. *Smart Cities, 5*(3), 979–993. doi:10.3390martcities5030049

Bu-Pasha, S. (2020). The controller's role in determining 'high risk' and data protection impact assessment (DPIA) in developing digital smart city. *Information &Communications Technology Law, 29*(3), 391-402. https://www.tandfonline.com/doi/full/10.1080/13600834.2020.1790092

BVerfGE. (1983). *1BVerfGE 65, 1 – Volkszählung Urteil des Ersten Senats vom 15. Dezember 1983 auf die mündliche Verhandlung vom 18. und 19. Oktober 1983 - 1 BvR 209, 269, 362, 420, 440, 484/83 in den Verfahren über die Verfassungsbeschwerden.* [Data Set]. http://www.servat.unibe.ch/dfr/bv065001.html

Cavoukian, A., & Popa, C. (2016). *Embedding Privacy Into What's Next: Privacy by Design for the Internet of Things*. Ryerson University. https://www.torontomu.ca/content/dam/pbdce/papers/Privacy-by-Design-for-the-Internet-of-Things.pdf

Chen, T. M. (2010). Smart Grids, Smart Cities Need Better Networks [Editor's Note]. *IEEE Network, 24*(2), 2–3. doi:10.1109/MNET.2010.5430136

Cheung, A. (2018). Moving beyond consent for citizen science in big data health and medical research. *Northwestern Journal of Technology and Intellectual Property*, 16.

Christofi, A. (2021). *Smart cities and the data protection framework in context*. Spectre project. https://lirias.kuleuven.be/retrieve/617624

Christofi, A., Wauters, E., & Valcke, P. (2021). Smart Cities, Data Protection and the Public Interest Conundrum: What Legal Basis for Smart City Processing? *European Journal of Law and Technology, 12*(1), 1–36.

Cró, I., & Roegiers, T. C. (2021). *Data protection in the smart city of Lisbon*. Flanders Investment & Trade. https://www.flandersinvestmentandtrade.com/export/sites/trade/files/market_studies/2021-Portugal-Data%20protection%20in%20the%20smart%20city%20of%20Lisbon-Website_2.pdf

EdwardsL. (2015). Privacy, Security and Data Protection in Smart Cities: a Critical EU Law Perspective. Zenodo. doi:10.5281/zenodo.34501

Galič, M. (2019). *Surveillance and privacy in smart cities and living labs: Conceptualising privacy for public space*. Optima Grafische Communicatie.

Gartner (n.d.). *Information Technology Gartner Glossary*. Gartner. https://www.gartner.com/en/information-technology/glossary/big-data

Halegoua, G. (2020a). *The Digital City: Media and the Social Production of Place*. NYU Press. doi:10.18574/nyu/9781479839216.001.0001

Halegoua, G. (2020b). *Smart Cities*. The MIT Press. doi:10.7551/mitpress/11426.001.0001

Hall, R., Bowerman, B., Braverman, J., Taylor, J., Todosow, H., & Wimmersperg, U. (2000). *The vision of a smart city. Proceedings of the 2nd International Life Extension Technology Workshop*, 1-16. Brookhaven National Laboratory.

International Telecommunication Union. (2016). *Recommendation L.1600 (06/16)*. ITU. https://www.itu.int/rec/dologin_pub.asp?lang=e&id=T-REC-L.1600-201606-I!!PDF-E&type=items

Ismagilova, E., Hughes, L., Dwivedi, Y. K., & Raman, K. R. (2019). Smart cities: Advances in research—An information systems perspective. *International Journal of Information Management, 47*, 88–100. doi:10.1016/j.ijinfomgt.2019.01.004

Ismagilova, E., Hughes, L., Rana, N. P., & Dwivedi, Y. K. (2022). Security, Privacy and Risks Within Smart Cities: Literature Review and Development of a Smart City Interaction Framework. *Information Systems Frontiers, 24*(2), 393–414. doi:10.100710796-020-10044-1 PMID:32837262

Laney, D. (2001). *3-D Data Management: Controlling Data Volume, Velocity and Variety*. MetaGroup.

Lin, J., Yu, W., Zhang, N., Yang, X., Zhang, H., & Zhao, W. (2017). A survey on internet of things: Architecture, enabling technologies, security and privacy, and applications. *IEEE Internet of Things Journal*, *4*(5), 1125–1142. doi:10.1109/JIOT.2017.2683200

Lombardi, P., Giordano, S., Farouh, H., & Yousef, W. (2012). Modelling the Smart City Performance. *Innovation (Abingdon)*, *25*(2), 137–149. doi:10.1080/13511610.2012.660325

Magare, S. S., Dudhgaonkar, A. A., & Kondekar, S. R. (2021). Security and Privacy Issues in Smart City: Threats and Their Countermeasures. In: Tamane, S.C., Dey, N., Hassanien, AE. (eds) Security and Privacy Applications for Smart City Development. Studies in Systems, Decision and Control, (vol. 308, pp. 37–58). Springer.

Manville, C. G., & Kotterink, B. (2014). *Mapping Smart Cities in the EU*. European Parliamentary Research Service. https://policycommons.net/artifacts/1339578/mapping-smart-cities-in-the-eu/1949353/

Marsal-Llacuna, M., Colomer-Llinàs, J., & Meléndez-Frigola, J. (2015). Lessons in urban monitoring taken from sustainable and livable cities to better address the Smart Cities initiative. [Elsevier.]. *Technological Forecasting and Social Change*, *90*, 611–622. doi:10.1016/j.techfore.2014.01.012

Naafs, S. (2018, March 1). 'Living laboratories': the Dutch cities amassing data on oblivious residents. *The Guardian*. https://amp.theguardian.com/cities/2018/mar/01/smart-cities-data-privacy-eindhoven-utrecht

National League of Cities. (2016). *Trends in Smart City Development*. NLC. https://www.nlc.org/wp-content/uploads/2017/01/Trends-in-Smart-City-Development.pdf

OECD. (2012). *Principles of Public Governance of Public-Private Partnerships*. Organisation for Economic Co-operation and Development – OECD.

Persoonsgegevens, A. (2021). *Smart Cities: Investigation Report on the Protection of Personal Data in the Development of Dutch Smart Cities*. Auto Rite IT. https://autoriteitpersoonsgegevens.nl/sites/default/files/atoms/files/investigation_report_development_of_dutch_smart_cities.pdf

Pina, P. (2011). Digital Copyright Enforcement: Between Piracy and Privacy. In C. Akrivopoulou & A. Psygkas (Eds.), *Personal Data Privacy and Protection in a Surveillance Era: Technologies and Practices* (pp. 241–254). IGI Global. doi:10.4018/978-1-60960-083-9.ch014

Qu, Y., Nosouhi, M. R., Cui, L., & Yu, S. (2019). *Privacy preservation in smart cities. Smart Cities Cybersecurity and Privacy*. Elsevier.

Rai, S. (2018). A Pragmatic Approach to Data Protection. *The Leap Blog*. https://blog.theleapjournal.org/2018/02/a-pragmatic-approach-to-data-protection.html

Rosadi, S.D., Suhardi, & Kristyan, S.A. (2021). Data privacy law in the application of smart city in Indonesia. *Journal of Legal. Ethical and Regulatory Issues*, *24*(S4), 1–9.

Singh, P., Dwivedi, Y. K., Kahlon, K. S., Sawhney, R. S., Alalwan, A. A., & Rana, N. P. (2019). Smart monitoring and controlling of government policies using social media and cloud computing. *Information Systems Frontiers*, 1–23. doi:10.100710796-019-09916-y

Stefanouli, M., & Economou, C. (2019). Data Protection in Smart Cities: Application of the EU GDPR. In: Nathanail, E., Karakikes, I. (eds) Data Analytics: Paving the Way to Sustainable Urban Mobility. CSUM 2018. Advances in Intelligent Systems and Computing, (vol 879). Springer, Cham. doi:10.1007/978-3-030-02305-8_90

Taylor, L., & Richter, C. (2015). *Big Data and urban governance. Geographies of urban governance, 175–191.* Springer International Publishing.

Theodorou, S., & Sklavos, N. (2019). Blockchain-Based Security and Privacy in Smart Cities. Smart Cities Cybersecurity and Privacy, 21-37. Elsevier.

Thierer, A. (2020). *Evasive Entrepreneurs and the Future of Governance: How Innovation Improves Economies and Governments.* Cato Institute.

Thomas, V., Mullagh, L., Wang, D., & Dunn, N. (2015). Where's Wally? In search of citizen perspectives on the smart city. *8th conference of the international forum on urbanism (IFoU),* (pp. 1–8). Multidisciplinary Digital Publishing Institute.

Tikkinen-Piri, C., Rohunen, A., & Markkula, J. (2018). EU general data protection regulation: Changes and implications for personal data collecting companies. *Computer Law & Security Review, 34*(I), 134–153. doi:10.1016/j.clsr.2017.05.015

Harvard Kennedy School. (2021). *Trends & 10 Calls to Action to Protect and Promote Democracy.* Belfer Center for Science and International Affairs - Harvard Kennedy School. https://www.belfercenter.org/sites/default/files/2021-08/WhoseStreets.pdf

Van Zoonen, L. (2016). Privacy concerns in smart cities. *Government Information Quarterly, 33*(3), 472–480. doi:10.1016/j.giq.2016.06.004

Viitanen, J., & Kingston, R. (2014). Smart cities and green growth: Outsourcing democratic and environmental resilience to the global technology sector. *Environment & Planning A, 46*(4), 803–819. doi:10.1068/a46242

Vojković, G. (2018). Will the GDPR slow down development of smart cities? *41st International Convention on Information and Communication Technology, Electronics and Microelectronics (MIPRO),* (pp. 1295-1297). IEEE. 10.23919/MIPRO.2018.8400234

#WhyID. (n.d.). *An open letter to the leaders of international development banks, the United Nations, international aid organisations, funding agencies, and national governments.* Access Now. https://www.accessnow.org/whyid/

Williams, R. (2021). *Whose Streets? Our Streets! 2020-21 "Smart City" Cautionary.* Belfer Center for Science and International Affairs. https://www.belfercenter.org/sites/default/files/2021-08/WhoseStreets.pdf

KEY TERMS AND DEFINITIONS

Big Data: A high-volume, high-velocity and/or high-variety collection of data that can be mined for information and used in machine learning projects, predictive modeling, and other advanced analytics applications.

Informational Self-Determination: The capacity of the individual to determine the disclosure and the use of his/her personal data, to control and to determine what others can, at every moment, know about his/her respect.

Internet of Things (IoT): The interconnection of computing devices embedded in everyday objects, enabling them to exchange data with other devices and systems over the Internet or other communications networks.

Personal Data breach: A breach of security leading to the accidental or unlawful destruction, loss, alteration, unauthorized disclosure of, or access to, personal data transmitted, stored, or otherwise processed (Article 4 of the GDPR).

Personal Data: Any information related to an identified or identifiable natural person, such as a name, an identification number, location data, an online identifier or to one or more factors specific to the physical, physiological, genetic, mental, economic, cultural, or social identity of that natural person.

Privacy by Design: A framework for preventing privacy harms by embedding the necessary privacy protective measures both at the time of the determination of the means for processing and at the time of the processing itself.

Chapter 14
Artificial Intelligence (AI)-based Intrusion Detection System for IoT-enabled Networks:
A State-of-the-Art Survey

Danish Javeed
Northeastern University, China

Tianhan Gao
Northeastern University, China

Zeeshan Jamil
The University of Agriculture, Peshawar, Pakistan

ABSTRACT

The quality of human existence is improving day by day, and the internet of things (IoT) has arisen as a new world of technology in the last two decades. It has aided the world through its applications in many sectors. However, while delivering several benefits, the extreme expansion of IoT devices makes them a potential target of attacks, which jeopardise the organisation if left unchecked. Cyber security analysts have recently been using the DL-based model to detect and investigate malware in order to keep the organization secure from cyber-attacks. This work describes how AI-based techniques are utilized to identify cyber threats in the IoT environments better while considering these devices' heterogeneous and resource-constrained nature so that no extra burden is imposed on them. This work comprehensively evaluated the current solutions, challenges, and future directions in IoT security.

DOI: 10.4018/978-1-6684-6914-9.ch014

1. INTRODUCTION

The term internet of things (IoT) is defined as an internet-based information service structure (Mendez Mena, Papapanagiotou, & Yang, 2018). It is also defined as a network of devices embedded in software programs and sensors that utilise the internet to communicate data. IoT device connections are now remotely accessed anytime, anywhere in the world with the utilisation of computing devices which includes laptops, phones, and watches, regardless of the network to which they are connected. Hardware and software are the two main components of computer networks. Both components may come with their own set of threats and drawbacks. Hardware attacks are simple to identify, as they only affect the device rather than the data. Physical, electrical, environmental, and maintenance threats are the four categories of hardware threats. Historically, only those with advanced programming abilities are engaged in the creation of hacking programmes but a person can also become a hacker by simply downloading some tools from the internet. An attack can be active or passive. In an "active attack," an attacker takes actions that could change system resources, such as: breaking or bypassing the protected system. In most cases, this leads to the disclosure of sensitive information, data changes, or complete data loss. Trojan horses, viruses, worms, malicious code injection, network data intrusions, and credential theft are examples of active attacks. This sort of attack is incredibly harmful to the system.

Active attack types are masquerading, session Replay, message modification, and denial of service (Hassija et al., 2019). A " passive attack" aims to recognize or use important information while causing no harm to system resources. The attacker employs a sniffer program to wait for sensitive information that might be utilised in another attack of this sort of assault. The assault includes traffic analysis software, package sniffer tools, and password filtering. Intrusions are a type of computer assault that includes any harmful action coordinated toward a computer framework or the services it delivers. Viruses, worms, and denial-of-service assaults are all forms of computer attacks. The acquisition of services that attempt to compromise privacy, integrity, or access to resources is known as access to intervention or Intrusion Detection. An intrusion detection system (IDS) is a hardware or software programme in which we scan a network or systems for malicious activity or policy violations (Lazarevic, Kumar, & Srivastava, 2005). IDS may be categorised in view of where detection (connection or host) and the detection mechanism are used (Deka et al., 2015; Hoque, 2012). An intruder can acquire unauthorised access to a system in a variety of ways. Some examples are:

1.1. Software Bug

Generally, the operating system or an application running as root is compromised to execute the inconsistent code of the attacker's choice. The code that the intruder will have the working framework or application run fluctuates, but some frequent activities include returning a command shell running as root or adding a client to the framework with a particular secret word and root permissions.

1.2. System Misconfiguration

This classification incorporates threats taking advantage of records without any passwords or documents with some unacceptable authorizations. Some systems come with a "guest" account that will take any password. Furthermore, a program, such as a web server, might be misconfigured to provide unauthorised users access to sensitive file system locations, such as the password file.

1.3. Social Engineering

Social engineering attacks occur when persons with access to the system are tricked into granting the attacker access. Calling corporate employees while claiming to be an official and requesting for a pin is only one example, as is mailing software purportedly from a provider who claims to have enhanced it. Once installed, this programme has a back door that allows an attacker to get access to the machine.

1.4. Password Sniffing

This approach often targets a computer on the local area network that the attacker has previously breached. This computer monitors all network activity and collects usernames and passwords when other people connect distantly.

1.5. Brute Force Strategy

When the attacker tries to guess the user's password, the attacker employs a brute force approach. An attacker can generally attempt to log in as a different user with multiple passwords (known as a dictionary attack) or copy the password file to his system and execute a password skipping application (Javeed, Gao, & Khan, 2021). It is intended to indicate that against various types of attacks, the system has to be able to protect itself. In recent years advanced mobile phones have become the prevailing method to get to the Web and internet. There are numerous distinctive, portable working frameworks utilized like iOS, Android, Windows Versatile, Blackberry, Palm operating system, etc. Android is the most mainstream versatile working framework, with 80% of the overall cell phone deals to end clients by the second quarter of 2018 (Sherasiya & Upadhyay, 2016), and more than 50 billion application downloads up until now. There will be 184 billion applications to be downloaded in 2024 (Ali et al., 2020). The ascent of the IoT has imagined a shrewd network of billions of fluctuated gadgets with high computational and handling abilities bringing about the advancement of the IoT. IoT devices may be utilised in a variety of industries, including smart homes, smartphones, transportation, health and medical care, agriculture, energy management, and manufacturing. Alexa and Google Home are just a few applications of IoT. Biometric cybersecurity scanners, durability monitors, Apple watches, medical sensors, and a range of other devices are all examples of IoT gadgets. The physical layer, the network layer, and the application layer make up the IoT architecture as shown in Figure 1.

Each layer is linked by a unique protocol of communication and threats (Ullah et al., 2021). The physical layer, often known as the perception layer, is the first. Booting, authentication, and information flow are all performed at this layer. The perception layer is made up of two parts: a perception node for data control and a perception network for data transmission to the controller (Atlam & Wills, 2020). It has senses for hearing and gathering information about the environment. The network layer (also known as the transport layer) which is the second layer is responsible for connecting to other smart devices, network devices, and servers. When communicating with objects such as sensors through protected lines, the network layer uses both wireless and wireless transmission methods. The system structure connects an IoT device to the network to which it is linked (Atlam et al., 2018; Maple, 2017). It manages data formatting and presentation and serves as a link between the performance of IoT devices and the network dissemination of the data they create. This IoT Architecture (NTP) layer employs protocols such as Network Time Protocol, Secure Shell Protocol (SSH), and Hypertext Transfer Protocol (HTTP).

Figure 1. The IoT three-layered architecture

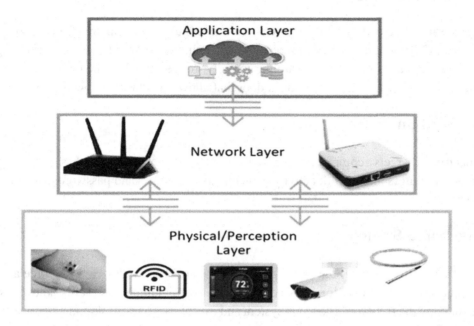

Android has a cross-sectional communication system (ICC) for interactive and diversified apps that prepares and modifies current segments and enables developers to construct rich and simple-to-understand applications (Pandita et al., 2013; Yu et al., 2017). Notwithstanding, this opens many entryways for vindictive hackers to misuse android's authorization system.

All in all, consent-based methodologies are grown principally for hazard assessment (Grace et al., 2012; Khan et al., 2020; Rastogi, Chen, & Jiang, 2013) instead of intrusion or malware identification. In general, permission-based approaches covered a little range of malware, intrusion, or threat identification. Understandably, malicious Android computer software with a high definition can accomplish more precision in their identification. (Poeplau et al., 2014) used a signature-based technique to demonstrate a computer-friendly programme by utilising certain patterns in bytecode calls and Application Program Interfaces (API). Nonetheless, bytecode-level transformation attacks can effectively leave these signature-based systems in the dust (Arp et al., 2014).

DL is a new era of ML and has received growing attention in natural language processing, image classification, and speech recognition. More recently, intervention detectors or malware experts have also been investigating DL separators to test malware for increased detection accuracy. A survey of countless real-world applications shows that deep learning makes sense, especially in demonstration interventions and can achieve 96.76% acquisition accuracy, thus far surpassing typical machine learning strategies, such as C4.5, Naive Bayes, Logistic Regression, Multi-layer Perceptron, and Support Vector Machine (SVM). Additionally, ML and DL techniques can be crucial in anticipating new assaults, which are frequently altered by earlier attempts, since they can shrewdly foresee unforeseen future attacks by cleverly learning from past ones.

2. LITERATURE REVIEW

2.1 Malware in Androids

Using a range of machine learning techniques, including reinforcement learning, genetic algorithms, and supervised learning with neural networks, decision trees, and SVM, security researchers have investigated the development of malware AEs (Anderson et al., 2017; Dang, Huang, & Chang, 2017; Grosse et al., 2016, 2017; Hu & Tan, 2017; Javeed et al., 2021). These methods, except for (Grosse et al., 2016), and (Grosse et al., 2017), are called black-box methods. The black box technique is one in which the user has no awareness of the detector's internal workings (e.g., network weights, gradients). The detector can only be questioned about the sample vectors' decisions. These strategies are all focused on identifying the best ways to escape machine learning models and succeed in doing so. Android has the greatest degree of malware, accounting for 47.15 percent of all susceptible devices (including Windows, macOS, and iOS), whereas iOS accounts for only approximately 1 percent. As reported in the global security threats statistics (2021) shown in Figure 2, these countries are most affected by malware programs.

Figure 2. Countries most targeted by mobile malware

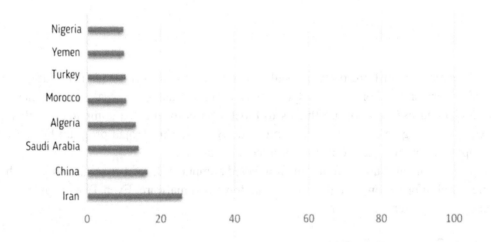

Login malware (Hu & Tan, 2017) for Android phones is divided into three categories: re-packing, downloading, and updating. Among these, re-packing legitimate apps and hiding malicious code in them is a common way to trick a user into installing malware. Customers accidentally update non-malware programs, insert malicious code fragments, and download malicious applications that hide them as malicious (e.g., Trojan horses). In trojan, an attacker may use highly effective renaming, use usable encryption, decrypt the source code, and conceal objects with a polymorphic code (Javeed et al., 2021). For example, an attacker might change the name of the malicious code into a single word in the system process so that the malicious code would appear to be normal. More importantly, the attacker can open the back door of the system that allows remote control.

Adware's unprofessional program comprises 61.43% of the malware program acquired in the first half of 2021. Riskware, which is widely employed by attackers, is in second place with 15.43 percent as shown in Figure 3. This programme is classified as malware that is maliciously abused by its attackers since it is used to distribute malware on other computers (Ullah et al., 2019).

Figure 3. Distribution of detected mobile application

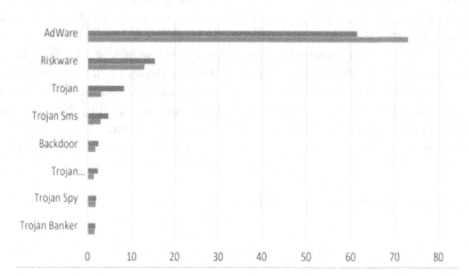

Trojan horse malware of third-party computers occupied third, fourth, and fifth place by 12.24%. Trojan can hide normal email or social media to attack computer users and steal users' money (Skoudis & Zeltser, 2004) and use ransomware threats to block access to injected computers so that injected computer users cannot gain access to their computers. Because this Trojan program blocks access to infected computers, removing it is difficult for injected computers.

Trojan spies can monitor user activity on an infected computer (Javeed et al., 2020). This threat can steal user personal information from hard disks and download malware. Even Trojan spy can send and receive sensitive files over the network.

2.2 Intrusion Detection System

Investing in intrusion detection systems (IDS) has been demonstrated to be a vital component of contemporary communication networks. The IDS feature detects unlawful or abusive network usage by users by identifying anomalous activities conducted by persons inside or outside the network. On the other hand, it ensures the overall security of the network and system by informing the administrator or central server of malicious activities and system breaches. Figure 4 depicts the IDS supply strategy. As can be seen, the firewall is the first layer of defence and the IDS is the second. The firewall provides limited defence against internal attacks and is primarily designed to protect against external threats (Razib et al., 2022). It is often built on consistent techniques that employ pre-defined rules to guard against known dangers and are hence consistent. The IDS can recognise and respond to internal and external threats in real-time, which distinguishes it from the fire protection system alone.

Figure 4. Intrusion detection system (IDS)

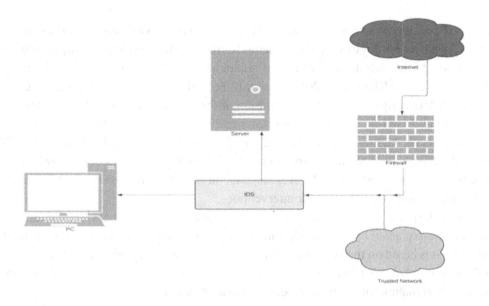

2.2.1 Network-based Intrusion Detection System (NIDS)

The network intrusion detection system (NIDS) as shown in Figure 5 is used to monitor the flow of data over the network from all linked systems. It analyses every subnet traffic and compares it to a website for that documented and known assault. After an intrusion or odd behaviour is discovered, the administrator will be alerted of a security issue. A system-based viewing framework prefers a planning perspective with an easy-to-see attack across the system. Detecting the opposite attack, the whole system, gives a complete indication of the distance at which the system is attacked (Ahmad et al., 2021).

Figure 5. Network intrusion detection system (NIDS)

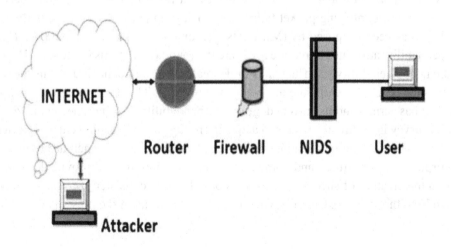

2.2.2 Intrusion Detection for Web Application

Web servers are considered an important test site to gain access to. While researchers are still testing the signature and behaviour of login acquisition methods, many companies are developing marketing tools to protect the use of the web using a variety of strategies as well. At the request level, most web IDs are special IDS (HIDS). (Khan et al., 2019) used this method's premise, which is based on the usage of well-known attack reading tactics and the definition of their signatures. Once the signatures have been created, an analogy based on a common phrase or pattern is utilised to identify assaults on question waves. It should also be highlighted that the study of (Ajjouri, Benhadou, & Medromi, 2015) falls within the scope of the intervention requirements and resulted in the creation of an IDS known as Web STAT. The attack is first represented in a high-level language in the STAT framework and then automatically integrated to be utilised as a signature for intervention.

(McHugh, 2000) present an approach that does not make use of any internal system information. These behaviours can be explained by the specification of the application or the conclusion of the study from the application. It is based on the system's ability to execute multiple system calls while also processing external data. The test result revealed that, depending on its position, a short-circuit system sequence creates a reliable signature for a typical process behaviour model.

2.2.3 Intrusion Detection in Android Platforms

Resiliency Oriented Secure (ROS) is a secure route devised by S. Shanmugavel and J Martin in 2006 that includes a route-finding phase to detect harmful places (Vigna et al., 2003). They used the number of changes in the routing database and set a limit for it to discover a malicious site. Whenever any node receives a router package with an update to its router table, it increases the value of each updated field. When the count numbers surpass the thresholds that cause the alert to sound. IDSX is a collection-based solution that uses an expanded architecture and serves as a protection mechanism; an individual node can be protected by an IDS solution (Khan, 2019). The IDSX solution works with any IDS solution that acts as the first line of defence. IDSX did not generate false scores based on imitation results. This is due to the fact that it allows for the synchronization of replies from various IDS systems deployed on nodes. Strangely based access schemes can be used as the first line of defence. IDSX operates within fixed limits.

(Javeed & Badamasi, 2020) introduced the IDS mobile network for multi-hop ad-hoc in their work. The authors describe a monitor node that may identify a node that is doing improperly. They also proposed a method for identifying packet failures and delays in packet delivery. Another type of IDS, known as HIDS, has been proposed by (Mitrokotsa, Komninos, & Douligeris, 2007). The reputation, trust, and dependability attributes of mobile notes are the foundation of this procedure. Depending on its behaviour, the node's reliability rate fluctuates or decreases. Normal behaviour earns the node-positive rewards; hazardous behaviour earns the node-negative rewards. The area's reliability is updated based on the rewards it has earned and its current degree of dependability. (Mohammed et al., 2011) presented an android app survey including research and acquisition stages. The learning category often comprises a training set of known dangerous samples and a set of Android apps, which are referred to together as the app corpus. The robustness and comparative analysis findings are provided, providing helpful information on the creation of successful solutions based on the consistent Bayesian analysis phase to detect new Android threats (Sen, Chaki, & Chaki, 2008). The limits of the present conventional system, as well as the option of screening applications for additional parallel or manual examination by security analysts, decrease the cost and effort necessary to collect fresh threat samples.

If any system can meet the needs of an active and inactive user, with stable performance and high efficiency in performing tasks, then that system is ineffective. The main problem is screen locking, which makes cell phone use difficult. The purpose of the application and to analyse the transfer of sensitive data to Android Privacy Leaked Discovery and specify the basic method (using a Digital calculator) as a series of events, which are carried out in the collection of agent performance (Yerima, Sezer, & McWilliams, 2014).

2.2.4 Host-based IDS

Host-based IDS shows an assessment of the data-monitoring context in the nearest host or operational framework. This can be achieved by a confused frame that determines the correct or indirect frame call, for example, to check frame log texts (Raza et al., 2022). The HIDS is shown in Figure 6.

Figure 6. Host-based intrusion detection system (HIDS)

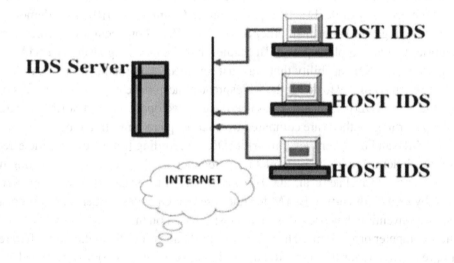

2.2.5 Protocol-Based Intrusion Detection System (PIDS)

PIDS is always linked to the front end of the server, storing agreements between devices and users, including translation. The system always controls the stream of HTTPS protocols regularly and accepts the related HTTP protocol while safeguarding the webserver.

2.2.6 Application Protocol-Based Intrusion Detection System (APIDS)

APIDS are often found on a central server. Interference is detected by tracking and recording certain application protocols (Ahmad et al., 2020).

2.2.7 Deep Learning-Based IDS

Deep learning has shown positive results in many areas of computer science. Since 2002, researchers have been including the use of ML approaches in identifying IoT infiltration and abnormalities (Jacobus & Sinsuw, 2015). These technologies is having the capability to detect the first phases of a network attack. However, the employment of DL strategies in confusing discovery has surpassed the use of ML methods over time (Ullah et al., 2022). GE Hinton is the first to introduce in-depth reading to in-depth networks (Chandola, Banerjee, & Kumar, 2009). Although in-depth reading has been demonstrated to be beneficial in NLP (Tahsien, Karimipour, & Spachos, 2020), graphical processing (Khan, Akhunzada, & Zeadally, 2022), signal analysis (Deng & Liu, 2018), and time series (Ahmad et al., 2020). There is a drawback when the training site is bigger. In-depth learning approaches, on the other hand, require a huge quantity of data to function successfully. It seems to perform improved than unexpected ML algorithms. (Elsayed, Zaghloul, & Li, 2021) designed and implemented four in-depth reading algorithms, including multilayer perceptron (MLP), CNN, and LSTM, as well as a combination of CNN and LSTM, for cyber-security on IoT networks. The goal is to compare these techniques to other machine learning approaches using the CICIDS2017 dataset (Elsayed, Maida, & Bayoumi, 2018). According to this study, the deep learning-based approach outperformed ML algorithms with 97.16 percent accuracy. The researchers have used precision, and accuracy metrics to work out the results. Although the amalgamation of LSTM and CNN has a very high accuracy of 98.44% (Roopak, Tian, & Chambers, 2019). This demonstrates that LSTM and CNN work together better than other algorithms. Based on accuracy and memory, LSTM can handle categories that are perplexing well. But rather than the repeating layers of LSTM, that effort focuses on leveraging the CNN capability that was just revealed. (Ghorbani, Lashkari, & Sharafaldin, 2018) proposed a deep study model to detect the widespread attack on the hog computer. This function is performed using the NSL-KDD dataset as well as the default developer code and SoftMax to distinguish attacks. These deep learning methods are compared to other deep learning strategies based on accuracy, false alarm level (FAR), and discovery level metrics (DR). According to the authors, the effectiveness and precision of attack detection in IoT networks might be increased by using deep learning models to identify dispersed assaults. (Tavallaee et al., 2009) proposed an advanced neural network-based technique to detect malware by using a three-way LSTM format based on Opcodes sequence. In contrast to other models tested using conventional metrics, this model test is based on the LSTM construction of new IoT data sets for a non-computer programme. The model used a database of 281 malicious software and 270 benign software, respectively, for training. (Raza, Wallgren, & Voigt, 2013) also revealed that LSTM as a classification model surpasses other methods. The methodology, however, is restricted to malware identification and necessitates numerous layers of data pre-processing.

The GRU-LSTM model based on DL is used in the SDN environment for network-based access (HaddadPajouh et al., 2018). (Irivbogbe, 2021) use advanced autoencoders to analyse the error of recreating network traffic records. Advanced autoencoder and large data viewing methods are used as well as statistical analysis methods to detect risk (Arora & Chauhan, 2017).

2.3 Intrusion Detection Techniques

The intrusion detection is categorized in the following as shown in Figure 7:

Figure 7. Types of intrusion detection techniques

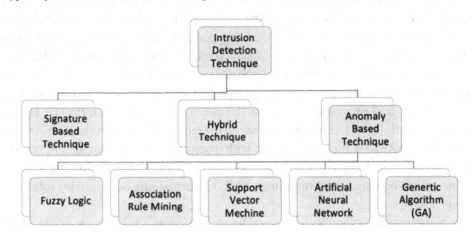

2.3.1 Signature-Based Intrusion Detection

Signature-based IDS detects threats based on certain network traffic patterns, for example, number bytes or by number 1 or 0 (Khan, Karim, & Kim, 2019). Additionally, it detects malicious computer programs based on a series of already known harmful commands. The signature-based words are derived from antivirus programs. Signatures of words given patterns obtained by IDS. While new malware attacks with an unknown pattern, such as a Zero-Day attack, are still challenging to detect, IDS-based IDS can quickly identify attacks with a known pattern (signature) both within and outside the system. As enemies become more capable, signature-based IDs are not enough to ensure safety.

2.3.2 Anomaly-Based Detection

New malware programmes are generated at an alarming rate, and intrusion detection systems (IDS) are used to detect unexpected malware threats. ML is used in anonymous IDS to develop a reliable behaviour model, and something input is connected to that model and is tagged as doubtful if it is not included in the model. Unlike the signature-based IDS, machine-based methods have similar properties, as these models can be trained in specific software and configured computer hardware.

2.3.3 Hybrid Technique

Several projects focus on building access systems for IoT systems. SVELTE, an IDS for IoT systems, was designed and deployed (Koo et al., 2013). Their primary goal is to compromise channels such as fake or manipulated information, sinkholes, and favoured transmission. (Pongle & Chavan, 2015) suggested a technique for detecting worm assaults and detecting signal intensity to identify attack locations by using node and neighbourhood information.

(Friedberg et al., 2015) created Kalis, a versatile, all-encompassing, information-driven IDS that can monitor a wide range of devices without jeopardizing existing IoT software. The method is suggested by

(Salama et al., 2012) to find out if a web page is malevolent or inappropriate. To speed up the analysis process, the static content of the web pages is first processed using the JAVA self-development system to process signatures in common terms. Next, the honeypot application is used to visit the websites, and lastly, the results are finalised as a web page. (Kaur, Singh, & Kaur, 2015) assured that the Advanced Persistent Threat (APT) employed a range of attack tactics in the initial phase to reach an unauthorised machine and slow down the network. This proposed technique is intended to improve the outcomes of any "package-level" IDS programmes. The model consists of Search Patterns (P), Hypothesis (H), Event Classes (C), and Rules (R). (Kour & Sharma, 2016) recommended that the Web Anomaly Misuse Intrusion Detection (WAMID) framework work with a sequence of harassment and confusing detection algorithms to detect SQL injection attacks. First, in the training phase, a structured data behaviour profile is created using organizational rules in an XML file containing SQL queries submitted from the application on the website.

Every time a user uses a web application, according to the (Seeber & Rodosek, 2015), all of the user's actions are automatically connected to weblog files. In essence, the system concentrated on certain log entries and recommended a blocking technique to safeguard them. The most frequent attacks are DoS and violent attacks. It also provides a secure file-sharing platform. This application has the ability to distinguish between users who are malevolent and non-malevolent users. XSS is a code injection attack that exploits the hazards of an online application by inserting HTML / Java tag script routines, according to (Ring et al., 2019). They introduced a variety of XSS attacks. This programme operates in two stages: To begin, monitor the danger of harmful site text in a web application. The PHP website has just been built, hosted on localhost (XAMPP server) and tests have been performed on modern browsers (Google Chrome49, IE11, Opera15 and Firefox 44.0.2) to use XSS risks. Reducing the attack is the next phase. (Gupta & Singh, 2017) proposed a new IDS-based approach for the detection of network attacks by processing data from the key components of networks using OpenFlow features in the SDN area. OpenFlow can elevate the event or update the flow counter during package arrival depending on the similarities or differences regarding the current or existing flow. on subnets or IP addresses.

3. SECURITY CHALLENGES IN CURRENT INTRUSION DETECTION TECHNIQUES

The existing solutions are proven to be very beneficial in IoT environments. However, these solutions still have some challenges and limitations. The limitation in the existing literature is summarized in Table 1 accordingly. (Le et al., 2012) characterise the puzzling discovery as a method of detecting patterns in data that do not match predicted behaviour. The puzzling discovery approach is utilised in a variety of applications, including network access detection, fraud detection, and health care. (Young et al., 2018) proposed a solution by employing machine learning methods to improve the security of IoT devices. Researchers tested vector support (SVM), K-nearest neighbours (KNN), retrieval, random forest, and XGBoost on IoT network login data. This research demonstrated that the random forest model produced extremely high matric schools. However, it has taken a lot of effort in the calculation process and the implementation of the model. Another study discusses the status of criminal gangs committing cybercrime (Zhao et al., 2015). They point out the meaning and possibility of cybercrime, theoretical challenges and the information encountered in dealing with these cyber criminals and conclude that profit-oriented cybercrime and cybercrime perpetrated by state actors are multifaceted. They say cy-

Table 1. Limitations in existing techniques

Ref	Algorithm	Achievements	Limitations
(Zhou et al., 2020)	K-Means Algorithm to Support Vector Machine	Implementation is simple, and training is completed quickly.	The proposed model uses other existing hybrid models for comparison and ignores feature dependencies.
(Thanthrige, Samarabandu, & Wang, 2016)	MLP Decision tree	Reduces the uncertainty of difficult judgments by assigning precise values.	In the proposed model performance of the classifier depends on the type of dataset. If the dataset is numeric, a sophisticated decision tree is generated.
(Jamadar, 2018)	Recursive Feature Elimination Method	Compatible with a plethora of models also the method does not require knowledge of what the feature represents.	It is observed that the methods used cannot handle a great deal of knowledge.
(Mazzariello, Bifulco, & Canonico, 2010)	Random Forest Zero R One R -k-star adaboost -Naïve Bayes -Multilayer perceptron	The random forest can accommodate tens of thousands of input variables without deleting any of them. -MLP yields the required decision function directly via training.	It is observed that the mentioned methods regain results with a reduced number of attributes.
(Bakshi & Dujodwala, 2010)	Correlation-based feature-selection-Bat-Algorithm (CFS-BA) Algorithm	Computationally cheap, fast running time, the ability of good generalisation.	It has been discovered that the technique indicated above cannot manage higher network traffic for the identification of uncommon assaults.
(Lo, Huang, & Ku, 2010)	lightweight Network IDSs in each physical machine, Signature-based	SIP flooding is one of the only known assaults.	Unknown threats are undetectable.
(Bharadwaja et al., 2011)	Anomaly signatures based on a network Every Virtual Switch	DDoS protection for virtual machines.	Only known attacks are detected.
(Kene & Theng, 2015)	Signature anomaly network based at each node	Defends against DoS, DDoS, and single point of failure attacks.	Unknown attacks are undetectable, and there is a large computational burden.
(Kene & Theng, 2015)	Based on VMM, distributed, and anomaly-based	Hyper-call-based attacks on VMM and the host OS can be detected.	Other sorts of attacks are undetectable.
(Lunt, 1993)	Hybrid Host-based	ANN has been used in known and unknown attacks.	Accurate detection needs additional training time, and there is a limit to the number of rules that may be used.
(Shelke, Sontakke, & Gawande, 2012)	At each node, there are two types of hosts: host-based and network-based.	ANN can identify all known attacks and may be able to detect undiscovered attacks.	The outcomes of the experiments are not disclosed.
(Viegas, Santin, & Oliveira, 2017)	At the processing server, there is a hybrid network.	All forms of threats are detected.	The integration of signatures and anomalies enhanced the complexity.
(Javeed et al., 2020)	Distributed Hybrid	Can assist a CSP in improving its service quality by detecting unknown attacks.	There is no implementation offered for the suggested idea.
(Broadhurst et al., 2014)	Deep learning NSL-KDD SGD	Accuracy has improved from 96 to 99 percent. The incidence of false alarms has dropped from 6.97 to 0.85. Recall increased from 97.50 to 99.27 percent.	It has been demonstrated that even simple deep learning algorithms can outperform efficient machine learning systems.

bercriminals operate on loose networks but are still found near each other, even if the attack affects the entire country. Because of the natural security vulnerabilities, (Sen et al., 2008) utilise the intervention detection system to obtain better insight and visibility in their 6LoWPAN. To safeguard IoT devices, they advise using cryptography/encryption as well as Intrusion Detection Systems. The issue with this strategy is the IoT devices, due to a lack of power, cannot handle extensive encryption. According to (Narmadha & Pravin, 2020), wireless nerve networks offer a wide range of possible uses, making them an attractive target for attackers. The authors argued that there is a need to employ access systems that can notify the end-user. They propose a law-based IDS to address the constraints of WSNs. Despite their success, their intrusion detection system (IDS) can only identify the following assaults: message delay, repetition, and wormhole attacks; jamming attacks; data conversion attacks; and message neglect, black hole, and selective transmission / submerge attacks.

(Praveena, Eriki, & Enjam, 2019) proposed an integrated access detection system for standard networks, with signature-based integration, Snort IDS and anonymous acquisition methods based on the Naive Bayes mining data algorithm. They chose the Naive Bayes data mining to find confusing after exploring different types of data mining techniques such as aggregation, segregation, and merging law. The authors examine their proposed mixed IDS using the Knowledge Discovery Data Mining (KDD) CUP 20 database and the Waikato Environment for Knowledge Analysis (WEKA) framework. In this paper, they explore 5 methods of data mining: neural networks, mysterious methods, Bayesian dividers, a neighbourhood near k, and cut trees. They replicate these data mining approaches and put them to the test in terms of accuracy, memory, and accuracy. (Shyry, 2014) proposed a system of access acquisition using neural transcription networks and an unconventional integration method, to increase the accuracy of acquisition and the stability of the acquisition, especially in rare attacks. The authors, on the other hand, did not focus on IoT network security, but the study employed the well-established KDD CUP 1999 database and outperformed alternative intervention acquisition methodologies such as decision trees and naive Bayes in terms of acquisition accuracy and stability.

4. CONCLUSION

The IoT is becoming an integral part of our daily life and aiding our lifestyle through various applications, i.e., smart homes, smart watches, smart cars, smartphones etc. However, such applications come with the cost of cyber threats. IoT devices continuously share data through the internet, and this extreme connectivity makes these devices vulnerable to cyber threats and malware. In the last decade, researchers are using automated techniques based on AI and DL to provide an efficient and scalable solution to identify and detect such threats. Further, cyber security analysts are continuously monitoring these networks and now adapting AI for threat detection in such environments. However, AI-based models for threat detection are still in their early stages. This chapter provided a detailed study of cyber threats and the role of AI-based threat detection systems, their limitations, and future direction.

REFERENCES

Ahmad, I., Liu, Y., Javeed, D., & Ahmad, S. (2020). A decision-making technique for solving order allocation problem using a genetic algorithm. *IOP Conference Series. Materials Science and Engineering, 853*(1), 012054. doi:10.1088/1757-899X/853/1/012054

Ahmad, I., Liu, Y., Javeed, D., Shamshad, N., Sarwr, D., & Ahmad, S. (2020). A review of artificial intelligence techniques for selection & evaluation. *IOP Conference Series. Materials Science and Engineering, 853*(1), 012055. doi:10.1088/1757-899X/853/1/012055

Ahmad, M. S., Javeed, D., Shoaib, M., Younas, N., & Zaman, A. (2021). *An Efficient Approach of Deep Learning for Android Malware Detection. United International Journal for Research & Technology.* UIJRT.

Ali, S., Javaid, N., Javeed, D., Ahmad, I., Ali, A., & Badamasi, U. M. (2020). A blockchain-based secure data storage and trading model for wireless sensor networks. *Paper presented at the International Conference on Advanced Information Networking and Applications.* IEEE. 10.1007/978-3-030-44041-1_45

Anderson, H. S., Kharkar, A., Filar, B., & Roth, P. (2017). Evading machine learning malware detection. *black Hat.*

Anto Praveena, M. D., Eriki, M. K., & Enjam, D. T. (2019). Implementation of Smart Attendance Monitoring Using Open-CV and Python. *Journal of Computational and Theoretical Nanoscience, 16*(8), 3290–3295. doi:10.1166/jctn.2019.8179

Arora, K., & Chauhan, R. (2017). Improvement in the performance of deep neural network model using learning rate. *Paper presented at the 2017 Innovations in Power and Advanced Computing Technologies (i-PACT).* ACM. 10.1109/IPACT.2017.8245184

Arp, D., Spreitzenbarth, M., Hubner, M., Gascon, H., Rieck, K., & Siemens, C. (2014). Drebin: Effective and explainable detection of android malware in your pocket. *Paper presented at the Ndss.*

Atlam, F., H., Alenezi, A., Khalid Hussein, R., & Wills, G. (2018). Validation of an Adaptive Risk-based Access Control Model for the Internet of Things. *International Journal of Computer Network and Information Security, 10*(1), 26–35. doi:10.5815/ijcnis.2018.01.04

Atlam, H. F., & Wills, G. B. (2020). IoT Security, Privacy, Safety and Ethics. In Digital Twin Technologies and Smart Cities (pp. 123-149).

Bakshi, A., & Dujodwala, Y. B. (2010). Securing Cloud from DDOS Attacks Using Intrusion Detection System in Virtual Machine. *Paper presented at the 2010 Second International Conference on Communication Software and Networks.* IEEE. 10.1109/ICCSN.2010.56

Bharadwaja, S., Sun, W., Niamat, M., & Shen, F. (2011). Collabra: A Xen Hypervisor Based Collaborative Intrusion Detection System. *Paper presented at the 2011 Eighth International Conference on Information Technology: New Generations.* IEEE. 10.1109/ITNG.2011.123

Broadhurst, R., Grabosky, P., Alazab, M., Bouhours, B., & Chon, S. (2014). An analysis of the nature of groups engaged in cyber crime. *An analysis of the nature of groups engaged in cyber crime. International Journal of Cyber Criminology, 8*(1), 1–20.

Chandola, V., Banerjee, A., & Kumar, V. (2009). Anomaly detection. *ACM Computing Surveys, 41*(3), 1–58. doi:10.1145/1541880.1541882

Dang, H., Huang, Y., & Chang, E.-C. (2017). Evading Classifiers by Morphing in the Dark. *Paper presented at the Proceedings of the 2017 ACM SIGSAC Conference on Computer and Communications Security.* ACM. 10.1145/3133956.3133978

Deka, R. K., Kalita, K. P., Bhattacharya, D. K., & Kalita, J. K. (2015). Network defense: Approaches, methods and techniques. *Journal of Network and Computer Applications, 57*, 71–84. doi:10.1016/j.jnca.2015.07.011

Deng, L., & Liu, Y. (2018). A Joint Introduction to Natural Language Processing and to Deep Learning. In Deep Learning in Natural Language Processing (pp. 1-22). doi:10.1007/978-981-10-5209-5_1

El Ajjouri, M., Benhadou, S., & Medromi, H. (2015). New collaborative intrusion detection architecture based on multi agent systems. *Paper presented at the 2015 International Conference on Wireless Networks and Mobile Communications (WINCOM).* IEEE. 10.1109/WINCOM.2015.7381338

Elsayed, N., Maida, A. S., & Bayoumi, M. (2018). Deep gated recurrent and convolutional network hybrid model for univariate time series classification. *arXiv preprint arXiv.07683.*

Elsayed, N., Zaghloul, Z. S., & Li, C. (2021). Arrhythmia Supraventricular Premature Beat Detection in Electrocardiography Signal using Deep Gated Recurrent Model. *Paper presented at the SoutheastCon 2021.* IEEE. 10.1109/SoutheastCon45413.2021.9401815

Friedberg, I., Skopik, F., Settanni, G., & Fiedler, R. (2015). Combating advanced persistent threats: From network event correlation to incident detection. *Computers & Security, 48*, 35–57. doi:10.1016/j.cose.2014.09.006

Ghorbani, A. A., Habibi Lashkari, A., & Sharafaldin, I. (2018). Toward Generating a New Intrusion Detection Dataset and Intrusion Traffic Characterization. *Paper presented at the Proceedings of the 4th International Conference on Information Systems Security and Privacy.* IEEE.

Grace, M., Zhou, Y., Zhang, Q., Zou, S., & Jiang, X. (2012). Riskranker: scalable and accurate zero-day android malware detection. *Paper presented at the Proceedings of the 10th international conference on Mobile systems, applications, and services.* IEEE. 10.1145/2307636.2307663

Grosse, K., Papernot, N., Manoharan, P., Backes, M., & McDaniel, P. (2016). Adversarial perturbations against deep neural networks for malware classification. *arXiv preprint arXiv.04435.*

Grosse, K., Papernot, N., Manoharan, P., Backes, M., & McDaniel, P. (2017). Adversarial examples for malware detection. *Paper presented at the European symposium on research in computer security.* IEEE.

Gupta, J., & Singh, J. (2017). Detecting Anomaly Based Network Intrusion Using Feature Extraction and Classification Techniques. *International Journal of Advanced Research in Computer Science, 8*(5).

HaddadPajouh, H., Dehghantanha, A., Khayami, R., & Choo, K.-K. R. (2018). A deep Recurrent Neural Network based approach for Internet of Things malware threat hunting. *Future Generation Computer Systems, 85*, 88–96. doi:10.1016/j.future.2018.03.007

Hassija, V., Chamola, V., Saxena, V., Jain, D., Goyal, P., & Sikdar, B. (2019). A Survey on IoT Security: Application Areas, Security Threats, and Solution Architectures. *IEEE Access: Practical Innovations, Open Solutions*, 7, 82721–82743. doi:10.1109/ACCESS.2019.2924045

Hu, W., & Tan, Y. (2017). Generating adversarial malware examples for black-box attacks based on GAN. *arXiv preprint arXiv.05983*.

Irivbogbe, I. J. (2021). *Securing Internet of things (IoT) using SDN-enabled Deep learning Architecture*. National College of Ireland.

Jacobus, A., & Sinsuw, A. A. (2015). Network packet data online processing for intrusion detection system. *Paper presented at the 2015 1st International Conference on Wireless and Telematics (ICWT)*. IEEE. 10.1109/ICWT.2015.7449259

Jamadar, R. A. (2018). Network Intrusion Detection System Using Machine Learning. *Indian Journal of Science and Technology*, *11*(48), 1–6. doi:10.17485/ijst/2018/v11i48/139802

Javeed, D., Badamasi, U. M., Iqbal, T., Umar, A., & Ndubuisi, C. O. (2020). Threat detection using machine/deep learning in IOT environments. *International Journal of Computer Networks & Communications Security*, *8*(8), 59–65.

Javeed, D., Gao, T., & Khan, M. T. (2021). SDN-Enabled Hybrid DL-Driven Framework for the Detection of Emerging Cyber Threats in IoT. *Electronics (Basel)*, *10*(8), 918. doi:10.3390/electronics10080918

Javeed, D., Gao, T., Khan, M. T., & Ahmad, I. (2021). A Hybrid Deep Learning-Driven SDN Enabled Mechanism for Secure Communication in Internet of Things (IoT). *Sensors (Basel)*, *21*(14), 4884. doi:10.339021144884 PMID:34300623

Javeed, D., Khan, M. T., Ahmad, I., Iqbal, T., Badamasi, U. M., Ndubuisi, C. O., & Umar, A. (2020). An efficient approach of threat hunting using memory forensics. *International Journal of Computer Networks Communications Security*, *8*(5), 37–45. doi:10.47277/IJCNCS/8(5)1

Javeed, D., & MohammedBadamasi, U. (2020). Man in the Middle Attacks: Analysis, Motivation and Prevention. *International Journal of Computer Networks and Communications Security*, *8*(7), 52–58. doi:10.47277/IJCNCS/8(7)1

Kaur, J., Singh, R., & Kaur, P. (2015). Prevention of ddos and brute force attacks on web log files using combination of genetic algorithm and feed forward back propagation neural network. *International Journal of Computers and Applications*, *120*(23).

Kene, S. G., & Theng, D. P. (2015). A review on intrusion detection techniques for cloud computing and security challenges. *Paper presented at the 2015 2nd International Conference on Electronics and Communication Systems (ICECS)*. IEEE. 10.1109/ECS.2015.7124898

Khan, M., Karim, M., & Kim, Y. (2019). A Scalable and Hybrid Intrusion Detection System Based on the Convolutional-LSTM Network. *Symmetry*, *11*(4), 583. doi:10.3390ym11040583

Khan, M. T., Akhunzada, A., & Zeadally, S. (2022). Proactive Defense for Fog-to-Things Critical Infrastructure. *IEEE Communications Magazine*, *60*(12), 44–49. doi:10.1109/MCOM.005.2100992

Khan, R., Ahmad, A., Alsayed, A. O., Binsawad, M., Islam, M. A., & Ullah, M. (2020). QuPiD Attack: Machine Learning-Based Privacy Quantification Mechanism for PIR Protocols in Health-Related Web Search. *Scientific Programming*, *2020*, 1–11. doi:10.1155/2020/8868686

Khan, R., Islam, M. A., Ullah, M., Aleem, M., & Iqbal, M. A. (2019). Privacy Exposure Measure: A Privacy-Preserving Technique for Health-Related Web Search. *Journal of Medical Imaging and Health Informatics*, *9*(6), 1196–1204. doi:10.1166/jmihi.2019.2709

Khan, T. U. (2019). Internet of Things (IOT) systems and its security challenges. *International Journal of Advanced Research in Computer Engineering*, *8*(12).

Koo, T. M., Chang, H. C., Hsu, Y. T., & Lin, H. Y. (2013). Malicious website detection based on honeypot systems. *Paper presented at the 2nd International Conference on Advances in Computer Science and Engineering (CSE 2013)*. IEEE. 10.2991/cse.2013.19

Kour, H., & Sharma, L. S. (2016). Tracing out cross site scripting vulnerabilities in modern scripts. *International Journal of Advanced Networking and Applications*, *7*(5), 2862.

Lazarevic, A., Kumar, V., & Srivastava, J. (2005). Intrusion detection: A survey. In *Managing cyber threats* (pp. 19–78). Springer. doi:10.1007/0-387-24230-9_2

Le, A., Loo, J., Lasebae, A., Aiash, M., & Luo, Y. (2012). 6LoWPAN: A study on QoS security threats and countermeasures using intrusion detection system approach. *International Journal of Communication Systems*, *25*(9), 1189–1212. doi:10.1002/dac.2356

Lo, C. C., Huang, C. C., & Ku, J. (2010). A Cooperative Intrusion Detection System Framework for Cloud Computing Networks. *Paper presented at the 2010 39th International Conference on Parallel Processing Workshops*. IEEE. 10.1109/ICPPW.2010.46

Lunt, T. F. (1993). A survey of intrusion detection techniques. *Computers Security and Communication Networks*, *12*(4), 405–418.

Maple, C. (2017). Security and privacy in the internet of things. *Journal of Cyber Policy*, *2*(2), 155–184. doi:10.1080/23738871.2017.1366536

Mazzariello, C., Bifulco, R., & Canonico, R. (2010). Integrating a network ids into an open source cloud computing environment. *Paper presented at the 2010 sixth international conference on information assurance and security*. IEEE. 10.1109/ISIAS.2010.5604069

McHugh, J. (2000). Testing intrusion detection systems: A critique of the 1998 and 1999 darpa intrusion detection system evaluations as performed by lincoln laboratory. *ACM Transactions on Information and System Security*, *3*(4), 262–294. doi:10.1145/382912.382923

Mendez Mena, D., Papapanagiotou, I., & Yang, B. (2018). Internet of things: Survey on security. *Information Security Journal: A Global Perspective*, *27*(3), 162-182. doi:10.1080/19393555.2018.1458258

Mitrokotsa, A., Komninos, N., & Douligeris, C. (2007). Intrusion detection with neural networks and watermarking techniques for MANET. *Paper presented at the IEEE International Conference on Pervasive Services*. IEEE. 10.1109/PERSER.2007.4283901

Mohammed, N., Otrok, H., Wang, L., Debbabi, M., & Bhattacharya, P. (2011). Mechanism Design-Based Secure Leader Election Model for Intrusion Detection in MANET. *IEEE Transactions on Dependable and Secure Computing*, *8*(1), 89–103. doi:10.1109/TDSC.2009.22

Narmadha, D., & Pravin, A. (2020). An intelligent computer-aided approach for target protein prediction in infectious diseases. *Soft Computing*, *24*(19), 14707–14720. doi:10.100700500-020-04815-w

Pandita, R., Xiao, X., Yang, W., Enck, W., & Xie, T. (2013). {WHYPER}: Towards automating risk assessment of mobile applications. *Paper presented at the 22nd USENIX Security Symposium (USENIX Security 13).*

Poeplau, S., Fratantonio, Y., Bianchi, A., Kruegel, C., & Vigna, G. (2014). Execute this! analyzing unsafe and malicious dynamic code loading in android applications. *Paper presented at the NDSS.*

Pongle, P., & Chavan, G. (2015). Real time intrusion and wormhole attack detection in internet of things. *International Journal of Computers and Applications*, *121*(9).

Rastogi, V., Chen, Y., & Jiang, X. (2013). Droidchameleon: evaluating android anti-malware against transformation attacks. *Paper presented at the Proceedings of the 8th ACM SIGSAC symposium on Information, computer and communications security.* ACM. 10.1145/2484313.2484355

Raza, A., Ayub, H., Khan, J. A., Ahmad, I. S., Salama, A., Daradkeh, Y. I., & Hamam, H. (2022). A Hybrid Deep Learning-Based Approach for Brain Tumor Classification. *Electronics (Basel)*, *11*(7). Advance online publication. doi:10.3390/electronics11071146

Raza, S., Wallgren, L., & Voigt, T. (2013). SVELTE: Real-time intrusion detection in the Internet of Things. *Ad Hoc Networks*, *11*(8), 2661–2674. doi:10.1016/j.adhoc.2013.04.014

Razib, M. A., Javeed, D., Khan, M. T., Alkanhel, R., & Muthanna, M. S. A. (2022). Cyber Threats Detection in Smart Environments Using SDN-Enabled DNN-LSTM Hybrid Framework. *IEEE Access : Practical Innovations, Open Solutions*, *10*, 53015–53026. doi:10.1109/ACCESS.2022.3172304

Ring, M., Wunderlich, S., Scheuring, D., Landes, D., & Hotho, A. (2019). A survey of network-based intrusion detection data sets. *Computers & Security*, *86*, 147–167. doi:10.1016/j.cose.2019.06.005

Roopak, M., Tian, G. Y., & Chambers, J. (2019). Deep learning models for cyber security in IoT networks. *Paper presented at the 2019 IEEE 9th annual computing and communication workshop and conference (CCWC).* IEEE. 10.1109/CCWC.2019.8666588

Salama, S. E., Marie, M. I., El-Fangary, L. M., & Helmy, Y. K. (2012). Web anomaly misuse intrusion detection framework for SQL injection detection. *International Journal of Advanced Computer Science and Applications*, *3*(3).

Sazzadul Hoque, M. (2012). An Implementation of Intrusion Detection System Using Genetic Algorithm. *International Journal of Network Security & Its Applications*, *4*(2), 109–120. doi:10.5121/ijnsa.2012.4208

Seeber, S., & Rodosek, G. D. (2015). Towards an Adaptive and Effective IDS Using OpenFlow. In Intelligent Mechanisms for Network Configuration and Security (pp. 134-139). doi:10.1007/978-3-319-20034-7_14

Sen, P., Chaki, N., & Chaki, R. (2008). HIDS: Honesty-Rate Based Collaborative Intrusion Detection System for Mobile Ad-Hoc Networks. *Paper presented at the 2008 7th Computer Information Systems and Industrial Management Applications.* IEEE.

Shelke, M. P. K., Sontakke, M. S., & Gawande, A. (2012). Intrusion detection system for cloud computing. *International Journal of Scientific Technology Research, 1*(4), 67–71.

Sherasiya, T., & Upadhyay, H. (2016). Intrusion detection system for internet of things. *Int. J. Adv. Res. Innov. Ideas Educ, 2*(3).

Shyry, S. P. (2014). Performance measurement in selfish overlay network by fuzzy logic deployment of overlay nodes. *Paper presented at the 2014 International Conference on Control, Instrumentation, Communication and Computational Technologies (ICCICCT).* IEEE. 10.1109/ICCICCT.2014.6993053

Skoudis, E., & Zeltser, L. (2004). *Malware: Fighting malicious code.* Prentice Hall Professional.

Tahsien, S. M., Karimipour, H., & Spachos, P. (2020). Machine learning based solutions for security of Internet of Things (IoT): A survey. *Journal of Network and Computer Applications, 161*, 102630. doi:10.1016/j.jnca.2020.102630

Tavallaee, M., Bagheri, E., Lu, W., & Ghorbani, A. A. (2009). A detailed analysis of the KDD CUP 99 data set. *Paper presented at the 2009 IEEE symposium on computational intelligence for security and defense applications.* IEEE. 10.1109/CISDA.2009.5356528

Thanthrige, U. S. K. P. M., Samarabandu, J., & Wang, X. (2016). Machine learning techniques for intrusion detection on public dataset. *Paper presented at the 2016 IEEE Canadian conference on electrical and computer engineering (CCECE).* IEEE. 10.1109/CCECE.2016.7726677

Ullah, M., Islam, M. A., Khan, R., Aleem, M., & Iqbal, M. A. (2019). ObSecure Logging (OSLo): A Framework to Protect and Evaluate the Web Search Privacy in Health Care Domain. *Journal of Medical Imaging and Health Informatics, 9*(6), 1181–1190. doi:10.1166/jmihi.2019.2708

Ullah, M., Khan, R. U., Khan, I. U., Aslam, N., Aljameel, S. S., Ul Haq, M. I., & Ullah, F. (2022). Profile Aware ObScure Logging (PaOSLo): A Web Search Privacy-Preserving Protocol to Mitigate Digital Traces. *Security and Communication Networks, 2022*, 1–13. doi:10.1155/2022/3083909

Ullah, R., Abbas, A. W., Ullah, M., Khan, R. U., Khan, I. U., Aslam, N., & Nazir, S. (2021). EEWMP: An IoT-Based Energy-Efficient Water Management Platform for Smart Irrigation. *Scientific Programming, 2021*, 1–9. doi:10.1155/2021/5536884

Viegas, E. K., Santin, A. O., & Oliveira, L. S. (2017). Toward a reliable anomaly-based intrusion detection in real-world environments. *Computer Networks, 127*, 200–216. doi:10.1016/j.comnet.2017.08.013

Vigna, G., Robertson, W., Kher, V., & Kemmerer, R. A. (2003). A stateful intrusion detection system for world-wide web servers. *Paper presented at the 19th Annual Computer Security Applications Conference, 2003. Proceedings.* IEEE. 10.1109/CSAC.2003.1254308

Yerima, S. Y., Sezer, S., & McWilliams, G. (2014). Analysis of Bayesian classification-based approaches for Android malware detection. *IET Information Security, 8*(1), 25–36. doi:10.1049/iet-ifs.2013.0095

Young, T., Hazarika, D., Poria, S., & Cambria, E. (2018). Recent Trends in Deep Learning Based Natural Language Processing [Review Article]. *IEEE Computational Intelligence Magazine*, *13*(3), 55–75. doi:10.1109/MCI.2018.2840738

Yu, Y., Kaiya, H., Yoshioka, N., Hu, Z., Washizaki, H., Xiong, Y., & Hosseinian-Far, A. (2017). Goal Modelling for Security Problem Matching and Pattern Enforcement. *International Journal of Secure Software Engineering*, *8*(3), 42–57. doi:10.4018/IJSSE.2017070103

Zhao, J.W., Hu, Y., Sun, L.M., Yu, S.C., Huang, J.L., Wang, X.J., & Guo, H. (2015). Method of choosing optimal features used to intrusion detection system in coal mine disaster warning internet of things based on immunity algorithm. *Vet. Clin. Pathol.: A Case-Based Approach*, 157.

Zhou, Y., Cheng, G., Jiang, S., & Dai, M. (2020). Building an efficient intrusion detection system based on feature selection and ensemble classifier. *Computer Networks*, *174*, 107247. doi:10.1016/j. comnet.2020.107247

Compilation of References

#WhyID. (n.d.). *An open letter to the leaders of international development banks, the United Nations, international aid organisations, funding agencies, and national governments.* Access Now. https://www.accessnow.org/whyid/

Abd El-Moghith, I. A., & Darwish, S. M. (2021). *A deep blockchain-based trusted routing scheme for wireless sensor networks.* Paper presented at the Proceedings of the International Conference on Advanced Intelligent Systems and Informatics 2020. Springer. 10.1007/978-3-030-58669-0_26

Abid, A., & Radoykov, B. (2003). *Access and preservation in the information society.* Blackwell.

Abu Al-Haija, Q., Krichen, M., & Abu Elhaija, W. (2022). Machine-learning-based darknet traffic detection system for IoT applications. *Electronics (Basel)*, *11*(4), 556. doi:10.3390/electronics11040556

Adar, E. (2007). *User 4xxxxx9: Anonymizing query logs.* Paper presented at the Proc of Query Log Analysis Workshop, International Conference on World Wide Web. IEEE.

Afflerbach, P. (2000). Verbal reports and protocol analysis. Handbook of reading research, 3, 163-179.

Agarwal, A. (2007). *Best Desktop Search Software – Reviews and Comparison.* Labnol. https://www.labnol.org/internet/tools/best-desktop-search-software-reviews-and-comparison/553/

Agarwal, R., & Tanniru, M. R. (1990). Knowledge acquisition using structured interviewing: An empirical investigation. *Journal of Management Information Systems*, *7*(1), 123–140. doi:10.1080/07421222.1990.11517884

Aggarwal, R. a. (2012). RFID security in the context of'' internet of things. *The First International Conference on Security of Internet of Things* (pp. 51-56). Association for Computing Machinery (ACM). 10.1145/2490428.2490435

Aggarwal, S., & Kumar, N. (2021). Attacks on blockchain []: Elsevier.]. *Advances in Computers*, *121*, 399–410. doi:10.1016/bs.adcom.2020.08.020

Ahmad, I., Liu, Y., Javeed, D., & Ahmad, S. (2020). *A decision-making technique for solving order allocation problem using a genetic algorithm.* Paper presented at the IOP Conference Series: Materials Science and Engineering. IOP Science. 10.1088/1757-899X/853/1/012054

Ahmad, I., Liu, Y., Javeed, D., Shamshad, N., Sarwr, D., & Ahmad, S. (2020). *A review of artificial intelligence techniques for selection & evaluation.* Paper presented at the IOP Conference Series: Materials Science and Engineering. 10.1088/1757-899X/853/1/012055

Ahmad, D., Lutfiani, N., Ahmad, A. D. A. R., Rahardja, U., & Aini, Q. (2021). Blockchain technology immutability framework design in e-government. *Jurnal Administrasi Publik*, *11*(1), 32–41.

Ahmad, M. S., Javeed, D., Shoaib, M., Younas, N., & Zaman, A. (2021). *An Efficient Approach of Deep Learning for Android Malware Detection. United International Journal for Research & Technology.* UIJRT.

Ahmad, Y., Ullah, M., Khan, R., Shafi, B., Khan, A., Zareei, M., Aldosary, A., & Mohamed, E. M. (2020). SiFSO: Fish swarm optimization-based technique for efficient community detection in complex networks. *Complexity*, *2020*, 2020. doi:10.1155/2020/6695032

Airehrour, D., Gutierrez, J., & Ray, S. K. (2017). A trust-aware RPL routing protocol to detect blackhole and selective forwarding attacks. *Journal of Telecommunications and the Digital Economy*, *5*(1), 50–69. doi:10.18080/jtde.v5n1.88

Al Nuaimi, E., Al Neyadi, H., Mohamed, N., & Al-Jaroodi, J. (2015). Applications of Big Data to smart cities. *Journal of Internet Services and Applications*, *6*(25), 25. doi:10.118613174-015-0041-5

Al Razib, M., Javeed, D., Khan, M. T., Alkanhel, R., & Muthanna, M. S. A. (2022). Cyber Threats Detection in Smart Environments Using SDN-Enabled DNN-LSTM Hybrid Framework. *IEEE Access : Practical Innovations, Open Solutions*, *10*, 53015–53026. doi:10.1109/ACCESS.2022.3172304

Alam, I., Khusro, S., & Khan, M. (2019b). *Usability barriers in smart TV user interfaces: A review and recommendations.* Paper presented at the 2019 international conference on Frontiers of Information Technology (FIT). IEEE. 10.1109/FIT47737.2019.00069

Alam, I., Khusro, S., & Naeem, M. (2017). *A review of smart TV: Past, present, and future.* Paper presented at the 2017 International Conference on Open Source Systems & Technologies (ICOSST). IEEE. 10.1109/ICOSST.2017.8279002

Alam, I., Khusro, S., Rauf, A., & Zaman, Q. (2014). Conducting surveys and data collection: From traditional to mobile and SMS-based surveys. *Pakistan Journal of Statistics and Operation Research*, 169-187.

Alam, I., Khusro, S., & Khan, M. (2019a). Factors affecting the performance of recommender systems in a smart TV environment. *Technologies*, *7*(2), 41. doi:10.3390/technologies7020041

Alam, I., Khusro, S., & Khan, M. (2021). Personalized content recommendations on smart TV: Challenges, opportunities, and future research directions. *Entertainment Computing*, *38*, 100418. doi:10.1016/j.entcom.2021.100418

Albino, V., Berardi, U., & Dangelico, R. M. (2015). Smart Cities: Definitions, Dimensions, Performance, and Initiatives. *Journal of Urban Technology*, *22*(1), 1, 3–21. doi:10.1080/10630732.2014.942092

Al-Hawawreh, M., Den Hartog, F., & Sitnikova, E. (2019). Targeted ransomware: A new cyber threat to edge system of brownfield industrial Internet of Things. *IEEE Internet of Things Journal*, *6*(4), 7137–7151. doi:10.1109/JIOT.2019.2914390

Alhawi, O. M., Baldwin, J., & Dehghantanha, A. (2018). Leveraging machine learning techniques for windows ransomware network traffic detection. In *Cyber threat intelligence* (pp. 93–106). Springer. doi:10.1007/978-3-319-73951-9_5

Ali, S., Javaid, N., Javeed, D., Ahmad, I., Ali, A., & Badamasi, U. M. (2020). *A blockchain-based secure data storage and trading model for wireless sensor networks.* Paper presented at the International Conference on Advanced Information Networking and Applications. 10.1007/978-3-030-44041-1_45

Ali, H., Batool, K., Yousaf, M., Islam Satti, M., Naseer, S., Zahid, S., Gardezi, A. A., Shafiq, M., & Choi, J.-G. (2022). Security Hardened and Privacy Preserved Android Malware Detection Using Fuzzy Hash of Reverse Engineered Source Code. *Security and Communication Networks*, *2022*, 1–11. doi:10.1155/2022/7972230

Alkhateeb, A., Catal, C., Kar, G., & Mishra, A. (2022). Hybrid blockchain platforms for the internet of things (IoT): A systematic literature review. *Sensors (Basel)*, *22*(4), 1304. doi:10.339022041304 PMID:35214212

Almutairi, K., Hosseini Dehshiri, S. J., Hosseini Dehshiri, S. S., Hoa, A. X., Arockia Dhanraj, J., Mostafaeipour, A., Issakhov, A., & Techato, K. (2022). Blockchain Technology application challenges in renewable energy supply chain management. *Environmental Science and Pollution Research International*, 1–18. doi:10.100711356-021-18311-7 PMID:34989989

Alnahari, M. S., & Ariaratnam, S. T. (2022). The Application of Blockchain Technology to Smart City Infrastructure. *Smart Cities*, 5(3), 979–993. doi:10.3390martcities5030049

Ambira, C & Kemoni, H. (2011). Records Management and risk management at Kenya Commercial Bank Limited, Nairobi. *Journal of Information Management*. 13(1), 475.

Anderson, H. S., Kharkar, A., Filar, B., & Roth, P. (2017). Evading machine learning malware detection. *black Hat*.

Anita, N., & Vijayalakshmi, M. (2019). *Blockchain security attack: A brief survey.* Paper presented at the 2019 10th International Conference on Computing, Communication and Networking Technologies (ICCCNT). Springer. 10.1109/ICCCNT45670.2019.8944615

An, K. (2012). Resource management and fault tolerance principles for supporting distributed real-time and embedded systems in the cloud. *Proceedings of the 9th Middleware Doctoral Symposium of the 13th ACM/IFIP/USENIX International Middleware Conference*, (pp. 1–6). ACM. 10.1145/2405688.2405692

Anto Praveena, M. D., Eriki, M. K., & Enjam, D. T. (2019). Implementation of Smart Attendance Monitoring Using Open-CV and Python. *Journal of Computational and Theoretical Nanoscience*, 16(8), 3290–3295. doi:10.1166/jctn.2019.8179

Arabie, P., Hubert, L., & De Soete, G. (1996). *Clustering and classification.* World Scientific. doi:10.1142/1930

Arampatzis, A., Drosatos, G., & Efraimidis, P. S. (2015). Versatile query scrambling for private web search. *Information Retrieval Journal*, 18(4), 331–358. doi:10.100710791-015-9256-0

Arampatzis, A., Efraimidis, P. S., & Drosatos, G. (2013). A query scrambler for search privacy on the internet. *Information Retrieval*, 16(6), 657–679. doi:10.100710791-012-9212-1

Aranda, G. N., Vizcaíno, A., Cechich, A., & Piattini, M. (2008). *A Methodology for Reducing Geographical Dispersion Problems during Global Requirements Elicitation.* Paper presented at the WER. IEEE.

Armando, A., Basin, D., Boichut, Y., Chevalier, Y., Compagna, L., Cuéllar, J., . . . Mantovani, J. (2005). *The AVISPA tool for the automated validation of internet security protocols and applications.* Paper presented at the International conference on computer aided verification. IEEE. 10.1007/11513988_27

Arora, A., Khanna, A., Rastogi, A., & Agarwal, A. (2017). *Cloud security ecosystem for data security and privacy.* Paper presented at the 2017 7th International conference on cloud computing, data science & engineering-confluence. IEEE. 10.1109/CONFLUENCE.2017.7943164

Arora, K., & Chauhan, R. (2017). Improvement in the performance of deep neural network model using learning rate. *Paper presented at the 2017 Innovations in Power and Advanced Computing Technologies (i-PACT).* ACM. 10.1109/IPACT.2017.8245184

Arp, D., Spreitzenbarth, M., Hubner, M., Gascon, H., Rieck, K., & Siemens, C. (2014). Drebin: Effective and explainable detection of android malware in your pocket. *Paper presented at the Ndss.*

Ashie-Nikoi, D. E. (2019). Ghana's Cultural Records in Diaspora: Perspectives from Papers held at the Schomburg Centre for Research in Black Culture, New York. African Journal Library, Archives and Informatio Science, 29(2), 143 – 155.

Aslanpour, M. S., Gill, S. S., & Toosi, A. N. (2020). Performance evaluation metrics for cloud, fog and edge computing: A review, taxonomy, benchmarks and standards for future research. *Internet of Things*, 12, 100273. doi:10.1016/j.iot.2020.100273

Atlam, H. F., & Wills, G. B. (2020). IoT Security, Privacy, Safety and Ethics. In Digital Twin Technologies and Smart Cities (pp. 123-149).

Atlam, F., H., Alenezi, A., Khalid Hussein, R., & Wills, G. (2018). Validation of an Adaptive Risk-based Access Control Model for the Internet of Things. *International Journal of Computer Network and Information Security, 10*(1), 26–35. doi:10.5815/ijcnis.2018.01.04

Aurum, A., & Wohlin, C. (2005). *Engineering and managing software requirements* (Vol. 1). Springer. doi:10.1007/3-540-28244-0

Aydoğdu, D., & Gündüz, M. (2016). Web Uygulama Güvenliği Açıklıkları ve Güvenlik Çözümleri Üzerine Bir Araştırma. *Uluslararası Bilgi Güvenliği Mühendisliği Dergisi, 2*(1), 1–7. doi:10.18640/ubgmd.56836

Aydos, M., Aldan, Ç, Coşkun, E., & Soydan, A. (2022). Security testing of web applications: A systematic mapping of the literature. *Journal of King Saud University - Computer and Information Sciences, 34*(9), 6775-6792. doi:10.1016/j.jksuci.2021.09.018

Ayres, D. L., Cummings, M. P., Baele, G., Darling, A. E., Lewis, P. O., Swofford, D. L., Huelsenbeck, J. P., Lemey, P., Rambaut, A., & Suchard, M. A. (2019). BEAGLE 3: Improved performance, scaling, and usability for a high-performance computing library for statistical phylogenetics. *Systematic Biology, 68*(6), 1052–1061. doi:10.1093ysbioyz020 PMID:31034053

Azzopardi, L., White, R. W., Thomas, P., & Craswell, N. (2020). *Data-driven evaluation metrics for heterogeneous search engine result pages.* Paper presented at the Proceedings of the 2020 Conference on Human Information Interaction and Retrieval. ACM. 10.1145/3343413.3377959

Babar, S. M. (2010). *Proposed security model and threat taxonomy for the Internet of Things (IoT).* In Recent Trends in Network Security and Applications: Third International Conference, CNSA 2010, (pp. 420-429). Springer Berlin Heidelberg.

Bakshi, A., & Dujodwala, Y. B. (2010). Securing Cloud from DDOS Attacks Using Intrusion Detection System in Virtual Machine. *Paper presented at the 2010 Second International Conference on Communication Software and Networks.* IEEE. 10.1109/ICCSN.2010.56

Baloyi, N., & Kotze, P. (2017). Are Organisations in South Africa Ready to Comply with Personal Data Protection or Privacy Legislation and Regulations? IST Africa. *Conference Proceedings.* Counsil for Scientific and Industrial Research.

Balsa, E., Troncoso, C., & Diaz, C. (2012). *OB-PWS: Obfuscation-based private web search.* Paper presented at the 2012 IEEE Symposium on Security and Privacy. IEEE. 10.1109/SP.2012.36

Balte, A. K. (2015). Security issues in Internet of things (IoT): A survey. *International Journal of Advanced Research in Computer Science and Software Engineering, 5*(4).

Barbaro, M., Zeller, T., & Hansell, S. (2006). A face is exposed for AOL searcher no. 4417749. *New York Times, 9*(2008), 8.

Bartlett, J. C., & Toms, E. G. (2005). Developing a protocol for bioinformatics analysis: An integrated information behavior and task analysis approach. *Journal of the American Society for Information Science and Technology, 56*(5), 469–482. doi:10.1002/asi.20136

Battisti, J. H., Koslovski, G. P., Pillon, M. A., Miers, C. C., & Gonzalez, N. M. (2022). *Analysis of an Ethereum Private Blockchain Network Hosted by Virtual Machines Against Internal DoS Attacks.* Paper presented at the Advanced Information Networking and Applications: Proceedings of the 36th International Conference on Advanced Information Networking and Applications (AINA-2022), Springer. 10.1007/978-3-030-99584-3_42

Baykara, M., & Daş, R. (2019). Saldırı tespit ve engelleme araçlarının incelenmesi. *Dicle Üniversitesi Mühendislik Fakültesi Mühendislik Dergisi, 10*(1), 57–75. doi:10.24012/dumf.44905

Beal, A. (2004). First Look at Ask Jeeves Desktop Search. *Web Pro News*. https://www.webpronews.com/first-look-at-ask-jeeves-desktop-search-2004-12

Beaman, C., Redbourne, M., Mummery, J. D., & Hakak, S. (2022). Fuzzing vulnerability discovery techniques: Survey, challenges and Future Directions. *Computers & Security*, *120*, 102813. doi:10.1016/j.cose.2022.102813

Begum, A., Tareq, A., Sultana, M., Sohel, M., Rahman, T., & Sarwar, A. (2020). Blockchain attacks analysis and a model to solve double spending attack. *International Journal of Machine Learning and Computing*, *10*(2), 352–357.

Berthold, O., Federrath, H., & Köpsell, S. (2001). *Web MIXes: A system for anonymous and unobservable Internet access*. Paper presented at the Designing privacy enhancing technologies. Springer. 10.1007/3-540-44702-4_7

Beyer, H. R., & Holtzblatt, K. (1995). Apprenticing with the customer. *Communications of the ACM*, *38*(5), 45–52. doi:10.1145/203356.203365

Bharadwaja, S., Sun, W., Niamat, M., & Shen, F. (2011). Collabra: A Xen Hypervisor Based Collaborative Intrusion Detection System. *Paper presented at the 2011 Eighth International Conference on Information Technology: New Generations*. IEEE. 10.1109/ITNG.2011.123

Bhat, O. S. (2017). Implementation of IoT in smart homes. *International Journal of Advanced Research in Computer and Communication Engineering*, ●●●, 149–154.

Blanchet, B. (2001). *An efficient cryptographic protocol verifier based on prolog rules*. Paper presented at the csfw. Springer. 10.1109/CSFW.2001.930138

Boel, J., Canavaggio, P., & Quintana, G. A. (2021). Archives and human Rights. A close relationship. Boel, J Canavaggio, P and Quintana, A.G (ed). Archives and Human Right. Routledge Taylor and Francis Group.

Bonetto, R., Bui, N., Lakkundi, V., Olivereau, A., Serbanati, A., & Rossi, M. (2012). Secure communication for smart IoT objects: Protocol stacks, use cases and practical examples. *2012 IEEE International Symposium on a World of Wireless, Mobile and Multimedia Networks (WoWMoM)*, (pp. 1–7). IEEE. 10.1109/WoWMoM.2012.6263790

Borky, J. M., & Bradley, T. H. (2019). Protecting Information with Cybersecurity. In *Effective Model-Based Systems Engineering*. Springer., doi:10.1007/978-3-319-95669-5_10

Boulila, N., Hoffmann, A., & Herrmann, A. (2011). *Using Storytelling to record requirements: Elements for an effective requirements elicitation approach*. Paper presented at the 2011 Fourth International Workshop on Multimedia and Enjoyable Requirements Engineering (MERE'11). IEEE. 10.1109/MERE.2011.6043945

Boutin, P. (2004). Keeper Finders. *Slate*. https://www.slate.com/articles/technology/webhead/2004/12/keeper_finders.html

Brachmann, M., Keoh, S. L., Morchon, O. G., & Kumar, S. S. (2012). End-to-end transport security in the IP-based internet of things. *2012 21st International Conference on Computer Communications and Networks (ICCCN)*, (pp. 1–5). IEEE.

Bradley, T. (2008). Desktop Search Tools. *Net Security*. http://netsecurity.about.com/od/secureyourcomputer/a/aa102904.htm

Bradley, P. (2000). Search Engines: 'Ixquick', a Multi-Search Engine With a Difference. *Ariadne*, 23.

Breiman, L. (2001). Random forests. *Machine Learning*, *45*(1), 5–32. doi:10.1023/A:1010933404324

Broadhurst, R., Grabosky, P., Alazab, M., Bouhours, B., & Chon, S. (2014). An analysis of the nature of groups engaged in cyber crime. *An analysis of the nature of groups engaged in cyber crime. International Journal of Cyber Criminology*, *8*(1), 1–20.

Bruning, S., Weissleder, S., & Malek, M. (2007). A fault taxonomy for service-oriented architecture. *10th IEEE High Assurance Systems Engineering Symposium (HASE'07)*, (pp. 367–368). IEEE. 10.1109/HASE.2007.46

BSIMM. (2008). *About the BSIMM*. BSIMM. https://www.bsimm.com/about.html

Bubenko, J. A., & Wangler, B. (1993). *Objectives driven capture of business rules and of information systems require-ments*. Paper presented at the Proceedings of IEEE Systems Man and Cybernetics Conference-SMC. IEEE. 10.1109/ICSMC.1993.384821

BugCrowd. (2023, February 28). Crowdsourced Cybersecurity Platform. https://www.bugcrowd.com/

Bu-Pasha, S. (2020). The controller's role in determining 'high risk' and data protection impact assessment (DPIA) in developing digital smart city. *Information &Communications Technology Law, 29*(3), 391-402. https://www.tandfonline.com/doi/full/10.1080/13600834.2020.1790092

Buran, A., & Filyukov, A. (2015). Mind mapping technique in language learning. *Procedia: Social and Behavioral Sci-ences, 206*, 215–218. doi:10.1016/j.sbspro.2015.10.010

Bu, S., Yu, F. R., Liu, X. P., & Tang, H. (2011). Structural results for combined continuous user authentication and intrusion detection in high security mobile ad-hoc networks. *IEEE Transactions on Wireless Communications, 10*(9), 3064–3073. doi:10.1109/TWC.2011.071411.102123

BVerfGE. (1983). *1BVerfGE 65, 1 – Volkszählung Urteil des Ersten Senats vom 15. Dezember 1983 auf die mündliche Verhandlung vom 18. und 19. Oktober 1983 - 1 BvR 209, 269, 362, 420, 440, 484/83 in den Verfahren über die Verfas-sungsbeschwerden*. [Data Set]. http://www.servat.unibe.ch/dfr/bv065001.html

Campigotto, P., Teso, S., Battiti, R., & Passerini, A. (2021). Learning Modulo Theories for constructive preference elicitation. *Artificial Intelligence, 295*, 103454. doi:10.1016/j.artint.2021.103454

Cao, J. C. (2010). Castle: Continuously anonymizing data streams. *IEEE Transactions on Dependable and Secure Computing, 8*(3), 337–352.

Cao, Z., Liu, L., & Yan, Z. (2016). An Improved Lindell-Waisbard Private Web Search Scheme. *International Journal of Network Security, 18*(3), 538–543.

Carrizo, D., Dieste, O., & Juristo, N. (2014). Systematizing requirements elicitation technique selection. *Information and Software Technology, 56*(6), 644–669. doi:10.1016/j.infsof.2014.01.009

Carrizo, D., Dieste, O., & Juristo, N. (2017). Contextual attributes impacting the effectiveness of requirements elicita-tion Techniques: Mapping theoretical and empirical research. *Information and Software Technology, 92*, 194–221. doi:10.1016/j.infsof.2017.08.003

Carter, P. A. (2018). SQL Injection. In *Securing SQL Server*. Apress. doi:10.1007/978-1-4842-4161-5_10

Casino, F., Politou, E., Alepis, E., & Patsakis, C. (2019). Immutability and decentralized storage: An analysis of emerg-ing threats. *IEEE Access : Practical Innovations, Open Solutions, 8*, 4737–4744. doi:10.1109/ACCESS.2019.2962017

Castellà-Roca, J., Viejo, A., & Herrera-Joancomartí, J. (2009). Preserving user's privacy in web search engines. *Computer Communications, 32*(13-14), 1541–1551. doi:10.1016/j.comcom.2009.05.009

Cavoukian, A., & Popa, C. (2016). *Embedding Privacy Into What's Next: Privacy by Design for the Internet of Things*. Ry-erson University. https://www.torontomu.ca/content/dam/pbdce/papers/Privacy-by-Design-for-the-Internet-of-Things.pdf

Cekerevac, Z., Dvorak, Z., Prigoda, L., & Cekerevac, P. (2017). Internet of things and the man-in-the-middle attacks–security and economic risks. *MEST Journal, 5*(2), 15–25. doi:10.12709/mest.05.05.02.03

Chandola, V., Banerjee, A., & Kumar, V. (2009). Anomaly detection. *ACM Computing Surveys*, *41*(3), 1–58. doi:10.1145/1541880.1541882

Chandrasekaran, M., Chinchani, R., & Upadhyaya, S. (2006). *Phoney: Mimicking user response to detect phishing attacks*. Paper presented at the 2006 International Symposium on a World of Wireless, Mobile and Multimedia Networks (WoWMoM'06). IEEE. 10.1109/WOWMOM.2006.87

Cha, S. C., Hsu, T.-Y., Xiang, Y., & Yeh, K.-H. (2018). Privacy enhancing technologies in the Internet of Things: Perspectives and challenges. *IEEE Internet of Things Journal*, *6*(2), 2159–2187. doi:10.1109/JIOT.2018.2878658

Chau, D. H., Myers, B., & Faulring, A. (2008). What To Do When Search Fails: Finding Information by Association. Paper presented at the *Proceedings of the SIGCHI Conference on Human Factors in Computing Systems,* Florence, Italy. 10.1145/1357054.1357208

Chaum, D. L. (1981). Untraceable electronic mail, return addresses, and digital pseudonyms. *Communications of the ACM*, *24*(2), 84–90. doi:10.1145/358549.358563

Chen, G., Bai, H., Shou, L., Chen, K., & Gao, Y. (2011). *UPS: efficient privacy protection in personalized web search*. Paper presented at the Proceedings of the 34th international ACM SIGIR conference on Research and development in Information Retrieval. ACM. 10.1145/2009916.2009999

Chen, J., Guo, H., Wu, W., & Xie, C. (2009). Search Your Memory! - An Associative Memory Based Desktop Search System. Paper presented at the *Proceedings of the 2009 ACM SIGMOD International Conference on Management of data,* Providence, Rhode Island, USA. 10.1145/1559845.1559992

Chen, J., Wu, W., Guo, H., & Wang, W. (2012). Context-Aware Search for Personal Information Management Systems. Paper presented at the *Proceedings of the 12th SIAM International Conference on Data Mining,* Anaheim, California, USA. 10.1137/1.9781611972825.61

Cheng, B. H., Eder, K. I., Gogolla, M., Grunske, L., Litoiu, M., Müller, H. A., & Rumpe, B. (2014). *Using models at runtime to address assurance for self-adaptive systems Models@ run. time*. Springer.

Cheng, C. F., & Lai, W. H. (2012). The Impact of Cloud Computing Technology on Legal Infrastructure within the Internet – Focusing on the Protection of Information Privacy, *International Workshop on Information and Electronics Engineering. Procedia Engineering*, *29*, 241–251. doi:10.1016/j.proeng.2011.12.701

Chen, J., Yan, Y., Guo, S., Ren, Y., & Qi, F. (2022). A system for trusted recovery of data based on blockchain and coding techniques. *Wireless Communications and Mobile Computing*, *2022*, 1–12. doi:10.1155/2022/8390241

Chen, T. M. (2010). Smart Grids, Smart Cities Need Better Networks [Editor's Note]. *IEEE Network*, *24*(2), 2–3. doi:10.1109/MNET.2010.5430136

Cheung, A. (2018). Moving beyond consent for citizen science in big data health and medical research. *Northwestern Journal of Technology and Intellectual Property*, 16.

Chirita, P.-A., Costache, S., Nejdl, W., & Paiu, R. (2006). *Beagle++: Semantically Enhanced Searching and Ranking on the Desktop*. Paper presented at the European Semantic Web Conference, Budva, Montenegro. http://www.springerlink.com/content/ 876p163v66873314/fulltext.pdf

Chor, B., Kushilevitz, E., Goldreich, O., & Sudan, M. (1998). Private information retrieval. [JACM]. *Journal of the Association for Computing Machinery*, *45*(6), 965–981. doi:10.1145/293347.293350

Christofi, A. (2021). *Smart cities and the data protection framework in context*. Spectre project. https://lirias.kuleuven.be/retrieve/617624

Christofi, A., Wauters, E., & Valcke, P. (2021). Smart Cities, Data Protection and the Public Interest Conundrum: What Legal Basis for Smart City Processing? *European Journal of Law and Technology*, *12*(1), 1–36.

Chze, P. L. R., & Leong, K. S. (2014). A secure multi-hop routing for IoT communication. *2014 IEEE World Forum on Internet of Things (WF-Iot)*, (pp. 428–432). IEEE.

CISA. (2023, Februrary 28). *Vulnerability Disclosure Policy Template*. CISA. https://www.cisa.gov/vulnerability-disclosure-policy-template

Citron, D. K., & Solove, D. J. (2022). Privacy harms. *BUL Rev.*, *102*, 793.

Claburn, T. (2006). Blinkx Changes Desktop Search. *Information Week*. http://www.informationweek.com/blinkx-changes-desktop-search/184417400

Cole, B. (2005). Search Engines Tackle the Desktop. *Computer*, *38*(3), 14–17. doi:10.1109/MC.2005.103

Conti, M., Dragoni, N., & Lesyk, V. (2016). A survey of man in the middle attacks. *IEEE Communications Surveys and Tutorials*, *18*(3), 2027–2051. doi:10.1109/COMST.2016.2548426

Cooper, A. (2008). A survey of query log privacy-enhancing techniques from a policy perspective. [TWEB]. *ACM Transactions on the Web*, *2*(4), 1–27. doi:10.1145/1409220.1409222

Corbridge, C., Rugg, G., Major, N., Shadbolt, N., & Burton, A. (1994). Laddering: Technique and tool use in knowledge acquisition. *Knowledge Acquisition*, *6*(3), 315–341. doi:10.1006/knac.1994.1016

Cox, D. R. (1958). The regression analysis of binary sequences. *Journal of the Royal Statistical Society. Series B. Methodological*, *20*(2), 215–232. doi:10.1111/j.2517-6161.1958.tb00292.x

Cró, I., & Roegiers, T. C. (2021). *Data protection in the smart city of Lisbon*. Flanders Investment & Trade. https://www.flandersinvestmentandtrade.com/export/sites/trade/files/market_studies/2021-Portugal-Data%20protection%20in%20the%20smart%20city%20of%20Lisbon-Website_2.pdf

Crowe, M., & Sheppard, L. (2012). Mind mapping research methods. *Quality & Quantity*, *46*(5), 1493–1504. doi:10.100711135-011-9463-8

Cumhurbaşkanlığı Dijital Dönüşüm Ofisi. (2021). Bilgi ve İletişim Güvenliği Denetim Rehberi. CDDO. https://cbddo.gov.tr/SharedFolderServer/Projeler/File/BG_Denetim_Rehberi.pdf

Dang, H., Huang, Y., & Chang, E.-C. (2017). Evading Classifiers by Morphing in the Dark. *Paper presented at the Proceedings of the 2017 ACM SIGSAC Conference on Computer and Communications Security*. ACM. 10.1145/3133956.3133978

Dan, O., & Davison, B. D. (2016). Measuring and predicting search engine users' satisfaction. [CSUR]. *ACM Computing Surveys*, *49*(1), 1–35. doi:10.1145/2893486

Dardenne, A., Van Lamsweerde, A., & Fickas, S. (1993). Goal-directed requirements acquisition. *Science of Computer Programming*, *20*(1-2), 3–50. doi:10.1016/0167-6423(93)90021-G

Daubert, J. W. (2015). A view on privacy & trust in IoT. *In 2015 IEEE International Conference on Communication Workshop (ICCW)* (pp. 2665-2670). IEEE. 10.1109/ICCW.2015.7247581

Dave, A., Sefika, M., & Campbell, R. H. (1992). Proxies, application interfaces, and distributed systems *Proceedings of the Second International Workshop on Object Orientation in Operating Systems* (pp. 212-220): IEEE. 10.1109/IWOOOS.1992.252978

Davey, B., & Cope, C. (2009). Consultants experience of requirements elicitation conversations-An empirical model.

De Hert, P., & Papakonstantinou, V. (2012). The proposed data protection Regulation replacing Directive 95/46/EC: A sound system for the protection of individuals. *Computer Law & Security Review, 28*(2), 130–142. doi:10.1016/j.clsr.2012.01.011

Deka, R. K., Kalita, K. P., Bhattacharya, D. K., & Kalita, J. K. (2015). Network defense: Approaches, methods and techniques. *Journal of Network and Computer Applications, 57*, 71–84. doi:10.1016/j.jnca.2015.07.011

Demertzis, K., Iliadis, L. S., & Anezakis, V.-D. (2018). An innovative soft computing system for smart energy grids cybersecurity. *Advances in Building Energy Research, 12*(1), 3–24. doi:10.1080/17512549.2017.1325401

Demertzis, K., Iliadis, L., & Bougoudis, I. (2020). Gryphon: A semi-supervised anomaly detection system based on one-class evolving spiking neural network. *Neural Computing & Applications, 32*(9), 4303–4314. doi:10.100700521-019-04363-x

Demertzis, K., Tsiknas, K., Takezis, D., Skianis, C., & Iliadis, L. (2021). Darknet traffic big-data analysis and network management for real-time automating of the malicious intent detection process by a weight agnostic neural networks framework. *Electronics (Basel), 10*(7), 781. doi:10.3390/electronics10070781

Deng, L., & Liu, Y. (2018). A Joint Introduction to Natural Language Processing and to Deep Learning. In Deep Learning in Natural Language Processing (pp. 1-22). doi:10.1007/978-981-10-5209-5_1

Derrick, D. C., Read, A., Nguyen, C., Callens, A., & De Vreede, G.-J. (2013). *Automated group facilitation for gathering wide audience end-user requirements.* Paper presented at the 2013 46th Hawaii international conference on system sciences. IEEE. 10.1109/HICSS.2013.109

Diaz, C., Seys, S., Claessens, J., & Preneel, B. (2002). *Towards measuring anonymity.* Paper presented at the International Workshop on Privacy Enhancing Technologies. Springer.

Dietrich, R., Opper, M., & Sompolinsky, H. (1999). Statistical mechanics of support vector networks. *Physical Review Letters, 82*(14), 2975–2978. doi:10.1103/PhysRevLett.82.2975

Dinu, D., Biryukov, A., Großschädl, J., Khovratovich, D., Le Corre, Y., & Perrin, L. (2015). FELICS-fair evaluation of lightweight cryptographic systems. *NIST Workshop on Lightweight Cryptography, 128.* ACM.

Domingo-Ferrer, J., & Bras-Amorós, M. (2008). *Peer-to-peer private information retrieval.* Paper presented at the International Conference on Privacy in Statistical Databases. Springer. 10.1007/978-3-540-87471-3_26

Domingo-Ferrer, J., Martínez, S., Sánchez, D., & Soria-Comas, J. (2018). Co-utile P2P anonymous keyword search Co-utility (pp. 51-70). Springer.

Domingo-Ferrer, J., Solanas, A., & Castellà-Roca, J. (2009). h (k)-private information retrieval from privacy-uncooperative queryable databases. *Online Information Review, 33*(4), 720–744. doi:10.1108/14684520910985693

Dominy, G. (2021). A long walk to Justice. Archives and the truth and reconciliation process in South Africa. Boel, J Canavaggio, P and Quintana, A.G (ed). Archives and human Rights. London. Routledge Taylor and Francis Group.

Donaldson, R. D., & Bell, L. (2018). Security, Archivist, Digital Collections. *Journal of Archival Organization, 15*(1-2), 1–19. doi:10.1080/15332748.2019.1609311

Dourish, P., Edwards, W. K., LaMarca, A., & Salisbury, M. (1999). Presto: An Experimental Architecture for Fluid Interactive Document Spaces. *ACM Transactions on Computer-Human Interaction, 6*(2), 133–161. doi:10.1145/319091.319099

Dowrey, E. A. (2017). *Processing to Protect Privacy and Promote Access. A study of Archival Processing in Medical Archives, Health Sciences Collections, and Hisotry of Medicine Collections. A Master's Paper for the Masters of Science in Library Science degree.* University of North Caroline.

Du, J., Wang, J., & Feng, X. (2014). *A safety requirement elicitation technique of safety-critical system based on scenario.* Paper presented at the International Conference on Intelligent Computing. IEEE. 10.1007/978-3-319-09333-8_15

Duan, J., Yang, D., Zhu, H., Zhang, S., & Zhao, J. (2014). TSRF: A trust-aware secure routing framework in wireless sensor networks. *International Journal of Distributed Sensor Networks*, *10*(1), 209436. doi:10.1155/2014/209436

Dumais, S., Cutrell, E., Cadiz, J., Jancke, G., Sarin, R., & Robbins, D. C. (2003). Stuff I've Seen: A System for Personal Information Retrieval and Re-Use. Paper presented at the *Proceedings of the 26th annual international ACM SIGIR conference on Research and development in informaion retrieval,* Toronto, Canada. 10.1145/860435.860451

Durach, C. F., Blesik, T., von Düring, M., & Bick, M. (2021). Blockchain applications in supply chain transactions. *Journal of Business Logistics*, *42*(1), 7–24. doi:10.1111/jbl.12238

Earp, J. B., Antón, A. I., Aiman-Smith, L., & Stufflebeam, W. H. (2005). Examining Internet privacy policies within the context of user privacy values. *IEEE Transactions on Engineering Management*, *52*(2), 227–237. doi:10.1109/TEM.2005.844927

EC Council. (2023, February 28). *Understanding the Five Phases of the Penetration Testing Process.* EC Council. https://www.eccouncil.org/cybersecurity-exchange/penetration-testing/penetration-testing-phases/

Edmundson, A., Holtkamp, B., Rivera, E., Finifter, M., Mettler, A., & Wagner, D. (2013). An Empirical Study on the Effectiveness of Security Code Review. In: Jürjens, J., Livshits, B., Scandariato, R. (eds) Engineering Secure Software and Systems. ESSoS 2013. Lecture Notes in Computer Science, vol 7781. Springer, Berlin, Heidelberg. doi:10.1007/978-3-642-36563-8_14

EdwardsL. (2015). Privacy, Security and Data Protection in Smart Cities: a Critical EU Law Perspective. Zenodo. doi:10.5281/zenodo.34501

EFF. (2023, Febraury 15). Coders' Rights Project. *EFF.* https://www.eff.org/issues/coders

El Ajjouri, M., Benhadou, S., & Medromi, H. (2015). New collaborative intrusion detection architecture based on multi agent systems. *Paper presented at the 2015 International Conference on Wireless Networks and Mobile Communications (WINCOM).* IEEE. 10.1109/WINCOM.2015.7381338

El-Ansari, A., Beni-Hssane, A., Saadi, M., & El Fissaoui, M. (2021). PAPIR: Privacy-aware personalized information retrieval. *Journal of Ambient Intelligence and Humanized Computing*, *12*(10), 9891–9907. doi:10.100712652-020-02736-y

ElGamal, T. (1985). A public key cryptosystem and a signature scheme based on discrete logarithms. *IEEE Transactions on Information Theory*, *31*(4), 469–472. doi:10.1109/TIT.1985.1057074

Elhakeem, Y. F. G. M., & Barry, B. I. (2013). *Developing a security model to protect websites from cross-site scripting attacks using ZEND framework application.* Paper presented at the 2013 International Conference on Computing, Electrical and Electronic Engineering (Icceee). IEEE. 10.1109/ICCEEE.2013.6634012

Elovici, Y., Glezer, C., & Shapira, B. (2005). Enhancing customer privacy while searching for products and services on the World Wide Web. *Internet Research*, *15*(4), 378–399. doi:10.1108/10662240510615164

Elsayed, N., Maida, A. S., & Bayoumi, M. (2018). Deep gated recurrent and convolutional network hybrid model for univariate time series classification. *arXiv preprint arXiv.07683.*

Elsayed, N., Zaghloul, Z. S., & Li, C. (2021). Arrhythmia Supraventricular Premature Beat Detection in Electrocardiography Signal using Deep Gated Recurrent Model. *Paper presented at the SoutheastCon 2021.* IEEE. 10.1109/SoutheastCon45413.2021.9401815

Elsey, C. (2021). *'This is my lesson': Ethnomethodological lessons in classroom order and social organization for adults with learning difficulties.* DeMontfort University.

Erik, H. (2017). *FRAM: the functional resonance analysis method: modelling complex socio-technical systems.* Crc Press. doi:10.1201/9781315255071

ERMProtect. (2023, February 28). *Penetration Testing for Compliance.* ERMProtect. https://ermprotect.com/blog/penetration-testing-for-compliance/

Erola, A., Castellà-Roca, J., Viejo, A., & Mateo-Sanz, J. M. (2011). Exploiting social networks to provide privacy in personalized web search. *Journal of Systems and Software, 84*(10), 1734–1745. doi:10.1016/j.jss.2011.05.009

Evans, N. S., Dingledine, R., & Grothoff, C. (2009). *A Practical Congestion Attack on Tor Using Long Paths.* Paper presented at the USENIX Security Symposium. IEEE.

Evans, D. &. (2012). Efficient data tagging for managing privacy in the internet of things. *In 2012 IEEE International Conference on Green Computing and Communications* (pp. 244-248). IEEE. 10.1109/GreenCom.2012.45

Ezra, P. J., Misra, S., Agrawal, A., Oluranti, J., Maskeliunas, R., & Damasevicius, R. (2022). Secured communication using virtual private network (VPN). *Cyber Security and Digital Forensics*, 309-319.

Farina, P. A. (2005). *A Comparison of Two Desktop Search Engines: Google Desktop Search (Beta) vs. Windows XP Search Companion.* Paper presented at the *21ᵗʰ Annual Computer Science Conference Hartford*, USA.

Farzaneh, B., Montazeri, M. A., & Jamali, S. (2019). *An anomaly-based IDS for detecting attacks in RPL-based internet of things.* Paper presented at the 2019 5th International Conference on Web Research (ICWR). IEEE. 10.1109/ICWR.2019.8765272

Fazio, M., Celesti, A., Puliafito, A., & Villari, M. (2014). An integrated system for advanced multi-risk management based on cloud for IoT. *Advances onto the Internet of Things: How Ontologies Make the Internet of Things Meaningful*, 253–269.

Felten, E. W., & Schneider, M. A. (2000). *Timing attacks on web privacy.* Paper presented at the Proceedings of the 7th ACM Conference on Computer and Communications Security. ACM.

Fertig, S., Freeman, E., & Gelernter, D. (1996). *Lifestreams: An Alternative to the Desktop Metaphor.* Paper presented at the *Conference Companion on Human Factors in Computing Systems,* Vancouver, British Columbia, Canada. 10.1145/257089.257404

Finn, R. L. (2013). Seven types of privacy. . *European data protection: coming of age*, 3-32.

Frantziou, E. (2014). Further Developments in the Right to be Forgotten: The European Court of Justice's Judgment in Case C-131/12, Google Spain, SL, Google Inc v Agencia Espanola de Proteccion de Datos. *Hum. Rts. L. Rev., 14*, 761.

Fränzle, M., Herde, C., Teige, T., Ratschan, S., & Schubert, T. (2006). Efficient solving of large non-linear arithmetic constraint systems with complex boolean structure. *Journal on Satisfiability. Boolean Modeling and Computation, 1*(3-4), 209–236.

Freund, Y., & Mason, L. (1999). The alternating decision tree learning algorithm. Paper presented at the *Proceedings of the Sixteenth International Conference on Machine Learning (ICML 1999),* Bled, Slovenia.

Friedberg, I., Skopik, F., Settanni, G., & Fiedler, R. (2015). Combating advanced persistent threats: From network event correlation to incident detection. *Computers & Security*, *48*, 35–57. doi:10.1016/j.cose.2014.09.006

Fromholz, J. M. (2000). The European Union data privacy directive. *Berk. Tech. LJ*, *15*, 461.

Fu, X., Lu, X., Peltsverger, B., Chen, S., Qian, K., & Tao, L. (2007). *A static analysis framework for detecting SQL injection vulnerabilities.* Paper presented at the 31st annual international computer software and applications conference (COMPSAC 2007). IEEE. 10.1109/COMPSAC.2007.43

Fuller, R. M., & Davis, C. J. (2017). *Requirements elicitation techniques as communication channels: a framework to widen the window of understanding Systems Analysis and Design.* Routledge.

Gad, A. G., Mosa, D. T., Abualigah, L., & Abohany, A. A. (2022). Emerging trends in blockchain technology and applications: A review and outlook. *Journal of King Saud University-Computer and Information Sciences*.

Galič, M. (2019). *Surveillance and privacy in smart cities and living labs: Conceptualising privacy for public space.* Optima Grafische Communicatie.

Gao, Y., Pan, Q., Liu, Y., Lin, H., Chen, Y., & Wen, Q. (2021). The notarial office in E-government: A blockchain-based solution. *IEEE Access : Practical Innovations, Open Solutions*, *9*, 44411–44425. doi:10.1109/ACCESS.2021.3066184

Garcia-Morchon, O., & Wehrle, K. (2010). Efficient and context-aware access control for pervasive medical sensor networks. *2010 8th IEEE International Conference on Pervasive Computing and Communications Workshops (PERCOM Workshops)*, (pp. 322–327). IEEE.

Garcia-Morchon, O., Gómez-Pérez, D., Gutiérrez, J., Rietman, R., Schoenmakers, B., & Tolhuizen, L. (2014). HIMMO-A lightweight collusion-resistant key predistribution scheme. *Cryptology EPrint Archive*.

Garcia-Morchon, O., Rietman, R., Sharma, S., Tolhuizen, L., & Torre-Arce, J. L. (2014). DTLS-HIMMO: Efficiently securing a post-quantum world with a fully-collusion resistant KPS. *Cryptology EPrint Archive*.

Garcia-Morchon, O., Tolhuizen, L., Gomez, D., & Gutierrez, J. (2012). Towards full collusion resistant ID-based establishment of pairwise keys. *Extended Abstracts of the Third Workshop on Mathematical Cryptology (WMC 2012) and the Third International Conference on Symbolic Computation and Cryptography (SCC 2012)*, (pp. 30–36).

Garcia-Morchon, O., Gómez-Pérez, D., Gutiérrez, J., Rietman, R., & Tolhuizen, L. (2014). The MMO problem. *Proceedings of the 39th International Symposium on Symbolic and Algebraic Computation*, (pp. 186–193). IEEE. 10.1145/2608628.2608643

Garcia-Morchon, O., Keoh, S. L., Kumar, S., Moreno-Sanchez, P., Vidal-Meca, F., & Ziegeldorf, J. H. (2013). Securing the IP-based internet of things with HIP and DTLS. *Proceedings of the Sixth ACM Conference on Security and Privacy in Wireless and Mobile Networks*, (pp. 119–124). ACM. 10.1145/2462096.2462117

Garcia-Morchon, O., Kuptsov, D., Gurtov, A., & Wehrle, K. (2013). Cooperative security in distributed networks. *Computer Communications*, *36*(12), 1284–1297. doi:10.1016/j.comcom.2013.04.007

Garcia-Morchon, O., Rietman, R., Shparlinski, I. E., & Tolhuizen, L. (2014). Interpolation and approximation of polynomials in finite fields over a short interval from noisy values. *Experimental Mathematics*, *23*(3), 241–260. doi:10.1080/10586458.2014.890918

Garg, N., Agarwal, P., & Khan, S. (2015). *Recent advancements in requirement elicitation and prioritization techniques.* Paper presented at the 2015 International Conference on Advances in Computer Engineering and Applications. IEEE. 10.1109/ICACEA.2015.7164702

Gartner (n.d.). *Information Technology Gartner Glossary*. Gartner. https://www.gartner.com/en/information-technology/glossary/big-data

Gausepohl, A., K., W Winchester, W., L Smith-Jackson, T., M Kleiner, B., & D Arthur, J. (. (2016). A conceptual model for the role of Storytelling in design: Leveraging narrative inquiry in user-centered design (UCD). *Health and Technology*, *6*(2), 125–136. doi:10.100712553-015-0123-1

Gemmell, J., Bell, G., Lueder, R., Drucker, S., & Wong, C. (2002). *MyLifeBits: Fulfilling the Memex Vision*. Paper presented at the *ACM international conference on Multimedia*, Juan-les-Pins, France. 10.1145/641007.641053

Genge, B., Haller, P., & Enăchescu, C. (2019). Anomaly detection in aging industrial internet of things. *IEEE Access : Practical Innovations, Open Solutions*, *7*, 74217–74230. doi:10.1109/ACCESS.2019.2920699

Gervais, A., Shokri, R., Singla, A., Capkun, S., & Lenders, V. (2014). *Quantifying web-search privacy*. Paper presented at the Proceedings of the 2014 ACM SIGSAC Conference on Computer and Communications Security. ACM. 10.1145/2660267.2660367

Ghorbani, A. A., Habibi Lashkari, A., & Sharafaldin, I. (2018). Toward Generating a New Intrusion Detection Dataset and Intrusion Traffic Characterization. *Paper presented at the Proceedings of the 4th International Conference on Information Systems Security and Privacy*. IEEE.

Gibbs, S. (2016). Google to extend 'right to be forgotten'to all its domains accessed in EU. *The Guardian, 11*.

Giotis, K., Argyropoulos, C., Androulidakis, G., Kalogeras, D., & Maglaris, V. (2014). Combining OpenFlow and sFlow for an effective and scalable anomaly detection and mitigation mechanism on SDN environments. *Computer Networks*, *62*, 122–136. doi:10.1016/j.bjp.2013.10.014

Girardi, R., & Leite, A. (2008). A knowledge-based tool for multi-agent domain engineering. *Knowledge-Based Systems*, *21*(7), 604–611. doi:10.1016/j.knosys.2008.03.036

Glissa, G., Rachedi, A., & Meddeb, A. (2016). *A secure routing protocol based on RPL for Internet of Things*. Paper presented at the 2016 IEEE Global Communications Conference (GLOBECOM). IEEE. 10.1109/GLOCOM.2016.7841543

Goguen, J. A., & Linde, C. (1993). *Techniques for requirements elicitation*. Paper presented at the [1993] Proceedings of the IEEE International Symposium on Requirements Engineering. IEEE.

Grace, M., Zhou, Y., Zhang, Q., Zou, S., & Jiang, X. (2012). Riskranker: scalable and accurate zero-day android malware detection. *Paper presented at the Proceedings of the 10th international conference on Mobile systems, applications, and services*. IEEE. 10.1145/2307636.2307663

Granjal, J., Monteiro, E., & Silva, J. S. (2012). On the effectiveness of end-to-end security for internet-integrated sensing applications. *2012 IEEE International Conference on Green Computing and Communications*, (pp. 87–93). IEEE. 10.1109/GreenCom.2012.23

Grant-Muller, S., & Usher, M. (2014). Intelligent Transport Systems: The propensity for environmental and economic benefits. *Technological Forecasting and Social Change*, *82*, 149–166. doi:10.1016/j.techfore.2013.06.010

Grosse, K., Papernot, N., Manoharan, P., Backes, M., & McDaniel, P. (2016). Adversarial perturbations against deep neural networks for malware classification. *arXiv preprint arXiv.04435*.

Grosse, K., Papernot, N., Manoharan, P., Backes, M., & McDaniel, P. (2017). Adversarial examples for malware detection. *Paper presented at the European symposium on research in computer security*. IEEE.

Gupta, M. K., Govil, M. C., & Singh, G. (2015). *Predicting Cross-Site Scripting (XSS) security vulnerabilities in web applications.* Paper presented at the 2015 12th International Joint Conference on Computer Science and Software Engineering (JCSSE). IEEE.

Gupta, J., & Singh, J. (2017). Detecting Anomaly Based Network Intrusion Using Feature Extraction and Classification Techniques. *International Journal of Advanced Research in Computer Science, 8*(5).

Gutwirth, S., Leenes, R., De Hert, P., & Poullet, Y. (2013). *European data protection: Coming of age* (Vol. 16). Springer. doi:10.1007/978-94-007-5170-5

HackerOne. (2023, February 28). *Bug Bounty.* Hacker Powered Security Testing. https://www.hackerone.com/

HaddadPajouh, H., Dehghantanha, A., Khayami, R., & Choo, K.-K. R. (2018). A deep Recurrent Neural Network based approach for Internet of Things malware threat hunting. *Future Generation Computer Systems, 85,* 88–96. doi:10.1016/j.future.2018.03.007

Hafid, A., Hafid, A. S., & Samih, M. (2022). A tractable probabilistic approach to analyze sybil attacks in sharding-based blockchain protocols. *IEEE Transactions on Emerging Topics in Computing.*

Haixia, Y., & Zhihong, N. (2009). *A database security testing scheme of web application.* Paper presented at the 2009 4th International Conference on Computer Science & Education. IOP Science.

Halegoua, G. (2020a). *The Digital City: Media and the Social Production of Place.* NYU Press. doi:10.18574/nyu/9781479839216.001.0001

Halegoua, G. (2020b). *Smart Cities.* The MIT Press. doi:10.7551/mitpress/11426.001.0001

Hall, R., Bowerman, B., Braverman, J., Taylor, J., Todosow, H., & Wimmersperg, U. (2000). *The vision of a smart city. Proceedings of the 2nd International Life Extension Technology Workshop,* 1-16. Brookhaven National Laboratory.

Hameed, S., Hameed, B., Hussain, S. A., & Khalid, W. (2014). Lightweight security middleware to detect malicious content in NFC tags or smart posters. *2014 IEEE 13th International Conference on Trust, Security and Privacy in Computing and Communications,* (pp. 900–905). IEEE.

Hameed, S., Jamali, U. M., & Samad, A. (2015). Integrity protection of NDEF message with flexible and enhanced NFC signature records. *2015 IEEE Trustcom/BigDataSE/ISPA, 1,* (pp. 368–375). IEEE.

Hameed, S., Jamali, U. M., & Samad, A. (2016). Protecting NFC data exchange against eavesdropping with encryption record type definition. *NOMS 2016-2016 IEEE/IFIP Network Operations and Management Symposium,* (pp. 577–583). IEEE.

Hameed, S., & Ahmed Khan, H. (2018). SDN based collaborative scheme for mitigation of DDoS attacks. *Future Internet, 10*(3), 23. doi:10.3390/fi10030023

Hameed, S., & Ali, U. (2018). HADEC: Hadoop-based live DDoS detection framework. *EURASIP Journal on Information Security, 2018*(1), 1–19. doi:10.118613635-018-0081-z

Handa, A., Negi, R., & Shukla, S. K. (Eds.). (2021). *Implementing enterprise cybersecurity with open-source software and standard architecture.* River Publishers. doi:10.1201/9781003338512

Hao, Y. (2022). *Research of the 51% attack based on blockchain.* Paper presented at the 2022 3rd International Conference on Computer Vision, Image and Deep Learning & International Conference on Computer Engineering and Applications (CVIDL & ICCEA).

Harvard Kennedy School. (2021). *Trends & 10 Calls to Action to Protect and Promote Democracy*. Belfer Center for Science and International Affairs - Harvard Kennedy School. https://www.belfercenter.org/sites/default/files/2021-08/WhoseStreets.pdf

Harzallah, M., Berio, G., & Opdahl, A. L. (2012). New perspectives in ontological analysis: Guidelines and rules for incorporating modelling languages into UEML. *Information Systems*, *37*(5), 484–507. doi:10.1016/j.is.2011.11.001

Hashemi, S. Y., & Shams Aliee, F. (2019). Dynamic and comprehensive trust model for IoT and its integration into RPL. *The Journal of Supercomputing*, *75*(7), 3555–3584. doi:10.100711227-018-2700-3

Hassan, A. N., Nihad, M., & Nife, N. (2019). The Internet of Things Privacy. *Journal of Computational and Theoretical Nanoscience*, *16*(3), 1007–1018. doi:10.1166/jctn.2019.7990

Hassija, V., Chamola, V., Saxena, V., Jain, D., Goyal, P., & Sikdar, B. (2019). A Survey on IoT Security: Application Areas, Security Threats, and Solution Architectures. *IEEE Access : Practical Innovations, Open Solutions*, *7*, 82721–82743. doi:10.1109/ACCESS.2019.2924045

Hayes, R. G., & Truong, N. K. (2009). *Selective Archving: A model for privacy Sensitive Capture and Access Technologies* (A. Seniro, Ed.). Protecting Privacy in Video Surveillenance.

Heck, M. (2010). dtSearch Desktop, Version 7.64 Powerful, Enterprise-Level Search Tool. *Network World*. https://www.networkworld.com/reviews/2010/072610-desktop-search-tools-test-dtsearch.html

Heer, T., Garcia-Morchon, O., Hummen, R., Keoh, S. L., Kumar, S. S., & Wehrle, K. (2011). Security Challenges in the IP-based Internet of Things. *Wireless Personal Communications*, *61*(3), 527–542. doi:10.100711277-011-0385-5

Henze, M. H. (2014). User-driven privacy enforcement for cloud-based services in the internet of things. *International Conference on Future Internet of Things and Cloud.*, (pp. 191–196). IEEE. 10.1109/FiCloud.2014.38

Herlocker, J. L., Konstan, J. A., Terveen, L. G., & Riedl, J. T. (2004). Evaluating collaborative filtering recommender systems. [TOIS]. *ACM Transactions on Information Systems*, *22*(1), 5–53. doi:10.1145/963770.963772

Hernandez-Ramos, J. L., Pawlowski, M. P., Jara, A. J., Skarmeta, A. F., & Ladid, L. (2015). Toward a lightweight authentication and authorization framework for smart objects. *IEEE Journal on Selected Areas in Communications*, *33*(4), 690–702. doi:10.1109/JSAC.2015.2393436

Hernán, M. A., & Robins, J. M. (2017). Per-protocol analyses of pragmatic trials. *The New England Journal of Medicine*, *377*(14), 1391–1398. doi:10.1056/NEJMsm1605385 PMID:28976864

Hicks, M. (2004). Desktop Search: The Ultimate Security Hole? *eWeek*. https://www.eweek.com/c/a/Enterprise-Applications/Desktop-Search-The-Ultimate-Security-Hole/

Himeur, Y., Sayed, A., Alsalemi, A., Bensaali, F., Amira, A., Varlamis, I., Eirinaki, M., Sardianos, C., & Dimitrakopoulos, G. (2022). Blockchain-based recommender systems: Applications, challenges and future opportunities. *Computer Science Review*, *43*, 100439. doi:10.1016/j.cosrev.2021.100439

Hu, W., & Tan, Y. (2017). Generating adversarial malware examples for black-box attacks based on GAN. *arXiv preprint arXiv.05983*.

Huang, X., Craig, P., Lin, H., & Yan, Z. (2016). SecIoT: A security framework for the Internet of Things. *Security and Communication Networks*, *9*(16), 3083–3094. doi:10.1002ec.1259

Hughes, L. E. (2022). SSL and TLS. In: Pro Active Directory Certificate Services. Berkeley, CA: Apress. doi:10.1007/978-1-4842-7486-6_11

Hughes, A., Park, A., Kietzmann, J., & Archer-Brown, C. (2019). Beyond Bitcoin: What blockchain and distributed ledger technologies mean for firms. *Business Horizons*, *62*(3), 273–281. doi:10.1016/j.bushor.2019.01.002

Hu, Y., Wu, Y., & Wang, H. (2014). Detection of insider selective forwarding attack based on monitor node and trust mechanism in WSN. *Wireless Sensor Network*, *6*(11), 237–248. doi:10.4236/wsn.2014.611023

IBM. (2023, February 28). *Cost of a data breach 2022 - A million-dollar race to detect and respond*. IBM. https://www.ibm.com/reports/data-breach

Indeed. (2023, February 28). *Penetration tester salary in United States*. Indeed. https://www.indeed.com/career/penetration-tester/salaries

Index, A. (1995). Communications of the ACM 1995 author index. *Communications of the ACM*, *38*(12), 91–99. doi:10.1145/219663.219693

International Telecommunication Union. (2016). *Recommendation L.1600 (06/16)*. ITU. https://www.itu.int/rec/dologin_pub.asp?lang=e&id=T-REC-L.1600-201606-I!!PDF-E&type=items

INTIGRITI. (2023, February 28). Bug Bounty & Agile Pentesting Platform. *Intigriti*. https://www.intigriti.com/

Iqbal, M., & Matulevičius, R. (2021). Exploring sybil and double-spending risks in blockchain systems. *IEEE Access : Practical Innovations, Open Solutions*, *9*, 76153–76177. doi:10.1109/ACCESS.2021.3081998

Irivbogbe, I. J. (2021). *Securing Internet of things (IoT) using SDN-enabled Deep learning Architecture*. National College of Ireland.

Ismagilova, E., Hughes, L., Dwivedi, Y. K., & Raman, K. R. (2019). Smart cities: Advances in research—An information systems perspective. *International Journal of Information Management*, *47*, 88–100. doi:10.1016/j.ijinfomgt.2019.01.004

Ismagilova, E., Hughes, L., Rana, N. P., & Dwivedi, Y. K. (2022). Security, Privacy and Risks Within Smart Cities: Literature Review and Development of a Smart City Interaction Framework. *Information Systems Frontiers*, *24*(2), 393–414. doi:10.100710796-020-10044-1 PMID:32837262

Jacobus, A., & Sinsuw, A. A. (2015). Network packet data online processing for intrusion detection system. *Paper presented at the 2015 1st International Conference on Wireless and Telematics (ICWT)*. IEEE. 10.1109/ICWT.2015.7449259

Jain, A., & Richariya, V. (2011). Implementing a web browser with phishing detection techniques. *arXiv preprint arXiv*.

Jakkaew, P., & Hongthong, T. (2017). *Requirements elicitation to develop mobile application for elderly*. Paper presented at the 2017 International Conference on Digital Arts, Media and Technology (ICDAMT). IEEE. 10.1109/ICDAMT.2017.7905013

Jamadar, R. A. (2018). Network Intrusion Detection System Using Machine Learning. *Indian Journal of Science and Technology*, *11*(48), 1–6. doi:10.17485/ijst/2018/v11i48/139802

Jarke, M. (1999). *CREWS: towards systematic usage of scenarios, use cases and scenes Electronic Business Engineering*. Springer.

Javeed, D., Badamasi, U. M., Iqbal, T., Umar, A., & Ndubuisi, C. O. (2020). Threat detection using machine/deep learning in IOT environments. *International Journal of Computer Networks & Communications Security*, *8*(8), 59–65.

Javeed, D., Badamasi, U. M., Iqbal, T., Umar, A., & Ndubuisi, C. O. (2020). Threat detection using machine/deep learning in IOT environments. *International Journal of Computer Networks and Communications Security*, *8*(8), 59–65.

Javeed, D., Gao, T., & Khan, M. T. (2021). SDN-enabled hybrid DL-driven framework for the detection of emerging cyber threats in IoT. *Electronics (Basel)*, *10*(8), 918. doi:10.3390/electronics10080918

Javeed, D., Gao, T., Khan, M. T., & Ahmad, I. (2021). A hybrid deep learning-driven SDN enabled mechanism for secure communication in Internet of Things (IoT). *Sensors (Basel)*, *21*(14), 4884. doi:10.339021144884 PMID:34300623

Javeed, D., Gao, T., Khan, M. T., & Shoukat, D. (2022). A hybrid intelligent framework to combat sophisticated threats in secure industries. *Sensors (Basel)*, *22*(4), 1582. doi:10.339022041582 PMID:35214481

Javeed, D., Khan, M. T., Ahmad, I., Iqbal, T., Badamasi, U. M., Ndubuisi, C. O., & Umar, A. (2020). An efficient approach of threat hunting using memory forensics. *International Journal of Computer Networks and Communications Security*, *8*(5), 37–45. doi:10.47277/IJCNCS/8(5)1

Javeed, D., & MohammedBadamasi, U. (2020). Man in the middle attacks: Analysis motivation and prevention. *International Journal of Computer Networks and Communications Security*, *8*(7), 52–58. doi:10.47277/IJCNCS/8(7)1

Jean-Francois. (2012). Cloud Computing: Weapon of Choice for DDoS? Khan, T. U. (2019). Internet of Things (IOT) systems and its security challenges. *International Journal of Advanced Research in Computer Engineering and Technology*, *8*(12).

Jeremy. (2006). The Fish That Was Ahead of Its Time. *Loose Wire Blog*. http://www.loosewireblog.com/2006/05/the_fish_that_w_1.html

Johnson, G. D., Regan, M. P., & Wayland, K. (2011). *Campaign Disclosure, Privacy, and Transparency*, 19. Wm. & Mary Bill Rts. J. https://scholarship.law.wm.edu/wmborj/19, 4/7.

Jones, W. P., & Dumais, S. T. (1986). The Spatial Metaphor for User Interfaces: Experimental Tests of Reference by Location versus Name. *ACM Transactions on Information Systems*, *4*(1), 42–63. doi:10.1145/5401.5405

Joo, M., Kim, S. H., Ghose, A., & Wilbur, K. C. (2023). Designing Distributed Ledger technologies, like Blockchain, for advertising markets. *International Journal of Research in Marketing*, *40*(1), 12–21. doi:10.1016/j.ijresmar.2022.08.004

Juárez, M., & Torra, V. (2013). *A self-adaptive classification for the dissociating privacy agent*. Paper presented at the 2013 Eleventh Annual Conference on Privacy, Security and Trust. IEEE.10.1109/PST.2013.6596035

Juarez, M., & Torra, V. (2015). *Dispa: An intelligent agent for private web search Advanced research in data privacy*. Springer.

Kaaniche, N., Masmoudi, S., Znina, S., Laurent, M., & Demir, L. (2020). *Privacy preserving cooperative computation for personalized web search applications*. Paper presented at the Proceedings of the 35th Annual ACM Symposium on Applied Computing. ACM. 10.1145/3341105.3373947

Kamal, R., Hong, C. S., & Choi, M. J. (2015). Autonomic Resilient Internet-of-Things (IoT) Management. *ArXiv Preprint ArXiv:1508.03975*.

Kanuparthi, A., Karri, R., & Addepalli, S. (2013). Hardware and embedded security in the context of internet of things. *Proceedings of the 2013 ACM Workshop on Security, Privacy & Dependability for Cyber Vehicles*, (pp. 61–64). ACM. 10.1145/2517968.2517976

Karlsson, J. (1997). Managing software requirements using quality function deployment. *Software Quality Journal*, *6*(4), 311–326. doi:10.1023/A:1018580522999

Karn, J. S., Syed-Abdullah, S., Cowling, A. J., & Holcombe, M. (2007). A study into the effects of personality type and methodology on cohesion in software engineering teams. *Behaviour & Information Technology*, *26*(2), 99–111. doi:10.1080/01449290500102110

Karpinski, M., Kovalchuk, L., Kochan, R., Oliynykov, R., Rodinko, M., & Wieclaw, L. (2021). Blockchain Technologies: Probability of Double-Spend Attack on a Proof-of-Stake Consensus. *Sensors (Basel)*, *21*(19), 6408. doi:10.339021196408 PMID:34640729

Kasauli, R., Knauss, E., Horkoff, J., Liebel, G., & de Oliveira Neto, F. G. (2021). Requirements engineering challenges and practices in large-scale agile system development. *Journal of Systems and Software*, *172*, 110851. doi:10.1016/j.jss.2020.110851

Kasinathan, P., Pastrone, C., Spirito, M. A., & Vinkovits, M. (2013). Denial-of-Service detection in 6LoWPAN based Internet of Things. *2013 IEEE 9th International Conference on Wireless and Mobile Computing, Networking and Communications (WiMob)*, (pp. 600–607). IEEE.

Kasinathan, P., Costamagna, G., Khaleel, H., Pastrone, C., & Spirito, M. A. (2013). An IDS framework for internet of things empowered by 6LoWPAN. *Proceedings of the 2013 ACM SIGSAC Conference on Computer & Communications Security*, (pp. 1337–1340). ACM. 10.1145/2508859.2512494

Kassen, M. (2022). Blockchain and e-government innovation: Automation of public information processes. *Information Systems*, *103*, 101862. doi:10.1016/j.is.2021.101862

Kaur, J., Singh, R., & Kaur, P. (2015). Prevention of ddos and brute force attacks on web log files using combination of genetic algorithm and feed forward back propagation neural network. *International Journal of Computers and Applications*, *120*(23).

Kausar, S., Tariq, S., Riaz, S., & Khanum, A. (2010). *Guidelines for the selection of elicitation techniques.* Paper presented at the 2010 6th International Conference on Emerging Technologies (ICET). IEEE. 10.1109/ICET.2010.5638476

Kendall, A. (2013). Best Free Desktop Search Utility. *Tech Support Alert.* https://www.techsupportalert.com/best-free-desktop-search-utility.htm

Kene, S. G., & Theng, D. P. (2015). A review on intrusion detection techniques for cloud computing and security challenges. *Paper presented at the 2015 2nd International Conference on Electronics and Communication Systems (ICECS)*. IEEE. 10.1109/ECS.2015.7124898

Khan, R., & Ali, S. (2013). Conceptual Framework of Redundant Link Aggregation. *arXiv preprint arXiv:1305.2708*.

Khan, R., & Islam, M. A. (2017). *Quantification of PIR protocols privacy.* Paper presented at the 2017 International Conference on Communication, Computing and Digital Systems (C-CODE). IEEE. 10.1109/C-CODE.2017.7918908

Khan, R., Ullah, M., & Islam, M. A. (2016). *Revealing pir protocols protected users.* Paper presented at the 2016 Sixth International Conference on Innovative Computing Technology (INTECH). IEEE. 10.1109/INTECH.2016.7845059

Khan, B., Naseem, R., Alam, I., Khan, I., Alasmary, H., & Rahman, T. (2022). Analysis of Tree-Family Machine Learning Techniques for Risk Prediction in Software Requirements. *IEEE Access : Practical Innovations, Open Solutions*, *10*, 98220–98231. doi:10.1109/ACCESS.2022.3206382

Khan, M. T., Akhunzada, A., & Zeadally, S. (2022). Proactive Defense for Fog-to-Things Critical Infrastructure. *IEEE Communications Magazine*, *60*(12), 44–49. doi:10.1109/MCOM.005.2100992

Khan, M., Karim, M., & Kim, Y. (2019). A Scalable and Hybrid Intrusion Detection System Based on the Convolutional-LSTM Network. *Symmetry*, *11*(4), 583. doi:10.3390ym11040583

Khan, R. (2020). *On the effectiveness of private information retrieval protocols*. Department of Computer Science, Capital University of Science and Technology.

Khan, R., Ahmad, A., Alsayed, A. O., Binsawad, M., Islam, M. A., & Ullah, M. (2020). QuPiD attack: Machine learning-based privacy quantification mechanism for PIR protocols in health-related web search. *Scientific Programming, 2020*, 2020. doi:10.1155/2020/8868686

Khan, R., Islam, M. A., Ullah, M., Aleem, M., & Iqbal, M. A. (2019). Privacy exposure measure: A privacy-preserving technique for health-related web search. *Journal of Medical Imaging and Health Informatics, 9*(6), 1196–1204. doi:10.1166/jmihi.2019.2709

Khan, R., Ullah, M., Khan, A., Uddin, M. I., & Al-Yahya, M. (2021). NN-QuPiD attack: Neural network-based privacy quantification model for private information retrieval protocols. *Complexity, 2021*, 2021. doi:10.1155/2021/6651662

Khan, T. U. (2019). Internet of Things (IOT) systems and its security challenges. [IJARCET]. *International Journal of Advanced Research in Computer Engineering and Technology*, 12.

Khan, T. U. (2019). Internet of Things (IOT) systems and its security challenges. *International Journal of Advanced Research in Computer Engineering, 8*(12).

Khoo, B. (2011). RFID as an Enabler of the Internet of Things: Issues of Security and Privacy. *2011 International Conference on Internet of Things and 4th International Conference on Cyber, Physical and Social Computing*, (pp. 709–712). IEEE. 10.1109/iThings/CPSCom.2011.83

Khusro, S., Naeem, M., Khan, M. A., & Alam, I. (2018). There is no such thing as free Lunch: An Investigation of Bloatware Effects on Smart Devices. *Journal of Information Communication Technologies and Robotic Applications*, 20-30.

Khusro, S., Ali, S., Alam, I., & Ullah, I. (2017). Performance Evaluation of Desktop Search Engines Using Information Retrieval Systems Approaches. *Journal of Internet Technology, 18*(5), 1043–1055.

Kilov, H., & Sack, I. (2009). Mechanisms for communication between business and IT experts. *Computer Standards & Interfaces, 31*(1), 98–109. doi:10.1016/j.csi.2007.11.001

King, N. (2006). Enfish Professional *Beta. PC Mag.* http://www.pcmag.com/article2/0,2817,939388,00.asp

Kirda, E., Kruegel, C., Vigna, G., & Jovanovic, N. (2006). *Noxes: a client-side solution for mitigating cross-site scripting attacks*. Paper presented at the Proceedings of the 2006 ACM symposium on Applied computing. ACM. 10.1145/1141277.1141357

Knauss, A., Damian, D., Franch, X., Rook, A., Müller, H. A., & Thomo, A. (2016). ACon: A learning-based approach to deal with uncertainty in contextual requirements at runtime. *Information and Software Technology, 70*, 85–99. doi:10.1016/j.infsof.2015.10.001

Knudsen, H., Notland, J. S., Haro, P. H., Ræder, T. B., & Li, J. (2021). *Consensus in blockchain systems with low network throughput: A systematic mapping study*. Paper presented at the Proceedings of the 2021 3rd Blockchain and Internet of Things Conference. ACM. 10.1145/3475992.3475995

Kolowrocki, K., & Soszynska-Budny, J. (2018). *Critical Infrastructure Safety Indicators*. Paper presented at the 2018 IEEE International Conference on Industrial Engineering and Engineering Management (IEEM). IEEE.

Kong, Q. L., Lu, R., Ma, M., & Bao, H. (2019). A privacy-preserving sensory data sharing scheme in Internet of Vehicles. *Future Generation Computer Systems, 92*, 644–655. doi:10.1016/j.future.2017.12.003

Koo, T. M., Chang, H. C., Hsu, Y. T., & Lin, H. Y. (2013). Malicious website detection based on honeypot systems. *Paper presented at the 2nd International Conference on Advances in Computer Science and Engineering (CSE 2013).* IEEE. 10.2991/cse.2013.19

Kote, T. (2005). Desktop Search Comparison. *The Jo.* http://thejo.in/2005/01/desktop-search-comparison/

Kothmayr, T., Schmitt, C., Hu, W., Brünig, M., & Carle, G. (2012). A DTLS based end-to-end security architecture for the Internet of Things with two-way authentication. *37th Annual IEEE Conference on Local Computer Networks-Workshops*, (pp. 956–963). IEEE. 10.1109/LCNW.2012.6424088

Kour, H., & Sharma, L. S. (2016). Tracing out cross site scripting vulnerabilities in modern scripts. *International Journal of Advanced Networking and Applications*, *7*(5), 2862.

Kulizhskaya, Y. (2017). *Snippet matching for click-tracking blocking.* Trinity College.

Kullback, S., & Leibler, R. A. (1951). On information and sufficiency. *Annals of Mathematical Statistics*, *22*(1), 79–86. doi:10.1214/aoms/1177729694

Kumar, J. S. (2014). 2014 A survey on internet of things: Security and privacy issues. *International Journal of Computers and Applications*, *90*(11).

Kunst, R., Avila, L., Binotto, A., Pignaton, E., Bampi, S., & Rochol, J. (2019). Improving devices communication in Industry 4.0 wireless networks. *Engineering Applications of Artificial Intelligence*, *83*, 1–12. doi:10.1016/j.engappai.2019.04.014

Kuptsov, D., Gurtov, A., Garcia-Morchon, O., & Wehrle, K. (2010). Brief announcement: Distributed trust management and revocation. *Proceedings of the 29th ACM SIGACT-SIGOPS Symposium on Principles of Distributed Computing*, (pp. 233–234). ACM. 10.1145/1835698.1835751

Kushilevitz, E., & Ostrovsky, R. (1997). *Replication is not needed: Single database, computationally-private information retrieval.* Paper presented at the Proceedings 38th annual symposium on foundations of computer science. IEEE. 10.1109/SFCS.1997.646125

Lamming, M. G., & Newman, W. M. (1992). *Activity-Based Information Retrieval: Technology in Support of Personal Memory.* Paper presented at the Proceedings of the IFIP 12th World Computer Congress on Personal Computers and Intelligent Systems. Springer.

Laney, D. (2001). *3-D Data Management: Controlling Data Volume, Velocity and Variety.* MetaGroup.

Lasla, N., Derhab, A., Ouadjaout, A., Bagaa, M., & Challal, Y. (2014). SMART: Secure Multi-pAths Routing for wireless sensor neTworks. *Ad-Hoc, Mobile, and Wireless Networks: 13th International Conference, ADHOC-NOW 2014, Benidorm, Spain.*

Lazarevic, A., Kumar, V., & Srivastava, J. (2005). Intrusion detection: A survey. In *Managing cyber threats* (pp. 19–78). Springer. doi:10.1007/0-387-24230-9_2

Le, A., Loo, J., Lasebae, A., Aiash, M., & Luo, Y. (2012). 6LoWPAN: A study on QoS security threats and countermeasures using intrusion detection system approach. *International Journal of Communication Systems*, *25*(9), 1189–1212. doi:10.1002/dac.2356

Lee, J., Lee, B., Jung, J., Shim, H., & Kim, H. (2021). DQ: Two approaches to measure the degree of decentralization of blockchain. *ICT Express*, *7*(3), 278–282. doi:10.1016/j.icte.2021.08.008

Lefaix-Durand, A., & Kozak, R. (2010). Comparing customer and supplier perceptions of value offerings: An exploratory assessment. *Journal of Business Market Management*, *4*(3), 129–150. doi:10.100712087-010-0038-0

Liebetrau, C. P. (2005). Gearing up for change: Building digital resources in a South African cultural heritage context. *Innovation, 30*, 22–30.

Lindell, Y., & Waisbard, E. (2010). *Private web search with malicious adversaries.* Paper presented at the International Symposium on Privacy Enhancing Technologies Symposium. IEEE. 10.1007/978-3-642-14527-8_13

Lin, H., & Bergmann, N. W. (2016). IoT privacy and security challenges for smart home environments. *Information (Basel), 7*(3), 44. doi:10.3390/info7030044

Lin, J., Yu, W., Zhang, N., Yang, X., Zhang, H., & Zhao, W. (2017). A survey on internet of things: Architecture, enabling technologies, security and privacy, and applications. *IEEE Internet of Things Journal, 4*(5), 1125–1142. doi:10.1109/JIOT.2017.2683200

Linn, E. (2021). *A Look into the Data Privacy Crystal Ball: A Survey of Possible Outcomes for the EU-U.S.* Privacy Shield Agreement 50. *Vanderbilt Law Review*, 1311.

Liou, Y. I., & Chen, M. (1993). Using group support systems and joint application development for requirements specification. *Journal of Management Information Systems, 10*(3), 25–41. doi:10.1080/07421222.1993.11518009

Liu, F., Cheng, X., & Chen, D. (2007). Insider attacker detection in wireless sensor networks. *IEEE INFOCOM 2007-26th IEEE International Conference on Computer Communications*, (pp. 1937–1945). IEEE.

Liu, Y., Tong, Y., & Yang, Y. (2018). The application of mind mapping into college computer programming teaching. *Procedia Computer Science, 129*, 66–70. doi:10.1016/j.procs.2018.03.047

Liu, Y., Yang, Y., Lv, X., & Wang, L. (2013). A self-learning sensor fault detection framework for industry monitoring IoT. *Mathematical Problems in Engineering, 2013*, 2013. doi:10.1155/2013/712028

Lo, C. C., Huang, C. C., & Ku, J. (2010). A Cooperative Intrusion Detection System Framework for Cloud Computing Networks. *Paper presented at the 2010 39th International Conference on Parallel Processing Workshops.* IEEE. 10.1109/ICPPW.2010.46

Lombardi, P., Giordano, S., Farouh, H., & Yousef, W. (2012). Modelling the Smart City Performance. *Innovation (Abingdon), 25*(2), 137–149. doi:10.1080/13511610.2012.660325

Lopez, J. R., Rios, R., Bao, F., & Wang, G. (2017). Evolving privacy: From sensors to the Internet of Things. *Future Generation Computer Systems, 75*, 46–57. doi:10.1016/j.future.2017.04.045

Lunt, T. F. (1993). A survey of intrusion detection techniques. *Computers Security and Communication Networks, 12*(4), 405–418.

Luong, N. C., Hoang, D. T., Wang, P., Niyato, D., Kim, D. I., & Han, Z. (2016). Data collection and wireless communication in Internet of Things (IoT) using economic analysis and pricing models: A survey. *IEEE Communications Surveys and Tutorials, 18*(4), 2546–2590. doi:10.1109/COMST.2016.2582841

Lu, X., Li, Q., Qu, Z., & Hui, P. (2014). Privacy information security classification study in internet of things. *2014 International Conference on Identification, Information and Knowledge in the Internet of Things*, (pp. 162–165). IEEE. 10.1109/IIKI.2014.40

Lv, J. Y. (2011). A new clock synchronization architecture of network for internet of things. In *International Conference on Information Science and Technology.* (pp. 685-688). IEEE.

Ma, J., Saul, L. K., Savage, S., & Voelker, G. M. (2009). *Beyond blacklists: learning to detect malicious web sites from suspicious URLs.* Paper presented at the Proceedings of the 15th ACM SIGKDD international conference on Knowledge discovery and data mining. ACM. 10.1145/1557019.1557153

Magare, S. S., Dudhgaonkar, A. A., & Kondekar, S. R. (2021). Security and Privacy Issues in Smart City: Threats and Their Countermeasures. In: Tamane, S.C., Dey, N., Hassanien, AE. (eds) Security and Privacy Applications for Smart City Development. Studies in Systems, Decision and Control, (vol. 308, pp. 37–58). Springer.

Mahmood, S., Chadhar, M., & Firmin, S. (2022). Cybersecurity challenges in blockchain technology: A scoping review. *Human Behavior and Emerging Technologies*, *2022*, 2022. doi:10.1155/2022/7384000

Mahmud, I., & Veneziano, V. (2011). *Mind-mapping: An effective technique to facilitate requirements engineering in agile software development.* Paper presented at the 14th International Conference on Computer and Information Technology (ICCIT 2011). IEEE. 10.1109/ICCITechn.2011.6164775

Malik, A., Gautam, S., Abidin, S., & Bhushan, B. (2019). *Blockchain technology-future of IoT: including structure, limitations and various possible attacks.* Paper presented at the 2019 2nd international conference on intelligent computing, instrumentation and control technologies (ICICICT). Springer. 10.1109/ICICICT46008.2019.8993144

Malina, L. S. (2019). A privacy-enhancing framework for internet of things services. In Network and System Security. *13th International Conference, NSS 2019* (pp. 77-97). Sapporo, Japan: Springer International Publishing. 10.1007/978-3-030-36938-5_5

Manceron, G., & Morin, G. (2021). France and the archives of the Algerian War. In Boel, J Canavaggio, P and Quintana, A.G. (eds.) Archives and Human Rights. Routledge Taylor and Francis Group. doi:10.4324/9780429054624-23

Manoj, M., & Jacob, E. (2012). Design and development of a programmable meta search engine.

Manville, C. G., & Kotterink, B. (2014). *Mapping Smart Cities in the EU.* European Parliamentary Research Service. https://policycommons.net/artifacts/1339578/mapping-smart-cities-in-the-eu/1949353/

Maple, C. (2017). Security and privacy in the internet of things. *Journal of Cyber Policy*, *2*(2), 155–184. doi:10.1080/23738871.2017.1366536

Markscheffel, B., Büttner, D., & Fischer, D. (2011, December 11-14, 2011). Desktop Search Engines - A State of the Art Comparision. Paper presented at the *Proceedings of the 6th International Conference for Internet Technology and Secured Transactions (ICITST-2011),* Abu Dhabi, UAE.

Marsal-Llacuna, M., Colomer-Llinàs, J., & Meléndez-Frigola, J. (2015). Lessons in urban monitoring taken from sustainable and livable cities to better address the Smart Cities initiative. [Elsevier.]. *Technological Forecasting and Social Change*, *90*, 611–622. doi:10.1016/j.techfore.2014.01.012

Marutha, S. N., & Mosweu, O. (2020). *Confidentiality and Security of information in the public health -care facilities to curb HIV/AIDS trauma among patients in Africa. HIV/AIDS trauma among patients.* Global Knowledge, Memory, and Communication. doi:10.1108/GKMC-06-2020-0089

Mathews-Hunt, K. (2016). CookieConsumer: Tracking online behavioural advertising in Australia. *Computer Law & Security Review*, *32*(1), 55–90. doi:10.1016/j.clsr.2015.12.006

Matzan, J. (2005). dtSearch 7.0 Review. *Software in Review.* http://www.softwareinreview.com/search_tools/dtsearch_7.0_review.html

Mayer, C. P. (2009). Security and privacy challenges in the internet of things. *Electronic Communications of the EASST, 17.*

Maynard, P., McLaughlin, K., & Haberler, B. (2014). *Towards understanding man-in-the-middle attacks on iec 60870-5-104 scada networks.* Paper presented at the 2nd International Symposium for ICS & SCADA Cyber Security Research 2014 (ICS-CSR 2014) 2. IOP Science.

Mayzaud, A., Badonnel, R., & Chrisment, I. (2017). A distributed monitoring strategy for detecting version number attacks in RPL-based networks. *IEEE eTransactions on Network and Service Management, 14*(2), 472–486. doi:10.1109/TNSM.2017.2705290

Mazzariello, C., Bifulco, R., & Canonico, R. (2010). Integrating a network ids into an open source cloud computing environment. *Paper presented at the 2010 sixth international conference on information assurance and security.* IEEE. 10.1109/ISIAS.2010.5604069

McHugh, J. (2000). Testing intrusion detection systems: A critique of the 1998 and 1999 darpa intrusion detection system evaluations as performed by lincoln laboratory. *ACM Transactions on Information and System Security, 3*(4), 262–294. doi:10.1145/382912.382923

Mendez Mena, D., Papapanagiotou, I., & Yang, B. (2018). Internet of things: Survey on security. *Information Security Journal: A Global Perspective, 27*(3), 162-182. doi:10.1080/19393555.2018.1458258

Miao, J., & Wang, L. (2012). Rapid identification authentication protocol for mobile nodes in internet of things with privacy protection. *Journal of Networks, 7*(7), 1099. doi:10.4304/jnw.7.7.1099-1105

Minssen, T. S., Seitz, C., Aboy, M., & Corrales Compagnucci, M. (2020). The EU-US Privacy Shield Regime for Cross-Border Transfers of Personal Data under the GDPR: What are the legal challenges and how might these affect cloud-based technologies, big data, and AI. *EPLR, 4*(1), 34–50. doi:10.21552/eplr/2020/1/6

Mishra, D., Mishra, A., & Yazici, A. (2008). *Successful requirement elicitation by combining requirement engineering techniques.* Paper presented at the 2008 First International Conference on the Applications of Digital Information and Web Technologies (ICADIWT). IEEE. 10.1109/ICADIWT.2008.4664355

Misra, S., Gupta, A., Krishna, P. V., Agarwal, H., & Obaidat, M. S. (2012). An adaptive learning approach for fault-tolerant routing in Internet of Things. *2012 IEEE Wireless Communications and Networking Conference (WCNC),* (pp. 815–819). IEEE. 10.1109/WCNC.2012.6214484

Mitrokotsa, A., Komninos, N., & Douligeris, C. (2007). Intrusion detection with neural networks and watermarking techniques for MANET. *Paper presented at the IEEE International Conference on Pervasive Services.* IEEE. 10.1109/PERSER.2007.4283901

Mohammed, N., Otrok, H., Wang, L., Debbabi, M., & Bhattacharya, P. (2011). Mechanism Design-Based Secure Leader Election Model for Intrusion Detection in MANET. *IEEE Transactions on Dependable and Secure Computing, 8*(1), 89–103. doi:10.1109/TDSC.2009.22

Mokhtar, S. B., Berthou, G., Diarra, A., Quéma, V., & Shoker, A. (2013). *Rac: A freerider-resilient, scalable, anonymous communication protocol.* Paper presented at the In Proceedings of the 2013 IEEE 33rd International Conference on Distributed Computing Systems, ICDCS'13. IEEE.10.1109/ICDCS.2013.52

Mokhtar, S. B., Boutet, A., Felber, P., Pasin, M., Pires, R., & Schiavoni, V. (2017). *X-search: revisiting private web search using intel sgx.* Paper presented at the Proceedings of the 18th ACM/IFIP/USENIX Middleware Conference. IEEE. 10.1145/3135974.3135987

Monrat, A. A., Schelén, O., & Andersson, K. (2019). A survey of blockchain from the perspectives of applications, challenges, and opportunities. *IEEE Access : Practical Innovations, Open Solutions, 7,* 117134–117151. doi:10.1109/ACCESS.2019.2936094

Monsalve, C., April, A., & Abran, A. (2012). *On the expressiveness of business process modeling notations for software requirements elicitation.* Paper presented at the IECON 2012-38th Annual Conference on IEEE Industrial Electronics Society. IEEE. 10.1109/IECON.2012.6389398

Monteleone, S. (2017). *Reform of the e-Privacy Directive: EPRS.* European Parliamentary Research Service, Members' Research Service.

Moore, D., Shannon, C., Brown, D. J., Voelker, G. M., & Savage, S. (2006). Inferring internet denial-of-service activity. [TOCS]. *ACM Transactions on Computer Systems, 24*(2), 115–139. doi:10.1145/1132026.1132027

Morchón, O. G., Baldus, H., & Sánchez, D. S. (2006). Resource-efficient security for medical body sensor networks. *International Workshop on Wearable and Implantable Body Sensor Networks (BSN'06).* IEEE. 10.1109/BSN.2006.45

Muñoz-Fernández, J. C., Mazo, R., Salinesi, C., & Tamura, G. (2018). *10 challenges for the specification of self-adaptive software.* Paper presented at the 2018 12th International Conference on Research Challenges in Information Science (RCIS). IEEE.

Murugesan, M., & Clifton, C. (2009). *Providing privacy through plausibly deniable search.* Paper presented at the Proceedings of the 2009 SIAM International Conference on Data Mining. SAIM. 10.1137/1.9781611972795.66

Mwasilu, F. J.-K.-W., Justo, J. J., Kim, E.-K., Do, T. D., & Jung, J.-W. (2014). Electric vehicles and smart grid interaction: A review on vehicle to grid and renewable energy sources integration. *Renewable & Sustainable Energy Reviews, 34*, 501–516. doi:10.1016/j.rser.2014.03.031

Naafs, S. (2018, March 1). 'Living laboratories': the Dutch cities amassing data on oblivious residents. *The Guardian.* https://amp.theguardian.com/cities/2018/mar/01/smart-cities-data-privacy-eindhoven-utrecht

Nair, S. M., Ramesh, V., & Tyagi, A. K. (2023). *Issues and challenges (Privacy, security, and trust) in blockchain-based applications Research Anthology on Convergence of Blockchain, Internet of Things, and Security.* IGI Global.

Nakamoto, S. (2008). Bitcoin: A peer-to-peer electronic cash system. *Decentralized business review*, 21260.

Narasimhan, V. L., & Lowe, M. (2010). *An Objective Comparison of Desktop Search and Visualization Tools.* Paper presented at the Proceedings of the 2nd International Conference on Trends in Information Sciences and Computing (TISC-2010). IEEE. 10.1109/TISC.2010.5714640

Nardi, B., & Barreau, D. (1997). "Finding and Reminding" Revisited: Appropriate Metaphors for File Organization at the Desktop. *SIGCHI Bull., 29*(1), 76–78. doi:10.1145/251761.248508

Narmadha, D., & Pravin, A. (2020). An intelligent computer-aided approach for target protein prediction in infectious diseases. *Soft Computing, 24*(19), 14707–14720. doi:10.100700500-020-04815-w

Nasa, C., & Suman, S. (2012). Evaluation of different classification techniques for web data. *International Journal of Computers and Applications, 52*(9), 34–40. doi:10.5120/8233-1389

National League of Cities. (2016). *Trends in Smart City Development.* NLC. https://www.nlc.org/wp-content/uploads/2017/01/Trends-in-Smart-City-Development.pdf

Navarro-Arribas, G., & Torra, V. (2014). *Advanced Research in Data Privacy* (Vol. 567). Springer.

Nawaz, A. (2012). A comparison of card-sorting analysis methods. Paper presented at *the 10th Asia Pacific Conference on Computer Human Interaction (Apchi 2012).* Matsue-city, Shimane, Japan.

Newman, A. L. (2015). What the "right to be forgotten" means for privacy in a digital age. *Science, 347*(6221), 507–508. doi:10.1126cience.aaa4603 PMID:25635090

Nissenbaum, H., & Daniel, H. (2009). TrackMeNot: Resisting surveillance in web search.

Nissenbaum, H., & Daniel, H. (2009). *TrackMeNot: Resisting surveillance in web search*. TrackMeNot.

Nissenbaum, H., & Daniel, H. (2009). TrackMeNot: Resisting surveillance in web search. In C. L. I. Kerr & V. Steeves (Eds.), *Lessons from the Identity Trail: Anonymity, Privacy, and Identity in a Networked Society*. Oxford University Press.

Nixon, R. (2021). *Learning PHP, MySQL & JavaScript* (6th ed.). O'Reilly Media.

Noda, T., & Helwig, S. (2005). *Benchmark Sutdy of Desktop Search Tools*. UW E-Business Consortium, University of Misconsin.

OECD. (1980). Recommendation of the council concerning guidelines governing the protection of privacy and trans border flows of personal data. Organisation for Economic Co-operation and Development (OECD).

OECD. (2012). *Principles of Public Governance of Public-Private Partnerships*. Organisation for Economic Co-operation and Development – OECD.

Ogonji, M. M., Okeyo, G., & Wafula, J. M. (2020). A survey on privacy and security of Internet of Things. *Computer Science Review*, *38*, 100312. doi:10.1016/j.cosrev.2020.100312

Ojha, R., & Deepak, G. (2022). *SAODFT: Socially Aware Ontology Driven Approach for Query Facet Generation in Text Classification*. Paper presented at the International Conference on Electrical and Electronics Engineering. 10.1007/978-981-19-1677-9_14

Ordóñez, H., Villada, A. F. E., Vanegas, D. L. V., Cobos, C., Ordóñez, A., & Segovia, R. (2015). *An impact study of business process models for requirements elicitation in XP*. Paper presented at the International Conference on Computational Science and Its Applications. IEEE.

Oriol, M., Stade, M., Fotrousi, F., Nadal, S., Varga, J., Seyff, N., & Schmidt, O. (2018). *FAME: supporting continuous requirements elicitation by combining user feedback and monitoring*. Paper presented at the 2018 ieee 26th international requirements engineering conference (re). IEEE. 10.1109/RE.2018.00030

OSEDA. (2023, February 28). *Exploit-DB*. Offensive Security's Exploit Database Archive. https://www.exploit-db.com/

OWASP. (2016). *Software Assurance Maturity Model v1.5*. OWASP. https://owasp.org/www-pdf-archive/SAMM_Core_V1-5_FINAL.pdf

OWASP. (2021). *OWASP Top Ten*. OWASP. https://owasp.org/www-project-top-ten/ https://owasp.org/

Paetsch, F., Eberlein, A., & Maurer, F. (2003). *Requirements engineering and agile software development*. Paper presented at the WET ICE 2003. Proceedings. Twelfth IEEE International Workshops on Enabling Technologies: Infrastructure for Collaborative Enterprises, 2003. IEEE. 10.1109/ENABL.2003.1231428

Palomares, C., Franch, X., Quer, C., Chatzipetrou, P., López, L., & Gorschek, T. (2021). The state-of-practice in requirements elicitation: An extended interview study at 12 companies. *Requirements Engineering*, *26*(2), 273–299. doi:10.100700766-020-00345-x

Pandey, S., & Batra, M. (2013). Formal methods in requirements phase of SDLC. *International Journal of Computers and Applications*, *70*(13), 7–14. doi:10.5120/12020-8017

Pandita, R., Xiao, X., Yang, W., Enck, W., & Xie, T. (2013). {WHYPER}: Towards automating risk assessment of mobile applications. *Paper presented at the 22nd USENIX Security Symposium (USENIX Security 13)*.

Parra-Arnau, J., Rebollo-Monedero, D., & Forné, J. (2014). Measuring the privacy of user profiles in personalized information systems. *Future Generation Computer Systems*, *33*, 53–63. doi:10.1016/j.future.2013.01.001

Parsania, V. S., Kalyani, F., & Kamani, K. (2016). A comparative analysis: DuckDuckGo vs. Google search engine. *GRD Journals-Global Research and Development Journal for Engineering*, *2*(1), 12–17.

Patriarca, R., Di Gravio, G., & Costantino, F. (2017). A Monte Carlo evolution of the Functional Resonance Analysis Method (FRAM) to assess performance variability in complex systems. *Safety Science*, *91*, 49–60. doi:10.1016/j.ssci.2016.07.016

Patriarca, R., Di Gravio, G., Woltjer, R., Costantino, F., Praetorius, G., Ferreira, P., & Hollnagel, E. (2020). Framing the FRAM: A literature review on the functional resonance analysis method. *Safety Science*, *129*, 104827. doi:10.1016/j.ssci.2020.104827

Patton, M. G. (2014). Uninvited connections: a study of vulnerable devices on the internet of things (IoT). *In 2014 IEEE Joint Intelligence and Security Informatics Conference* (pp. pp. 232-235). IEEE.

Peddinti, S. T., & Saxena, N. (2010). On the privacy of web search based on query obfuscation: A case study of trackmenot. Paper presented at the *Privacy Enhancing Technologies: 10th International Symposium, PETS 2010,* Berlin, Germany. 10.1007/978-3-642-14527-8_2

Peddinti, S. T., & Saxena, N. (2011). *On the effectiveness of anonymizing networks for web search privacy.* Paper presented at the Proceedings of the 6th ACM Symposium on Information, Computer and Communications Security. ACM. 10.1145/1966913.1966984

Peddinti, S. T., & Saxena, N. (2014). Web search query privacy: Evaluating query obfuscation and anonymizing networks. *Journal of Computer Security*, *22*(1), 155–199. doi:10.3233/JCS-130491

Pekala, S. (2017). Privacy and User Experience in 21st Century Library Discovery. *Information Technology and Libraries*, *36*(2), 48–58. doi:10.6017/ital.v36i2.9817

PereraG. T. (n.d.). Identification of the Optimum Light Conditions and Development of an Iot Based Setup to Monitor a Household Indoor Hydroponic Tomato Cultivation. *Available at:* SSRN 4167457. doi:10.2139/ssrn.4167457

Peretti, G., Lakkundi, V., & Zorzi, M. (2015). BlinkToSCoAP: An end-to-end security framework for the Internet of Things. *2015 7th International Conference on Communication Systems and Networks (COMSNETS)*, (pp. 1–6). IEEE.

Perez, J. C. (2004). Ask Jeeves Previews Desktop Search Tool. Utility Software. *PC World*. https://www.pcworld.com/article/118932/article.html

Persoonsgegevens, A. (2021). *Smart Cities: Investigation Report on the Protection of Personal Data in the Development of Dutch Smart Cities.* Auto Rite IT. https://autoriteitpersoonsgegevens.nl/sites/default/files/atoms/files/investigation_report_development_of_dutch_smart_cities.pdf

Petit, A. (2017). *Introducing privacy in current web search engines.* Université de Lyon; Universität Passau (Deutscheland).

Petit, A., Cerqueus, T., Mokhtar, S. B., Brunie, L., & Kosch, H. (2015). *PEAS: Private, efficient and accurate web search.* Paper presented at the 2015 IEEE Trustcom/BigDataSE/ISPA. IEEE. 10.1109/Trustcom.2015.421

Petit, A., Cerqueus, T., Boutet, A., Mokhtar, S. B., Coquil, D., Brunie, L., & Kosch, H. (2016). SimAttack: Private web search under fire. *Journal of Internet Services and Applications*, *7*(1), 1–17. doi:10.118613174-016-0044-x

Pina, P. (2011). Digital Copyright Enforcement: Between Piracy and Privacy. In C. Akrivopoulou & A. Psygkas (Eds.), *Personal Data Privacy and Protection in a Surveillance Era: Technologies and Practices* (pp. 241–254). IGI Global. doi:10.4018/978-1-60960-083-9.ch014

Pires, R., Goltzsche, D., Mokhtar, S. B., Bouchenak, S., Boutet, A., Felber, P., & Schiavoni, V. (2018). *CYCLOSA: Decentralizing private web search through SGX-based browser extensions.* Paper presented at the 2018 IEEE 38th International Conference on Distributed Computing Systems (ICDCS). IEEE. 10.1109/ICDCS.2018.00053

Piro, G., Boggia, G., & Grieco, L. A. (2014). A standard compliant security framework for IEEE 802.15. 4 networks. *2014 IEEE World Forum on Internet of Things (WF-IoT)*, (pp. 27–30). IEEE.

Platt, M., & McBurney, P. (2021). Sybil attacks on identity-augmented Proof-of-Stake. *Computer Networks*, *199*, 108424. doi:10.1016/j.comnet.2021.108424

Poeplau, S., Fratantonio, Y., Bianchi, A., Kruegel, C., & Vigna, G. (2014). Execute this! analyzing unsafe and malicious dynamic code loading in android applications. *Paper presented at the NDSS.*

Polyakov, A., Efimov, D., Perruquetti, W., & Richard, J.-P. (2013). Output stabilization of time-varying input delay systems using interval observation technique. *Automatica*, *49*(11), 3402–3410. doi:10.1016/j.automatica.2013.08.012

Pongle, P., & Chavan, G. (2015). A survey: Attacks on RPL and 6LoWPAN in IoT. *2015 International Conference on Pervasive Computing (ICPC)*, (pp. 1–6). IEEE. 10.1109/PERVASIVE.2015.7087034

Pongle, P., & Chavan, G. (2015). Real time intrusion and wormhole attack detection in internet of things. *International Journal of Computers and Applications*, *121*(9).

Pour, M. S., Mangino, A., Friday, K., Rathbun, M., Bou-Harb, E., Iqbal, F., Samtani, S., Crichigno, J., & Ghani, N. (2020). On data-driven curation, learning, and analysis for inferring evolving internet-of-Things (IoT) botnets in the wild. *Computers & Security*, *91*, 101707. doi:10.1016/j.cose.2019.101707

Preibusch, S. (2015). The value of web search privacy. *IEEE Security and Privacy*, *13*(05), 24–32. doi:10.1109/MSP.2015.109

PrivacyAffairs. (2023, February 15). *Dark Web Price Index 2021 - Dark Web Prices of Personal Data.* Privacy Affairs. https://www.privacyaffairs.com/dark-web-price-index-2021/

Priyantha, N. B., Kansal, A., Goraczko, M., & Zhao, F. (2008). Tiny web services: Design and implementation of interoperable and evolvable sensor networks. *Proceedings of the 6th ACM Conference on Embedded Network Sensor Systems*, (pp. 253–266). ACM. 10.1145/1460412.1460438

Pufahl, L., Ohlsson, B., Weber, I., Harper, G., & Weston, E. (2021). Enabling Financing in Agricultural Supply Chains Through Blockchain: Interorganizational Process Innovation Through Blockchain *Business Process Management Cases Vol. 2: Digital Transformation-Strategy, Processes and Execution* (pp. 41-56). Springer.

Qu, Y., Nosouhi, M. R., Cui, L., & Yu, S. (2019). *Privacy preservation in smart cities. Smart Cities Cybersecurity and Privacy.* Elsevier.

Rai, S. (2018). A Pragmatic Approach to Data Protection. *The Leap Blog.* https://blog.theleapjournal.org/2018/02/a-pragmatic-approach-to-data-protection.html

Raikwar, M., & Gligoroski, D. (2022). DoS Attacks on Blockchain Ecosystem. Paper presented at *the Euro-Par 2021: Parallel Processing Workshops: Euro-Par 2021 International Workshops*, Lisbon, Portugal. 10.1007/978-3-031-06156-1_19

Rajan, M. A., Balamuralidhar, P., Chethan, K. P., & Swarnahpriyaah, M. (2011). A self-reconfigurable sensor network management system for internet of things paradigm. *2011 International Conference on Devices and Communications (ICDeCom)*, (pp. 1–5). IEEE. 10.1109/ICDECOM.2011.5738550

Rajendran, S. S. (2020). Security and Privacy for Internet of Things (IoT): Issues and Solutions. [IJSREM]. *International Journal of Scientific Research in Engineering and Management, 4*(11).

Ram, C., Montibeller, G., & Morton, A. (2011). Extending the use of scenario planning and MCDA for the evaluation of strategic options. *The Journal of the Operational Research Society, 62*(5), 817–829. doi:10.1057/jors.2010.90

Ramgovind, S. M. (2010). The management of security in cloud computing. 2010 Information Security for South Africa, (pp. 1-7). IEEE.

Ranjan, S., Swaminathan, R. P., Uysal, M., & Knightly, E. W. (2006). DDoS-Resilient Scheduling to Counter Application Layer Attacks Under Imperfect Detection. *Proceedings IEEE INFOCOM. 25TH IEEE International Conference on Computer Communications*, (pp. 1-13). IEEE. 10.1109/INFOCOM.2006.127

Rao, K. N. (2008). Application domain and functional classification of recommender systems—A survey. *DESIDOC Journal of Library and Information Technology, 28*(3), 17–35. doi:10.14429/djlit.28.3.174

Rasheed, A., Zafar, B., Shehryar, T., Aslam, N. A., Sajid, M., Ali, N., Dar, S. H., & Khalid, S. (2021). Requirement engineering challenges in agile software development. *Mathematical Problems in Engineering, 2021*, 2021. doi:10.1155/2021/6696695

Rastogi, V., Chen, Y., & Jiang, X. (2013). Droidchameleon: evaluating android anti-malware against transformation attacks. *Paper presented at the Proceedings of the 8th ACM SIGSAC symposium on Information, computer and communications security.* ACM. 10.1145/2484313.2484355

Rauhofer, J (2014). What do the proposed changes to the purpose limitation principle mean for public boides rights to access third party data?. *International Rev of Law, Computers and Technology, 28* (2), 144 – 158: Doi:.2013.801592. doi:10.1080/13600869

Raza, A., Ayub, H., Khan, J. A., Ahmad, I. S., Salama, A., Daradkeh, Y. I., & Hamam, H. (2022). A Hybrid Deep Learning-Based Approach for Brain Tumor Classification. *Electronics (Basel), 11*(7). Advance online publication. doi:10.3390/electronics11071146

Raza, A., Han, K., & Hwang, S. O. (2020). A framework for privacy preserving, distributed search engine using topology of DLT and onion routing. *IEEE Access : Practical Innovations, Open Solutions, 8*, 43001–43012. doi:10.1109/ACCESS.2020.2977884

Raza, S., Wallgren, L., & Voigt, T. (2013). SVELTE: Real-time intrusion detection in the Internet of Things. *Ad Hoc Networks, 11*(8), 2661–2674. doi:10.1016/j.adhoc.2013.04.014

Rebollo-Monedero, D., Forne, J., & Domingo-Ferrer, J. (2012). Query profile obfuscation by means of optimal query exchange between users. *IEEE Transactions on Dependable and Secure Computing, 9*(5), 641–654. doi:10.1109/TDSC.2012.16

Redmond, W. (2004). Microsoft Introduces MSN Toolbar Suite Beta with Desktop Search. *Microsoft.* http://www.microsoft.com/en-us/news/press/2004/dec04/12-13searchtoolbarpr.aspx

Reed, J., & Payton, V. R. (1997). Focus groups: Issues of analysis and interpretation. *Journal of Advanced Nursing, 26*(4), 765–771. doi:10.1046/j.1365-2648.1997.00395.x PMID:9354990

Reiter, M. K., & Rubin, A. D. (1998). Crowds: Anonymity for web transactions. [TISSEC]. *ACM Transactions on Information and System Security*, *1*(1), 66–92. doi:10.1145/290163.290168

Renault, S., Méndez-Bonilla, Ó., Franch, X., & Quer, C. (2009). *PABRE: pattern-based requirements elicitation.* Paper presented at the 2009 Third International Conference on Research Challenges in Information Science. ACM.

Rhodes, B. J. (1997). The Wearable Remembrance Agent: A System for Augmented Memory. *Personal Technologies*, *1997*(1), 218–224. doi:10.1007/BF01682024

Ribeiro, C., Farinha, C., Pereira, J., & da Silva, M. M. (2014). Gamifying requirement elicitation: Practical implications and outcomes in improving stakeholders collaboration. *Entertainment Computing*, *5*(4), 335–345. doi:10.1016/j.entcom.2014.04.002

Richardson, J., Ormerod, T. C., & Shepherd, A. (1998). The role of task analysis in capturing requirements for interface design. *Interacting with Computers*, *9*(4), 367–384. doi:10.1016/S0953-5438(97)00036-2

Ringel, M., Cutrell, E., Dumais, S. T., & Horvitz, E. (2003). *Milestones in Time: The Value of Landmarks in Retrieving Information from Personal Stores.* Paper presented at the INTERACT. http://dblp.uni-trier.de/db/conf/interact/interact2003.html#RingelCDH03

Ring, M., Wunderlich, S., Scheuring, D., Landes, D., & Hotho, A. (2019). A survey of network-based intrusion detection data sets. *Computers & Security*, *86*, 147–167. doi:10.1016/j.cose.2019.06.005

Rodrigues, A., Caldas, R. D., Rodrigues, G. N., Vogel, T., & Pelliccione, P. (2018). *A learning approach to enhance assurances for real-time self-adaptive systems.* Paper presented at the 2018 IEEE/ACM 13th International Symposium on Software Engineering for Adaptive and Self-Managing Systems (SEAMS). ACM. 10.1145/3194133.3194147

Rodríguez, G. E., Torres, J. G., Flores, P., & Benavides, D. E. (2020). Cross-site scripting (XSS) attacks and mitigation: A survey. *Computer Networks*, *166*, 106960. doi:10.1016/j.comnet.2019.106960

Roman, R., Fernandez-Gago, C., López, J., Chen, H. H., Gritzalis, S., Karygiannis, T., & Skianis, C. (2009). Trust and reputation systems for wireless sensor networks. In Security and Privacy in Mobile and Wireless Networking.

Romero-Tris, C., Castella-Roca, J., & Viejo, A. (2011). *Multi-party private web search with untrusted partners.* Paper presented at the International Conference on Security and Privacy in Communication Systems. IEEE.

Romero-Tris, C., Castella-Roca, J., & Viejo, A. (2014). Distributed system for private web search with untrusted partners. *Computer Networks*, *67*, 26–42. doi:10.1016/j.comnet.2014.03.022

Romero-Tris, C., Viejo, A., & Castellà-Roca, J. (2015). *Multi-party methods for privacy-preserving web search: survey and contributions Advanced research in data privacy.* Springer.

Roopak, M., Tian, G. Y., & Chambers, J. (2019). Deep learning models for cyber security in IoT networks. *Paper presented at the 2019 IEEE 9th annual computing and communication workshop and conference (CCWC).* IEEE. 10.1109/CCWC.2019.8666588

Rosadi, S.D., Suhardi, & Kristyan, S.A. (2021). Data privacy law in the application of smart city in Indonesia. *Journal of Legal. Ethical and Regulatory Issues*, *24*(S4), 1–9.

Rostow, T. (2017). What happens when an acquaintance buys your data: A new privacy harm in the age of data brokers. *Yale Journal on Regulation*, *34*, 667.

Rouncefield, M. (2011). Fieldwork, ethnography and ethnomethodology. LSCITS Socio-Technical Systems Engineering Handbook. University of St Andrews, 44-48.

Ruan, N., & Hori, Y. (2012). DoS attack-tolerant TESLA-based broadcast authentication protocol in Internet of Things. *2012 International Conference on Selected Topics in Mobile and Wireless Networking*, (pp. 60–65). IEEE. 10.1109/iCOST.2012.6271291

Ruan, N., Sun, H., Lou, Z., & Li, J. (2022). A General Quantitative Analysis Framework for Attacks in Blockchain. *IEEE/ACM Transactions on Networking*, 1–16. doi:10.1109/TNET.2022.3201493

Rubenking, N. J. (2005). *MSN Toolbar Suite Beta*. Retrieved January 16, 2022, 2022, from http://www.pcmag.com/article2/0,2817,1741498,00.asp

Ruse, M., Sarkar, T., & Basu, S. (2010). *Analysis & detection of SQL injection vulnerabilities via automatic test case generation of programs*. Paper presented at the 2010 10th IEEE/IPSJ International Symposium on Applications and the Internet. IEEE. 10.1109/SAINT.2010.60

Saad, M., Cook, V., Nguyen, L., Thai, M. T., & Mohaisen, A. (2019). *Partitioning attacks on bitcoin: Colliding space, time, and logic*. Paper presented at the 2019 IEEE 39th international conference on distributed computing systems (ICDCS). IEEE. 10.1109/ICDCS.2019.00119

Sadeghi, A.-R., Wachsmann, C., & Waidner, M. (2015). Security and privacy challenges in industrial internet of things. *Proceedings of the 52nd Annual Design Automation Conference*, (pp. 1–6). ACM. 10.1145/2744769.2747942

Sağıroğlu, Ş. (Ed.). (2019). *Siber Güvenlik ve Savunma: Standartlar ve Uygulamalar*. Grafiker Yayınları.

Sahay, R., Geethakumari, G., & Modugu, K. (2018). *Attack graph—Based vulnerability assessment of rank property in RPL-6LOWPAN in IoT*. Paper presented at the 2018 IEEE 4th World Forum on Internet of Things (WF-IoT). IEEE. 10.1109/WF-IoT.2018.8355171

Saint-Jean, F. (2005). *Java implementation of a single-database computationally symmetric private information retrieval (cSPIR) protocol*. Yale Univ New Haven Ct Dept Of Computer Science.

Salah, K., Rehman, M. H. U., Nizamuddin, N., & Al-Fuqaha, A. (2019). Blockchain for AI: Review and open research challenges. *IEEE Access: Practical Innovations, Open Solutions*, 7, 10127–10149. doi:10.1109/ACCESS.2018.2890507

Salama, S. E., Marie, M. I., El-Fangary, L. M., & Helmy, Y. K. (2012). Web anomaly misuse intrusion detection framework for SQL injection detection. *International Journal of Advanced Computer Science and Applications*, 3(3).

Sanderson, M., & Croft, W. B. (2012). The History of Information Retrieval Research. *Proceedings of the IEEE, 100*(Special Centennial Issue), 1444-1451. 10.1109/JPROC.2012.2189916

Santoro, F. M., Borges, M. R., & Pino, J. A. (2000). *CEPE: cooperative editor for processes elicitation*. Paper presented at the Proceedings of the 33rd Annual Hawaii International Conference on System Sciences. IEEE. 10.1109/HICSS.2000.926587

Sarıman, G., & Çelikten, H. (2021). Yeni bir güvenli yazılım geliştirme uygulama modeli: GYG-MOD. *Uluslararası Teknolojik Bilimler Dergisi*, 13(1), 39–49.

Sazzadul Hoque, M. (2012). An Implementation of Intrusion Detection System Using Genetic Algorithm. *International Journal of Network Security & Its Applications*, 4(2), 109–120. doi:10.5121/ijnsa.2012.4208

Schalken, J., Brinkkemper, S., & van Vliet, H. (2004). *Assessing the effects of facilitated workshops in requirements engineering*. Paper presented at the Proceedings of the 8th Conference on Evaluation & Assessment in Software Engineering (EASE 2004), IEE Press. 10.1049/ic:20040406

Schlatt, V., Guggenberger, T., Schmid, J., & Urbach, N. (2022). Attacking the trust machine: Developing an information systems research agenda for blockchain cybersecurity. *International Journal of Information Management*, ●●●, 102470.

Schneider, F., & Berenbach, B. (2013). A literature survey on international standards for systems requirements engineering. *Procedia Computer Science*, *16*, 796–805. doi:10.1016/j.procs.2013.01.083

Schurmann, T. (2005). The Beagle Desktop Search Engine SNIFFER DOG. *Linux Pro Magazine*. http://www.linuxpro-magazine.com/content/download/62688/485752/ version/1/file/Beagle_Search_Tool.pdf

Schütze, H., Manning, C. D., & Raghavan, P. (2008). *Introduction to information retrieval* (Vol. 39). Cambridge University Press Cambridge.

SearchLogistics. (2023, February 28). Cybersecurity Statistics 2023: The Alarming Truth. *Search Logistics*. https://www.searchlogistics.com/grow/statistics/cybersecurity-statistics/

Sebastiani, R., & Tomasi, S. (2015). Optimization modulo theories with linear rational costs. [TOCL]. *ACM Transactions on Computational Logic*, *16*(2), 1–43. doi:10.1145/2699915

Seeber, S., & Rodosek, G. D. (2015). Towards an Adaptive and Effective IDS Using OpenFlow. In Intelligent Mechanisms for Network Configuration and Security (pp. 134-139). doi:10.1007/978-3-319-20034-7_14

Seid, H. A., & Lespagnol, A. (1998). *Virtual private network: Google Patents*.

Seitz, L., Selander, G., & Gehrmann, C. (2013). Authorization framework for the internet-of-things. *2013 IEEE 14th International Symposium on" A World of Wireless, Mobile and Multimedia Networks"(WoWMoM)*, (pp. 1–6). IEEE.

Sen, P., Chaki, N., & Chaki, R. (2008). HIDS: Honesty-Rate Based Collaborative Intrusion Detection System for Mobile Ad-Hoc Networks. *Paper presented at the 2008 7th Computer Information Systems and Industrial Management Applications*. IEEE.

Serjantov, A., & Danezis, G. (2002). *Towards an information theoretic metric for anonymity*. Paper presented at the International Workshop on Privacy Enhancing Technologies. IEEE.

Shahid, J., Hameed, M. K., Javed, I. T., Qureshi, K. N., Ali, M., & Crespi, N. (2022). A Comparative Study of Web Application Security Parameters: Current Trends and Future Directions. *Applied Sciences (Basel, Switzerland)*, *12*(8), 4077. doi:10.3390/app12084077

Shapira, B., Elovici, Y., Meshiach, A., & Kuflik, T. (2005). PRAW—A PRivAcy model for the Web. *Journal of the American Society for Information Science and Technology*, *56*(2), 159–172. doi:10.1002/asi.20107

Shapiro, M. (1986). *Structure and encapsulation in distributed systems: The proxy principle*. Paper presented at the Int. Conf. on Distr. Comp. Sys.(ICDCS). IEEE.

Sharma, S. (2010). Beagle. *Tech Radar*. http://www.techradar.com/news/software/applications/6-of-the-best-desktop-search-tools-for -linux-666158/2

Sharma, V. a. (2016). A review paper on "IOT" & It's Smart Applications. *International Journal of Science, Engineering and Technology Research (IJSETR)*, (pp. 472-476). ACM.

Sharma, S., & Pandey, S. (2013). Revisiting requirements elicitation techniques. *International Journal of Computers and Applications*, *75*(12).

Shelke, M. P. K., Sontakke, M. S., & Gawande, A. (2012). Intrusion detection system for cloud computing. *International Journal of Scientific Technology Research*, *1*(4), 67–71.

Sherasiya, T., & Upadhyay, H. (2016). Intrusion detection system for internet of things. *Int. J. Adv. Res. Innov. Ideas Educ*, 2(3).

Sherman, C. (2005). Yahoo Launches Desktop Search. *Search Engine Watch*. http://searchenginewatch.com/article/2048664/Yahoo-Launches-Desktop-Search

Shin, Y., Williams, L. A., & Xie, T. (2006). *SQLUnitgen: Test case generation for SQL injection detection*. Retrieved from Thomas, S., Williams, L., & Xie, T. (2009). On automated prepared statement generation to remove SQL injection vulnerabilities. *Information and Software Technology*, 51(3), 589–598.

Shirey, R. (2000). *RFC 2828: Internet Security Glossary.*.

Shugrue, D. (2017). Fighting application threats with cloud-based WAFS. *Network Security*, 2017(6), 5–8. doi:10.1016/S1353-4858(17)30059-4

Shukla, M., Lin, J., & Seneviratne, O. (2022). Blockchain and IoT enhanced clinical workflow. Paper presented at the *Artificial Intelligence in Medicine: 20th International Conference on Artificial Intelligence in Medicine, AIME 2022*, Halifax, NS, Canada.

Shyry, S. P. (2014). Performance measurement in selfish overlay network by fuzzy logic deployment of overlay nodes. *Paper presented at the 2014 International Conference on Control, Instrumentation, Communication and Computational Technologies (ICCICCT)*. IEEE. 10.1109/ICCICCT.2014.6993053

Silva, B. N., Khan, M., & Han, K. (2018). Internet of things: A comprehensive review of enabling technologies, architecture, and challenges. *IETE Technical Review*, 35(2), 205–220. doi:10.1080/02564602.2016.1276416

Singh, P., Dwivedi, Y. K., Kahlon, K. S., Sawhney, R. S., Alalwan, A. A., & Rana, N. P. (2019). Smart monitoring and controlling of government policies using social media and cloud computing. *Information Systems Frontiers*, 1–23. doi:10.100710796-019-09916-y

Singhvi, V., Krause, A., Guestrin, C., Garrett, J. H. Jr, & Matthews, H. S. (2005). Intelligent light control using sensor networks. *Proceedings of the 3rd International Conference on Embedded Networked Sensor Systems*, (pp. 218–229). IEEE. 10.1145/1098918.1098942

Skoudis, E., & Zeltser, L. (2004). *Malware: Fighting malicious code*. Prentice Hall Professional.

Sohaib, O., & Khan, K. (2010). *Integrating usability engineering and agile software development: A literature review*. Paper presented at the 2010 international conference on Computer design and applications. IEEE. 10.1109/ICCDA.2010.5540916

Solanas, A. P.-B., Patsakis, C., Conti, M., Vlachos, I., Ramos, V., Falcone, F., Postolache, O., Perez-martinez, P., Pietro, R., Perrea, D., & Martinez-Balleste, A. (2014). Smart health: A context-aware health paradigm within smart cities. *IEEE Communications Magazine*, 52(8), 74–81. doi:10.1109/MCOM.2014.6871673

Sommerville, I. (2011). Software engineering 9th Edition. 18.

Sosnowski, M., Bereza, M., & Ng, Y. Y. (2021). *Business-Oriented Approach to Requirements Elicitation in a Scrum Project*. Paper presented at the International Conference on Lean and Agile Software Development. IEEE. 10.1007/978-3-030-67084-9_12

Sousa-Zomer, T. T., & Miguel, P. A. C. (2017). A QFD-based approach to support sustainable product-service systems conceptual design. *International Journal of Advanced Manufacturing Technology*, 88(1), 701–717. doi:10.100700170-016-8809-8

Srinivasan, V. S. (2008). Protecting your daily in-home activity information from a wireless snooping attack. *In Proceedings of the 10th International Conference on Ubiquitous Computing*, (pp. 202-211).

Statista. (2023, March 10). *Number of monthly active Facebook users worldwide as of 4th quarter 2022 (in millions)*. Statistia. https://www.statista.com/statistics/264810/number-of-monthly-active-facebook-users-worldwide/

Stefanouli, M., & Economou, C. (2019). Data Protection in Smart Cities: Application of the EU GDPR. In: Nathanail, E., Karakikes, I. (eds) Data Analytics: Paving the Way to Sustainable Urban Mobility. CSUM 2018. Advances in Intelligent Systems and Computing, (vol 879). Springer, Cham. doi:10.1007/978-3-030-02305-8_90

Stokes, K., & Bras-Amorós, M. (2010). Optimal configurations for peer-to-peer user-private information retrieval. *Computers & Mathematics with Applications (Oxford, England)*, *59*(4), 1568–1577. doi:10.1016/j.camwa.2010.01.003

Stone, M. (2022a). Understanding and Evaluating Search Experience. *Synthesis Lectures on Information Concepts, Retrieval, and Services*, *14*(1), 1–105. doi:10.1007/978-3-031-79216-8

Sullivan, D. (2004). Privacy and Desktop Search: A Closer Look. *Search Engine Watch*. http://searchenginewatch.com/article/2065797/A-Closer-Look-At-Privacy-Desktop-Search

Sundmaeker, H. G. (2010). Vision and challenges for realising the Internet of Things. *Cluster of European research projects on the internet of things. European Commision*, *3*(3), 32–36.

Sutcliffe, A., & Maiden, N. (1998). The domain theory for requirements engineering. *IEEE Transactions on Software Engineering*, *24*(3), 174–196. doi:10.1109/32.667878

Swanson, C. M., & Stinson, D. R. (2011). Extended combinatorial constructions for peer-to-peer user-private information retrieval. *arXiv preprint arXiv:1112.2762*.

Syverson, P., Dingledine, R., & Mathewson, N. (2004). *Tor: The secondgeneration onion router*. Paper presented at the Usenix Security.

Szekely, I. (2014). The right to be forgotten and the new archival paradigm. In Ghezzi A. Pereira, A. G., & Vesnic-Alujevic, L. (eds) The ethics of memory in a digital age. Interrogating the right to be foforgetten, pp 28 – 49. Palgrve Macmillan. doi:10.1057/9781137428455_3

Tahsien, S. M., Karimipour, H., & Spachos, P. (2020). Machine learning based solutions for security of Internet of Things (IoT): A survey. *Journal of Network and Computer Applications*, *161*, 102630. doi:10.1016/j.jnca.2020.102630

Tandon, A., Kaur, P., Mäntymäki, M., & Dhir, A. (2021). Blockchain applications in management: A bibliometric analysis and literature review. *Technological Forecasting and Social Change*, *166*, 120649. doi:10.1016/j.techfore.2021.120649

Tang, D., Li, T., Ren, J., & Wu, J. (2014). Cost-aware secure routing (CASER) protocol design for wireless sensor networks. *IEEE Transactions on Parallel and Distributed Systems*, *26*(4), 960–973. doi:10.1109/TPDS.2014.2318296

Tanha, F. E., Hasani, A., Hakak, S., & Gadekallu, T. R. (2022). Blockchain-based cyber physical systems: Comprehensive model for challenge assessment. *Computers & Electrical Engineering*, *103*, 108347. doi:10.1016/j.compeleceng.2022.108347

Tariq, U., Ibrahim, A., Ahmad, T., Bouteraa, Y., & Elmogy, A. (2019). Blockchain in internet-of-things: A necessity framework for security, reliability, transparency, immutability and liability. *IET Communications*, *13*(19), 3187–3192. doi:10.1049/iet-com.2019.0194

Tavallaee, M., Bagheri, E., Lu, W., & Ghorbani, A. A. (2009). A detailed analysis of the KDD CUP 99 data set. *Paper presented at the 2009 IEEE symposium on computational intelligence for security and defense applications.* IEEE. 10.1109/CISDA.2009.5356528

Taylor, L., & Richter, C. (2015). *Big Data and urban governance. Geographies of urban governance, 175–191.* Springer International Publishing.

Thanthrige, U. S. K. P. M., Samarabandu, J., & Wang, X. (2016). Machine learning techniques for intrusion detection on public dataset. *Paper presented at the 2016 IEEE Canadian conference on electrical and computer engineering (CCECE).* IEEE. 10.1109/CCECE.2016.7726677

Theodorou, S., & Sklavos, N. (2019). Blockchain-Based Security and Privacy in Smart Cities. Smart Cities Cybersecurity and Privacy, 21-37. Elsevier.

Thierer, A. (2020). *Evasive Entrepreneurs and the Future of Governance: How Innovation Improves Economies and Governments.* Cato Institute.

Thomas, V., Mullagh, L., Wang, D., & Dunn, N. (2015). Where's Wally? In search of citizen perspectives on the smart city. *8th conference of the international forum on urbanism (IFoU),* (pp. 1–8). Multidisciplinary Digital Publishing Institute.

Threats Disclosed. (2023, February 15). Security Research Threats. https://threats.disclose.io/

Thurrott, P. (2004). *MSN Toolbar Suite Preview.* Win SuperSite. http://winsupersite.com/windows-live/msn-toolbar-suite-preview

Tian, J., Wu, J., Yang, Q., & Zhao, T. (2016). FRAMA: A safety assessment approach based on Functional Resonance Analysis Method. *Safety Science, 85,* 41–52. doi:10.1016/j.ssci.2016.01.002

Tikkinen-Piri, C., Rohunen, A., & Markkula, J. (2018). EU general data protection regulation: Changes and implications for personal data collecting companies. *Computer Law & Security Review, 34*(I), 134–153. doi:10.1016/j.clsr.2017.05.015

Torres, A., Galante, R., Pimenta, M. S., & Martins, A. J. (2017). Twenty Years of object-relational mapping: A survey on patterns, solutions, and their implications on application design. *Information and Software Technology, 82,* 1–18. doi:10.1016/j.infsof.2016.09.009

Tough, AG. (2009). Archives in Sub–Saharan Africa Half a century after independence. *Archival Science 9,* 187–201.

Trujillo, A., & Buzzi, M. C. (2016). *Participatory user requirements elicitation for personal menopause app.* Paper presented at the Proceedings of the 9th Nordic Conference on Human-Computer Interaction. IEEE. 10.1145/2971485.2996737

Truyen, F., & Waelde, C. (2016). Copyright, cultural heritage and Photography: A Gordian Knot? Borowiecki, J.K; Forbes, N and Fresa, A (ed). Cultrual Heritage in a Changing World. Springer. doi:10.1007/978-3-319-29544-2_5

Tschabitscher, H. (2007a). *Blinkx 2.0.5 - Email Search Tool.* Microsoft. http://email.about.com/od/outlookaddons/gr/blinkx.htm

Tschabitscher, H. (2007b). *Enfish Find 6.1.3 - Email Search Tool.* Microsoft. http://email.about.com/od/outlookaddons/gr/enfish_find.htm

Tsumaki, T., & Tamai, T. (2006). Framework for matching requirements elicitation techniques to project characteristics. *Software Process Improvement and Practice, 11*(5), 505–519. doi:10.1002pip.293

TÜBİTAK-BİLGEM. (2018). Güvenli Yazılım Geliştirme Kılavuzu. Tübitak-Bilgem. Https://Siberakademi.Bilgem.Tubitak.Gov.Tr/Pluginfile.Php/6115/Mod_Page/Content/26/Sge-Klv-Guvenliyazilimgelistirmekilavuzu_R1.1.Pdf

Ullah, M. (2020). '*Obsecure logging: A framework to protect and evaluate the web search privacy* [Ph. D. dissertation, Dept. Comput. Sci., Capital Univ., Telaiya, India].

Ullah, M. (2020a). *Obsecure logging: A framework to protect and evaluate the web search privacy.* [Ph. D. dissertation, Dept. Comput. Sci., Capital Univ., Telaiya, India].

Ullah, M., Khan, R., & Islam, M. A. (2016a). *Poshida II, a multi group distributed peer to peer protocol for private web search.* Paper presented at the 2016 International Conference on Frontiers of Information Technology (FIT). IEEE. 10.1109/FIT.2016.022

Ullah, M., Khan, R., & Islam, M. A. (2016b). *Poshida, a protocol for private information retrieval.* Paper presented at the 2016 Sixth International Conference on Innovative Computing Technology (INTECH). IEEE. 10.1109/IN-TECH.2016.7845060

Ullah, M., Islam, M. A., Khan, R., Aleem, M., & Iqbal, M. A. (2019). ObSecure Logging (OSLo): A framework to protect and evaluate the web search privacy in health care domain. *Journal of Medical Imaging and Health Informatics, 9*(6), 1181–1190. doi:10.1166/jmihi.2019.2708

Ullah, M., Khan, R. U., Khan, I. U., Aslam, N., Aljameel, S. S., Ul Haq, M. I., & Islam, M. A. (2022). Profile Aware ObScure Logging (PaOSLo): A Web Search Privacy-Preserving Protocol to Mitigate Digital Traces. *Security and Communication Networks, 2022,* 2022. doi:10.1155/2022/2109024

Ullah, M., Khan, R., Haq, M. I. U., Khan, A., Alosaimi, W., Uddin, M. I., & Alharbi, A. (2021). Multi-group ObScure logging (MG-OSLo) A privacy-preserving protocol for private web search. *IEEE Access : Practical Innovations, Open Solutions, 9,* 79005–79020. doi:10.1109/ACCESS.2021.3078431

Ullah, R., Abbas, A. W., Ullah, M., Khan, R. U., Khan, I. U., Aslam, N., & Nazir, S. (2021). EEWMP: An IoT-Based Energy-Efficient Water Management Platform for Smart Irrigation. *Scientific Programming, 2021,* 1–9. doi:10.1155/2021/5536884

USD Commerce. (2012). *The U.S.-EU & U.S. - Swiss Safe Harbor Frameworks.* Retrieved from US Department of Commerce http://export.gov/safeharbor/

Valaski, J., Reinehr, S., & Malucelli, A. (2014). *Environment for requirements elicitation supported by ontology-based conceptual models: a proposal.* Paper presented at the Proceedings of the International Conference on Software Engineering Research and Practice (SERP). IEEE.

Van Heesch, U., Avgeriou, P., & Hilliard, R. (2012). *Forces on architecture decisions-a viewpoint.* Paper presented at the 2012 Joint Working IEEE/IFIP Conference on Software Architecture and European Conference on Software Architecture. IEEE. 10.1109/WICSA-ECSA.212.18

Van Zoonen, L. (2016). Privacy concerns in smart cities. *Government Information Quarterly, 33*(3), 472–480. doi:10.1016/j.giq.2016.06.004

VDP vs BBP. (2023, February 2023). HackerOne Platform. https://docs.hackerone.com/organizations/vdp-vs-bbp.html

Velásquez, I., Caro, A., & Rodríguez, A. (2018). Authentication schemes and methods: A systematic literature review. *Information and Software Technology, 94,* 30–37. doi:10.1016/j.infsof.2017.09.012

Viegas, E. K., Santin, A. O., & Oliveira, L. S. (2017). Toward a reliable anomaly-based intrusion detection in real-world environments. *Computer Networks, 127,* 200–216. doi:10.1016/j.comnet.2017.08.013

Vieira, E. R., Alves, C., & Duboc, L. (2012). *Creativity patterns guide: support for the application of creativity techniques in requirements engineering.* Paper presented at the International Conference on Human-Centred Software Engineering. IEEE. 10.1007/978-3-642-34347-6_19

Viejo, A., Castella-Roca, J., Bernadó, O., & Mateo-Sanz, J. M. (2012). *Single-party private web search.* Paper presented at the 2012 Tenth Annual International Conference on Privacy, Security and Trust. IEEE. 10.1109/PST.2012.6297913

Viejo, A., & Castellà-Roca, J. (2010). Using social networks to distort users' profiles generated by web search engines. *Computer Networks, 54*(9), 1343–1357. doi:10.1016/j.comnet.2009.11.003

Vigna, G., Robertson, W., Kher, V., & Kemmerer, R. A. (2003). A stateful intrusion detection system for world-wide web servers. *Paper presented at the 19th Annual Computer Security Applications Conference, 2003. Proceedings.* IEEE. 10.1109/CSAC.2003.1254308

Viitanen, J., & Kingston, R. (2014). Smart cities and green growth: Outsourcing democratic and environmental resilience to the global technology sector. *Environment & Planning A, 46*(4), 803–819. doi:10.1068/a46242

Vikas, B. O. (2015). Internet of things (iot): A survey on privacy issues and security. *International Journal of Scientific Research in Science, Engineering and Technology,* 168–173.

Vojković, G. (2018). Will the GDPR slow down development of smart cities? *41st International Convention on Information and Communication Technology, Electronics and Microelectronics (MIPRO),* (pp. 1295-1297). IEEE. 10.23919/MIPRO.2018.8400234

Wahab, F., Zhao, Y., Javeed, D., Al-Adhaileh, M. H., Almaaytah, S. A., Khan, W., Saeed, M. S., & Kumar Shah, R. (2022). An AI-Driven Hybrid Framework for Intrusion Detection in IoT-Enabled E-Health. *Computational Intelligence and Neuroscience, 2022,* 2022. doi:10.1155/2022/6096289 PMID:36045979

Wallen, J. (2010). *Efficient Desktop Searching with Beagle.* Linux. https://www.linux.com/news/software/applications/277970:efficient-desktop-searching-with-beagle

Wallgren, L., Raza, S., & Voigt, T. (2013). Routing attacks and countermeasures in the RPL-based internet of things. *International Journal of Distributed Sensor Networks, 9*(8), 794326. doi:10.1155/2013/794326

Wang, H., Liu, W., & Wang, J. (2020*). Achieve web search privacy by obfuscation.* Paper presented at the Security with Intelligent Computing and Big-Data Services 2019: *Proceedings of the 3rd International Conference on Security with Intelligent Computing and Big-data Services (SICBS),* New Taipei City, Taiwan.

Wang, X., Wang, J., Zheng, Z., Xu, Y., & Yang, M. (2009). Service composition in service-oriented wireless sensor networks with persistent queries. *2009 6th IEEE Consumer Communications and Networking Conference,* (pp. 1–5). IEEE.

Wang, L., Guo, S., Li, X., Du, B., & Xu, W. (2018). Distributed manufacturing resource selection strategy in cloud manufacturing. *International Journal of Advanced Manufacturing Technology, 94*(9), 3375–3388. doi:10.100700170-016-9866-8

Wang, T., Hua, H., Wei, Z., & Cao, J. (2022). Challenges of blockchain in new generation energy systems and future outlooks. *International Journal of Electrical Power & Energy Systems, 135,* 107499. doi:10.1016/j.ijepes.2021.107499

Wang, Y. (2011). *A privacy enhanced dns scheme for the internet of things.*

Wang, Y., Jia, P., Liu, L., Huang, C., & Liu, Z. (2020). A systematic review of fuzzing based on machine learning techniques. *PLoS One, 15*(8), e0237749. doi:10.1371/journal.pone.0237749 PMID:32810156

Westin, A. F. (1968). Privacy and freedom. *Washington and Lee Law Review,* 166.

Westin, F. A. (2003). Social and Political Dimensions of Privacy. *The Journal of Social Issues, 59*(2), 431–453. doi:10.1111/1540-4560.00072

Whitmore, A., Agarwal, A., & Da Xu, L. (2015). The Internet of Things—A survey of topics and trends. *Information Systems Frontiers*, *17*(2), 261–274. doi:10.100710796-014-9489-2

Williams, R. (2021). *Whose Streets? Our Streets! 2020-21 "Smart City" Cautionary.* Belfer Center for Science and International Affairs. https://www.belfercenter.org/sites/default/files/2021-08/WhoseStreets.pdf

Winder, D. (2007). *Yahoo Desktop Search review.* PC Pro. http://www.pcpro.co.uk/reviews/office/102280/yahoo-desktop-search

Wisser, M. K., & Blanco-Rivera, A. J. (2015). Surveillance, Documentation and Privacy: An international comparative analysis of state intelligence records. *Archival Science*. doi:10.100710502-015-9240-x

Wolinsky, D. I., Corrigan-Gibbs, H., Ford, B., & Johnson, A. (2012). *Dissent in numbers: Making strong anonymity scale.* Paper presented at the 10th USENIX Symposium on Operating Systems Design and Implementation (OSDI 12). IEEE.

Wright, M. K., Adler, M., Levine, B. N., & Shields, C. (2004). The predecessor attack: An analysis of a threat to anonymous communications systems. [TISSEC]. *ACM Transactions on Information and System Security*, *7*(4), 489–522. doi:10.1145/1042031.1042032

Wu, H.-H., & Shieh, J.-I. (2010). Applying repertory grids technique for knowledge elicitation in quality function deployment. *Quality & Quantity*, *44*(6), 1139–1149. doi:10.100711135-009-9267-2

Xing, B. C., Shanahan, M., & Leslie-Hurd, R. (2016). Intel® software guard extensions (Intel® SGX) software support for dynamic memory allocation inside an enclave. *Proceedings of the Hardware and Architectural Support for Security and Privacy*, *2016*, 1–9. doi:10.1145/2948618.2954330

Xing, L., Demertzis, K., & Yang, J. (2020). Identifying data streams anomalies by evolving spiking restricted Boltzmann machines. *Neural Computing & Applications*, *32*(11), 6699–6713. doi:10.100700521-019-04288-5

Xu, G., Guo, B., Su, C., Zheng, X., Liang, K., Wong, D. S., & Wang, H. (2020). Am I eclipsed? A smart detector of eclipse attacks for Ethereum. *Computers & Security*, *88*, 101604. doi:10.1016/j.cose.2019.101604

Yang, D., Usynin, A., & Hines, J. W. (2006). Anomaly-based intrusion detection for SCADA systems. *5th Intl. Topical Meeting on Nuclear Plant Instrumentation, Control and Human Machine Interface Technologies (Npic&hmit 05)*, (pp. 12–16). IEEE.

Yang, H., Luo, H., Ye, F., Lu, S., & Zhang, L. (2004). Security in mobile ad hoc networks: Challenges and solutions. *IEEE Wireless Communications*, *11*(1), 38–47. doi:10.1109/MWC.2004.1269716

Yang, J., Onik, M. M. H., Lee, N.-Y., Ahmed, M., & Kim, C.-S. (2019). Proof-of-familiarity: A privacy-preserved blockchain scheme for collaborative medical decision-making. *Applied Sciences (Basel, Switzerland)*, *9*(7), 1370. doi:10.3390/app9071370

Yan, H., Feng, L., Yu, Y., Liao, W., Feng, L., Zhang, J., Liu, D., Zou, Y., Liu, C., Qu, L., & Zhang, X. (2022). Cross-site scripting attack detection based on a modified convolution neural network. *Frontiers in Computational Neuroscience*, *16*, 981739. doi:10.3389/fncom.2022.981739 PMID:36105945

Yan, X., Xu, Y., Cui, B., Zhang, S., Guo, T., & Li, C. (2020). Learning URL embedding for malicious website detection. *IEEE Transactions on Industrial Informatics*, *16*(10), 6673–6681. doi:10.1109/TII.2020.2977886

Ye, S., Wu, F., Pandey, R., & Chen, H. (2009). *Noise injection for search privacy protection.* Paper presented at the 2009 International Conference on Computational Science and Engineering. ACM. 10.1109/CSE.2009.77

Yerima, S. Y., Sezer, S., & McWilliams, G. (2014). Analysis of Bayesian classification-based approaches for Android malware detection. *IET Information Security*, *8*(1), 25–36. doi:10.1049/iet-ifs.2013.0095

Yıldız, A. K., Atmaca, A., Solak, A. Ö., Tursun, Y. C., & Bahtiyar, S. (2022). *A Trust Based DNS System to Prevent Eclipse Attack on Blockchain Networks.* Paper presented at the 2022 15th International Conference on Security of Information and Networks (SIN). Springer. 10.1109/SIN56466.2022.9970533

Young, T., Hazarika, D., Poria, S., & Cambria, E. (2018). Recent Trends in Deep Learning Based Natural Language Processing [Review Article]. *IEEE Computational Intelligence Magazine*, *13*(3), 55–75. doi:10.1109/MCI.2018.2840738

Yu, E. S. (1997). *Towards modelling and reasoning support for early-phase requirements engineering.* Paper presented at the Proceedings of ISRE'97: 3rd IEEE International Symposium on Requirements Engineering. IEEE. 10.1109/ISRE.1997.566873

Yu, S., Tian, Y., Guo, S., & Wu, D. O. (2013). Can we beat DDoS attacks in clouds? *IEEE Transactions on Parallel and Distributed Systems*, *25*(9), 2245–2254. doi:10.1109/TPDS.2013.181

Yu, Y., Kaiya, H., Yoshioka, N., Hu, Z., Washizaki, H., Xiong, Y., & Hosseinian-Far, A. (2017). Goal Modelling for Security Problem Matching and Pattern Enforcement. *International Journal of Secure Software Engineering*, *8*(3), 42–57. doi:10.4018/IJSSE.2017070103

Zahid, S., Abid, S. A., Shah, N., Naqvi, S. H. A., & Mehmood, W. (2018). Distributed partition detection with dynamic replication management in a DHT-based MANET. *IEEE Access : Practical Innovations, Open Solutions*, *6*, 18731–18746. doi:10.1109/ACCESS.2018.2814017

Zahid, S., Ullah, K., Waheed, A., Basar, S., Zareei, M., & Biswal, R. R. (2022). Fault Tolerant DHT-Based Routing in MANET. *Sensors (Basel)*, *22*(11), 4280. doi:10.339022114280 PMID:35684901

Zargar, S. T., Joshi, J., & Tipper, D. (2013). A survey of defense mechanisms against distributed denial of service (DDoS) flooding attacks. *IEEE Communications Surveys and Tutorials*, *15*(4), 2046–2069. doi:10.1109/SURV.2013.031413.00127

Zavala, E., Franch, X., Marco, J., Knauss, A., & Damian, D. (2015). *SACRE: A tool for dealing with uncertainty in contextual requirements at runtime.* Paper presented at the 2015 IEEE 23rd International Requirements Engineering Conference (RE). IEEE. 10.1109/RE.2015.7320437

Zhang, B., Li, J., Ren, J., & Huang, G. (2022b). Efficiency and Effectiveness of Web Application Vulnerability Detection Approaches: A Review. *ACM Computing Surveys*, *54*(9), 190. doi:10.1145/3474553

Zhang, H., Kishore, R., Sharman, R., & Ramesh, R. (2007). Agile Integration Modeling Language (AIML): A conceptual modeling grammar for agile integrative business information systems. *Decision Support Systems*, *44*(1), 266–284. doi:10.1016/j.dss.2007.04.009

Zhang, W., Li, Y., Li, X., Shao, M., Mi, Y., Zhang, H., & Zhi, G. (2022a). Deep Neural Network-Based SQL Injection Detection Method. *Security and Communication Networks*, *2022*, 4836289. doi:10.1155/2022/4836289

Zhao, J. W., Hu, Y., Sun, L. M., Yu, S. C., Huang, J. L., Wang, X. J., & Guo, H. (2015). Method of choosing optimal features used to intrusion detection system in coal mine disaster warning internet of things based on immunity algorithm. *Vet. Clin. Pathol.: A Case-Based Approach*, 157.

Zhao, K., & Ge, L. (2013). A survey on the internet of things security. *2013 Ninth International Conference on Computational Intelligence and Security*, (pp. 663–667). IEEE. 10.1109/CIS.2013.145

Zhou, Y., Cheng, G., Jiang, S., & Dai, M. (2020). Building an efficient intrusion detection system based on feature selection and ensemble classifier. *Computer Networks*, *174*, 107247. doi:10.1016/j.comnet.2020.107247

Ziegeldorf, J. H., Morchon, O. G., & Wehrle, K. (2014). Privacy in the Internet of Things: Threats and challenges. *Security and Communication Networks*, *7*(12), 2728–2742. doi:10.1002ec.795

ZipRecruiter. (2023, February 28). *Junior Penetration Tester Salary in LaCoste, TX*. ZipRecruiter. https://www.ziprecruiter.com/Salaries/Junior-Penetration-Tester-Salary-in-LaCoste,TX

Zowghi, D., & Coulin, C. (2005). *Requirements elicitation: A survey of techniques, approaches, and tools Engineering and managing software requirements*. Springer.

Zuiderveen Borgesius, F. J., Kruikemeier, S., Boerman, S. C., & Helberger, N. (2017). Tracking walls, take-it-or-leave-it choices, the GDPR, and the ePrivacy regulation. *Eur. Data Prot. L. Rev.*, *3*(3), 353–368. doi:10.21552/edpl/2017/3/9

About the Contributors

Rafi Ullah Khan was born in Peshawar, Pakistan, in 1984. He completed his PhD (Computer Science) from the Capital University of Science and Technology (CUST), Islamabad, Pakistan. He completed his M.S. in IT from the Institute of Management Sciences, Peshawar, Pakistan and B.S. in Computer Science from Islamia College. His area of interest includes Privacy, Internet of Things, Sentiment Analysis, Text Mining, and Machine Learning. His research papers have been published in international journals, conferences, and book chapters. He is also an Editor-in-Chief of the book: Protecting User Privacy in Web Search Utilization. He worked as Lecturer at Preston University Peshawar, Iqra National University Peshawar, and Farabi College Peshawar from 2007 to 2011. He has been working as a Senior Lecturer at the University of Agriculture Peshawar, since 2011. He is a former member of the PCN Group at CUST, Islamabad and a Lead and Founding member of Zero One Research Group at the ICS&IT, The University of Agriculture Peshawar. He is also a part of the S2MILE research group and currently working as Visiting Fellow at the School of Computing, Macquarie University Sydney, Australia.

***

Arbab Waseem Abbas is a Ph.D. Scholar in Computer Systems Engineering UET Peshawar, Master of Science in Computer Systems Engineering, UET Peshawar. Teaching Courses at Under-graduate and Post-graduate level, Post graduate Co-ordinator, Member BoS, Advisor post-graduate and under-graduate studies; duties include guiding students in the selection of their projects, and coordination of the overall research and co-curricular activities carried out in the department.

Said Ul Abrar is a Computer Research Student And President Of Shining Star Special People Welfare Society, The University Of Agriculture Peshawer.

Iftikhar Alam is working as Associate Professor of Computer Science since 2022. He has done PhD in Computer Science from Department of Computer Science, University of Peshawar, Pakistan. His filed of interests include Semantic Web, Web Engineering, User Modeling, Recommender Systems, Machine Learning and Artificial Intelligence.

Shaukat Ali is working as Lecturer of Computer Science and member of the Information and Web Semantics Research Group at the Department of Computer Science, University of Peshawar, Peshawar, Pakistan. He has completed his post-doctoral from the School of Computing and Communications, Lancaster University, UK under the supervision of Prof. Dr. Corina Sas and has done his Ph.D. from the Department of Computer Science, University of Peshawar under the supervision of Prof. Dr. Shah Khusro. Earlier he did his MS(IT) from the Institute of Management Sciences (IMSciences), University of Peshawar. He is the author of several research paper published in national and international reputed journals and conferences. He has conducted and attended several international conferences and workshops. His research interests include web semantics, web engineering, information retrieval, ontology engineering, linked open data, and mobile-based lifelogging systems for the people with memory impairments and special needs.

Zulfiqar Ali is working as Assistant Professor of Computer Science. His filed of interests include software testing, and requirement engineering.

Muhammad Arshad is working as Associate Professor. His filed of interests are software engineering, web engineering, and networking.

Tianhan Gao graduated from Northeastern University in China with a B.E. in computer science and technology, as well as M.E. and Ph.D. degrees in computer application technology, in 1999, 2001, and 2006. He started as a Lecturer at Northeastern University's Software College in 2006, and was quickly promoted to Associate Professor in 2010. From 2011 to 2012, he was a Visiting Scholar at Purdue University's Department of Computer Science. In 2016, he was awarded the title of doctoral tutor. He has authored or co-authored of over 60 research publications. Next-generation network security, security and privacy in ubiquitous computing, and virtual/augmented reality are among his key research interests.

Shahab Haider received his M.Sc. degree in Computer Science (16 years) from University of Peshawar, Pakistan in 2003, and the M.S. degree in Information Technology (18 years) from Institute of Management Sciences, Pakistan in 2014. He completed his PhD in Computer Engineering in 2020 from the Faculty of Computer Sciences and Engineering, GIK Institute of Engineering Sciences and Technology, Pakistan. Shahab was with the Institute of Business and Management Sciences, University of Agriculture, Peshawar, Pakistan as a Lecturer from 2006 to 2010. He also served at the KPK Ministry of Health, Pakistan as Network Administrator from 2011 to 2016. After his services at KPK Ministry of Health, he worked at Ghulam Ishaq Khan Institute (GIKI) of Engineering Sciences and Technology, Pakistan as Lecturer from September 2016 to June 2019. In August 2019, he joined City University of Science and Information Technology (CUSIT), Pakistan as Lecturer, Computer Science. He was promoted to Assistant Professor, Computer Science at CUSIT in September 2020. After being further promoted, he is currently working as Associate Professor, Computer Science at CUSIT since June 2022. Moreover, he is a member of the Telecommunications and Networking (TeleCoN) Research Lab at GIKI. His research interests include vehicular Mobile Ad hoc Networks, Vehicular Ad hoc Networks, Network security, and routing and switching.

Muhammad Hamad received his MS Computer Sciences degree with a specialization in Information Security from Pakistan Institute of Engineering and Applied Sciences (PIEAS), Islamabad, Pakistan. He is currently working as a research assistant and Ethical Hacker in the Department of Computer Science, KICSIT Kahuta Campus, Institute of Space Technology, Islamabad, Pakistan. His prior experience includes diverse domains of software development, computer networks, and Artificial Intelligence. His main research interests are Ethical Hacking, Artificial Intelligence, and the Internet of things

Muhammad Inam Haq graduated from University of Peshawar and did PhD from Jean Monnet University Saint Etienne, France in 2013. He is currently working as an Assistant Professor with the Department of Computer Science & Bioninformatics, Khushal Khan Khattak University, Karak. His research interests include image processing, computer vision, computer graphics, security, and privacy.

Altaf Hussain received the Ph.D. degree with the Capital University of Science and Technology, Islamabad. He is an Associate Professor and serving as the Head of Computer Science Department, KICSIT Kahuta Campus, Institute of Space Technology, Islamabad, Pakistan. His main research interests include software testing, data mining and distributing computing comprises performance analysis, and cloud computing.

Imran Ihsan conducts research, and the main research interests are knowledge representation and reasoning through Ihsan's Ph.D on Semantic Web Technologies. Ihsan enjoys working with the whole spectrum from deep epistemological problems through the application of semantic computing, to practical solutions in terms of writing computer programs. Ihsan's involvement with Web and Semantic Web technologies extends back to 1996 and 2005 respectively. Most recently, Ihsan has developed and implemented Ontology for Citation Reasons that can provide classification of bibliometric citations in a research paper. Ihsan is also extending LaTEX for research papers to be written using RDF and RDFS Semantics using Ontology for Citation Reasons.

Zeeshan Jamil obtained a B.S. in computer science from The University of Agriculture Peshawar Pakistan in 2022. His research interests include cyber security, deep learning, Intrusion detection, and prevention system

Danish Javeed is currently pursuing a Ph.D. degree in Software Engineering, specializing in Information Security with the Software College, Northeastern University, China under prestigious fellowship of Ministry of Education funded by the Government of China. He got his M.E degree in Computer Applied Technology from Changchun University of Science and Technology, China, under the same fellowship in 2020. His research interests include Internet of Things, Information Security, Network Security, Augmented Intelligence, Deep learning, Intrusion Detection and Prevention System, Software-defined Networking and Edge Computing. He has authored or coauthored over 10+ publications in high-ranked journals and conferences. He is also an IEEE Member.

Irfan Khan received the Ph.D. degree from Middlesex University, London. He is currently an Assistant Professor with the College of Computer Science and Information Technology, Imam Abdulrahman Bin Faisal University (IAU), Saudi Arabia. His research interests include machine learning, data mining, big data processing, image processing, computer vision, and specifically the application of AI in health.

Majida Khan received his MS degree from FAST National University of Computer and Emerging Sciences, Islamabad Campus. She is currently Lecturer in Department of Computer Science, KICSIT Kahuta Campus, Institute of Space Technology, Islamabad, Pakistan. Her main research interests are networks, communication, information and cyber security.

Mumtaz Khan has received MS degree in Computer Science from the Department of Computer Science, University of Peshawar, Pakistan. He is pursuing his PhD in Computer Science from the Department of Computer Science, University of Peshawar, Pakistan. He is the author of several research papers published in national and international reputed journals and conferences. His research interests includes recommender systems, user modelling, group modelling, user-friendly interfaces and personalization for smart TV, ubiquitous computing, web mining, search engines, augmented reality, and mobile-based systems for people with special needs.

Shah Khusro is working as Professor of Computer Science and Head of Information and Web Semantics Research Group at the Department of Computer Science, University of Peshawar, Pakistan. He has done his PhD from the Institute of Software Technology & Interactive Systems, Vienna University of Technology, Vienna, Austria under the supervision of Prof. Dr. A Min Tjoa. Earlier he did his M.Sc. from the Department of Computer Science, University of Peshawar with a Gold Medal. He is a member of different academic bodies of several universities in the region. He has attended/organized several international conferences. He is working on some real world projects in eGovernance, Health, and for Blind and Elderly People. His research interests include web semantics, web engineering, information retrieval, web mining, search engines, augmented reality, mobile-based systems for people with special needs.

Nkholedzeni Sidney Netshakhuma is currently the Postdoctoral Research Fellowship with the University of Cape Town, Centre for African Studies effective from January 2023. His research interest includes Records Management, Archives management and Heritage management, and Political and liberation movements archives. He has published more than 60 articles and book chapters. He currently served as a Deputy Chairperson of the South Africa Higher Education Records and Archives Management Forum. He reviewed more than 60 research articles and book chapters. He obtained Ph.D. Information Science, Masters of Information Science, Post Diploma in Archival Studies, BTECH (Archival Studies at the University of South Africa (UNISA), BPHIL (Information Science at the University of Stellenbosch), BA (History and Political Studies at the University of Venda.

Pedro Pina is a lawyer and a law teacher at the Technology and Management School of Oliveira do Hospital - Polytechnic Institute of Coimbra. He holds a law degree from the University of Coimbra Law School and a post-graduation in Territorial Development, Urbanism and Environmental Law from the Territorial Development, Urbanism and Environmental Law Studies Center (CEDOUA) at the University of Coimbra Law School. He holds a master degree in Procedural Law Studies from the University of Coimbra Law School and the title of Specialist in Law granted by the Polytechnic Institute of Coimbra. Pedro Pina is a researcher at the SUScita – Nucleus for Research Center on SUStainability, Cities, and Urban Intelligence of the Polytechnic Institute of Coimbra.

Tayyaba Riaz is currently pursuing MS Degree in Computer Science from City University of Science and Information Technology, Peshawar, Pakistan. She is working on blockchain technology since 2020.

Muhammad Shahid Saeed is pursuing his Ph.D. at Software College, Dalian University of Technology. He acquired a Masters' degree in "Telecommunication & Networking" from Bahria University Islamabad (Pakistan) in 2020, after earning a Bachelor's degree in "Information Technology" from The Islamia University of Bahawalpur (Pakistan) in 2016. He is currently working as a research associate at Cyber Reconnaissance and Combat lab, Bahria University Islamabad. He is also working on various state-of-the-art projects in collaboration with senior scientists and researchers from Northeastern University China. His research interests mainly encompass network & system security, intrusion detection & prevention, digital forensics & investigation, internet of things, software-defined-networking, artificial intelligence, deep learning, and security protocols. He possesses 5 years of research experience and has several publications in highly ranked international journals and specialized conferences in the applications of network security, intrusion detection, and artificial Intelligence. Additionally, he is on the editorial boards of several international Journals.

Zartasha Saeed is working as Lecturer in City University of Science and Information Technology, Peshawar, Pakistan. She has done MS and working actively in Software Engineering field since 2019.

Bushra Shafi received the Ph.D. degree in Social Work from University of Peshawar in 2010 and she is currently perusing Post Doctorate from University of Dundee, Scotland. Her research interest include Social Work, Sociology, and Gender Studies.

Gurkan Tuna is a Professor at the Department of Computer Programming of Trakya University (2006–. . ..). He has authored several papers in international conference proceedings and refereed journals, and has been actively serving as a reviewer for international journals and conferences. His current research interests include smart grid, ad hoc and sensor networks, cyber security, and machine learning.

Ufuk Uçak has an MSc degree in Cyber Security from Ahmet Yesevi University, Turkey.

Index

A

B

C

D

E

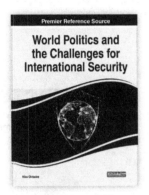

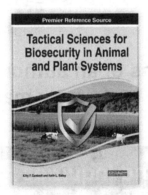

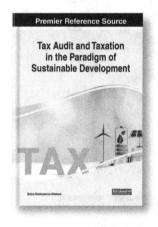

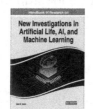

Printed in the United States
by Baker & Taylor Publisher Services